DATE DUE

3/18/08			

Demco

A Companion to the Regional Literatures of America

Blackwell Companions to Literature and Culture

This series offers comprehensive, newly written surveys of key periods and movements, and certain major authors, in English literary culture and history. Extensive volumes provide new perspectives and positions on contexts and on canonical and post-canonical texts, orientating the beginning student in new fields of study and providing the experienced undergraduate and new graduate with current and new directions, as pioneered and developed by leading scholars in the field.

A COMPANION TO

THE REGIONAL LITERATURES OF AMERICA

EDITED BY **CHARLES L. CROW**

Blackwell
Publishing

Editorial material copyright © 2003 by Blackwell Publishing Ltd

350 Main Street, Malden, MA 02148-5018, USA
108 Cowley Road, Oxford OX4 1JF, UK
550 Swanston Street, Carlton South, Melbourne, Victoria 3053, Australia
Kurfürstendamm 57, 10707 Berlin, Germany

The right of Charles L. Crow to be identified as the Author of the Editorial Material in this
Work has been asserted in accordance with the UK Copyright, Designs, and Patents Act 1988.

First published 2003 by Blackwell Publishing Ltd

Library of Congress Cataloging-in-Publication Data

A companion to the regional literatures of America / edited by Charles L. Crow.
p. cm. — (Blackwell companions to literature and culture ; 21)
Includes bibliographical references and index.
ISBN 0–631–22631–1 (alk. paper)
1. American literature—History and criticism—Handbooks, manuals, etc. 2. Regionalism
in literature—Handbooks, manuals, etc. I. Crow, Charles L. II. Series.

PS169.R45 C66 2003
810.9—dc21
2002038288

A catalogue record for this title is available from the British Library.

Set in 11 on 13 pt Garamond 3
by Graphicraft Limited, Hong Kong
printed and bound in the United Kingdom
by T.J. International, Padstow, Cornwall

For further information on
Blackwell Publishing, visit our website:
http://www.blackwellpublishing.com

Contents

Illustrations

Notes on Contributors

Lawrence I. Berkove is Professor of English at the University of Michigan-Dearborn and Director of its American Studies Program. He has published extensively within his field of nineteenth- and early twentieth-century American literature, but has specialized in Mark Twain, Ambrose Bierce, Jack London, and the writers of the Sagebrush School.

Mark Busby is Director of the Center for the Study of the Southwest and Professor of English at Southwest Texas State University. He is author of *Larry McMurtry and the West: An Ambivalent Relationship* (1995), and author, editor, or co-editor of seven other volumes on southwestern authors. He is also co-editor of the journals *Southwestern American Literature* and *Texas Books in Review*. His first novel, *Fort Benning Blues*, was published in 2001. He is currently President of the Texas Institute of Letters.

Donna Campbell is Associate Professor of English at Gonzaga University. She is the author of *Resisting Regionalism: Gender and Naturalism in American Fiction, 1885–1915* (1997) and articles on Edith Wharton, Sarah Orne Jewett, Jack London, and Frank Norris, as well as the annual "Fiction: 1900–1930" chapter for *American Literary Scholarship*.

Lauren Coats is a doctoral candidate in English at Duke University. She examines the inter-sections between literature and cultural geography in eighteenth- and nineteenth-century America. Her work concentrates on the geographical imagination, specifically the mapping of literary constructions of national and regional identities.

Krista Comer is an Assistant Professor of English at Rice University. She is the author of *Landscapes of the New West: Gender and Geography in Contemporary Women's Writing*, and has written on West Coast writers such as Wanda Coleman and Joan Didion, California's surfing culture, environmental issues, third-wave feminism, and youth culture.

Rosemary D. Cox is Professor of English at Georgia Perimeter College, where she teaches composition, literature, and creative writing, and serves as a faculty editor for *The Chattahoochee Review*. Her primary research and publication interests are in nineteenth-century American literature, particularly antebellum Southern humor, and writers of the modern South.

Richard H. Cracroft is Nan Osmond Grass Professor Emeritus in English at Brigham Young University, where he was Chair of the English Department, Dean of the College of Humanities, and Director of the Center for the Study of Christian Values in Literature. He has published extensively on literary subjects in nineteenth-century American literature, Mark Twain, the literature of the American West, literature of the German-American West, American humor, and the literature of the Latter-day Saints. He has been editor of *Literature and Belief* (1993–2001) and of eight books, including *A Believing People: The Literature of the Latter-day Saints*, *Colloquium: Essays in Literature and Belief*, and three volumes of the *Dictionary of Literary Biography* series on *Twentieth-Century American Western Writers*.

Charles L. Crow, Professor Emeritus of English at Bowling Green State University, has written and edited studies of nineteenth-century American literature, American naturalistic fiction, California writers, and the American Gothic. His most recent book is *American Gothic: An Anthology, 1787–1916* (Blackwell, 1999).

Suzanne Disheroon-Green serves as Assistant Professor of American Literature at Northwestern State University in Natchitoches, Louisiana. She is the author, editor, or co-editor of four books on Southern literary and cultural topics, including, most recently, *Songs of the Reconstructing South: Building Literary Louisiana, 1865–1945* (2002). She currently is editing a comprehensive anthology of Southern literature, titled *Voices of the American South*, is co-editing a volume in the *Dictionary of Literary Biography* series titled *Twenty-First Century American Novelists*, and is working on a book-length study of Kaye Gibbons.

Nihad M. Farooq, a doctoral candidate in English at Duke University, is particularly interested in literary and cultural manifestations of racial anxiety in the late nineteenth and early twentieth centuries. Her work addresses parallels between the treatment of African Americans and immigrants in America and the depiction of colonized 'others' in Britain.

David Fine is Professor of English at California State University, Long Beach. His publications include the books *The City, the Immigrant and American Fiction, 1880–1920* (1977) and *Imagining Los Angeles: A City in Fiction* (2000) and five edited critical anthologies, including *Los Angeles in Fiction* (1985; 2nd edn. 1995), *San Francisco in Fiction* (1995), and *John Fante, a Critical Gathering* (1998).

Stephanie Foote is Associate Professor of English, Women's Studies, and Critical Theory at the University of Illinois at Urbana-Champaign. She is the author of *Regional Fictions: Culture and Identity in Nineteenth-Century American Literature* (2001) and is currently at work on a study of parvenus, shame, and class mobility in US culture.

Sarah E. Gardner is Associate Professor of History at Mercer University. She holds a Ph.D. from Emory University and has received awards from the American Historical Association, Duke University, and the Mellon Foundation. Her book *"Blood and Irony:" Southern White Women's Narratives of the Civil War, 1861–1937* is forthcoming from the University of North Carolina Press.

P. Jane Hafen (Taos Pueblo) is an Associate Professor at University of Nevada, Las Vegas. She is a Frances C. Allen Fellow at the D'Arcy McNickle Center for History of the American

Indian, the Newberry Library. Her most recent publication is an edition of *Dreams and Thunder: Stories, Poems and the Sun Dance Opera by Zitkala Ša*.

Bev Hogue, formerly a newspaper editor and feature writer, is now Assistant Professor of English at Marietta College in Ohio, where she teaches American and postcolonial literatures, film, and courses on gender. She is currently revising the manuscript of a book on the Old Northwest in literature.

Betsy Klimasmith is Assistant Professor of English at the University of Massachusetts-Boston. She co-edited *Exploring Lost Borders: Critical Essays on Mary Austin* with Melody Graulich (1999), and has published other articles on Austin, Louisa May Alcott, and Edith Wharton. She won a National Endowment for the Humanities Fellowship to complete a book on urban domesticity in modern American literature and culture.

Susan Kollin is Associate Professor of English at Montana State University in Bozeman. Her essays on Western American literature and environmental cultural studies have appeared in *American Literary History, Modern Fiction Studies, Contemporary Literature, Isle*, and *Arizona Quarterly*. Her book, *Nature's State: Imagining Alaska as the Last Frontier*, was published by the University of North Carolina Press in 2001.

Annette Kolodny is Professor of Comparative Cultural and Literary Studies at the University of Arizona. Her most recent book is *Failing the Future: A Dean Looks at Higher Education in the Twenty-First Century*. Her previous works include *The Land Before Her: Fantasy and Experience of the American Frontiers, 1630–1860* and *The Lay of the Land: Metaphor as Experience and History in American Life and Letters*.

Michael Kowalewski teaches courses in American literature and culture at Carleton College. He is the Director of American Studies, active in the Environmental and Technology Studies program, and the creator and Director of Carleton's "Visions of California" seminar. He is a former President of the Western Literature Association, and the author or editor of five books, including *Reading the West: New Essays on the Literature of the American West* (1996) and *Gold Rush: A Literary Exploration* (1997). His essays and reviews have appeared in more than a dozen periodicals.

Vera M. Kutzinski is a Professor of African American Studies, English, and American Studies at Yale University. Her publications include numerous articles and two critical studies – *Against the American Grain* (1987) and *Sugar's Secrets: Race and the Erotics of Cuban Nationalism* (1993) – as well as the translation of Nicolás Guillén's *El diario que a diario* (*The Daily Daily*, 1989). She has also published on Afro-Hispanic literature in *The Cambridge History of Latin American Literature* and on Caribbean literary theory in *The Johns Hopkins Guide to Literary Theory and Criticism*, and has both contributed and edited essays on anglophone Caribbean writers as part of a three-volume *History of Literature in the Caribbean* sponsored by the International Comparative Literature Association (2001). Her research and teaching focus on comparative American and postcolonial literatures. She is at work on *Translating Modernisms*, a comparative study of modernist writing from the United States, the Caribbean, and Latin America.

Brenda Kwon was born and raised in Honolulu, Hawai'i. She is the author of *Beyond Ke'eaumoku: Koreans, Nationalism, and Local Culture in Hawai'i*, and her poetry has appeared in *Amerasia Journal*, *dis.Orient Journalzine*, and the anthology *Making More Waves*. She currently lives in Hawai'i, where she teaches at Honolulu Community College and writes.

James Kyung-Jin Lee is an Assistant Professor of English and Asian American Studies at the University of Texas at Austin. He is currently completing a book entitled *Urban Triage: Racial and Urban Crisis in Contemporary US Fiction*.

David Mazel is Associate Professor of English at Adams State College in Colorado, where he teaches courses in American Literature and American Studies. He is the author of *American Literary Environmentalism* and the editor of several anthologies, including *A Century of Early Ecocriticism* and *Mountaineering Women: Stories of Early Climbers*.

Farrell O'Gorman is currently Visiting Assistant Professor of English at Wake Forest University. He has published articles on Walker Percy, Flannery O'Connor, Tom Wolfe, and other postwar writers in such journals as *Mississippi Quarterly*, *Carolina Quarterly*, and the *Southern Literary Journal*, and has also contributed to *American National Biography* and *The Companion to Southern Literature*. His interests include religion, region, and ethnicity in contemporary American literature.

Diane D. Quantic is an Associate Professor of English at Wichita State University. The author of *The Nature of the Place: A Study of Great Plains Fiction* and *William Allen White*, she also edited the Midwest section of *Updating the Literary West*. She is co-editor (with P. Jane Hafen) of *A Great Plains Reader* (2003). Quantic is a past President of the Western Literature Association and serves as first Vice-President of the Mari Sandoz Heritage Society.

Lori Robison is Assistant Professor of English at the University of North Dakota. She has published articles on the representation of race in Whitelaw Reid's journalistic treatment of the postwar South and in Grace King's post-Reconstruction Southern stories. She is currently at work on a book, *Domesticating Difference: Gender, Race, and the Birth of a New South*, which examines how literary representations of the postbellum South contributed to the national construction of race.

Kent C. Ryden is an Associate Professor in the American and New England Studies Program at the University of Southern Maine. He is the author of *Landscape with Figures: Nature and Culture in New England* (2001) and *Mapping the Invisible Landscape: Folklore, Writing, and the Sense of Place* (1993), as well as many essays and reviews which collectively focus on the interrelationships among landscape, literature, and regional identity. He is a recipient of the American Studies Association's Ralph Henry Gabriel Prize.

Gary Scharnhorst is Professor of English at the University of New Mexico, and is the author or editor of 18 books. He co-edits the journal *American Literary Realism* and edits in alternating years the research annual *American Literary Scholarship*. His *Bret Harte: Opening the American Literary West* (2000) won the Thomas J. Lyon Award for "Outstanding Book in Western American Literary Criticism."

Robert Thacker is Professor and Director of Canadian Studies at St. Lawrence University, and Executive Secretary of the Western Literature Association. He is the author of *The Great Prairie Fact and Literary Imagination*, and author and editor of works on Willa Cather, Alice Munro, and other US and Canadian authors.

Nicolas Witschi is Assistant Professor of English at Western Michigan University. His interests include American realism and modernism, the American West, culture studies, and film. He is the author of *Traces of Gold: California's Natural Resources and the Claim to Realism in Western American Literature* (2002), and of articles on Mary Austin, John Muir, and Sinclair Lewis. He is presently working on a much-needed recovery of the life and letters of Alonzo Delano, the California Gold Rush chronicler and humorist also known as Old Block.

Acknowledgments

The editor's greatest debt is to the community of scholars who created these chapters. He would also like to recognize helpful suggestions from Sandra Zagarell, Melody Graulich, and Chad Rohman.

The book and its editor benefited from the encouragement, good judgment, and patience of Andrew McNeillie, Emma Bennett, and Alison Dunnett at Blackwell.

Text Credits

Robert Davis, "The Albino Tlinglit Carving Factory" and "Saginaw Bay: I Keep Going Back," from *Soul Catcher*. Sitka: Raven's Bones Press, 1986. Reprinted by permission of the author.

Norah Marks Dauenhauer, "Village Tour: Nome Airport" and "Genocide" from *The Droning Shaman*. Haines: Alaska: Black Current Press, 1988. Reprinted by permission of the author.

Annette Kolodny, "Letting Go Our Grand Obsessions: Notes Toward a New Literary History of the American Frontiers," *American Literature* 64: 1 (March 1992), pp. 1–18. Copyright © 1992, Duke University Press. Reprinted with permission.

Vera M. Kutzinsky, "Borders and Bodies: The United States, America, and the Caribbean." This work originally appeared in *CR: The New Centennial Review* 1: 2 (2001), published by Michigan State University Press. Reprinted with permission.

Illustration Credits

Figure 1.1: Map of Native California. From Malcolm Margolin, *California Indian Stories, Songs and Reminiscences*. Copyright © 1993. Used with permission of Heyday Books, Berkeley, California, publisher.

Figure 5.1: "Darkies Shelling Corn." From *North Carolina: A Guide to the Old North State* by the Federal Writers' Project, WPA of North Carolina. Copyright © 1939 by the North Carolina Department of Conservation and Development. Published by the University of North Carolina Press.

Figure 12.1: Actor Joshua Silsbee as the Yankee character Jonathan Ploughboy in Samuel Woodworth's *The Forest Rose*. Courtesy of the Harvard Theater Collection, the Houghton Library, Harvard University.

Figure 12.2: John Barber engraving of Traunton, Massachusetts, from his 1839 book *Historical Collections of Massachusetts*. Courtesy of the Maine Historical Society.

Figure 14.1: Photography of cornfield and power plant in southeast Ohio, by Bev Hogue. Courtesy Bev Hogue.

Figure 15.1: "Major Jones's Courtship." Courtesy Special Collections and Archives, Robert W. Woodruff Library, Emory University.

Figure 18.1: Map of Louisiana, 1895. Courtesy Special Collections, Tulane University Libraries.

Figure 19.1: Photograph of Joseph Thompson Goodman (1838–1917). Courtesy Lawrence I. Berkove.

Figure 20.1: "Callin' Ahead," by Greg Keeler. Courtesy of the artist.

Figure 21.1: "Winter Sunrise in the Sierra," by Ansel Adams. Courtesy of the Trustees of the Ansel Adams Publishing Rights Trust.

Figure 24.1: Photograph of tourists on a cruise ship in the Glacier Bay National Park, by Susan Kollin. Courtesy Susan Kollin.

Figure 25.1: "J. Frank Dobie at Joe Small's BBQ, ca. 1957," by Russell Lee. Courtesy the University of Texas Center for American History.

Figure 25.2: Photograph of Leslie Marmon Silko, by Don Anders. Courtesy of Don Anders, Media Services, Southwest Texas State University.

Figure 27.1: Photograph of Bret Harte. Courtesy of the Bancroft Library, University of California, Berkeley.

Figure 28.1: Photograph of Mark Twain at his childhood home, Hannibal, 1902. Courtesy the Mark Twain Project, the Bancroft Library, University of California, Berkeley.

Figure 29.1: Photograph of Willa Cather at Mesa Verde, 1915. Courtesy Archives and Special Collections, University of Nebraska-Lincoln Libraries.

Figure 30.1: Photograph of Mary Austin. Courtesy of the Bancroft Library, University of California, Berkeley.

Figure 31.1: Photograph of Wallace Stegner. Photographer unknown. Courtesy of Mary Stegner.

Figure 31.2: "Writing class meeting at Wallace Stegner's house, about 1958," by John C. Lawrence. Courtesy of Mary Stegner.

Introduction

Charles L. Crow

This Blackwell *Companion* reveals the rich heritage of regional literatures in the United States. Our goal is twofold: to show the scope and history of regional literatures, and to understand their importance, as revealed by several theoretical approaches.

Regional literatures usually have been undervalued by literary historians, and by university textbooks and courses, until recently. Two trends have altered this situation. The first, born in the marketplace, is the spectacular appeal to readers today of books with a regional emphasis. As our first chapter will discuss in detail, bookstores today are filled with acclaimed and bestselling books from authors like Cormac McCarthy, Charles Frazier, E. Annie Proulx, Barbara Kingsolver, and many others, that are deeply grounded in local culture and landscape. In an age of corporate-produced mass culture, of identical shopping malls and fast-food restaurants, regionalism has staged a defiant comeback.

The second trend, born in the academy, is the re-evaluation of the canon of American literature. This process began as long ago as the 1960s (when so many important changes began), unearthed many lost or undervalued authors, and overturned many of the assumptions by which we once judged literary texts. Among the baggage of the old orthodoxy was the assumption that regional writing was inherently minor, an art of the miniature, the commonplace, the local, and often the feminine. The term "local color" was used dismissively, as a diminutive, in contrast to works embodying the big slam-bang national themes of exploration, adventure, and conquest. Through the lively discussions of the sixties and seventies, these positions became increasingly difficult to maintain. Feminist scholars, especially, challenged the belief that the literature of "small and private lives" was necessarily less important than stories about seafaring or fighting Indians. Regional writers of manifestly superior quality, like Kate Chopin, were rescued from obscurity. By the 1990s, Judith Fetterley and Marjorie Pryse had defined a tradition of "women's regional realism" extending from Harriet Beecher Stowe through Sarah Orne Jewett and Mary E. Wilkins Freeman to Mary Austin and Willa Cather. Fetterley and Pryse, in their introduction to *American*

Women Regionalists, 1850–1910 (1992) defined common interests and themes shared by these writers, and raised awareness of their artistic achievement. Some scholars suggested later that Fetterley and Pryse paid too little attention to the respective regional concerns of their regionalists, made them seem too much alike, and ignored their interaction with other authors and traditions. Whatever the merit of these objections, the work of Fetterley and Pryse opened the way for a resurgence of scholarship on regional literatures, and its importance cannot be overstated.

As a result of these debates of the last few decades, we now better understand the achievements of regionalist authors, and the importance of the traditions in which they wrote. Indeed, it is difficult to understand the large issues of American culture and literature, we can now assert, without understanding the literature of regions. Thus, while the chapters of this book are devoted to sections of the country, the reader will recognize the major problems and concerns of national history: slavery, sectional rivalries, the place of indigenous people, the natural landscape, the meaning of frontier experience, the rise of cities, progress and change, women's rights. At the same time, as we will see, the regional approach offers unique insights, and at times even challenges the wisdom of studying literature packaged according to nation-states. Is there really an American literature, or is there only a collection of regional literatures? And do these literatures always stop at national borders?

"Regional literature," as used here, is a very large and inclusive term. We are concerned with regions before the existence of the nation, from early attempts by colonists to describe their lives in a new place, with literatures of new regions as the country moved west, and with stories of those the settlers displaced. We include the tradition of women's regionalism defined by Fetterley and Pryse, the rowdy masculine humor of the Old Southwest, the literature of cities and small towns and farms and wilderness. We move through the realistic movement, which was largely defined by regionalist writers, into and through the twentieth century.

Readers of this *Companion* will encounter familiar and famous names, as well as many new writers they may wish to read for the first time, and will learn of histories and traditions from many regions.

Our book is divided into three parts. The eleven chapters of part I are designed to show several theoretical approaches to our subject, and to indicate how the concepts of region and regional literatures have changed over time. A key issue, which runs throughout the book, is introduced in the second chapter. What is the "cultural work" that is performed by regional literatures? What does such writing *do* within our evolving national experience? The folk ways of a region are often described in texts which are read, or consumed, by members of another, dominant class. Is this commodification of regional culture inherently demeaning or condescending, reducing it to the quaint and picturesque, like souvenir snapshots of summer vacations in the mountains or at the seashore? A related question concerns the issue of nostalgia in regional literature. Do pictures of simple life in Maine fishing villages, Midwestern small towns, or (an even more challenging instance) antebellum Southern plantations pander to the reader's desire to escape to an imagined simpler time? And, if so, is this always wrong? Or, on the contrary, can the perspective of a region offer a useful minority view, a healthy subversion, of dominant values?

Other chapters in part I will develop this question of cultural work in various ways. The "work" of region often involves both place and race, and race may be the key issue of American life, as important as class is in Britain. Regional writers make implicit claims about the region as a homeland to the peoples within it. Much regionalism is the story of colonial peoples learning to regard themselves as native to a place. As we would expect, the original native peoples have found ways to write back, to place themselves again in the landscape through their own literatures (see chapter 10). Much of the literature of the South, especially, is a continuing debate over the relationship of several cultures to the place, and the legitimacy of the stories they have written of their lives there.

Inherently, regional literature is placed at the intersection of human culture and natural landscape. People define this relationship through lines drawn by surveyors and politicians, through laws and texts, and through social and personal histories. These human constructions often fit imperfectly with the watersheds, shorelines, and ecological systems of the landscape. Repeatedly in part I, and in later chapters as well, our writers use the key terms "borders" and "boundaries" in discussing this relationship of people and place. Chapter 3 asks us to replace the powerful myth of the frontier, a westward-moving line of settlement, with a regional approach, in which we consider particular regions and and the interaction of cultures within them. Chapters 7 and 11 both ask us to consider ways in which cultures cross borders (as will some essays in part II, especially chapter 13); chapter 7 also brings the study of region into contemporary suburban culture, and, like several of these chapters, uses tools of contemporary feminist theory. Chapters 8 and 9 study the literature of ecology and the literature of the city (the latter usually invisible to the regional approach).

Part II, the largest section of the book, is a survey of several of the regional literatures of the United States. No such survey can ever claim to be complete, since it is always possible for a region to be subdivided or defined in an alternative way. Nonetheless, the fifteen chapters in this section provide a very full survey of the regions of the country and their respective literary histories. As would be expected, there is careful treatment of regions long recognized for their literary traditions, such as the South and New England; but the Old Northwest, a region whose identity has faded over time, is also represented. The Great Plains, the Southwest, the Rocky Mountain West, and California, which from an Eastern perspective might blur into one generalized West, are here separated into distinct regions requiring individual treatment. Likewise, the Pacific Northwest and Alaska are given a separate chapter, as is the state of Hawai'i, often ignored or considered too foreign or exotic for discussion as an American region.

The final section, part III, presents studies of a small number of important regional authors. This list could be extended almost indefinitely, of course, and the section fill another volume. The five authors represented here – Bret Harte, Mark Twain,

Willa Cather, Mary Austin, and Wallace Stegner – were each important in defining and representing regions to American and world audiences. Harte began the craze for "local color" in the years immediately after the Civil War, and was for a time the most popular fiction writer in the English language. Mark Twain, his one-time friend, transformed American fiction through his close observation of place and regional language. Mary Austin and Willa Cather, each in her own way, brought the tradition of women's regionalism into the twentieth century and (to use words handed like magical tokens from Sarah Orne Jewett to Cather) brought the parish to the world. Wallace Stegner not only was a masterful writer himself, a border-crosser grounded in the American and Canadian Wests, but through his creative writing classes at Stanford shaped generations of new regional writers. These five writers, then, are offered as specific and detailed studies of the issues raised and explored earlier in the book.

*

The chapters in this *Companion* are all original work, except the pieces by Annette Kolodny and Vera M. Kutzinski, which were revised by the authors for inclusion here.

PART I
History and Theory of Regionalism in the United States

1

Contemporary Regionalism

Michael Kowalewski

"The idea of a regional literature is an odd one," the novelist Marilynne Robinson contends, because it is "the product of a cultural bias that supposes books won't be written in towns you haven't heard of before." But it contains a blessing, in her opinion, because "it makes people feel that they live in a peculiar place. Of course, people, by definition, do live in a peculiar place. But if they become aware of this peculiarity as something exceptional they are stimulated to an enriching interest in the particulars of their own lives" (Robinson 1992: 65–6). American regionalism is steeped, like strong tea, in the details of particular places as they have been filtered through a writer's imagination. In fact, one of the central impulses in American literature – one shared by Thoreau and Cather, Faulkner and Silko, Stevens and Didion, Hurston and Welty – has been to evoke what Frederick Turner (echoing D. H. Lawrence) calls a "spirit of place." These evocations involve more than simply background color or a little local seasoning. The "spirit of place" in literature springs from a sense of belonging and human attachment. It also tends to be refracted through the "spirit of time," whether in human history or in the deeper temporal reaches of geology and forests. This is what makes for "deep," "thick," or "dense" descriptions that create a three-dimensional sense of memory and life and that capture what might be called the local metabolism of American places. The best American regional writing tends to be less about a place than *of* it, with a writer's central nervous system immersed in the local ecology, subcultures, hidden history, and spoken idioms of a given location.

Yet we sometimes forget that American authors were often driven to evoke this kind of "spirit" precisely because it was felt to be absent and uncelebrated in American life. The gradual creation of a national literary landscape of specific places (Faulkner's Mississippi, Twain's Hannibal, Steinbeck's Salinas, and so on) was largely a response to a more general belief that the landscape Americans inhabited was, as Turner says, "an ahistorical landscape, one without spirit and without life" (1989: x). Regional authors still have to combat historical amnesia, but a sense of historical belatedness now further muddies the waters in which they swim. They still have to shoulder aside American ignorance or misperceptions about local places, but they also have to do so in ways that haven't yet been done in classic evocations of "place" in American literature. ("The presence alone of Faulkner," Flannery O'Connor once remarked, "makes a great difference in what the [Southern] writer can and cannot permit himself to do. Nobody wants his mule and wagon stalled on the same track the Dixie Limited is roaring down" [O'Connor 1969: 45].) In addition, regional authors often have to wrench their work free from popular, overpublicized representations of regional identity. A writer eager to catch the texture of contemporary life in Minnesota, for instance, may have to contend less with the ghosts of Sinclair Lewis and Ole Rólvaag than with the melodious ironies of Garrison Keillor's radio shows on Lake Woebegon or the regional stereotypes in movies like *Grumpy Old Men* (1993) and *Fargo* (1996). We don't tend to hear, after all, about Hmong culture, or prairie restoration, or tribal spearfishing rights, or grids of genetically engineered soybeans in Lake Woebegon.

Contemporary literary regionalism in the United States – a rich, capacious body of work that resists easy classification – might best be defined by two contradictory cultural attitudes encapsulated as follows: "Region Matters" and "Yes, Isn't It Pretty to Think So?" Regional art and identity have never seemed stronger in American society, yet there is a nagging suspicion that they may be increasingly peripheral in a postmodern "Planet Reebok" world of convenience, mobility, and postindustrial economies that run on global flows of information and capital. High claims are made for "living in place," for digging in and staying put, and becoming native to the places we inhabit. At the same time, increasingly large numbers of Americans feel less tied to and less aware of the places in which they live. As Pico Iyer puts it in *The Global Soul*, the question " 'Where do you come from?' is coming to seem as antiquated an inquiry as 'What regiment do you belong to?'" (2000: 11). A recent statewide survey of the public by the California Council for the Humanities, for example, reported that only 21 percent of Californians strongly agreed that their city or town had a strong sense of community; 65 percent of the survey respondents said they knew only a "little or nothing at all about the history of their communities,"[1] and 67 percent said they knew "little or nothing at all about the cultural backgrounds of the people in their communities." (Robert Putnam's exhaustive and much-discussed new study of the decline of community and "social capital" in America, *Bowling Alone* [2000], suggests that this is a strong national trend.) How are we to understand such contradictions? And how do they inform or deform American regional art and identity?

The signs of a strong, expansive interest in and support for regional identity are effervescing in any number of venues: in successful regional theaters and art museums; in expanding membership in local historical societies and watershed partnerships; in Chautauquas, "living history" exhibits, and touring one-man or one-woman shows focused on local historical figures; in "multicultural" urban food-fests and community-building cultural pride festivities; in centennial, sesquicentennial, and bicentennial celebrations of statehood or historical events like the California Gold Rush or the Lewis and Clark expedition; in popular regional magazines, from *Sunset* to *Southern Living*; in active state humanities councils, as well as in land conservation and historical restoration projects that seek to protect and restore the natural resources and historical "treasures" of a region; in Ken Burns's high-profile documentary series on the Civil War and the West; in local jazz concerts and folk festivals; even in the plethora of local wineries, farmers' markets, Community Supported Agriculture cooperatives, brewpubs, and microbreweries that now dot the map, most celebrating some aspect of local history or ecology and capitalizing on a taste for regional cuisine.

Every major region of the country now also boasts a large research center, like the Center for the Study of Southern Culture at the University of Mississippi and the Center of the American West at the University of Colorado. The National Endowment for the Humanities is presently in the process of helping fund a number of new regional centers of research and public outreach around the country. Regional writing in particular seems to be enjoying a renaissance of interest. New regional book awards honor local (as well as international) talent. Regional book festivals, conferences, and benefits bring together authors and (often first-time) readers. New and old literary journals and magazines with a strong regional flavor (*Zyzzyva, Ruminator Review, Northern Lights, Sewanee Review,* and *Great Plains Quarterly,* to name a few) continue to flourish. Professional organizations like the Western Literature Association (founded in 1965) are thriving. Despite the incursions of corporate chain stores and online ordering companies, many independent regional bookstores somehow manage to hold on and sponsor active reading series. Radio programs like David Dunaway's series *Writing the Southwest* (1995), or the American Library Association's regional literature series, entitled "StoryLines America" (begun in 1999), or joint audio/book projects like *Texas Bound* (1993), in which Texas actors like Tommy Lee Jones read Texas stories, continue to introduce important works of regional literature to a wide audience. Many regional publishers (Heyday Books in Berkeley, for instance, or Milkweed Editions in Minneapolis) continue to publish high-quality literary works. Many reputable university presses either reprint regional classics, as in the University of California's "California Fiction" series, or sponsor regional series, like the "Literature of the American West" series at the University of Oklahoma Press. Local literary festivals and cultural events (or extravaganzas, like the Cowboy Poetry Festival in Elko, Nevada) frequently gain national attention. Guides to regional art and culture are readily available. *The Encyclopedia of Southern Culture* was a national bestseller, while *The Literary History of the American West,* in 1987 – which weighed in at 1,353 pages: longer than most literary histories of the United States as a whole – was followed by *Updating the Literary West* (1997). Recent anthologies like *The Literature of California* (2000), *Great and Peculiar Beauty: A Utah Reader* (1995), *Georgia Voices* (begun 1992), and *The Last Best Place: A Montana Anthology* (1988) have expanded and enriched the sweep of American literature. This *Companion* itself is a sign of the continuing interest and vitality of regional writing and criticism.

It would be small-minded not to feel heartened in some way by this outpouring of regional energy. The resurgence of interest in regional history, identity, and culture might be seen, in its most promising light, as America's coming of age. The United States, one might hope, is finally beginning to acknowledge and appreciate the fascinating intricacies of its landscape and history. Yet much of the popular focus on regional identity, as Hal Rothman has shown, relies heavily on "scripted space" (Rothman 1998: 12). Touting of regional identity – whether in Salt Lake City or Williamsburg – frequently partakes of the "heritage" movement: a promotional impulse that often has more to do with kitsch, nostalgia, and economic "growth coalitions" than with any deep-rooted or stabilizing sense of community. The packaging and marketing of regional history and experience as commodities tends, unsurprisingly, to be distrusted by historians and writers because that process too often casts history in a soft-focus celebratory vein that downplays discordance and conflict, ignores racial and ethnic diversity, and simplifies natural features into familiar icons (wheatfields, Spanish Moss swamps, mitten buttes) that hide regional distinctiveness more than they reveal it. "I do not know what 'reality' really is," the historian Daniel J. Boorstin says in his book *The Image: A Guide to Pseudo-Events in America*, "but somehow I do know an illusion when I see one" (1961: ix). Regional writers might heartily agree, as many of them see regional promotion and the clamor for regional distinctiveness as so much snakeoil, a kind of commercial flotsam that usually interferes with rather than facilitates in-depth understandings of a region. Barry Lopez has used the term "false geographies" to refer to a congeries of romantic preconceptions by means of which the "essential wildness" and "almost incomprehensible depth and complexity" of the American landscape have been reduced to "attractive scenery" (1990: 55). Many Americans, he says, now think about their country in terms of a "memorized landscape" (visually memorized – in a television ad, a calendar, or a computer screen saver – *before* it has been actually experienced). This creates a homogenized national geography that seems to operate independently of the land, Lopez says; "a collection of objects rather than a continuous bolt of fabric" (1990: 62).

Regional writers often have to deal not only with selective historical memory, but with a plethora of predigested and preassigned images and characters which eclipse other, more searching evocations of a place. When Lyman Ward, the maimed and cranky historian who narrates Wallace Stegner's novel *Angle of Repose* (1971), starts out to record the story of his grandparents' lives in the American West, he encounters a problem familiar to regional writers. He wishes to avoid writing the kind of book his son Rodman – whose "notion of somebody interesting is numbingly vulgar" – would like him to do:

> Having no historical sense, [Rodman] can only think that history's interest must be "color." How about some Technicolor personality of the Northern Mines, about which I already know so much? Lola Montez, say, that wild girl from an Irish peat bog who became the mistress of half the celebrities of Europe, including Franz Liszt and Dumas,

père or *fils* or both, before taking up with King Ludwig I of Bavaria, who made her Countess of Landsfeld. And from there, in 1856, to San Francisco, where she danced the spider dance for miners and fortune hunters (*No, Lola, no!*) and from there to Grass Valley to live for two years with a tame bear who couldn't have been much of an improvement on Ludwig. That's Rodman's idea of history. Every fourth-rate antiquarian in the West has panned Lola's poor little gravel. My grandparents are a deep vein that has never been dug. They were *people*. (Stegner 1971: 22)

Lyman knows the details of Lola Montez's life (which makes his dismissal of them more convincing), but he also knows that a fascination with self-dramatizing regional "color" obscures an interest in establishing the historical depth that might complicate or reconfigure such one-dimensional historical portraiture. As Cynthia Shearer notes, *à propos* of the South, "the Southern writers' rage to explain . . . is mostly a feeling that if you want something done right, you have to do it yourself" (2000: 55).

The "vulgar" or overly dramatic attempt to establish regional distinctiveness often seems to prompt a response in an opposite direction: a deliberate deflation of scenic or mythic preconceptions of a landscape and its people. The Wyoming of Jackson Hole and Yellowstone, for instance, is nowhere in sight in Annie Proulx's short-story collection *Close Range*, though we do get a glimpse of some tourists on a dude ranch, who are taken "up into the mountains where tilted slopes of wild iris aroused in them emotional displays and some altitude sickness" (Proulx 1999: 154). For the most part, however, Proulx's Wyoming is at "the bunchgrass edge of the world." She creates a memorable, hardscrabble rogue's gallery of knotheads, troublemakers, lonely hearts, and dreamers, pink-slipped somewhere else in a company downsizing and drifting through town. Proulx's stories are peopled with ne'er-do-well antiheroes who are unlikely to appear in brochures from the Wyoming Visitors' Bureau. This kind of antimythic puncturing of regional stereotypes appears around the country, like bullet holes in rural traffic signs, in much hard-edged regionalist writing: in New England (in Russell Banks's novels *Affliction* [1989] and *Continental Drift* [1985]); in the South (in Cormac McCarthy's novel *Child of God* [1973] or Dorothy Allison's novel, *Bastard Out of Carolina* [1992]), in the Midwest (in Jane Smiley's novel *A Thousand Acres* [1991]); and in the West (in collections of stories like Sherman Alexie's *The Lone Ranger and Tonto Fistfight in Heaven* [1993], Sharon Doubiago's *The Book of Seeing with One's Own Eyes* [1988], novels such as Cormac McCarthy's *Blood Meridian* [1985], and poetry like Adrian Louis' *Blood Thirsty Savages* [1994]). Contemporary regional authors often resist regional preconceptions in an intentionally discomforting or raunchily comic manner – and, as in the case of Proulx, they cannot always extricate themselves successfully from the myths and stereotypes with which they wrestle.[2]

If the Scylla of the regional imagination is too much identity (the overdone or stereotypical), the Charybdis is no identity at all: the fear, in Gertrude Stein's notorious formulation, that there's no there there in American regionalism. How can a writer celebrate the uniqueness of local places when they begin to feel less and less distinctive? Writers must now face the fact that large portions of the United States, from Tucson to Milwaukee and from Seattle to Tampa Bay, look and feel largely identical. James Howard Kunstler has characterized much of the contemporary American landscape as "the geography of nowhere." If you were to be kidnapped today in Southern California, the journalist Ray Suarez wryly hypothesizes, "your captors might not even have to blindfold you. You could drive for hours and not think you had gone anywhere. If you were to break away and reach a phone, your surroundings – a 76 gas station, a Taco Bell, a Pep Boys, a used-car lot, and mountains in the smoggy distance – would be of no use at all to the police" (Suarez 1999: 18). Contemporary evocations of place in America often seem embattled, unsettled, and besieged: at odds – often overwhelming odds – with attitudes and economic, technological, and social forces that threaten the local distinctiveness of the American landscape, both rural and urban. Overscheduled and overstimulated Americans, the feeling goes, have grown numb to the importance of place in their lives. Members of an "attention deficit disorder" society, they have increasingly opted for privacy, convenience, and consumption over community, shared public spaces, and a dense street culture. Distracted by information technologies that claim to connect but that frequently replace human contact, they have fallen prey to an image-based "hyper-capitalism," in which brand names replace products. ("The universities now offer only one serious major," Wes Jackson quips: "upward mobility" [1994: 3].) Habitable communities become commodities to be purchased rather than entities to be created through collective effort. Americans are increasingly surrounded by a Velveeta landscape of sprawling, look-alike suburbs, traffic-choked expressways full of drivers on cellphones, and huge, corporate superstores with acres of parking lots. The spiritual as well as physical "macadamization" of contemporary America has eroded the distinctiveness of individual places and pre-emptively discouraged people from caring about them.

To put this another way, if one were to update the end of Willa Cather's novel *My Ántonia* (1918), Ántonia Cuzak's children, instead of helping make *kolaches*, planting hollyhocks, or showing guests a new "fruit cave" with barrels of pickled watermelon rinds, might be checking their palm pilots and sipping from Nalgene water bottles before heading to the Black Hawk mall to rent DVDs. (Leo might be listening to Bohemian hip-hop and wondering whether Black Hawk is ready for a tattoo parlor; Anna and Yulka might be dreaming of SUVs or a new dot.com start-up in Omaha; Nina might tend to Britney Spears and Pokémon cards.) In other words, pop culture and hip consumerism might have so saturated the children as to overwhelm or displace the experience of growing up in rural Nebraska towns, "buried in wheat and corn," as Cather's Jim Burden puts it, where "burning summers" alternate with "blustery winters . . . when the whole country is stripped bare and gray as sheet-iron" (Cather 1918: 1).

This kind of (admittedly exaggerated) juxtaposition is perhaps easiest to make with regard to children, because of the importance of a child's formative years, when memory, place, and identity are inextricably intertwined. Children, Mary Austin declared, are "at heart the most confirmed regionalists. What they like as background for a story is an explicit, well mapped strip of country, as intensively lived into as any healthy child lives into his own neighborhood" (1932: 102). The occasion for this remark was an article entitled "Regionalism in American Fiction," hardly a peripheral topic by Austin's lights. For her, "the source of all art" arose "as people truly and rudely say, in our 'guts,' the seat of life and breath and heartbeats, of loving and hating and fearing" (Austin 1932: 98). The "guts" of art arose not only from physiology and emotion, but from the local environmental factors that had already molded them: "No sort of experience . . . works so constantly and subtly upon man as his regional environment. It orders and determines all the direct, practical ways of his getting up and lying down, of staying in and going out, of housing and clothing and food-getting; it arranges by its progressions of seed times and harvest, its rain and wind and burning suns, the rhythms of his work and amusements. It is the thing always before his eye, always at his ear, always underfoot" (Austin 1932: 97).

Austin's emphasis upon "regional environment" was proportional to her concern that Americans did not care about it. Opposing the rhythms of seed times and harvest and loving evocations of the land was the American reading public's preference for "something less than the proverbial bird's-eye view of the American scene, what you might call an automobile eye view, something slithering and blurred, [with] nothing so sharply discriminated that it arrests the speed-numbed mind to understand, characters like garish gas stations picked out with electric lights" (Austin 1932: 107). This image of urban anonymity and anesthesia (for which a bird's eye is an unsuitably organic metaphor) invokes a phantom opposite that has historically helped define "regional" experience, especially as regionalism has been associated with rural culture. The Southern Agrarians had voiced similar concerns two years earlier in *I'll Take My Stand* (1930). The "speed-numbed" mind of contemporary – typically urban – society has for some time now been deemed particularly unsuited to an appreciation of the slower rhythms and local nuances of rural locales, whether agrarian or not. This is an idea inherited from a late nineteenth-century conception of "local color," which conceived of regional writers as provincials writing at a remove from the centers of commerce and culture. Regionalism in this guise is also tied to that "complex blend of accommodation and protest" that T. J. Jackson Lears calls "antimodernism" (1981: xiii), which, in the early twentieth century, recoiled from "overcivilized" modern existence and looked for more intense and more authentic forms of physical and spiritual experience.

Yet contemporary regionalism is not best thought of by excluding writers who write about urban areas. No longer can we claim that when we are discussing regional writers we are "really" talking about, say, Ivan Doig or Louise Erdrich or Mary Oliver or Wendell Berry, and not Walter Mosley or Amy Tan or Tom Robbins or Gwendolyn Brooks or Joan Didion, all of whom write with loving detail about specific urban areas. Given the nation's expanding population, a regional writer interested in capturing the texture of contemporary existence would be hard put *not* to address some aspect of urban life, even if not necessarily the life of a congested metropolis. Most regional writers are likely to alternate between the city and the country, often in the same story or poem. The work of Southern writers like Doris Betts, Jill McCorkle, Kaye Gibbons, Lee Smith, Larry Brown, and Reynolds Price often shuttles between rural and metropolitan settings and between the Old and New South. (Some, like Betts in her novels *Heading West* [1981] and *The Sharp Teeth of Love* [1997], also write about regions other than the South: a kind of transregional cross-pollination that deserves to be more widely studied.) The novelist Jon Hassler, the essayist Scott Russell Sanders, and the poet Ted Kooser have all produced significant bodies of Midwestern writing. While all grounded in rural areas, they are as likely to set their work in a leafy college town as in a wetland or a limestone quarry. The urban/rural distinction seems less and less crucial to much contemporary regionalism. Jane Hamilton's engaging novel, *A Map of the World* (1994), should quiet the voice of skeptics who think that serious fiction cannot be written today about agrarian life in Midwestern "fly-over" country. Maxine Hong Kingston's novel *Tripmaster Monkey* (1989) might counter the charge that urban fiction cannot somehow be "regional." Kingston's protagonist, the fifth-generation Chinese American Wittman Ah Sing (whose name slyly alludes to "Song of Myself"), embodies an ironic trans-Pacific consciousness that mixes Rilke, Kerouac, and Chinese legends of the Monkey King, none of them out of place on the foggy streets of San Francisco. Ana Castillo, for her part, writes with equal adeptness about Mexican Americans both in Chicago, in *Peel My Love like an Onion* (1999), and in sleepy hamlets in New Mexico (*So Far From God*), where a young girl can fly up onto a church roof and, in the words of Castillo's narrator, "nobody could say nothing about it" (Castillo 1993: 21).

Yet despite this greater inclusiveness in contemporary American regionalism, there is still often an undeniable thread of antimodernist (or antipostmodernist) recoil in much contemporary regional writing. Urban and suburban America, as glimpsed through a regional lens, often looks increasingly bland, intolerant, unhealthy, and consumer-oriented. As William Bevis has noted about the West, the rootedness and uniqueness of rural places in many Western works – particularly those by Native Americans and dry-land realists – are often set against a mainstream culture of individualism, freedom, mobility, and interchangeability that Bevis calls "liquidity." In American culture, liquidity often takes shape as "freedom in the form of license, the right to do anything one wishes, free of background, race, kinship, place, and fate" (Bevis 1996: 31). Certain Western writers remind us, as Bevis says, that the antiprogressive aspects of the West have not always been "primitivist, nostalgic, or anti-civilization." Rather, they often originate in "marginal but informed cultural points of view" (Bevis 1996: 35) that show the problems of capitalist modernity to be not only problems of multinational corporations and global profits, but problems of identity that arise from conflicting conceptions of the self.

One could do worse, in reaching for a fresh understanding of contemporary regionalism, than to look at a tribal map of the state perhaps most associated with rootlessness, transience, and unchecked growth: California (see figure 1.1). The general

Figure 1.1 Map of Native California. From Malcolm Margolin, *California Indian Stories, Songs and Reminiscences*.

public's relative unfamiliarity with California tribes helps make this an eye-opening revelation. The twisting boundaries of tribal units are provisional demarcations determined by language, culture, and natural features rather than by abstract governmental designations: the whole is a loose confederacy of biocultural locales. The value of learning to envision California this way is not to satisfy a primitivist longing for prelapsarian images of a Native American "harmony with nature." Native Californians use chainsaws and food processors to prepare for traditional ceremonies, and Greg Sarris, in his fine memoir of the renowned Cache Creek Pomo basketweaver and medicine woman, *Mabel McKay: Weaving the Dream* (1994), recounts an incident at Stanford University when a student asked Mabel, in an auditorium where she was being interviewed as a native healer, "What do you do for poison oak?" "Calamine lotion," she replied, with no hint of sarcasm (1994: 1).

The value of visualizing California not as a single entity but as a mosaic of interdependent, interlocking microregions, each with its distinctive landforms, climate zones, history, and blendings of culture, is that it brings the true richness of the state into sharper clarity. The historical and biological continuum within which to imagine California widens, not in spite of but because of the particularities of individual places. The more carefully we train ourselves to superimpose California's human history and culture onto its natural history, like overlaid transparencies, the more likely we are to approximate the imaginative equivalent of deep focus in film. An awareness of "place" as a living, interactive force in human identity helps create a more richly textured and multilayered sense of volume and depth in any region's history and art.

Visualizations of place that frequently use natural features rather than recently imposed political demarcations are a central element of a contemporary environmental movement called bioregionalism. Bioregionalism emphasizes the fact that human behavior and ethical deliberation take place within the context of local communities, both human and biotic. Individuals and communities, in such a view, come into consciousness *through*, not apart from, the natural environments they inhabit. Bioregional definitions of healthy communities rely on downsized ecological systems and local relationships with the land, seeing identity as bound up in a specific terrain defined by natural boundaries rather than abstract governmental designations.

As Kirkpatrick Sale puts it in explaining the ethics of environmental action in *Dwellers in the Land*, "The issue is not one of morality . . . but of *scale*" (1985: 53). The optimal scale at which ecological consciousness and healthy human communities can be developed, Sale argues, is the bioregional. The earth is organized, he asserts, not into artificial states but into natural areas, or bioregions, that are defined by "particular attributes of flora, fauna, water, climate, soils, and landforms, and by the human settlements and cultures those attributes have given rise to" (Sale 1985: 55). Sale quickly adds that the borders of bioregions are inevitably indistinct and interpenetrating. Bioregions "are not only of different sizes but often can be seen to be like Chinese boxes, one within another [morphoregions within georegions within ecoregions], forming a complex arrangement from the largest to the smallest, depending

upon which natural characteristics are dominant" (1985: 56). Bioregionalists generally seek to stress not the common qualities of American places but the distinctive
ones, the aspects of local identity taken to be most indelible and unreproducible elsewhere. They are particularly wary of what Wendell Berry calls "a regionalism of the
mind" (1990: 81), one which can result in "a map without a territory" (1990: 82), a
literature of place without a place – in a physical sense – to evoke.

Bioregional "mappings" of local environments have increasingly involved an
interest in metaphors of depth, layering, resonance, root systems, habitats, and
interconnectedness – factors that not only connect different aspects of a place but
seem to put them into motion, making them move within their own history (both
human and nonhuman). The effect, as Patricia Hampl puts it, is to pitch us harder
into the landscape: "There is no forest, but there is the sensation that now we're
going deeper. The *deeper* of characters in fairy tales who set off from home and, sooner
or later, must enter a deep wood" (Hampl 1987: 40).

Barry Lopez's exploration of Arctic tundras and icefloes in *Arctic Dreams* (1986);
Linda Hasselstrom's writings from the ranches and coffee shops in the interior of the
American West, *Land Circle* (1991); Wendell Berry's profusion of essays, poetry, and
fiction from his Kentucky hill farm; Terry Tempest Williams's account of birdlife
and self-healing at the Great Salt Lake, *Refuge: An Unnatural History of Family and
Place* (1991), and her explorations of eroticism in the canyon country of Southern
Utah, *Desert Quartet* (1995); John McPhee's geological tetralogy (*Basin and Range*
[1981], *In Suspect Terrain* [1983], *Rising From the Plains* [1986], and *Assembling
California* [1993]); John Hanson Mitchell's explorations of "deep time" in patches of
remnant countryside outside Boston in *Ceremonial Time* (1984) and *Living at the End
of Time* (1990); Keith Basso's masterly exposition of landscape and language among
the Western Apache *Wisdom Sits in Places* (1996); David Rains Wallace's meditations
on myth and evolution in *The Klamath Knot* (1983) or his description of a unique area
of Florida woodlands in *Bulow Hammock: Mind in a Forest* (1988); William Least
Heat-Moon's *Prairy-Erth* (1991), a 600-page exploration of a single county of tallgrass prairie in the Kansas Flint Hills; Rick Bass's description of land conservation
efforts in the far northwestern corner of Montana in *The Book of Yaak* (1996); Gary
Nabhan's southwestern ethnobotanical studies in *The Desert Smells Like Rain* (1982) –
the sense of place that emerges from these and dozens of other contemporary works
that might be termed bioregional is informed by an ecological understanding of the
interdependence, interconnectedness, and adaptation of all living systems. Bioregional
writers picture specific localities as complex, multilayered palimpsests of geology,
meteorology, history, myth, etymology, family genealogy, agricultural practice, storytelling, and regional folk ways.

Bioregional writing offers a multidimensional vision of identity and landscape. It
does not imagine "place" in literature as a conceptual index of social attitudes, or a
receding backdrop for the actions of isolated selves in the foreground, but rather as
a form of depth perception. Less a formalized movement in recent American writing
than an impulse or a turn of mind, bioregionalism represents, in Gary Snyder's

words, "the entry of place into the dialectic of history" – but not "place" defined in exclusively human terms. "We might say," Snyder asserts, "that there are 'classes' which have so far been overlooked – the animals, rivers, rocks, and grasses – now entering history" (Snyder 1990: 41).

Replacing larger, more homogeneous entities (whether states or regions) with the more flexibly defined microregions that bioregional writers propose might seem a form of Balkanization to some, a form of fashionable fragmentation in imagining the self. Strangely enough, the opposite seems to be the case, at least insofar as a contemporary literature of place implicitly testifies. Imagining "deep maps" of smaller, more specific places actually offers what W. J. Keith calls "a welcome limitation of possibility" (1988: 10), one that allows for a richer understanding of individual wholeness – one, in Hampl's words, that feels like sanity. The most compelling bioregional works attempt to establish imaginative title to specific American places, to reimagine a numinous landscape beneath a desacralized, irradiated, and overdeveloped one. One of the most ambitious of these is Snyder's book-length poem, *Mountains and Rivers without End.* Forty years in the making, the poem is an exploration of whether it is possible to imagine a bioregional vision of the planet, with various places in the American West connected – like images in an East Asian painter's hand scroll – to sites in Japan, Australia, China, and Taiwan: all of them linked by "the dynamics of mountain uplift, subduction, erosion, and the planetary water cycle" (Snyder 1996: 155).

Snyder's multifaceted interests in Buddhism, plate tectonics, Japanese Noh drama, and calligraphy offer an apt example of the blending of science, art, and spirituality in the bioregional imagination. They also reveal the increasing cultural eclecticism of American regional writing, which now often embodies a hybrid collage of multiple voices, memories, and cross-cultural exchange. There has been a healthy and long overdue recognition that every region of the United States is criss-crossed by vectors of inward and outward migration. Every area of the country teems with the historical and cultural "footprints" of multiple populations (some recent, many long-established over generations). As the Chicano playwright and film-maker Luis Valdez puts it, "we must cross the 'T,' we must square the circle, in order to understand who it is we are" (1990: 169). Writers and scholars now find it more difficult to characterize something as large as, say, "the Mind of the South" and tend to focus on what Krista Comer calls "competing geographical and historical imaginations" (1999: ix) of a given place. Works like Victor Villaseñor's epic family chronicle, *Rain of Gold* (1991), the poetry of New Mexico native Simon Ortiz (Acoma Pueblo), and the play *Tea* (1987) by Velina Hasu Houston (who is of mixed Japanese, African-American, and Native American ancestry), a work which explores the lives of Japanese "war brides" who settled after World War II with their ex-GI husbands in rural Kansas, all demonstrate how many regional writers stretch out to non-European cultures, via bloodlines and cultural affiliations, in imagining their local places. These writers negotiate bicultural, even tricultural identities in locating themselves and their characters. Many create what might be called "placed" evocations of displacement:

dramatizations of cultural disorientation, cultural vertigo, or deracinated yearnings for distant places or the lost comfort of traditional ways. Their works often powerfully remind readers that culture shock can be experienced at home as well as abroad.

Biologists, ethnobotanists, and environmental historians have altered our notion that the American wilderness was pristine and untouched prior to the arrival of European settlers. Lands once thought of as unaltered by human culture have now been shown to reveal complex signs of early indigenous agriculture and land management. Similarly, many authors have re-imagined aspects of the regional past that have deepened our understanding of regional society and culture. Some of these – for instance, William Kennedy's Albany cycle (*The Ink Truck* [1969], *Legs* [1975], *Billy Phelan's Greatest Game* [1978], *Ironweed* [1983], and *Quinn's book* [1988]), Leslie Marmon Silko's *Almanac of the Dead* (1991), Charles Frazier's *Cold Mountain* (1997), and David Guterson's *Snow Falling on Cedars* (1995) – have received widespread, often award-winning attention. But other, less well-known works deserve equal consideration. Andrew Hudgins's book-length narrative poem, *After the Lost War* (1988), vividly re-imagines the life of nineteenth-century poet Sidney Lanier; Shannon Applegate relates the history and lore of her Oregon pioneer family in *Skookum* (1988); Jonathan Raban explores the lives of early twentieth-century homesteaders in the Dakotas and eastern Montana in *Bad Land* (1996); Larry Watson explores some of the same territory in his Montana trilogy, which begins with the novel *Montana 1948* (1993); James D. Houston chronicles the life of Patty Reed, a member of the Donner Party of 1846, in his novel *Snow Mountain Passage* (2001); Peter Matthiessen dramatizes the life of an early twentieth-century outlaw entrepreneur in the Florida Everglades in *Killing Mr. Watson* (1991); Frank Chin re-imagines the building of the Transcontinental Railroad through the eyes of a young Chinese-American boy in San Francisco in his coming-of-age novel *Donald Duk* (1991); and Patricia Hampl's *Spillville* (1987) pays lyrical tribute to Czech composer Antonin Dvorak's 1893 summer stay in a wedge of farm and forest in northeastern Iowa, sometimes called Little Switzerland.

In addition to these renderings of regional history, anyone interested in the true scope of contemporary regionalism should also sample the explosion of literary nonfiction that deals with place, in memoir, autobiography, and personal narrative. The recent outpouring of American memoirs and autobiographies is a larger, national phenomenon having to do with the popularity of literary nonfiction, and not all of this writing focuses on place; but much of it does, providing fresh new understandings of what it means to dwell, or have dwelt, in specific places, for varying lengths of time. Dan Duane's account of a surfer's year on the central California coast in *Caught Inside* (1996); Larry McMurtry's account of his ambivalent love affair with Texas in *Walter Benjamin at the Dairy Queen* (1999); Tim McLaurin's account of growing up in North Carolina, *Keeper of the Moon* (1991); Kathleen Norris's portrait of life on the high plains in *Dakota: A Spiritual Geography* (1993); Verlyn Klinkenborg's agrarian adventures in *Making Hay* (1986); Bobbie Ann Mason's memoir of her Kentucky childhood in *Clear Springs* (1999); Western ranch narratives like Mary Clearman

Blew's *All But the Waltz* (1991) and William Kittredge's *Hole in the Sky* (1992); Bill Holm's tribute to his home town in *The Heart Can Be Filled Anywhere on Earth: Minneota, Minnesota* (1996); Eudora Welty's autobiographical musings in *One Writer's Beginnings* (1984); James Galvin's lyrical delving into the history of a postage-stamp pasture on the Colorado/Wyoming border in *The Meadow* (1993); Henry Louis Gates's remembrances of growing up in the "segregated peace" of Piedmont, West Virginia, in *Colored People* (1994); Jane Brox's account of living on her family farm in the Merrimack Valley in Massachusetts in *Here and Nowhere Else* (1995); Darryl Babe Wilson's memoir of growing up with the Achumawe and Atsugewi Indians in northeastern California in *The Morning the Sun Went Down* (1998); Paul Gruchow's collection of Minnesota memories in *Grass Roots: The Universe of Home* (1995); and Luis Rodriguez's account of growing up amidst the gang warfare of East Los Angeles in *Always Running* (1993): these and dozens of other personal narratives are infused with the sometimes tender, sometimes harrowing details that help create the patch-work quilt of local places that makes up contemporary regionalism.

One other form of literary nonfiction – travel writing – also deserves mention here. At least since Henry David Thoreau's exploration and mapping of his own backyard, American travel writing has been intimately tied to the literature of place. While travel narratives are not "regional" in the sense of springing from extended residence in a place, and while their authors have sometimes been disparaged (in W. E. B. DuBois' memorable phrase) as "car window sociologists" (quoted in Rampersad 1990: 25), contemporary travel writing about the United States has nevertheless resulted in some remarkable accounts of regional landscapes and cultures. The extraordinary success of William Least Heat-Moon's account of his backroads circuit of the country in *Blue Highways* (1982) helped create the sense that much of the rural landscape and history of the United States had been lost on the American public, and that, in Heat-Moon's words, if a traveler but has the perception, he can become "a *perpetual* stranger in a strange land" (1992: 21, emphasis in original). Jonathan Raban's trip down the Mississippi in a 16-foot aluminum boat in *Old Glory* (1981); Eddy Harris's report of what the same trip was like for a young African American in *Mississippi Solo* (1988), followed by his motorcycle tour of the South in *South of Haunted Dreams* (1993); Douglas Brinkley's rollicking account of taking college students around the country for an on-the-road exploration of American history in *The Majic Bus: An American Odyssey* (1993); Mary Morris's description of wandering through the New Age groups of southern California in *Angels and Aliens* (1999); Charles Bowden's explorations of the Santa Catalina Mountains in Arizona in *Frog Mountain Blues* (1994); Kent Nerburn's journeys along the Pacific Coast highway in *Road Angels* (2001); Dayton Duncan's renderings of the American West in *Out West* (1987) and *Miles from Nowhere* (1993); Joan Didion's portrait of urban tension, fast money, and the center of Cuban exile in *Miami* (1987); Thurston Clarke's journeys along earthquake rifts in *California Fault* (1996); Kenneth Lincoln and Al Logan Slagle's journeys through Native America in *The Good Red Road* (1987); Linda Niemann's railroad memoir, *Boomer* (1990); Sallie Tisdale's search for "home" in the Pacific

Northwest, in *Stepping Westward* (1991); Heat-Moon's chronicle of his trip across America by boat in *River-Horse* (1999); Tim Palmer's exploration of American waterways, from the Penebscot to the Sheenjek, in *America by Rivers* (1996): these and other recent travel narratives bear alternately marveling and cranky witness to the prodigal variety of contemporary regionalism.

Writers have not always been anxious to be thought of as "regional writers," not least because that tag has often denoted small-press status and the chance of only local, sometimes uncritical, recognition. "Regional fiction at its best" is a blurb emblazoned on any number of remaindered novels. Many regional writers have an animating ambivalence about being considered "Western" or "Southern" or "Midwestern," because while they may believe that regional identity and a sense of place can crucially shape and inform a writer's sensibilities, they are wary of notions of geographical determinism. Regional identity is something that a number of writers try somehow to both embody and escape. Also, an intimate connection between landscape and writing can sometimes be more a wished-for condition than an actuality, and it is not always clear what kind of causal relationship can be established between the two.

When remembering her childhood in northern Idaho, Marilynne Robinson says she preferred old, thick, dull, and hard books that had nothing Western about them – books about "Constantinople and the Cromwell revolution and chivalry." "Relevance was precisely not an issue for me. I looked to Galilee for meaning and to Spokane for orthodonture, and beyond that the world where I was I found entirely sufficient" (Robinson 1993: 165). "Do you feel a strong sense of connectedness between yourself and the land?" an interviewer once asked Robinson. "Less than I wish I did," she replied, "but that's often the way it is. You imagine what it would be like if you felt the way you wished you did feel, and that becomes a sort of feeling in itself" (Robinson 1987: 229). Yet, as many readers know, Robinson's novel *Housekeeping* (1980) is one of the most richly rendered regional works of the last two decades. Not knowing what kind of link can be established between self and environment is clearly not the same as asserting that there is nothing there to be known.

"The idea that [one's] style is rooted to the landscape just sounds sort of quaint to me," the poet William Stafford once remarked (1987: 236). "Our country is so fluid for travel and access that a regional recognition is more a matter of convenience than it is any kind of valid movement" (1993: 65). In discussing the importance of natural sounds in his poetry, however, Stafford mentions precisely the kind of detail regional writers often evoke: "there is a mossy, deadened sound here [in the Northwest]. So you listen more carefully: you're an owl. You don't have to put on earmuffs to keep from damaging your hearing. It's nice and quiet, so you listen . . ." (1993: 68). Literary critics (like myself) who wish to show that region and "place" are important – even crucially formative – elements of a writer's sensibility sometimes skip over remarks like Stafford's disavowal of "quaintness" and look for places where writers say their writing has been influenced by landscape and local communities. But if we are not careful, we may do at least two kinds of disservice to Stafford, Robinson, and other authors. First, we ignore or downplay the fact that many regional writers do not consider their writing "regional," at least not unequivocally so; and second, we may miss some of the nuances of how a regional writer's understanding of "place" might actually manifest itself in language and in his or her verbal imagination.

Stafford actually *does* suggest – as in his remark about the "mossy, deadened sound" of the Northwest – that the sensory texture of a region may somehow be capable of getting into a writer's nervous system or into his verbal temperament. But he tends to suggest this deflectingly, by indirection and with humor. "My attitude is this," he says in an interview conducted in Portland: "where you live is not crucial, but how you *feel* about where you live is crucial. . . . In some ways, let me say, the most minimal scenery is my kind of scenery. This [Portland] is too busy a place. I stand it very well. It doesn't make me nervous. It's just that it's superfluous. Any Kansan knows that Oregon is a little too lavish" (Stafford 1987: 235). If there is a unity to Northwest writing, Stafford says, it is attributable less to "scenery and a mystique" and more to the kind of company writers keep. "If Theodore Roethke hadn't moved to Seattle," Stafford says, "the scene would be the same, but the literary scene wouldn't be the same. I think he had a great effect on that. But I hit all that too late for it to do anything to me. I was already an Osage orange, hedgewood Kansan" (1987: 236). Stafford's logic is elfishly circular here. Landscape doesn't influence writing, the argument goes, *writers* do; but I'm too much a product of my landscape (a Kansan) to have it affect me. I'm too serious to be anything but playful, Robert Frost once said, and we might adapt the phrase in Stafford's case. Region and place may be too indelible to lend themselves to direct statements or to social movements. Having self-doubts about the possibility of adequately conveying a sense of regional identity is not the same as asserting that it does not exist.

Flannery O'Connor, prescient as always, said as much in 1963, in an essay entitled "The Regional Writer." "I have a friend from Wisconsin who moved to Atlanta recently and was sold a house in the suburbs. The man who sold it to her was himself from Massachusetts, and he recommended the property by saying, 'You'll like this neighborhood. There's not a Southerner for two miles'" (O'Connor 1969: 56–7). "At least we can be identified when we do occur," O'Connor added. The prospect of regional identity at the time was not encouraging:

> The present state of the South is one wherein nothing can be taken for granted, one in which our identity is obscured and in doubt. . . . It is not a matter of so-called local color, it is not a matter of losing our peculiar quaintness. Southern identity is not really connected with mocking-birds and beaten biscuits and white columns any more than it is with hookworm and bare feet and muddy clay roads. Nor is it necessarily shown forth in the antics of our politicians . . . An identity is not to be found on the surface; it is not accessible to the poll-taker; it is not something that *can* become a cliché. . . . It is not made from what passes, but from those qualities that endure, regardless of what passes, because they are related to truth. It lies very deep. In its entirety, it is known only to God, but of those who look for it, none gets so close as the artist. (O'Connor 1969: 57–8)

Some forty years later, O'Connor's double vision seems more pertinent than ever: Never underestimate the American penchant for attempting to turn *everything* into a cliché or into a "memorized landscape." But, by the same token, never underestimate the willingness of American writers to stand their ground against that impulse. Regional authors continue to send their verbal imaginations into the vortex of contemporary life, and they continue to return and to speak of what endures: one neighborhood, one river basin, one metropolis, one region at a time.

NOTES

1 See "Survey: Californians believe sharing stories strengthens community" (June 15, 2001), http://www.thinkcalifornia.net/news/.

2 See my review of *Close Range* in "Losing Our Place: An Essay Review," *Michigan Quarterly Review* 40: 1 (Winter 2001), 242–56.

REFERENCES

Austin, Mary (1932). "Regionalism in American Fiction." *English Journal* 21, 97–107.

Berry, Wendell (1990). "Writer and Region." In *What Are People For?* San Francisco: North Point. 71–87.

Bevis, William (1996). "Region, Power, Place." In Michael Kowalewski (ed.), *Reading the West: New Essays on the Literature of the American West*, 21–43. New York: Cambridge University Press.

Boorstin, Daniel J. (1961). *The Image: A Guide to Pseudo-Events in America*. New York: Vintage.

Castillo, Ana (1993). *So Far From God*. New York: Plume.

Cather, Willa (1918). *My Ántonia*. Boston: Houghton Mifflin.

Comer, Krista (1999). *Landscapes of the New West: Gender and Geography in Contemporary Women's Writing*. Chapel Hill: University of North Carolina Press.

Hampl, Patricia (1987). *Spillville*. Minneapolis: Milkweed Editions.

Heat-Moon, William Least (1992). "Journeys into Kansas." In Michael Kowalewski (ed.), *Temperamental Journeys: Essays on the Modern Literature of Travel*, 19–24. Athens, Ga: University of Georgia Press.

Iyer, Pico (2000). *The Global Soul: Jet Lag, Shopping Malls, and the Search for Home*. New York: Knopf.

Jackson, Wes (1994). *Becoming Native to this Place*. Washington DC: Counterpoint.

Keith, W. J. (1988). *Regions of the Imagination: The Development of British Rural Fiction*. Toronto: University of Toronto Press.

Kunstler, James Howard (1993). *The Geography of Nowhere: The Rise and Decline of America's Man-Made Landscape*. New York: Simon & Schuster.

Lears, T. J. Jackson (1981). *No Place of Grace: Antimodernism and the Transformation of American Culture, 1880–1920*. New York: Pantheon.

Lopez, Barry (1990). "The American Geographies." In Robert Atwan and Valeri Vinokurov (eds.), *Openings: Original Essays by Contemporary Soviet and American Writers*, 55–69. Seattle: University of Washington Press.

O'Connor, Flannery (1969). *Mystery and Manners: Occasional Prose*, ed. Sally and Robert Fitzgerald. New York: Farrar, Straus & Giroux.

Proulx, Annie (1999). *Close Range: Wyoming Stories*. New York: Scribner.

Putnam, Robert (2000). *Bowling Alone: The Collapse and Revival of American Community*. New York: Simon & Schuster.

Rampersad, Arnold (1990). "V. S. Naipaul: Turning in the South," *Raritan* 10 (Summer), 24–47.

Robinson, Marilynne (1987). Interview. In Nicholas O'Connell (ed.), *At the Field's End:*

Interviews with Twenty Pacific Northwest Writers, 220–30. Seattle: Madrona.

Robinson, Marilynne (1992). "Talking about American Fiction: A Panel Discussion with Marilynne Robinson, Russell Banks, Robert Stone, and David Rieff." *Salmagundi* 93, 61–77.

Robinson, Marilynne (1993). "My Western Roots." In Barbara Howard Meldrum (ed.), *Old West – New West: Centennial Essays*. Moscow, Idaho: University of Idaho Press.

Rothman, Hal (1998). *Devil's Bargains: Tourism in the Twentieth-Century American West*. Lawrence: University Press of Kansas.

Sale, Kirkpatrick (1985). *Dwellers in the Land: The Bioregional Vision*. San Francisco: Sierra Club Books.

Sarris, Greg (1994). *Mabel McKay: Weaving the Dream*. Berkeley: University of California Press.

Shearer, Cynthia (2000). "Notes on Southern Literature." *Hungry Mind Review* 52, 54–6.

Snyder, Gary (1990). *The Practice of the Wild*. San Francisco: North Point.

Snyder, Gary (1996). *Mountains and Rivers without End*. Washington DC: Counterpoint.

Stafford, William (1987). Interview. In Nicholas O'Connell (ed.), *At the Field's End: Interviews with Twenty Pacific Northwest Writers*, 231–47. Seattle: Madrona.

Stafford, William (1993). "The Art of Poetry LXVII," *Paris Review* 129, 51–78.

Stegner, Wallace (1971). *Angle of Repose*. New York: Doubleday.

Suarez, Ray (1999). *The Old Neighborhood: What We Lost in the Great Suburban Migration, 1966–1999*. New York: Basic Books.

Turner, Frederick (1989). *Spirit of Place: The Making of an American Literary Landscape*. Washington DC: Island.

Valdez, Luis (1990). "Envisioning California." *California History* 68, 162–71.

2

The Cultural Work of American Regionalism

Stephanie Foote

I

Regional writing might be the great comeback story of American literature. Extraordinarily important in the late nineteenth and early twentieth centuries, it has been the subject of a fascinating and widespread critical rediscovery during the past thirty or so years. The genre of regional writing, dismissed for much of the twentieth century as a "minor" element within the canon of American letters, has provided an ideal vantage point from which contemporary scholars can examine how a national literature was constructed. As a genre, regional writing is deeply concerned with what is remembered and what forgotten, and how; with how local, particular people and places are incorporated or discarded. Concerned with forgetting and remembering, having been forgotten and then remembered itself, regional writing is an object lesson in how national literary traditions are constructed through powerful, ideologically driven mechanisms of inclusion and exclusion. Regional writing's new prominence in American Studies has attracted a great deal of critical attention to the genre's range and depth, but even more importantly, it has given critics a template on which to map the cultural work of other "minor" texts and "local" concerns within the field of American literature.

Structurally and substantively, regional writing is especially able to help critics understand the meaning of local lives, local ideas, and local traditions. Regional writing, imaginatively devoted to the concerns of discrete localities, is also therefore committed to asking what place local knowledges have in the construction of a national tradition. While it would be impossible to say that every text that can be assigned to the genre of regional writing arrived at the same response to the pressing question of how to evaluate the category of the local, it is fair to say at the very least that almost all regional texts have as an organizing principle a deep desire to understand what the local is, and what the local does. It is precisely its dedication to illuminating the often contradictory meanings of the local that made regional writing so important in its own era, and that continues to make it so important to ours.

In this essay, I will look at regional writing's transformative engagement with the idea of the local, focusing on two interrelated stories. First, I will trace the consolidation of regional writing as one of the late nineteenth century's most important literary forms, considering how its circulation and reception in its own era were charged with a variety of complex cultural work. I shall pay special attention to the terms under which early twentieth-century critics, seeking to create a monolithic national literary tradition, untangled regional writing from its own cultural moment, making it a genre whose importance was aesthetic rather than political. But I will also tell another story about regional writing. In this story, itself one of forgetting and remembering, I examine the terms under which regional writing has been resuscitated. I focus especially on what current interest in regionalism tells us about our own era's concerns with the place of local knowledges and persons. I will argue that focusing on the shifting, historically contingent category of the local can help us find in regional writing an important, still-vital model for understanding cultural difference in the early twentieth-first century. Telling the story of regionalism's changing meaning for different historical eras, paying attention to the conditions of its production and consumption, taking account of the ways its subject-matter shaped and was shaped by the concerns of its own era, is a painstaking process. Telling these interrelated stories is like creating a regional text of our own, for we shall be using a small slice of literary history to illuminate the cultural importance not just of regional literature, but of literature more broadly.

Literature was only one among a multitude of ways in which people engaged with culture, but in both its consumption and its production it is one of the most important and complex means by which people struggled over basic issues of representation. That small area of the cultural field in the nineteenth century that was occupied by literature is an especially interesting and useful site through which to examine how conflicts over the meaning and the place of new kinds of people were staged, circulated, and consumed. Writing, especially the kind studied in English courses at universities, is usually seen as supporting a very narrow definition of culture. Writing that is institutionally valued is called "literature," and is therefore understood as part of high culture. But we need to broaden the definition of culture to include all forms of narrative that attempted to make sense of the world. Literature in this reading does cultural work: it does not simply express or reflect the concerns of its author or its time period, but rather is a gregarious element of culture; it interprets its complex moment, and it is interpretable within its framework. Like all cultural forms, literature engages in a complicated and conflicted relationship with its own cultural moment, transforming and being transformed by a dense field of social concerns. This view of literature's relationship to culture has been very fruitfully explored in relationship to the genres of realism and naturalism, long understood as the major genres of the late nineteenth century. But during a moment in which so much conflict revolved around the *place* of new persons, no genre was more important than regional writing. Regional writing is a genre that is on its face dedicated to elaborating the meaning of places and of the people who inhabited them. It is therefore the genre most efficient at discussing and mediating the place of social and cultural difference itself.

The cultural work of regional writing has not always been immediately accessible, because regional writing has suffered from two antithetical critical judgments. From its consolidation as a respectable genre in the late nineteenth century until its "rediscovery" in the mid-twentieth century, regional writing was associated with the interests of persons who, for a variety of reasons, were themselves considered minor or marginal. Women, minority writers, provincials, sexual dissidents, and village dwellers – all of whom have been understood to be outside of the normative category of American readers and writers – have been closely associated with the producers and the subject-matter of regional literature. But while regional writing has been partially understood as an expression of the interests of these varied and non-normative groups, it has also, paradoxically, been subject to a seemingly opposite reading. In aesthetic terms, regional writing has been considered a narrow, static, elegaic, eminently predictable genre.

Regionalism performed some of the most important cultural work of the nineteenth and early twentieth centuries, and it set the agenda for many of the cultural concerns about multiculturalism that we see in late twentieth-century literature. But it has only been very recently that it has been analyzed as participating in rather than commemorating its own cultural moment. Part of the long critical tradition of diminishing regional writing can be traced to a common error: the conflation of a regional *sensibility* with the work of regional writing itself. Because regional writing seems to be nostalgic, it has sometimes been understood as dealing with elements of culture whose power is diminishing. But, as I shall show, nothing could be further from the truth. Conflating regionalism's concerns with its formal properties has also led to another – odd and often unremarked – error: because critics believe they know what regional writing *is*, they believe they know what regional writing *does*. In other words, critics have taken regionalism at its word as a genre that deals with merely local or regional concerns. Few critics would argue that realism is "real" or naturalism "natural," but the term "regional" has maintained a privileged status as a transparent signifier. In fact regional writing, as I shall show, rather than shoring up and abetting the transparency of the term "regional," radically reconfigures it, making it as contentious as "the real" or "the natural."

Regionalism, by definition, concentrated on regions that were spatially remote from its largely urban, middle-class readers. But regional writing's focus on places that were geographically remote tends to translate into an understanding of those regions as *temporally* remote, too. Regional writing, then, seems to be about not only the folk ways of people inhabiting remote geographical places, but also, and more crucially, about fast-disappearing folk ways. Highlighting the genre's careful inscription of the cadences of village life, the dialect of remote village-dwellers, the rustic concerns of persons seemingly untouched or ignored by the spread of urbanization and modernization, critics have maintained an informal consensus that regional writing seeks to preserve what is in danger of being lost. As a chronicle of places that might be understood to be teetering on the edge of decline, regionalism has therefore been understood as a genre in decline itself. And because it seems to deal faithfully with the minute matters of everyday life, regional writing has been considered somewhat staid, even, according to some of its critics, formulaic. Yet it is partially because the production and the subject-matter of regional writing (associated with non-normative persons) and the formal attributes of regional writing (associated with a predictable and delicious kind of nostalgia) are so apparently contradictory that regional writing has been able to develop its most powerful cultural strategies of mediating cultural difference.

Regionalism is the signal genre of the late nineteenth century, not simply because it was the bearer of so much of its culture's otherwise half-expressed anxiety and wonder about the role of the strange and the local in its own self-conception, but because it was itself a genre dedicated to culturalizing all forms of difference. The cultural work of American regionalism is, paradoxically, its dedication to the importance of culture itself, its commitment to finding a language to express political and social difference in the discourse of cultural variation. How did a genre whose practitioners were almost always marginal figures in the literary marketplace, and whose subject-matter appeared to be so disengaged from its contemporary world, achieve such enormous cultural status? How did regionalism manage to comment, however obliquely, on the most sensitive political issues of its era? How has it helped critics reconceive the work of culture in the late nineteenth century? How has its sensibility helped to ground the work of marginal writers in the late twentieth century? How does regional writing help us to understand the culture that produced it? What are the lessons it can teach the late twentieth-century critics who have rediscovered it?

II

The heyday of regional writing was roughly between the Civil War and the early years of the twentieth century. Regional writers tended to work in the short-story form, and their work detailed the lives of characters from a variety of mainly rural geographical areas. Although its choice of subject-matter was often assumed by its contemporary readers to be a conservative or antimodern response to the material conflicts of an urbanizing nation, regional writing was deeply implicated in the social contests of its own era. Regional writing was produced at one of the most volatile moments in American history, and it was a form of writing particularly well suited to the task of processing and mediating the social and political conflicts that occurred with surprising rapidity at the turn of the century.

In the years following the Civil War and Reconstruction, the United States was engaged in two broad political endeavors. On the one hand, it was recovering from the sectionalism of the Civil War and was therefore formalizing the relationship of the states to a central government. On the other hand, it was extending its reach beyond its own western territory, making its first concerted ventures as a serious imperial power overseas. Both the project of nation-building and the project of imperialism involved often brutal confrontations with new people within and outside the borders of the United States.

Yet the consolidation of a national identity is a task that is always more or less underway in the United States. To say that regional writing was deeply implicated in the logic of nation-building is to read the past as if it were a smooth narrative with a single object. But nothing could be further from the truth. Depending on their different situations, people in the nineteenth century experienced the culture and politics of their nation very differently. All kinds of people in the United States found that their world was changing at an unprecedented rate, but those changes did not register in the same way for everyone. During the late nineteenth century, the country witnessed one of the most profound economic changes in its history, as an integrated and complex consolidation of capitalism happened unevenly across the nation. This ragged process of consolidation was enabled and spurred by technological advances in almost all forms of industry and communication. But while the emergence of a national economy promised to improve the lives of the nation's citizens by standardizing and rationalizing production and consumption, it also compounded the stark social and political inequalities that were troubling the nation in the political sphere.

Many of those inequalities were most visible in urban centers, as the economic growth of the late nineteenth century brought in its wake increased immigration, urbanization, and class divisions. These signs of inequality also became signs of urban decay, and produced powerful nativist sentiments among politicians and intellectuals. But cities did more than produce a sense of anxiety; they produced a powerful form of nostalgia. In the heart of an increasingly anonymous urban existence, many people began to see in the countryside the source of a national wholeness. Although they might never have lived there, or might have only recently left it for the economic opportunities of the city, a growing segment of the population yearned for the country. Rural centers became imaginatively valuable because they provided an image of what Raymond Williams (1977) has called "knowable communities" in contradistinction to the fragmented world of big cities. Nostalgic desire for the countryside had as its object an idealized rural life, in which traditional virtues always obtained, and in which its citizens knew their place, and knew the place of their compatriots. As Raymond Williams has also pointed out, such an image of the countryside covers over tensions within rural areas, and also covers over the very tensions between rural areas and urban centers that generate the need for an image of the rural in the first place.

The nostalgia that urbanization produced was not, however, the only response to the rapid changes of the nineteenth century. Although the economic shifts in the United States produced, as T. J. Jackson Lears (1981) has argued, a powerful sense of anxiety and unreality among its citizens, it also nourished a climate in which new kinds of narratives about identity and community could flourish. If urbanization motivated a sense that a generic version of "the country" represented a culture in itself, a "whole way of life" in the words of Raymond Williams, it also produced the sense that there were new and emerging cultures in the national polity. The public sphere – expanding, unevenly accessible, and always fractious and multiple – became the site of unprecedented demands for political and social recognition by immigrants, women and African-American citizens. Literary critics and historians like Amy Kaplan have argued that the nineteenth-century genre of realism, with its narrative complexity and detailed inventory of objects and desires, was crucially important in helping to mediate "competing social realities" (Kaplan 1988), but the genre of regionalism was engaged with narrating and transforming its culture's pleasures and anxieties in an equally complex way. Nation-building, immigration, and imperialism demanded mechanisms for making sense of foreigners, or for assimilating new kinds of people within a narrative of American identity. Regional writing was a genre that was especially interested in representing non-normative communities or cultures to a national audience.

How did regional writing come to occupy this role? How was it able to mediate between nostalgia for a lost rural culture and the simultaneous fascination with emerging cultures? One way to understand how it performed such a delicate narrative maneuver is to look at its history. We are used to thinking of regional writing as a genteel, staid, lyrical genre, but it is important to recognize that it developed from a more popular form. Before its publication in elite periodicals, regional writing circulated in local venues like newspapers and penny press publications. In the early and mid-nineteenth century, regional writing comprised tall tales, broad dialect sketches, and frontier stories. With the rise of national magazines and a national readership in the later part of the century, regional writing became more refined, shedding the rougher narrative signs of the frontier humor tradition. In the mid-nineteenth century, regional writing might have been emblematized by the broadly comic genre of Sut Lovingood's escapades on the frontiers of the known and knowable national world, but by the late nineteenth century it had reconsidered the very idea of the frontier. It had become the resolutely literate and literary testament to the lives of the "folk" who were in danger of disappearing in the face of the very nationalizing tendencies also responsible for bringing them to the notice of the national public. In the late nineteenth century, regional writing (especially the writing that we read today) circulated in some of the most elite periodicals in the nation, and when it was released in book form, it came out from equally elite presses. *Scribners*, *Harper's*, and the *Atlantic Monthly* all featured regional writing as staple work by the end of the nineteenth century. Indeed, regionalism as we know it today was a product of elite national periodicals; but more generally, its popularity can be traced to standardizing and nationalizing modes of production and consumption.

Within the arena of elite national periodicals, regional writing – regardless of the specificity of its setting, presumptively its most important feature – shared certain stylistic features. It is important to see that those stylistic features were developed in conversation with the periodicals, which made certain assumptions about the kinds of things their wealthy and privileged audiences wanted to read. The regional writing published in such periodicals generally narrated the story of an incident in the life of a town, or the surprising effect of an outsider on a village or town. It featured copious use of dialect and the strategic use of local, homespun wisdom. Its stories proceeded with a measured, elegiac tone; either the characters of the village were very old, and unable to regenerate or reproduce themselves, or the village folk were directly threatened by the incursions of modernity in some form or another. Regional stories in the *Atlantic* and its peer magazines tended to operate according to binaries such as nation and region, primitive and civilized, rural and urban, literary and vernacular, childhood and maturity, use and exchange, nature and culture, community and individualism. Because they represented a synthesis of these binaries, it became easy to read not only the cultural work of regional writing, but the cultural work of the region itself, as conservative. That is to say, regional writing seemed to be the antidote for the very predations of capital that generated it.

The formal features of regional writing that elite, nationalizing periodicals helped to standardize were also implicated in the volatile social and political anxieties that troubled social actors in the late nineteenth century. The culture that witnessed the solidification of regional writing as writing with more than regional scope and value also witnessed some of the most concentrated demographic shifts in the nation's history. Historians like John Higham (1963) report that the expansion of cities became a serious problem when the steady arrival of new immigrants began to tax the resources and governmental infrastructure of urban centers. Divisions between capital and labor, the growth of sedimented classes and class practices, the increasing professionalization of knowledge, the development of opportunities for women's advancement, the growth of urban popular cultures, the continued problem of the color line and the failures of Reconstruction, imperialist ventures into the southern hemisphere, and the gradual assimilation and incorporation of all territory and persons west of the Rockies made the idea of a national culture highly contested. All of these issues were covered in the journalistic portions of the periodicals in which regional writing appeared. Regional writing was not only part of the cultural conversation about these issues, it was, quite literally, proximate to these issues for readers. A reader could, in the same journal issue, imaginatively visit a region and then read about its contemporary race problems. It was precisely the energetic and seemingly ubiquitous claims of the local that made the national press at once so important, and so interested in negotiating the various particularized claims that local interests attempted to assert.

Together, the national magazines' construction of an enlightened and elite reading audience, and a series of demographic shifts in the United States, ensured the success of regional writing. This is because the periodicals marketed it as a genre devoted to describing new kinds of persons within a conventional epistemological form. This, at least, was the assessment of William Dean Howells. Howells, regionalism's biggest and most influential fan, used his editorial position at the *Atlantic* and at *Harper's* to publicize and disseminate the virtues of regional writing. In his monthly column, "From the Editor's Study," Howells proclaimed in his best Whitmanesque tone that "no one writer, no one book, represents [America] for that is not possible, our social and political decentralization forbids this, and may forever forbid it. But a great number of very good writers are instinctively striving to make each part of the country and each phase of our civilization known to all the other parts; and their work is not narrow in any feeble or vicious sense" (Howells 1983: 98). In perhaps his most famous passage from this column, he wrote that "Men are more like than unlike one another: let us make them know one another better, that they may be all humbled and strengthened with a sense of their fraternity" (Howells 1983: 96). In other words, regional writing would not only help to democratize the field of literature, it would actually help to advance democracy itself.

The democratic potential of regional fiction that so inspired Howell was not, however, the aspect of regional writing that was most celebrated by critics in the early part of the next century. When the first literary critics attempted to summarize the tradition of American literature and make a smooth narrative of the nation, they included nineteenth-century local color fiction. But despite their quite genuine-seeming admiration for much of the writing, these critics attended to its aesthetic dimensions first and only secondarily, if at all, to its social components. They therefore missed how completely regionalism's expansive social concerns and conventional narrative strategies enabled its innovative engagement with new cultural formations in its own day.

The first literary evaluations of local color writing focused on the nostalgia of the local colorists' stories. Vernon Parrington, Fred Lewis Pattee, and Werner Berthoff understood realism to be the most important genre of the late nineteenth century. Accordingly, in considering regional writing they focused on its relationship to realism, presenting it as a dimension of realism, a feminized version of its more serious, thematically capacious, and formally developed parent. The first generation of American literary critics thus did not read regionalism's innovative responses to the very themes that had preoccupied the realists. Early twentieth-century critics also made a series of distinctions about regional writers that has endured even in the work of later critics specifically set on refuting their claims.

Most seriously, critics like Parrington, Berthoff, and Pattee made distinctions between *kinds* of regional writers. Focusing on what they perceived to be purely aesthetic concerns (derived, as we have seen, from their primary allegiance to realism), they privileged Sarah Orne Jewett above all, and tended to concentrate on the work of women local colorists. For example, Werner Berthoff, who devotes a good deal of *The Ferment of Realism* to dialect fiction and local color, sees regionalism as an ideologically transparent genre. He argues that the best local colorists are "historians" (1981: 94), and explains that "at its most compelling, American local-color realism . . . points toward an imaginative sociology that is at once objective and visionary. The images it yields up compose the fragments of a book of the people, an essential history of their lives' common conditioning. Paradoxically, at this level of realization the particular local circumstances begin to appear incidental. The same stories are told, in more or less detail, on all sides" (Berthoff 1981: 100).

Fred Lewis Pattee argues in a chapter entitled "Recorders of New England Decline" that the best local colorists were women, and that, despite the polish of their art, the power of their fiction derives from its emotional intensity; those writers like Sarah Orne Jewett who could intellectualize their subjects are faintly disdained as too careful of their art, as though they had betrayed the transparency expected of the regional recorder. Of Harriet Beecher Stowe's local color, he writes, "she wrote simple little stories of commonplace people in a commonplace environment, and she treated them with the sympathy of one who shares, rather than as one who looks down upon a spectacle . . . there is no bookish flavor about the stories" (Pattee 1915: 230). Of Sarah Orne Jewett, he writes, "she is a writer of little books and short stories, the painter of a few subjects in a provincial little area" (p. 234). Alice Brown, who "if she were to paint the picture at all she must paint it as it was in her heart. To add to it or to subtract from it were to violate truth itself" (p. 241) is an example of someone who balances women's need to express themselves emotionally with regionalism's project of faithful, nearly photographic representation. Critiques of women's local color writing served an odd double function; by imagining women as the finest of the local colorists, and by imagining local color as a subset of realism, they divided nineteenth-century literary history in terms of gender. Local color was thus consigned to be the literary version of the housework of realism, its cultural work reduced to mere preservation.

It was precisely this categorization that made regional writing ripe for re-evaluation by feminist literary critics. Pointing to the conjunction between the domestic and the feminine, between the diminution of regionalism's subject-matter and the perceived narrowness of its practitioners' lives, feminist critics argued that regional writing ought not to be evaluated against standards inimical to its subject-matter and hostile to its creators. Feminist critics argued that regional writing was not a failed version of realism, but a genre with its own aesthetic concerns, narrative strategies, and broad-ranging political ramifications. In this reading, regional writing opened up a forgotten or suppressed view of the nineteenth century in which women and their "proper sphere" had been actively contested. Marjorie Pryse, Sandra Zagarell, Josephine Donovan, Judith Fetterley, and Elizabeth Ammons, among others, used regional writing to challenge the implicit gender, class, and racial bias of the American canon, arguing that regional writing itself was an incipient critique of the values of that canon. Feminist retrievals of individual women regional writers focused on the alternative literary tradition that women's regionalism might help critics to imagine. The values of such a tradition – community, nature, family, cooperation, communication, and a tradition of feminine knowing – are alternatives to the values of an urban, competitive, male-dominated sphere. If regionalism posited such altern-ative values in its texts, it also, for these critics, helped to redefine the importance of a feminine tradition of women's writing, moving to its center people and places who had once been considered marginal. Indeed, one of the most important texts in the recovery of nineteenth-century regional writing was the 1992 Norton anthology, *American Women Regionalists*, edited by Judith Fetterley and Marjorie Pryse.

Such a project of reclamation did much to reintroduce a new generation of readers to regional fiction by women, and it made great strides in demonstrating that regional writing, in its major texts, achieved more than a nostalgic rendition of the lost world. Judith Fetterley has recently argued that regionalism's commitment to women's experiences makes it an "unAmerican" genre (Fetterley 1994). In this view, it is hard to overestimate how deeply indebted to feminist criticism recent readings of regional writing's relationship to nationalism really are. The most recent critiques of regionalism have, each in its own way, been predicated on the implicit belief that regional writing was far more than a nostalgic genre. Eric Sundquist and Amy Kaplan have argued that regional writing was one of the signal genres of the nation's consolidation of its territories in the late nineteenth century, and that it was therefore deeply implicated in a corollary logic of empire. Sundquist argues, for example, that "in the realism of both city and country, there is an anthropological dimension in which new 'regions' are opened to fictional or journalistic exploration and analysis" (1988: 503). Richard Brodhead has followed the logic of regionalism as a form of cultural imperialism by arguing that regional writing was intimately related to "the post-bellum elite and its adherents [who] made other ways of life the objects of their admiration and desire, objects which they then felt free to annex; the upper class vacation, thus, entails crossing out of one's own culture into another culture (not just place) to the end of living another way of life. Regionalism can be guessed to have ministered especially effectively to the imagination of acquisitiveness" (Brodhead 1993: 133).

Even more recently, critics have argued that regional writing helped to develop complex strategies for representing and circulating emerging forms of identity. Kate McCullough (1999) has argued that regional writing helps to construct sexual difference as one of its most powerful narrative engines because it privileges women's relationships. Gavin Jones, in his study of dialect literature (1999), has examined the ways in which attention to distinct, carefully transcribed accents and their assignation to liminal figures like immigrants pervades the nineteenth century's understanding of a normative "American" identity. The arguments of the newest generation of regional critics maintain that the idea of the local needs to be expanded to encompass all forms of deviation from the normative. Regional fiction's idea of the local, therefore, has not only expanded in the reading of contemporary critics, it has become one precursor of what we might think of as identity. In this view, regional fiction does not decide on who has the "right" or the "best" or the "real" identity; rather, it understands those notions as contingent, as meaningful only locally.

Regional writers, for better or for worse, helped to introduce the production and consumption of local differences and local identities into a national vocabulary. In this way regional writing was able to figure difference as both a commodity and a positive value in itself. But regional writing also helped to introduce other kinds of "new" people to the nation. As Richard Brodhead has pointed out, regional writing offered an access point to writers who were previously marginalized in American letters. Regionalism's ability to broker the emergence of new authors is a crucial factor in understanding its cultural work. Indeed, regional writing's ability to represent new people extends to the very persons who were engaged in writing regional fiction.

Regional writing came from a diverse set of geographical locations, but it was also the product of writers who had not previously enjoyed especial cultural status in American letters. A mere sampling of standard writers of regional fiction demonstrates its reach: Bret Harte, Sarah Orne Jewett, Harriet Beecher Stowe, Mary E. Wilkins Freeman, Rose Terry Cooke, Mary Noailles Murfree, Siu Sin Far, Alice Cary, Hamlin Garland, Edward Eggleston, Grace King, Kate Chopin, George Washington Cable, Edward Kirkland, Gertrude Atherton, Alice Brown, Charles Chesnutt, Joel Chandler Harris, Thomas Nelson Page, and Mary Halleck Foote, among others, released collections of short stories and regional sketches in the late nineteenth century. Their work ranged in setting from the New England scenes conventionally associated with local color to the mountains of Tennessee, to the bayou of Louisiana, to the empty plains of the Midwest, to the wilds of California.

While many of the writers I have listed secured and maintained some level of fame, at least as fame might be measured by appearances on university syllabi, many of them have fallen into obscurity. Nonetheless, it is important to note not only the geographical distribution they represent, but their distribution in terms of gender, social background, and racial identification. Certainly, the late nineteenth century saw an increase in the number of writers across the board – and also, because of the explosion of venues in which writers could publish their work, an increase in the number of writers who were professionalized – that is to say, who made a living from writing. Many of these wrote in a kind of literary factory system, and were paid by the word (the dime novel, for example, was a genre especially hospitable to members of the emerging middle class who had not had the benefits of a Boston-bred, Harvard-educated youth), and still others made a credible living by writing sentimental or popular literature (genres especially hospitable, but by no means limited to, women writers).

While regional writing took up the question of social difference within its own major texts, it was also deeply involved in suggesting that racial, gender, and even sexual difference had a place within the literary marketplace. Because it was a genre that was, above all, dedicated to elaborating the day-to-day lives of the citizens of discrete, quasi-rural locales, one of the most distinctive textual marks of local color fiction was its strong investment in reproducing the "folk" of any given location. While regional writing's subject-matter, then, tracks the meeting line of the nation's immigrants and the timeless folk in whom it has a larger interest, its marketing tracks the line between the nation's solid citizens and the citizens on its periphery. Regionalism was overdetermined as the "natural" home for variously marginalized writers. Indeed, it was a genre in which marginalization itself was a positive virtue.

Of what exactly was the regional writer's value made? Regional writing afforded a special kind of authorial identity to its writers – personal authority, personal expertise, and authenticity. In an era in which educational and professional opportunities for women and minorities were limited, regional writing became a venue in which they could advance their own expertise in what it was like to be themselves. The desire for authentic experience, according to historian T. J. Jackson Lears, underwrote much of the late nineteenth century's cultural preoccupations. But regionalism was a genre especially important in mediating a larger cultural desire for the real. As I have said, it gave its practitioners the ability to market their very difference from the mainstream as the source of their writerly value; but it also gave audiences, preoccupied with national problems regarding the proper constitution of the citizen, a way to negotiate fear of foreigners alongside a romantic longing for rural countrymen. Regional writers, seeking to enter a national literary marketplace, found that they were in possession of a number of particularly marketable kinds of differences. As non-standard Americans, they were in a fascinating position. Unsurprisingly, many of them took up exactly those problems in the constitution of communities of which they were understood to be the arbiters. Although regional writing as a genre extended the authority of personal experience to its practitioners, we should not simply see them as embracing that authority unproblematically. While audiences and editors may have invested a certain kind of personal authority in regional writers, those writers often resisted such schematic readings of "real" and "unreal" and "insider" and "outsider."

Take, for example, the work of Mary E. Wilkins Freeman, lauded by many critics, even those who diminish regional writing, as one of the technically finest artists of the genre. In her regional stories, communities are initially unable to accommodate the demands of the misfits within them. Often focusing on single women who have slender or no means of support, Freeman's stories question the limits of communities that are assumed to be democratic. She queries, in other words, the ability of any community to absorb members who challenge its sense of who counts. And yet Mary Wilkins Freeman was slyly aware of the conventions of the very genre in which she first rose to national prominence. In her novella "The Jamesons" (see Freeman 2000), she organizes the events of the region in question around the arrival of an outsider who seeks to alert the townsfolk to the value of their rural community. Schooled in an urban style of reading regions, the officious but good-hearted interloper, Mrs. Jameson, appears to her amused neighbors as an outlandish parody. No longer a normative urban citizen, the visitor's very identification with an abstract ideal of regionalism seals her separation from the community. And yet, at the end of the text, the outsider becomes one of the community because her daughter marries a local boy. Mrs. Jameson's inclusion in the region is not, therefore, founded on the endogamous logic of blood ancestry, but on an exogamous logic of intermarriage. Even regions have immigrants, in this reading, and can learn to accommodate them.

Such commentaries on the role of the region in conducting fine and complex negotiations about past and present, outsider and insider, the real and the inauthentic are not unusual in regional fiction. Because it is concerned with place, regional writing is deeply concerned with who is a native and who a stranger. This narrative concern is often manifested in the relationship between urban narrators and regional folk. Sarah Orne Jewett, for example, while often lauded by feminist critics for her ability to figure a world in which "feminine" virtues of compassion and care take precedence over such masculinized traits as individualism and aggression, is deeply concerned with basic issues of belonging. Her most famous work, *The Country of the Pointed Firs*, is constructed around vignettes dramatizing how easily strangers and natives alike can find themselves outside of their communities. This general textual interest extends to a more specific sense of inclusion and exclusion: many of the text's most contentious characters are constructed through racial discourses, and they therefore challenge the ways in which the novel's community comes to understand on whom it should lavish its care.

The cultural work of regionalism in deciding how communities are constituted and how the value of local persons ought to be determined extends to another crucial element of regional writing. Earlier in this essay, I said that I would tell two stories in order to illuminate the cultural work of American regionalism. In the first story, I looked at the history of regional writing, and its changing critical reception; in the second story, I looked at the terms of its recovery in the late twentieth century. That recovery, focused on the retrieval of what had been forgotten, alerts us to another, crucial element of that second story. Regionalism was one of the first genres to think about the meaning of difference itself, and it often understood individual regions as very different from the nostalgic "home" or "childhood," to use Susan Stewart's terms, of the nation. It understood regions as internally complex, as including within them their own secret or suppressed histories of racial or ethnic difference. We can see, for example, the important role of racial difference in the work of regionalists as diverse as Sarah Orne Jewett, George Washington Cable, Kate Chopin, and Hamlin Garland.

Following the suggestion of Richard Brodhead and Eric Sundquist, among others, it is therefore important to look not only at the ways in which much regional writing devotes itself to understanding the variety within even presumably small and homogeneous local communities, but also at how it provided a way for ethnic writers and subjects to enter into the mainstream of American literature. Writers like Siu Sin Far (Edith Maude Eaton), most famous for the collection of stories *Mrs. Spring Fragrance* (1912), and Charles Chesnutt, for example, seized the conventions of regional writing to introduce themselves to the literary market. Doubtless, regional writing's stylistic conventions softened some of the more radical critiques that Chesnutt, for one, went on to make in his later long fiction. Even if regional writing as it was created by the national periodicals could not accommodate the "real" of ethnic writers, it offered them an initial entryway into the world of publication. As Chesnutt found, writers might find themselves reduced to a single explanatory element, like race; but for others this was less of a problem. Abraham Cahan, for example, was "discovered" by William Dean Howells. During his long tenure as a political activist and editor of the *Jewish Daily Forward*, Cahan also wrote what we might think of as regional fiction. Like Howells, he understood it as a way to address himself to an audience

already primed to consume his "authentic" culture. But because regional writing –
predicated on faithful representations of regions – made a homology between the
value of what a writer knew and who a writer was, it provided an initial, if imperfect,
way for the literary market to recognize and value identities that still struggled for
representation in other areas.

III

The vitality of regional writing makes it an especially useful genre through which to
consider the relationship of literary forms to the audiences that read them. It helps to
tell the story of literature's relationship to culture because it indexes the constantly
changing interaction between literary forms and a broader discussion over what constitutes "America" in an American literary tradition. Despite the nostalgia that seems
to motivate critical work on regional writing (a nostalgia that mimics the tone of
much of its object), regional writing has never disappeared. It has retained a toehold
in the American canon throughout the nineteenth and twentieth centuries, and has,
for some critics, become the source of the most productive contemporary ruminations on imperialism, cosmopolitanism, nationalism, and the spread of a potentially
homogenizing global economy. Though it is these very elements that are often
charged with threatening the local culture that regionalism represents, regional writing rarely dismisses or ignores them; on the contrary, it is a genre constituted by the
desire to address, confront, critique, and even transform them. Like the places and
people it portrays, regional writing has proven itself to be remarkably enduring and
flexible because it is capable of accommodating and transforming the very elements
that seemed to most threaten it.

Regional writing helped to imagine a nation that was composed of discrete and
complex subcultures. In doing so, it worked to represent all forms of social difference
as dynamic cultural variations that could be assimilated into an idea of Americanness
and that, according to its logic, already traversed the idea of the nation. Regional
writing is therefore one of the first genres that tried to understand the nation itself as
an ideologically inflected cultural construct, and that tried to supplement the official
story of what counted as American by providing "unofficial" histories of the nation's
inhabitants.

It is a large claim to say that regional writing, so often seen as the dreamy
spinster-lady of the nineteenth century, is vitally concerned with demystifying the
nation's understanding of itself. It is an especially large claim to make on behalf of a
style of writing and a genre that does not, compared to other genres like sentimental
fiction or even realism, its more esteemed colleague, comprise a very large number of
texts. If regionalism's focus on the idea of community and the place of nonstandard
individuals within various communities helped to transform the terms of the late
nineteenth century's discussion of the meaning of place and local cultures, it also
provided a map to help us follow some of the ways in which cultural relativism and

social difference were imagined. Indeed, it gives us a way to understand some of the deep concerns of our own era about the meaning of the local. Just as the late nineteenth century was experiencing an erosion of what it considered national wholeness (an erosion, as we have said, that was always more or less operative in the history of the United States), it was also experiencing the influx of new people. As I understand the work of regionalist fiction, its most powerful cultural work was the culturalization of difference itself; and the transformation of political difference into cultural differences that could be managed is its most important legacy to the United States.

While the cultural work of late nineteenth-century regional writing is specific to its own place and its own time, it can be understood as having helped to inaugurate and solidify some of the concerns that most troubled the late twentieth century. Specifically, the question of identity and cultural difference links late twentieth-century literature to its nineteenth-century predecessor. Like the late nineteenth century, the late twentieth century was troubled by claims for recognition on the part of figures who have been seen as "alien" or as somehow minor. Late twentieth-century literature is far more hospitable to cultural, social, and racial difference than was that of the nineteenth century. Can we make a connection between regional fiction's strategies and the strategies employed by contemporary fiction that discusses difference and identity?

If we understand regionalism's narrative strategies of faithful representation of regional dwellers as an attempt to understand and re-imagine, rather than simply assimilate and preserve, social differences, the answer is yes. Contemporary fiction about regional, racial, or ethnic concerns may or may not have been written by people who have read the small corpus of regional writing from the late nineteenth century. But that genre nevertheless helped to establish a small, stylized strategy for understanding local concerns, and contemporary discourses about multiculturalism are in its debt. Regionalism was fascinated by – and fascinated its audiences because of – the very fact of social difference itself. Over and over again, regional texts told the story of local differences, and told them in such a way that such a story would become part of a larger story about who "we" were. Regionalism traced a multitude of origins for the United States: it sometimes located the past of the nation in New England, but it more often showed that the nation's past was fractured by a series of hidden histories, ranging from those of the African slaves who populated the stories of the Southern regionalists to those of the German and Scandinavian farmers who populated the stories of Midwestern regionalists. Fundamentally challenging a coherent definition of what it meant to be an "American," regionalism provided a vocabulary to account for and to culturalize difference.

There is no doubt that it was not the only available vocabulary, and there is no doubt that it was insufficient and often problematic. But it is a legacy that has meant a great deal to the development in the late twentieth century of a literary tradition centralizing sexual, gender, regional, and racial difference. In an age in which an increasing global circulation of commodities and ideas has not mitigated fundamental structural inequalities – has not, in other words, made everyone equally valuable – interest in regions and regional identity is on the rise. As in the nineteenth century, regions might be figured as the sites of nostalgia, as the sources of an imaginary wholeness and simplicity, or imagined as a complex source of positive, rather than strictly nostalgic and conservative, resistance against the perceived anonymity of capitalism. What regions mean and do varies from person to person, from era to era; but in the late twentieth century, as in the late nineteenth, regions are imaginatively linked with particularized kinds of knowledges. The local knowledges that regionalism first helped to publicize fracture any monolithic narrative of American literature and American identity. Because it held open the meaning of America and Americanness, regional writing helped to create a way to understand and value social differences, and helped to establish a way of imagining communities that interrupted even as they sustained a national culture.

REFERENCES AND FURTHER READING

Ammons, E. E. (1983). "Going in Circles: The Female Geography of Jewett's *Country of the Pointed Firs.*" *Studies in the Literary Imagination* 16, 83–92.

Berthoff, W. (1981). *The Ferment of Realism: American Literature, 1884–1919.* Cambridge, Mass.: Cambridge University Press. (First publ. 1965.)

Brodhead, R. (1993). *Cultures of Letters: Scenes of Reading and Writing in Nineteenth-Century America.* Chicago: University of Chicago Press.

Far, S. S. (1995). *Mrs. Spring Fragrance and Other Writings,* ed. A. Ling and A. White-Parks. Urbana: University of Illinois Press.

Fetterley, J. (Dec. 1994). "'Not in the Least American': Nineteenth-century Literary Regionalism." *College English* 56, 877–95.

Fetterley, J. (1998). "On 'Reading New Readings of Regionalism.'" *Legacy: A Journal of American Women Writers* 15: 1, 45–52.

Fetterley, J., and Pryse, M., eds. (1992). *American Women Regionalists, 1850–1910.* New York: Norton.

Foote, S. (2001). *Regional Fictions: Culture and Identity in Nineteenth-Century American Literature.* Madison: University of Wisconsin Press.

Freeman, M. E. W. (2000). *A New England Nun and Other Stories,* ed. S. Zagarell. New York: Viking Penguin. (First publ. 1891.)

Gellner, E. (1983). *Nations and Nationalism.* Oxford: Blackwell.

Higham, J. (1963). *Strangers in the Land: Patterns of American Nativism, 1860–1925.* New York: Atheneum.

Hobsbawm, E. (1990). *Nations and Nationalism since 1780: Programme, Myth, Reality.* Cambridge: Cambridge University Press.

Howard, J. (1994). "Sarah Orne Jewett and the Traffic in Words." In *New Essays on* The Country of the Pointed Firs, ed. J. Howard. Cambridge: Cambridge University Press.

Howells, W. D. (1898). "Confessions of a Summer Colonist." *Atlantic Monthly* 82 (May), 443, 742–50.

Howells, W. D. (1983). "Editor's Study Columns." In *Editor's Study,* ed. J. W. Simpson Troy. New York: Whitson Publishing.

Jewett, S. O. (1981). *The Country of the Pointed Firs and Other Stories,* ed. M. E. Chase. New York: Norton. (First publ. 1896.)

Jones, G. (1999). *Strange Talk: The Politics of Dialect Literature in Gilded Age America.* Berkeley: University of California Press.

Kaplan, A. (1988). *The Social Construction of American Realism.* Chicago: University of Chicago Press.

Lears, T. J. J. (1981). *No Place of Grace: Antimodernism and the Transformation of American Culture, 1880–1920.* New York: Pantheon.

McCullough, K. (1999). *Regions of Identity: The Construction of America in Women's Fiction, 1885–1914.* Stanford: Stanford University Press.

Morgan, P. (1887). "The Problems of Rural New England." *Atlantic Monthly* 79 (May), 465, 577–87.

Pattee, F. L. (1915). *A History of American Literature since 1870.* D. Appleton-Century Co. Inc.

Pryse, M. (1998). "Sex, Class, and 'Category Crisis': Reading Jewett's Transitivity." *American Literature* 70, 517–49.

Sanborn, A. (1897). "The Future of Rural New England." *Atlantic Monthly* 79 (July), 477, 577–98.

Stewart, S. (1991). *Crimes of Writing: Problems in the Containment of Representation.* New York: Oxford University Press.

Sundquist, E. (1988). "Realism and Regionalism." In Emory Elliott (ed.), *The Columbia Literary History of the United States*, 501–24. New York: Columbia University Press.

Trent, W. P. (1897). "Tendencies of Higher Life in the South." *Atlantic Monthly* 79 (June), 476, 766–78.

Ulrich, L. T. (2001). *The Age of Homespun: Objects and Stories in the Creation of an American Myth.* New York: Knopf.

Williams, R. (1977). *The Country and the City.* New York: Oxford University Press.

Zagarell, S. (1994). "*Country*'s Portrayal of Community and the Exclusion of Difference." In *New Essays on* The Country of the Pointed Firs, ed. J. Howard. Cambridge: Cambridge University Press.

3

Letting Go our Grand Obsessions: Notes toward a New Literary History of the American Frontiers

Annette Kolodny

Situada entre fronteras, en los problemáticos intersticios culturales y lingüísticos creados
en el choque e interacción de varias culturas en tensión.
        Carmen M. Del Río, "Chicana Poets: Re-visions from the Margin"

A history may be conceptualized as an ideologically or imaginatively governed catalog
of figurative elements. The catalog is inconceivable in the absence of ideology, and a
shift, or rupture, in ideological premises promotes strikingly new figurations.
        Houston A. Baker, Jr., "Archeology, Ideology, and African American Discourse"

Those societies which cannot combine reverence to their symbols with freedom of
revision must ultimately decay either from anarchy, or from the slow atrophy of a life
stifled by useless shadows.
        Alfred North Whitehead, *Symbolism: Its Meaning and Effect*

On the sunny morning of October 4, 1553, in a gesture meant to translate physical
borders into cultural and political boundaries, an old man carrying "'his bow and
arrows, and a wooden staff with a very elaborate handle'" "drew a line on the ground
as a demarcation, threatening death to any intruder who dared cross it." Impressive
in his "'black robe . . . studded with pearls, and surrounded by dogs, birds and
deer,'" the old man nonetheless faced a formidable adversary: an exploratory expedition dispatched by the Spanish adventurer Nuño Beltrán de Guzmán, notorious
for pillaging the villages of the Indies and enslaving all captives. Tracing the first
contacts between Europeans and the Yaqui nation, historian Evelyn Hu-DeHart has
translated the anonymous first-person expedition report. "'Aiming our heaviest cannon at them,'" the Spaniards attacked the warriors who accompanied their robed
leader and, in the words of the Spanish scribe, quickly concluded that "'These Indians
fought as well and as energetically as any Indians I have seen since I have been in the
Indies, and I have seen none fight better than they.'" Deciding that they could not

afford to sustain additional heavy losses, "the Spaniards turned back," according to Hu-DeHart (1981: 15–16).

> While one motley band of Spanish slavers was driven off, however, the mark intended to inscribe inviolable borders finally came to denote permeable margins. By the 1620s, Jesuit missionaries had established churches and schools within Yaqui enclaves and translated rituals, the mass for the dead, and various prayers into the Yaqui language. As anthropologist Edward Spicer has noted, "the ideas in these prayers were therefore a part of Yaqui thought in the Yaqui language." (1981: 326)

At the same time, *maehtom*, Yaqui lay priests, were developing a species of priestly literacy that preserved elements of distinctly precontact religious beliefs and involved writing in Spanish, Latin, and Yaqui. The old man's line, in short, was quickly contained within a zone of successive interpenetrations which – on all sides – were variously hostile, welcomed, policed, suppressed, acknowledged, and subversive.

To recover and reconstruct the linguistic and textual encodings of seriate interpenetrations such as these would allow us, at last, to embark on a long-overdue literary history of the American frontiers. My aim here is to initiate just such a project. Building on the work of Norman Grabo, William Spengemann, Francis Jennings, William Cronon, Carolyn Merchant, Tzvetan Todorov, and Howard Lamar and Leonard Thompson,[1] I propose extending the implications of their investigations beyond European colonial beginnings; and, in the case of the historians, I want to reinforce their debt to concentrated textual analysis – all in an effort to reconceive what we mean by "history" when we address literary history, and to reconceptualize what we mean by "frontier" when we consider the Americas. My strategy is to offer an approach that allows for a more inclusive interdisciplinarity. This approach mitigates the condescension with which we have traditionally treated the impact of region on the construction of literary texts, and at the same time frees American literary history from the persistent theories of continuity that have made it virtually impossible to treat frontier materials as other than marginalia or cultural mythology. For scholars of early American literature – the field in which I was trained – my approach necessarily complicates the notion of *earliness* but, at the same time, promises liberation from the stultifying habit of regarding that literature merely as precursor to an authentic literature yet to follow, or as transition pieces between British forebears and American identities.

To effect this project will require that we let go our grand obsessions with narrowly geographic or strictly chronological frameworks and instead recognize "frontier" as a locus of first cultural contact, circumscribed by a particular physical terrain in the process of change *because of* the forms that contact takes, all of it inscribed by the collisions and interpenetrations of language. My paradigm would thus have us interrogating language – especially as hybridized style, trope, story, or structure – for the complex intersections of human encounters with other humans and with the physical environment. It would enjoin us to see the ways in which the collision of languages encodes the physical terrain as just as much a player in the drama of contact as the human participants, with the landscape variously enabling, thwarting, or even evoking human actions and desires.

The Yaqui "Testamento" provides an apt example. As Larry Evers and Felipe Molina speculate in the introduction to their translation, "some time perhaps long after the Yaqui elder inscribed that line on the earth before the Spanish slave-traders, other Yaquis wrote a narrative on paper as a way of re-inscribing the same boundary."[2] Describing the origins of what the Yaquis have come to call the Holy Dividing Line, the "Testamento" represents what Evers and Molina call "a layered discourse in a combination of Spanish and Yaqui," with inflections from Latin and Hebrew. At the heart of the "Testamento" is the authorizing of Yaqui land boundaries and the prophesied threats to their security. Prophets, or originating elders, sing "the Holy Dividing Line" into being and then predict that

> in the course of some years will come
> some wicked men from
> Gethsemane, that is New Spain, those men,
> the image of Lucifer, are
> invaders and enemies of our life and they do not respect
> others and they will keep these properties.
> . . .
> They will ask you: "Whose land is this kingdom?"

Clearly, as Evers and Molina point out, establishing the boundaries of Yaqui lands has become "part of a story that evokes the Bible as much as any aboriginal Yaqui narratives." It thus participates in a long tradition "of cross-cultural interpretation" in which the Yaquis write and rewrite "their own culture in a dialogue with . . . European history and Christian religion" – and, I would add, in dialogue with European concepts of ownership and landholding.

In asserting a mythic history for legalistic claims to "our poor inheritance, the earth that was given," the Yaqui "Testamento" renders the landscape ardently, albeit passively, possessed. In other texts that I would designate as integral to a literary history of the frontiers, by contrast, the physical terrain becomes an "active partner" in Carolyn Merchant's terms, "acquiesce[ing] to human interventions through resilience and adaptation or 'resist[ing]' human actions through mutation and evolution." In the works of Willa Cather, just as in Leslie Marmon Silko's *Ceremony*, "nature . . . is not passive, but," as Merchant describes it, "an active complex that participates in change over time and responds to human-induced change" (Merchant 1989: 23, 8). Indeed, Alexandra Bergson confronts the palpably sentient presence of the Nebraska prairies in Cather's *O Pioneers!* (1913), while what Tayo comes to understand as part of his healing in *Ceremony* is that he loves, and is loved by, the mountains that surround his New Mexico pueblo: "They were close; they had always been close. And he loved them then as he had always loved them, the feeling pulsing over him as strong as it had ever been. They loved him that way; he could still feel the love they had for him . . . This feeling was their life, vitality locked deep in blood memory, and the people were strong, and the fifth world endured, and nothing was ever lost as long as the love remained." When the bond between the people and their land is threatened by uranium mining, by atomic testing laboratories "deep in the Jemez Mountains, on land the Government took from Cochiti Pueblo," and by the Los Alamos installations, fencing off the "mountain canyon where the shrine of the twin mountain lions had always been" (Silko 1978: 230, 257) Silko provides story and symbol for Merchant's insistence that "the relation between human beings and the nonhuman world is . . . reciprocal" (Merchant 1989: 8).

Although the figurative elements of such contacts do not concern them, historians Howard Lamar and Leonard Thompson similarly "regard a frontier not as a boundary or line, but as a territory or zone of interpenetration between . . . previously distinct societies." For them, "there are three essential elements in any frontier situation . . . : territory; two or more initially distinct peoples; and the process by which the relations among the peoples in the territory begin, develop, and eventually crystallize" (Lamar and Thompson, eds. 1981: 7, 8). My own definition incorporates theirs, asserting that there always stands at the heart of frontier literature – even when disguised or repressed – a physical terrain that, for at least one group of participants, is newly encountered and is undergoing change because of that encounter; a currently indigenous population and at least one group of newcomers or "intruders"; and the collisions and negotiations of distinct cultural groups as expressed "en el choque e interacción" of languages and texts (Del Río 1990: 431). Whether written or oral, the texts that comprise this new literary history of the frontiers would be identified by their articulation of these initial encounters. Thus, the literature of the frontiers may be identified by its encoding of some specifiable first moment in the evolving dialogue between different cultures and languages, and in their engagement with one another and with the physical terrain.

The materials that qualify as the primary or proto-texts of frontier literary history would be those that themselves participate in that first moment of contact – for example, the Eskimo legends of the Tunnit, the strangers who came from afar and erected stone buildings;[3] Christopher Columbus's "Letter to Lord Sanchez . . . on his first voyage"; Amerigo Vespucci's *Mundus Novus*; Gaspar Pérez de Villagrá's *Historia de la Nueva Mexico*; William Bradford's *History of Plimmoth Plantation*; Mary White Rowlandson's captivity narrative; and Daniel Boone's putative autobiography. The secondary – but no less important – texts of frontier literary history would be those composed after the fact, reworking for some alternative audience or future generation the scene and meaning of original contact, or "recovering" the primary texts so as to give them new readings in a newly imagined and reconstructed past. Examples in English include Joel Barlow's *Columbiad* (1807) and even J. N. Barker's high-pitched melodrama *The Indian Princess; or, La Belle Sauvage* (1808), the first play by a US author to focus on Indian characters. Reworking incidents from John Smith's *General History of Virginia* (1624), a primary text in my schema, *The Indian Princess* is also the first play to utilize the story of Pocahontas. Among novels that represent examples of significant secondary texts in English, I would certainly include James Fenimore Cooper's Leatherstocking series; Willa Cather's *Death Comes for the Archbishop*; and Leslie Silko's *Ceremony*, with its subtext evoking a twentieth-century nuclear culture intruding itself into the sacred sites of the Indian Southwest.

What makes the paradigm so appealing is that English texts, by themselves, could never constitute a sufficient history. Indeed, the new frontier literary history that I envisage might well begin with a comparative analysis of the Eskimo legends of the Tunnit and the Icelandic Norse sagas detailing the discovery and attempted colonization of Vinland, on the North American coast, by Scandinavian explorers from Greenland and Iceland about the year 1000. Recording clashes between Vikings and "Skraellings" (a pejorative Norse term for the indigenous peoples), the sagas describe "a fair, well-wooded country" and the appeal "of all the valuable products of the land, grapes, and all kinds of game and fish." The dramatic elements center on the frustrated attempts of the Skraellings to barter with the Europeans, and the Europeans' frustration at the fact that "neither (people) could understand the other's language."[4]

Without question, a revised literary history of the frontiers would also include the foundational corpus of the hispanoamerican written tradition, the *crónicas de Indias*, with texts by *criollo* and *mestizo* authors alike.[5] Examples include not only the letters and diaries of the more notorious explorers and conquistadores from Columbus on but, as well, the journal of Cabeza de Vaca's wanderings from Florida to Texas (1555), Bartolemé de las Casas' *Historia de las Indias* (1527–61), and Gaspar Pérez de Villagrá's *History of New Mexico* (1610), arguably the first epic poem composed in what is now the United States.[6] A key text for examining the way in which frontiers inevitably give rise to hybridized forms would be the massive two-volume *Royal Commentaries of the Incas and General History of Peru* (published in Spain in separate segments in 1609 and 1616–17). Claiming noble Spanish blood from his father and descent from the royal Inca line on his maternal side, Garcilaso de la Vega, El Inca, intentionally took on the name of the great medieval Spanish warrior-poet Garcilaso de la Vega (c.1502–36) in order to compose a text that at once justifies and mourns the demise of the Inca empire. By employing narrative structures from Incan *haravi* (oral verse histories), chivalric romance, and European discovery narratives, the Inca Garcilaso pits the narrative impulse of the Quechua *haravi* chants to celebrate the victories and glories of the ancestors against a distinctly Spanish golden age impulse to retell epic victories and reveal epic betrayals:

> When the Spaniards saw how generously Titu Atauchi and his companions had treated them while in confinement, and how attentively they had been cared for and given their freedom, gifts of gold, silver, and precious stones, and provided with a large escort of natives to accompany them back to Spanish quarters, though the Indians might easily have cut them to pieces out of rage and indignation at the death of their king, and finally how the Indians asked for negotiations on such fair and reasonable terms, they were confounded and amazed. (de la Vega 1966: II, 745)

Moreover, like the (presumably) later and much shorter Yaqui "Testamento," de la Vega's *Royal Commentaries* demonstrates the dynamic and reciprocal relationship between a prior oral tradition and the intrusion of a written literature. The oral (or folkloric) elements have not been simply appropriated or incorporated into the European structures. Rather, their inclusion has fundamentally altered the narrative patterns that previously governed the written genres.

Similarly, the moral dialogues composed by mendicant friars in the Nahuatl language would become frontier texts. In the years following the Spanish conquest, from Mexico through the present day Southwest, missionaries rendered catechistic texts into language and terminology by which (they hoped) Old World Catholicism might convert New World Aztec thought. Resembling no catechism then available in Latin or Spanish, but decidedly influenced by the traditions of Aztec "flower songs," these texts offer a rich body of proto-literary material that amply plays out – for both Spanish and Nahuatl – the consequences of the encounter of the two languages and the confrontation of two widely variant systems for constructing a cosmology of spiritual meaning and responding, on its basis, to the physical environment.

But the interplay between European and indigenous traditions alone is inadequate to any comprehensive understanding of the literary history of the American frontiers. There were, after all, as Thompson and Lamar remind us, "frontier processes in precolonial America . . . as when Pueblo-dwelling agriculturists and Apachean hunter-collectors confronted one another in present-day New Mexico and Arizona" (1981: 11). With perhaps 550 different languages and dialects in use north of the Rio Grande, rooted in at least nine distinct linguistic stocks, the peoples of precolonial North America repeatedly engaged in exchanges of vocabulary, stories, and oral lore as they traded with or invaded one another, or simply migrated into another group's territory. This hybridizing process was only accelerated when, under pressure from land-hungry Euro-Americans, native peoples withdrew – or, more often, were forcibly removed – from traditional territories to new areas or reservations. In some instances, as with the Delawares, previously separate peoples came together for the first time after contact with Europeans, forging wholly new cultural patterns.

Additionally, the encounter of African languages with English-, Dutch-, French-, and Spanish-speaking slaveholders must certainly figure in any meaningful understanding of the songs, narrative play, and captivity (or slave) narratives which recall African Americans' original forced removal to a frontier defined by chattel slavery. The hybridized vernacular traditions that Houston Baker, Jr. and Henry Louis Gates, Jr. have identified as intrinsic to African-American literary expression enjoy linguistically complex frontier antecedents. Baker's proposition that any "shift, or rupture, in ideological premises" necessarily "promotes strikingly new figurations" in the historical catalog underscores my point here (Baker 1990: 165). When "frontier" is reconceptualized in terms of initial encounters between distinct peoples and the accompanying environmental transitions, then neither the black cowboys nor the Black Seminoles of the nineteenth century are any longer anomalous (see Porter 1971; Littlefield 1977). And the engagement of fiction writers – from Charles Chesnutt onward – with recapturing the voices and cadences of antebellum landscapes emerges clearly as a succession of projects to reconstitute for later generations an oral tradition's remembered meaning of first contact.

Equally importantly, with neither chronology nor geography defining the historical frame, an entire corpus of what we now loosely term "immigrant literature" might be given fresh analysis because it could, on the one hand, be uncoupled from the imputed continuities of a New England "errand," and, on the other, be anchored to a landscape in the process of change, regardless of what kind of landscape is involved. Thus, some of the "American" materials in Yiddish by Sholem Aleichem (the pen name of Solomon Rabinowitz), Mary Antin's original Yiddish *From Plotzk to Boston* (which she edited and translated into English for publication in 1899), and the work of Anzia Yezierska would enter a literary history that recognized the concept of urban frontiers. Yezierska's *Bread Givers* (1925) could profitably be read as an anticipation of Edward Rivera's 1982 fictionalized autobiography of growing up Puerto Rican in Harlem, *Family Installments: Memories of Growing Up Hispanic*, while Aleichem's World War I-era evocation of fledgling Jewish communities newly removed from rural *shtetls* in eastern Europe to teeming tenements on Manhattan's Lower East Side might resonate with new meanings when compared to Carlos Bulosan's World War II-era revulsion at fleeing the Philippines only to find in America

> . . . the city where
> The streets scream for life, where men are hunting
> Each other with burning eyes, mountains are made of sand.
> Glass, paper from factories where death is calling
> For peace; hills are made of clothes, and trees
> Are nothing but candies.[7]

In a related move, to get at yet another set of complex frontier responses, scholarship would seek to recover letters, diaries, poems, and fictions composed by Chinese and other Asians brought to labor in the silver mines or on the railroads in the nineteenth century. Here we could study the Asians grappling both with their own preconceptions of America and with the language and conceptual patterns of the Euro-Americans who employ them, even as they help to transform the dominant culture's already mythologized agrarian landscape into an industrial frontier.

There are, of course, other examples, but the point is made: to establish a truly comprehensive frontier literary history, both geography and chronology must be viewed as fluid and ongoing, or as a continuously unfolding palimpsest that requires us to include Old Norse, Papago, Nahuatl, Quechua, Spanish, Yaqui, Tewa, Gullah, French, Dutch, Chinese, Japanese, German, Yiddish, and so on – as well as English – within our textual canon. Hybridized forms and tropes constitute the focus of textual analysis, and the resultant attentiveness to "code switching" radically alters our understanding of style and aesthetics. As Gloria Anzaldúa announces in *Borderlands/La Frontera* (itself a study in intercultural hybridized forms), "the switching of codes in this book from English to Castillian Spanish to the North Mexican dialect to Tex-Mex to a sprinkling of Nahuatl to a mixture of all of these, reflects my language, a new language – the language of the Borderlands. There, at the juncture of cultures, languages cross-pollinate and are revitalized; they die and are born" (Anzaldúa 1987: preface, n.p.).

In effect, in my reformulation the term "frontier" comes to mean what we in the Southwest call *la frontera*, or the borderlands: that liminal landscape of changing meanings on which distinct human cultures first encounter one another's "otherness" and appropriate, accommodate, or domesticate it through language. By concentrating on frontier as an inherently unstable locus of (generally unacknowledged – at least at the outset) environmental transitions and cultural interpenetrations, however, I have purposefully dropped two features which previously were assumed: population scarcity, and either primitive technology or a site where a more developed or superior technology overwhelms an inferior one. Both are willfully ahistorical.

The population densities of precontact peoples in the Americas are now being radically reassessed as the full implications of European diseases are better understood. Recent evidence suggests that the imported diseases not only decimated native populations but, more crucially, may have left a portion of the survivors sterile or infertile. As a result, many European colonizers encountered dramatically diminished numbers of indigenous inhabitants, the diseases often traveling the native trade routes well ahead of actual direct contact. The immediate consequences were exaggerated reports back to Europe of an empty "wilderness" there for the taking, and the tenacious grip of a mythology of sparsely settled frontiers. In fact, the Black Death that swept Europe in the fourteenth century, killing as much as three-quarters of the population in some areas, probably left Europe with a population density roughly equivalent to that of North America at the same period. In any event, the precontact population north of the Rio Grande alone has recently been revised upwards from estimates of four million to twelve million or more. That population had developed extensive and sophisticated trade routes, with major trade centers established from South America to the present-day Midwest – the intricate road system branching out from Chaco Canyon (in north-central New Mexico) being only one example. The frontier contacts of these peoples included constant exchanges of technology, from building techniques to basketweaving and pottery. Moreover, in the first recorded contact with European peoples, the Skraellings effectively repulsed the Norse colonizing effort, forcing the Scandinavians to abandon the Vinland settlement after only three years. As Wilcomb Washburn observes, at this point "the technological levels of the two peoples were not far apart." "Even Columbus and his followers did not arrive with overwhelming technological superiority," Washburn continues. "The native inhabitants of the New World had the same bow-and-arrow technology from which Europeans had only recently graduated to crude firearms. Both sides had shields and protective clothing, but Europeans had iron, which gave their sharp weapons and durable household utensils . . . a decisive advantage" (Washburn 1986: 269).

Even so, the Spanish chronicles of conquest are filled with awe at the accomplishments of Incan stonework (which even today cannot be replicated); and the letters
and diaries of seventeenth- and eighteenth-century English colonists contain repeated
references to the Indians' ability to produce rich harvests with only a digging stick,
as compared to the meager crops that resulted from metal tools. Soon enough, of
course, Europeans learned to adapt Indian fertilizing techniques, while the Indians
appropriated iron cooking pots, firearms, and metal instruments useful for hunting,
gathering, and planting. Therefore, rather than defining a frontier as a site of primitive or disparate technologies, it might prove more useful to think in terms of competing appropriate technologies and rapid technological exchange and innovation.
This allows us to encompass all frontiers – "wilderness," agricultural, urban, and
industrial alike. And it prevents us from ignoring, as part of our frontier equation,
the impact of technological exchange on the physical environment.

*

For critics and scholars, for historians of literature, and even for those who create
literature out of them, borderlands are never "a comfortable territory to live in." Too
often, "the prominent features of this landscape," as Gloria Anzaldúa attests, are
"hatred, anger and exploitation" (1987: preface, n.p.). Nonetheless, there are compelling reasons to adopt the reformulation I have outlined here. First, by understanding
the frontier as a specifiable first moment on that liminal borderland between distinct
cultures, we forever decenter what was previously a narrowly Eurocentric design. As
such, we constrain the continuing assertion of vast unsettled or uninhabited areas,
no matter how powerfully that notion permeates the texts we would analyze; we
afford ourselves the scholarly occasion to examine a variety of contacts between native
peoples; and we inhibit the tendency to develop frontier models that exclude certain
groups from their rightful place in an ongoing pioneering process on a variety of
landscapes.[8] Second, we engage energizing interdisciplinary challenges that demand
comparative cultural and literary analyses in which anthropology, geography, ecology,
and literary history can work together in new ways. At the very least, in Paul Lauter's
view, literary scholars will come "to appreciate a broader range of conventions, to set
form more fully into historical and functional context[s], and to comprehend how
audience expectation and assumption mandate formal priorities" (Lauter 1990: 29).
And third, by acknowledging the many different configurations of indigenous peoples,
immigrants, and emigrants who came in contact over time on a variety of landscapes,
we allow the literatures of the frontiers to stand – accurately, at last – as multi-
lingual, polyvocal, and newly intertextual and multicultural. In consequence, we find
ourselves better able to understand the meanings and trace the genesis of hybridized
forms and usages – whether they occur as a borrowing of vocabulary from indigenous
peoples, as in John Smith; as an adaptation by *mestizo* generations of European
discovery tracts, as in Garcilaso de la Vega, El Inca; or as an incorporation by native
peoples of European religious narratives, as in the Yaqui "Testamento."

What most appeals to me in this reformulation, however, is that it necessarily de-stabilizes easy assumptions about centers and margins in the construction of literary history. As I stated at the outset, the persistence of theories of continuity in the study of American literary history has repeatedly distorted its capacity to treat frontier texts as anything other than marginalia or cultural mythology, because the frontier is displaced always to the geographical edges, regarded as transitory, and its texts scoured for signs of hegemonic purposes or anxieties.[9] Obsessed with its own myth of origins, the scholarship that comprises most literary histories is always seeking some defining beginning (usually Puritan New England, sometimes the Virginia Plantation, in rare instances the European voyages of discovery) in whose texts may be discerned something peculiarly or characteristically "American" – American by current criteria, of course.[10] Understandably, "the stakes are high in this struggle for the defining origins of the American temperament." As Donald Weber explains, "whoever can follow the reverberations of the American voice from the seventeenth century to the nineteenth and beyond can claim an authorizing vision of the culture, and thus impose a compelling paradigm" (1990: 102).

But the limitations of this kind of literary history are obvious: the works produced are patently ahistorical, tacitly reading some version of the present back into the past. They are univocal and monolingual, defining origins by what later became the tropes of the dominant or conquering language. And, by imputing "profound con-tinuities between early American literary expression and the classic literature of the United States in the mid-nineteenth century," they necessarily obscure any text that cannot be accommodated to whatever are currently accepted as the features of the mature national literary consciousness. It is notions like these, moreover, adds Philip Gura, that give rise to "the concomitant belief in American 'exceptionalism,' both literary and cultural" (1988: 309). Furthermore, in terms of their adequacy to accom-modate a literary history of discontinuous frontiers, these studies tend to characterize all productions outside major urban cultural centers as merely regional, and to underestimate the influence of place and physical environment on any writer's con-struction of reality.

Although in 1992 we marked the one-hundredth anniversary of the supposed closing of the frontier, I am recommending that we reopen it, thematizing frontier as a multiplicity of continuing first encounters over time and land, rather than as a linear chronology of successive discoveries and discrete settlements. Remembering the passionately contested meanings of the five-hundredth anniversary of Columbus's first landing, I am asking that we once and for all eschew the myth of origins – with its habits of either fetishizing or marginalizing race, place, and ethnicity – and, by returning to serious study of the frontiers, adopt a model of literary history that privileges no group's priority and no region's primacy. In the frontier literary history I have projected here, there can be no Ur-landscape because there are so many border-lands, and, over time, even the same site may serve for seriatim first encounters. There can be no paradigmatic first contact because there are so many different kinds of first encounters. And there can be no single overarching story.

To be sure, no literary history of the frontiers will fail to note resonances, affinities, and semantic and symbolic resemblances across texts. But at the same time, by its very definition, no literary history of the frontiers will naïvely conflate the Spanish search for cities of gold, the Chinese belief in the Golden Mountain, and the sale of human beings in the trade to supply Europeans with the New World's golden rum into a flattened narrative of unproblematic discovery, settlement, and progress. Similarly, the crush of languages and cultures on a single day at Ellis Island in 1905 represents a frontier with features – and consequences – radically different from the landing at Plymouth Rock. The texts that attempt to delineate these frontier moments – like the literary histories generated to accommodate them – will tell many different stories. Indeed, the study of frontier literary history – like American literary history in general – should properly be marked by endlessly proliferating, multiple, competing narrative designs. The singular identities and unswerving continuities that Americanists have regularly claimed for our literary history are no longer credible.

Nevertheless, the scope of the project outlined here will make many literary historians nervous because it appears to beg the question of "literariness." In asking that we study Norse sagas and the Yaqui "Testamento" as assiduously as we study texts by James Fenimore Cooper and Willa Cather, I threaten to sustain the premise, always suspected by William Spengemann, that American literature is "an altogether imaginary subject." But only by opening up the question of literariness can we ever take on Spengemann's "task of reconstructing the foundations on which our collective enterprise rests" (Spengemann 1989: 2, 3). In elaborating a literary history of the frontiers, the challenge is not to decide beforehand what constitutes literariness, but rather to expose ourselves to different kinds of texts and contexts so as to recover the ways they variously inscribe the stories of first contact. Inevitably, the interdisciplinary and multilingual skills required for such an undertaking will tend, in Cary Nelson's words, to "destabilize distinctions between quality and historical relevance by making them self-conscious" (Nelson 1989: 41).

The same Norse sagas whose stylistic conventions were lauded in my literature courses at the University of Oslo in 1961, for example, had been available to me previously (in bad translations and excerpted, to be sure) in my high-school and college world history courses only to signify the historical exploits of the Vikings. Similarly, Larry Evers and Felipe Molina's examination of "conventional Yaqui rhetorical pattern[s]" and the evidence of an ever-evolving text written "in a dynamic relation with Yaqui oral tradition" invite literary treatments of the Yaqui "Testamento" in the ways we generally define such procedures. By contrast, for the Yaquis themselves, as one of Evers and Molina's consultants explains to them, "a 'testamento' is a sacred word that is continually affirmed by the community as it goes about the day-to-day business of its governance, a sacred word that provides authority in what non-Yaquis might factor out as legal, moral, and theological realms." Of course, none of these textual usages is incompatible with any other. They are merely functionally variable and context-dependent. The point here is that what we commonly think of as "literariness" may be too narrow to encompass – or may even wholly distort – the functionally variable roles of texts in different societies. By forcing us to become self-conscious about how we distinguish the literary from the "merely" historical or ethnographically relevant, the project of frontier literary history (to quote Cary Nelson again) can eventually "establish varied cultural roles for literariness – as opposed to a single, dominant notion of literariness overseen by the academy." And this, in turn, could produce "different, even contradictory, subject positions from which literariness can be valued" (Nelson 1989: 41).

Finally, while I would not argue that a literary history of the frontiers could adequately account for all of the many different kinds of literature and literary forms produced in the United States (or in its precolonial past), I would suggest that such a project will radically alter both what we recognize as "literature" and how we define its historical processes. The literature of the frontiers may not be the only kind of literature produced in the Americas, but it is surely inherent in all the rest.

Too little of what I have outlined here can come to fruition, however, as long as American literary specialists remain trapped within Departments of English. For if we are ever to have what Andrew Wiget calls "a new literary history that is both just and useful" (1991: 228), then American literary specialists must move beyond the training that prepares us to analyze only texts written in English or to recognize only European (or "Western") antecedents. And we must become the intellectual colleagues of those, from a variety of disciplines, who can teach us to read across cultural boundaries. In order to properly study a literature that for so long has been formed and reformed "en el choque e interacción de varias culturas en tensión," American literary scholars must begin to create their own new frontiers, openly declaring their agenda as radically comparativist, demandingly interdisciplinary, and exuberantly multilingual. We must, in short, propose an endlessly proliferating diversity over which no school or theory, no ethnic, racial, or cultural enclave, and no political or scholarly party could ever again take control.

NOTES

1 In conference papers too numerous to list here, in personal correspondence and conversations, Norman S. Grabo generously shared his study of the first European writings produced within what is now the continental United States, examining works in Spanish, French, and Dutch, as well as English; although none of this work has yet appeared in print, we can nonetheless catch a glimpse of his scholarly intentions in his "Villagrá: Between a Rock and Other Hard Places" (1990). See also Spengemann 1989; Jennings 1975; Cronon 1983; Merchant 1989; Todorov 1984; and Lamar and Thompson, eds. 1981.

2 Throughout this essay, all discussion of the Yaqui "Testamento" is indebted to Evers and Molina 1992. This publication offers a comprehensive introduction to the text, a transcription of the handwritten Yaqui document provided to them, and a full English translation. I am enormously grateful to Evers and Molina for giving me a typescript in advance of publication, and I thank Larry Evers for his generosity in discussing this material with me.

3   See Gathorne-Hardy (1970: viii–ix), which makes the provocative suggestion that Eskimo legends of the people they call the "Tunnit" refer to contacts with Vikings from Greenland. My own forthcoming *In Search of First Contact* examines Norse contacts with Algonquian-speaking peoples in the Canadian maritimes and the northeastern United States.

4   Quoted in Gray 1972: 46, 59; Gray offers serviceable translations of most extant texts dealing with the Vikings in Vinland. His comparison of the different versions is useful, and his argument that Vinland was actually in the vicinity of Cape Cod is tantalizing.

5   An excellent overview of this material is Promis 1991, to which I am much indebted for my discussion here.

6   Like much of the material listed here, until recently Gaspar Peréz de Villagrá's *History of New Mexico* was available only in a limited-edition inadequate prose translation by Gilberto Espinosa (Peréz de Villagrá 1933). An *en face* edition with an updated scholarly and critical introduction is now available (Peréz de Villagrá 1992).

7   Bulosan 1942: 20. For an analysis of the poem and its provenance, see Campomanes and Gernes 1988: 15–46.

8   An example of this kind of exclusionary model appears in Spiller 1980. Although Spiller acknowledges their "great importance to the American literary identity today," he nonetheless excludes "three kinds of ethnic groups" from "the main frontier movement. These are the immigrant groups which came

to this country comparatively late; the blacks who were brought to this country under special circumstances; and the Jews who in all their history have mingled with, but rarely become totally absorbed into, any alien culture." As Spiller explains, "only immigrations from European countries other than Great Britain followed a course close enough to our model to suggest inclusion here" (1980: 15). Spiller eliminates any discussion of Asian immigrants by ignoring the mining, urban, and industrial frontiers; he appears ignorant of the numbers of blacks who escaped their "special circumstances" to relative safety on the frontiers; and he appears equally ignorant of the Latino-speaking Spanish Jews (or Sephardim) who escaped the long arm of the Inquisition by fleeing to the New World as *conversos* and establishing communities in what is now the United States Southwest. For a useful introduction, see Hernandez 1990.

9   Susman (1984) illustrates this process succinctly in his examination of post-Turnerian intellectual debates over the meaning and import of the frontier.

10 Until quite recently, a similar tendency ruled the study of Latin American literary history. As Rolena Adorno points out, "Following Alfonso Reyes and Pedro Henríquez Ureña, the goal has been to attach a 'literary vocation' to the historiographical writings about the conquest of America, seeking 'to place the literary origins of Latin American literary discourse in the chronicles of the conquest of America'" (1990: 175).

References and Further Reading

Adorno, Rolena (1990). "New Perspectives in Colonial Spanish American Literary Studies." *Journal of the Southwest* 32 (Summer), 173–91.

Anzaldúa, Gloria (1987). *Borderlands/La Frontera: The New Mestiza*. San Francisco: Spinsters/Aunt Lute.

Baker, Houston A., Jr. (1990). "Archeology, Ideology, and African American Discourse." In A. LaVonne Brown Ruoff and Jerry W. Ward Jr. (eds.), *Redefining American Literary History*, 157–195. New York: Modern Language Association.

Budd, Louis J., Cady, Edwin H., and Anderson, Carl L., eds. (1980). *Toward a New American Literary History*. Durham: Duke University Press.

Bulosan, Carlos (1942). *Letter from America*. Prairie City, Ill.: Decker.

Campomanes, Oscar V. and Todd S. Gernes (1988). "Two Letters from America: Carlos Bulosan and the act of writing." *MELUS* 15 (Fall), 15–46.

Cronon, William, Jr. (1983). *Changes in the Land: Indians, Colonists, and the Ecology of New England.* New York: Hill and Wang.

de la Vega, Garcilaso, El Inca (1966). *Royal Commentaries of the Incas and General History of Peru,* trans. Harold V. Livermore. Austin: University of Texas Press. (Pt. I, 1609; Pt. II, 1617.)

Del Río, Carmen M. (1990). "Chicana Poets: Re-visions from the Margin," *Revista Canadiense de Estudios Hispánicos* 14 (Spring), 431–45.

Evers, Larry and Molina, Felipe S. (1992). "The Holy Dividing Line: Inscription and Resistance in Yaqui Culture." *Journal of the Southwest* 34: 1 (Spring), 3–46.

Gathorne-Hardy, G. M. (1970). *The Norse Discoverers of America: The Wineland Sagas.* London: Oxford University Press. (First publ. 1921.)

Grabo, Norman S. (1990). "Villagrá: Between a Rock and Other Hard Places." *Ideas* 6 (Spring), 86–92.

Gray, Edward F. (1972). *Leif Eriksson: Discoverer of America, AD 1003.* New York: Kraus. (First publ. 1930.)

Gura, Philip E. (1988). "The Study of Colonial American Literature, 1966–1987: A Vade Mecum." *William and Mary Quarterly* 3rd ser., 45 (April), 301–51.

Hernandez, Frances (1990). "The Secret Legacy of Christopher Columbus in the Southwest." *Password* 35 (Summer), 55–70.

Hu-DeHart, Evelyn (1981). *Missionaries, Miners, and Indians: Spanish Contact with the Yaqui Nation of Northwestern New Spain, 1533–1820.* Tucson: University of Arizona Press.

Jennings, Francis (1975). *The Invasion of America: Indians, Colonialists, and the Cant of Conquest.* Chapel Hill: University of North Carolina Press.

Kolodny, Annette (forthcoming). *In Search of First Contact.* The Vikings of Vinland and the Peoples of the Dawnland. Durham, NC: Duke University Press.

Kopper, Philip, ed. (1986). *The Smithsonian Book of North American Indians: Before the Coming of the Europeans.* Washington: Smithsonian Books.

Lamar, Howard and Thompson, Leonard, eds. (1981). *The Frontier in History: North America and Southern Africa Compared.* New Haven: Yale University Press.

Lauter, Paul (1990). "The Literatures of America: A Comparative Discipline." In A. LaVonne

Brown Ruoff and Jerry W. Ward Jr. (eds.), 9–34. *Redefining American Literary History.* New York: Modern Language Association.

Littlefield, Daniel E., Jr. (1977). *Africans and Seminoles: From Removal to Emancipation.* Westport, Conn.: Greenwood.

McReynolds, Edwin C. (1957). *The Seminoles.* Norman: University of Oklahoma Press.

Merchant, Caroline (1989). *Ecological Revolutions: Nature, Gender, and Science in New England.* Chapel Hill: University of North Carolina Press.

Nelson, Cary (1989) *Repression and Recovery: Modern American Poetry and the Politics of Cultural Memory, 1910–1945.* Madison: University of Wisconsin Press.

Peréz de Villagrá, Gaspar (1933). *History of New Mexico,* trans. Gilberto Espinosa. Los Angeles: Quivira Society. (First publ. 1610.)

Peréz de Villagrá, Gaspar (1992). *Historia de la Nueva Mexico: English and Spanish,* ed. and trans. Miguel Encinias, Alfred Rodríguez, and Joseph P. Sánchez. Albuquerque: University of New Mexico Press. (First publ. 1610.)

Porter, Kenneth W. (1971), *The Negro on the American Frontier.* New York: Arno.

Promis, José (1991). *The Identity of Hispanoamerica: An Interpretation of Colonial Literature,* trans. Alita Kelley and Alec E. Kelley. Tucson: University of Arizona Press.

Ruoff, A. LaVonne Brown and Ward Jerry W., Jr., eds. (1990). *Redefining American Literary History.* New York: Modern Language Association.

Silko, Leslie Marmon (1978). *Ceremony.* New York: Signet/New American Library.

Spengemann, William C. (1989). *A Mirror for Americanists: Reflections on the Idea of American Literature.* Hanover, NH: University Press of New England.

Spicer, Edward H. (1989). *The Yaquis: A Cultural History.* Tucson: University of Arizona Press.

Spiller, Robert E. (1980). "The Cycle and the Roots: National Identity in American Literature." In Louis J. Budd, Edwin H. Cady, and Carl L. Anderson (eds.), *Toward a New American Literary History,* 3–18. Durham, NC: Duke University Press.

Susman, Warren I. (1984). *Culture as History: The Transformation of American Society in the Twentieth Century* (1973). New York: Pantheon.

Thompson, Leonard, and Lamar, Howard (1981). "Comparative Frontier History." In *The Frontier in History: North America and Southern Africa Compared*. New Haven: Yale University Press.

Todorov, Tzvetan (1984). *The Conquest of America: The Question of the Other*, trans. Richard Howard. New York: Harper & Row.

Washburn, Wilcomb E. (1986). "Epilogue." In Philip Kopper (ed.), *The Smithsonian Book of North American Indians: Before the Coming of the Europeans*. Washington: Smithsonian Books.

Weber, Donald (1990). "Historicizing the Errand." *American Literary History* 2 (Spring) 101–18.

Wiget, Andrew (1991). "Reading against the Grain: Origin Stories and American Literary History." *American Literary History* 3 (Summer), 209–31.

4

Region and Race: National Identity and the Southern Past

Lori Robison

The phrase "region and race" evokes, in the American consciousness, the South. Regional identity in the United States, almost a century and a half after the Civil War, is still most often defined in terms of northern or southern identifications. While many geographical regions of the country continue to maintain a distinctive regional culture, despite the enduring American fear of an impending national homogeneity, the South has somehow become "the most regional region" (Dew 1994: 745). It is not that the South is the only place in contemporary America where one can find differences in speech, or food, or values, or how history is told; nor is it that these differences are necessarily more pronounced in the South than they are in any other region. It is that the American South continues to provide the mythic space for the working out of a national identity. And the South has provided that space precisely because of its continued connection to the nation's racial conflicts. As historian Grace Elizabeth Hale has said, "The American South has most often provided the metaphorical and actual settings, the playgrounds of the American racial drama, the locations of American racial meanings" (1998: 282).[1]

This is not to say that the South is more racist than the rest of the country. In which part of the nation we would currently find the most racism, or even how one would define racism (as overt racial violence? as peaceful segregation? as unspoken hatred? as unequal access?), are issues that are under continuous debate in American life. It is not to say, either, that other regions of the country have not staged their own racial dramas: African Americans, Hispanic Americans, Asian Americans, and Native Americans have both contributed to the regional cultures of the West, the Southwest, the Midwest, and the East and, at various times in American history, been cast in the role of outsider, providing an other against which regional (and national) identity can be formed. American regional identity is, to an extent that we have only begun to uncover, caught up in our understanding of racial identity and racial difference. As we consider American regionalisms, we must also examine the mutual construction of region and race. We must consider how discourses of race have informed our understanding of region and, conversely, how our way of speaking and writing about region has shaped our approach to race. The goal of such work would not be to merely point out the racist messages of regional texts, nor would it be to dismiss texts with racist messages from literary study. Instead, the goal would be to begin to unravel these interwoven discourses. If we can understand more about how we have constructed race, perhaps we can avoid replicating the racism that has shaped the American past. With this goal in mind, I want, in this essay, to draw attention to the complex interrelatedness of region and race. Because of its central role in the creation of American regional and racial identity, I will focus here on the American South. And yet, notwithstanding this focus, I believe that this kind of discussion can – and should – take place in examinations of other American regionalisms.

Nation-building and the South

Throughout American history, the South has been represented as a place apart from mainstream American culture. In the popular imagination the region has been understood to be hotter, more exotic, more mythic, more romantic, more unified, more anachronistic, and more brutal than the rest of the country. And this image of Southern excess has served in the creation of a national identity. At times, this image of the South has forged a sense of national unity by giving the nation something to react against; all of that excess can allow the "North" (or actually the non-South, the rest of the country) to understand itself as kinder and gentler, as superior because of its moderation. At other times in the American past, the South has been used in the opposite manner; instead of being the other against which the nation unites, it has provided the symbolic landscape through which national reunion can occur. Though still represented, at these times, as excessive, the region provides a national ideal. All of its heat, myth, and history offer an exaggerated reflection of what America wants to become.

In the late twentieth century, the South was used in both of these ways. The media representation of its regressive, racist laws and social policies during the Civil Rights Movement gave the nation the impetus to develop an emancipatory federal program and thus a new, more liberatory national identity. Depictions of the South in films like *Deliverance* and *Cool Hand Luke* re-presented this repressive brutality and provided a stark contrast against which the developing Great Society could complacently measure itself. Yet, as Peter Applebome has demonstrated, by the 1990s mainstream national culture had embraced a "Southern" worldview. Pointing to the national prominence of Southern politicians and conservative political and social values, and the increased popularity of traditional Southern pastimes (such as stock car racing and country music), Applebome finds a South that is no longer a national outsider. Now, the very issues that distanced the region have come to characterize the nation as a whole; antigovernment sympathies, strong individualism, and race as "a constant subtext to daily life" have become the issues through which the nation has begun to define itself (Applebome 1996: 8). These twentieth-century uses of the

South mirror the nineteenth-century shift in national perceptions of the region. During the antebellum period, because of the debate over slavery, the North understood the South as the "silent Other" against which national identity could be formed; the region "provided a screen on which [the rest of the population] could project all that they wished to repress, deny, and purge from the national body politic" (Porter 1988: 351). By the end of the century, however, the nation was "distinctly Confederate in sympathy" (Tourgée 1978: 402). In the wake of the Civil War, national reconciliation was achieved as the culture embraced images of a noble, pastoral Southern civilization.

If, as Applebome has noted, the national view of "the South as a hellhole of poverty, torment, and depravity" has long competed with a view of the region as "an American Eden of tradition, strength, and grace" (1996: 10), this vacillation has rested on the region's – and, ultimately, the nation's – relationship to race. It is, after all, institutionalized racism, in the form of nineteenth-century slavery and twentieth-century segregation, that has served to position the South outside of American cultural values. The Civil War and the Civil Rights Movement both called attention to the contradictions inherent in maintaining a legally sanctioned racism in a democratic society, and both resulted in federal attempts to eradicate that institutionalized racism by bringing the errant region back into the national fold. And in the historical moments that have followed, in the periods in which the South becomes "an American Eden," here too we see a national preoccupation with racial identity. In the Reconstruction period, the questions about the terms and conditions of citizenship (for Southerners and for African Americans) that faced the newly reconstituted nation were fundamentally tied to issues of racial difference. In present-day American culture we can again detect a profound cultural discussion underway about the nature of race that coexists – through no coincidence, I would argue – with the current cultural appropriation of a Southern ethos. It seems no accident that we can again see, in a culture which is becoming increasingly heterogeneous and in which policies like affirmative action are fiercely debated, an increased investment in traditionally Southern values.

When we see the United States embrace the "family values" and conservative individualism that are traditionally associated with the South, we can imagine that this is, at least in part, an attempt to construct a nationalizing whiteness. Having rejected the explicit racism of slavery or segregation, the nation, assured of its own beneficence, may feel that it is reconciling with a "New South," a South that has moved beyond the racism of its past. But the desire for regional reunion may, in fact, be a reaction against the new visibility of racial difference. The nation, disturbed by the new, more subtle, forms of racial negotiations demanded by the end of slavery or the end of legal segregation, wants to retreat back into an "American Eden" in which racial threats seem to disappear. But that "Eden" is not a racially neutral landscape, and when there is no examination of the ways in which its traditional values could be tied to racist thought, the issues of race are not confronted; they are merely forced back into invisibility. This is not to say that continued regional antagonism would be the only way to combat national racism. The problem is that regional reconciliation has typically been effected through cultural amnesia, through the repression of the South's recent past. As the nation retreats back into the South, there is a naïve desire to stabilize racial meaning, to neutralize what has become threatening about race; but all that is accomplished is a muting of racial difference. With the assumption that race can be unmarked, that it will no longer be disruptive or noticeable, comes the unexamined assumption that the dominant culture lacks a racial identity. The desire to embrace regional difference, then, has served in the construction of a national identity in which whiteness remains normative.

Reconstruction and the Rise of Regional Writing

American Reconstruction brought the inextricable issues of national, regional, and racial identity to the fore of American consciousness. After the dissolution of the nation, the questions of what it meant to be an American citizen, who could be a citizen, and how white Southerners and black Americans would rejoin the Union were very much under public debate. Even as the war came to an end, daily life dramatically underscored these continuing regional and racial negotiations: federal troops occupied the South to enforce Reconstruction policy; the constitutional amendments guaranteeing the end of slavery and the rights of citizenship to African Americans were debated and ratified; and African Americans pursued those rights by voting, by seeking public education and elected office, and by becoming landowners. In the postwar years, deciding what it meant to be an American meant deciding what it meant to be a Northerner or a Southerner; and, conversely, definitions of regional identity were necessarily articulated through an allegiance to or a disavowal of the national government – including the federal position on race. To be an American in this period also meant confronting race in new ways. Before the war, the difference between black and white identity rested primarily on the distinction between slave and citizen. Once citizenship was granted to all African Americans, once the assumed relationship between national and racial identity was destabilized, Americans were challenged to think again about racial difference. What would it mean to be black and a citizen? What would it mean to be white if whiteness was no longer the marker of national privilege? The new national order would also complicate the intersections of regional and racial identity. Would identification with the South assume loyalty to the Confederacy and, therefore, assume whiteness? Or would the nation continue to equate the North with "the progressive forces of the Anglo-Saxon race" and the South with "blackness and barbarism" (Porter 1988: 356)?

   As historian Eric Foner has pointed out, Reconstruction was a productive and even revolutionary period in American political life that witnessed the "emergence of a national state possessing vastly expanded authority and a new set of purposes, including an unprecedented commitment to the ideal of a national citizenship whose equal rights belonged to all Americans regardless of race" (Foner 1988: xxvi). The promise of Reconstruction diminished, however, very quickly, and was in fact completely dismantled by the last decade of the nineteenth century. (Reconstruction is generally considered to have ended in 1877 following the Hayes–Tilden compromise, which resulted in the withdrawal of federal troops from the South.) In 1883 the Supreme Court overturned the Civil Rights Act of 1875, and in 1896 it affirmed that "separate but equal" public facilities were constitutional in *Plessy* v. *Ferguson*. One way to explain this remarkable reversal is to understand the final 25 years of the century, the post-Reconstruction period, as a time in which the nation wanted to stabilize the increasingly fluid nature of regional, racial, and national identity. In the social policies of this period we can see an attempt to reassert an earlier definition of racial difference. Southern segregation culture made it difficult for African Americans to vote or to own land, and thus the connections between servitude and blackness, and citizenship and whiteness, were maintained. Segregation itself was an extreme attempt to codify racial meaning: in the marking of public spaces with the words "white" or "colored," we can see the desire to repress any ambiguity surrounding what it means to be white or black, or how to define who is white or black.

That the nation came to betray its egalitarian political goals is traditionally explained by the national interest in reunion; because of the desire for regional reconciliation, the North, according to conventional history, increasingly accepted – and finally replicated – the institutionalized racism practiced by the post-Reconstruction South. And yet, we can productively understand this dynamic as working in the opposite manner: an already present national racism may have led the nation to embrace the South. Threatened by the shifting grounds of racial identity, the North would have seen in the segregated South a return to racial definitions that cohered to well-drawn social relationships. If the Civil War and its aftermath had profoundly challenged how Americans understood themselves and their nation, then we see in the post-Reconstruction period a re-investment in an imagined past in which identity appeared to have been fixed. It is in this cultural context that regional literary forms became critically acclaimed and widely popular. Just as the federal presence in the South was in retreat, local color literature achieved national prominence, and by the turn of the century, popular plantation romances signaled the cultural re-investment in a mythic South. Participating in the cultural work of containing the threat of regional and racial difference, these literatures took part in the creation of a stable sense of regional, racial, and therefore national identity.

Amy Kaplan has convincingly demonstrated that post-Civil War literature was involved in the project of rebuilding the fractured nation. Drawing on Benedict Anderson's notion that nations are created through "imagined communities," most prominently through a common print culture that lends a sense of shared values, Kaplan notes that postbellum fiction escaped the splintered present by re-imagining a unifying past. In a wide variety of literary genres popular at this time, Kaplan detects an obsession with revising the American past: "all enact a willed amnesia about founding conflicts, while they reinvent multiple and contested pasts to claim as the shared origin of nation identity" (1991: 241). The literature of this period, in addition to creating a mythic past, contributed to national reunion, Kaplan asserts, through an emphasis on spatial and cultural borders and other borders against which to imagine American nationhood. In local color literature, the regional literature most often produced in this period, we see both of these dynamics. Local color stories often seem to be set in a simpler past, or at least, as Kaplan points out, in a present that seems like the past because it "eludes historical change" (1991: 242). And regional writing is fundamentally about borders, about the spatial locations that make people – even people who claim the same nationality – different from one another.

Local color emerged in the pages of American journals – most notably the *Atlantic Monthly* and *Harper's Monthly* – in the 1870s and 1880s, and was very popular with contemporary critics and readers. Traditional literary history has attributed the genre's appeal to a cultural appreciation of quaint, out-of-the-way locales. Fear of an impending homogeneous national, urban culture, the usual argument goes, resulted in literary texts that preserved on paper the unique peoples and regions of the country that could potentially disappear. Yet Richard Brodhead, like Kaplan, understands this regional literature to have been not resisting the creation of a national culture but participating in it. The genre, according to Brodhead, marked the coalescing of a dominant, "cultured" American upper class: "its public function was not just to mourn lost cultures but to purvey a certain story of contemporary cultures and of the relations among them: to tell local cultures into a history of their supersession by a modern order now risen to national dominance" (1993: 121).

For Brodhead too, local color aided in the coming together of this "modern order" by providing a sense of cultural difference against which it could ally. Though this literature has often been assumed to have represented an implicit appreciation of heterogeneity, it played to "an imagination of acquisition" by making the culture of "primitive" or "exotic" locales something that could be entered into, possessed, and then subsumed by the reader's literate, elite culture (Brodhead 1993: 133). And thus this literature did acknowledge cultural difference, but did not come to terms with the more threatening national heterogeneity precipitated by late nineteenth-century immigration, or by the postwar status of African Americans: "this fiction produced the foreign only to master it in imaginary terms . . . by substituting less 'different' native ethnicities for the truly foreign ones of contemporary reality." Brodhead, then, understands this genre to have performed a kind of "wishful thinking" for its bourgeois readers: "Nineteenth-century regional writing produced a real-sounding yet deeply fictitious America that was not homogeneous yet not radically heterogeneous either and whose diversities were ranged under one group's normative sway" (Brodhead 1993: 137).

"Our Contemporary Ancestors"

By nostalgically investing in a place in which heterogeneity is contained and made safe, local color literature created an imagined community, a nation that need never fully recognize its racist present. We can see this dynamic at work in Mary Murfree's Southern regional writings and in the late nineteenth-century cultural construction of the people of Appalachia. Murfree, writing under the pen name Charles Egbert Craddock, was one of the most popular of the local color writers. From 1878 to 1884 eight of Murfree's stories of the mountain people of eastern Tennessee were accepted for publication in the *Atlantic Monthly*. In 1884, these stories were collected as *In the Tennessee Mountains*, which became so popular that the collection went through 14 editions within two years. The collection, coinciding with the "discovery" of Appalachia, made Murfree, for the larger culture, an expert on the mountain people. In reality, Murfree, who grew up in her family's wealthy plantation home near Nashville, learned about the mountain people only through visits to a vacation home at the prestigious Beersheba Springs resort (which is located in the Cumberland mountains, though this range, the Great Smoky Mountains, and the Appalachians all blend indiscriminately in the stories).

Part of the new, leisured class of vacationers that Brodhead sees as wanting to "possess" exotic or primitive locales, Murfree was able to write stories that spoke to – and even created – a cultural fascination with this southern locale. Historians of Appalachia have argued that Murfree's stories were responsible for creating a pervasive stereotype of the mountain people. These stereotypes of a "wily people who believed in witchcraft," and people of "low domestic morality," would have served to locate the mountain people completely outside the values of the dominant American culture (Klotter 1980: 835). And yet the otherness of Appalachia did not serve to threaten that sense of dominance. Henry Shapiro understands local color depictions of the region to be a nostalgic investment in a past that supports an imagined national community in the present: the regions thus depicted "were separated from the bourgeois, urban present by an ethnic or chronological distance which transformed the potential challenge to the idea of a dominant national culture . . . into additional evidence of the reality of such a national culture" (Shapiro 1978: 15). The discovery of Appalachia – a distinct, but American, culture – could have fractured the developing sense of a homogeneous, middle-class America. But Appalachia was made safe through representations that emphasized distance, both distant borders and a distant past.

It is not that Murfree's stories are actually set in the past. Rather, contained within the very genre in which Murfree writes are particular assumptions that create an "ethnic or chronological distance" between the reader and the people represented in the text. Murfree's stories are consistently told by a literate narrator whose stilted, formal prose provides a clear contrast to the dialect her mountain characters speak. And the author's frequent focus on the perceptions of a visiting outsider reinforces the sense that the mountain characters are quite different from the story's central consciousness and thus from the assumed reader. As recent work in anthropology tells us, this rhetorical distance has persistently shaped traditional written representations of the other. Murfree's fiction served much the same function in her culture that ethnography serves in ours – to provide mainstream readers with an authoritative introduction to a new culture. Traditional ethnography, the travel narrative (from which many of ethnography's generic conventions were derived), and local color fiction are all rhetorically structured through an outsider's perceptions of a different place or culture. These written representations are thus shaped through metaphors of sight: those who approach the new culture write from the experience of "seeing," "observing," "looking at," "perceiving," or "objectifying" it. Anthropological theorists have noted that these metaphors imply distance between the I and the other; all "presuppose a standpoint outside" (Clifford 1986: 11). And this outside standpoint, this distance, suggests the powerful position of the observer: the metaphors that dominate the writing of ethnography take the "scientific" position "of an observer fixed on the edge of a space, looking in and/or down upon what is other" (Pratt 1986: 32). Thus, unless these textual representations of cultural difference become willing to challenge or call attention to these metaphors, they replicate the very fear of heterogeneity that they would seem to challenge. They enact, through their very form, a hierarchical relationship between observer and observed that assumes the superiority of the voice that "looks down upon what is other."

This textual hierarchy also has an impact on readers, and thus on the larger culture's perceptions of the marginalized culture. It is the perspective of the "observer" that the text implicitly invites us to share, and contemporary reviews of Murfree's collection reveal that the reading public took her up on that invitation. *The Dial*, for example, writes:

> [Murfree's stories] deal with the rudest and humblest class of people – the inhabitants of the rough mountain regions of Tennessee who, never descending to the valleys or meeting with a higher grade of civilization, live on from generation to generation, destitute of learning, of religion, of every refining influence of civilization. (*Dial* 1884: 43)

There is a strong sense here of an assumed cohesiveness among narrative voice, reviewer, and reading public – those who share "the refining influence of civilization." By focusing on the differences of the mountain culture (differences that already have been shaped through the "observing" narrative voice of Murfree's fiction, and that already have been filtered through Murfree's own leisure-class assumptions), this review participates in the creation of that imagined, "civilized," cohesive community.[2]

The desire to write Appalachia into a region that could be possessed by the larger culture happened just at the close of Reconstruction, just as the federal presence was leaving the South. Through these literary texts, this white, Southern region was contained and made safe just at the moment when the larger culture wanted to distance itself from the challenges to regional and racial identity that Reconstruction had made possible. Represented as a region set apart from the nation, Appalachia was understood to be part neither of the Union nor of the Confederacy; and thus perhaps part of the cultural fascination with the region stemmed from its ability to elide Reconstruction's challenges to regional identity. And yet, at the same time, the newly discovered region was identified with the South – not only through its geographic borders, but also because the mountain people were represented through the already recognizable stereotype of the poor white Southerner. If Appalachia came, through these literary depictions, to have a metonymic relationship to the larger South, then we can detect, in the cultural fascination with the mountains, the project of regional reconciliation. The South's threat to national unity was disarmed by equating the region with a backwoods, primitive culture that had no power to shape the present. And, once the South's threat was nullified in this manner, the nation could again embrace it.

Implicit in the move to possess the mountain culture (and to imaginatively repossess the South) was the desire to turn away from the racial differences that marked the present. James C. Klotter points out that in much of the late nineteenth-century nonfiction that was written about Appalachia there is an emphasis on the whiteness of the mountain people. An 1898 sociological study of the mountains assures readers that "the population of this region is singularly free from what we are wont to call 'foreign' elements. The mountaineers are predominantly, if not exclusively, of English, Irish, and Scotch origin" (Vincent 1898: 4). Klotter has uncovered numerous essays from this period that reveal a cultural insistence on the Anglo-Saxon ancestry of the mountain people. One asserts that this "purest Anglo-Saxon stock in all the United States" was "free from the tide of foreign immigrants which ha[d] been pouring in." Another sets the mountain people against the "mob of strikers born in other lands." And yet another argues for the preservation of "the valorous stock of native-born Anglo-Saxons of our mountains" (quoted in Klotter 1980: 840). The whiteness of the mountain people is set up, in these articles, against a present in which immigration and Reconstruction have disrupted the usual assumptions that made whiteness and citizenship synonymous. These essays reveal a racist belief in the superiority of whiteness, and they also reveal the culture's desire to restabilize racial (and national) identity. The mountain people are constructed not only as white but also as racially pure. The race of the mountain people is lauded, in part, because it is knowable, it is easy to define. Not part of the confusing, unknowable "tide" or "mob" of "foreign elements," the mountain people are depicted instead with the clear racial identity of the "native-born." Embracing the white, Southern mountain-dweller as the "purest American type" thereby reasserts whiteness as the marker of membership in the national community (Klotter 1980: 840).

The distant past, in which mountain people were assumed to live, was thus represented as a past with clear racial identities. These late nineteenth-century discussions of Appalachia, Klotter finds, tended to characterize its inhabitants as representatives of the hearty pioneers and frontiersmen of America's previous century, or as descendants of Elizabethan Anglo-Saxons. It was not uncommon for Appalachian people to be represented as "our contemporary ancestors" (Klotter 1980: 837): a phrase that encapsulates the strange contradictions and the racist impulses contained within the cultural fascination with Appalachia. Through this phrase, the distance between national, urban present and the mountain people is maintained: "ancestors" are not threatening because they belong to the past and their influence in the present is limited. And yet there is also a sense of connection; they are ancestors who provide a sense of biologic continuity between the past and the present. And they are "our" ancestors – ancestors possessed by the collective, national community. The culture that is coalescing by defining itself against Appalachia can also validate itself through a shared racial history. The discovery of Appalachia, with the accompanying belief that the mountain people "have our best blood in their veins," aids in the construction of national identity by historically grounding the homogeneity (and the assumed racial superiority) of the emerging bourgeoisie (quoted in Klotter 1980: 843). By equating the mountain people with racial purity and with America's noble ancestry, and then by embracing the mountain people as family, the imagined national community both creates itself and asserts its dominance. In the process, it constructs whiteness as an identity that supersedes regional affiliation; the white Southerner shares the same Elizabethan and pioneer ancestors that the white Northerner claims. The Anglo-Saxon is re-inscribed as the quintessential American.

Local color literature like that written by Murfree could have had the potential to unravel the assumption that American culture was homogeneous. But, as Brodhead points out, by "substituting less 'different' native ethnicities for the truly foreign ones of contemporary reality," the genre actually participated in the creation of an imagined homogeneity (Brodhead 1993: 137). The people of Appalachia may have been represented as outside the culture's dominant values; but, as Klotter's research demonstrates, they were also championed as part of the national family because their race kept them from being "truly foreign." This desire to embrace the mountain people in reaction to more threatening cultural difference was enacted by post-Reconstruction reform efforts. As literary texts stirred cultural interest in the mountain region, philanthropists increasingly made the case that the nation needed to turn its money and attention to the Appalachian people. And that case was made, Klotter reports, by very explicitly comparing the mountain people to African Americans. He reports that "accounts made it clear that mountain whites in many ways resembled blacks in their needs, their lives, and their living conditions," and yet the assumption was that the "racism, frustration, and disappointment of white reformers who dealt with blacks after slavery would not be a factor in this society" (Klotter 1980: 841). In an 1884 article, significantly titled "Mountain White Work in Kentucky," Mrs. A. A. Myers of the American Missionary Society pits the mountain-dwellers against the former slaves in order to argue that the white people have not received the charitable attention they deserve:

> "Our brother in black" has been held up to a view of two continents for the last fifty years. And what is America going to do with and for him, has been a question which has interested the whole civilized world. . . . But until recently it has escaped the notice of these Christian workers that we have another class as needy perhaps as any. No spice of romance is connected with them. No barbarous tale of cruelty could be told to awaken sympathy in them. They are simply poor people. (Myers 1884: 12–13)

To call for help for the mountain people depends here on devaluing the oppression suffered by African Americans; slavery and its legacy are dismissed as a romantic attention-getting device.

There is, of course, no real reason why aid for the white people of Appalachia would have needed to be contingent upon the social and political neglect of African Americans. That the argument for support of the mountain people takes this form reveals just how culturally entangled were the discourses of region and race. If the cultural interest in this American region was, as I have been suggesting, inflected from the start by a desire to contain Reconstruction's fracturing of antebellum racial identity, then there would be a strange cultural logic to supporting the mountain people by dismissing the oppression faced by African Americans. According to Klotter, William Goodell Frost, the president of Berea College at the turn of the century, understood the political efficacy of playing Appalachian whites against African Americans when requesting financial support for his institution: "'The education of the Negro, momentous as that duty is, cannot solve the southern problem – we must deal with the white people of the South'" (Klotter 1980: 846). Race and region become even more fully tangled in Frost's plea; not only does he set up the needs of the mountain people against the needs of African Americans, but he also places that conflict back into the context of regional reconciliation. The people of Appalachia are now fully identified as "the white people of the South," and by supporting their education Frost's audience can "solve the southern problem." Only by turning away from the reforms of Reconstruction, away from the challenges of race, Frost implies, can the nation achieve regional and national reunion; the "southern problem" will only be solved through white solidarity. And, in the process, the national community has been constructed as white.

Constructing a (White) Nation

This essay has asserted that the American cultural investment in region, specifically in the South, can serve larger ideological projects. Particularly, I have wanted to suggest that our ways of representing regional identity have been inextricably caught up in the construction of national and racial identities. And with this assertion, I am operating under the assumption that nations and races are constructed – that they have been produced through social and historical forces. Postmodern cultural theorists have demonstrated that social groups, no matter how cohesive their identity or their "difference" appears to be, are not constituted by nature. According to this paradigm, social groupings – like region, race, and nation – are always in flux, always in the process of being constructed and negotiated. Social groupings therefore become strangely interdependent and mutually constructing; we understand groups only through their relationship to other groups. Regional identity, for example, is defined against the identity that has been posited for or by another region, or against a perception of national identity; or, as I have been suggesting here in the case of

American regional identity, through and against the culture's understanding of racial identity.

For Etienne Balibar, the social grouping of individuals into the imagined community of a nation happens through the construction of "fictive ethnicity." Balibar argues that "no modern nation possesses a given 'ethnic' base," but a group can "produce itself continually as national community" through an imagined ethnicity (1991: 93–4). Fictive ethnicity has the power to create a seemingly natural unity. The creation of a fictive ethnicity is effective in the construction of national identity because it seems to precede the creation of the state; there is a sense that nations have seamlessly evolved out of social groups that have been naturally constituted. A population that has been "ethnicized," Balibar says, is "represented in the past or in the future *as if* they formed a natural community, possessing of itself an identity of origins, culture and interests which transcends individuals and social conditions" (1991: 96).

These "ethnicized" communities, Balibar asserts, have been produced through language and race; the ethnicity does not appear to be fictitious because language and race seem to "root historical populations in a fact of 'nature.'" Race is particularly effective in this role because the notion of race contains within it that of "genealogy" or "the idea that the filiation of individuals transmits from generation to generation a substance both biological and spiritual and thereby inscribes them in a temporal community known as 'kinship'" (Balibar 1991: 100). Race and nation thus become inextricably connected; the concept of race (which is itself another social grouping that has no natural or biologic origins) serves in the production of an ethnic "kinship" – something like a large, extended family that seems to extend back into the past – which in turn creates the "we the people" who understand themselves as a nation. For Balibar, then, "every discourse on the fatherland or nation which associates these notions with the 'defense of the family' . . . is already ensconced in the universe of racism" (1991: 106). If national identity (or, I might add, regional identity; the North and South certainly understood themselves as two separate nations) depends upon fictive ethnicity, race, or family – upon social groupings that seem to have always existed on the basis of what are perceived as natural or somatic characteristics – then, nationalism (or regionalism) comes to rest on racist logic. It would seem no accident, then, that the cultural moment in which African-American citizenship challenged American national identity was also the moment in which the imagined national community began reconstructing itself through regional reconciliation and through an investment in region. It follows, too, that this national reconstitution would have been aided by making the Appalachian people – and the larger South – part of the white, Anglo-Saxon "family." Balibar's analysis serves to clarify the strange cultural logic that caused the rights of African Americans to be sacrificed to "our contemporary ancestors" of the mountains and of the larger South. When the fictive ethnicity of the nation was challenged, it was restored, in part, through an emphasis on the collective family of white Americans, and as a result racism was re-inscribed by the newly linked discourses of region and nation.

If, as Balibar asserts, every social community is "based on the projection of individual existence into the weft of a collective narrative, on the recognition of a common name and on traditions lived as the trace of an immemorial past" (1991: 93), we can see Americans in the post-Reconstruction and early twentieth-century periods attempting to stabilize identity by writing themselves into a collective narrative that holds up an imagined past against the challenges of the present. Grace Elizabeth Hale reads the culture of Southern segregation as just such a narrative: a narrative that participates in the making of race as well as in the creation of region. According to Hale, two late nineteenth-century social changes precipitated segregation culture: "a black middle class was rising, with its unhinging of black race and class identities, and hierarchies of personalized power were being subverted in the move to a more urban, less locally grounded, mass society" (1998: 284).

In the new mass culture, identity became more fluid: class and race were not necessarily connected, and class itself was not as easily recognized because a new consumer culture made it possible for Americans of different classes and races to use the same products and to wear the same clothes. Segregation thus became a way to "ground" racial identity by asserting white supremacy: "Since southern black inferiority and white supremacy could not, despite whites' desires, be assumed, southern whites created a modern social order in which this difference would instead be continually performed" (Hale 1998: 284). The culture of segregation was not, then, about social antipathy between black and white Southerners, as we so often assume. For Hale, the culture of segregation was about constructing or, as she says, "making" whiteness. The process of marking public spaces, denying African Americans the privileges of citizenship, and limiting black mobility resulted in a culture that made blackness highly visible. The collective white identity that was forged against that visibility could then become invisible, and through that invisibility could become normative and powerful.

Segregation culture created Southern whiteness and it participated in the creation of a national white identity. It also, Hale points out, created Southern regional identity: "the culture of segregation turned the entire South into a theater of racial difference, a minstrel show writ large upon the land. . . . And southern whites commanded this performance of segregation for both a local and a national audience, to maintain both white privilege at home and a sense of southern distinctiveness within the nation" (1998: 284). This sense of Southern distinctiveness and a voyeur nation, Hale suggests, has endured. That the South has continued to supply a "collective narrative" through which Southern, racial, and national identity are mutually constructed prompts Hale to issue a final challenge to her readers:

> All of us . . . would have to think of "the South," the "race problem," and the "burden of history," not as the weight of some other, of a dark and distant place and time, but as a burden that we still carry and as a history that we have not agreed to face or acknowledge as a source of our subjectivities. We would have to remember that "the South," the romance, the place of not now, the space of safety and mooring for whatever we imagine we have lost, lies not south of anywhere but inside us. (1998: 295)

Hale's sense of how we might begin to unmake race, of how we might begin to rewrite "the immemorial past" of our collective regional and national narratives, is particularly important as we consider the pervasive hold that regionalisms, particularly those invested in the American South, continue to have over our culture.

Present Uses of the Southern Past

We are continuously writing our collective national identity: "The myth of origins and national continuity . . . is therefore an effective ideological form, in which the imaginary singularity of national formations is constructed daily, by moving back from the present into the past" (Balibar 1991: 87). The American South has retained its cultural associations with the American past; the stories Americans still like to tell about the region, about its homey simplicity and its sometimes brutal, sometimes reassuring primitiveness place the region back into an "immemorial past." Taking part in "the myth of origins and national continuity," these stories continue to use the South to form national identity. These cultural uses of the region are apparent in the popular and critically acclaimed film *Forrest Gump*.

Winner of the 1994 Oscar for best picture and one of the highest-grossing films in US history, *Forrest Gump*, with its insistent retelling of the recent American past, attempts to write a national collective narrative. The film is often perceived as not just depicting the turbulent national disruptions of the second half of the twentieth century – the Civil Rights movement, the Vietnam War, the antiwar movement, and the assassinations associated with those events – but as also actively taking part in the process of national healing, in the process of bringing closure to these national dramas. But the problem is that the film itself seems uncomfortable with national divisions, even if those divisions could be understood as a productive crux of democratic society. The scene in the film, for example, in which Forrest, the war hero, embraces Jenny, the counterculture flower child, in front of the Lincoln Memorial reveals the film's investment in national reconciliation. Any productive cracks in the façade of national cohesion are erased in this scene when the war protestors end their oppositional critique to cheer for the reunion of Forrest and Jenny. Though the film depicts the fracturing of the easy nationalism that marked the country at midcentury, it does so only to regain an imagined homogeneous unity.

The wide appeal of the film comes from its ability to neutralize the very traumas that it depicts. Even as it depicts events that reveal an always fractured, never whole nation, the film attempts to forge a new national collectivity in reaction to those very events. In part, the film achieves this sense of national wholeness by making Forrest, who never articulates a political position and who never fully recognizes these cultural fissures, the central consciousness of the film. The viewer is invited, at least to an extent, to identify with Forrest who, because of his low IQ, can be only a passive, uncritical observer of the traumatic history he witnesses. In addition, the film engineers a sense of national unity through its use of region. If Forrest represents the relationship with the national past through which an imagined community can be created, then, given the historical relationship between Southern and national identity, it is perhaps inevitable that Forrest is depicted as a Southerner.

But just as the film does not come to terms with the traumas of the recent past, neither does it come to terms with the South's actual history. Early in the film, for example, Forrest reveals that he was named for Nathan Bedford Forrest, the Confederate general and early Ku Klux Klan leader. Forrest says of his naming, "Mama said that the Forrest part was to remind me that sometimes we all do things that, well, just don't make no sense." This is a new South, the film seems to say, in which the name Forrest conjures up not images of Confederate heroism, the Klan, or violence against African Americans, but instead the nonsensical mistakes of the past. The implication here is that the past can be erased. Forrest and his mother don't have to come to terms with the past or with the legacy of Southern racism; they only need to make it mean something else. As Forrest narrates, telling of his naming, the viewer is shown an image of the Klan taken from *Birth of a Nation*. Forrest's naïve, uncritical explanation of the Klan is then juxtaposed with scenes from Griffith's racist film. While the disjunction between what the viewer knows of the Klan and what Forrest knows is certainly meant to make the Klan look ridiculous, the scene also serves to defuse the historical legacy of Griffith's film. The images from *Birth of a Nation* for most viewers evoke the horrifying and violent racism of the post-Reconstruction South, and yet Forrest's narration revises the viewer's relationship to this story of the South by making the Klan members, like Nathan Bedford Forrest, merely a nonsensical mistake of the past. Just as Forrest's mother attempts to empty the name "Forrest" of its original meaning, in other words, *Birth of a Nation* is emptied of its historical significance by this scene.

The film thus writes a collective national narrative by revising the Southern past; "moving back from the present into the past," the film, shaped by the present desire for national reunion, inscribes a new, less threatening South into American history. And the film also forges national unity by reinvesting in a mythic Southern past. Forrest's antebellum house in Greenbow, Alabama becomes a central and recurring image in the film. The film is structured around Forrest's movement out into the public sphere, where he witnesses the traumatic events of national life, and his return home. The house, which is set symbolically apart from the community, is placed in opposition to public life; when Forrest returns to this house it is as if he has gone back into a safe, nurturing past. Jenny, too, in two different scenes of the film, goes home with Forrest to escape the destructive forces of the present. With its use of the culturally and historically resonant image of the antebellum plantation house, the film thus locates the mythic space of national reconciliation and healing squarely in the South. In the film's aesthetically appealing opening scenes, the camera focuses on the front exterior of the house, which is illuminated against the evening sky. With its open windows, large front porch, and the Spanish moss that hangs from the large trees in its front yard, the house evokes the "moonlight and magnolias" and the warm summer nights of the mythic southern past. If *Forrest Gump* works to heal the nation, it does so by making the viewer feel at home in the mythic South – in a South whose real history has been obscured.

It is not that *Forrest Gump* is an overtly racist film. But the issue is that by calling on the regional tropes of the past to provide a sense of national community, the film recapitulates the very narratives that have served so well in the construction of an invisible whiteness. The film re-inscribes "the myth of origins and national continuity" with which the South has provided American culture without examining, at least in any sustained way, the mutual dependence of those myths and the making of race. But this raises a question: Is it possible to celebrate, or even to invest in, the South and Southern identity without participating in the continued construction of polarized racial identities? It is possible; but, as Hale suggests, such a regionalism could not rest on unexamined Southern myths. It would need to come to terms with the present – not by rewriting the past to fit present needs and not by writing a mythic past that provides an escape from the present, but rather by recognizing that the present continues to be shaped by the past, that regional and racial identity are not "of a dark and distant place and time, but . . . a burden that we still carry." As we reread the regional literature from the past and as we begin to examine the recent flowering of contemporary regional literature, our critical practice needs to attend to these questions: Does the text rely on culturally resonant images from the past, a kind of cultural shorthand, allowing us to feel secure in our national identity by retelling a false collectivity? Or does it provide an opportunity to revise that collectivity by disrupting our regional space of "safety and mooring"? We can begin to unmake race by challenging the continued conflation of national, regional, and racial identity.

Notes

1 Throughout this essay, I am indebted to Hale's thoughtful, persuasive analysis of the construction of race in Southern segregation culture. I will discuss her work in greater detail later in this essay.

2 There is evidence that this cultural strategy went beyond the textual. Even political interventions into Appalachia, which followed the literary discovery of the region, worked to distance and tame the threat of heterogeneity while, perhaps unknowingly, supporting the superiority of the "bourgeois, urban present" (Shapiro 1978: 15). See David E. Whisnant's study of the discovery of Appalachia by New England teachers (1983). Whisnant argues that the national investment in nostalgically containing the disruptive heterogeneity of American subcultures dispossessed the Appalachian people of their land, and thus of any economic power. And this dispossession, in turn, ensured the continuing dominance of the urban, mainstream culture.

References and Further Reading

Anderson, B. (1983). *Imagined Communities*. London: Verso.

Applebome, P. (1996). *Dixie Rising: How the South is Shaping American Values, Politics, and Culture*. San Diego: Harcourt Brace.

Ayres, E. L. (1992). *The Promise of the New South: Life after Reconstruction*. New York: Oxford University Press.

Balibar, E. (1991). "The Nation Form: History and Ideology." In E. Balibar and I. Wallerstein,

Race, Nation, Class: Ambiguous Identities, trans. Chris Turner, 86–104. New York: Verso.

Brodhead, R. H. (1993). *Cultures of Letters: Scenes of Reading and Writing in Nineteenth-Century America*. Chicago: University of Chicago Press.

Clifford, J. (1986). "Introduction: Partial Truths." In J. Clifford and G. E. Marcus (eds.), *Writing Culture: The Poetics and Politics of Ethnography*, 1–26. Berkeley: University of California Press.

Dew, C. B. (1994). "The Most Regional Region." *New York Times Book Review*, 20 Nov., 745.

Dial, The (1884). Review of *In the Tennessee Mountains*. 5, 43.

Foner, E. (1988). *Reconstruction: America's Unfinished Revolution 1863–1877*. New York: Harper & Row.

Forrest Gump (1994). Dir. Robert Zemeckis. Paramount.

Guillaumin, C. (1995). *Racism, Sexism, Power, and Ideology*. London: Routledge.

Hale, G. E. (1998). *Making Whiteness: The Culture of Segregation in the South, 1890–1940*. New York: Vintage.

Kaplan, Amy (1991). "Nation, Region, and Empire." In Emory Elliot (ed.), *The Columbia History of the American Novel*, 240–66. New York: Columbia University Press.

Klotter, J. C. (1980). "The Black South and White Appalachia." *Journal of American History* 66, 832–49.

Morrison, T. (1992). *Playing in the Dark: Whiteness and the Literary Imagination*. New York: Vintage.

Murfree, M. (1970). *In the Tennessee Mountains*. Knoxville: University of Tennessee Press. (First publ. 1884.)

Myers, Mrs A. A. (1884). "Mountain White Work in Kentucky." *American Missionary* 38, 12–16.

Porter, C. (1988). "Social Discourse and Nonfictional Prose." In Emory Elliot (ed.), *The Columbia History of the American Novel*, 345–63. New York: Columbia University Press.

Pratt, M. L. (1986). "Fieldwork in Common Places." In J. Clifford and G. E. Marcus (eds.), *Writing Culture: The Poetics and Politics of Ethnography*, 27–50. Berkeley: University of California Press.

Roberts, D. (1994). *The Myth of Aunt Jemima: Representations of Race and Region*. New York and London: Routledge.

Shapiro, H. D. (1978). *Appalachia on Our Mind: The Southern Mountains and Mountaineers in the American Consciousness, 1870–1920*. Chapel Hill: University of North Carolina Press.

Sundquist, E. J. (1993). *To Wake the Nations: Race in the Making of American Literature*. Cambridge, Mass.: Belknap.

Tourgée, A. (1978). "The South as a Field for Fiction", ed. L. M. Simms, Jr. *Southern Studies* 17, 399–409. (First publ. 1888.)

Vincent, G. E. (1898). "A Retarded Frontier." *American Journal of Sociology*, July, 1–20.

Whisnant, D. (1983). *All That is Native and Fine: The Politics of Culture in an American Region*. Chapel Hill: University of North Carolina Press.

5

Regionalism in the Era
of the New Deal

Lauren Coats and Nihad M. Farooq

Regionalism . . . is the true native ground. The perception of that home truth is an act of politics, cultural politics, a seizing of imaginative power, and the construction or re-construction of institutions . . . It is not a denial or a retreat from realities and issues – it is a way through and into them.

L. Honnighausen, "The Old and New Regionalism," p. 17

Regionalism in the era of the New Deal worked at the intersections of government, academia, politics, literature, and nationalism. Regionalists of the 1930s recognized their work as something different from the art and fiction of the late nineteenth-century literary regionalists. While the literary and aesthetic were not divorced from regionalism in this later era, the movement was explicitly interested in the inter-sections of such aesthetic practices with political practices. Regionalism explored the possibilities of transforming social theory into social action, whether through scholarly research, literary production, or politics. Self-proclaimed regionalists of the time used the idea of regionalism to confront the problems of the Great Depression. In so doing, they enacted a central tenet of regionalism in this period: that it would result in effective programs and policies. The question, then, is how regionalists of this era conceived of revitalizing the American nation.

Participants in debates about regionalism came from numerous disciplines, worked within various institutions, and identified with different regions. What is perhaps most striking about the debate is that it never presented a uniform version of what regionalism was or what it might accomplish. The debate and disagreement over the principles and practices of regionalism, however, illuminate how this conceptual framework was built in response to the exigencies of the period. This essay will look to two locations in the regionalist debate to trace the various practices and effects of the investment in repairing the nation. First, we will look to a social science per-spective and its incorporation within New Deal planning; then we will turn to the

Federal Writers' Project, one of the New Deal programs, to consider how regionalism operated in the literary landscape.

I

At the time Franklin D. Roosevelt first took office as President in 1933, the economy had collapsed, one-third of the US labor force was unemployed, and the world of finance and industry was in disarray. According to historian Monty Penkower, "the Depression challenged the very mythology that had buttressed what Jefferson had termed 'the great experiment.' The sense of America's uniqueness, of a land where hopes become realities and paupers self-made men, seemed to vanish" (1977: 2). Roosevelt began his 12-year tenure as President with a buoyant optimism and a pledge to lift the nation out of the Great Depression – the most profound and enduring economic crisis it had ever faced. In the first 115 days of his presidency, Roosevelt began to make good on his pledge, authorizing the creation of several new programs designed to usher in a long season of relief, reform, and recovery known as the New Deal era.

The federal government's involvement with regionalism was never formalized or wholesale; rather, it was more a matter of influence and a shared interest in developing an ideology by which to guide the nation out of the Depression. In 1931, FDR gave the keynote address at the University of Virginia Round-Table Conference on Regionalism, one of the major regionalist conferences of the era. The audience included several key figures in the movement, such as Howard Odum, a sociologist from the University of North Carolina at Chapel Hill; H. C. Nixon and John Gould Fletcher, Vanderbilt Agrarians; and Benton MacKaye and Lewis Mumford, colleagues from New York. Promising that an interest in national planning would balance the rural and urban, Roosevelt seemed to be in at least some accord with the visions of regionalists, and indeed, several regionalists participated quite literally in New Deal legislation and programs (Dorman 1993: 275, 292). Benton MacKaye worked with the Tennessee Valley Authority, John Collier with the Bureau of Indian Affairs, B. A. Botkin and John Lomax on the Federal Writers' Project, Rupert Vance with the National Resources Committee, Paul Taylor with the Resettlement Administration, Howard Odum with the Civil Works Administration (Wilson 1998: 14; Challen 1992: 52). Yet the New Deal was far from a programmatic implementation of regionalist principles, and the individuals named above were far from unified in their vision of what regionalism was and how it would function.

The development of folklore and social science in the decade preceding the New Deal era informed the rise of regionalism. Universities witnessed a resurgent interest in folklore. This interest in an American folk was not new; the American Folklore Society had been founded in 1888, and the impulse to recognize a native cultural tradition, folk or otherwise, can be traced back to authors such as Irving, Hawthorne, and Longfellow (Bauman 1976: 361). With the work of early twentieth-century folklorists, including B. A. Botkin and John Lomax, the interest in an American folk culture intersected with the interest in an American regionalism. That is, regionalism can be understood as a "science with an agenda, . . . an attempted fusion of the modern with the traditional," an attempt to find a balance between the older folk ways of regions and the forces of modernization (Dorman 1993: 138). Folklore, then, was a tool by which such folk ways could be salvaged from the threat of dissolution. Just as folklorists attempted to locate a uniquely American folk tradition out of the array of transplanted Old World customs, so regionalists, too, negotiated a singular definition of "America" within the array of regional differences. Regionalism, like the New Deal itself, assayed a broad-scale recultivation not only of the economy but also of the national psyche. For the first time, Americans sought to "understand and interpret American *character*" (Mangione 1972: 47). The effort to locate the national psyche carried with it the hope of ultimately reviving, and in some instances creating, an American folk culture. This turn to an American folk sought a model of national integration in the present by invoking a vision of the American past. Regionalism's task of creating a usable past provided a framework for understanding American difference. In the words of a prominent regionalist, Lewis Mumford: "under the even whitewash of 'national unity' the colors of the underlying geographic, economic, and cultural realities are beginning to show through" (Odum and Moore 1938: 46). Regionalism, then, would counteract the tendentious claims of national unity that ignored such differences by creating a nation integrated by the recognition and celebration of them.

Regionalism was also informed by the rise of the social sciences, which increasingly were institutionalized in universities in the earliest years of the twentieth century (Grantham 1968: 3–4). Disciplines such as sociology were active in the several regional institutes which contributed to the growing influence of and interest in regionalism in American during the 1920s and 1930s. For example, the Institute for Research in Social Science at the University of North Carolina headed regionalist scholarship in the South (Grantham 1968: 7–8). Philanthropic institutions, such as the Rockefeller Foundation, also funded studies that worked within regional boundaries, particularly studies of race and rural poverty. University presses, including those at the University of North Carolina and Oklahoma, followed a policy of publishing books of regional interest. The variety of regionalist projects ranged from Nebraska's new state capitol to regional journals across the Midwest, Southwest, and Northwest, to books such as Walter Prescott Webb's *The Great Plains* (1931), Lewis Mumford's *The Culture of Cities* (1938), and Mary Austin's *Earth Horizon* (1932), to the National Folk Festival in 1934. These projects, in addition to the numerous regionalist conferences in the early 1930s, all testify to the growing importance of regionalism in this era (Wilson 1998: 6–7).

Howard Odum, one of the most significant figures of regionalism during the New Deal era, had a career that both influenced and mirrored the gradual development of this movement. More specifically, Odum's career speaks to the influence of social science on the conceptualization of regionalism. Born in rural Georgia, Odum first received a doctorate in psychology before studying under Franklin Giddings at Columbia. He then went on to earn his second doctorate, this time in sociology, in 1910. G. Stanley Hall, as well as psychologist Thomas Bailey, introduced Odum to the burgeoning social science discipline. Some of Odum's first scholarly publications, before World War I, included studies on contemporary racial debates (such as his *Social and Mental Traits of the Negro*) and the rural South. It was not until he joined the faculty at the University of North Carolina at Chapel Hill in 1920 that Odum became involved with the work for which he is most remembered. Odum's first task at UNC was to organize the new School of Public Welfare. Odum optimistically envisioned the school as providing a platform for reform of social problems that plagued the South, most particularly through cooperation with government agencies. This combination, a productive partnership between the academy and the government, was central to Odum's hopes for a program of Southern social planning (O'Brien 1979: 31–40).

In the 1920s, Odum wrote a description of the role of social workers that accurately prefigures his own later sociological studies of American regions:

> Studying facts, making them applicable to folks with human interests and social instincts, utilizing methods, principles, convictions. . . . Among his [the social worker's] many other characteristics is his ability to influence leadership in various fields – the men and women interested in civic endeavor, the capitalist interested in philanthropy, leaders in labor reform, the law makers of the land, college professors, university presidents. (Quoted in O'Brien 1979: 40–1)

Odum thus expressed his faith in the potential of his social science work to make a quite tangible impact. Regionalism, for Odum, was "a framework for social planning and social action" (Grantham 1968: 16). In his first years at UNC he also established the *Journal of Social Forces*, as well as helping to organize the Institute for Research in Social Science. In addition, he served as the first chairman of the Southern Regional Committee, a division of the Social Science Research Council. It was under this group's auspices that Odum conducted the research that resulted in his 1936 *Southern Regions of the United States*. Odum's activities speak to the intersection of different institutional locations, forces, and capital – from the university, philanthropic foundations, and the government – that fueled the more explicit elaboration of regionalist ideology. Odum's work, as well as that of his colleagues, also reveals the way in which the social science studies of rural farming conditions, African-American life, and Southern folklore coalesced in Southern regional thought. Works produced by Odum's colleagues during his tenure at UNC include Rupert Vance's *Human Geography of the South: A Study in Regional Resources and Human Adequacy* (1932), Arthur Raper's *Preface to Peasantry: a Tale of Two Black Belt Counties* (1936), and Guy B. Johnson's *Folk Culture on St. Helena Island, South Carolina* (1930). Gradually, Odum's interests in the folk, sociology, and social planning coalesced into a formulation of a regionalist creed.

The demarcation of regions was, of course, a major question of regionalism. A region, as Odum defined it in his 1938 *American Regionalism* (written with Henry Moore), should "[embody] the fewest contradictions, the greatest flexibility, and the largest degree of homogeneity for all purposes of study and planning" (Odum and Moore 1938: 29). This entity could be found by employing indices that measured regional characteristics, "both natural factors and societal factors which must, of course, include the American states and prevailing historic, economic, and culture traits" (Odum and Moore 1938: 30). Thus Odum's 1936 study carved the nation into six distinct regions, based on the over 700 indices of cultural, economic, and social factors it incorporated: the Southeast, the Southwest, the Northeast, the Middle States, the Northwest, and the Far West.

American Regionalism outlines the tenets of Odum's version of regionalism. His conception of the utility and vision of this movement reflected the widespread belief by regionalists across disciplines and institutions (sociologists, novelists, city planners, folklorists, and more) that regionalism would find an " 'accommodating middle ground' between the modern and the traditional" (Dorman 1993: 50). The idea of finding a middle ground was central to Odum's conception of regionalism:

> The significance of regionalism as the key to equilibrium is reflected in an extraordinarily wide range of situations, such as the conflict between nationalism and internationalism, between sectionalism and federalism, and the imbalance between agrarian and urban life, between agriculture and industry, between individuation and socialization in governmental trends, between a quantity civilization of standardizing forces and a quality world, between machines and men. (Odum and Moore 1938: 5)

Odum's formulation of regionalism suggests that this equilibrium was contingent on decentralization. Working against consolidations of power in urban centers, big businesses, and the government, Odum instead offered a vision of the nation that would reside in the balance across and within regions – a balance of scale, between individuals and large governments or corporations, between natural resources and human resources, between the past and the present.

The ideas of decentralization and balance turned upon Odum's conceptualization of the folk. He believed "the folk-society, the folk-culture, is the elemental and basic culture definitive of all societies in process" (Odum and Jocher 1945: 16). However, Odum's understanding of the definition and parameters of "the folk" was vague; for Odum, the folk was both the South as a whole as well as smaller groups, such as tenant farmers or African Americans, within the South. Regionalism, though, would succeed only insofar as it found a way to incorporate this folk into the nation. Odum distinguished between the "folkway," the threatened ways of the past, and the "stateways" or "technicways," the increasingly powerful ways of the present. The major distinction was that the former was an organic, "extra-organization" expression of a society and culture, while stateways and technicways "regulated the informal ways of the folk" (O'Brien 1979: 65). This reliance of regionalism on the folk does not translate into a completely nostalgic longing for the past, nor does it assume that the folk is necessarily outdated. Rather, regionalism would mediate among these various forces, "providing technical ways for the reintegration of agrarian culture in American life" (Odum and Jocher 1945: 12). Regionalism would provide "a new equilibrium between culture and civilization" where culture is the folk and civilization is the state and technology (Odum and Jocher 1945: 3).

One of the most trenchant sources of criticism of Odum's regionalism is its theorization of the folk. More specifically, Odum's studies often focused on African Americans and small farmers, yet did not address the issue of how these folk might be included in regionalism, not as objects of study, but as participants. That is, he believed that improvements and reform in Southern agriculture and education would mitigate the economic crisis and ameliorate the worst of class and race conflict in the South. Regionalist reform "was not a revolutionary program, so much as an attempt to make a platonic agrarian ideal workable and eliminate the immense waste in Southern society" (O'Brien 1979: 67).

Odum's call for reform of the Southern economy seemed to advocate a radical restructuring of the tenant farm system, and indeed, offered an incisive critique of it. However, his program reveals an underlying conservative politics of race and class. It is useful to see the ways in which Odum's social science sought both to confront and to occlude racial and class difference through its reliance on the valuation of the folk. "By pitching institutions of geographical control against class divisions," regionalism would circumvent class divisiveness. Even Odum's euphemistic vocabulary, the use of the term "folk" for middle- and lower-class farmers, "divert[ed] attention from the possibility of analyzing the region in terms of class relationships" (King 1980: 47). That is, the fetishization of these tenant farmers as "folk" – the same folk whose existence was so integral to the region – belied the purported attempt to reform the Southern culture and economy and bring these "folk" out of the poverty of the Depression. On the question of race, Odum did not advocate a policy of equality: he supported segregation, and assumed that improved structures, for example in agriculture and education, would improve not only the South as a whole, but also its constituent parts, among them the African-American community. Regionalism, by this critique, could offer only a limited response to the inequalities of class and race in the South. As Richard King notes:

Odum and [Rupert] Vance . . . did not analyze the exploitative class relationships within the region. This is not to say that they neglected poverty; far from it. Rather they tended to talk of general income levels or to point to the rise of tenancy and share-cropping; and their solutions were either very general – the call for regional economic planning – or quite specific – the call for better vocational and higher education. They assumed that if the masses received better education, they would receive better jobs and improve their lives. The rising tide of future Southern prosperity would lift all boats. Education took the place of politics, planning the place of participation. (King 1980: 48)

This impulse to generalize both the concept and management of the folk thus ultimately constrained Odum's otherwise radical attempt to re-imagine the structure of the nation through regionalism.

As a result, regionalist reform perpetuates certain racial and class inequalities. Odum believed that "[d]emocracy assumes opportunity and representation for the individual, but it is too often overlooked that the same guarantee applies to the group or state or race or region" (Odum and Moore 1938: 10). Yet a focus on the group tended to present a homogeneous, fetishized typology of its members. "Odum was committed to the 'folk' without desiring their direct participation in the development of the South . . . Once economic problems had been solved, racial and class conflicts would disappear" (King 1980: 48–9). By this critique, Odum's regionalism was a palliative, alleviating rather than confronting class inequalities within regions, obviating divisiveness through an appeal to an American folk.

Thus, regionalism would serve as a model by which to integrate the nation and ensure its economic, social, and cultural security. "It is true that the unity of the nation is found in the integration of its diversities," admitted Odum, "but also the organic union of the nation is found in the continuing rediscovery and reintegration of its regions. Still more, each of the diversities or regions is fabricated of historical and cultural developments, of geographic and physiographic characteristics, of the folk quality and culture of the people" (Odum and Moore 1938: 423). Regionalism seemed to offer a vision of national integration that used the region as the fulcrum on which to balance old and new, poor and rich, state and federal, folk and technology. Regionalism, then, is not opposed to nationalism, but rather a means to achieve a more perfect union within the nation.

The interest in regionalist perspectives on national issues was not new to the Roosevelt administration. Hoover had created the Research Committee on Social Trends on which Howard Odum served and which resulted in a lengthy sociological study. However, the study was never translated into political action (Baldwin 1968: 43). It was not until the New Deal that a more active symbiosis of regionalist thought and government planning occurred. The interest in enacting regionalist thought in governmental policy suggests the extent to which the New Deal provided a testing ground for the efficacy of regionalism.

New Deal programs promoted numerous studies of the various regions – the Great Plains, the South, the Tennessee Valley – to gather information that would assist in the implementation of policies to ameliorate the effects of the Depression. The Agricultural Adjustment Administration commissioned studies of rural and agricultural life, using the social sciences that were so deeply imbricated in regionalism as a tool in forming policy. The AAA was one of the first recovery efforts of Roosevelt's administration that took a particular interest in the plight of farmers and attempted to provide relief and reform through policies of price parity and production control, among others. In the actual implementation of policy, however, the AAA did not adhere to regionalist philosophy. Many of its detractors complained that "farmers were merely being advised to manage production as industrial corporations did in their quest for profit" – a tactic that worked against Odum's regionalist vision of balancing old and new agrarian methods and practices rather than simply making the old ways obsolete.

Another criticism of the AAA illustrates the ways in which both regionalism and the AAA bolstered extant and oppressive class structures. The AAA provided government subsidies to farmers (as direct relief, as compensation for reduced production, and as incentive to find alternative farming methods), but the money was not always distributed equally. "Landlords often refused to give their tenants shares of the government checks, demoted sharecroppers to day laborers so as to free themselves from any obligation to share the benefits from Washington, and cut back on the number of sharecroppers as they cut back on the cotton acreage" (Graham and Wander 1985: 2). While the AAA tried to combat such discrepancies, to a certain extent its failures highlight the ways in which the New Deal's policies of reform toed the line between radical restructuring and the status quo. Thus, the effect of these policies was to reinforce rather than alter class relationships among farmers. Likewise, as critiques of Odum's regionalism reveal, the movement's obfuscation of the entrenched structures of class avoided the issue of whether such class inequalities would forestall the large-scale economic improvement it envisioned. That is, the way in which class structures were themselves a cause of the socioeconomic crisis was often neglected by the New Deal agencies, such as the AAA, thereby limiting the effectiveness of their proposed solutions.

In another intersection of the New Deal and regionalism, Frederic A. Delano, the head of the National Planning Board created in 1933, had been closely involved with the Regional Plan of New York and its Environs (RPNY) in the 1920s (Reagan 1999: 45–6). Regionalists such as Odum and Mumford lauded regional planning boards of this kind, and indeed Odum saw these organizations as a central mechanism in the implementation of regionalist ideals. Another 1933 creation was the Federal Emergency Relief Administration (FERA) headed by Harry Hopkins, who had been involved in social welfare work in New York (Reagan 1999: 59). FERA's structure can be seen as the implementation, at least in part, of regionalist principles. Hopkins established "four operation divisions: The Division of Research, Statistics and Finance; the Works Division; the Division of Rural Rehabilitation; and the Division of Relations with States" to aid in the distribution of relief (Graham and Wander 1985: 132). The emphasis on research and the rural as key to creating an effective relief program echo regionalist sentiment. Moreover, FERA operated with regional offices that served as vehicles for liaison between the central organization and the states. FERA participated in regionalist concerns, and can be seen as incorporating regionalist sentiment, but was never explicitly conceived as being a regionalist agency.

Even with the Tennessee Valley Authority (TVA), which Odum and many of his regionalist contemporaries lauded as the great regionalist experiment, the establishment of regionalist ideas in public policy was provisional, at best. The TVA sought to develop the resources in the area along the Tennessee River through programs that would manage flood control, hydroelectric power, soil erosion, industrial development and diversification, and the retirement of marginal land from agriculture (Graham and Wander 1985: 421–422). The TVA supported research studies of the region, using a model akin to that supported by Odum that would integrate scholarly research with political action (Grantham 1968: 18). In addition, as Roosevelt's description of the TVA emphasizes, it followed a regionalist mission of decentralization: "It is time to extend planning to a wider field, in this instance comprehending in one great project many states directly concerned with the basin of one of our greatest rivers" (Graham and Wander 1985: 422). Although the TVA was hailed as the pinnacle of regionalist experiments, it had to operate by "framing its program within the existing pattern of government, including the powers and the traditional prerogatives of the local units" (Dorman 1993: 298). While it did approach a radical reconceptualization of the relationship between the states and the federal government, as well as of relationships among the various individuals and local interests within the region itself, its reformist tendencies were attenuated by the exigencies of political efficacy. That is, its reforms could work only insofar as they did not upset the existing political structures. When, in 1937, Roosevelt submitted to Congress "a proposal for seven 'regional authorities or agencies' to plan for the integrated use and conservation of water, soil, and forests" modeled on the TVA, the plan never was entered into serious debate. The demise of the "seven little TVA's" testifies to the severe limitations which regionalism suffered in government policy (Graham and Wander 1985: 78). "Thus were the agendas of the regionalist movement attenuated by the politics of the New Deal" (Dorman 1993: 297).

II

The New Deal's plans for relief, reform, and recovery soon extended to the arts. Through the Works Progress Administration, a work-relief agency designed to preserve and develop skills among people outside the agricultural and manual trades, Roosevelt authorized funding for Federal Project Number One, a subunit which gave work relief to artists, actors, musicians, and writers. On November 1, 1935, the Federal Writers' Project was launched under the directorship of journalist Henry G. Alsberg as a catch-all for unemployed white-collar workers, such as teachers, preachers, journalists, doctors, lawyers, and recent college graduates. The Writers' Project aspired not to the conventional literary goals of producing poetry and fiction, but rather to the more socially, politically, and economically *useful* objectives of providing the country with "a survey of varying aspects of everyday life as it is lived in all parts of the US" – a nonfiction American Guide Series that would provide a state-by-state portrait of the nation. The utilitarian function of the Project was threefold. First, it would provide work for needy writers and other professionals; second, it would help bolster the tourist economy, and third, it would promote national pride in regional roots by "mapping an uncharted America" (Penkower 1977: 13; Graham and Wander 1985: 135, 461).

It was the Authors' League, a group organized by the Communist Party and deeply invested in working-class radicalism, which first suggested to the Roosevelt administration in 1934 that a guidebook series focusing on the varied lives and landscapes of American regions might be a project of "social usefulness" to the government and its citizens, to readers and writers alike (Penkower 1977: 13). Thus began an unlikely partnership between the left-wing literary community, which had spent a decade denouncing capitalism and the bourgeois mentality of the 1920s, and the federal government, which for the first time viewed the arts as instrumental to national recovery, both economic and psychological. For who was better suited, in this troubled moment, to help this newly introspective nation find its character than its most scrutinizing observers, its citizen-artists?

The American Guide Series modeled itself on the European Baedeker guidebooks. But the organizers of the FWP wanted to give the nation something more than just a bland text of charts, statistics, and maps. Instead, they sought to narrate a lively journey that would unearth the hidden histories and unique characters of each state and serve as an indispensable tool for both historians *and* travelers. Each guide was divided into three sections. The first section brought to life the history and peculiarities of the people, politics, arts, and economy of each state. The second section focused on the major cities, and the final section, filled with map routes and landmarks, represented the motor-tour section of each guidebook (Graham and Wander 1985: 135). These comprehensive volumes represented rich chapters in the nation's first autobiography and attempted to restore a sense of national unity by promoting regional self-awareness and introspection. "As domestic unrest tested the Republic's foundation," explains Monty Penkower, "the guides helped make this inspection fruitful . . . by placing the particular within the framework of a whole" (1977: 241).

Despite the media's initial censure of the government's patronage of the arts, the guides were received favorably by a literary community already focused on the theme of American rediscovery. Regarded by one reviewer as "the biggest, fastest, most original research job in the history of the world," the Writers' Project was praised for performing a valuable national service and for presenting the country with its first true self-portrait (Penkower 1977: 135). *The New Republic* echoed this sentiment, stating that "of all the good uses of adversity, one of the best has been the conception and execution of a series of American guidebooks . . . the first attempt, on a comprehensive scale, to make the country itself worthily known to Americans" (Mangione 1972: 216).

As one might imagine, the Project's field workers and writers produced an enormous amount of research on each state, which spilled into additional city guides and over 150 books in a *Life in America* series. But beyond these guidebooks, the Federal Writers' Project also had an extremely important alternate role, as a research group concerned with collecting and narrating the unwritten history of America's vanishing folklore as well as the stories of former slaves. Through their nationwide search for folklore, the federal writers helped unearth "a rich and significant part of the American past which was in immediate danger of being lost" as the generation of early settlers died out, and the acceleration of mechanical means of communication altered oral traditions of storytelling. Writers emphasized the speech and ways of the common people and the contributions of minorities as a way of revealing a "genuinely native" American culture (Mangione 1972: 238, 68). "Without the misleading tinsel of prosperity," explains Jerre Mangione:

> with the country ripped at the seams by the Great Depression, the variegated parts of America became more visible, and these writers understood the country as they never had before. They saw, for the first time, that the population did not live solely under the influence of the Protestant ethic, with its inhibiting bourgeois vision, but that it was a mixture of different groups – blacks, Irish, Italian, German, Russian, etc. – all interacting with one another in a struggle for survival and assertion and generating their own special influence. (1972: 50)

Benjamin Botkin, who assumed the post of folklore editor in 1938, advocated that the folk movement break away from its scholarly past. He firmly believed that such a movement should "come from below upward . . . otherwise it may be dismissed as a patronizing gesture, a nostalgic wish, an elegiac complaint, a sporadic and abortive revival – on the part of paternalistic aristocrats . . . going back to the soil, and anybody and everybody who cares to go collecting" (Mangione 1972: 270). But it seems that Botkin's desire to cultivate "folk fantasy rather than folk knowledge" may have resulted in just this type of nostalgia and paternalism, as writers of varying levels of "creative listening" and writing skills had free range to collect, depict, and, indeed, *reconstruct* folk stories and culture according to their own designs. Although these writers were able to investigate the lives of "Connecticut clock makers . . . Oklahoma oil field workers . . . Vermont granite workers from Italy . . . and brick-layers from Chicago," the depth and diversity of this collection of "living lore" was contingent on the writers' own interests, intuition, and influences, as well as the Washington office's final editorial revisions (Mangione 1972: 272).

Botkin soon joined forces with Morton Royse, a national consultant for socio-ethnic studies, to gather material from both recent immigrants and indigenous folk in each state. Botkin and Royse worked together to produce "intensive studies on single groups and cross-section analyses of whole communities" (Penkower 1977: 150). But once again, their "functional approach," which stressed cultural back-grounds and activities instead of peculiarities and "contributions," seemed primarily interested in providing a broad, static picture of American "types" that could be easily captured by Project writers and tidily incorporated into the national fabric. The American folklore study, though concerned with collecting the stories of *all* Americans, had a more complicated relationship to the individual histories and voices it attempted to present. More than just "an agency of conservation and re-habilitation of threatened personalities," the folklore program could be seen as an agency concerned with the management of personalities whose diverse regional and cultural affiliations and undocumented status could otherwise be seen as a threat to the project of national cohesion.

The federal writers, emboldened by the cause of documenting and salvaging the histories of "local" folk across the varied regions of America, entered the process of literary production in a way that conveyed to them their own power to make "a genuine indigenous art" (Penkower 1977: 68–9). Let us pause for a moment to examine this endeavor. What does it mean, after all, to reveal a genuinely native American culture? To *create* an art that is *indigenous*? Is it the act of molding something that one already possesses (such as an understanding of a particular region or people) into a piece of art? Or is it the act of taking something that is foreign and transforming it, through narrative, into something that becomes a beloved artifact of the nation? This discussion of the Federal Writers' Project and its treatment of specific minority "folk" groups, such as African Americans, provides a necessary framework for the examination of broader questions about how specific localities and persons can influence and are influenced by a larger national narrative. It is with such questions in mind that we turn to the socioliterary movement of regionalism, which made a radically inspired but federally controlled return to the national scene in this era of the New Deal.

Much like the language of the New Deal itself, regionalist literature of the 1930s seemed to offer its own pledge of relief, recovery, and reform. It offered immediate relief by providing employment as well as a focal point for writers who might already be making connections between space and identity, allowing them to document their regional cultures and heritage; it spawned a recovery in helping writers cultivate a sense of pride in a utilitarian art; and its ultimate aim seemed – at least on the surface – to be the larger project of welcoming minorities and folk into the national narrative, thereby fostering a reformed sense of national cohesion.

Michael Szalay examines the literary regionalism of this era through the lens of the 1929 crash and the ensuing crisis of "social legitimacy" faced by the nation. He parallels this with a similar crisis facing the literary world, as "writers looked to reconcile conflicting impulses toward individual agency and collective affiliation" (2000: 2). Many writers on the left initially viewed modernism's "fascination with form as a solipsistic refusal of the hardship occasioned by the Great Depression." Portraying art for art's sake in such a time, stated Diego Rivera in 1932, served "to limit the use of art as a revolutionary weapon" (Szalay 2000: 47). However, the Depression changed the political connotations of existing literary conventions, and new accounts began to emerge that addressed "how modernist concerns with form and audience might engage in political and economic experience" (Szalay 2000: 3). The renaissance of literary regionalism in this era of federally sponsored artistic production merged the aesthetic concerns of modernists with the utilitarian concerns of the radical left.

Thus, despite their political and ideological quarrels with a government they felt overemphasized individuality over collective struggle, the radical left put aside their grudges to work with the administration toward a revolutionary program in the arts. Radical writers hoped, through the Project, to produce an art that might reconceive the national structure as a series of regional, or collective, movements. But the

ideology that inspired the creation of the Federal Writers' Project and the subsequent flurry of regional research and literary endeavor was quickly subsumed and
transformed into a government-mechanized machine that glossed over class struggle.
As Malcolm Cowley reflected on the Writers' Project in 1954, the "democratic"
method of employment by the government took the radical writer, "initially allied
with the working class, and turned him into the 'salaried writer' – a new figure in
American society" (Szalay 2000: 28). Through the Writers' Project, the radical left
thus seems not only to have begrudgingly reconciled itself to New Deal politics, but
actually to have converged, in a sense, with a government ideology of conservatism
through the exploitation and fetishization of the "folk," masked in a desire to assist
them by giving voice to them.

The regionalist aim of the Project sought to convey the heterogeneity of American people through the documentation and preservation of traditions, customs, and
languages that made each landscape "uniquely" American. But the standardizing
quality of these depictions eventually erased the individual quirks and personalities
of folks in order to portray a sense of group consistency – that is, homogeneity. This
erasure of difference not only discounted the inherent diversity that can exist among
even those of the same race and region, but, in a much more harmful way, often
confirmed and perpetuated racist stereotypes about minority groups. The notion of
giving voice to the people of a region served to patronize and ventriloquize them,
as the writer's translation of a particular encounter often led to a complete re-
contextualization (especially since all copy went through the central Washington
editorial office for approval, censorship, or rewording). Also, the very endeavor of
researching, unearthing, and publishing these regional voices to share them with the
rest of the nation has a tone of objectification and exoticization that is not easily
countered. Nowhere is this fetishization more flagrant than in the Project's depiction
of African Americans, who, like other minority "folk" depicted in the guide series,
were invited to enter this regionalist project not as subjects of the nation's history,
but as *objects* of the nation's lore.

It is useful to pause here in order to examine the political and historical impact of
the New Deal on African Americans, as this may help us understand the viewpoint
of the black writers on the Project, as well as the skewed testimony of those African
Americans interviewed by Project members. African Americans witnessed the in-
auguration of FDR with little hope for the relief, reform, and recovery promised by
the New Deal. They associated FDR with his Democratic Party – the same party
that had voted against emancipation and reconstruction, and supported segregation
and white supremacy (Graham and Wander 1985: 281). Roosevelt's initial indifference to African Americans manifested itself quite clearly in the National Recovery
Administration (NRA), a New Deal agency that assisted large-scale entrepreneurs
and unionized workers, forcing many black business-owners to close shop (leading
many African Americans to refer satirically to the NRA as the "Negro Run Around").
Racial exclusion, discrimination, and segregation also dominated many other New
Deal agencies, including the AAA, which allowed white landowners to dominate the

county communities, the Civilian Conservation Corps, which did not allow African Americans to enroll in training programs that would have led to advanced positions, and the Federal Housing Authority, which encouraged residential segregation (Graham and Wander 1985: 281–2).

But by 1934, as a result of pressure from labor groups, the radical left, intellectuals, and Southern liberals, the Roosevelt administration began to focus at least some of its attention on African Americans. Black Americans were assigned to more government positions, more work facilities were desegregated, and the President appointed several new Supreme Court justices who played key roles in dismantling discriminatory laws. Although these changes were tentative, and although racism still dominated New Deal programs, the tide appeared to be turning, at least on the surface, for African Americans.

The Federal Writers' Project mirrored the government's slow but increasing investment in African Americans. Within the original plan of the FWP, Henry Alsberg intended to include a separate section in each guide called "Negro Culture in America." However, this plan was later altered to include just one essay on black culture and folklore in the first section of each state guide. Although Alsberg's plan may have been a noble attempt at highlighting the role of African Americans within the national narrative, the essays constantly evoked racist stereotypes and derogatory references to black Americans, and were a source of great shame to many of the employees of the FWP, including the 106 black writers it employed – out of a staff of over 4,500 writers (Penkower 1977: 66). The Project's concerns with providing a lively representation of the nation's various regions often did so at the expense of African Americans and other minorities, replacing agency with visibility.

In the guidebooks, African Americans were represented not as agents of the state, but as "named absences, a people without lived culture or history" (Bold 1996: 202). In her study of the North Carolina guidebook, Christine Bold explains how African Americans, though often representing more than half of a city's population, were frequently reduced to a single paragraph of description, characterized "in group terms without further differentiation or details." For example, within the guide, buildings are often described as "Negro dwellings" as if the buildings themselves represent "racial characteristics." Two adjacent photographs of a smiling black man and a straw-hatted black woman are each marked "Negro field hand." A photograph of a family husking corn labels them as "Darkies" (Bold 1996: 202–14). These homogenizing images did not *reform* the nation's racist stereotypes of African Americans, but rather seemed to *reiterate* them, discounting the individuality of the black experience and cultural heritage in America, and denying African Americans a crucial privilege and major tenet of the Federal Writers' Program: regional self-expression.

As Benjamin Botkin stated, the federal writer was to "live the life of the people he writes about . . . not as an interpreter, but a voice, their voice, which is now his own." In the attempt to "restore America to herself," the writer was to act simply as "a catalyst in the linguistic self-incarnation of America" (Szalay 2000: 74). This voicing of America, however, relied on the marginalization and fetishization of African

Figure 5.1   "Darkies Shelling Corn." From *North Carolina: A Guide to the Old North State* by the Federal Writers' Project, WPA of North Carolina.

Americans and other American folk. The objective of regionalist representation in this era, it seems, was to maintain a subtle play between the *emphasis on difference*, on the one hand, as a means of keeping racial and socioeconomic hierarchies in place, and an *erasure of difference*, on the other hand, as a means of codifying and preserving stereotypes – thereby keeping these "threatened" (and threatening) personalities at a safe distance from "mainstream" white society.

This dual objective of the 1930s literary regionalist project is strikingly evident in the FWP's compilation of 2,194 interviews with ex-slaves conducted between 1936 and 1938 in 17 Southern states across America. In the most obvious sense, the relationship between (usually white) interviewer and (black) interviewee automatically set up a position of hierarchy, as black interviewers were virtually excluded from conducting these interviews in Southern states. As John Blassingame explains in his study of black testimony in the ex-slave narratives, "1930s caste etiquette generally impeded honest communication between southern blacks and whites." But personal reserve was much more than a matter of etiquette for black informants – it was a matter of survival. In just four years from 1931 to 1935, there were 70 lynchings in the South; the constant threat of violence forced African Americans into silence about the truth of slavery (Blassingame 1985: 85). The highly personal and often offensive nature of questions such as "Which was best, slavery or freedom?" or

"Were there sex relations between slaves and whites on your plantation?" also made silence the wisest and most dignified response (Young 1993: 65).

Just as the above scenario reveals the *emphasis* on difference as a vital component of a regionalist project that sought to separate the "objects" of national study from the predominantly white reading "subjects," so the government's role in "editing" these narratives depicts the desire to homogenize racial groups through the *erasure* of individual difference. The government played an active part in the perpetuation of racist stereotyping in these interviews through the editing of each testimony to fit a "uniform pattern" of black dialect. The Washington office gave the interviewers a "standard dialect form" to use when transcribing the interviews. Dialect was attributed to *all* African Americans as a way of creating uniformity in speech patterns, even in instances where informants spoke "standard" English (Young 1993: 62). Although these interviews purported to convey the history and narratives of those who suffered through the bonds of slavery, it seems the final product succeeded only in *preserving* the racist images of this peculiar institution in order to protect a white readership from its nation's shameful past. Black citizens were not empowered to reveal the truth of their experiences, but were instead fetishized as objects of study – as artifacts of the nation's lore. It seems, in this sense, that the aim of the Project was indeed to *"restore* America to herself" – not to recreate or reform the image of America as a nation in constant flux, but to indulge a nostalgic vision of a simpler, more unified nation.

III

In the early 1940s, as the nation's attention and funding efforts turned toward more global concerns, the rise of fascism and the approaching war, regionalist movements in the arts and social sciences experienced a slow decline. What was it exactly that prevented this resurgence of regionalism from effecting a permanent and lasting social change in America? It seems the shortcomings of New Deal regionalism lay in the hands of those who tried to channel its lofty goals through a legislative bureaucracy. The regionalist movement of the 1930s was, like its practitioners in the university, the government, and the arts, vigorously optimistic and persistent. But in the end, this optimism translated into a rather conservative vision of national reform and recovery. Yet the question of the relative success or failure of New Deal regionalism echoes its own preoccupations with the "utility" and relevance of scholarly and artistic endeavors. Perhaps the more important question lies not in the fate of regionalism, but rather in the incipient forces that lead to its repeated resurgence at moments when American nationalism seems threatened by cultural pluralism (Dorman 1993: xiii). The ebb and flow of these regionalist tendencies throughout American literature offers valuable insights into the conflicting claims of nation and region. There is an inherent tension in the myth of a nation whose unity is contingent upon the social and geographic particularities of its various regions.

Robert Dorman argues that the interwar period in America represented a "critical juncture in the transformation of the country from a rural, frontier, decentralized, producerist, agrarian society to the modern commercialized, consumerist, mechanized mass society of the metropolis" (1993: xiii). This moment of crisis and transition intensified an orientation toward regionalism, as the local seemed to promise "a more reliable basis for social and cultural values" (Honnighausen 1996: 4). Regional sociology envisioned that such a focus on the local would provide a new politics of the folk, that "regionalism might serve not only as a tool for progress but as a medium for portraying the new pluralism of the American nation" (Odum and Moore 1938: v). Likewise, the Federal Writers' Project, despite its flaws, led to a new way of imagining the role of literature through this regional lens, which incorporated both a (seemingly) decentralized methodology and a (proposed) depiction of the collective struggle of "folk" across America.

If nineteenth-century regionalism lamented a past that was beyond recovery, then New Deal regionalism can be viewed as an attempt not only to revive a dying past through the documentation of oral traditions, folklore, and the heritage of African Americans and other "folk" — as well as through sociological research and governmental policy — but also to *transform* a past of exclusion and shame into a future of inclusion and welcome. Unfortunately, this inclusion came with a high price. For regionalism, in this sense, begins by celebrating difference only to erase it in service of *creating* or *manufacturing* a sense of indigenous belonging to the pre-existing architecture of a national narrative.

REFERENCES AND FURTHER READING

Baldwin, Sidney (1968). *Poverty and Politics: The Rise and Decline of the Farm Security Administration.* Chapel Hill: University of North Carolina Press.

Bauman, Richard, et al. (1976). "American Folklore and American Studies." *American Quarterly* 28: 3, 360–77.

Blassingame, John W. (1985). "Using the Testimony of Ex-slaves: Approaches and Problems." In Charles T. Davis and Henry Louis Gates, Jr. (eds.), *The Slave's Narrative*, 78–112. New York: Oxford University Press.

Bold, Christine (1996). "Mapping the Color Line: The WPA Guidebook to North Carolina." In Theo D'haen and Hans Bertens (eds.), *"Writing" Nation and "Writing" Region in America*, 197–216. Amsterdam: VU University Press.

Challen, Paul (1992). *A Sociological Analysis of Southern Regionalism: The Contributions of Howard W. Odum.* Lewiston, NY: Edwin Mellen.

Davidson, Donald (1938). *The Attack on Leviathan: Regionalism and Nationalism in the United States.* Chapel Hill: University of North Carolina Press.

Dorman, Robert L. (1993). *Revolt of the Provinces: The Regionalist Movement in America, 1920–1945.* Chapel Hill: University of North Carolina Press.

Eysberg, C. D. (1996). "Regionalism in North America." In Theo D'haen and Hans Bertens (eds.), *"Writing" Nation and "Writing" Region in America*, 21–34. Amsterdam: VU University Press.

Graham, Otis L., Jr., and Wander, Meghan Robinson, eds. (1985). *Franklin D. Roosevelt: His Life and Times: An Encyclopedic View.* Boston: G. K. Hall.

Grantham, Dewey W., Jr. (1968). "The Regional Imagination: Social Scientists and the American South." *Journal of Southern History* 34: 1 (Feb.), 3–32.

Hobson, Archie, ed. (1985). *Remembering America: A Sampler of the WPA American Guide Series*. New York: Columbia University Press.

Honnighausen, L. (1996). "The Old and New Regionalism." In Theo D'haen and Hans Bertens (eds.), *"Writing" Nation and "Writing" Region in America*, 197–216. Amsterdam: VU University Press.

Jensen, Merrill, ed. (1951). *Regionalism in America*. Madison: University of Wisconsin Press.

King, Richard H. (1980). *A Southern Renaissance: The Cultural Awakening of the American South, 1930–1955*. New York: Oxford University Press.

Kirkendall, Richard S. (1966). *Social Scientists and Farm Politics in the Age of Roosevelt*. Columbia: University of Missouri Press.

McDonald, William F. (1969). *Federal Relief Administration and the Arts: The Origins and Administrative History of the Arts Projects of the Works Progress Administration*. Columbus: Ohio State University Press.

Mangione, Jerre (1972). *The Dream and the Deal: The Federal Writers' Project, 1935–8*. Boston: Little, Brown. (First publ. 1943.)

Mumford, Lewis (1938). *The Culture of Cities*. New York: Harcourt, Brace.

O'Brien, Michael (1979). *The Idea of the American South: 1920–1941*. Baltimore: Johns Hopkins University Press.

Odum, Howard W. (1936). *Southern Regions of the United States*. Chapel Hill: University of North Carolina Press.

Odum, Howard W., and Jocher, Katharine (1945). *In Search of the Regional Balance of America*. Chapel Hill: University of North Carolina Press.

Odum, Howard W., and Moore, Harry Estill (1938). *American Regionalism: A Cultural-Historical Approach to National Integration*. New York: Henry Holt.

Penkower, Monty N. (1977). *The Federal Writers' Project: A Study in Government Patronage of the Arts*. Urbana: University of Illinois Press.

Rawick, George P., ed. (1972–3). *The American Slave: A Composite Autobiography*, 19 vols. Westport: Greenwood.

Reagan, Patrick B. (1999). *Designing a New America: The Origins of New Deal Planning, 1890–1943*. Amherst: University of Massachusetts Press.

Sitkoff, Harvard (1978). *A New Deal for Blacks: The Emergence of Civil Rights as a National Issue*. New York: Oxford University Press.

Szalay, Michael (2000). *New Deal Modernism: American Literature and the Invention of the Welfare State*. Durham: Duke University Press.

Weisberger, Bernard A., ed. (1985). *The WPA Guide to America*. New York: Pantheon.

Weiss, Nancy J. (1983). *Farewell to the Party of Lincoln: Black Politics in the Age of FDR*. Princeton: Princeton University Press.

Wilson, Charles Reagan, ed. (1998). *The New Regionalism*. Jackson: University Press of Mississippi.

Young, Melvina Johnson. (1993). "Exploring the WPA Narratives: Finding the Voices of Black Women and Men." In Stanlie M. James and Abena P. A. Busia, eds., *Theorizing Black Feminisms: The Visionary Pragmatism of Black Women*, 55–74. London: Routledge.

6

Realism and Regionalism

Donna Campbell

In 1915, as he took stock of his long career, William Dean Howells wrote to his friend Henry James, "I am comparatively a dead cult with my statues cast down and the grass growing over them in the pale moonlight" (1983: 31). The "dead cult" was, as Howells recognized, the cult of realism that he had championed as critic and novelist for nearly fifty years. Featured in a host of literary journals after the Civil War, among them the *Atlantic Monthly*, *Harper's New Monthly Magazine*, and *The Century*, works by Howells, Henry James, Mark Twain, and others exposed the educated, urban, middle-class audience of these periodicals to the principles of realism. Focusing on ordinary characters and situations with which the audience could identify rather than emphasizing extraordinary events and exotic locales, realism sought to position identifiably flawed human beings within the complex webs of economic forces and American social class. As nineteenth-century audiences saw it, realistic fiction placed less emphasis "upon the extraordinary, the mysterious, the imaginary" than did the romance; it is "that which does not shrink from the commonplace (although art dreads the commonplace) or from the unpleasant (although the aim of art is to give pleasure) in its effort to depict things as they are, life as it is," and is used "in opposition to conventionalism, to idealism, to the imaginative, and to sentimentalism" according to Bliss Perry, editor of the *Atlantic Monthly* from 1899 to 1909 (B. Perry 1903: 269, 229, 222). As Howells defined it more simply in his November 1889 "Editor's Study" column for *Harper's New Monthly Magazine*, "Realism is nothing more and nothing less than the truthful treatment of material" (Howells 1889: 966), and for a time the idea of truthful treatment held sway as realism dominated American literary fiction during the 1880s. Despite its seeming simplicity, however, that definition and others like it actually came to be ammunition for what was called on both sides of the Atlantic the "realism war," in which proponents of the romance and those of the realistic novel waged a fierce battle through essays and reviews in the *Dial*, the *Forum*, *Harper's*, and the *North American Review*.

Equally significant is the parallel growth of regional or local color fiction, terms usually used interchangeably in the nineteenth century, with "local color" being predominant before "regionalism" was redefined by Judith Fetterley and Marjorie Pryse in the twentieth century as a more serious, more sympathetic, and less stereotypical way of writing about region. An important literary force during the last quarter of the nineteenth century, local color stories focused on the unique locales of what the authors saw as a vanishing American past whose customs, dialect, and characters the authors of the movement sought to describe and preserve. In *Crumbling Idols*, arguing for a new kind of realism that he called "veritism," Hamlin Garland declared that "Local color in fiction is demonstrably the life of fiction" (1960: 49). Garland added that "Local color in a novel means that it has such quality of texture and back-ground that it could not have been written in any other place or by any one else than a native" (1960: 53–4), emphasizing that "[i]t cannot be done from above nor from the outside" (1960: 61). Garland thus grants himself authority to write – as Joseph Kirkland tells him, he is the "first actual farmer in literature" – and distinguishes authentic regional writers from the "literary tourists," to use Amy Kaplan's term, charmed by a village's eccentricities or appalled by the squalor of a slum. Making local color authentic (written by a native) and regional in focus, as Garland suggests, would ensure its fidelity to real life and fascinate readers eager to learn about other regions. In his essay "On the Theory and Practice of Local Color," W. P. James confirms the attraction: Local color "has been used on the one hand to signify the magic of the unfamiliar, the romance of the unknown regions 'over the hills and far away'; it is used, on the other hand, to signify the intimate touch of familiarity, the harvest of the quiet eye and loving spirit in their own little corner of earth" (James 1897: 748). An emphasis on the local, an interest in the exotic or unusual features of a region, detailed descriptions of setting, the use of dialect, and the use of a shorter form for fiction – usually sketches or stories as opposed to novels – distinguish local color or regional fiction from mainstream realism, although Eric Sundquist suggests a more subtle distinction in that "economic or political power can itself be seen to be definitive of a realist aesthetic, in that those in power (say, white urban males) have more often been judged 'realists,' while those removed from the seats of power (say, Midwesterners, blacks, immigrants, or women) have been categorized as regionalists" (Sundquist 1988: 503). Later cast by its detractors as a lighter, more comforting version of realism, one in which descriptive detail and the humorous depiction of quaint customs painted over its lack of serious themes, local color or regional fiction faced a different sort of struggle for acceptance as the public first embraced the genre and then dismissed it as irrelevant.

The story of the complex relationship between realism and regionalism is exactly what was lost in the generations after Howells, when those iconoclasts who cast down the statues of his "dead cult" smoothed over the difficulties and dissensions that characterized realism and regionalism in the nineteenth century. Once the standard-bearer for the brave new movement of realism, by 1915 Howells had become a straw man for the attacks of H. L. Mencken and other twentieth-century writers opposed to what they charged were realism's flaws. According to the new generation, these included realism's self-censorship, practiced to avoid bringing a blush to a young girl's cheek; its worship of New England as a literary center; its stylistic timidity; and its willingness to follow Howells' much-misunderstood admonition for American writers to write of "the smiling aspects of life, which are the more American" (Howells 1886: 641). Damning him with faint praise, Mencken wrote that as an official representative of American literature Howells "looked well in funeral garments" and "made a neat and caressing speech" (1955: 1238), but "[h]is psychology is superficial, amateurish, often nonsensical" (1919: 54) and his later prose "simpering, coquettish, overcorseted English" (1968: 179). For Mencken, Hemingway, Sinclair Lewis, and the rest, genteel Howellsian realism was the repressive force that ruined courageous literary roughnecks like Mark Twain and tamed vigorous regionalists like Hamlin Garland. This reaction against Howells resembled a similar reaction against local color fiction. In what Carl Van Doren described in 1922 as "the revolt from the village," writers such as Carl Sandburg, Edwin Arlington Robinson, Zona Gale, and, most famously, Sinclair Lewis in *Main Street* (1920) rebelled against an idealized version of small-town life. The idealized vision arose not from the spare and often grim works of local color writers like Mary E. Wilkins Freeman but from bestsellers that sentimentalized rural life, such as E. N. Westcott's *David Harum* (1898) and Irving Bacheller's *Eben Holden* (1900), yet the stigma of unreality attached itself to both. In clearing the path for a new American literature, one modern in subject-matter but not necessarily modernist in style, Mencken, Lewis, and the rest promoted their characterizations of insipid, repressive realism and irrelevant, sentimentalized local color so effectively that these judgments held sway for much of the twentieth century.

To see realism and regionalism as the powerful forces they were for their nineteenth-century audiences, then, we need to set aside Mencken's prejudices and look at them from the dual perspective of literary documents of the time and recent work on the deeper significance of regionalism and realism. To begin with, realism and regionalism were not necessarily or exclusively literary palliatives to soothe a nation's fractured psyche after the Civil War, although they did serve this purpose. In the 1970s and 1980s, as women's regional writing began to be studied, one branch of interpretation that gained credence through the works of Marjorie Pryse, Judith Fetterley, Josephine Donovan, Elizabeth Ammons, Sarah Way Sherman, and others was the analysis of the genre's sophisticated narrative strategies and the vision of women's community that exists in local color fiction, especially as that community suggests a timeless or healing realm. Others, such as June Howard, Richard Brodhead, Amy Kaplan, and Sandra Zagarell, have shown that realistic and regional fiction functioned in part as narrative spaces in which ideological conflicts about immigration, industrialization, urbanization, race, and above all national identity could be negotiated, if not resolved. Brodhead and Kaplan emphasize the relations between cultural tourist and regional spectacle, and Zagarell and Kaplan examine local color's racially conservative, nativist vision of community. Regional literature defines itself as necessarily distinct from the whole, a literature of margins, as many critics have noted. It exists in tension with mainstream works even when, as in the late nineteenth century, American regional fiction became highly visible through the sheer number of stories published. As the tangible site of an imagined national past, regional fiction provided a temporary respite from the incursions of modernity represented by an increasingly industrialized and urban national landscape. By representing itself as a site of exclusion from and, implicitly, opposition to the dominant national culture, the region as it is constructed in local color fiction paradoxically resisted integration into mainstream American life even as it represented itself as uniquely and purely American, a bastion of unadulterated American lineage and perfectly preserved rituals. As June Howard points out, however, "the claim to cultural authority based on deep roots in the past is itself a distinctively modern one" (1996: 368), based on an awareness of the inherent factitiousness of a regionally constructed past. It is within these paradoxes and this space between "region" and "America" that the "cultural work" of regionalism, to use Jane Tompkins's term, is accomplished. From the emergence of a regional sensibility and the rise of realism after the Civil War, through the "realism war" of the 1880s and the return to romance in the 1890s, the "genteel" movements of realism and regionalism served as the staging ground for a heated debate about what American literature could or should be.

The Beginnings of Regionalism

The traditional point of departure for local color literature is the end of the Civil War, but interest in regions as a subject for writing began much earlier. From the earliest days of the republic, American writers had called for a truly American literature, a call typically combined with an admonition to avoid imitation of foreign models. The first problem was to define not only the nature of American literature but also the nature of its audience. In the January 1820 issue of the *Edinburgh Review*, Sydney Smith, a frequent contributor, had posed a rhetorical question that, as Margaret Fuller later commented, spurred "patriotic vanity" (Fuller 1999: 42) and stung American authors into response, namely: "In the four quarters of the globe, who reads an American book?" Criticism of America's failure to produce authentically American and authentically excellent literary works was not confined to British commentators, however. In the same year, James Kirke Paulding, a friend of Washington Irving and already a defender of American frontier culture in such works as *The Diverting History of John Bull and Brother Jonathan* (1812) and *The Backwoodsman* (1818), charged that "[w]e have imitated where we might often have excelled; we have overlooked our own rich resources, and sponged upon the exhausted treasury of our impoverished neighbors" (Paulding 1999: 24). Paulding's complaint is echoed later in writings by Poe and, most famously, by Ralph Waldo Emerson, who in "The American Scholar" complained that "We have listened too long to the courtly muses of Europe" and challenged his listeners to "walk on [their] own feet" and "speak [their] own minds"

(Emerson 1998a: 1113–14). In speaking of architecture in "Self-reliance," Emerson proposed a method equally applicable to the nation's literature: "If the American artist will study with hope and love the precise thing to be done by him, considering the climate, the soil, the length of day, the wants of the people, the habit and form of the government, he will create a house in which all of these will find themselves fitted, and taste and sentiment will be satisfied also" (Emerson 1998b: 1141). The growing consensus in the fitness of a nation's building its own literature, like Thoreau's argument for the fitness of a man's building his own house, increased with the growth of national consciousness, a consciousness that even at an early date retained a sense of distinct regions.

By the 1840s American writers were already evaluating the work of earlier genera-tions and proposing the shape of regional literatures to come. In the early decades of the century, Washington Irving had won fame abroad and at home for works such as *The Sketch Book* (1819–20), which included "Rip Van Winkle" and "The Legend of Sleepy Hollow," both adaptations of German folk tales transposed into an American setting. As literary historian Henry A. Beers wrote in his pioneering survey of American literature, *Initial Studies in American Letters* (1895), "Washington Irving (1783–1859) was the first American author whose books, as *books*, obtained recogni-tion abroad" (Beers 1895: 74). With the publication of *The Pioneers* (1823), the first in the Leatherstocking series, James Fenimore Cooper had defined what reviewers hailed as a genuinely American character and iconic figure of the frontier, Natty Bumppo. Cooper's success encouraged other regional writers, such as William Gilmore Simms of South Carolina, who won the title "the James Fenimore Cooper of the South" with his historical romances, including *Guy Rivers* (1834) and *The Yemassee: A Romance of Carolina* (1844). In his 1844 Phi Beta Kappa address at the University of Georgia, Simms said that he "rejoiced to behold symptoms of [. . .] independent intellectual working, simultaneously, in remote regions of the country" and had a "vision of a generous growth in art and letters, of which tokens begin to make themselves felt from the Aroostook to the Rio Brave" (Simms 1999: 28). As more of the regional writers Simms envisioned were heard from, the reverence that an earlier generation had felt for Washington Irving and James Fenimore Cooper as supreme interpreters of the American experience began to wear thin. For example, in assessing past and current American writers, Margaret Fuller dispatched Washington Irving with left-handed compliments – he is "just what he ought to be" and has a "niche" that no one else could occupy – before dispensing with Cooper's hitherto inflated reputation: Cooper's achievement in preserving the "noble romance of the hunter-pioneer's life" almost makes one forget "the baldness of his plots, shallowness of thought, and poverty in the presentation of character" (1999: 41). Similarly, in *A Fable for Critics* (1848) James Russell Lowell echoed Fuller's general assessment of Cooper's characterization, complaining that, having created one new character in Natty Bumppo, Cooper "has done naught but copy it ill ever since" (Lowell 1867b: 57). But Lowell heartily approved of Cooper's use of American materials and advised other American writers to follow the same course:

Though you brag of your new World, you don't half believe in it;
And as much of the Old as is possible weave in it;

. . .

You steal Englishmen's books and think Englishmen's thought,
With their salt on her tail your wild eagle is caught;
Your literature suits its each whisper and motion
To what will be thought of it over the ocean;

. . .

Forget Europe wholly, your veins throb with blood,
To which the dull current in hers is but mud

. . .

O my friends, thank your god, if you have one, that he
'Twixt the Old World and you set the gulf of a sea;
Be strong-backed, brown-handed, upright as your pines
By the scale of a hemisphere shape your designs.

(Lowell 1867b: 59–60)

From Emerson to Lowell and Simms, and, later, Walt Whitman, the consensus was building: The American bard would be vigorous, tanned, and red-blooded; he would fashion literature with his bare hands from the soil of his region and not from corrupt European traditions.

Indeed, several writers had already taken up the challenge of regional writing, although most were far from the romanticized American bard that Lowell had pictured. The regional fiction of the era was typically humorous and unofficially divided along gender lines. The most conspicuous group of writers, the Southwestern humorists, introduced two elements that remained a consistent presence in local color literature: the convention of the frame story, often with an educated listener or narrator who responds to lower-class local characters; and the use of dialect to represent differences in class as well as differences in region. Along with the stories of other regions, those of Southwestern humor were published primarily in William T. Porter's New York-based sporting weekly the *Spirit of the Times* as well as in local newspapers; they were irreverent and decidedly not genteel enough for general consumption. Noting that some Southwestern humor extols traditional virtues but that much of it was anti-establishment, Walter Blair and Hamlin Hill explain that such "subversive humor portrayed indelibly drawn characters whose code of behavior affirmed disorder, violence, and amorality" (1978: 163). In this way, the stories served as an antidote to the strictures of civilization for their largely white male audience. Many of the tales feature crude humor, prankster or trickster behavior, conservative political views, and cruelty ranging from eye-gouging to mutilation and death. Some authors drew on the tall-tale tradition that transformed real figures into folk heroes: thus Davy Crockett not only encouraged his larger-than-life status in his own *Narrative of the Life of David Crockett* (1834) but also was mythologized as the hero of the *Crockett Almanacs*; and braggart keelboatman Mike Fink boasted his way into legend as the "Mississippi roarer." Other notable characters include the "ring-tailed roarer" Ransy

Sniffle of Augustus Baldwin Longstreet's *Georgia Scenes* (1835) and George Washington Harris's cruel prankster, the Tennessee frontiersman Sut Lovingood, of *Sut Lovingood: Yarns Spun by a "Nat'ral Born Durn'd Fool"* (published in the *Spirit of the Times* and local papers; collected in 1867). Among the characters that influenced later authors is Johnson Jones Hooper's confidence man Simon Suggs of *Some Adventures of Simon Suggs, Late of the Tallapoosa Volunteers* (1845), whose experiences in "The Captain Attends a Camp-meeting" prefigure those of the King at the revival meeting in *The Adventures of Huckleberry Finn*. Another figure, the "mighty hunter" Joe Doggett, of Thomas Bangs Thorpe's "The Big Bear of Arkansas" (1841), tells of an impossibly fruitful "creation state" of Arkansas where beets grow to the size of cedar stumps and an "unhuntable bar" cannot be killed but only dies "when his time come," a comic quest later given mythic resonance in William Faulkner's "The Bear" (*Go Down, Moses*, 1942).

Regional humor from other areas appeared as well in the years before the Civil War, some of it employing dialect traditions and a satiric wit less crude but no less pointed than that of Southwestern humor. As in Southwestern humor, even those tales that lacked an overt political purpose praised, poked fun at, or deplored the incursions of democracy and the peculiarities of the region. In the Northeast, for example, the humorist Seba Smith commented on the workings of the Maine legislature through the dialect letters of his alter ego, the innocent bumpkin Jack Downing, in *The Life and Writings of Major Jack Downing of Downingville, away Down East in the State of Maine, Written by Himself* (1833). Other tales poked fun at the character of the sharp, wily Yankee peddler such as Thomas Halliburton's Sam Slick, of *The Clockmaker; or, The Sayings and Doings of Samuel Slick* (1836), whose sharp dealings cause one of his victims to call him "a yankee pedlar, a cheatin vagabond, a wooden nutmeg" (Halliburton 1836: 117), the last from the stereotypical Yankee peddler's supposed habit of selling wooden rather than real nutmegs to unsuspecting farm wives on his route. More significant for later regionalists is James Russell Lowell's first series of dialect poems in *The Biglow Papers* (1848), which criticized the Mexican War through the blunt speech of New England countryman Hosea Biglow and the stuffy, pedantic commentary of his ostensible editor, the Reverend Homer Wilbur. Lowell resurrected the characters to comment on the Civil War in *The Biglow Papers, Second Series* (1867), a volume that Howells praised as expressing "the genuine vernacular, the true feeling, the racy humor, and the mother-wit of Yankee-land" (1993: 69). In his introduction to the second series, Lowell defends his use of dialect on linguistic grounds, seeking to rescue the racy natural idiom from both the schoolmaster who has been "busy starching our language and smoothing it flat" and the newspaper reporter who puffs out the language with grandiose circumlocutions (1867a: xi). Both in the perceived accuracy of his use of dialect and in his defense of its use, Lowell was a significant figure for later realist writers such as Howells, Hamlin Garland, and Edward Eggleston. In "Folk-speech in America," Eggleston quotes from one of Lowell's letters emphasizing the importance of dialect for the American language: "I hope you will persevere [in collecting dialect] . . . Remember that it will soon be too late . . . When the lumberer comes out of the woods he buys him a suit of store-clothes and flings his picturesque red shirt into the bush. Alas! we shall soon have nothing but store-clothes to dress our thoughts in, if we don't look sharp" (Eggleston 1894: 875).

Regional humor focusing on women, although less evident, added another dimension. As in Southwestern humor and most other local color fiction, the common thread is the use of oral tradition: storytelling as action and as voice predominates, and the liberal use of dialect ensures the illusion of orality even at the risk of overwhelming the reader with unorthodox and unpronounceable spellings. In 1854, Benjamin P. Shillaber introduced Mrs. Partington and her malapropisms in *Life and Sayings of Mrs. Partington, and Others of the Family*. Earlier, however, Frances Miriam Whitcher, the "first significant woman prose humorist of the nation" according to Linda A. Morris (1992: 10), had published sketches in *Godey's Lady's Book* and other periodicals that featured the outspoken Widow Bedott and Aunt Maguire (published posthumously as *The Widow Bedott Papers*, 1855). Whitcher's portrayal of this independent and wryly unsentimental woman influenced another upstate New York author, Marietta Holley, sometimes called "the female Mark Twain." Beginning in 1873 with *My Opinions and Betsy Bobbet's*, Holley would go on to write her own hugely popular series of dialect-based novels centered on a strong female character, Samantha Allen or "Josiah Allen's wife." Holley pits the sentimental ideals of pure womanhood and the sacredness of marriage spouted by the spinster Betsy Bobbet and the traditional pronouncements on woman's place of Josiah Allen against Samantha's commonsense realism, managing in the process to comment on everything from temperance and women's suffrage to religion (*Samantha among the Brethren*, 1890), Gilded Age conspicuous consumption (*Samantha at Saratoga*, 1887), and race relations (*Samantha on the Race Problem*, 1892).

Although not strictly regional humor, Caroline Kirkland's *A New Home – Who'll Follow? or, Glimpses of Western Life* (1839) interfuses vivid character types and humor in what is essentially a women's frontier narrative in novel form, one comparable to but more realistic than Mary Austin Holley's *Texas* (1833) or Eliza Farnham's *Life in Prairie Land*, as Annette Kolodny notes in *The Land Before Her: Fantasy and Experience of the American Frontiers, 1630–1860* (1984). Praising the "spirited delineations of Mrs. Kirkland," Margaret Fuller had commented that "[t]he features of Hoosier, Sucker, and Wolverine life are worth fixing; they are peculiar to the soil and indicate its hidden treasures" (1999: 41). Seen from a woman's perspective, these hidden treasures of the frontier adventure consist of mud, rain, and a cramped house continually invaded by every kind of pest, from flies to the horde of inquisitive neighbors whose criticism of the narrator's furniture and way of life does not prevent them from borrowing everything she owns. The humor consists in the ironic contrast between the narrator's ideal vision of democracy and her confrontation with its grubby reality: the pipe-smoking, tobacco-spitting women and hard-drinking men who are oblivious to her genteel hints about privacy and class distinctions. When she has coaxed one of these exceedingly independent villagers into being her servant for a time,

Kirkland's narrator comments, "Granting the correctness of the opinion which may be read in their countenances that they are 'as good as you are,' I must insist, that a greasy cook-maid, or a redolent stable-boy, can never be, to my thinking, an agreeable table companion" (Kirkland 1990: 53). Kirkland heightens the class disparity and consequently the humor through contrasting characters whose social pretensions render them ridiculous; she also contrasts the local characters' dialect with her own standard English and extravagant use of classical allusion and literary quotations. She ridicules the romantic vision and pastoral tradition of simplicity and gentility as the natural state of human beings by bestowing classical names on her neighbors: "My rosy-haired Phillida[,] who rejoiced in the euphonius [*sic*] appellation of Angeline, made herself entirely at home, looking into my trunks, &c., and asking the price of various parts of my dress" (Kirkland 1990: 45). Like Sarah Orne Jewett, Kirkland emphasizes community, but her view of its power is more acerbic than reverent. In Montacute, the frontier town, communal feeling and democratic manners are born of necessity rather than of similar values and sympathy, for "[w]hat can be more absurd than a feeling of proud distinction, where a stray spark of fire, a sudden illness, or a day's contre-temps, may throw you entirely on the kindness of your humblest neighbor?" (Kirkland 1990: 65). *A New Home – Who'll Follow?* is, as Sandra Zagarell argues in her introduction, a highly original work that does not resemble other contemporary work by American women writers, but it does anticipate later local color fiction in its episodic structure, detailed descriptions, and interest in the dynamics of communities.

By the 1850s, then, the necessary elements of regional or local color literature were in place: a sense of regional differences as an interesting and sufficiently exotic subject-matter to arouse readers' interest; a rural or frontier setting that plausibly explains the inhabitants' lack of sophistication and their colorful behavior; an established dialect tradition that had both popular and scholarly support; well-established character types through which writers could evoke laughter; and the device of the frame story and storytelling as an important element of the structure. It was lively and interesting in its language and plots, and it was decidedly American. What it did not have was access to publication in culturally elite journals and critical respectability; but that would change during the age of realism and regionalism.

Regional Realism or Local Color Fiction

Regional realism emerged as a dominant literary force in the last quarter of the nineteenth century, although fiction by regional authors had appeared earlier. The two writers traditionally credited with establishing local color as a genre were Bret Harte and Harriet Beecher Stowe. Part of a new breed of Western humorists whose ranks included Mark Twain, Charles Foster Brown or "Artemus Ward," and Dan De Quille, Harte contributed sketches to the *Golden Era* and the *Californian* before assuming editorship of the newly established *Overland Monthly* and publishing his most famous stories there, including "The Luck of Roaring Camp," "The Outcasts of Poker Flat," and "Tennessee's Partner." Collected in *The Luck of Roaring Camp and Other Stories* (1870), Harte's tales caught the public's attention and, because they eschewed the more overt violence and crudity of the earlier generation of Southwestern humorists, they could be read by a broader audience. By mixing realistic details and unusual characters from the mining camps with a morally conventional, sometimes sentimental, vision of human nature and community, Harte expanded the realm of possibilities for local color writers and sparked public interest in a form that was at once alien and familiar.

Most famous as the author of *Uncle Tom's Cabin* (1852), Harriet Beecher Stowe also wrote of regional character types such as the drawling Yankee storyteller Sam Lawson of *Oldtown Folks* (1869) and *Sam Lawson's Oldtown Fireside Stories* (1872); her *Pearl of Orr's Island* (1862) inspired Sarah Orne Jewett and is often cited as the beginning of the tradition of women's local color fiction. As Marjorie Pryse points out, however, Stowe's regionalism began with her first published story, "A New England Sketch" (1834), in which she created "the possibility of regionalism itself as a literary form capable of conferring literary authority on American women" (Pryse 1997: 20) – in part, argues Pryse, to counter the male-dominated traditions of Southwestern humor. In the tradition of women's local color fiction, stories focus on women's lives and their ability to endure hardship through the bonds of friendship and community; the quotidian round of activities that comprise women's work becomes a kind of meditation if not a means to transcendence, as past meets present and is passed down through storytelling and ritual feasts such as the Bowden family reunion in Jewett's *The Country of the Pointed Firs*.

The popularity of local color arose from a complex series of social and literary forces. First, in part because of the returning veterans who had traveled to other regions, especially the South, during their campaigns, and in part because the conflict heightened awareness of sectional differences more generally, the Civil War had made the country conscious of itself as a land full of disparate regions. Curiosity about the South as the site of the conflict was followed by interest in the Midwest as the site of farmers, homesteaders, and "free land," and in the West as a half-tamed country from which unimaginable wealth from mining could flow into the hands of those adventurous enough to seek it. Advances in transportation helped to break down the isolation of communities, whether for good or ill, and advances in communication completed the process. The railroad during this era extended not only across the continent (1869) but also into interurban and suburban branch lines that made travel between small communities and cities easier than ever before. The adoption of faster presses, cheaper paper, and the Mergenthaler typesetting machine ensured a more rapid dissemination of printed information, facilitated by the ubiquity of telegraph offices and even, after 1883, the reality of long-distance telephone service between New York and Chicago. Also, increasing industrialization and creeping urbanization bred a middle-class population nostalgic for an imagined past, a pastoral landscape where traditional country folk plied their trades and provided a living link to national history and memory. As Richard Brodhead points out in *Cultures of Letters* (1993), the rise in cultural tourism at this time also added to the popularity of local color, for although upper-class tourists had always been able to travel abroad and to visit fashionable spas, even middle-class city-dwellers now had it within their power to visit the sites about which they read. Since local color fiction could construct in print the rural villages of New England or the ruined plantations of the South as sites of spectacle and living tropes of the past, the middle-class tourist could now visit the past and enjoy an "authentic" rather than vicarious experience of a place at once exotic and non-threatening.

Authenticity was the keynote; and it became a sought-after trait in other fields as well as in the realist and regionalist fiction of the time. The late nineteenth century and early twentieth century saw a growing interest in the artifacts of American history and culture: for example, an interest in antiques and handcrafts as tangible evidence of an American past increased until writers like Rollin Lynde Hartt complained of the plundering of New England villages for their antiques. Driven indirectly by the evolutionary theories of Charles Darwin and the scientific application of those theories to social laws by Herbert Spencer and others, the era also saw an increasing interest in family heritage as "native" American families sought to differentiate themselves from the hordes of immigrants pouring through Castle Garden and, after 1892, Ellis Island. Genealogical societies that required members to prove their American roots sprang up at this time: the Sons of the American Revolution was founded in 1889, gaining, among other members, the otherwise iconoclastic writer Stephen Crane in April 1896. The national organization of the Daughters of the American Revolution was founded in 1890, followed by the incrementally more restrictive Colonial Dames of America (1891) and the Mayflower Society (1897); not to be outdone, the United Daughters of the Confederacy organized their national group in 1894. Authenticity in heritage called for authenticity in language as well, as "native" American rural dialects and phrases in literature implicitly became a means for shutting out the Irish, Yiddish, Italian, and east European dialects that could be heard everywhere in the great cities. In reviews of realistic fiction, authenticity of character, situation, and motive became a touchstone against which works were judged; in reviews of local color fiction, the additional criteria of authenticity in dialect and setting were added. As Gavin Jones notes, the use of dialect was a double-edged sword: insufficient dialect in a work rendered dialogue inauthentic and inexpressive of the region, but too much dialect risked not only vulgarity but the more long-term possibility "that the encouragement of dialect would produce a situation in which speakers 'of the same race . . . can communicate only through an interpreter'" (Jones 1999: 49). As a child during this era, for example, Edith Wharton recalled reading the dialect stories of Mark Twain and Mr. Dooley with her parents' approval, but with a clear understanding of the limits: "We spoke naturally, instinctively good English, but my parents always wanted it to be better, that is, easier, more flexible and idiomatic," more attuned to "racy innovations" – as long as "pure English" was preserved (Wharton 1990: 821). Jones notes that the quest for authenticity in speech could mask or legitimize an attempt to naturalize differences in class and race, especially in the attempt to reproduce black dialect for a white audience. However scientifically minded the ethnographer or recorder of dialect may be, however great the degree of sympathy on the part of the observer, the very fact that the dialect of a region is being transcribed as something other than standard speech legitimizes inequality. As Stephanie Foote points out, regional writing's "formal concern with assigning to different kinds of people a place in relation to the standard, national culture demonstrates that regional writing was a powerful method of understanding not just the 'place' where certain people lived but also the 'place' they inhabited in a social hierarchy" (2001: 11).

The showcase for this "authentic" American literature, and one of the reasons for its popularity, was the group of monthly literary magazines that Nancy Glazener has called the "Atlantic group," most of them owned by major publishing houses. Among others, the "Atlantic group" included the *Atlantic* (founded 1857); *Harper's New Monthly Magazine* (founded 1850); the *North American Review* (1815–1939); *Scribner's Monthly* (1870–1930), which became the *Century* in 1881; *Scribner's Magazine* (1887–1939), which was started after *Scribner's Monthly* ceased publication; and the review periodicals the *Critic* (1881–1906) and the *Forum* (1886–1916). In *Reading for Realism*, Glazener suggests that "high realism" began as a collaboration between "the belletristic branch of the publishing industry, which was defining its market position by defining an American literary high culture aimed at the bourgeoisie and its aspirants; and Boston's bourgeoisie, which used its sponsorship and consumption of high culture to justify its privileged status" (1997: 24). The magazines of this group had a self-defined role as cultural gatekeepers; in addition to emanating from New York or, better still, Boston, they carefully guarded their tone of high seriousness (except for the light or humorous pieces that appeared in well-defined sections like *Harper's* "Editor's Drawer"), their sense of setting a tone as well as setting a trend, and their keen sense of an audience that wished to be enlightened but never shocked. Separating themselves early on from the sensational weeklies or popular publications like *Frank Leslie's Illustrated Newspaper*, and later from the cheaper popular magazines and muckraking journals like *McClure's*, the Atlantic group guaranteed certain standards for a middle class willing to purchase the kind of literary taste that was formerly the carefully cultivated and strenuously guarded aesthetic province of the leisured and highly educated upper class. The importance of this was clear for the local colorists as well as for the realists: instead of publishing their work only in local newspapers or specialty publications like the *Spirit of the Times*, regional writers were now granted access to the most literary of the high-culture journals. The *Atlantic*, in fact, published a story by Rose Terry Cooke, a prominent early local colorist, in its inaugural issue. The standards of the group bred a kind of tautological reading: If a story appeared in the *Atlantic* or *Harper's*, the audience could be sure that it was literature; and if an unpublished story deserved to be called literature, it would, the readers felt, surely be selected to appear in one of the Atlantic group magazines. However, as the *Century* admitted in 1885, "[t]here is some truth" in the charge that "our literature may lose in frankness and in force" by catering to a hypersensitive audience, and "much of the world's most valuable literature . . . could never reach the public through the pages of the 'family magazine'" (*Century* 1885: 164). As Kenneth Warren argues in *Black and White Strangers* (1994), these restrictions guaranteed a level of moral protection for works with an edge, such as Howells's "divorce novel" *A Modern Instance*, which was serialized in the *Century*. However, the policy of avoiding revolutionary sentiments meant that touchy issues of racial equality could be addressed only in certain ways, if at all, to avoid alienating Southern readers; Charles W. Chesnutt "The Negro's Answer to the Negro Question" could not be published because it was "so partisan" that the magazine would not print it – a kind of censorship that valued social order over "'truly' subversive political activity" (Warren 1994: 55, 53).

Once the doors to a truly national if still middle- and upper-class audience had been opened by these journals, local color stories appeared alongside travel articles, essays on politics, poetry, memoirs, and serial novels. The December 1885 issue of *Harper's*, for example, contains a farce (*The Garroters*) by Howells; poems by C. P. Cranch and R. P. Blackmore; essays in art criticism; stories by Elizabeth Stuart Phelps and the local color writer Mary Noialles Murfree (the real name of Charles Egbert Craddock); serial fiction from Howells (*Indian Summer*) and local color writer Constance Fenimore Woolson (*East Angels*); and some travel and nature essays. As is evident even from this brief list, the "Atlantic group" magazines, despite their reputation for high culture and supposed timidity, were more welcoming to women and writers of color during this era than were other mainstream periodicals. Beginning with "The Goophered Grapevine" in the August 1887 issue, Charles W. Chesnutt published four stories in the *Atlantic* by the turn of the century: the first African-American fiction writer to publish in a high-culture literary review. In addition to a story in the *North American Review*, Paul Laurence Dunbar published several poems in the *Atlantic* – not merely the popular poems in dialect that had earned him praise from Howells, but sonnets on Harriet Beecher Stowe and Robert Gould Shaw, the latter of which concludes that Shaw and the others "[h]ave died, the Present teaches, but in vain!" (Dunbar 1900: 488) because of rights denied to African Americans. *The Atlantic* also published the Sioux writer Zitkala-Ša's autobiographical articles, starting with "Impressions of an Indian Childhood" in January 1900.

Regional works helped both to confirm the position of Boston and later New York as cultural centers and to dislodge them as the most appropriate literary subjects for fiction. Although approximately 150 volumes of collected local color stories had appeared before 1900, magazines were the main publication outlet for the regional fiction that poured in from around the country (Simpson 1960: 8). Local color thrived in the context of a steady diet of book reviews, critical essays, colloquy in letters and notes columns, and occasionally articles that grouped and assessed the writers' work to guide the taste of the reading public. For example, Thomas Sargent Perry warned equally against the vapid dialogue of Harriet Beecher Stowe's *My Wife and I*, the "weird visions of the Southern novelist," and the "innocently prattling stories for which *Harper's Magazine* is famous" (T. S. Perry 1872: 378), and George Parsons Lathrop measured the region's fiction and concluded that "New York writers are not actuated by any impulse in common; . . . and that they do not concern themselves about making a special New York literature" (Lathrop 1886: 833). Charles W. Coleman, Jr. (1887) gave extended treatment to Cable, King, Johnston, Harris, Page, and especially Mary Noailles Murfree or "Charles Egbert Craddock," author of *In the Tennessee Mountains* (1884) and *The Prophet of the Great Smoky Mountains* (1885); critically acclaimed in her time, she is also the only female regional writer mentioned in Beers's *Initial Studies in American Letters* (1895).

From New England, the writers that followed the earlier generation of Harriet Beecher Stowe and Rose Terry Cooke included Sarah Orne Jewett, whose *Country of the Pointed Firs*, published in the *Atlantic* in 1896, was widely acknowledged then as now to be a masterpiece of regional fiction; Mary E. Wilkins Freeman, of *A Humble Romance and Other Stories* (1887) and *A New England Nun and Other Stories* (1891); Alice Brown of New Hampshire (*Tiverton Tales*); Rowland E. Robinson; and Celia Thaxter. Further west and south were Philander Deming of New York (*Adirondack Stories*, 1880) and Margaret Deland of Pennsylvania (*Old Chester Tales*, 1898). Mid-western writers produced a number of works debunking the pioneer myth, among them E. W. Howe's *Story of a Country Town* (1883) and Edward Eggleston's *The Hoosier Schoolmaster* (1871). Joseph Kirkland, the son of Caroline Kirkland, carefully reproduced authentic dialect in his contribution to Midwestern literature, *Zury: The Meanest Man in Spring County* (1887). A few years later, Hamlin Garland wrote of farms crushed under mortgages and debt in *Main-Traveled Roads* (1891), later taking up the cause of local color fiction in *Crumbling Idols* (1894). Constance Fenimore Woolson, who also wrote of the South in *For the Major* (1883) and *Rodman the Keeper: Southern Sketches* (1886), recorded the life of the Michigan lake country in *Castle Nowhere: Lake Country Sketches* (1875). The Far West could, and did, boast of Bret Harte and Mark Twain, whose works soon transcended the tradition of regional, frontier humor represented by the early pieces collected in *The Celebrated Jumping Frog of Calaveras County and Other Sketches* (1867); another larger-than-life figure was the self-promoting poet Joaquin Miller (Cincinnatus Heine Miller), whose *Songs of the Sierras* (1871) won praise from the British press. Mary Hallock Foote contributed novels such as *The Led-Horse Claim: A Romance of the Silver Mines* (1882) and stories of the northern Idaho mining district to the *Century*, where stories of Mormon women and other Western subjects by Helen Hunt Jackson, best known for her California romance *Ramona* (1884), also appeared. In addition to Zitkala-Ša's memoirs and her retellings of Native American myths, the *Atlantic* published stories about Native Americans by Mary Austin, whose sketches of the Southwest appeared in *The Land of Little Rain* (1903).

In the South, several traditions of regional fiction developed, some based on the memories, real and imagined, of times before the war and the romantic idea of the "Lost Cause," others addressing current issues in a region destabilized by impoverishment, industrialization, reintegration with the nation, and conflicts over race. Among the early works in this tradition were John W. DeForest's *Miss Ravenel's Conversion from Secession to Loyalty* (1867) and Albion Tourgée's *A Fool's Errand, by One of the Fools* (1879), a story of Reconstruction. As James Herbert Morse summed them up for the *Century*, "J. W. De Forest, in his Southern stories, attempted the bloody side of society there; Tourgée, the darkly passionate and political" (Morse 1883: 367). George Washington Cable's unflinching look at the tangled racial inheritance of the south in *Old Creole Days* (1879) and *The Grandissimes* (1880) brought protests from another non-Creole Louisianan, Grace King, who, when lamenting Cable's perspective on the region, was challenged by editor Richard Watson Gilder to write stories of the region as she saw it. Her response included *Monsieur Motte* (1888), *Balcony Stories* (1893), and works of Louisiana history. A different perspective is that of Alice Moore Dunbar-Nelson, who purposefully sidestepped racial issues in *Violets and Other Tales* (1895) and *The Goodness of St. Rocque and Other Stories* (1899), although she addressed them at length in later works and unpublished stories like "The Stones of the Village." Other Louisiana writers included Sherwood Bonner (*Dialect Tales*, 1883), and later Kate Chopin, who published *Bayou Folk* (1894) and *A Night in Acadie* (1897), among other works, before she abandoned writing fiction after *The Awakening* (1899). Thomas Nelson Page's stories, such as *In Ole Virginia* (1887), exemplified what came to be called the "plantation tradition" that romanticized life before the war; the Uncle Remus stories of Joel Chandler Harris (*Uncle Remus: His Songs and Sayings*, 1880) are often grouped with Page's as part of the tradition despite the content of the tales themselves, which undercut the idealized view of master–slave relations. A more overt challenge to the plantation tradition is the work of Charles W. Chesnutt, whose short story collections *The Conjure Woman* (1899) and *The Wife of His Youth and Other Tales of the Color Line* (1899) gathered wider acceptance than more pointedly political later novels such as *The Colonel's Dream* (1905).

The "Realism War," the Retreat into Romance, and the Decline of Local Color

As the nineteenth century drew to a close, so too did the public's interest in local color fiction, driven by impatience with a style that had run its course, a retreat into historical romance, and, indirectly, fallout from the "realism war." Significantly, the critical discourse surrounding regionalism did not dispute the category within which a work was placed (realism or local color), evaluate works based on region, or, with few exceptions, rate regional writing based on gender. Instead, the principal terms for debate were authenticity, faithfulness to life, truthfulness of incidents, and realistic representation of character, all terms borrowed from the "realism war" of the 1880s and 1890s.

The realism war began early, with a shot across the bow from William Dean Howells, who in an 1882 essay on Henry James for the *Century* declared that "[t]he art of fiction has, in fact, become a finer art in our day than it was with Dickens and

Thackeray" (Howells 1882: 28), following it a few years later with a strong state-ment of realism in his first "Editor's Study" column for *Harper's* (January 1886). For the next six years in this column, Howells steadily promoted realist and local color fiction, prodding his audience with analogies (learning to prefer a "real grasshopper" over an ideal one, however beautiful), with examples (the sincerity of Mary E. Wilkins Freeman), and with sweeping pronouncements: "We must ask ourselves before we ask anything else, Is it true? . . . In the whole range of fiction we know of no *true* picture of life – that is, of human nature – which is not also a masterpiece of literature, full of divine and natural beauty." But the real battle began, as Edwin H. Cady suggests, in the late 1880s, with George Pellew's "The Battle of the Books" (1888); among the responses back and forth was William Roscoe Thayer's "The New Story-tellers and the Doom of Realism," which commented acidly, "It took fortitude, until custom made us callous, to watch Mr. Howells, like another Tarquin, go up and down the poppy-field of literature, lopping off head after head which had brought delight to millions" (Thayer 1894: 162). Thayer also blasted "the dialect story" or local color fiction as "another product of Epidermism," or the obsession with externals that Thayer believed characterized realism (1894: 166). Others on the romance or idealism side of the debate included authors from both sides of the Atlantic, such as Robert Louis Stevenson, Andrew Lang, Maurice Thompson, H. C. Vedder, and, more moderately, Horace Scudder, who wrote that "if our ancestors could read some of the microscopic fiction of the present day, we suspect they would cry out for something more in mass, less in detail. . . . Grasshoppers do not interest us, however truthful. We prefer leopards" (Scudder 1891: 568). Those defending Howells and realism included formidable critics and writers such as Hjalmar Horth Boyesen, Henry James, Hamlin Garland, Joseph Kirkland, Richard Watson Gilder, Brander Matthews, and W. P. Trent; but the realism war nonetheless "raged with deadly fury for eight years [1886–1894]," according to Garland, who dated its origins to Howells' first "Editor's Study" column in 1886 (Garland 1930: 248).

By the late 1890s the tide had already turned toward adventure fiction or histor-ical romance and away from realism and local color, with even local color writers like Sarah Orne Jewett, Mary E. Wilkins Freeman, Hamlin Garland, and Mary Hartwell Catherwood writing historical romances. "A large number of readers, who have wearied of minute descriptions of the commonplace, are to-day often found con-demning an author who does not keep his hero in imminent danger of death through at least seventy-five percent of his pages," wrote John Kendrick Bangs. "Realism and romance both have their champions, and doughty ones, and a watching world . . . must decide that the supremacy of the one over the other can never be established as a settled fact . . ." (Bangs 1898: 1). Another measure of local color's decline appears in essays by Charles Dudley Warner of *Harper's*, who succeeded Howells as writer of the "Editor's Study." In the June 1892 column he briefly derides local color as "some-thing you could buy, like paint," but praises Grace King's *Tales of a Time and Place* for not using "local color as a varnish" (Warner 1892: 155, 156). Four years later, he extended the paint metaphor by saying that "so much color was produced that the market broke down" but added that "we do not hear much now of 'local color'; that has rather gone out" (Warner 1896: 961). By 1893, even the realism–romanticism debate had moved from the pages of the *Dial*, the *Forum*, *Harper's*, and other magazines to become a kind of publicity stunt for Eugene Field's "Sharps and Flats" column in the *Chicago News*. Applauding Mary Hartwell Catherwood's romances, Field began an exchange of letters with Hamlin Garland and Catherwood that led to a public debate at the Chicago World's Fair in 1893. As Garland tells it, he responded to Catherwood's assertion that he "over-emphasized the dirt and toil and loneliness of the farmer's life" by challenging her with "What do you know of the farm realities I describe? . . . I have bound my half of eight acres of oats . . . You city folk can't criticize my stories of farm life – I've lived them" (Garland 1930: 255). Despite his unchallengeable authenticity and his populist politics, in later years Garland, like the rest, retreated into writing Western historical romances. Although writers such as Garland, Mary Wilkins Freeman, Mary Austin, Grace King, and Howells himself, among others, would continue to publish fiction well into the first few decades of the twentieth century, the era of local color's greatest popularity was over.

Thus, despite its supposed position on the margins, regional fiction kept pace in its various forms with the country's continued quest for self-definition and national identity. Like Thoreau's multiple perspectives of Walden Pond, when viewed from the decentered perspective of regional fiction the trajectory of nineteenth-century literature looks very different. What emerges is a series of partial views of region, seen through the lenses of regional humor, romance, realism, and the rest until they comprise not a "whole" in American literature but a series of partial portraits. As Carrie Tirado Bramen writes, "It was precisely this embrace of the partial that made local color such a popular genre for representing the modern nation" (2000: 128). In spite of its quest for authenticity, authority, completion, and simplicity, regional fiction reveals its modern roots through its "embrace of the partial" – the disarticulated language that constitutes its representation of dialect, the sketches and stories from disparate regions – that finally suggests its denial of the myth of wholeness and its contribution to an American literature that recognizes and celebrates, rather than denying, its imperfections.

References and Further Reading

Ammons, Elizabeth (1983). "Going in Circles: The Female Geography of Jewett's *Country of the Pointed Firs*." *Studies in the Literary Imagination* 16: 2, 83–92.

Bangs, John Kendrick (1898). "Literary Notes." *Harper's New Monthly Magazine* 97 (Nov.), 1–2.

Beers, Henry A. (1895). *Initial Studies in American Letters*. Meadville, NY: Flood & Vincent.

Blair, Walter, and Hill, Hamlin Lewis (1978). *America's Humor: From Poor Richard to Doonesbury*. Oxford: Oxford University Press.

Bramen, Carrie Tirado (2000). *The Uses of Variety: Modern Americanism and the Quest for National Distinctiveness*. Cambridge, Mass.: Harvard University Press.

Brodhead, Richard H. (1993). *Cultures of Letters: Scenes of Reading and Writing in Nineteenth-*

Century America. Chicago: University of Chicago Press.

Century (1885). "A New Volume of 'The Century,'" July, 164–5.

Coleman, Charles W., Jr. (1887). "The Recent Movement in Southern Literature." *Harper's New Monthly Magazine* 74 (May), 837–56.

Donovan, Josephine (1983). *New England Local Color Literature: A Women's Tradition*. New York: F. Ungar.

Dunbar, Paul Laurence (1900). "Robert Gould Shaw." *Atlantic Monthly* 86 (Oct.), 488.

Eggleston, Edward (1894). "Folk-speech in America." *Century* 48, 867–75.

Emerson, Ralph Waldo (1998a). "The American Scholar." In Nina Baym (ed.), *Norton Anthology of American Literature*, vol. I, 1101–14. New York: Norton. (First publ. 1837.)

Emerson, Ralph Waldo (1998b). "Self-Reliance." In Nina Baym (ed.), *Norton Anthology of American Literature*, vol. I, 1126–44. New York: Norton. (First publ. 1841.)

Fetterley, Judith, and Pryse, Marjorie, eds. (1992). *American Women Regionalists, 1850–1910*, 1st edn. New York: Norton.

Foote, Stephanie (2001). *Regional Fictions: Culture and Identity in Nineteenth-Century American Literature*. Madison: University of Wisconsin Press.

Fuller, Margaret (1999). "American Literature." In Gordon Hutner (ed.), *American Literature, American Culture*, 37–47. New York: Oxford University Press. (First publ. 1859.)

Garland, Hamlin (1930). *Roadside Meetings*. New York: Macmillan.

Garland, Hamlin (1960). *Crumbling Idols: Twelve Essays on Art Dealing Chiefly with Literature, Painting, and the Drama*. Cambridge: Harvard University Press. (First publ. 1894.)

Glazener, Nancy (1997). *Reading for Realism: The History of a US Literary Institution, 1850–1910*. Durham: Duke University Press.

Halliburton, Thomas (1836). *The Clockmaker; or, the Sayings and Doings of Samuel Slick*. Halifax, Nova Scotia: Joseph Howe.

Hartt, Rollin Lynde (1899). "A New England Hill Town: Its Condition." *Atlantic Monthly* 83 (April), 561–74.

Howard, June (1996). "Unraveling Regions, Unsettling Periods: Sarah Orne Jewett and American Literary History." *American Literature* 68: 2, 365–84.

Howells, William Dean (1882). "Henry James, Jr." *Century* 25 (Nov.), 24–9.

Howells, William Dean (1886). "Editor's Study." *Harper's New Monthly Magazine* 73 (Sept.), 639–44.

Howells, William Dean (1889). "Editor's Study." *Harper's New Monthly Magazine* 79 (Nov.), 962–7.

Howells, William Dean (1983). *Selected Letters: 1912–1920. A Selected Edition of W. D. Howells*, ed. William Merriam Gibson and Christoph K. Lohmann, vol. VI. Boston: Twayne.

Howells, William Dean (1993). *Selected Literary Criticism*, vol. I. Bloomington: Indiana University Press.

James, W. P. (1897). "On the Theory and Practice of Local Color." *Living Age* 213 (June 12), 743–8.

Jones, Gavin Roger (1999). *Strange Talk: The Politics of Dialect Literature in Gilded Age America*. Berkeley: University of California Press.

Kaplan, Amy (1991). "Nation, Region, and Empire." In Emory Elliott (ed.), *The Columbia History of the American Novel*, 240–66. New York: Columbia University Press.

Kirkland, Caroline M. (1990). *A New Home – Who'll Follow? Or, Glimpses of Western Life*, ed. Sandra A. Zagarell. New Brunswick: Rutgers University Press. (First publ. 1839.)

Kolodny, Annette (1984). *The Land Before Her: Fantasy and Experience of the American Frontiers, 1630–1860*. Chapel Hill: University of North Carolina Press.

Lang, Andrew (1887). "Realism and Romance." *Littell's Living Age* 5th ser., vol. 60 (Dec. 10), 618–24.

Lathrop, George Parsons (1886). "The Literary Movement in New York." *Harper's New Monthly Magazine* 73 (Nov.), 831–3.

Lowell, James Russell (1867a). *The Biglow Papers, Second Series*, 1st edn. Boston: Ticknor & Fields.

Lowell, James Russell (1867b). "A Fable for Critics." In Edmund Wilson (ed.), *The Shock of Recognition*, 21–78. New York: Farrar, Straus, & Cudahy, 1955. (First publ. 1848.)

Mencken, H. L. (1919). "The Dean." *Prejudices, First Series*. New York: Knopf. 52–8.

Mencken, H. L. (1955). "Want Ad." In Edmund Wilson (ed.), *The Shock of Recognition*, 1238–41. New York: Farrar, Straus, and Cudahy. (First publ. 1926.)

Mencken, H. L. (1968). "Twain and Howells." In *H. L. Mencken's Smart Set Criticism*, ed. William H. Nolte, 178–9. Ithaca: Cornell University Press. (First publ. 1911.)

Morris, Linda (1992). *Women's Humor in the Age of Gentility: The Life and Works of Frances Miriam Whitcher*, 1st edn. Syracuse: Syracuse University Press.

Morse, James Herbert (1883). "The Native Element in American fiction: Since the War." *Century* 26 (July), 362–75.

Paulding, James Kirk (1999). "National Literature." In Gordon Hunter (ed.), *American Literature, American Culture*, 24–5. New York: Oxford University Press. (First publ. 1815.)

Pellew, George (1888). "The New Battle of the Books." *Forum* 5 (July), 564–73.

Perry, Bliss (1903). *A Study of Prose Fiction*. Boston: Houghton Mifflin.

Perry, Thomas S. (1872). "American Novels." *North American Review* 115 (Oct.), 366–78.

Pryse, Marjorie (1997). "Origins of American Literary Regionalism: Gender in Irving, Stowe, and Longstreet." In Sherrie A. Inness and Diana Royer (eds.), *Breaking Boundaries: New Perspectives on Women's Regional Writing*, 17–37. Iowa City: University of Iowa Press.

Scudder, H. E. (1891). "Mr. Howells's Literary Creed." *Atlantic Monthly* 68 (Oct.), 554–6.

Sherman, Sarah Way (1989). *Sarah Orne Jewett, an American Persephone*. Hanover: University Press of New England.

Simms, William Gilmore (1999). "Americanism in Literature." In Gordon Hutner (ed.), *American Literature, American Culture*, 26–36. New York: Oxford University Press. (First publ. 1845.)

Simpson, Claude M. (1960). *The Local Colorists: American Short Stories, 1857–1900*. New York: Harper.

Sundquist, Eric J. (1988). "Realism and Regionalism." In Emory Elliott (ed.), *Columbia Literary History of the United States*, 501–24. New York: Columbia University Press.

Thayer, William R. (1894). "The New Storytellers and the Doom of Realism." *Forum* 18 (Dec.), 470–80.

Thompson, Maurice (1894). "The Analysts Analyzed." *Critic* 6 (July), 19–22.

Tompkins, Jane (1985). *Sensational Designs: The Cultural Work of American Fiction, 1790–1860*. Oxford: Oxford University Press.

Van Doren, Carl (1985). *Contemporary American Novelists*. New York: Macmillan.

Vedder, Henry C. (1985). *American Writers of To-Day*. New York: Silver Burdett.

Warner, Charles Dudley (1892). "Editor's Study." *Harper's New Monthly Magazine* 85 (June), 155–6.

Warner, Charles Dudley (1896). "Editor's Study." *Harper's New Monthly Magazine* 92 (May), 961–2.

Warren, Kenneth W. (1994). *Black and White Strangers: Race and American Literary Realism*. Chicago: University of Chicago Press.

Wharton, Edith (1990). *Novellas and Other Writings*. (Library of America.) New York: Literary Classics of the United States, distrib. Viking.

Zagarell, Sandra A. (1997). "Crosscurrents: Registers of Nordicism, Community, and Culture in Jewett's *Country of the Pointed Firs*." *Yale Journal of Criticism: Interpretation in the Humanities* 10: 2, 355–70.

7

Taking Feminism and Regionalism toward the Third Wave

Krista Comer

As both a social movement and a many-sided scholarly project, feminism breathed new life into regional studies in the 1970s, transforming the terms by which regional writing has since been regarded. For much of the twentieth century up to this point, American regionalism had been taken by critics to mean local color writing, or, loosely, regional realism. As a genre ostensibly motivated by appeal of the local and vernacular, one moreover with the mark of commercial success and mass appeal upon it, regionalist undertakings generally had failed in American letters to meet the litmus test of literary accomplishment. To be "serious" in American high culture as critic, thinker, or writer was to be modernist, interested not in the supposedly quaint and picturesque but in literary innovation and the robust transcendental landscape of universals. To the extent that the rare regional writer surpassed the limits of the local – Twain or Faulkner being the favorite examples – regionalism operated as a micro template for macro concerns. By and large, especially at the foundational midcentury period, twentieth-century critical judgment held that regionalism constituted less of a rich, politically suggestive and influential, formal tradition, than of an undeniably large but still minor literature of smatterings, sketches, and escapist novels, even if one granted the occasional satisfying short story. Regional realism served as historical precursor to the more evolved intellectual and creative achievement of modernism. As such, it was tolerated as a fact of literary history, forgiven by the flowering that came after.

Feminist interventions into literary studies, including regional studies, have changed the prominence of the above attitude at the same time that the attitude itself has changed less than one might have anticipated. Much of what follows in this essay will be devoted to investigating why this is so. For if, as I noted above, feminist critics revived and transformed regional studies starting in the 1970s, it simultaneously is true that a larger group of feminist critics, with more institutional clout, have regarded regionalism with indifference. This fact should puzzle both groups of thinkers, since the enabling premises of so many evolving feminist knowledge projects have been articulated through and sustained by metaphors of place, space, location, and migration; by attention to private and to public spheres, to segregations as well as to the hopes for integrations of many kinds. For example, what feminist Americanist has not somehow encountered Nina Baym's "Melodramas of Beset Manhood," Adrienne Rich's "Notes Toward a Politics of Location," or Gloria Anzaldúa's *Borderlands/La Frontera*? If key canonical texts of feminist literary history and theory show investments in what I would liberally associate with "regional thinking" – that is, if feminist knowledge production has from its contemporary inception drawn from this theoretical resource – how might "regional thinking" be more explicitly acknowledged? What is to be gained by such an embrace? Or, maybe, who is to gain, what social groups (to deploy Bourdieu's sense of the political import of the region) will be made, remade, unmade?

To address these questions, I have structured this essay around a series of textual examples designed to reveal and intervene upon different critical attitudes about "the regional." I begin with a text that has in feminist studies been widely read, taught, and retaught, Gloria Anzaldúa's *Borderlands/La Frontera* (1987). The novelty of my argument here issues less from attention to this text's narrative of border crossings than from attention to its discursive debts to the genre of regionalism. I then move to a work critically understood and commercially promoted as a Western regionalist text, Judith Freeman's novel *The Chinchilla Farm* (1989), in which I am interested to show the unusual working-class quasi-anti-intellectual feminist Mormonism at work. My last texts include the novel and film *Gidget* (1957 and 1958 respectively) and a recent surf novel by Joy Nicholson, *The Tribes of Palos Verdes* (1997). I engage these not only as regional texts, but also as texts whose various "regional moves" open up, rather than confirm, dominant understandings of feminism and regionalism. Through these examples I want to showcase just a few of the wealth of rich, new, and different feminisms that might be brought into focus were "regionalism" taken seriously by university feminism at large.

Critical to unlocking the dynamic between regionalism and feminism is an investigation of the presumed relationship between the regional and "the national." Common sense has it that regional literature functions as a subset to, or of, national literature. In my own field, that of Western studies, critics and historians have often remarked upon the West *as* America (as the controversial Smithsonian exhibit of Western art declared in 1991), meaning that Western mythology signifies for a particular kind of American nationalism. Regionalism thus operates in some kind of service to representations, including critical ones, of the nation-state. To the extent anyone ponders regionalism's marginal status, that status would probably be judged to derive from regionalism's role as a kind of "under" literature – under the sign of the nation, subsumed within or by "larger," more central, or seemingly efficacious discursive fields.

However valuable this analysis, I am not producing my own version of regional thinking quite along these lines. Instead I am interested in innovating the category and analytic practice of regionalism so that it does not inevitably bounce back to critics in the form of the nation-state; in exploring the possibility that regionalism offers one method by which to render literary studies more postnational and transnational. I want to put into play, in the context of that very vexed, evolving problematic called globalization, what have been usually understood as "American subregions." Whereas global studies "does" region (although not US regions), American regional studies rarely "goes global." Hence a major task faced by scholars of the regional today – a task already well advanced in American literary studies, the interdisciplinary field of American Studies, the fields of history, both Western and Southern, and in feminist studies across the humanities – is to reckon with and displace the centrality of the nation-state in accounts of US cultural production. Regional studies is by no means in the vanguard of this effort, though it may be positioned, because of its curious liminality, to enter it, and alter it, in interesting and productive ways.

In order to demonstrate ways in which the regional might be deployed alternatively, let me turn now to the West, as I promised. A Western emphasis, I hope, forces scholars out of certain habitual narratives about the region and the nation likely to impede the changes I advocate. Perhaps the dominant one is to claim that the Civil War is *the* central fact of nineteenth-century nation-building efforts, a claim re-institutionalized every time an American literature survey course ends at 1865. Since the defeat of Mexico in 1846 and the annexation of its northern lands added over a third to the territorial mass of the evolving nation, shouldn't scholars redesign the political unconscious of nineteenth-century studies so that its spatial unconscious – its north/south bias – does not "space out" that "other" nation-building effort? A similar spatial unconscious exists in American feminist studies as well. Elsewhere I have elaborated the north/south geographical imagination mapping much of American women's history, as well as women's studies pedagogies about the contemporary US women's movement (Comer 1999: 34–59). The role these knowledge projects play in continually recentering narratives of the nation over north/south imaginative terrains poses problems for scholars' abilities to grasp the global *as it strategically figures in representations of the regional*. I am interested in displacing the hold that the north/east spatial field exerts on university feminisms and in forwarding the different political imaginations that come out of such a displacement. I wonder: what might happen if from this day forward American feminism reconceptualized itself through other than north/south geographical imaginations? How might it differently imagine the political?

Embracing Greater Mexico

To say that the north/south spatial axis dominates narratives of the nation is not to say that the classic east-to-west tale is without powerful social effect. But what if "the West" were *not* about America, or anyway, not only and finally about the "America" that Wallace Stegner or A. B. Guthrie or Henry Nash Smith or Frederick

Jackson Turner or Teddy Roosevelt or Ronald Reagan understood to be constituted by the process of westward migration itself? What processes or social effects might "the West" then signify? I have talked about these matters elsewhere, though not to this end, in formulating what I call the alternative and competing geographical imaginations produced by civil rights and feminist literatures of the 1960s, 1970s, and 1980s (Comer 1999: 34–49). One obvious alternative to dominant east–west spatial renderings underwriting that social space known as "the West" can be found in the geographical imagination of Aztlán – meaning the lands, generally, lost by Mexico to the United States in the war of 1846, and imaginatively reclaimed by many Mexican-American writers of the Chicano cultural renaissance. Of course, this is the "Greater Mexico" to which the founding figure of Mexican-American scholarship, Américo Paredes, referred in the 1950s and 1960s (Limón 1998). The spatial field of "Greater Mexico" is generally considered to extend from Texas to California, from the southern points of Arizona and New Mexico to portions of Colorado and Utah.

Suppose that critics reframed regionalism so that, for instance, the American Southwest signaled alternatively, as Paredes claimed it did, Greater Mexico? Such a remapping would at the minimum take regionalism *trans*national. But how else might the map of "the West" be re-imagined – say, the map of southern California? I will offer some thoughts toward this end centered on textual examples that encourage us to take the Greater Mexico paradigm seriously, not just for its *trans*national implications but – the harder task – for its *post*national applications, as well as its consequences for all (not only Mexican Americans) who make their daily lives in the nexus of those social geographies. If, as Américo Parades had it, Greater Mexico remains active and alive in Mexican Americans, is it not also true that "Greater Mexico," *as a residual structure of feeling*, is likely to be present in those parts of the United States previously designated "Mexican space" (R. Saldívar, forthcoming)? As one example alone, think of the Spanish place names that are spoken millions of times daily throughout the so called "American West." Can it entirely escape one's notice that the street where one grows up bears a Spanish name, as does one's school, one's town, and so on? The claim has to do with the ways in which regional subject formation, in western American contexts, is thoroughly if unconsciously inscribed with Spanish and Mexican cultural and colonial legacies.

The "Greater Mexico" paradigm appears prominently in Anzaldúa's *Borderlands/La Frontera*, starting with the text's initial enunciatory gesture: its title, represented in both English and Spanish. The title's bilingualism links Anzaldúa's ability to speak to the ability of a reading audience to comprehend both languages, a gesture which at the same time, for Anzaldúa, is inseparable from the speech act's spatial location on the literal and figurative geopolitical border between Mexico and the United States, specifically Texas. So the method by which this text announces its existence, its articulation of its own conditions of possibility, *requires* the invocation of "the regional." But the regional at play here refers readers to that prior historical moment and memory when Texas was Mexican, which is to say that its signification of the regional is also and at once transnational. In the late 1980s, *Borderlands/La Frontera* produced an enormously influential respatialization of the South Texas/Mexico regional imaginary, one both responsive and responsible to the larger inter-American hemispheric context and structure of feeling that it likewise attempts to name. Out of this text (not exclusively owing to it, of course) the 1990s buzzword "borderlands" was born.

The above argument is likely more familiar than the one I advance now: namely, that Anzaldúa's narrative could be articulated only *through* recourse to the regional (even while she innovates it) and therefore owes much more than has been appreciated to the possibilities for representing difference afforded by the regional genre. That is, the text recalls a basic premise of feminist regionalism: that regional writing is a "form *about* the representation of difference" (Foote 2001: 4; see also Ammons 1992, Fetterley and Pryse 1995). This claim is in keeping with the general thesis of feminist regionalism, which, with ever more sophistication over the years, has demonstrated that regionalist discourse historically empowered those at a distance from the power centers of culture to speak – writers such as Mary Wilkins Freeman, Sarah Orne Jewett, Alice Cary, Kate Chopin, Celia Thaxter, Mary Hallock Foote, Mary Austin, and Edith Eaton (Sui Sin Far). By invoking "the regional," writers enfranchised and authorized their "local" and "female" knowledges, transforming them, in the process, into legitimate public knowledges which then were more strategically situated to contest the reigning masculinism of the "official" national sphere (Brodhead 1993; Kolodny 1985; Graulich 1989). Were there no tradition of regional discourse in US cultural history, Anzaldúa would have had no discursive location or "place" from which to speak.

This is no ancillary argumentative point, even if it is the one most elided when critics and teachers recuperate *Borderlands/La Frontera* as a Mexican-American version of a "US third world woman/lesbian of color text," one which, with refreshing novelty, theorizes hybridity and postmodern subjectivity. While such a recuperation is understandable enough, it does not remain faithful to – on the contrary, it even silences – the other differences through which Anzaldúa is trying to write her way: namely, that the principal models for representing US woman-of-color subjectivity rely on black/white oppositions and invocations of the historical memory of slavery. No comparable national memory is at stake when one invokes the Mexican–American War. Keeping the analytic pressure on the regional also forces the issue as to Anzaldúa's own regional influences, most obviously Américo Paredes, whose own south Texas upbringing figured largely in what he would produce as a folklorist, social historian, novelist, and public intellectual. Paredes provides an ethnoregional frame for *Borderlands/La Frontera* just as much as the Chicano, gay liberation, or women's movements framed the terms by which "borderlands" subjectivity might be newly narrativized.

I would emphasize that the "Greater Mexico" model of regionalism that I am sketching here is not an attempt to erase the "American," for it is precisely "the American" – but conceived as a whole symbolic region, *not as a set of subregions* – that enables Anzaldúa, and especially other Chicanas and Asian-American Western women writers of this moment (e.g. Maxine Hong Kingston, Jeanne Wataksuki Houston, Sandra Cisneros) to speak in feminist ways *about* "Greater Mexico" or about the Chinatowns or Japanese internment camps of their female youths. (I would not extend this claim generally to the cultural production of Western African-American women or for Native American women writers.)

The above is a less difficult analytic step than the one we have to take next; for once one is persuaded that the combination of Greater Mexico and American geographical imaginaries seems more relevant for understanding Anzaldúa than ones conceived as "Western" or even "counter-Western" or "alternatively Western," then we have to ask: where do we go from there? By what established method and analytic logic does one understand "Mexico"? For one thing, as Amy Kaplan has noted, "the study of American culture has traditionally been cut off from a study of foreign relations" (Kaplan and Pease 1993: 11). Even this problem, however daunting, pales next to the larger one of how to represent Mexico, since the dominant spatial understanding of "Mexico" itself is emplotted by nationalist imaginaries, and hence provides no answer to the goal of *post*national analyses.

Regionalism and the Postnational

How might we in regional studies pursue *post*national thinking? Most critical work on Chicano/a literature, including my own, has framed Mexican-American writers more or less exclusively through the analytic vehicle of the nation-state, trying desperately to make Mexican Americans *present* in narratives of the nation. And the reason for this can be traced quite clearly, I think, to the "field-imaginary" of 1968. By the term "field-imaginary" I mean Donald Pease's sense of "the field's fundamental syntax – its tacit assumptions, convictions, primal words, and the charged relations binding them together" (Pease 1990: 11–12). From 1968 until the Berlin Wall came down in 1989 and the Cold War was officially over, claims for civil rights upon the state were uppermost in the mind of many new academics who made their way into English departments, and founded Women's Studies, Ethnic Studies, and Cultural Studies programs. The "charged words" often in play in those conversations had to do with oppression, claims upon the state for redress of oppression, and minority and/or female victimization and empowerment.

For many complex reasons these knowledge projects have found such a field-imaginary an increasing hindrance, for do they not owe more to the exceptionalist paradigms that founded American Studies in 1950 than is obvious at first glance? Doesn't the 1968 field-imaginary leave us "alone with America" (Amy Kaplan's phrase) after all? If we follow up on the idea of American Studies, of America itself as one more player in the international field of area studies, an idea implicit in so much of the work on (almost exclusively non-American) regional studies within globalization studies today – that is, if we abandon the exceptionalist premises so crucial to the founding of American Studies and also to Western Studies – would scholars then not be obliged to figure regions and regionalism in far more comparative and multi-lingual ways than we are used to doing? Certainly this kind of practice motivates much of postcolonial studies, as well as critical interventions like José David Saldívar's *Border Matters*, Lisa Lowe's *Immigrant Acts*, and the essays in this volume by Annette Kolodny and Vera Kutzinski (chapters 3 and 11). Importantly, these new renderings of the regional show radical internationalist underpinnings *not* because the post-1989 moment is more global than previous ones, but because the post-1989 moment has forced a recasting of "the American experience" as more transcultural, multiply national, and internationally imbricated than Americanist critics, including canon-busters, had managed to impress upon historical memory.

Following a trajectory invoked by Anzaldúa herself – that of the chain-link fence of the Tortilla Curtain, stretching from the flatlands of Texas to the sea where Tijuana meets San Diego – I want now to address the claims I've made about southern California as part of Greater Mexico. Though many Western novels or films could make the case, I will begin by way of Judith Freeman's *The Chinchilla Farm* (1989). As I noted before, though this novel is generally framed through "the regional," my goal here is to demonstrate how Freeman's regionalism expands the boundaries of "the feminist" by innovating both the places where, and the logic by which, feminists go about their business of changing the world. The ethics of the text, while rooted in a Mormon upbringing, reveal a Mormonism fundamentally retooled, denationalized or, rather, transnationalized. The exceptionalist claims of Mormon history are renounced in favor of an embrace of something like postnational feminist solidarity – but on terms that do not reproduce the problems of the "sister-hood is global" ideal of 1970s feminism. This solidarity is not one exclusively among women, but is also based on the shared *economic* status of those characters – homeless men, the working poor, the nonwhite – who are represented in the novel as having been hardest hit by the emergent global economies of the 1980s. Key to *this* kind of feminist project is Freeman's insistence that men, like the recurrent white homeless men about whom the novel cares very much, are "natural" constituents of any fem-inisms reconceived in the wake of globalization.

The Chinchilla Farm structures its movement by way of its regional imagination: it names Part One, "Utah," Part II, "Los Angeles," Part III, "Mexico." Listen to the bookjacket blurb, which sets out to locate and promote the text's presumed reader-ship as well as to build a consumer base for a particular "brand" of the Western female regional:

> Raised a Mormon in a small town in Utah, married to a stiflingly conventional adulterer, Verna Flake has gotten tired of pretending. So she heads for Los Angeles, where people have the freedom to find themselves over and over again. In this lyrical and keenly observant novel Judith Freeman captures the solitude, the dislocation, and the offbeat optimism of the American West in a way that raises comparison with writers like Louise Erdrich and Bobbie Ann Mason.

At the end of *The Chinchilla Farm* a couple of surprising events occur. First, two of the text's American protagonists remain in Mexico to start new lives, make new homes, even as the central protagonist, Verna Flake, returns to Los Angeles. Second, Verna Flake announces things have turned out happily for her back in Los Angeles because, as she tells us, "I am writing this book, aren't I?" (Freeman 1989: 308). She also marries a rich man, and has a baby whom she names "Silvia" after her dead brother's Mexican-American wife (one of those who stay south of the border). Thus, in the book's last pages, readers are invited to imagine Americans who permanently relocate themselves in Baja, California. We are also to understand our transplanted protagonist as a budding writer and, by extension, to understand Judith Freeman herself as the partial subject of this book, since on the final page she intrudes without preparation into the narrative with a new "I" persona (I am writing this book, aren't I?). We also know, from the jacket and other biographical information, that Freeman is, in "real life," married to a Mexican-American man, Anthony Hernandez, to whom in fact the book is dedicated. The first point here is that the regional imaginary concluding this text – written not by a south Texas Chicana lesbian feminist like Gloria Anzaldúa but by a white working-class woman from Salt Lake City with Mormon communitarian convictions – is actually less compatible with that of Bobbie Ann Mason or Louise Erdrich than with that of Anzaldúa, because Freeman locates herself, as a working-class subject, "a real woman," and a writer, within the imaginative space of Greater Mexico.

In that Greater Mexican space, the story takes its most dramatic feminist turns. Verna Flake ferries her sister-in-law Silvia across the border toward her extended family in Bahía de los Angeles in order to escape Silvia's violent, gun-toting new second husband Jim, who has also (when she was younger) molested Silvia's retarded daughter, Cristobel. A kind of post-1989 version of Steinbeck's Joad family, these three women and their homeless, newly sober companion Duluth, journey, in a rickety truck, nothing short of desperate. When Jim catches up with them, as of course the reader knows he must, the shocking resolution happens: Cristobel pushes him to his death in a villager's well. The Mexican local authorities call it an "accident," and the reader, unsure as to the event's status as accident or not, concurs perhaps uneasily with what seems a Mexican willingness to say: Well, we'll leave it at that. He was a bad man. The women and Duluth, thereafter, evidence new and different kinds of personal empowerments. Silvia and her daughter decide to stay south, a more forgiving environment for these particular women than is Los Angeles, the reader agrees. Duluth too will stay, because in Mexico he finds a new health. Verna understands something about the interconnectedness of all things, but in ways that seem less Zen than postnational, and with such a knowledge she can return to Los Angeles with a very changed grasp of that city as well as definitions of the global. This empowerment, I want to stress, is quite *mutual*. A transnational and cross-cultural exchange takes place, and all of the parties give and gain. This is not a story of bourgeois Anglo womanhood saving global womankind from indignities "they" supposedly haven't the sense to perceive.

The fact that Verna returns to LA with a different grasp of "the global" is significant. Verna's "Western road trip" – that is, Freeman's strategic use of a classic masculine regional convention – has moved both the convention and Western characters in ever more postnational and feminist directions. Whatever one's opinion about the justice of the tale's resolution, my point is to emphasize its location in non-American contexts, figuratively outside of the moral logics of the nation-state. This assault on the inevitability of nation-statehood is only the most obvious, however, since from the tale's beginning, Freeman figures Verna's departure from Utah as itself a break with nation-based community affinities: a break, as the narrator notes, with "Zion." Mormonism, like American exceptionalism, works from its sense of Mormons (like Puritans) as persecuted, chosen, as well as compelled to convert, evangelize. It is precisely these last duties Verna refuses when she stops wearing her white undergarments – clothing which, she says, in combination with all of the other white clothing that must be worn in temple, *makes* people feel exceptional (Freeman 1989: 22). The initial move from Utah to Los Angeles effects the first transnational shock, for when the sheltered Verna, a woman accustomed to cultural homogeneity, arrives in Los Angeles, she has arrived in what appears to her a foreign country. Particularly when she makes her home in low-end, often Spanish-speaking MacArthur Park, she has essentially renounced the Mormon symbolic investment in whiteness, linking the rhythms of the everyday with the spaces of Greater Mexico.

This renovation of the Western imaginary is not the end of the matter, however, for the last lines of the book ask the reader to broaden further the remappings going on, to turn our sense of "the regional" toward the Far East. The explicit language of "the Pacific Rim" articulates the horizon of the final landscape which defines our protagonist's new family and new life. Verna Flake looks out, from the picture window of a beach-front home, to observe that "the water beyond them [the husband and baby Silvia] is coming in in fanciful rows, small, lacy waves. They just keep coming, row after row of flowing ripples, these endless waves. The Pacific is such a wide, fathomless ocean, and here we are, still on the rim" (Freeman 1989: 308). Greater Mexico always "touches upon" or navigates the Pacific Rim, thus, the waves bringing into conversation with one another a different triangle from that operating in a transnational imaginary like that named by Paul Gilroy's *The Black Atlantic*. Call this the Bronze Pacific? I don't know, but the relevant spatial poles are Asia, Spain, and the Pacific coastal region, expansively understood. Importantly, this "Pacific Rim" discussion begins mid-book, and there Verna dismisses it, by saying, in her anti-intellectual way, "I don't find this talk [about LA as the capital of the Pacific Rim] all that interesting. I'd rather look at the scenery [of the Malibu coastline]" (Freeman 1989: 180). It is only after Verna's journey to Baja, and her epiphanic postnational moment, that she can extend that embrace of Greater Mexico to the Far East.

One could take off in a million directions from here, for this ending to Freeman's book recalls F. Scott Fitzgerald's "boats against the current, borne back ceaselessly into the past" – but from a colonial perspective more Spanish than Dutch or English, an immigrant perspective not as familiar as is that of Jimmy Gatz, whom Fitzgerald memorializes as Jay Gatsby. One could think about Los Angeles not just as the city that (as Mike Davis reminds us) intellectuals love to hate, or, as Ed Soja has identified it, as a space of paradigmatic postmodernity, but as James Clifford might notice it, as a place, like *all places*, whose inhabitants' "roots," that is their claim upon an identity based in place, result from "practices of displacement [which] might emerge as *constitutive* of cultural meanings rather than as their simple transfer or extension" (Clifford 1997: 3). Their "roots" come from "routes." Clifford's point is that "place" is defined not only by way of rootedness but by way of travel, by the fact of "routes" and the traversal of boundaries that give rise to discrete cultural identity. Regional identities do not exist, that is, before they encounter "others" against whom they define themselves.

Gidget: A Case Study in a New Feminist Geography

One intriguing cultural location – that of surfers – witnesses the literal movement of the ground upon which "place-based" identities are formed. The geographical imagination of surfers, I want to argue, has from the beginning, at least in its American versions, been trained upon a larger (sometimes colonialist) internationalism, perhaps providing some explanation as to why surfers historically have marched to a different drum, one not so preoccupied with the goings-on of the nation-state, one not so easily grasped or valued by a 1968 field-imaginary. Surfers spend large parts of their days (and daydreams) "offshore," waiting for waves on the liminal zones of nations' territorial boundaries, their cognitive maps attuned to swells arriving or delayed from down south or points northwest. But even the "gremmiest" of novices in *some* way grasps that the wave that breaks at, say, Rincon, below Santa Barbara, began its trek across the ocean from some distant place, perhaps as distant as Japan, traveling a great formative distance before it encountered a shallow enough place to reshape it from swell to breaking wave face. This wave thus connects the American surfer – always, every day – to the bigger horizon of the wide world, and the link-up moment, the moment of the breaking wave, is always the moment of his own global enunciation, his location in social space, his play.

In the space that remains to me, I turn to southern California surf culture as an example of what it means to inhabit that "bigger horizon." Greater Mexico may seem in what follows to signify in far more ghostly ways than in the discussions of Anzaldúa and Freeman. Like the sound of surf itself, one detects its presence as "background noise," an informing rhythm shaping surf culture's sense of time, play, work, community purpose. But if surfers themselves are inclined to register the transnational most often in explicitly Far Eastern terms – through reference to the legendary surf spots of Hawaii, Bali, Java (Mexico's surf, by comparison, lacks) – it would be a mistake to underestimate the "background noise" effect. In surf culture's renunciation of a WASPy work ethic, its pleasure in group activity and collective identity, its love of sport and the outdoors, we see remnants of nineteenth-century Old Californio culture. Surfers straddle southern California's regional identity, its location as a Cliffordian "route" or global crossroads. Surfers, like so very many alternative communities throughout California history, locate or invent themselves through a spatial logic often strikingly isolated from mainstream ideas about the nation and national normativity. My point here is not to idealize surfers' community formations, but to emphasize that theirs is a space, because of its literal edginess, positioned to foster one kind of postnational subject formation.

Female surfers, too, for reasons different from those motivating their male counterparts, have found the pleasures of the global horizon enormously appealing. To get at this difference, I explore the transnational endings of several surf texts: the recently reissued 1957 novel *Gidget* (on which the hugely popular 1958 film *Gidget*, starring Sandra Dee, was based),[1] and the 1997 first novel of southern Californian Joy Nicholson, *The Tribes of Palos Verdes*. I will save my discussion of "the regional" in these texts for the conclusion.

The film *Gidget*, the most widely circulated of surf images to date, concludes with its heroine dancing on the shoreline, happily matched with one of the love objects she has desired over the course of the tale: Moondoggie. She wears a 1950s party dress, and twirls about the shoreline in a kind of carefree, rapturous splendor. We might well assume that whatever opening the film has produced for athletic, flat-chested young women has just been effectively contained. But this is not, I think, the whole of it. Yes, Gidget has been removed from the water as able surfer and appears on the brink of female initiation into her prescribed relationship to the state, that of consuming mother of a "nuclear" or Cold War family. But if Gidget is not figured atop her board, neither is she within the domestic frame of the suburban home at movie's end, as is, implicitly, her mother. Gidget remains out of doors, playing at the edge of national femininity. In the terms I suggested above: the conditions of possibility are present for her enunciation as an international and transnational subject.

I owe part of my reading of the film's conclusion to my reading of the novel's conclusion. There, the tale also resolves by way of consummation of a romance plot: Gidget is pinned to Moondoggie. But the difference is that here, even while the romance plot is "successfully" realized (the girl gets her guy), it is also subverted. The final page of the text proclaims Gidget's "big love is still out Malibuways with some bitchen surf going." Gidget second-guesses the truth of her feelings for each of the text's male love objects, and contrasts those "maybe" feelings with this statement: "But with the board and the sun and the waves it was for real." In a text quite concerned with a young woman's coming of age, with being a woman in love, Gidget concludes: "maybe I was just a woman in love with a surfboard" (Kohner 2001: 154).

What I find so telling about the Gidget novels as a series (there are five) is their general disregard of the nation's Cold War "need" for mother/soldiers. Often the rhetoric of Cold War aggression appears quite parodically. For example, several novels, in their different opening gambits, explicitly figure Cold War contexts. In *Gidget* we get a description of a bay next to the Malibu pier, "where the waves coming from Japan crush against the shore like some bitchen rocket bomb" (Kohner 2001: 2). Or, in *Cher Papa*, we learn that Gidget's family goes to the ski town of Sun Valley to ski, "a yearly ritual in our family, come hell or sputnik" (Kohner 1960: 1). The state of the nation and national identity certainly are at issue – the opening scene of *Gidget* pivots upon young Francie's rescue by Moondoggie at sea on the fourth of July.

But Gidget's response to the serious business of fighting the Cold War is to play. She surfs, skis, swims, rages, laughs; she kisses, she cuddles, she longs. This a world which revolves around "some bitchen surf going," meaning a world driven by tides, swells, healthy air, above all, desire – and the desired envisioned here is counter to that promoted for women by a militarist state. In her bodily love affair with the Pacific, Gidget engages in something like a traitorous international border crossing, for its waters don't obey the logic of geopolitical boundaries. Hers is a form of female subjectivity based *not* on the reproduction of Cold Warriors but on some more vague and pacifist sense of female possibility, articulated through healthy, sexual, internationalist, physically powerful, playful, and free female bodily experience.

In the figure of Gidget, we have one example of a regional feminism whose political work and practical influence has gone underestimated by university feminism. To be sure, Gidget is not representative of a feminism that anticipates Betty Friedan, the Redstockings, or the Combahee River Collective Statement; but must she be, in order to be "seriously" feminist? If not through a feminist lens, how is one to make sense of an iconic figure which has empowered countless young women as athletes and *subjects* (rather than objects) of California stories, which encourages young women to script their bodies according to a narrative of female strength, persistence, and risk-taking? Perhaps the question should be instead: What does this debate say about *us*, meaning university feminists, rather than about Gidget? One thing it says, to my mind, is that definitions of "the political" remain appropriately heated. But they also evidence a dated predictability, for this particular debate about a nonintellectual heroine returns us to tensions unresolved in early second wave feminism. Here I'm talking about the skepticism of especially Northeastern self-identified political activists toward the idea that various, usually West Coast, counter-cultures (like surf culture) might indeed create feminist political consciousness. Linked to this unresolved debate is another: over the political import of "pleasure" or "desire" or "play." For university feminism to come at a figure like carefree noncerebral Gidget with anything approaching a fresh perspective, it would have to revisit its judgment that countercultural subjectivity ultimately produces protopolitical and unactivist feminist political subjectivity; which is to say that it would have to revise the geography, the north/south bias, of US feminism's political imagination. The West Coast as a transnational regional imagination – not only the "capital" of the

Pacific Rim but the capital of the counterculture as well as a crossroads space with Greater Mexico — will simply have to figure more earnestly in feminist formulations of the political.

Surfing the Third Wave

Indeed, this new geography is visible in, even dominates, the recent hard-to-read political imaginations laid out by writers who often are referred to as members of "Generation X" (b. 1960–80). A great many of the highest-profile Generation X novels, and also television shows and films, locate their particular pathos and X-er sensibility from within "Western" contexts. Sometimes it is Texas (think of the film *Reality Bites*, or of Richard Linklater's *Slacker* and *Dazed and Confused*). Sometimes it's the Bay area, with incursions farther northwest into Vancouver (the TV series *Party of Five*, and *X-Files*). But most often Los Angeles provides the premier site of Generation X cultural production, with gestures toward Mexico and the Pacific Rim, or upward into Canada. Take as examples the novels *Less Than Zero*, by the king of the Brat Pack Bret Easton Ellis, or *Generation X*, by Canadian writer Douglas Coupland; films like *Clueless*; or any number of super-successful TV series like *Buffy the Vampire Slayer*, *Moesha*, *The Fresh Prince of Bel Air*, *Melrose Place*, or *Beverly Hills 90210*. The transnational cultural landscapes of the West Coast/borderlands regions permit writers, TV producers and film-makers to raise a relatively new set of questions about American race relations (not so black/white), gender relations (feminism as concerning others than the female professional), and about the relative noncentrality of the nation-state in young people's sense of themselves and their communal identifications. In all of the above examples, and of course in youth culture today more generally, the status of "the political" is profoundly up for grabs.

Perhaps more familiar to university feminists is the recent, hugely publicized phenomenon of the young American woman (across race, though mostly middle-class) who "is not a feminist, but . . ." Usually, popular magazines and news media position second-wave feminists as caricatures of political rigidity, nay-sayers of young women's life choices, their supposed apoliticism, hyperconsumerism, and so on. Young women are thereby invited to reject the feminism of their second-wave figurative and literal mothers, confident they have not disposed of a crucial life ally. In many ways, the figure of Gidget (like Buffy the Vampire Slayer or Ally McBeal) is precisely the kind of figure that young women might embrace without having simultaneously to acknowledge overt feminist commitments; which means that the Gidget or Buffy phenomena can potentially be staged in such a way as to drain them of their most edgy contents. In making this observation I only state the obvious, which is that the promotion of certain feminisms within pop culture cuts both ways (Meglin and Perry 1996; Radner and Luckett 1999). The Gidget legacy is truly upon university feminism, layering older tensions about "the political" within the counterculture atop newer ones about how to effectively reach young women who, however suspicious they are of feminism, have no intentions of playing second fiddle to men. But not all young women refuse the political identification of feminist, and no feminists are more aware of the complex "bite the hand that feeds it" tendency of pop culture than those young women who call their movement "third wave." At pains to distinguish their politics from those of young antifeminist or so-called "postfeminist" writers (Roiphe, Denfield, Sommers, Paglia), third-wavers like Leslie Heywood and Jennifer Drake or Rebecca Walker embrace second-wave or "boomer feminism" (b. 1940–60) even while they locate their own feminist sensibilities in different historical contexts, having come of age in the late 1970s and 1980s.

It is within the above third-wave frame that I want to consider my last chosen text, Joy Nicholson's *The Tribes of Palos Verdes*. To locate our discussion, let me invoke for a second time a series of dustjacket promotional blurbs. A *Los Angeles Times* reviewer describes *Tribes of Palos Verdes* as "the wise, funny, adolescent voice of a female Holden Caulfield, noble and honest. . . . A vibrant book, brave and true to a young girl's voice." On the back cover, we read: "This is the moving story of growing up 'different,' of the love between siblings, and one girl's power to save herself." Other blurbs repeatedly emphasize the "youth" of this female protagonist. The pitch here is a respectful one to the currently very lucrative, "girl market segment." By way of analogy to Caulfield, St. Martin's Griffin hopes to persuade the reader that girls' challenges occupy a central place in culture today – as did 1950s male adolescence in *Catcher in the Rye*. The "Holden Caulfield analogy" is an interesting one, indicative of the bookseller's intention to target a "Generation X" buying population. Consider other recent blockbuster Gen. X books that have been sold by way of the same Caulfield analogy: the aforementioned Bret Easton Ellis's *Less Than Zero* and Douglas Coupland's *Generation X*.

But Medina Mason, the protagonist of *The Tribes of Palos Verdes*, will never be a "Holden Caulfield," the main reasons being that she is a female from southern California and that the year is not 1950. Like Ellis and Coupland (and unlike Salinger's Holden Caulfield), Nicholson chronicles, through thematics very common to Generation X cultural production, the absolute shock of the post-1989 cultural order. On a personal level, Medina Mason's family is shattered. Her twin brother and mother die in the course of her fourteenth and fifteenth years, both implicit suicides. Her father comes and goes, as he will. In lieu of a family, Medina Mason relies upon her "tribe," comprised of the local surfers in Palos Verdes. If one of the reviewers applauds the "power" of a young girl to save herself, I would applaud less and note the utter necessity of her saving herself. There is little triumph in self-preservation for Medina Mason, and much heartache. In the text's representation of friends-as-family, and the complete "on one's own" status of children in this particular American family, *Tribes of Palos Verdes* is a one of the most frequently told of Gen. X tales.

The text also illustrates well many of the defining differences between second- and third-wave feminist cultural norms. In implicit defiance of the second-wave tradition of "women-identified women," Medina Mason's best friend is her brother (indeed, she has not a single girlfriend). She has no intention of affirming female athletic difference, insisting she will "forget [she's] a girl" and surf "like a man, aggressive and fierce" (Nicholson 1997: 24). Medina reflects casually upon surfing as sometimes akin to "religious experience," sometimes "pure domination" (Nicholson 1997: 48). No doubt Medina Mason would prefer calling herself not a feminist but, in the tradition of TV queen Roseanne Arnold, a "killer bitch." But "bitch" is not the hardest self-affirmation for a second waver to swallow. In a moment when she fears her brother will not go out into the surf with her, she chides him: "oh Jim, don't be such a pussy, just close your eyes and go in" (Nicholson 1997: 15). There it is: "pussy," uttered by a young women angry at a man! Third-wavers, one might say, have much stronger stomachs than their older feminist allies ever did.

In her sexual behavior in particular, Medina illustrates the third wave's very expansive sense of female sexual agency, its affirmation (to the dismay of many second-wavers) of even sex work. At the beginning of the text, Medina makes a deal with a neighborhood boy to lift up her shirt for ten seconds in exchange for a surfboard. She gets enough of what she wants out of that deal that she makes it again, with another neighborhood boy, and takes home proudly her own version of a trophy – another surfboard, a gift to her brother so she now has surfing company! If a second-wave reading of this text might wonder about Medina's status as a victim or object of masculinist sexual discourse, asking whether this isn't a form of "sex work" (vaguely like prostitution), a third-wave reading – which the narrator and most student readers seem to prefer – might understand Medina's act as one in which it is not she who has been exploited, but the sexual attitudes about girls of the neighborhood boys. Indeed, we might read this moment as a 1990s innovation of the 1960s "feminist zap," for Medina Mason's parents are rich, and probably, at her request, would have bought her a surfboard. Since much of the text is given to narrating Medina's sexual coming-of-age, and probably only one sexual relationship falls into the category of a "good" or mutually respectful relationship, the second-wave reader is again tempted to frame analyses with the word "victimization" in mind. But such a frame would have to answer to the claim, implicit in a character like Medina Mason, that young women now feel less victimized than "we," their second-wave predecessors, felt; that indeed the world for girls has been bettered.

Still, a world in which one's mother and twin brother commit suicide is hardly a good world, and in testimony to that stark fact, this book ends accordingly. Medina Mason paddles herself, along with her brother's empty board, out past the surf break, and then, in a ritualized goodbye to him, she lets the board go. As she does so we get the remarks, "I'll be surfing in Hawaii soon. After that, Bali, Java, Thailand. I have no itinerary, no plans to return. I'm going to surf until I die." The final departing sentence, five lines later: "No one knows I'm crying" (Nicholson 1997: 218).

As I noted earlier, this text, like the *Gidget* texts, ends with a distinctly transnational reach. I have hoped to suggest some of the peculiarly "Gen. X" tropes underwriting this very solitary conclusion, the feeling, in Generation X cultural works, that (as is said in International Studies sometimes) the time we live in, instead of being one of Cold War, is one of "hot peace." I would also remind us that if the transnational landscape most beloved by surfers is the one Nicholson names in Java, Bali, and so on, we only have to return to the fact of the novel's title, drawn from the place where Medina lives, "Palos Verdes," to resurrect and keep therefore alive the trace of Greater Mexico.[2]

CONCLUSION

The analytic curve of this essay has moved from a regional emphasis on Anzaldúa's *Borderlands/La Frontera* to a third-wave text about a California surfergirl – in other words, a long way into relatively unexplored "territory" for contemporary feminist history. I concede some reservation, as I close, about forwarding, without qualification, the newer feminist geographies at work in texts like *Gidget*, *Chinchilla Farm*, or *The Tribes of Palos Verdes*. I too am beholden to feminisms conceived over north/south spatial terrains, to critiques of institutional sites of oppression and committed activist interventions upon them. These are the political forms feminists in the United States know best; their kinds of politics have covered a great distance in a relatively short time.

At the same time, I am thoroughly persuaded that feminism needs new political forms more responsive to the media-saturated culture of today, where feminism itself is a powerful player. Some of the fresher ideas in recent memory, to my way of thinking, come out of Gen. X and third-wave culture, from regions not generally studied or considered to be in the avant-garde of political movements. For X-ers, "messy" politics, a politics shorn of 1960s idealism, is normative. Normative, too, are more just gender and race relations, and a distance from statist or nation-based political paradigms. Perhaps because Generation X is the first generation to actually suffer a decline in its standard of living (X today has a lower percentage of middle-class people than at any point in twentieth-century American history), their politics may ultimately, and paradoxically, be both more conservative and more class-sensitive. Perhaps a new kind of anticorporatism is on the rise, this time one not so obtuse to gender and racial difference. In any event, the hand has not been played out, the movie is still running. In the interim there is always, only, the now.

ACKNOWLEDGMENT

Many thanks go to Eric Lott. Informing this essay's conceptualization of "field-imaginaries" is his informal think-piece "American Studies in the Age of Free Trade: Some Points for a Discussion of 19th-century Studies," presented at Rice University in the fall of 2001.

Notes

1 Many people will be surprised to learn there are Gidget novels, penned by the father of surfergirl Kathy "Gidget" Kohner. The author, Frederick Kohner, a German Jewish intellectual turned Hollywood screenwriter, arrived in California in 1938, fleeing the Holocaust. I have not taken up the provocative implications of the text's authorship here. For a full analysis see Comer, *Gidget to Surfergrrls* (forthcoming).

2 Due to space limitations I have not elaborated here other evidence offered by this novel about its implication in Greater Mexico.

References and Further Reading

Ammons, Elizabeth (1992). *Conflicting Stories: American Women Writers at the Turn into the Twentieth Century*. New York: Oxford University Press.

Anzaldúa, Gloria (1987). *Borderlands/La Frontera: The New Mestiza*. San Francisco: Spinsters/Aunt Lute.

Baym, Nina (1985). "Melodramas of Beset Manhood: How Theories of American Fiction Exclude Women Authors." In Elaine Showalter (ed.), *Feminist Criticism: Essays on Women, Literature, Theory*, 63–80. New York: Pantheon.

Brodhead, Richard (1993). *Cultures of Letters: Scenes of Reading and Writing in Nineteenth-Century America*. Chicago and London: University of Chicago Press.

Clifford, James (1997). *Routes: Travel and Translation in the Late Twentieth Century*. Cambridge, Mass.: Harvard University Press.

Comer, Krista (1999). *Landscapes of the New West: Gender and Geography in Contemporary Women's Writing*. Chapel Hill: University of North Carolina Press.

Comer, Krista (forthcoming). *From Gidget to surfergrrls: Cultural History and Gender Formations in an Era of Globalization*.

Fetterley, Judith, and Pryse, Marjorie (1995). *American Women Regionalists, 1850–1910*. New York and London: Norton.

Foote, Stephanie (2001). *Regional Fictions: Culture and Identity in Nineteenth-Century American Literature*. Madison: University of Wisconsin Press.

Freeman, Carla (2001). "Is Local: Global as Feminine: Masculine? Rethinking the Gender of Globalization." *Signs: Journal of Women in Culture and Society* 26: 4, 1007–37.

Freeman, Judith (1989). *The Chinchilla Farm*. New York: Vintage.

Graulich, Melody (1989). " 'O beautiful for spacious guys': An Essay on the 'Legitimate Inclination of the Sexes.' " In David Mogen, Mark Busby, and Paul Bryant (eds.), *The Frontier Experience and the American Dream*, 186–204. College Station: Texas A&M University Press.

Heywood, Leslie, and Drake, Jennifer (1997). *Third Wave Agenda: Being Feminist, Doing Feminism*. Minneapolis: University of Minnesota Press.

Inness, Sherrie, and Royer, Diana (1997). *Breaking Boundaries: New Perspectives on Women's Regional Writing*. Iowa: University of Iowa Press.

Jameson, Frederic and Miyoshi, Masao (1998). *The Cultures of Globalization*. Durham: Duke University Press.

Kaplan, Amy, and Pease, Donald P. (1993). *Cultures of United States Imperialism*. Durham: Duke University Press.

Kohner, Frederick (1960). *Cher Papa*. New York: Bantam.

Kohner, Frederick (2001). *Gidget*. New York: Berkeley. (First publ. 1957.)

Kollin, Susan (2001). *Nature's State: Imagining Alaska as the Last Frontier*. Chapel Hill: University of North Carolina Press.

Kolodny, Annette (1985). "Dancing through the Minefield: Some Observations on the Theory, Practice, and Politics of a Feminist Literary Criticism." In Elaine Showalter (ed.), *Feminist Criticism: Essays on Women, Literature, Theory*, 144–67. New York: Pantheon. (First publ. 1980.)

Limón, José (1998). *American Encounters: Greater Mexico, the United States, and the Erotics of Culture*. Boston: Beacon Press.

Lowe, Lisa (1996). *Immigrant Acts: On Asian American Cultural Politics*. Durham: Duke University Press.

Meglin, Nan Dauer, and Perry, Donna (1996). *"Bad Girls"/"Good Girls": Women, Sex, and Power in the Nineties*. New Brunswick: Rutgers University Press.

Nicholson, Joy (1997). *The Tribes of Palos Verdes*. New York: St Martin's Griffin.

Pease, Donald (1990). "New Americanists: Revisionist Interventions into the Canon." *boundary 2/17* (Spring), 1–37.

Radner, Hilary, and Luckett, Moya (1999). *Swinging Single: Representing Sexuality in the 1960s*. Minneapolis: University of Minnesota Press.

Rich, Adrienne (1985). "Notes toward a Politics of Location." In Myriam Díaz-Diocaretz and Iris M. Zavala (eds.), *Women, Feminist Identity and Society in the 1980s: Selected Papers*, 7–22. Amsterdam: Benjamins.

Roberts, Diane (1994). *The Myth of Aunt Jemima: Representations of Race and Region*. New York and London: Routledge.

Saldívar, José David (1997). *Border Matters: Remapping American Cultural Studies*. Berkeley: University of California Press.

Saldívar, Ramón (forthcoming). *Americó Paredes and the Transnational Imaginary*.

8

Regionalism and Ecology

David Mazel

In her 1932 essay "Regionalism and American Fiction," Mary Austin criticized writers who set their work in a generic, homogenized locale intended to represent the United States as a whole. The result was "fiction shallow enough to be common to all regions, so that no special knowledge of other environments than one's own is necessary to the appreciation of it" (Austin 2001: 265). The best American fiction, by contrast, was concretely set in particular, vividly evoked regions, and its appreciation *did* call for a "special knowledge" of varied environments. One of the engines producing and popularizing such knowledge – and thereby shaping an audience for regional literature – has been what is now broadly called "ecology."

Literary regionalism and ecology in fact emerged more or less simultaneously in response to the various upheavals of modernity, and they have since interacted with each other in ways scholars are just beginning to explore. Our understanding of those interactions is complicated by the fact that "ecology" names at once a science, a politics, and a sensibility. Ecological science is the study of the biological relationships between organisms and their environment. Ecological politics concerns itself with the prevention of air and water pollution and the preservation of natural landscapes and ecosystems. The ecological sensibility manifests itself, among other ways, as an aesthetic appreciation of the beauty and "rightness" of nature, and an ethical compulsion to minimize environmental damage by living more "naturally."

All three of these senses of "ecology" are deeply intertwined and at times contradictory. Ecological science, for example, is based like any other natural science on the rigid conceptual separation of the observer from the object being studied. Green politics and its attendant sensibility, by contrast, tend to see this human/nature split as the root of our environmental predicament, even as they necessarily and paradoxically make copious use of the data provided by ecological science. Green movements generally occupy the left end of the political spectrum, yet what would now be considered "ecological" thinking has also lent considerable ideological support to imperialism, nativism, and fascism.

Regionalism is haunted by similar contradictions. At its best, regionalism's careful attention to local peoples and environments can endow its subjects with dignity and agency while also illuminating the complex relations between culture and place. But that same attention always entails the risk of degenerating into the sort of environmental determinism that has so often underwritten dehumanizing theories of racial difference and national superiority. Under the spell of such a determinism, even so perceptive and progressive a thinker as Austin could write that "everything an Indian does or thinks is patterned by the particular parcel of land which is his tribal home" (2001: 268). Like ecology, regionalism has been put to political uses both progressive and regressive.

In all three of its senses – as science, politics, and sensibility – ecology has roots in many of the same aspects of modernity that gave rise to regionalism, particularly the growth of imperialism and colonialism and the onset of nationalism. As a science – as the branch of biology grounded in the work of Linnaeus and Darwin and culminating in the rigorous and sophisticated theories of twentieth-century ecologists like Frederic Clements and Eugene Odum – ecology is part of the Baconian project of transforming all of nature so as to put it to human use. It is in this sense, to borrow Donald Worster's term, an "imperial ecology" (1994: 30); it is also "imperial" in the sense that imperialism created the global network of explorers and collectors who stocked the great natural history collections essential to the founding of modern biology. Many of the naturalists who amassed this scientific capital during America's colonial and early national periods wrote extensively about their travels, and writers such as Mark Catesby, William Bartram, and John James Audubon, though not typically classed as American regionalists, demonstrated early on the potential of America's natural environments as literary material. Later, the figure of the wandering naturalist–collector would itself be portrayed in regional fiction, sometimes sympathetically and sometimes as part of a critique of the imperial sensibility – as is the case, for example, with the ornithologist in Sarah Orne Jewett's "A White Heron."

If Jewett's gun-toting ornithologist represents the imperial strand of ecology, then Sylvia embodies what Worster has termed "arcadian ecology" (1994: 11): a sensibility that intuitively understands the human and the natural as elements of an integrated community. Like its imperial cousin, arcadian ecology stresses close observation of local particulars – not in order to amass a foundation of data upon which to construct an edifice of scientific theory, but in order to express a felt, holistic understanding of a specific place. Its ancient forebear is Virgil's *Eclogues*, but it made its modern debut as a species of literary regionalism with the 1789 publication of Gilbert White's *Natural History of Selbourne*. In the United States this arcadian strain characterizes the work of writers ranging from Henry David Thoreau, who read and enjoyed White's book, to Celia Thaxter, Mary Austin, Wendell Berry, and Edward Abbey. Such work celebrates rural simplicity and authenticity in the face of the wholesale dislocations – both geographical and psychological – incurred by modernity. It is no coincidence that White began his *Natural History* precisely as a newly industrializing England was beginning the destruction of the organic, rural life the book would celebrate. Just as the *Eclogues* were written during imperial Rome's expropriation of rural landholders like Virgil, so White initiates the modern ecological fetish of rural organicism during the time the Enclosure Acts were decimating the yeomanry and swelling the ranks of the urban proletariat. Behind Selbourne stood Birmingham and Manchester, just as behind Walden Pond stood the Fitchburg Railroad and the factories of Lowell. Similarly, in "A White Heron" it is the existence of the "crowded manufacturing town" (Jewett 1886: 140) – scarcely mentioned in the story, but looming large in any modern reader's consciousness – that produces the specifically arcadian appeal of Sylvia's country retreat.

In its most feverish, wilderness-oriented mode, arcadian ecology has also contributed to the creation of a recognizably American literary and cultural type. Blending the sensibility of Henry David Thoreau with that of John Wayne – the sensitive wilderness-lover with the rugged individualist – this type was brought to perhaps its ultimate expression by Edward Abbey. In predictably arcadian fashion, Abbey's *Desert Solitaire* (1968) announces that the Utah landscape it so lovingly depicts "is already gone or going under fast"; the book "is not a travel guide but an elegy." In addition to memorializing that landscape, however, the book also calls for its spirited defense, figuring itself as a "tombstone" and a "bloody rock" that the reader is invited to "throw . . . at something big and glassy" (Abbey 1968: xiv). Thus does the narrator of *Desert Solitaire* anticipate George Washington Hayduke, the radical anarcho-environmentalist protagonist of *The Monkey Wrench Gang* (1975) and hero to legions of readers – some of whom would go on to undertake the "direct action" ecological politics of radical green groups such as Earth First!

The developing ideology of nationalism typically called for the creation of national literatures that, if only imaginatively, might distinguish the writer's own nation from others and unify its diverse peoples. In practice, such a "national" literature was often simply the literature of a dominant region elevated and universalized into that of the whole; writing rooted in outlying perspectives was demoted to the status of regional rather than national. But in the case of the United States this characteristic subordination of the regional was complicated by the way the early republic conceived of itself as "Nature's Nation." The raw, wild splendor of the American environment was held to set the country apart from overcivilized Europe even as it molded a unique and supposedly definitive American identity. Intellectuals from Hector St. Jean de Crèvecoeur to Frederick Jackson Turner encouraged Americans to imagine themselves as deriving their "Americanness" from their continuing contact with the frontier – a habit which gave ecology a patriotic basis and helped prompt its institutionalization in the form of the national parks, whose creation was motivated as much by nationalism as by what we today think of as environmentalism. It also cultivated an audience eager for writing set in vividly realized natural settings. American writers aspiring to national status had both an ideological and a commercial stake in paying close attention to precisely those ecological specificities that in other nations might have completely marginalized their work; in the United States, writing could be at once local *and* national. Generic characters and settings never succeeded in epitomizing Americanness so well as such regionalist creations as Natty Bumppo and his forest or Huck Finn and his river.

Such was the case, at least, for male writers, to whom the nineteenth century's gender ideology of "separate spheres" had delegated the cultural work of defining an American identity. To the other half of the population was reserved the "woman's sphere" of home and hearth – a fact that did not by any means eliminate ecology as a concern of women writers. The root of the word "ecology" is after all the Greek *oikos*, or "house," and a recognizably domestic strand of ecology informed American women's regional writing from the beginning. This domestic ecology did not view the environment as an object of scientific study, an arcadian retreat, or a wellspring of national identity, but rather understood it quite pragmatically as the setting of people's workaday lives. As early as 1839, in *A New Home – Who'll Follow?*, Caroline Kirkland was depicting and analyzing what might be called the ecological gender politics of pioneering, noting, for example, that life on the Michigan frontier could enrich the lived environmental experience of men while impoverishing that of women. On the frontier, a man finds a more exuberant and fertile soil for his plow and a higher quality of fishing and hunting for his leisure hours; in general "he gazes on the same book of nature he has read from his infancy, and sees only a fresher and more glowing page." A woman, however, faces the challenge of making a comfortable home out of a rude cabin lacking "the cherished features of her own dear fireside." Acutely feeling "a thousand deficiencies which her mate can scarce be taught to feel as evils," it is the pioneer woman who is first motivated to think proactively about the local environment: "Bye and bye a few apple-trees are set out; sweet briars grace the door yard, and lilacs, and currant bushes; all by female effort" (Kirkland 1840: 262, 264). Hand in hand with such environmental improvement goes an early ethic of environmental preservation. Observing how rapidly new construction was ruining the "grand esplanade" of her own frontier community, for example, Kirkland asks "that the fine oaks which now graced it might be spared," and then complains bitterly that "these very trees were the first to be sacrificed in the new development" (1840: 24).

On the heels of this domestic ecological sensibility there emerged a domestic ecological science: human ecology, also known as home economics. This pragmatic field was largely the brainchild of Ellen Swallow, the first woman to graduate from the Massachusetts Institute of Technology. Deploying her scientific expertise in the domestic sphere then thought proper to her, Swallow invented techniques for detecting harmful substances in the home environment and then tracing them to their sources in polluted air and contaminated water. In a series of books written around the turn of the nineteenth century she detailed the now familiar web of relationships linking the human body to its surrounding environment. Her work helped create the environmental awareness that would blossom in the 1960s into concerted protests against the poisoning of the nation's food, air and water – protests that were led, not coincidentally, by significant numbers of women, such as *Silent Spring* author Rachel Carson and Love Canal activist Lois Gibbs.

By the 1980s this strongly gendered ecological sensibility, with its emphasis on the relations among environment, home, family, and body, had begun to shape a new and more self-consciously environmentalist regional literature by women authors. Much of this work features human beings deeply rooted in places whose outward beauty is belied by the sinister presence of invisible but deadly pollutants. In Jane Smiley's *A Thousand Acres* (1991), the polluted well water of a prosperous Iowa farm is suspected of causing miscarriages; in *Refuge: An Unnatural History of Family and Place* (1991), Terry Tempest Williams suspects fallout from nuclear tests as the cause of the "Clan of One-Breasted Women" – her term for the unusually high number of breast cancer victims in her Utah family. Reflecting the recent ecofeminist analysis of the patriarchal exploitation of women and nature, both books associate damaged environments with damaged female bodies.

The increasing importance of ecology as a theme in America's regional literatures has created a new scholarly niche currently being occupied by a still-evolving species of ecologically informed literary critic. The now well-established term "ecocriticism" was apparently first used in 1978, in William Rueckert's essay "Literature and Ecology: An Experiment in Ecocriticism." By the latter half of the 1980s a number of professional journals had dedicated special issues to the study of literature and ecology, and the critical practice that Rueckert had rather cautiously termed an "experiment" steadily grew in both popularity and professional acceptance. It reached a milestone of sorts in 1989, when Glen Love delivered a speech, "Revaluing Nature: Toward an Ecological Literary Criticism," as the past president's address at the annual meeting of the Western Literature Association. (It should not be surprising that the first organization to thus officially validate ecocriticism would be one dedicated to the study of regional literature.) The next few years saw the rapid solidification of the field in the academy, with special sessions devoted to ecocriticism at the annual meeting of the Modern Language Association; the creation of a professional organization, the Association for the Study of Literature and Environment; the founding of a professional journal, *Interdisciplinary Studies in Literature and Environment*; and the publication of *The Ecocriticism Reader: Landmarks in Literary Ecology* (Glotfelty and Fromm 1996), a definitive anthology featuring a wide variety of ecocritical work.

As a cursory glance at any contemporary ecocriticism will reveal, neither regionalism nor ecology has been immune to the late twentieth century's postmodern turn, part of which has entailed a searching critique of that protean term "nature." In *The End of Nature* (1989), Bill McKibben popularized the idea that we live now in a "postnatural" world – nature having "ended" in the sense that such trends as global warming, the ubiquity of environmental pollution, and the eradication of wilderness have nullified any grounds for continuing to understand nature as operating independently of human intervention. More recently, the population ecologist Daniel Botkin has argued that natural ecological processes are not harmonious, progressive, and predictable – as the science of ecology has typically assumed – but, rather, unpredictable and chaotic. Thus, Botkin says, even the most carefully preserved wilderness cannot provide a sure guide to what nature "should" be like elsewhere;

conversely, we cannot be sure what a disturbed ecosystem would be like in the present had it not been subjected to human intervention in the past. Hence it makes little sense for environmentalism to pin its hopes on "restoring" damaged ecosystems to their "natural" state. Instead, it should embrace science and technology and use them consciously to "manage nature wisely." Given the extent to which we have already affected the biosphere, we really have little choice: whether we like it or not, says Botkin, "nature in the twenty-first century will be a nature that we make" (Botkin 1991: 193, 200).

This idea of "nature" as something we *make* has been echoed by a growing body of postmodern philosophers, environmental historians, geographers, and literary and cultural theorists. Critics such as William Cronon understand "wilderness" as a "self-conscious cultural construction" (1995: 39) and argue that environmentalism's refusal to think critically about this most fundamental of ecological concepts has led to an *ideological* abuse of nature that is ultimately as objectionable as its *physical* destruction. To the extent that radically biocentric philosophies, such as the "deep ecology" championed by Arne Naess, consider wilderness to be a self-evident "moral imperative," nature is liable to be valued for its ability to make existing social and economic structures "seem innate, essential, eternal, nonnegotiable" – and, therefore, all too easily invoked to close off legitimate political debates such as those concerning environmental justice (Cronon 1995: 36). Andrew Ross has taken a similar line, analyzing the many ways in which contemporary environmentalism finds itself complicit with the destructive politics of late capitalism.

But "nature" is a slippery concept, and it can be used to underwrite progressive ideologies as well. Gregg Mitman, for example, has chronicled the development in the first half of the twentieth century of ecological theories that, in contrast to then-prevailing models, understood evolution as favoring cooperative groups rather than competitive individuals. Leading this movement was University of Chicago ecologist and liberal pacifist Warner Clyde Allee, who hoped ecology might naturalize the values of nonviolence and community – values that also tend to resonate strongly in America's regional literatures. Toward midcentury, this "socialist ecology" fell victim to the anticollectivist intellectual climate of the Cold War and, as Mitman demonstrates, Allee's vision of the "ecologist as social healer" gave way to that of "the ecologist as environmental engineer" (Mitman 1992: 7). His progressive ecological sensibility lives on, however, in the many contemporary "green" movements that see environmentalism as inextricably bound up with social justice.

The postmodern reconceptualization of nature and ecology is far from over, but several distinct themes can now be seen emerging from the ongoing intellectual ferment: an acute sense of the global nature of environmental problems; a blurring of the once-clear line distinguishing nature from culture and history; a sensitivity to nature's political and ideological uses in a multicultural society; an awareness of nature's textuality or social construction; and a deep suspicion of nature as a source of stability, authenticity, and reliable meaning. These themes have informed American regional writing since at least the 1960s. In Richard Brautigan's *Trout Fishing in*

America (1967), for example, seemingly pristine waterfalls turn out to be stairways (Brautigan 1989: 4–5) – that is, what the narrator had thought to be natural turns out all along to have been a cultural artifact. Elsewhere, a trout stream is broken down into sections, stored in the Cleveland Wrecking Yard, and offered for sale "by the foot length." The book's figurative language also works to blur the boundary dividing natural from artificial: a small stream is "like 12,845 telephone booths," and when the narrator fishes the stream he feels "just like a telephone repairman." Other passages call the reader's attention to nature's textuality, as when the narrator muses on "what a lovely nib trout fishing in America would make" with its "wild flowers and dark fins pressed against the paper" (Brautigan 1989: 104, 55, 110).

The tendency of modernity was to subordinate history and culture to the universal hegemony of nature. (In thinking that a culture's thoughts and actions are largely "patterned by the particular parcel of land" in which it was formed, Mary Austin typified this propensity.) The postmodern sensibility, by contrast, sees nature as the product of history and culture – nowhere more so, perhaps, than in Leslie Marmon Silko's sweeping novel of the contemporary Southwest, *Almanac of the Dead* (1992). Relentlessly driven by the pressure of history, this novel's plot reveals an Arizona landscape deeply enmeshed in the global drug trade, ancient Aztec prophecies, and simmering Latin American and Native American revolutions. In a similar vein, Rebecca Solnit's *Savage Dreams* (1993) frames the contemporary landscape of the intermountain West in terms of interrelated battles over nuclear testing and long-running disputes over Paiute and Shoshone Indian land rights. In good postmodern fashion, Solnit's landscapes are *contested*: interpretive questions about what places *mean* are inseparable from ethical questions about who will *own* and *benefit from* them.

In another postmodern regional work, *The Last Cheater's Waltz*, Ellen Meloy summarily dismisses the idea that the Southwestern desert might serve as a "kind of cosmic navel, an inexhaustible well-spring of mystery and transcendence" (Meloy 1999: 6). The region's spiritual center is no longer to be found, as it was for modernist writers like Austin, in the purity of its wild mountains or the authenticity of its Pueblo Indians, but is located rather at Ground Zero in the Jornada del Muerto of New Mexico's White Sands Missile Range. It was there, Meloy writes, that a rare desert thunderstorm brought thousands of spadefoot toads out of a lengthy dormancy; invigorated by the rain, the toads "unburied themselves" for an orgy of mating that "filled the desert with song." This occurred before dawn on July 16, 1945, just hours before "an elite tribe of scientists" detonated the world's first nuclear bomb and thereby "spawned the primary death anxiety of all time" (Meloy 1999: 26). The exuberant procreation of the toads and the horrific destruction wrought by nuclear weapons are utterly unassimilable opposites, and their juxtaposition renders Meloy's desert landscape not *authentic*, but – again in good postmodern fashion – brutally *ironic*.

It is frequently said that such postmodern phenomena as globalization, the internet, and the end of nature are rendering physical place increasingly obsolete. Yet the power and relevance of the most recent regional writing suggest that the alliance of regionalism and ecology remains as fruitful as ever. Ecology doubtless will continue to inform the themes of regional literature, and that literature will continue to give powerful voice to the insights and concerns of ecology.

REFERENCES AND FURTHER READING

Abbey, E. (1968). *Desert Solitaire: A Season in the Wilderness*. New York: McGraw-Hill.

Abbey, E. (1975). *The Monkey Wrench Gang*. Philadelphia: Lippincott.

Austin, M. H. (2001). "Regionalism in American Fiction." In David Mazel (ed.), *A Century of Early Ecocriticism*, 261–71. Athens, Ga.: University of Georgia Press. (First publ. 1932.)

Botkin, D. (1991). *Discordant Harmonies: A New Ecology for the Twenty-First Century*. New York: Oxford University Press.

Bramwell, A. (1989). *Ecology in the 20th Century: A History*. New Haven: Yale University Press.

Brautigan, R. (1989). *Richard Brautigan's* Trout Fishing in America, The Pill versus the Springhill Mine Disaster, *and* In Watermelon Sugar. Boston: Houghton Mifflin.

Clarke, R. (1973). *Ellen Swallow: The Woman Who Founded Ecology*. Chicago: Follett.

Cronon, W. (1995). *Uncommon Ground: Rethinking the Human Place in Nature*. New York: Norton.

Devall, Bill, and Sessions, George (1985). *Deep Ecology: Living as if Nature Mattered*. Salt Lake City: Gibbs Smith.

Egerton, F. (1977). *History of American Ecology*. New York: Arno.

Fetterley, J. (1994). "'Not in the Least American': Nineteenth-Century Literary Realism." *College English* 56, 877–95.

Glotfelty, C. and Fromm, H. (1996). *The Ecocriticism Reader: Landmarks in Literary Ecology*. Athens, Ga: University of Georgia Press.

Jewett, S. O. (1886). *A White Heron and Other Stories*. Boston: Houghton Mifflin.

Kirkland, C. (1840). *A New Home – Who'll Follow? or, Glimpses of Western Life*. New York: C. S. Francis. (First publ. 1839.)

Loriggio, F. (1994). "Regionalism and Theory." In D. Jordan (ed.), *Regionalism Reconsidered: New Approaches to the Field*, 3–27. New York: Garland

Love, G. "Revaluing Nature: Toward an Ecological Literary Criticism." In C. Glotfelty and H. Fromm (eds.), *The Ecocriticism Reader: Landmarks in Literary Ecology*, 225–240. Athens, Ga: University of Georgia Press.

McKibben, B. (1989). *The End of Nature*. New York: Random House.

Meloy, E. (1999). *The Last Cheater's Waltz: Beauty and Violence in the Desert Southwest*. Tucson: University of Arizona Press.

Miller, P. (2001). "Nature and the National Ego." In David Mazel (ed.), *A Century of Early Ecocriticism*, 314–28. Athens, Ga: University of Georgia Press. (First publ. 1955.)

Mitman, G. (1992). *The State of Nature: Ecology, Community, and American Social Thought, 1900–1950*. Chicago: University of Chicago Press.

Ross, A. (1991). *Strange Weather: Culture, Science, and Technology in the Age of Limits*. New York: Verso.

Rueckert, W. (1978). "Literature and Ecology: An Experiment in Ecocriticism." In C. Glotfelty and H. Fromm (eds.), *The Ecocriticism Reader: Landmarks in Literary Ecology*, 105–23. Athens, Ga: University of Georgia Press.

Smiley, J. (1991). *A Thousand Acres*. New York: Ballantine.

Solnit, R. (1993). *Savage Dreams: A Journey into the Hidden Wars of the American West*. San Francisco: Sierra Club.

Soulé, M. and Lease, G. eds. (1995). *Reinventing Nature? Responses to Postmodern Deconstruction*. Washington DC: Island.

Williams, T. T. (1991). *Refuge: An Unnatural History of Family and Place*. New York: Pantheon.

Worster, D. (1994). *Nature's Economy: A History of Ecological Ideas*. Cambridge: Cambridge University Press.

9
The City as Region
James Kyung-Jin Lee

The American city begets literary casuists: those who, like screaming street-corner preachers, toll God's wrath, natural disaster, or blank lives to readers who might have eyes to see. Always fallen from that fictive origin on the Hill, the city makes machines of men, wearies its women, and pours enervating concrete and tar everywhere else. Conceived from the mind of man, the city cannot satiate its edifice complex and builds itself toward Faustian heights on top of the bones of countless arrested breaths. Yet just as our conception of the American urban landscape brings us to that point of exhausted resignation, where the city's universe implodes into atomized existence or explodes in riotous violence, there emerges from the city's streets those who view the city, their home, with slanted vision. They give us eyes to see that cannot see all, but whose special line of vision jiggles us out the despair derived from the idealized fiction of urban worlds always tumbling, even before the first stone crumbles. Two cities, one conceived from mythic perpetuation, the other perceived with nothing more than partial glance, jostle in American literature, each supplying the other with countertext, their juxtaposition prompting readers to pause before capitulating to the dogma of the city's inevitable decay.

It is now more than three-quarters of a century since T. S. Eliot – whom Lisa New aptly designates one of "these modernists who happen to be American" (1998: 177) – published *The Waste Land*. And while Eliot would later claim that this poem, which secured his place in modern poetry, represented little more than a "piece of rhythmical grumbling," few readers and writers since 1922 have heeded his admonition not to view this work as a definitive distillation of an exhausted twentieth-century experience. Out of the images and sounds of falling towers tolling "reminiscent bells" and disembodied voices "singing out of empty cisterns and exhausted wells" arises Eliot's Unreal City, a ruinous place where mythic shards serve as the only buttress against the ruins of history for its dulled citizens. Such a vision of an urban wasteland pervades so much of American literature (this despite its material moorings in London), that Fitzgerald's direct reference to Eliot's "valley of the ashes" in *The Great*

Gatsby (1925) to convey the detritus produced by roaring Manhattan is only the most obvious literary resurrection of the Unreal City. Thanks largely to *The Waste Land*, the city incarnates both tenor and vehicle for the writer's social, and often moral, vantage; the city warehouses its own metaphorical material, fashions its own desperate rhetoric, and pulses its own monotonous heartbeat. Generations of American writers since have struggled against or acceded to the solipsism of Eliot's wasteland, whether by burrowing underneath, setting out, or fighting within.

Yet for all the palpable images of urban *ennui* that Eliot invokes – the baked beans tin and hooded hordes holding disparate but corresponding sensibilities of civilization lost – the poem more conceives than it perceives. It announces social ruin and psychic fragmentation in a metaphorical clutch, but such sure-sightedness of this objective correlative is only momentarily apparent. Put on another lens, or rather admit that all sight and sound are *mediated* senses, and the power of particular, contingent experience – the eye perceiving – casts new light on Eliot's vision. This is not to say that Eliot's city is false; it is simply "Unreal." The pathetic characters of *The Waste Land* are tethered to this unreality, a London layered by the remnants of past "glorious," mythic cities, but in whose shattered parts can never be put back together the organic "*shanti*" that the end of poem whimpers in distressed longing. Eliot's speaker finishes this chant in perpetual grimace, the city calcifying his face into an unreal pose.

Why Eliot's Unreal City of London sticks in the consciousness of those writing about (and, unlike Eliot, living in) US cities has partly to do with the conception – and again, not exactly perception – that American writers have traditionally held bias against the city. Notwithstanding the routine formulation of the Puritans' New Jerusalem, John Winthrop's proverbial "city on a hill," American writers and other culture-makers seem to have been prejudiced against the city long before and well after Eliot wrote *The Waste Land*. From Jefferson's dream of an agrarian republic to Turner's oft-cited "frontier thesis" of social release, to Daniel Patrick Moynihan's ill-crafted prescription of "benign neglect" for the nation's black inner-city residents, standard bearers of US culture have repeatedly conceived of the American city as both real and rhetorical space of social dissolution and danger. From the city, so it goes, emerge excess and poverty. Jefferson's recoil from an urban republic sprang from his fear of an industrializing nation's dependence on an encroaching centralized state, but he also mistrusted the extremities of emotion and behavior, both individual and collective, that the city fostered and that cultivated land (not the wilderness) could temper. Of even more concern for Jefferson, and corroborated by other writers, was the excess of number in the city. Cramped together in compacted space, city-dwellers could easily degenerate into the mob, which in turn justified autocracy as the primary means of social control: "The mobs of great cities add just so much to the support of pure government, as sores do to the strength of the human body." Echoing Jefferson's concern, Alexis de Tocqueville, the Frenchman who taught Americans what to think of themselves, warned his readers that a growing population in US cities, both in number and in kind, presented a "real danger" for the burgeoning democracy. Racial, national, and economic diversity in cities would require, in de Tocqueville's analysis, a national armed force simply to "repress its excesses."

Unable to gain the more "mature observations" gained "through country," that which Jefferson saw as requisite experience to produce the "men of most learning," residents of the city were held in sway by the extremities of greed and the machinations of commerce, excesses which in turn abetted poverty, both in material and in mind. By the end of the nineteenth century, writers deemed the social contradictions of the poverty of many and the riches of the few a natural occurrence in the city, a determinism as sure as Theodore Dreiser's "equation inevitable" in *Sister Carrie* (1900). Dreiser borrowed extensively from Herbert Spencer's recalibration of Darwin's theory of evolution to arrive at the belief that the world was governed by a system of laws and forces, all of which immured a person's social options and, indeed, forecast his inner values. Dreiser's novel relies upon this scientific, zero-sum *deus ex machina*: in order for Carrie to rise in wealth and ambition, Hurstwood must fall. Eighty years later, James Baldwin depicted this inevitable vector of urban poverty and privilege in crueler terms, as a collective "divorce" that would lead us down the Unreal path. "When I got to the city," he consequently recalls, "I met slaughter" (1981: 134).

But if Baldwin's experience demonstrates a city of terrible divorce, he also reminds his readers that for many what was outside the urban landscape menaced greater danger, surer slaughter than troubles within city limits. Outside the city, there was no social divorce; people there lived in a deathly embrace: "[T]he reason my father left the land and came to the city," Baldwin reflects, "was because he was driven by the wave of terror which overtook the South after the First World War when soldiers were being lynched in uniform, slaughtered like flies" (Baldwin 1981: 134–5). The terror of "the land," which propelled thousands of blacks into US cities during the first half of the twentieth century, was limited neither in geography nor to African Americans. In the West, between 1889 and 1939, 166 lynchings occurred; of these, 12 were black, while more than 150 Asians were murdered. And the redemptive myth of the frontier, Turner's "Great West" – even, too, Arthur Schlesinger's revision of this thesis, that cities and the frontier constituted a symbiotic relationship – belied even further the conception of a renewing soil in the territory. For those already living in this New World Canaan, the visionary and actual drive westward as a way to relieve the neurasthenia of city life amounted to little more than genocide. If the fears of the city enhanced the belief in an idyllic land beyond, it was the faith of a privileged few. For others, pushed out, hanged up, or beaten down, grim life in an Unreal city was preferable to the frightening realities of the plains and fields.

Still others inveighed against the current of antiurbanism that otherwise seems to flow unhampered in the main stream of American literature. While Gertrude Stein distilled her invective against Oakland into the infamous putdown, "There is no there there," writers such as Carl Sandburg turned a "hell of a place" like Chicago into a celebration of urban monstrosity. Aiming to "sing, blab, chortle, yodel, like people," Sandburg's "Chicago" (1916) returned the sneer laid against "this my city" with brawny language:

Come and show me another city with lifted head singing so proud to be alive
    and coarse and strong and cunning.
Flinging magnetic curses amid the toil of piling job on job, here is a tall bold
    slugger set vivid against the little soft cities;
Fierce as a dog with tongue lapping for action, cunning as a savage pitted
    against the wilderness,
        Bareheaded,
        Shoveling,
        Wrecking,
        Planning,
        Building, breaking, rebuilding . . .

Sandburg's formal clumsiness in "Chicago" actually, perhaps unintentionally, illuminates his ideal figure set almost as a monument against an industrial landscape tender-
ized. A committed socialist, Sandburg's man of the city is a worker, active in his
transforming of Chicago's built environment. Indeed, the "tall bold slugger" creates
even as he is created by the city, ideally and ruggedly masculine in his efforts to tame
the urban just as the pioneer would subdue the wildness of the frontier. Whereas
Eliot's city enervates, producing a foppish and fastidious Prufrock ("Prufrock" was
written one year before "Chicago"), in Sandburg's city resides the resilient worker
who, even as he suffers from the "terrible burden of destiny," laughs "the stormy,
husky, brawling laughter of Youth." Sandburg strikes a tone a little too emphatic
here. But like other "regionalist" writers, who sought to reclaim and liberate verse
and fiction from a settled gentility, he roared a sweaty, half-naked poetry precisely to
extol the very extremities of sentiment that American writers supposedly found
inherent and abhorrent in the city.

    Sandburg's poems about the city, of course, favored a singular figure acting on his
surroundings; one who, despite the burdens of destiny, seems to worry little about
how the city acts on him. Sacrificed here is the slumped but more complex interiority
of Eliot's Prufrock and Fitzgerald's Gatsby, both of whom display a social impotence
as a halcyon myth of pastoral prudence gives way to the urban vortex. Sandburg's
own anxiety stems rather from the relative ease with which his laughing worker
could be re-imagined without a face and degenerate into a seething mob, a wholly
more conventional yet still compelling construction of the working classes. Thus,
Sandburg opts to incarnate an organized proletariat in the worker, a collective "he"
or "I" through which Chicago and its residents form a symbiotic, albeit often contested, relationship in the service of its industrial and cultural productivity as the
"Hog Butcher, Tool Maker, Stacker of Wheat, Player with Railroads and Freight
Handler to the Nation."

    Against this distillation of the industrial and industrious hewers of wood into the
singular arises the alienated "we" of Fitzgerald's New York at the end of *The Great
Gatsby*: "So we beat on, boats against the current, borne back ceaselessly into the
past." This past, the lost and depleted "frontier" from where Gatsby hails, gives way
to the urban farmland turned to wasteland, Fitzgerald's insertion of Eliot's valley of

ashes. Ensconced between West Egg and Manhattan, Queens emerges from the gray forms of houses, chimneys, and smoke and the "men who move dimly and already crumbling through the powdery air." Had he lived in New York, Sandburg's ideal worker would likely dwell in such a cinereous region. Queens is New York's "solemn dumping ground," just as the borough's poor and immigrant residents constitute the threatening detritus for *Gatsby*'s urbanites. Geography and class, citizenship and ethnicity: when these and other social categories are harnessed in the 1920s – the decade in which the US passed its most restrictive immigration laws to date – the "we" of the polis unravels, as in *Gatsby*, forewarning the very dangers of the dissolved "I" that Sandburg emphatically tries to keep together. As Lewis Mumford observes when tracing the disappearing communal ethic, "When [the] primary bonds dissolve, when the intimate visible community ceases to be a watchful, identifiable, deeply concerned group, then the 'We' becomes a buzzing swarm of 'Is', and secondary ties and allegiances become too feeble to halt the disintegration of the urban community" (1968: 15). Interiority in urban literature privileges alienation at the expense of social pathos, the "primary bonds" of a visible community. This, when coupled with "secondary allegiances" of nationality, race, and economics as ways to further carve the city, renders soulless Fitzgerald's West Eggers, just a mirror-image away from the blank blindness of Doctor Eckleburg's billboard eyes gazing lifelessly over the ashen cavity of Queens.

Scholars remain divided over the prevailing image of the urban wasteland. For Richard Lehan, the logic of the modern city, of which American versions represent the endpoint, concludes with apocalypse, then slides in epilogue toward social entropy. Focusing on different historical moments and geographical centers, Leo Marx (1981) and Charles Crow (1995) counter, and insist that American writers do not harbor antiurban sentiment as such, but merely wage a larger cultural contest – over the coercion of the market economy or the sterility of the modern world – within city limits. But if the ontological flux of cityness persists, the problem of finding meaningful social anchorage in urban landscape also endures. Just as Henry Adams laments the moral and inspiring feminine force of the Virgin giving way to the "abysmal fracture" of the dynamo during the Great Exposition of 1900 in Paris, so too does Henry James feel an age passing when, in *The American Scene* (1907), his eyes struggle to find New York's Trinity Church amidst the "thousand glassy eyes" of the city's newer skyscrapers. "Where, for the eye," James pleads, "is the felicity of simplified Gothic, of noble pre-eminence, that once made of this highly-pleasing edifice the pride of the town and the feature of Broadway? The answer is, as obviously, that these charming elements are still there, just where they ever were, but that they have been mercilessly deprived of their visibility" (James 1993: 420–1). Later, James recalls that the obsolescence of this older landmark in the daunting face of Wall Street's newer buildings, the "monsters of the mere market . . . crushing the old quite as violent children stamp on snails and caterpillars," compresses history and signals his own anachronism: "this impact of the whole condensed past at once produced a horrible, hateful sense of personal antiquity" (James 1993: 422). He likens the spatial deprivation of sight to the temporal violence of the new on the old, and such geographical distillation of time hurtles him beyond history, into "antiquity." James's anxiety stems not simply from his feeling old; it is that his age provides no historical mooring and, like Trinity Church, renders him socially useless in his contemporary moment.

But every city undergoes periodic facelift. Buried underneath Manhattan lies the skeleton of its former self, as today's subway lines traverse the island over the remains of an older version. In Los Angeles, the ubiquitous freeways cover sections of land not much different from or larger than the Pacific Electric Car system of the early twentieth century. To this extent, the city as palimpsest is intrinsic to its development and maintenance. Quarry this landscape, and the writer can surely save herself from Eliot's unredeemable present. Still, James's correlation between an ocular poverty and subjective crisis registers a deep fear among writers that architecture out of sight would surely lead to historic consciousness out of mind. And in a new era ruled, it seems, by Mammon, urban palimpsest might appear an irretrievable, impossible archaeology, especially when the modern transformation of the city's built environment also coincided with the birth of modern psychology and its attendant fracturing of the "we." Sandburg may praise his worker's active participation in helping to recreate Chicago anew with the cyclical expectation of "building, breaking, rebuilding," but the poem would end quite differently, and less defiantly, perhaps, if this bold slugger built a city in which he would be no longer welcome or could not afford to live.

Even a poet like Walt Whitman, whose various editions of *Leaves of Grass* suffuse the city, particularly New York, with lines unforgettable in their celebration, struggled against the sinister approach of urban transformation. Between 1820 and 1860, New York's population rose almost tenfold, from a mere 123,000 to more than one million. As David Reynolds (1996) unearths, "constant flux" was a term used in the day to describe the demographic and physical changes underway in the city. Whitman himself was not immune to such dynamism. Steeped in the political furor of US politics during the mid-nineteenth century, Walt Whitman aligned much of his poetry before the 1855 edition of *Leaves of Grass* with his mercurial attraction to various political parties before the Republican ascendancy of Lincoln set the nation on the path to civil war. He began as a devoted Jacksonian Democrat when he worked for the *Brooklyn Daily Eagle* in the 1840s, but by 1848 was attending the first convention of the Free Soil party in Buffalo. When the "Great Compromise" of 1850 essentially destroyed the Free Soilers, Whitman flirted with nativism, attracted by the nationalist platform of the Know-Nothing party, which he tempered later because of the party's stringent antiforeigner rhetoric that targeted predominantly Irish Catholic immigrants. By the time *Leaves of Grass* was published Whitman had given up political affiliation, claiming that he would be "no tied and ticketed democrat, whig, abolitionist, republican, – no bawling spokesman of natives against foreigners." Instead, poets would save America; where politics was rotten to its core, poetry could rescue and reclaim the morality and vibrancy of a nation at the brink of social collapse.

If Whitman had given up on organized politics, he took artistic sustenance from the cacophonous social debates swirling around New York City in the 1840s and 1850s. Yet how could a writer take into himself and articulate the disparate sensibilities that the city held? Besides the warring political factions struggling over the soul-wrenching issues of slavery, immigration, labor, women, and religion, New York encapsulated the highbrow writing of the Knickerbocker school and Boston Brahmin transplants as well as the seemingly more organic slang of the "b'hoys" located in the Bowery and African-American dialect coming from the South. Searching for a literary version of the Kantian categorical imperative, Whitman simply shorthanded the contradictory voices in New York with his all-powerful "I." The famous first lines of "Song of Myself" embody his belief in the restorative power of poetic language to bring together the city and by extension the entire nation:

> I celebrate myself,
> And what I assume you shall assume
> For every atom belonging to me as good belongs to you.

It is easy now to miss the political implications of such an adamantly affirmative statement in American poetry, even as one might celebrate its implied democratic impulse. Earlier visions of the singular individual, most notably Thoreau's "community of one" at Walden Pond, sought liberation from the corruption of mass society, the injustice of unfettered economic greed, and the immorality of political life by proposing that the individual determine his own destiny by untethering himself from this tangled network of compromise and collaboration. Thoreau probably would have agreed with the first line of "Song of Myself," but would have found disagreeable the impulse to see his atoms in, say, those of James Polk, who instigated the war with Mexico and occupied what is now called the American Southwest. For Whitman, however, the "good" of the individual must be the "good" of the other – whether that other is another person or another group *unlike* himself. Buried within the consciously contradictory "I" in the poem lie more ominous lines such as "the fury of roused mobs," or the audible "groans of overfed or half-starved who fall on the flags sunstruck or in fits." But the poem recuperates each group of people otherwise dispossessed: "I mind them or the resonance of them. . . . I come again and again." As Reynolds notices, "Throughout his poetry, the disturbing aspects of urban experience are nested between positive, refreshing ones" (1996: 110).

Yet even Whitman, in later years, would feel overtaken by the rapacity of urban change. The vulpine features of the postbellum US culture of material greed and collective fragmentation pervade *Democratic Vistas*, even though Whitman ostensibly wrote the essay to counter Thomas Carlyle's vision of an American democracy gone demonic in the Scotsman's essay "Shooting Niagara" (1867). Striving to imagine a "programme of culture" radically transformed "with an eye to practical life" and not merely shut in the parlors and lecture-rooms – in a phrase, calling for an elevated public sphere – Whitman nonetheless conceives of this dream at the same time as he concedes to Carlyle the "lamentable conditions" of US culture, most particularly in the cities. Despite an undying faith in the possibility of social contradictions "harmoniously blending," Whitman's vista is besieged with images of wasteland:

> Confess that to severe eyes, using the moral microscope upon humanity, a sort of dry and flat Sahara appears, these cities, crowded with petty grotesques, malformations, phantoms, playing meaningless antics. Confess that everywhere, in shop, street, church, theatre, bar-room, official chair, are pervading flippancy and vulgarity, low cunning, infidelity – everywhere the youth puny, impudent, foppish, prematurely ripe – everywhere an abnormal libidinousness . . . with a range of manners, or rather lack of manners, (considering the advantages enjoy'd,) probably the meanest in the world. (Whitman 2002: 2962)

The anaphoric injunction – "Confess" – suggests an admission full of anxiety that even poetry might prove insufficient as an antiseptic against the desecration of the American democratic experiment. For, as Whitman observes, the very success of the United States in "uplifting the masses out of their sloughs" fills American society with a "dyspeptic depletion." This "confessional" paragraph contains palpable satire directed at the "severe eyes" of Carlyle. But that Whitman gives ground here to Carlyle's charge of an America tumbling toward its national demise, ruined most of all by its morally bankrupt cities, signals a tearing away of the poet's careful Adamic impulse in the earliest poems of *Leaves of Grass*. Instead of paradisal Eden or redemptive Canaan, Whitman encounters wilderness, "Sahara," a desert in whose continuous present (note the use of the present progressive in "are pervading") he finds a manner of people and culture not unlike the flat, empty hollow men of Eliot's urban tableau of ennui.

Whitman's indefatigable belief in the democratic impulse and its creation of a "new and greater literatus order," in the face of the meanness of American cities, suggests to critics like Leo Marx that his earlier triumphalism depends on transmogrifying real urban landscapes into what Richard Chase calls "a paradoxically urban-pastoral world of primeval novelty" (1955: 95). In essence, Marx argues, Whitman's depiction of New York is able to contain its multitudes and contradictions because it is *unlike* the real New York. Yet this sketch of Whitman writing a spatial version of Emerson's "original relation" – the ideal poet of the "Divinity School Address," in which "poetry was all written before time was" – levels the complexity of the city's palimpsest into an urban vision of American Romantic correspondence. The transformation of American cities then would make more difficult, perhaps impossible, the task of writers to realign themselves with an original universe alienated: how can you manage "correspondence" when objects and landscapes appear in sight only momentarily, rapidly disappearing for newer architecture, preventing a totality of vision? The city thus resembles fallen Sahara, empty save the litter that accumulates on its streets, feebly gathered up in the final lines of Eliot's wasteland.

If this discussion of cityscapes has come full circle back to Eliot's poem, it has done so because the axis upon which the analysis rests, the individual in urban space, whether for or against, demands a kind of fullness of scope that in the end leads to disillusioned vision. Even Sandburg's reclamation of the bold slugger relies upon a logic and poetics that yearns to know the city fully, to enfold urban landscapes into a cognitive map which a writer's speakers and characters can traverse and imbue with meaning. One might argue that the amoral universe of urban determinism, whose Spencerian laws seem to overwhelm the characters of Dreiser's Chicago and New York, Norris's San Francisco, or Stephen Crane's Lower East Side, comes closest to dislodging the centrality of the urban figure's ability to know the world. But naturalism remains tied to a certain kind of correspondence: this time, the universe's indifference to humanity puts in place forces and signs that chart a character's social ascendancy or demise. The conception of the city is in these cases a desire outstripped by the city's perceptual vortex. Always changing, it grants no quarter to its observers, even those who struggle to construct out of urban grit what Richard Poirier (1966) calls "a world elsewhere." A transparent eyeball is left gaping, points of reference refuse objective correlatives, stylized consciousness peters out in the din of urban cacophony. The realities of the American city, as these writers observe and grope to understand, place urban landscapes squarely in time and space.

Climbing out of such solipsism depends upon a willingness to concede that cities are regenerate only insofar as we view these spaces as fractured, contradictory, but altogether democratic process of struggle. Against social forces and institutions that further alienate their inhabitants is the differentiated, divided agglomeration of city-dwellers struggling to find and be community. There is no original relation to living in the city now lost, no prior commonality that one can return to, no City of God within the City of Man except one built on faith. In a word, or rather in a letter, we lose the City, but we gain the city. And it is in this city, one which must bear its name and release its history, its palimpsest, that the work of experience, of mediated perception, replaces the Ideal correspondence of the fallen, unreal City.

In the city of perception, the paucity of singular vision and impossibility of perfect cohesion are taken for granted. Built on conflict and contradiction, the terrain that meets a writer's character or speaker limits, but it also limns. People walk the streets without security, but also without pretension. Presented in mythic terms, the city offers no promise of union or gnosis, either past or future. Yet from this point of ignorance springs knowledge that is willed into existence, born of the stuff observed. As William Carlos Williams, who homespun a poetics from the industrial furnace of Paterson, New Jersey, famously pronounced, "no ideas but in things" (1995: 6). Notwithstanding his excoriation of Eliot's *The Waste Land* as "the great catastrophe of our letters," Williams's determined effort to metamorphose local landscapes and people into consummating male and female personifications proposes no great statement about the city as a measure of Western civilization's or democracy's decline. Likewise, Hart Crane, the ostensible "inheritor" of Whitman's poetic impulse to unite all things, inveighs against the primacy of the Idea over things. His most well-known poem, *The Bridge* (1930), is often misread for its "failure" to enact a connecting myth that brings together past and present, nature and technology, the rural and the urban, East and West. Crane's work is usually socketed in the Romantic legacy of

Emerson and Whitman, as attempts to discover invisible transcendent power in an increasingly urban America. And in this vein, Crane's poem misses the mark; his own suicide seems almost fitting to a poet incarnating the timeless "poet-hero" falling victim to the failed ecstasy of his vision. In a letter to Waldo Frank in 1926, he seems to suggest this failure of total union, as he ruminates on the apparent inability to find in his extended apostrophe to the Brooklyn Bridge anything more than a "delusion" that would bind past and future to the present: "The bridge as a symbol today has no significance beyond an economical approach to shorter hours, quicker lunches, behaviorism and toothpicks."

Actually, Crane's "Proem: To Brooklyn Bridge" anticipates the seeming pessimism of his letter, but does so without the pretense of vision that sees, and by extension, captures all. Consider the speaker's attempt at insight into the seagull that flies above the "chained bay waters Liberty" at the beginning of the poem, which

> Then, with inviolate curve, forsake our eyes
> As apparitional as sails that cross
> Some page of figures to be filed away;
> – Till elevators drop us from our day . . .

Another well-known waterfowl, whose wings are driven by an unseen "Power whose care / Teaches thy way along that pathless coast," provides for William Cullen Bryant's speaker assurance of divine, transcendent guidance "in the long way that [he] must tread alone." Crane's bird, in contrast, enjoys no definitive flight plan. With wings that "dip and pivot," the seagull frustrates straight lines of sight, its "inviolate curve" metamorphosing the bird first into fluttering pages, then a plummeting elevator. Unable to follow its airy arc, Crane's speaker is left without clarity; as an emblem of Romantic spirit, the seagull rather "forsakes" his eyes. Even the syntax of this stanza, as Lisa New notices, trembles in ambiguity: is it the seagull or the speaker's eyes that are "apparitional?" New regards these lines as Crane's entry into a "nexus of the unknown" (1993: 206), where poetic perspicacity is undone by slanted sight. When the bridge does finally come into view, Crane's speaker addresses not the bridge's glimmer in the sunlight, but its full reckoning through slivers of observation. With almost a Dickinsonian lens, his eye focuses not on the brightness of "Noon," but the aura of Circumference:

> Under thy shadow by the piers I waited;
> Only in darkness is thy shadow clear.
> The City's fiery parcels all undone,
> Already snow submerges an iron year . . .

Clarity emerges not through the sun's freedom, but by the restraint of shadow and darkness. Moreover, with our eye moving vertically, the bridge's "shadow clear" is aligned with the city's "iron year," time and space fettering – and thus enabling – the pull and counterpull of the bridge's tenor of longed-for union and its visceral vehicle of metal and cable. Hope and gravity, clarity and haze: Crane's prologue to his mythical bridge is bound by its palpable representation in the Brooklyn Bridge. This poem tethers urban abstraction by posing the very limits of its vision: the speaker's singular sight.

More than 60 years later, novelist Fae Ng would write of another bridge in her eerie portrait of a Chinese-American family. Set in contemporary San Francisco, *Bone* brings together the city as perceptual palimpsest in a story that centers on a family broken by the catalytic suicide of Ona, the middle daughter of Leon, a "paper son" who came to the United States in the period of the nation's most restrictive immigration laws (some specifically directed against Chinese), and Mah, a more recent immigrant. The eldest daughter Leila, the novel's narrator, struggles to come to terms with her sister's death, keep the family together, and blaze her own path in the midst of these familial burdens. As the characters of *Bone* traverse San Francisco, particularly its Chinatown, they wrestle with contending markers, each of them asserting one history over another, none of them fixing a proprietary stamp on any landscape. The seeming fixity of the Chinese-American community in Chinatown is uprooted as new stores and institutions replace the remnants of the bachelor society. Early in the novel, Leila searches for her father on Waverly Place, the heart of Chinatown that Leon still refers to as "Fifteen-Cent Alley," now replete with churches, Buddhist temples, restaurants, and travel agencies. A community's regeneration, then, contains the ironic tale of erasing another's story. At the very least, *Bone* documents a city in which no totality exists nor any given polity is assumed. Instead, the very idea of community is premised on contingency, contest, and even sheer will of memory. The power of perception of the novel's characters creates compelling and competing visions of San Francisco. And while each person's eye reveals a certain narrowness, even provincialism, of singular scope, the *collective* effect of Ng's aggregated landscape presents a dynamic vision of San Francisco whose only constancy is that people remain to battle over its meaning.

In the following passage, Leila's boyfriend Mason drives Leon and Mah to view the Golden Gate Bridge. The same landmark evinces crucially different responses, different memories, according to the first time each observer encountered the bridge. And, like Hart Crane's vision of the Brooklyn Bridge, the Golden Gate emerges into consciousness as much by the shadow of Mah's and Leon's particularities of vision, as by the light of its importance to each. Leila reflects:

> Late afternoon, Mason came and took us all for a ride. He drove over the Golden Gate Bridge because he knew Mah loved how the light bounced off the cables, copper, and bright gold, and Leon liked to remember the first time he sailed into San Francisco, how when his ship passed under the Golden Gate, the light disappeared for a long moment. (Ng 1993: 109)

The different memories that Leon and Mah harbor come from their different moments of entry; points in different histories in which the Golden Gate Bridge serves as a "gateway," as it does for thousands of Asian immigrants. Vantage also constrains and gives sight. Mah's love of the light bouncing off the bridge's copper and gold cables illuminates a bird's-eye, or, more accurately, plane's-eye view of the landmark and the city. As a mode of transport, the plane not only signals the rapidity of modern transportation and social mobility; it also conveys, like the glittering light of the bridge, Mah's initial optimism of her new life in the United States. Leon, on the other hand, sails under the bridge and, like Crane's speaker in "Proem," sees as much shadow as light as the ship passes underneath the illuminated span. The Golden Gate, for Leon, is not so much a symbol of America's promise as a visible reminder of the humiliating detention and examination that he, as an early immigrant and "paper son," had to endure at Angel Island to even pass under the bridge. But Leon's remembrance of a darker past has prepared him for a difficult life as a Chinese American, for, as he remarks, "In this country, paper is stronger than blood." He had already had to suffer the "paper" of legal restriction (the Chinese Exclusion Acts), which relegated whole communities of Chinese Americans to perpetual "bachelor-hood" before 1965, an experience that taught him to regard all promises – whether of paper (legal status) or blood (kinship) – with skepticism. Mah's vision of the bridge's glitter casts ironic light on her eventual life of extreme toil and misery, as a degraded sweatshop worker in Chinatown. Even in an era of relaxed immigration law, race and gender impinge on her social options, her initial effervescence dampened by the betrayal of her adopted land and her disintegrating family. Later, at the point of breakdown, Mah looks again to the bridge, but this time as a bitter reminder of her dreams, dashed by her life in the city for which no plane passing overhead could equip her: "Her cries told the whole story: the runaway husband, the child, the shame in her face. Her heavy heavy face . . . 'Death. I will jump from the Golden Gate.'" (Ng 1993: 188).

Instead of seeking death, Leon seems to embrace his marginal status, always on the move, cut off from all but the barest of associations. He thus embodies in the novel a figure not unlike Robert Park's "marginal man," a social type freed from bonds of tradition and custom, enabled by his cosmopolitan vision to observe different cultures and communities without the imprimatur of any one group's social control. For Park, this marginal man gave a new language of hope in the early twentieth century to the apparent dissolution of filial networks brought about by rapacious urban transformation. That Park and his cohorts of the famed Chicago School derived this marginal man from their investigation of the "Oriental" and "Negro Problem," as Henry Yu has demonstrated, suggests Leon's affinity with this prototypical observer.

The marginal man has many other names: Benjamin's *flâneur*, George Simmel's "stranger." Each formulation of this detached walker of the city shares the common attribute of its ability to observe through detachment, to experience the city without falling prey to its forces. He makes uncanny what appears familiar in the mundane life of the urban; he himself is uncanny, a personification of the landscape's repressed, which brings to light the darker forces that gird and energize the city. Park's marginal man is in many ways the logical conclusion of extensive and comprehensive creation of human ecology in urban setting. With Ernest Burgess, Park affixed the natural "law" of society propounded by Herbert Spencer into the city's geography, and provided a portrait of an internally divided landscape in which a city's residents clustered to form a functional social system (see Park and Burgess 1984). "The city," Park describes repeatedly in his landmark 1916 essay "The City: Suggestions for the Investigation of Human Behavior in the Urban Environment," "is . . . a state of mind, a body of customs and traditions, and of organized attitudes and sentiments . . . it is a product of nature, and particularly of human nature . . . a kind of psychophysical mechanism in and through which private and political interests find not merely a collective but a corporate expression" (Park and Burgess 1984: 1). Park's rather pensive remarks about the city are complemented by Ernest Burgess's more schematic representation of Chicago's ecological system, the famous ring of concentric circles comprising the city's different social classes. For both Park and Burgess (and most of the Chicago School), this urban form as "psychophysical mechanism" through differentiated space and neighborhood constituted a dynamic equilibrium through which people could anchor themselves, even as larger forces compelled change, growth, and progress.

But if in achieving this social equilibrium residents of the city congregate in areas where like-minded individuals share common goals and interests – Burgess's zones – then how might anyone move beyond his specific space, in which everyone in the neighborhood holds similar worldviews? This is not very far from a Lukácsian vision of a reified society. Against the typical man of the city, who lives in his functional subgroup, emerges Park's "marginal man," the figure whose social transience enables him to move among all groups and who is able to observe the whole city. The marginal man is Park's personified sublation. It is thus no surprise that the Chicago School would quickly adopt the marginal man figure to stand in as the eminent urban ethnographer, the incipient sociologist who is friend and family of no one and observer of all. Like Benjamin's *flâneur*, Park's marginal man gives permission to bring objective credence to subjective perception. Drawing from his earlier description of the "hobo," Park grants authority to these migrant souls; but unlike the hobo, a "man without a cause or country" and without "vocation," the marginal does serve the crucial purpose of gathering knowledge of the city and its inhabitants. Whereas the hobo is pure subjective, solipsistic existence, the marginal man transforms particular perception into realized conception.

Park developed his theory of the marginal man after attending lectures in Berlin given by Georg Simmel, who at the beginning of the twentieth century offered one of the first portraits of the "metropolitan psyche." It was Simmel's notion of the "stranger," based on these lectures and in his seminal essay "The Metropolis and Mental Life," that Park and the other members of the Chicago School used to begin their work on creating an American discourse of the urban. Like the marginal man, Simmel's stranger exhibits the cosmopolitan qualities of belonging to no group. And like the *flâneur*, the stranger adopts the characteristic attitude of "blasé" toward relating to others, a result of the intense, constant, and compressed stimuli exuding from the city. But unlike Park's marginal man, who achieves a special vantage through his detachment, Simmel's stranger, his blasé, his very cosmopolitanism, is an expression of the emptiness of the city's increasingly dominant money economy: "Money, with all its colorlessness and indifference, becomes the common denominator of all values; irreparably it hollows out the core of things, their individuality, their specific value, and their incomparability" (Sennett 1970: 52). The stranger is not above money or other exigencies of the city; the stranger's lens is hazed by it. Intrinsic to the stranger, then, is a fundamental contradiction that Park attempts to overlook in developing his marginal man. Where the marginal man is, in the final instance, transhistorical in his homelessness, the stranger is homeless because of his participation and complicity in history.

Perhaps because they have suffered continuous and *real* social marginality, blacks in US literature have become quintessential figures of the stranger since Park's formulation of the marginal man, whether this figure look like Wright's Bigger, Ellison's Invisible Man, Petry's Lutie, or Brooks's personae in "We Real Cool." But as John Edgar Wideman highlights throughout his work, African-American marginality also shares some of the complicity that Simmel locates in his figure of the stranger. Thus a central problem emerges, one which Wideman's characters struggle with, but almost always fail to resolve: what happens when the stranger, the marginal man, achieves the capacity to put himself at the center of power? What are the consequences to those who remain on the periphery, not merely in metaphoric but also in material terms? In *Philadelphia Fire* (1990), Wideman engages this dilemma, externalizing onto Philadelphia's changing landscape the internal contradictions of Simmel's stranger – his simultaneous detachment from and participation in the political economy of the city. In the novel, Cudjoe, Wideman's protagonist who is traversing Philadelphia to find a lost boy of the infamous MOVE bombing of 1985 and to write a story about that tragedy, meets Timbo, an old friend and now the "cultural attaché" to the mayor, the city's first black chief executive. Sitting in a five-star Center City restaurant, Cudjoe and Timbo enjoy a momentary, multicultural oasis, where wealth and power celebrate cross-racial cosmopolitanism. But what enables this new black power in Philadelphia, the rise of a new black elite in the city, are the mayor's initiatives to "revitalize" the city through purported urban "redevelopment." As he and Cudjoe drive throughout the city, Timbo rehearses the mayor's plans:

> All this mess around here, warehouses, garages, shanties, all these eyesores got to go. When redevelopment's finished, a nice, uncluttered view of the art museum. That's the idea. Open up the view. With universities just a hop skip down the way what we're trying to create here is our little version of Athens, you dig? (Wideman 1990: 78)

A clownish parody of the talented tenth, that term that DuBois – another writer of Philadelphia – coined almost a century earlier, Timbo's remarks reflect the blasé attitude of a marginal man with the means to level the city's palimpsest into an urban environment that harnesses culture and civilization at the expense of Philadelphia's black residents. Timbo juxtaposes future hellenistic glory with its necessary social consequence: "them that ain't got and never had, they worse off than ever . . . Some these pitiful bloods off the map, bro. And they know it" (Wideman 1990: 79). If Timbo and the mayor seek to instill the conceptual city that might save the existing city from its ostensible wasteland present, they do so by deliberate, even if creative, destruction of its layered history, and by still excluding the vast majority of people who will never touch the refreshing palms of multicultural paradise. Timbo's mapping of the new Philadelphia makes clear that urban devastation is not a natural process, nor even a spatial example of Moynihan's famous "benign neglect" thesis. Instead, this vision of the city marks the latest of what urban theorists call "urban triage." Attending to the demands of a deindustrialized city core, urban triage harnesses corporate interests and city government to level old physical markers of Philadelphia's industrial past to make room for its postindustrial, service-driven economic future. And Wideman figuratively links this vision of Philadelphia as the new Athens with the structural connections between black destitution and the rise of these latter-day talented tenth: Timbo likens the city's new map to "thin ice . . . damn thin ice and we all dancing on it" (Wideman 1990: 80).

Wideman's novel suggests that the conceived city – whether imaged as a present wasteland or future Athens – buries the city of perception, those partial glimpses that narrate slivers of urban life. Those who perceive rather than conceive do not allow the city to tumble down the slope of urban apocalyse or utopian ecstasy, despite the occasional hope that springs from existential crisis in city space. Seen not from above, but rather from underneath a bridge or a freeway, the city of perception remains partial and provisional, never spinning a vision of the city with a semblance of totality, nor taking for granted that there is, has been, or should be an ideal polity. Instead, those who perceive the city uncover the layers of its palimpsest, marking its spatial transformations, recovering its lost histories, and engaging in the contested terrain where others will perceive differently. It is through this contest that the polis emerges; not the presumption of a given public space, but the active creation of the public space, that resists the Idea of the city, for those who still clamor for a voice in it. Underneath the bridge or freeway, as Karen Tei Yamashita's recent novel about Los Angeles, *Tropic of Orange* (1997), demonstrates, people watch the city through shadow, where other eyes have forsaken them. But Yamashita's character Buzzworm watches from below, and in a rare moment on the freeway, on which people pass by, trapped in their fantasies of this most stereotyped city – as an example of a city feeding on its own simulacra – he reflects on this oldest of the modern American cities and its dominant plant: the omnipresent palm tree. Against the soil of Eliot's wasteland, Yamashita's character offers the advice of the peripheral perceiver, the stranger at home in his city, to remind us that perception mandates that all objects of the city be looked upon anew, and to tell us something about the strangeness of ours:

One day, Buzzworm got taken for a ride on the freeway. Got to pass over the Harbor Freeway, speed over the hood like the freeway was a giant bridge. He realized you could just skip out over his house, his streets, his part of town. You never had to see it ever. Only thing you could see that anybody might take notice of were the palm trees. That was what the palm trees were for. To make out the place where he lived. To make sure that people noticed. And the palm trees were like the eyes of his neighborhood, watching the rest of the city, watching it sleep and eat and play and die. There was a beauty about those palm trees, a beauty neither he nor anybody down there next to them could appreciate, a beauty you could only notice if you were far away. Everything going on down under those palm trees might be poor and crazy, ugly and beautiful, honest or shameful – all sorts of life that could only be imagined from far away. This was probably why the palm trees didn't need any water to speak of. They were fed by something else, something only the streets of his hood could offer. It was a great fertilizer – the dankest but richest of waters. It produced the tallest trees in the city, looking out over everything, symbols of the landscape, a beauty that could only be appreciated from afar. (Yamashita 1997: 33)

REFERENCES AND FURTHER READING

Adams, Henry (1999). *The Education of Henry Adams*. New York and Oxford: Oxford University Press. (First publ. 1918.)

Baldwin, James (1981). "The Language of the Streets." In Ann Chalmers Watts and Michael C. Jaye, eds., *Literature and the Urban Experience: Essays on the City and Literature*. New Brunswick: Rutgers University Press.

Benjamin, Walter (1973). *Illuminations*. London: Fontana.

Bridge, Gary and Watson, Sophie, eds. (2002). *A Companion to the City*. Oxford and Malden, Mass.: Blackwell.

Chase, Richard (1955). *Walt Whitman Reconsidered*. London: Victor Gollancz.

Crane, Hart (1970). *The Bridge*. New York: Liveright. (First publ. 1930.)

Crane, Stephen (1960). *Maggie: A Girl of the Streets*. New York: Fawcett. (First publ. 1893.)

Crow, Charles (1995). "Home and Transcendence in Los Angeles Fiction." In David Fine, ed., *Los Angeles in Fiction: A Collection of Essays*. Albuquerque: University of New Mexico Press.

de Tocqueville, Alexis (2000). *Democracy in America*. Chicago: University of Chicago Press. (First publ. 1841.)

Deutsche, Rosalyn (1996). *Evictions: Art and Spatial Politics*. Cambridge, Mass.: MIT Press.

Dreiser, Theodore (1991). *Sister Carrie*. New York: Norton. (First publ. 1900.)

Eliot, T. S. (2000). *The Waste Land*. New York: Penguin. (First publ. 1922.)

Ellison, Ralph (1982). *Invisible Man*. New York: Random House. (First publ. 1952.)

Fine, David, ed. (1995). *Los Angeles in Fiction: A Collection of Essays*. Albuquerque: University of New Mexico Press.

Horne, Gerald (1997). *Fire this Time: The Watts Uprising and the 1960s*. Cambridge, Mass.: De Capo.

James, Henry (1993). *Collected Travel Writings: Great Britain and America*. New York: Library of America.

Jefferson, Thomas (1998). *Notes on the State of Virginia*. New York: Penguin. (First publ. 1787.)

Lehan, Richard (1998). *The City in Literature: An Intellectual and Cultural History*. Berkeley: University of California Press.

Marx, Leo (1981). "The Puzzle of Anti-Urbanism in Classic American Literature." In Ann Chalmers Watts and Michael C. Jaye, eds., *Literature and the Urban Experience: Essays on the City and Literature*. New Brunswick: Rutgers University Press.

Mumford, Lewis (1968). *The City in History: Its Origins, its Transformations, and its Prospects*. San Diego and New York: Harvest.

New, Elisa (1993). *The Regenerate Lyric: Theology and Innovation in American Poetry*. New York: Cambridge University Press.

New, Elisa (1998). *The Line's Eye: Lyric Experience, American Sight*. Cambridge, Mass.: Harvard University Press.

Ng, Fae (1993). *Bone*. New York: Hyperion.

Norris, Frank (1981). *McTeague*. New York: Signet. (First publ. 1899.)

Park, Robert and Burgess, Ernest (1984). *The City*. Chicago: University of Chicago Press.

Petry, Ann (1974). *The Street*. Boston: Houghton Mifflin. (First publ. 1946.)

Poirier, Richard (1966). *A World Elsewhere: The Place of Style in American Literature*. New York: Oxford University Press.

Reynolds, David S. (1996). *Walt Whitman's America: A Cultural Biography*. New York: Vintage.

Rotella, Carlo (1998). *October Cities: The Redevelopment of Urban Literature*. Berkeley: University of California Press.

Sandburg, Carl (1970). *The Complete Poems of Carl Sandburg*. New York: Harcourt Brace.

Sennett, Richard, ed. (1970). *Classic Essays on the Culture of Cities*. New York: Knopf.

Simmel, Georg (1997). *Simmel on Culture: Selected Writings*, ed. David Frisby and Mike Featherstone. Thousand Oaks, Calif.: Sage.

Watts, Ann Chalmers, and Jaye, Michael C., eds. (1981). *Literature and the Urban Experience: Essays on the City and Literature*. New Brunswick: Rutgers University Press.

Whitman, Walt (1994). *Leaves of Grass and Democratic Vistas*. New York: Everyman.

Whitman, Walt (2002). "Democratic Vistas." In *Selections from Walt Whitman and Emily Dickinson: A Supplement to the Heath Anthology of American Literature*. Boston: Houghton Mifflin. (First publ. 1871.)

Wideman, John Edgar (1990). *Philadelphia Fire*. New York: Vintage.

Williams, William Carlos (1995). *Paterson*. New York: New Directions. (First publ. 1946.)

Winthrop, John (1996). *The Journal of John Winthrop, 1630–1649*, ed. Richard S. Dunn and Laetitia Yandle. Cambridge, Mass.: Belknap.

Wright, Richard (1940). *Native Son*. New York: Harper & Bros.

Yamashita, Karen Tei (1997). *Tropic of Orange*. Minneapolis: Coffee House.

Yu, Henry (2002). *Thinking Orientals: Migration, Contact, and Exoticism in Modern America*. New York: Oxford University Press.

10
Indigenous Peoples and Place
P. Jane Hafen

Nothing defines indigenous peoples more than belonging to a place, a homeland. No single political issue has been more important to indigenous peoples than the effort to retain land bases, recover lost territories, and hang on to hunting, water, mineral, and other rights associated with living in a particular place. Yet "home" also functions metaphorically to refer to a future place of self-esteem (on the individual level), and self-governance, cultural maintenance, revitalization, and sovereignty (on the collective level).

> Kathryn Shanley (Nakota), "'Born from the need to say': Boundaries and Sovereignties in Native American Literary and Cultural Studies"

The literature of indigenous peoples in regard to place or region has an imperative more compelling than any other American literatures. As original inhabitants of this continent and with a history of dispossession and removal and government-sanctioned attempts at cultural assimilation, contemporary American Indian writers have a unique perspective and responsibility. In the words of Louise Erdrich (Turtle Mountain Chippewa, b. 1954), "Contemporary Native American writers have therefore a task quite different from that of other writers . . . In the light of enormous loss, they must tell the stories of contemporary survivors while protecting and celebrating the cores of cultures left in the wake of the catastrophe" (Erdrich 1985).

Although generalizations are hazardous when speaking of American Indians, one common thread among the various tribal nations (more than 550 recognized by the United States federal government), is a direct connection to place. This connection is much more complicated than the romantic notion of native ties to "Mother Earth." Native peoples are inextricably connected with place in terms of history and identity. The specific locus defines the existence of diverse tribal communities. Also distinguishing those individual tribal communities are unique, sovereign worldviews and governing structures, disparate cultures and languages. Nevertheless, a primary concern is always the land.

This connection to place is evident in many of the indigenous literatures of the North American continent. American Indian writings have garnered much attention in recent years, yet literary traditions predate European encounters. Of course, most of these literatures were in the oral tradition and included the sacred stories that define cosmology, songs, rituals, and oratory. These oral modes continue among many tribal peoples today. Inevitably they represent their places of origin. As Jeannette Armstrong (Okanagan, b. 1948) notes in her essay, "Land Speaking," "My own experience of the land sources . . . arises in my poetry and prose and . . . the Okanagan language shapes that connection. . . . As I understand it from my Okanagan ancestors, language was given to us by the land we live within" (Armstrong 1998: 175).

While some tribes, including the Cherokee, developed their own systems of literacy, most American Native peoples did not enter the written realm of literature until the nineteenth century. Much of this early writing involved life histories, autobiography, and written collections of oral literatures by ethnographers. These writings, like Sarah Winnemucca's *Life Among the Piutes: Their Wrongs and Claims* (1883), also spoke to protecting land rights.

The United States government developed policies to deal with American Indians and land policies. In 1887 the Dawes General Allotment Act was a major attempt to detribalize Indians by dividing commonly held tribal lands into 160-acre tracts. Tribal members were to become individual landholders and farmers. The bill was enacted without regard to differences in geography and the viability of farming in various locations. The intended outcome was a "civilizing" program to make American Indians like other citizens of the United States.

In addition to the land policies, the government made a systematic effort to remove Indian children from their families and place them in residential boarding schools. Inspired by Richard Pratt's motto "Kill the Indian, Save the Man," Indian children were forbidden to speak their own languages, Christianized, given new names, and taught skills of manual labor. While many of these children did assimilate into mainstream society and others perished, a cadre of boarding-school educated Natives took their training and used it to establish a forum within which they argued for American Indian rights. Sioux writers Luther Standing Bear (1868–1939), Charles Eastman (1858–1939), and Zitkala-Ša (Gertrude Simmons Bonnin, 1876–1938) each told stories from their youth and recounted the enormous transitions in their lives. In each case, their writing surrenders to their specific places of origin.

For example, Zitkala-Ša begins her "Impressions of an Indian Childhood," first published in the *Atlantic Monthly* in 1900 and 20 years later collected in her volume, *American Indian Stories*: "A wigwam of weather-stained canvas stood at the base of some irregularly ascending hills. A footpath wound its way gently down the sloping land till it reached the broad river bottom; creeping through the long swamp grasses that bent over it on either side, it came out on the edge of the Missouri" (Zitkala-Ša 1986: 7). Rather than beginning as many traditional autobiographies do with a declaration of self or individual history, Zitkala-Ša begins with the geographic place that defines her as a Yankton Sioux. Demonstrating the skills imposed upon her, her use of the English language shows that she is aware of her audience. Throughout her literary and political career she would return physically and metaphorically to the Great Plains that shaped her perceptions of the world. With Standing Bear, Eastman, and others, she would turn her writing to political agendas which included a campaign for American Indian citizenship (accomplished in 1924) and respect for land rights.

At the same time that American Indians were experiencing political changes early in the twentieth century, some tribal nations in Oklahoma and Minnesota were fighting fraudulent and violent efforts to deprive them of their land and natural resources. Zitkala-Ša, along with Charles Fabens and Matthew Sniffen, investigated the circumstances and prepared a report, "Oklahoma's Poor Rich Indians." Linda Hogan (Chickasaw, b.1947) fictionalizes this "reign of terror" in Osage Indian Country in her novel *Mean Spirit* (1990).

The Osage people fight for their very existence in this historical novel. In the first few pages a major character is murdered and a plot set in motion to deprive the victim's daughter of her oil and land rights. At the time, the Osage were among the most wealthy Americans because of royalties from oil exploration. While the story revolves around racism, conflicts over land and natural resources, and survival, Hogan's graceful language also gives life to the earth:

> Up the road from Grace's sunburned roses was an enormous crater a gas well blowout had made in the earth. It was fifty feet deep and five hundred feet across. This gouge in the earth, just a year earlier, had swallowed five workmen and ten mules. The water was gone from that land forever, the trees dead, and the grass, once long and rich, was burned black. The cars passed by this ugly sight, and not far from there, they passed another oil field where pumps, fueled by diesel, worked day and night. These bruised fields were noisy and dark. The earth had turned oily black. Blue flames rose up and roared like torches of burning gas. The earth bled oil. (Hogan 1990: 53–4)

Every time a human being is assaulted in the novel, the earth responds indignantly with tornados, crickets or bats. As Hogan's later writings additionally have shown, the earth is a living entity.

John Joseph Mathews' early novel, *Sundown* (1934) also deals with Osage matters of rights and inheritances. Often viewed as a coming-of-age novel with a conflicted mixed-blood hero, it is also tied to its locale. Despite cultural confrontations and experiences out in the world, the main character is continually drawn home to the prairie and blackjacks. This novel, too, begins with emphasis on place, similar to Zitkala-Sa's autobiography, and an invocation to the Osage deity:

> The god of the Great Osages was still dominant over the wild prairie and the blackjack hill when Challenge was born.
>
>   He showed his anger in fantastic play of lightning, and thunder that crashed and rolled among the hills; in the wind that came from the great tumbling clouds which appeared in the northwest and brought twilight and ominous milk-warm silence.

His beneficence he showed on April mornings when the call of the prairie chicken came rolling over the awakened prairie and the killdeer seemed to be fussing; on June days when the emerald grass sparkled in the dew and soft breezes whispered, and the quail whistled; and the autumnal silences when the blackjacks were painted like dancers and dreamed in the iced sunshine with fatalistic patience. (Mathews 1988: 1)

In his discussion and reassessment of early American Indian authors, Osage critic Robert Allen Warrior observes: "The immediate importance of what Mathews achieves is his ability to discuss American Indian religious ecology without slipping into sentimental romanticism" (Warrior 1995: 65). Indeed, Mathews represents the spirituality of the place by melding the power of deity with the lyricism of the land.

In another novelistic rendering of land losses from the early twentieth century, Louise Erdrich begins her North Dakota cycle of novels with *Tracks* (1988). Erdrich's series of novels is a complex intertwining of characters and families connected to an imaginary reservation but with events and descriptions that resonate with the nature of the northern Great Plains and the woodlands culture of the Ojibwe. She describes her own sense of developing character and place: "In a tribal view of the world, where one place has been inhabited for generations, the landscape becomes enlivened by a sense of group and family history. Unlike most contemporary writers, a traditional storyteller fixes listeners in an unchanging landscape combined of myth and reality. People and place are inseparable" (Erdrich 1985: 1).

Erdrich's novels are set primarily in the twentieth century. They witness tremendous changes among Ojibwe peoples, including land losses and cultural adaptations through conversion to Christianity and popular influences. These tribal peoples cannot remain unchanged, yet they maintain a sense of who they are as Ojibwes, and they remain tied to the land, even as their place names are adapted by the ever-encroaching dominant society. "Anishinaabeg" is the traditional name the Ojibwe peoples called themselves, a name that utilizes the image of Ojibwe-specific puckered moccasins:

White people usually name places for men – presidents and generals and entrepreneurs. Ojibwe name places for what grows there or what is found. . . . If we call ourselves and all we see around us by the original names, will we not continue to be Anishinaabeg? Instead of reconstituted white men, instead of Indian ghosts? Do the rocks here know us, do the trees, do the waters of the lakes? Not unless they are addressed by the names they themselves told us to call them in our dreams. Every feature of the land around us spoke its name to an ancestor. Perhaps in the end, that is all that we are. We Anishinaabeg are the keepers of the names of the earth. And unless the earth is called by the names it gave us humans, won't it cease to love us? And isn't it true that if the earth stops loving us, everyone, not just the Anishinaabeg, will cease to exist? (Erdrich 2001: 359–61)

The earth and tribal peoples have a symbiotic relationship; they are mutually self-defining. Forgetting reciprocal dependence leads to destruction. Survival as indigenous peoples is predicated on the land. Erdrich is refuting assimilation and the Vanishing American through adherence to the earth. Yet, through the stories and the places, the Ojibwe continue to exist as one of the largest indigenous cultures in North America. Erdrich depicts the modulations and accommodations through her Ojibwe characters as they struggle to survive.

In an essay that preceded the publication of *Tracks*, Erdrich and her husband, Michael Dorris (Modoc, 1945–97), discuss the historical land loss of the White Earth Chippewa Nation that is central to the novel:

> Not content with the General Allotment Act's provision that Indians had to wait 25 years before they could be deprived of their parcels, [Moses E.] Clapp [a lumber baron and lawyer who became a Minnesota Senator] pushed through a rider to the Indian Appropriations Bill of 1906 which declared that mixed-blood adults on White Earth were "competent" to dispose of them immediately.

> What followed was a land-grab orgy so outrageous that to this day local people, regardless of ethnic heritage speak of it with a sense of bewildered shame. Threatened, duped or plied with drink, many Chippewa signed away their deeds with an X or a thumb print.... The effect on the band was devastating. While lumber companies clear-cut millions of dollars' worth of pine from forests located within White Earth, dispirited and broken Indian families clustered ten or more to single-room cabins on the allotment left to them. (Dorris and Erdrich 1988: 35)

The final description also parallels Erdrich's North Dakota saga's family groups or clans, the Kashpaws, Nanapushes, Pillagers, Lazarres, and Morrisseys, who, in addition to land forfeitures, face disease, starvation, yet manage to survive.

When the Dawes General Allotment Act turned Native peoples into private landholders, there was little consideration for how they would subsist, or, more importantly, pay taxes to keep their land titles. In *Tracks*, the main characters are considering their allotments and the lands lost to other, more entrepreneurial Indians and lost to industrial interests:

> With her fingernail, Margaret traced the print she could not read, polished first the small yellow Kashpaw square, then tapped the doubled green square of Morrisseys, and gestured at Fleur and Eli to compare.
> "They're taking it over."
> It was like her to notice only the enemies that she could fight, those that shared her blood however faintly. My concern was the lapping pink, the color of the skin of lumber-jacks and bankers, the land we would never walk or hunt, from which our children would be barred. (Erdrich 1988: 173–4)

The map represents the whole construct of land ownership and legal validation. It becomes the concrete emblem of colonization and loss. As the land changes hands, the social situations deteriorate as well. Alcoholism becomes rampant, children are abandoned, "dressed in nothing but snow." Nanapush laments, "I am a man, but for years I had known how it was to lose a child of my blood. Now I also knew the uncertainties of facing the world without land to call home" (Erdrich 1988: 184, 187).

Nanapush faces the world by mediating his traditional ways with new skills that would facilitate survival for his people. He becomes literate and uses the power of literacy to protect tribal members. "To become a bureaucrat myself was the only way that I could wade through the letters, the reports, the only place where I could find a ledge to kneel on" (Erdrich 1988: 225). His example sets in motion a pattern for Nector Kashpaw and Lyman Lamartine who, in subsequent novels, will both become cultural brokers in their positions of power and keepers of the land.

Erdrich's next book in the narrative sequence, *The Beet Queen* (1986), does not focus on American Indian characters, although their presence is palpable. The setting moves from the unidentified reservation to the town of Argus, North Dakota. The novel begins with a description of the locale: "Long before they planted beets in Argus and built the highways, there was a railroad. Along the track, which crossed the Dakota–Minnesota border and stretched on to Minneapolis, everything that made the town arrived. All that diminished the town departed by that route, too" (Erdrich 1986: 1).

Like its Greek counterpart, Argos, the town contains life-giving elements central to each character and his/her personality. Argos is inextricably intertwined with Jason in preindustrial Greek sacred stories. Likewise, Argus is a source of identification and a repository of values that each character seeks or rejects. According to protagonist Mary Adare, the town has its own poetic association and is named for its Indian predecessors (Erdrich 1986: 278).

As with peoples and cultures, the land transforms. The images of adaptability include the implied transfer from Native American to Euro-American, and conversions from railway to highway and from grain production to sugar beets, providing an economic means for people to continue on the land. The emphasis on transportation metaphors suggests transition and connection between destinations. Because the railroad is fixed, basic assumptions about progress are questioned. When the butcher shop suffers because of the infusion of supermarkets, values of personal service are lost in conveniences gained.

One of the characters who wanders in and out of the plot is Karl Adare. Near the end of *The Beet Queen*, Karl returns to Argus. His description reveals Erdrich's perceptions of the northern plains:

> I left Rapid City by route of that endless stretch of highway that runs beneath the border between the two Dakotas. During long drives my trick was usually to hit on a catchy tune or talk back to the radio, but after a while I switched it off. I found it pleasant to have the peace of the afternoon around me, to be at the center of unchanging fields of snow and brown branches. The landscape stayed so much the same, in fact, that at one point I seemed suspended, my wheels spinning in thin air. I hung motionless in speed above the earth like a fixed star. (Erdrich 1986: 320)

Although Karl is one of Erdrich's memorable non-Indian characters, he differs from mainstream literary characters, like James Joyce's Stephen Daedalus, who leave home in search of self-definition. He follows the compulsion of many indigenous characters to return to homeland, what critic William Bevis calls "homing in."

The next novel in Erdrich's series, *Love Medicine*, was actually published first in 1984 to much acclaim, including the National Book Critics Circle Award. The North Dakota story continues with the families introduced in *Tracks*, and shows their complex relationships among one another and with the land. In 1993 Erdrich reissued the novel with additions that broadened connections with other novels in the cycle. *Love Medicine* has a familiar beginning, with June Morrissey Kashpaw compelled by the call of home and risking her life to the natural elements and capricious spring weather of the northern plains:

> The wind was mild and wet. A Chinook wind, she told herself. She made a right turn off the road, walked up a drift frozen over a snow fence, and began to pick her way through the swirls of dead grass and icy crust of open ranchland. Her boots were thin. So she stepped on dry ground where she could and avoided the slush and rotten gray banks. . . . She crossed the wide fields swinging her purse, stepping carefully to keep her feet dry.

> Even when it started to snow she did not lose her sense of direction. Her feet grew numb, but she did not worry about the distance. The heavy winds couldn't blow her off course. She continued. Even when her heart clenched and her skin turned crackling cold it didn't matter, because the pure and naked part of her went on.

> The snow fell deeper that Easter than it had in forty years, but June walked over it like water and came home. (Erdrich 1993b: 6–7)

June's presence hovers over the novel, her death bringing together other characters as they remember her and clarify their own relationships with her. In a stunning narrative twist, Erdrich revisits the same opening scene in *Tales of Burning Love* (1996), where with similar but not identical language she narrates from the point of view of Jack Mauser, an Ojibwe man who had picked up June in a bar:

> He turned away, and still the shadows rode across the icy crust of open ranch land, the pastures, pure and roadless, the fields, the open spaces. . . . The storm had blown over with the speed of all spring lapses. . . . [June had] gotten tired of walking in those thin shoes, and sat down against a fence post. To wait for the bus, he thought. She was looking to the east, her hair loaded with melting stars. No one had touched her yet. Her face was complex in its expectations. A fist of air punched Jack to earth and he knelt before her with his hands outstretched. But then the officer reached past him, thumbed her eyelids down, took her purse from her lap, knocked off her blanket of snow. (Erdrich 1996: 13)

While altering the perspective, Erdrich keeps consistent the images associated with the character June. The reader never encounters her without some sort of geographical signifier. This style of character shorthand might not be so unusual if June were not indigenous. The land of her ancestors reclaims her; the elements that her ancestors survived overwhelm her. June's demise contrasts with and contradicts the survival of other Ojibwe characters in the novels.

The final gesture of *Love Medicine* occurs when June's son, Lipsha Morrissey, comes to a reconciliation of his relationship with her and with other members of the tribal community. Standing on a bridge, Lipsha observes:

> The sun flared. I'd heard that this river was the last of an ancient ocean, miles deep, that once had covered the Dakotas and solved all our problems. It was easy to still imagine us beneath them vast unreasonable waves, but the truth is we live on dry land. I got inside [June's car]. The morning was clear. A good road led on. So there was nothing to do but cross the water and bring her home. (Erdrich 1993b: 367)

Lipsha is a trickster character who uncovers his true parentage and demonstrates intergenerational ties in *Love Medicine*. In the next novel in the series, *The Bingo Palace* (1993), Lipsha seeks to find a purpose in life, and like many Erdrich characters has comic adventures on the way. Through the intervention of his dead mother, June, Lipsha wins a grand prize bingo van. Immediately he runs into a group of guys from Montana he had previously insulted. Their plan is to tattoo an image of Montana on Lipsha's derrière. Lipsha tries to talk his way out of the situation:

> [I] ask Marty in a polite kind of way, to beat me up instead. If that fails, I will tell him that there are many states I would not mind so much, like Minnesota with its womanly hourglass for instance, or Rhode Island which is small, or even Hawaii, a soft bunch of circles. I think of Idaho. The panhandle. That has character.
> "Are any of you guys from any other state?" I ask, anxious to trade.
> "Kansas."
> "South Dakota."
> It isn't that I really have a thing against those places, understand, it's just that the straight-edged shape is not a Chippewa preference. You look around, and everything you see is round, everything in nature. There are no perfect boundaries, no natural borders except winding rivers. Only human-made things tend toward cubes and square – the van, for instance. That is an example. Suddenly I realize that I am driving a four-wheeled version of North Dakota. (Erdrich 1993a: 80)

Indeed, Lipsha, in essence, temporarily loses his soul to the sharp angles and materialism of the bingo van. He later attempts a ritual reconciliation through a vision quest, but like his thwarted application of love medicine to his grandfather Nector, this ceremony does not go as planned. After spending time in the wilderness, his animal helper and spiritual guide appears as "the mother of all skunks." The voice that follows proclaims: *"This ain't real estate."* Lipsha ponders: "This ain't real estate, I think, and then I am surrounded and inhabited by a thing so powerful I don't even recognize it as a smell" (Erdrich 1993a: 200–1).

This "skunk dream" speaks to Lipsha in a discourse he understands, colloquial and profound in its absurdity, and indeed it helps steer Lipsha back toward a tribal path. The cultural mediator is the land, the place that defines him; it is not mere "real estate" but a life-giving force.

In *A Reader's Guide to the Novels of Louise Erdrich*, Peter G. Beidler and Gay Barton attempt to locate precise locations in the books, including the town of Argus. They painstakingly extract clues from *Tracks*, *The Beet Queen*, and *Tales of Burning Love* to situate the town just north of Fargo and note that it is "modeled roughly after the real town of Argusville" (Beidler and Barton 1998: 12). The location of Argus is key to placing the site of the imaginary reservation of Erdrich's novels. Finally, though, Beidler and Barton admit:

> Readers should not be upset by the indeterminate location of the reservation and Argus. It may well be that Erdrich did not want us to identify the reservation in her novels with the Turtle Mountain Indian Reservation and thus purposefully worked in some inconsistencies. The world she creates is, after all, a fictional world. Like Garrison Keillor's Lake Wobegon, it need not be expected to coincide exactly with real locations in real states. (1998: 13)

In their quest to determine exact geographical locations of both the border town and the reservation, Beidler and Barton, in a manner that exemplifies their general approach, fail to recognize the luminous fluidity of Erdrich's writing. With locations and characters alike they impose a rubric that represents a desire for linear order and finite and fixed interpretation in an attempt to straighten the crooked and entangled complexities of the novels. The specific location of settings in Erdrich's novels is less significant than their implications of history and tribal definitions. Even the tendency of many critics to focus on Erdrich's exquisite writing overlooks her subtle representations of political connections between indigenous peoples and their lands. By frequently attending to structure, language, aesthetics, and narrative strategies, tribal foundations of land, sovereignty, and Native rights become colonized. Erdrich writes because she is a survivor of colonization, as are her tribal people, the Turtle Mountain Chippewa of North Dakota. She *is* where she is from, Turtle Mountain.

In an endnote to *The Last Report on the Miracles at Little No Horse*, Erdrich comments: "the reservation depicted in this and in all of my novels is an imagined place consisting of landscapes and features similar to many Ojibwe reservations. It is an emotional collection of places dear to me, as is the town called Argus" (2001: 357). While her descriptions of place are as realistic as literature can be, she understands and demonstrates throughout her works that land is inextricable from culture and people: *"Land is the only thing that lasts life to life"* (Erdrich 1993a: 148).

Erdrich's fiction spans a century. Her own formal education and training have the benefit of an established core of American Indian writing. The terrain of American literature changed when N. Scott Momaday (Kiowa, b. 1934) won a Pulitzer Prize for *House Made of Dawn* (1968). With the novel's sophisticated structure, Momaday introduced the literary mainstream to Native traditions of orality, politics and place. According to critic Louis Owens (Choctaw/Cherokee), "*House Made of Dawn* assumes a place within a Native American literary tradition in which stories have serious responsibilities: to tell us who we are and where we come from, to make us whole and heal us, to integrate us fully within the world in which we live and make that world inhabitable" (Owens 1992: 94). Momaday explains the relationship between that inhabitable world and the imagination:

> I am interested in the way that a man looks at a given landscape and takes possession of it in his blood and brain. For this happens, I am certain, in the ordinary motion of life. None of us lives apart from the land entirely; such an isolation is unimaginable. We have sooner or later to come to terms with the world around us – and I mean especially the physical world; not only as it is revealed to us immediately through our sense, but also as it is perceived more truly in the long turn of seasons and of year. And we must come to moral terms . . . I am talking about an act of the imagination essentially and the concept of an American land ethic. (Momaday 2001: 85–6)

Momaday creates this land ethic in all of his writings, but most particularly in *House Made of Dawn*. The main story of the novel centers on World War II veteran Abel, and his dissociation from his traditional tribal home, Walatowa (Jemez Pueblo). In the course of his journey of reconciliation, Abel encounters a Kiowa trickster, the Right Reverend John Big Bluff Tosamah, and a traditional Navajo, Ben Benally. The novel is framed by the timelessness of Jemez, yet the events and time markers are connected specifically to the landscape. The cycles of the earth acknowledge Pueblo cultural life in the Feast Day, a celebration of the harvest, and the winter ceremonial races that prepare for spring planting. A "Prologue" introduces the place before presenting the main character. The first word and final word of the novel are in Towa, Jemez language for ritual beginning and ending of a story:

> Dypolah. *There was a house made of dawn. It was made of pollen and* of rain, and the land was very old and everlasting. There were many colors on the hills, and the plain was bright with different-colored clays and sands. Red and blue and spotted horses grazed in the plain, and there was a dark wilderness on the mountains beyond. The land was still and strong. It was beautiful all around. (Momaday 1999: 1)

The consistency of the land is one factor that assists Abel in his healing and in his finding of his own voice and gestures.

As part of the federal government's relocation program that transferred reservation Indians to urban centers, Abel is sent to Los Angeles in 1952. There he is trained in labor and he encounters a pan-tribal group of Indians from across the nation. They band together and participate in communal ceremonies, such as a peyote ritual. Although they are tribally distinct, they find commonalities as minorities in the larger population. In this section of the novel Tosamah assumes the narrative voice and tells of his Kiowa background in Oklahoma. The language is nearly identical to that of Momaday's autobiographical *The Way to Rainy Mountain* (1969), where Momaday/Tosamah recounts returning to Oklahoma after the death of his grandmother, Aho. Rainy Mountain is synonymous with Momaday/Tosamah's identity:

> A single knoll rises out of the plain in Oklahoma, north and west of the Wichita range. For my people it is an old landmark, and they gave it the name, Rainy Mountain. There, in the south of the continental trough, is the hardest weather in the world. . . . Loneliness is there as an aspect of the land. All things in the plain are isolate; there is no confusion of objects in the eye, but *one* hill or *one* tree or *one* man. At the slightest elevation you can see to the end of the world. To look upon that landscape in the early morning, with the sun at your back, is to lose the sense of proportion. Your imagination comes to life, and this, you think, is where Creation was begun. (Momaday 1969: 5)

Momaday goes on to explain that the Kiowas were relative latecomers to the place and how they acquired aspects of Plains cultures along the way. Part of their mythology includes a story about Devil's Tower in Wyoming, a sacred place to the Sioux as well.

The novel's title stems from the Navajo Night Chant that Abel learns in Los Angeles from Navajo Ben Benally. The traditional Navajo song acknowledges the wholeness of the earth. Ben's relocation seems less tumultuous than Abel's, in part because Ben seems to have closer ritual ties to his Navajo homeland. He performs the Night Chant for Abel. It demonstrates the Navajo concept of *hozho*, or balance and beauty, that is required for a person to live in harmony with him/herself and the world.

> *Tségihi.*
> House made of dawn,
> House made of evening light,
> House made of dark cloud,
> House made of male rain,
> House made of dark mist,
> House made of female rain,
> House made of pollen,
> House made of grasshoppers,
> Dark cloud is at the door.
>
> . . .
>
> May it be beautiful before me,
> May it be beautiful behind me,
> May it be beautiful below me,
> May it be beautiful above me,
> May it be beautiful all around me.
> In beauty it is finished. (Momaday 1999: 129–30)

The wholeness represented in the chant emblematizes the healing Abel is seeking. He returns home to Jemez, where he finds the power and strength to perform ritual and to find his own voice. He becomes one of the ritual dawn runners and, having come to a sense of self, returns to the place where the novel begins.

Momaday's pioneering novel and growing interest in American Indian Studies programs paved the way for a number of young writers in the early 1970s. James Welch (Blackfeet/GrosVentre, b. 1940), Simon Ortiz (Acoma Pueblo, b. 1941), Joy Harjo (Muscogee Creek, b. 1951), and Leslie Marmon Silko (Laguna Pueblo, b. 1948) were among the most prominent emerging voices. Each addressed compelling political issues including land rights, identity, and sovereignty, and each continues to produce important literature.

Silko, in particular, integrates place into her storytelling. She reworks narratives in various publications, such as the multiple versions of the Yellow Woman tales. Her tales are geographically and culturally specific, most set in the arid Southwest. Of the Laguna Pueblo stories, she observes:

> One of the other advantages that we Pueblos have enjoyed is that we have always been able to stay with the land. Our stories cannot be separated from their geographical locations, from actual physical places on the land. We were not relocated like so many Native American groups who were torn away from their ancestral land. And our stories are so much a part of these places that it is almost impossible for future generations to lose them – there is a story connected with every place, every object in the landscape. (Silko 2001: 165)

Those stories and geographical markers are most prominent in Silko's novel *Ceremony* (1977). Much like Abel in *House Made of Dawn*, the main character, Tayo, is an alienated war veteran whose ceremonial journey takes place so he can be whole and healed. The ceremony of Tayo's healing merges with the telling of the story itself. However, the novel has been criticized by Paula Gunn Allen, who is also Laguna Pueblo, for revealing sacred stories that should not be disclosed outside their cultural context.

Tayo recalls the humid jungles of the Pacific theater where, in the horrors of war, he "prayed the rain away" (Silko 1977: 14). Upon his return to Laguna Pueblo and the dry landscape of the American Southwest, a lack of even a little rain means drought. Tayo associates the dust and dryness with the death of his mother. "The day they buried her the wind blew gusts of sand past the house and rattled the loose tin on the roof. He never forgot that sound and the sand, stinging his face at the graveyard" (Silko 1977: 93). He realizes that redemptive rains are associated with the sacred mountains:

> He knew the holy men had their ways during the dry spells. People said they climbed the trails to the mountaintops to look west and southwest and to call the clouds and thunder. They studied the night skies from the mountaintops and listened to the winds at dawn. When they came back down they would tell the people it was time to dance for rain. (Silko 1977: 93)

In his quest for peace and a quenching to his and the land's thirst, Tayo encounters helpers: Night Swan, Ts'eh Montaño, and the Navajo medicine man, Betonie. After having adventures in the four cardinal directions, Tayo is drawn to the navel of the earth, a sacred place in Pueblo cosmology (Owens 1992: 187):

> He was aware of the center beneath him; it soaked into his body from the ground through the torn skin on his hands, covered with powdery black dirt. The magnetism of the center spread over him smoothly like rainwater down his neck and shoulders; the vacant cool sensation glided over the pain like feather-down wings. It was pulling him back, close to the earth, where the core was cool and silent as mountain stone, and even with the noise and pain in his head he knew how it would be: a returning rather than a separation. . . . he was sinking into the elemental arms of mountain silence. (Silko 1977: 201)

Tayo's commune with the mother earth leads him not only to re-enter Laguna ceremonial traditions, but also to unveil his understanding to the horrors of the atomic age. He realizes that the uranium mining on the Laguna reservation has led to the creations of the most horrible destruction humankind has wrought upon the earth. He remembered the detonation of the first atomic bomb at Trinity Site, that "the laboratories where the bomb had been created were deep in the Jemez Mountains, on land the Government took from Cochiti Pueblo." He went to the mine at Laguna (Paguate), where the "powdery yellow uranium, bright and alive as pollen" was extracted "from deep within [the] earth" (Silko 1977: 246). He enters the ceremonial kiva with his wisdom and is reimmersed into Laguna traditions.

Silko's treatments of landscape in *Ceremony* and her numerous short fictions are consistent with other Native writers in connecting place and being. However, her vision places these elements in a more global context. She fuses ancient traditions and peoples with the implications of the atomic age. More recently, with her epic novel *Almanac of the Dead* (1991), Silko expands her concerns to hemispheric indigenous issues of land and human rights.

Another, perhaps lesser-known writer from the American Southwest is Luci Tapahonso (Navajo, b. 1953). The Navajo reservation is the largest in the United States, and the Navajo population is second in number only to the Cherokees. Primarily a poet, Tapahonso incorporates her native language into many of her works. Several of her poems are inspired by Navajo cosmology. "A Song for the Direction of North" tells the story of mother and daughter as they examine the night sky. In a matrilineal culture and matrilineal mythology, the mother proclaims her devotion to the daughter and the desire to remain in the locale of the poem, Tsaile, Arizona.

> My beloved baby, if only we could stay here.
> There is no end to this clear, sweet air.
> To the west, immense rocks lie red and stark in the empty desert.
> Somewhere my daughters' smooth laughter
> deepens the old memory of stars.
> (Tapahonso 1998: 6)

Tapahonso dedicates another poem to the four sacred mountains of the Navajo in "This Is How They Were Placed for Us." In "Conversations at the Gila River Arts Center" she recalls the ancient people who once lived in a place that is paved over by the urban sprawl of Phoenix.

Perhaps Tapahonso's most complex poem connecting past, present, and place is "In 1864" from her 1993 collection, *Sáanii Dahataał the Women are Singing* (7–10), which recounts the Navajo Long Walk, when the people were driven from their lands by Kit Carson and the US army. The poem begins with a contemporary setting:

> While the younger daughter slept, she dreamt of mountains,
> the wide blue sky above, and friends laughing.
>
> We talked as the day wore on. The stories and highway beneath
> became a steady hum. The center lines were a blurred guide.
> As we neared the turn to Fort Sumner, I remembered this story.

The speaker's story is associated with a specific place. The memory is sparked on a trip, and the details of the trip suggest the freedom of traveling through open spaces. That freedom will be contrasted by the story of captivity. The specific story the speaker remembers is of a Navajo man who was working construction in the area:

> The land was like he had imagined it from the old stories – flat and dotted with shrubs.
> The arroyos and washes cut through the soft dirt.
> They were unsuspectingly deep.

They were so deep that they harbored the sorrows of his ancestors. At night he could hear them crying, so he left the job without even collecting his pay.

The narration segues into a family story of the narrator's great-grandmother, and shifts into first person. The great-grandmother tells how Carson came and burned the crops and killed the sheep. Many people hid in the canyons and mountains, but without crops and sheep they knew they would starve. So they agreed to leave their homeland:

> We didn't know how far it was or even where we were going.
> All that was certain was that we were leaving Dinetah, our home.

"Dineh" is what Navajos call themselves in their own language. In a footnote Tapahonso indicates that "'Dinetah' means 'Navajo country' or 'Homeland of The People'" (1993: 7). Place and identity are inseparable.

She tells of the hardships of the walk. Those who straggled, old ones and expectant mothers, were shot. Some drowned when they crossed the Rio Grande River.

> There were many who died on the way to Hwééldi. All the way
> we told each other, "We will be strong, as long as we are together."
> I think that was what kept us alive. We believed in ourselves

> and the old stories that the holy people had given us.
> "This is why," she would say to us. "This is why we are here.
> Because our grandparents prayed and grieved for us."

Tapahonso not only establishes an imperative for survival, she renders the poem out of the place and its history. She shows how the people had to adapt, how they created Navajo fry bread from the rations they were given, how they learned to love coffee, how they adapted their dress to the cloth that was given them, and how they hammered coins into decorations such as concha belts. Those material items were forced upon them and have now come to represent aspects of Navajo culture. Like the deep arroyos, their meaning is subtle and profound.

Also from the American Southwest, Acoma poet Simon Ortiz sees both the historical violation of the land and its people and contemporary exploitation in his essay "Our Homeland, a National Sacrifice Area." In the autobiographical piece, Ortiz describes growing up in New Mexico. Like Erdrich, he distinguishes between the traditional place names and the names imposed by colonizers:

> I was raised in McCartys which is one of the small villages in the Acoma community. The people say Aacqu. Aacqumen hanoh, we call ourselves. New Mexico and U.S. maps say Acoma, The Sky City. . . . Those Aacqumeh names do not appear anywhere except in the people's hearts and souls and history and oral tradition, and in their love. (Ortiz 1992: 337–8)

Ortiz effectively delineates differences in perceptions and power created by language, and he also shows the endurance of orality, tradition, and place. Ortiz continues to describe the changes in the area as he grows up – the economy changes, more and more businesses and people enter the area. Yet the Acoma adapt, just as oral tradition modifies the stories, to the changes. He reflects back to the history of the first European encounters and how the Pueblo peoples rose up to defend themselves and their lands against the "Spanish oppressor" in the revolt of 1680. While the revolt was immediately successful, the Spanish "swept back brutally in bloody reconquest." After 1821 the "Mericanos" came: "They were so shrewd, talkative, even helpful, and so friendly they didn't look like thieves. As the Mericano stole unto the land, claiming it, the people didn't even feel like anything was being taken away from them" (Ortiz 1992: 347).

What happened to the Pueblo peoples was not unique. As Ortiz summarizes,

> Thomas Jefferson and Alexander Hamilton had spelled it out in political and economic theory: the U.S. needed capital for it to be really considered a free and independent national power. Land was the only real asset the U.S. had, and it would be the commodity used to raise capital. And in the early 19th century, most of the present land was in the possession of Indian People. So in the 1820s and the 1830s, Andrew Jackson was sent to remove Indians from the land, and he was made President because he was successful at it. (Ortiz 1992: 349)

As the land base was consumed, first by the railroads, then by mines and other industries based on natural resources, American Indians were caught in a whirlpool of growing economic dependence. Ortiz speaks of transitions from subsistence cultures to market-dependent cultures. As a little boy, he farmed with his father; as a young man, he worked in the mines in order to purchase basic goods that were no longer self-sufficiently accessible. He saw the water tables drop, mines expand, the air polluted by the Four Corners power plant. He witnessed a huge natural gas explosion in 1966 that impacted both the local economy and the environment. As Silko fictionalized in *Ceremony*, the atomic industry grew out of Indian lands. The industrial environmental hazards and their consequences have a direct impact on indigenous peoples of the Southwest. Ortiz concludes:

> Only when we are not afraid to fight against the destroyers, thieves, liars, exploiters who profit handsomely off the land and people will we know what love and compassion are. Only when the people of this nation, not just Indian people, fight for what is just and good for all life, will we know life and its continuance. And when we fight, and fight back those who are bent on destruction of land and people, we will win. We will win. (Ortiz 1992: 363)

Ortiz's passionate plea grows from his understanding of the symbiotic and ontological relationship between people and place.

> The land. The people.
> They are in relation to each other.
> We are in a family with each other.
> The land has worked with us.
> And the people have worked with it.
> This is true:
> Working for the land
> and the people – it means life
> and its continuity.
> Working not just for the people,
> But for the land too.
> We are not alone in our life;
> We cannot expect to be.
> The land has given us our life,
> And we must give life back to it.
> (Ortiz 1992: 324–5)

American Indian authors write about land with an imperative that goes beyond establishing setting or creating a descriptive backdrop for action and characters. Land gives life, identity, and wisdom to tribal communities. Land is the center of language, culture, and existence. The word "indigenous" implies native to a place. Descendants and survivors of the original peoples of this hemisphere know that being and place are inseparable.

References

Allen, Paula Gunn (Laguna Pueblo) (1998). "Special Problems in Teaching Leslie Marmon Silko's *Ceremony.*" In Devon A. Mihesuah (ed.), *Natives and Academics: Researching and Writing about American Indians*, 55–64. Lincoln: University of Nebraska Press.

Armstrong, Jeanette C. (Okanagan) (1998). "Land Speaking." In Simon J. Ortiz (ed.), *Speaking for Generations: Native Writers on Writing*, 174–94. (Sun Tracks: An American Indian Literary Series, vol. 35, ed. Ofelia Zepeda.) Tucson: University of Arizona Press.

Beidler, Peter G., and Barton, Gay (1998). *A Reader's Guide to the Novels of Louise Erdrich.* Columbia: University of Missouri Press.

Bevis, William (1993). "Native American Novels: Homing In." In Richard F. Fleck (ed.), *Critical Perspectives on Native American Fiction*, 15–45. Washington DC: Three Continents.

Dorris, Michael (Modoc), and Erdrich, Louise (Turtle Mountain Chippewa) (1988). "Who Owns the Land?" *New York Times Magazine*, 4 Sept., pp. 32ff.

Erdrich, Louise (Turtle Mountain Chippewa) (1985). "Where I Ought to Be: A Writer's Sense of Place." *New York Times Book Review*, 28 July, 1, 24–5.

Erdrich, Louise (Turtle Mountain Chippewa) (1986). *The Beet Queen.* New York: Holt.

Erdrich, Louise (Turtle Mountain Chippewa) (1988). *Tracks.* New York: Holt.

Erdrich, Louise (Turtle Mountain Chippewa) (1993a). *The Bingo Palace.* New York: HarperCollins.

Erdrich, Louise (Turtle Mountain Chippewa) (1993b). *Love Medicine*, new and expanded version. New York: Holt. (First publ. 1984.)

Erdrich, Louise (Turtle Mountain Chippewa) (1996). *Tales of Burning Love.* New York: HarperCollins.

Erdrich, Louise (Turtle Mountain Chippewa) (2001). *The Last Report on the Miracles at Little No Horse.* New York: HarperCollins.

Hogan, Linda (Chickasaw) (1990). *Mean Spirit.* New York: Atheneum.

Mathews, John Joseph (Osage) (1988). *Sundown.* Norman: University of Oklahoma Press. (First publ. 1934.)

Momaday, N. Scott (Kiowa) (1969). *The Way to Rainy Mountain.* Albuquerque: University of New Mexico Press.

Momaday, N. Scott (Kiowa) (1999). *House Made of Dawn.* New York: Perennial Classics. (First publ. 1968.)

Momaday, N. Scott (Kiowa) (2001). "The Man Made of Words." In John L. Purdy and James S. Ruppert (eds.), *Nothing but the Truth: An Anthology of Native American Literature*, 82–93. Upper Saddle River, NJ: Prentice-Hall.

Ortiz, Simon J. (Acoma Pueblo) (1992). *Woven Stone.* (Sun Tracks: An American Indian Literary Series, vol. 21, ed. Ofelia Zepeda and Larry Evers.) Tucson: University of Arizona Press.

Owens, Louis (Choctaw/Cherokee) (1992). *Other Destinies: Understanding the American Indian Novel.* (American Indian Literature and Critical Studies Series, ed. Gerald Vizenor, vol. 3.) Norman: University of Oklahoma Press.

Shanley, Kathryn W. (Nakota) (2001) "'Born from the need to say': Boundaries and Sovereignties in Native American Literary and Cultural Studies." *Paradoxa* 15, 3–16.

Silko, Leslie Marmon (Laguna Pueblo) (1977). *Ceremony.* New York: Viking.

Silko, Leslie Marmon (Laguna Pueblo) (1991). *Almanac of the Dead.* New York: Simon & Schuster.

Silko, Leslie Marmon (Laguna Pueblo) (2001). "Language and Literature from a Pueblo Indian Perspective." In John L. Purdy and James S. Ruppert (eds.), *Nothing but the Truth: An Anthology of Native American Literature*, 159–65. Upper Saddle River, NJ: Prentice-Hall.

Tapahonso, Luci (Navajo) (1993). *Sáanii Dahataał the Women are Singing.* Tucson: University of Arizona Press.

Tapahonso, Luci (Navajo) (1998) *Blue Horses Rush In: Poems and Stories.* Tucson: University of Arizona Press.

Warrior, Robert Allen (Osage) (1995). *Tribal Secrets: Recovering American Indian Intellectual Traditions.* Minneapolis: University of Minnesota Press.

Zitkala Ša (Gertrude Simmons Bonnin, Yankton Sioux) (1986). *American Indian Stories.* Lincoln: University of Nebraska Press. (First publ. 1921.)

11

Borders, Bodies, and Regions: The United States and the Caribbean

Vera M. Kutzinski

Since national borders regulate the movements of individual bodies and the shape of collective ones, the ways in which they are imagined, enforced, and (one hopes) rethought have palpable ramifications for how many Americans live their daily lives, both within and outside of that nation José Martí was fond of calling "the colossus of the North." How national borders are viewed also has a profound impact on the formation of literary canons, intellectual constructs that, in the United States and elsewhere, have traditionally been deployed to sustain fictions of national impermeability. One of the centerpieces of the American literary canon constructed during the post-World War II institutionalization of American Studies was 1949 Nobel laureate William Faulkner, a regionalist with roots in the Old South. To the US Cold War academy, Faulkner's novels epitomized the moral integrity of liberal humanism and, along with it, a coherent vision of the nation, with all of its borders intact. What such canonizing readings conveniently ignored, however, was that Faulkner's major novels push hard against the very values they were deemed to sustain, including the idea of national integrity.

I define "nation" as a provisional political construct that delineates, and restricts, cultural kinship; a "closed world," in Wilson Harris's phrase. A nation, then, is a political construct without a necessarily coincident cultural entity (the latter changes, the former remains static). Culture pulls at politics, at institutions, while politics tries to bring perceived cultural chaos back in line, violently if need be. The trouble that nationalisms cause, both practically and theoretically, has to do with the fact that the political entities we call nations are not static at all but change all the time, in relation to each other as well as internally, as certain borders become more permeable. In response to such permeability, nations try to limit our ability to imagine kinship beyond familial boundaries.

Regionalism, much maligned because of the parochialism with which it has often been associated in literary study, may, ironically enough, offer interesting ways in which to rethink nationalism, for, as Michael Kowalewski points out in chapter 1 of this volume, "Every area of [the United States] teems with the historical and cultural footprints of multiple populations (some recent, many long-established over generations)" – and, one might add, too many of them neglected or forgotten. What I have in mind is a sort of hemispheric regionalism, one that allows us to look at how cultural regions do *and* do not overlap with the actual geographic shape of political entities such as the United States. The hemispheric region of particular interest to me, because of its remarkable cultural diversity, is the Caribbean basin whose rimlands include not only Colombia, Venezuela, and a variety of Central American countries but also, notably, Faulkner's South. From a Northern perspective, the Caribbean has been home to many shadowy images, images that, though attractively exotic, also raise the specter of unsafe, and hence undesirable, mixing, cultural and especially racial. One particularly active specter that has haunted the United States' colossal northern body politic has been Haiti, which in 1804 became "the second country in the New World to declare itself independent from colonial Europe" and "the first state in the New World to declare itself 'other'" (Dash 1998: 43). Representative of the Caribbean to many, Haiti has affected New World writers' literary imaginations in unexpected ways. Faulkner, as we shall see, is no exception.

Bodies, individual and collective, stabilize not only political ideologies but also literary representations and ways of reading them. What sorts of bodies are called upon to ground literary representations of America and Americanness, and how did those bodies change during the course of the twentieth century? Because the space of one essay is far too limited to provide anything even close to a full account of these changes, I focus on two prominent examples. The first one, from fairly early in the last century, is the body of the notorious Thomas Sutpen from William Faulkner's 1936 novel *Absalom, Absalom!*, whose persistent ghost can easily be placed in the illustrious company of James Weldon Johnson's not-quite-autobiographical Ex-Colored Man (1912), Edith Wharton's ruddy-faced Donald Trump figure Elmer Moffat (from *The Custom of the Country* [1913]), Fitzgerald's "gorgeous" Jay Gatsby (1925), and Hemingway's "sick" Jake Barnes from *The Sun Also Rises* (1926). My second example is Jamaican novelist Erna Brodber's young African-American ethnographer Ella Townsend, from *Louisiana* (1994), whose literary company includes figures such as Michelle Cliff's interstitial Harry/Harriet from *No Telephone to Heaven* (1986) and Maryse Condé's crafty Tituba from *Moi Tituba sorcière noire de Salem* (*I, Tituba, Black Witch of Salem* [1986]). More specifically, I want to know what exactly happens to the assumed integrity of the identities of humans and nations alike when the bodies that are supposed to stabilize, or ground, surreptitiously "turn" into someone, or something, else. Such figurative turning (or troping) is easily imagined as an act of trespass that, especially in contexts marked by cultural/racial differences, is cast, more often than not, in the vocabulary of adulteration and contamination. Through my readings of Faulkner's and Brodber's respective texts, I suggest that bodies – of persons, characters, texts, and nations – become perhaps not so much other but equivocal when they are exposed to repressed cultural memories. In the particular hemispheric context of the Americas, this equivocation registers on bodies as barely legible traces of memories of "collaborative interdependence across imaginary borders of race, nation, and origin" (Roach 1996: xi).

The traces of collaborative interdependence that concern me most in this essay have to do with the varied, vexing, and obscured cultural relationships between the United States and the Caribbean, which the fictions of both Faulkner and Brodber address. I particularly want to call attention to the ways in which writers from different parts of the Caribbean, such as Wilson Harris from Guyana and Edouard Glissant from Martinique, redraw the southernmost borders of the imperiously capitalized American "South" in their respective critical/theoretical rereadings of novels by Faulkner,[1] in *The Womb of Space: The Cross-Cultural Imagination* (1983) and *Faulkner, Mississippi* (1996). What both Harris and Glissant value in Faulkner's writing is that it "takes on the risk of revelation rather than simply being an expose, a presentation, an analysis, a description, a story" (Glissant 1996: 141), and I would add that this "risking" of revelation is precisely the reason why Faulkner's novels have had such a tremendous impact on twentieth-century African-American, Latin American, and Caribbean writers, including Erna Brodber. By retelling the life of Zora Neale Hurston, a contemporary of Faulkner's and another "Southern" writer who trespassed into Caribbean regions, Brodber's 1994 novel *Louisiana* renders more explicit the kind of inter-American cultural traffic that Faulknerian narrative often only implies.

I

Most striking about the Sutpen saga in Faulkner's *Absalom, Absalom!* is its insistently trans-American reach: the novel's geography extends both northward to Canada and southward to the Caribbean (culturally speaking, this may well be the same direction, given the history of Caribbean immigration to Canada since the nineteenth century). It is the Americas, not just the southern parts of the United States, that constitute Faulkner's literary and cultural "region," and he, in turn, is reconstituted by the perspectives and claims of this larger territory.[2] Acknowledging that a trans-American context is either implicitly or explicitly relevant to many of Faulkner's fictions enables us to read him as a different kind of regionalist: the kind who crosses national boundaries with impunity even as he stays within his own county. As is clear from the work of other prominent US American modernists, notably Williams Carlos Williams and Hart Crane, both of whom had family connections to the Caribbean (see Kutzinski 1987: ch. 1; Mariani 1999: 261ff.), one need not be an expatriate to participate in such transnational crossings. Even Fitzgerald's Gatsby ventures to the West Indies at some point (see Niessen de Abruña 1989: 136). Critics' traditional preoccupation with the specifically trans-*Atlantic* aspects of modernism have kept modernists in the Americas oddly separate from one another, and from political and cultural events in other parts of the New World.[3] Yet, as I have insisted elsewhere (Kutzinski 1987), inter-American readings are vital to understanding American (literary) modernisms and hence contemporary literary production in the Americas. I imagine both as a series of partly obscured conversations that serve to remind us that "America," that ever-slippery space that is always both "ours" and other, was never really a "nation." Nor is it likely to become one in the future; and herein lies a (to me) welcome opportunity for re-imagining processes of cultural affiliation beyond familiar, that is, familial, notions of identity.

"For the Faulknerians," Glissant points out in *Faulkner, Mississippi*, "wandering is a person's destiny. . . . Wandering . . . is the capacity to maintain oneself in living suspension, far from foundational and systematic certainties. . . . Wandering is a confused setting down of roots: This is a precaution that the great, foundational works established, something their partisans forget when they focus only on the excluding elements of the works" (Glissant 1996: 113–17). The "strong sense of interconnected roots and plantings, of a new poetics," that wandering/migration confers upon Faulkner's characters is linked to the difficulty of criticizing one's community and yet remaining part of it, which runs through all of his major novels, fraught as they are with contradictions and inconsistencies (Glissant 1996: 227). Barbara Ladd's suggestion that Faulkner himself was most interested in "the persistence of history in the New World – in the discourse of New World speakers – and its capacities to undermine official U.S. innocence" (Ladd 1996: 144) is entirely consistent with Glissant's claims. This "persistence of history" within Faulkner's unreconciled strivings makes available for critical scrutiny the cultural and political isolationism out of which myths of national innocence are wrought. Glissant's discussion of Faulkner's failure to reclaim the epic mode in his narrative fictions suggests the centrality of concepts such as disequilibrium and disunity to such an investigation: "Epic song and tragic disclosure have traditionally had as their purpose a restoration of a lost unity. Through their intervention, we are guaranteed to regain it. The Faulknerian intervention accepts the impossibility of a return to equilibrium. This is the source of its originality and force. . . . It is in the realist prose of the Snopeses that epic interrogation is extinguished and erased" (Glissant 1996: 98–100). In the acceptance of this impossibility, an "unwritten epic of the fabulous cocreation" of circum-Atlantic cultures (Roach 1996: 286) begins to articulate itself. Here, revisionist readings can take hold and work to implode myths of national innocence and cultural purity by exposing such myths to the unruly bodies of others – unruly in their darkness, unquiet in their association with the Caribbean, that supposed place of magic and sorcery. If Euro-American modernism's at once most troubling and most fascinating racial others are typically of African descent, in fictions about the Southern United States especially, they are often very specifically nonwhite West Indians – really a redundant formulation to my mind – entering the country through the portals of New Orleans, the "foreign" city where Faulkner's *Absalom* meets Brodber's *Louisiana* (see Roach 1996: 63; Tallant 1962: 19–22).[4]

New Orleans has functioned historically and imaginatively as link between the United States and the West Indies, that problematic territory even more south than the "South," a region so persistent in its capitalization that it does not admit the existence of anything beyond its southern borders. Glissant notes: "in many respects, Louisiana is close to the Caribbean and especially to the Antilles: the plantation system, the thrilling persistence of Creole language, a linguistic background of French, and, most blatantly in all of these slave societies, the insistent suffering and the Negro runaways . . . one emphatically says 'the South,' with a capital 'S,' as though it represents an absolute, as though we other people of the south, to the south of the capitalized South, never existed" (Glissant 1996: 29–30). In *Absalom*, "the South" is pulled into the Caribbean in ways that undermine, even reverse, the US imperialist ambitions that are part of the historical record; in the novel, the "South" is part of the Caribbean, not vice versa. Faulkner's Yoknapatawpha county, to Glissant, "is linked with its immediate surroundings, the Caribbean and Latin American, by the damnation and miscegenation born of the rape of slavery – that is, by what the county creates and represses at the same time" (1996: 87–8). In the same way that the living are not entirely free to remember and to forget as they please, the Caribbean and Latin America are no longer just a potential political possession, a territory parts of which have variously been invaded or annexed by the United States since the Spanish–American War: Cuba, Haiti, Grenada, and of course Puerto Rico and the US Virgin Islands. In cultural terms, the southernmost parts of the United States are really rimlands of the Caribbean, and have been so ever since slaves were traded between the two areas, well before the Louisiana Purchase in 1803. Their unacknowledged rimland status has all kinds of imaginative, political implications. Wilson Harris was one of the first to call attention to them.

In *The Womb of Space*, Harris explicitly claims Faulknerian narrative for the Caribbean – or has the Caribbean claim it for itself – through a "cross-cultural" reading of *Intruder in the Dust* (1948) in which Harris speculates on the possibility of "subterranean" links between the American South and the Caribbean islands. By locating the source of racial conflict in *Intruder* beyond the American South, Harris makes it quite clear that racialism is a hemispheric concern. Specifically, Harris connects *Intruder* with the Haitian phenomenon of the "sent dead" (more popularly known as zombies) in a reading that complicates George Lamming's more nostalgic perspective on West Indian peasant cultures as gateways into authenticity, in *The Pleasures of Exile* (1960) and elsewhere. Harris's purpose is to uncover the "hidden *rapport* between Faulkner's intuitive imagination and Lucas Beauchamp's anonymous black kith and kin in the Caribbean," the site, or image, of which is Gowrie's corpse and its function as a voodoo spell cast on Beauchamp:

> That the corpse of Vinson Gowrie may be interpreted as ceaseless nightmare of history or institutionalized spectre of prejudice 'sent against' Lucas Beauchamp enriches the depth potential of *Intruder in the Dust* and suggests an activity of image beyond given verbal convention into non-verbal arts of the imagination in the womb of cultural space as though an *unstructured force* arbitrates or mediates between articulate or verbal signs and silent or eclipsed voices of nemesis in folk religions whose masks or sculptures subsist upon implicit metaphors of death-in-life, life-in-death. (Harris 1983: xix)

In this and other readings throughout *Womb*, Harris is interested in the "activity of image" (that is, image clusters) to suggest what he calls an "irrational coherence" between New World cultures in "the womb of cultural space" represented here by the dead body of a white Southerner. To read this unquiet, soulless body, presumed by most of the other characters to have been slain by a black man's bullet, as the specter of a violent, nightmarish history of racial conflict makes good sense. Gowrie's corpse, or better, the twin corpses found in his grave, represents the "evil" conscience of institutionalized Southern racism, and the body's uncertain location in *Intruder* unsettles characters' (and readers') race-based biases and social hierarchies. When Harris re-animates Faulkner's textual effigy by making it speak, if you will, of "black arts" of Haitian vodun in a conversation mediated by Alfred Métraux's famous ethnographic study *Voodoo in Haiti* (1958),[5] he turns Vinson Gowrie's corpse into the composite archetype of the "magic corpse." This "magic corpse" is sent against Lucas Beauchamp, "the Intruder who disturbs the order of things" and who can now be read, with the help of his French Creole surname, as a black Jacobin (see Glissant 1996: 89).[6] This is the other, apparently dead, tradition with which Faulkner's "magic corpse" is also invested and which it makes again accessible as an imaginative resource.[7] As Harris puts it,

> To arrive in a tradition that appears to have died is complex renewal and revisionary momentum *sprung from originality and the activation of primordial resources within a living language*. We arrive backwards even as we voyage forwards. This is the phenomenon of simultaneity in the imagination of times past and future, a future that renews time in its imaginary response to gestating resources in *the womb of the present and the past*. It is unlike the linear biases that prevail in conventional fiction. To arrive in a place where we are not brings into play transitive chords within densities, transitive dimensionalities that unlock doors within the body of language itself. Arrival then differs from photographic description. Arrival then is a concert between unfathomable psyche and place-in-depth, place displaced, recovered in the living Word. (Harris 1999: 187, emphases added)

Harris connects "arrival" to epic in ways reminiscent of Kamau Brathwaite's poetic trilogy *The Arrivants* (1973) and implicitly, proleptically, takes Glissant's point about Faulkner's acceptance of disequilibrium a step further. Where Glissant talks about Faulkner's poetics of failure, which may result in stasis, Harris perceives possibilities for conversion and renewal. "Epic," Harris writes, "is an *arrival* in an architecture of space that is *original* to our age, an *arrival* in multi-dimensionality that alerts us to some kind of transfiguration of appearances. . . . [Epic] offers a renewed scrutiny . . . of the unfulfilled promises of tradition and of a descent and ascent all over again into inequalities, unequal cultures. It offers in stages a conversion of such inequalities into numinous inexactitudes" (1999: 187–94). In contemporary literatures, especially those of Latin America and other regions of postcolonization (in Patrick Hogan's term), we have come to know such "numinous inexactitides" under a different name, a misappellation perhaps: magical realism. The "shadow" of Charles Bon in *Absalom* is the residue of a dead body that may well belong to this realm of the "subterranean quakings of everyday life," in Glissant's turn of phrase. For Bon's shadowy existence marks an imperfection within Thomas Sutpen's obsession with "absolute lineage" in the form of racial purity and within the "absolute linearity" of his American Dream narrative (Glissant 1996: 191).

"Absolute linearity" is as divisive as "pure lineage" – what Hemingway's Jake Barnes, in *The Sun Also Rises*, calls "purity of line" – and as imaginatively deficient. In fact, we may say that Sutpen suffers from an "illiterate imagination." He will not imagine himself outside of the Hegelian master–slave paradigm. Despite himself, he replicates that paradigm and its binarisms, and misses whatever opportunity he might have had to modify it or reject it outright. Sutpen's peculiar obsession is perhaps best described in Harris's words, as a "perverse commitment to privileged frame or family, a hidden authoritarianism" (1999: 238). Ironically, Sutpen is the one who remains in bondage, and the significance of illegitimate son "Bon" 's last name regresses from the possible "bonding" (as in kinship, potentially non-familial), back into "bondage" – bondage to a past made up of an entrenched system of social and racial divisions (see also Blake 1985: 136). Carolyn Porter notes that "Sutpen not only refuses to give his son the name of his own father, but denies him the name of any father, as the antebellum code dictated for all black sons, who thus remained legally 'boys'" (1995: 191). The slippage between linearity and lineage helps connect Sutpen's denial of his oldest son, the (by some accounts) racially mixed Charles Bon, to Sutpen's revisionist account of Haitian history, and to Faulkner's deliberate mis-dating of the Haitian Revolution.[8] Sutpen's is an astonishing tale, doubly mediated by Quentin's father and grandfather, of how he went to the West Indies and defeated a slave rebellion there in order to establish his claims to whiteness and to empire. This struggle is ritualistically re-enacted throughout the novel in recurring scenes of Sutpen fighting with his "niggers" whom he comes to resemble more and more in the process, a resemblance of which he seems oddly unaware. Rosa, through a slip of her syntax, identifies Sutpen as "one of the negroes himself" (Faulkner 1990: 21). So inextricably is Sutpen tied to *Absalom*'s Haitian episode that, in spite of his willful, almost desperate claims to whiteness throughout the novel, his position in the text is equivalent to that of an other, specifically a racial other. (Class, in this novel, is almost always represented in terms of race – which is not unusual.[9]) Sutpen misrecognizes himself by repeatedly pledging allegiance to closed systems – dynasties – and to linearity in the form of genealogy. He seems unaware that he, Thomas Sutpen, represents the very element that all these systems seek to exclude, indeed, on whose exclusion their very coherence depends. Sutpen, in fact, is what James Snead calls "the carrier of an originless blackness that clandestinely inserts its way into the presumably pure genealogies of Southern whiteness" (1986: 113). Sutpen's social and racial position, and with it his potential "lineage," is highly unstable from the very start, much as he would like for it not to be once he has cut himself off from his poor white (West) Virginian past.[10] The more he tries to stabilize his lineage and the identity he seeks to derive from it, the more unstable both become, and Sutpen has to devise strategies to keep things under control. One such strategy is the attempt to reproduce himself in the shape of sons; but, like Wallace Stevens's comedic Crispin, Sutpen turns out to be the fallen paterfamilias who, with his sons either dead or otherwise absent, is left with "daughters with curls" (Faulkner 1990: 43),[11] a phrase with a surprisingly apt meaning, especially when one considers not only Judith but also the conspicuously "motherless" Clytie.

Of course, as Richard Godden points out, Thomas Sutpen could not possibly have suppressed a slave revolt in Haiti in 1827, where slavery had been abolished in 1803. The island where Sutpen should have gone (might have gone?) at that time is Cuba – for where else would one travel to buy slaves (illegally) in the 1820s and 1830s, and where else might one have been involved in suppressing a slave revolt around that time? Charles Bon, whose French name affiliates him with the "gens libres de couleur" of New Orleans, even has the requisite Hispanic Caribbean connections – his mother Eulalia Bon is purportedly a "Spaniard" – to make such a rereading plausible.[12] But the historic connections between Cuba and Haiti – and there were many – do not get us around the fact that Faulkner either deliberately or unwittingly misdates the Haitian Revolution (1791–1804) in *Absalom*, a novel published only two years after the US occupation of Haiti (1915–34) ended (see Godden 1994a: 489). Haiti displaced, some have argued, becomes the kind of "wild alien space" traditionally conducive to romance and adventure, as well as to colonial (and more contemporary) encounters of the imperialistic kind with which we have ample familiarity. It would seem that *Absalom* does little to defamiliarize that picture when it casts Sutpen in the role of the American colonizer who suppresses (single-handedly!) a full-fledged slave revolt, buys his slaves for export, and "innocently" marries a girl of "Spanish" blood, who promptly bears him a "mulatto" son, or what Glissant, arguing that "there are no mulattos in Faulkner," would call a "Black-and-White character" (1996: 90).

But there may be a more productive way to read Haiti in this novel than as a "wild alien space," and a way to think differently about Faulkner's blatant and entirely unsurprising disrespect for linear history.[13] This disrespect in *Absalom* effectively loosens the first black republic from its moorings in place and in a certain kind of historical specificity and, conceptually speaking, sets it afloat in the Sargasso Sea. We can well imagine that it even drifts into the Atlantic, where it travels north and east on faster, even more treacherous currents. It is not difficult to see how Haiti, as a floating structure, almost a projectile, comes to represent the entire Caribbean in ways familiar from Antonio Benítez Rojo's postmodernist "repeating island." In the process of drifting, seemingly without destination, without purpose, this structure, now a vessel, reproduces itself (and mutates) upon entering different spaces, temporal and geographic. Haiti, unable to be contained geographically and temporally, becomes an archetype grafted onto those other spaces, where it leaves traces of Jacobin rebellion and spreads cultural Africanisms of various kinds that, surreptitiously but persistently, call into doubt paradigms that encode and disseminate beliefs in racial purity, as well as attempts to separate the edifice of white culture from its foundation of slave labor. Godden suggests that "Haiti seeps associatively from 'shadow' into the very fabric of the master's house" and that it escapes "through 'Bon' into the very goods that Rosa would inherit" (1993: 56). What is made available through this floating signifier is an entirely different kind of history, one in which "Haiti," rather than being merely the "dumping ground for all Southern white anxiety" (Stanchich 1996: 607), becomes a dynamic chronotope (in M. M. Bakhtin's coinage) constituted by both inter-American and interoceanic cultural and political relations. That Faulkner, by referencing Haiti as the only successful black revolutionary country at the time, may have wished "to foreground the continuous potential for revolution within the institution of slavery" (Godden 1994a: 494) strikes me as too optimistic a reading of a novel that does, after all, end on a striking note of tautology, or autism.

Because of his association with the place/space where he literally remakes himself and which thus becomes his substitute origin, Sutpen must be read as a metonym of the "West Indies." It is this particular bon(d) that the novel's narrators seek to withhold or deny; in order for them to separate Sutpen from "blackness," the narrators (and Sutpen himself) create the shadowy figure of Charles Bon as Sutpen's "black" double. So Quentin and Shreve, in whose narrative Bon most manifests himself most clearly, "as a last resort, restore the black, whose import as repeated absence everyone had overlooked all along" and thus produce a (to some) more credible narrative in which Sutpen's whiteness is ultimately safeguarded, no longer equivocal, or "shadowy." As it is racially inscribed, Bon's body not only becomes visible in its blackness; it also becomes an object. As Godden notes, "Eulalia does not give birth to a son but to goods, and in naming him as such Sutpen declares Bon dead, and himself an owner not a father"; Quentin and Shreve's narrative choices repeat, and consolidate, Bon's initial translation from "nominal son into real property" (Godden 1994b: 708). The historical legacy of slavery tends to make racially marked bodies – be they persons, fictional characters, or nations – behave as if they were objects in relation to other, racially unmarked, and hence invisible bodies, that is, bodies perceived as white. Racial "mixing," then, would describe a situation in which a person and an object enter into messy, politically undesirable contact, sexual or otherwise. The knowledge (and progeny) incurred by such contacts is placed in the realm of the uncanny, or "unhomely," as Homi Bhabha has it (1994: 9), because it threatens to unravel the fabric of marriage, family, region, and nation – all, of course, closely intertwined. To see *Absalom* as an inter-American text, we only have to extend this idea of politically undesirable contact from human bodies to bodies politic.

If, however, we do not follow Quentin and Shreve in reading Bon as black, some intriguingly different possibilities emerge. "If Bon is one of the white men, as he says," argues Snead,

> then the reversal of the novel's standard reading is complete. It is incorrect to say that the white Thomas Sutpen rejects his black son Charles Bon. Rather, Sutpen (like Burch in *Light in August*) may be considerably "blacker" than we thought – and perhaps most

black where he wishes to be most white. In turning his black Caucasian son away from his door, Sutpen has simply merged with the same "monkey dressed nigger" who first rebuffed him at a front door as a child. He, the father, has become black by turning back his putatively black son (we never learn whether in fact Bon had black blood). (Snead 1986: 116–17)

The focus of the novel, then, is on Sutpen's being precisely what he thinks he is not: he is neither father nor white, at least not in relation to Charles Bon. Glissant argues that "Creolization is the very thing that offends Faulkner: metissage and miscegenation, plus their unforeseeable consequences. . . . The Caribbean, land of Creolization, would not attract Faulkner. The inextricable is not the same as mixture. Sutpen encounters his first failure to found a dynasty in Haiti. . . . Sutpen speaks Creole, as do all Planters in Haiti and Guadeloupe. This represents the very things he wants to kill in himself" (Glissant 1996: 83). That Sutpen misrecognizes himself in his "innocence," and that the narrators perpetuate this situation of misrecognition, highlights the dire need for the reader's "heightened self-reflexion," lest she be caught up in this novelistic "study in implication" (Reichardt 1997: 623; Ladd 1996: 155). My point is this: If only Thomas Sutpen had embraced his purported mulatto son Charles Bon across racial divides, all still would not have been well in Yoknapatawpha County. For *Absalom, Absalom!* is not just family romance gone sour because the rejected firstborn son refuses to be denied – much in the same way, for instance, that Cirilo Villaverde's irrepressible mulatta Cecilia Valdés does, gender differences notwithstanding. Nor is Faulkner's novel simply "an American imperialist representation of the Caribbean" in which the foreign-born Charles Bon plays the role of the "Caribbean homeless son" desirous of, and of course prevented from, "naturalization," that is, from being legally assimilated into the US American body politic (see Stanchich 1996: 613, 611). Affiliation is a much more complicated affair than that, for in Faulkner's novel the family, and with it the nation-state in all of its romantic certitude, is very much representative of a doomed order (Nichols 1995: 167), one marked by rejection, vengeance, and fratricide. The problem of/in this novel is ultimately the difficulty of accepting the existence of strangers within in the self, and this makes it a very untidy endeavor. If *Absalom* is a novel about the failure of self-sufficiency, it is also a novel about the failure of Romantic individualism's denial of "the life of strangers in the self." It shows how the latter failure tears at the fabric of the novel whose development runs parallel to that of the nation-state. Harris renders the connection in this way:

Inadequacies began to surface in conventional narratives of stereotypical purity and these evolved into numinous inexactitudes within which the Imagination was empowered by the sacred to pitch its parameters of vision into unsuspected places, unsuspected heights and depths. As a consequence a simultaneity occurred not only between a variety of features and pigmentations in variable identity but between intimate reality and stranger reality. That simultaneity broke a purely linear persuasion, it broke a linear addiction to a progressive chasm between the past and the present. It revealed that however determined we are to maintain absolute linearity in fictions of reality the past is still active in the present moment, it still arrives in the future, and continues to store ambivalent pressures that fall below the level of creative and re-creative consciousness, pressures that continue to cement our fears and biases within the institutional life of the nation-state. (Harris 1999: 206)

This tearing at the fabric of the novel is, as Harris well recognizes, tantamount to an exposure of the nineteenth-century novel's pretension to exact representation in the form of literary realism. To readmit "strangers," notably racial strangers, into constructions of both individual and communal selves, the novel has to negotiate what Glissant, commenting on Faulkner's poetics, calls the "relationship between what is narrated and what is unsayable" (1996: 140). As a result of such negotiations, literary realism comes to acknowledge the uncanny (Harris's "numinous inexactitudes") as an integral part of its internal makeup, and this acknowledgment "turns" realism into magical realism. Godden hints at such an acknowledgment of the unspeakable when he calls "Bon . . . a revenant living among the inferences of Rosa's narrative; which is to say, he haunts her lower semantic levels" (Godden 1993: 58). In *Louisiana*, the haunting is not confined to those levels but encompasses the entire narrative.

II

In *Louisiana*, Erna Brodber revisits the dead's intensely complicated modes of address in the fictionalized context of ethnographic fieldwork by exploring what happens to narrative when scientific "detachment" fails and the anthropologist-as-observer turns into a full-fledged participant, and an involuntary one at that. Lamming's account of the Haitian Ceremony of Souls at the beginning of *The Pleasures of Exile* helps us understand what is at stake in this novel's representations of New World cultural memory as spirit possession.

This Ceremony of the Souls is regarded by the Haitian peasant as a solemn communion; for he hears, at first hand, the secrets of the Dead. The celebrants are mainly relatives of the deceased who, ever since their death, have been locked in Water. It is the duty of the Dead to return and offer, on this momentous night, a full and honest report of their past relations with the living. . . . It is the duty of the Dead to speak, since their release from that purgatory of Water cannot be realized until they have fulfilled the contract which this ceremony symbolizes. The Dead need to speak if they are going to enter that eternity which will be their last and permanent Future. The living demand to hear whether there is any need for forgiveness, for redemption; whether in fact there may be any guide which may help them towards reforming their present condition. Different as they may be in their present state of existence, those alive and those now Dead – their ambitions point to a similar end. They are interested in their Future. (Lamming 1992: 9–10)

That the dead *must* speak to the living, who, in fact, "demand to hear" them, is but a different way of talking about the transfigurative "arrival in multi-dimensionality," in Harris's phrasing, that is at the center of Brodber's novel, in which anthropological fieldwork unexpectedly turns into just such an arrival. In a crucial passage in *Louisiana*, budding ethnographer Ella Townsend Kohl reflects on her involuntary crossing of the line one expects more decisively to separate the living from the dead: "At least now I know from the horse's mouth what St. Mary has been expecting of me. I know too from that same horse, that there is a name for that state in which your body is depressed into physical collapse and something else is activated, rather like an injection needle is pushed forward and the shell in which it resides, recedes. 'Getting over.' I prefer to call it hegemony of the spirit. I had experienced hegemony of the spirit, I could again and would" (Brodber 1994: 98). Although Ella's account of her experience as "hegemony of the spirit" seems to maintain the mind/body duality whose applicability to non-Western cultures has rightly been questioned, the body's depression into "physical collapse" during spirit possession is not figured as "rigid asceticism" (Deren 1970: 9). Instead, it is a process of activation, in which the body behaves as if it had been injected with the drug-like substance of cultural memory. The dramatic changes in such a body's behavior cause problems that compel us, among other things, to re-imagine the relationship between bodies and writing. For if the writing that Ella produces stands in for her own materially absent body – an absence accentuated because she is deceased by the time her manuscript finds a public readership – it follows that this textual body would also manifest uncanny traces of "collaborative interdependence," both between the living and the dead, and, more specifically, between the Southern United States and the Caribbean. In *Louisiana*, the Caribbean, like Faulkner's Haiti, is located somewhere in between the United States and Europe, and the United States and Africa, and its liminality affects that national body known as the United States in ways similar to what happens to Ella's body, and what happens to Vinson Gowrie's body in Harris's reading of *Intruder*: namely, it is dislocated, or, as Brodber's novel has it, it "is depressed into physical collapse and *something else* is activated" (emphasis added).

"Getting over" – or being carried across – signals Brodber's interest in disorienting narrative by way of dislocating cultural identity. From an historical perspective, Brodber's trope calls attention to the processes of migration that undergird the myriad conversations about the imagined cultural space of "America" among writers and texts separated by the waters of the Gulf of Mexico and the Sargasso Sea: conversations that appropriately temper the pretensions to exceptionalism which have a tendency to resurface periodically in US history. "Getting over" is an intertextual crossing of political – that is, national, though not necessarily linguistic – divides drawn and redrawn by ongoing practices of colonization and imperialism. Theoretically speaking, "getting over" is what Bhabha might call a "term of cultural engagement" (1994: 2) or what Harris apprehends as a sign of intercultural dialogue "beyond exact representation or seizure" (1999: 207). Influence paradigms cannot adequately account for what appear to be literal and figurative wanderings of the spirit, or "numinous inexactitudes," because such paradigms work to unify bodies of writing into literary traditions, defined usually along national or hemispheric lines. For that purpose, they channel intellectual traffic into the sorts of closed systems Brodber's novel seeks to break open by restaging the past and injecting, and animating, the present with the traces of the unspeakable, the uncanny, the numinously inexact.

Brodber's novel looks back from 1978, the date of the fictitious "Editor's Note," to the 1930s, when Ella first arrives in Louisiana, and the narrative's setting shifts between St. Mary's parish in rural Louisiana and a New Orleans alive with the legacy of legendary hoodoo priestess Marie Laveau.[14] Its text, as the "Editor's Note" informs us, is comprised of Ella's field notes, arranged in the form of a manuscript that "appeared on our desk" in "the early 1970s" (Brodber 1994: 3). In the manuscript, which is really a series of narrative fragments, Ella's notes and transcriptions are supplemented occasionally by her husband Reuben's comments – most notably, in an "Epilogue" dated April 1954 – and, even more significantly, by the voices of the dead women who "ride" her: Sue Anne Grant-King, Ella's deceased "native inform-ant," and her friends, notably Miss Lowly. The novel's "Prologue" already offers ample encouragement to read the character of Ella as a fictional version of Zora Neale Hurston:[15]

> We [the fictitious editors of The Black World Press] have not spent time verifying the existence of all the parties mentioned in this manuscript. We stopped at Ella Townsend. She did exist. Her last publication, according to our research, appeared in *Crisis* Vol XLVII 1935. [Note: There is no such volume of the *Crisis*; the year 1935 corresponds to volume 42, not 47.] We have also found evidence that she was one of the writers employed to the WPA, so be she in her last days petty thief, conjure woman, anthro-pologist, we do know that she started public life as a writer and was employed officially as such. (Brodber 1994: 4)

Though Hurston, unlike Brodber's character, had a patron who supported her finan-cially, she, like Ella Townsend, studied anthropology with Franz Boas at Columbia University (18), or, more accurately, at Barnard College, and, being short of money, signed on the Works Progress Administration's Federal Theater Project in New York City in the fall of 1935 (see Hemenway 1977: 218, 223, 225). Although Hurston never published in the *Crisis*, she, like Ella, conducted field work in the American South, not in Louisiana but in her native Florida. *Louisiana* places itself quite explicitly in the context not so much of Hurston's novels – although Ella makes a point of telling Mammy that she is "also a writer" (Brodber 1994: 18) – as of Hurston's anthropological writings in *Mules and Men* (1935) and *Tell My Horse* (1938). Much as these texts did well before professional anthropologists started to question their disciplinary constructs of scientific objectivity and to take seriously the distortions of what Hurston, in *Mules*, memorably calls "the spy glass of Anthro-pology" (Hurston 1990a: 1), Brodber's novel imagines what happens when an an-thropologist becomes an unwitting participant in the very cultural processes she observes. For Ella, not unlike the Hurston we encounter in the second part of *Mules*, which details her initiation as a hoodoo priestess in New Orleans, is chosen to be a "horse" by Sue Anne Grant-King (aka Mammy King) and Miss Lowly, who function as *loas* would in Haitian vodou. "Who is this gal with some bits of me and some bits of you?" asks Lowly of Mammy King in the first part of the novel, and their dialogue continues, somewhat mysteriously, since we do not yet know anything about these speakers and their position in Ella's narrative.

> "This be the kid?"
> "This is the horse. Will you ride?"
> "Will she do?"
> "Best I have ever seen. Will you ride?"
> "Let's see if she will."
>   (Brodber 1994: 17)

In clipped lines that theatrically intone and repeat key phrases, Brodber blurs the line between the living and the dead in a textual Ceremony of Souls in which the ancestors speak not to but *through* the voices, and the bodies, of the living. In *Louisiana*, even more so than in Brodber's second novel, *Myal* (1988), hemispheric spirit-world religions, such as Haitian vodou, Cuban santería, New Orleans hoodoo, and Jamaican kumina, or pukkumina, inspire narrative experiments with voices from different realms, or layers, of existence. Here, as in Pauline Melville's 1996 novel *The Ventriloquist's Tale*, narrative turns into a self-conscious site of ventriloquism as the dead struggle over the possession of the living. "These struggles," says Roach, "take many forms, of which the most remarkable are those in which the participatory technique of orature – people speaking in one another's voices – predominate" (1996: 69). But orature is deliberately participatory – it implies choice – whereas Brodber's Ella, at least initially, appears to have little choice in the matter, for, in *Louisiana*, memory seems even less deliberate than Rosa Coldfield suggests it is in Faulkner's *Absalom*, when she blurs the line between memory and dream: *"there is no such thing as memory: the brain recalls just what the muscles grope for: no more, no less: and its resultant sum is usually incorrect and false and worthy only of the name of dream"* (Faulkner 1990: 115; italics in original).

But even if Ella's lack of agency cannot but raise the question "of how far the state of possession is consciously willed and artfully crafted by the adept performer and how far it happens 'spontaneously' without the active collaboration of the cultist concerned" (Burton 1997: 223), the novel leaves ultimately no doubt about the theatrical nature of spirit possession as a public performance. Possession does not, as Burton argues, "consist . . . of some uncontrolled frenzy or trance but of a conventionally codified and crafted performance" that is a "a triadic phenomenon involving a spirit, a 'horse,' and spectators who may at some point in the proceedings be 'ridden' themselves" (1997: 225, 223). This implies, significantly, that the positions of spectator and performer are but temporarily assigned roles, because any member of the audience is potentially a "horse," a performer. Such characteristic lack of difference, or distance, between subject positions in this specific performative context helps us understand the seemingly involuntary aspect of Ella's own experience of being "ridden." It is not that Brodber's protagonist moves from having a detached, stable identity as Ella Townsend to the state of participatory instability that her name-change marks (Ella eventually becomes Lousiana). The difference between detachment and participation is but one of degree. What Ella experiences as involuntary "hegemony of spirit" is a function of her being initially unaware that what she, in her role of anthropologist, observes is a performance of community in which she, as audience, is already involved as a potential spirit vessel and performer. Ella's journal, then, chronicles her increasing awareness of the precise degree of her involvement.

While the "Editor's Note" in *Louisiana* offers a familiar perspective on anthropological fieldwork as a series of interviews, complete with realist props like a "recording machine" (Brodber 1994: 14), the novel's first chapter presents those interviews as a chaotic jumble of voices that we have, at that point, no way of identifying and distinguishing. What might be understood as a transition from a realist to a magical realist literary mode is rendered astonishingly clear as we move from the novel's prologue to its first chapter. In that chapter, it is as if we have been thrown right into the middle of a sort of jazz funeral (see Roach 1996: 277–81), reported from the perspective not of the living but of the one being buried, the spirit "cut loose" from its body.

> Anna do you remember? Can you still hear me singing it?
> It is the voice I hear
> the gentle voice I hear
> that calls me home?

They sang it for me Anna. They sang it for me, and Anna, had I any doubts about how they saw me and that in coming home I had done the right things, I could now lay them to rest along with that crumbled old body to keep in one piece had taken too much from many people these past four years. (Brodber 1994: 9)

Roach's observation that "Death often provided the occasion for the public performance of semisecret memories" (1996: 59) helps us appreciate the purpose of this intense and confounding instance of written orature, a nonlinear, dramatic combination of speech and song which, though highly stylized, seems curiously unmediated – straight from the horse's mouth, as it were. The beginning of our own readerly journey, in medias res, is the suspicion, the hope perhaps, that a "hidden agenda" – that is, some sort of plot – resides within these cryptic utterances. This is confirmed when we later learn that this chapter represents a transcription of the "other frequencies" that Ella's "black box" recorded above and beyond the expected voices of interviewer and interviewee. Ella, for instance, hears Mammy's recorded voice, as well as her own voice, articulate things that were never actually spoken between them, and she comments simply on what Harris would call a de-individualized manifestation of composite archetype: "Somebody spoke" (Brodber 1994: 28).

In *Louisiana*, voices tend to stray from their assigned bodies, physical and written, and in doing so strip those bodies of the constraints of assigned identities. Because voices can be connected to and inhabit more than one body, they become radically unlocatable, or unhomely, in the novel's narrative. Bodies, instead of grounding identities, function more as animate effigies in a collective memory play. The following scene is particularly poignant in this regard because it suggests an unsettling, objectifying proximity between Ella's physical body and the tape-recording machine. As her bones painfully echo others' voices, a severe strain is placed on Ella's physical body. In the end, the kind of remembering that she calls "hegemony of the spirit" renders the individual material body unnecessary, a broken and dispensable vessel.

> Pain. Bone breaking pain, shooting from my bones, silver bullets dead set on freedom, liberated, fill my room with lightening bugs and I am become Christmas, starlights, fireworks, holiday, *no flesh*. I have become a hot silver tree melted to a single conduit that courses through the gap above my temples from left to right, bending and fitting itself and doubling back to the center of my pendant. I am a silver stethoscope. Anyday now that line will be a silver thread, a strand, will slip through my pendant, be a streak of lightning. What a relief then to be making my way over the rainbow's mist! Til then, I am a metal aerial conductor tuned to the rainbow and this is the day of the pentecost. Must be. (Brodber 1994: 161; emphasis added)

Ella Kohl dies in January 1954, in the same month Hurston did six years later. All that is left for Reuben Kohl, for the editors of her manuscript, and for us to *touch* are papers – Ella's transcripts and journal entries: things that exist in the place of a body that, during the course of the novel, is gradually turning into an object. It is a "hot silver tree" turned into a "metal aerial conductor tuned to the rainbow." Ella's body is attenuated, transformed into a triangular line of "silver thread" that represents an abstract map of circum-Atlantic commerce and thus measures the triangular diasporic dimensions of her (and our) listening. As this image unravels and straightens into a "streak of lightning," Ella's body is reshaped into images of intense electrical brain activity. Ella's death and the ascension of her spirit on the symbolic day of the Pentecost is figured earlier in the novel, by the voice that used to reside in the now deceased body of Louise Lowly, as a state of "being translated" (Brodber 1994: 10), which is not so very different from what Ella calls "getting over." Ella's writing, like her husband's, is a substitute for her absent human body (hers more than his); all that remains of them, or all that in fact ever existed of them, is a collection of notes and fragments assembled into a manuscript, a body of writing that temporarily, and precariously, houses spirits and memories. This textual body is "magical" in the same way, in the same sense, that the spirit-injected body becomes a "magical thing" at the moment of possession (Roach 1996: 69). What New World African religions understand as spirit possession can also be described as a body's "numinous inexactitude." That moment of possession, then, is also the moment when field notes in a journal are translated into a novel, which is analogous to the transition from realism into the "numinous inexactitudes" of magical realism.

In literary situations, human bodies are necessarily displaced by textual bodies, which have a materiality all their own; but not all such displacements amount to arguments about performance and against realism. Nor do they all have the geocultural specificity on which Brodber's novel insists. Geography, as I mentioned earlier, is crucial in her novel, for what triggers the (to many readers) unexpected exchange between interviewer and subject is the fact that Ella is displaced, the "child" of two places: St. Mary's parish, Louisiana,[16] and St. Mary's parish, Jamaica, the very place Hurston visits in the opening chapters of *Tell My Horse*. Brodber, herself from Jamaica, makes the Islands part of her characters' imagined geo-genealogy. Ella, unlike Hurston, is Jamaican-born, which is why, according to Mammy, "she talk[s] in two different ways. Can't figure it –" (Brodber 1994: 19). "I left Jamaica when I was an infant," Ella admits to Anna, who really is the interviewer and is "totally in charge." "My parents had already migrated. They came back for me. They don't say very much about the place that they came from –" (p. 19). But the novel makes the Caribbean function as an image of kin independent of the conventional genealogies to which Ella appeals when she excitedly tells Mammy King: "Miss Anna, you are my family. My mother was a Grant. Her grandfather a Grant. All Grants are my cousins. They all born and grow where I come from" (p. 16). It is consistent with the fact that Ella is practically an orphan without any connections to her parents that Anna and Miss Lowly articulate kinship in alternative terms, terms that simultaneously emphasize the importance of geography, of the memory (or spirit) of place, and acknowledge the possibility for non-heterosexual structures of reproduction: "Two places can make children! Two women sire another?" (p. 17). That "in Vodou all 'horses,' male and female, are known by the female term *hounsi*" (Burton 1997: 225) is important to reading the transtemporal American communities Brodber constructs in *Louisiana* as feminine, quite regardless of the gender of their members. While this feminization is historically grounded in the prominence of women in positions of authority in vodou, it thematically extends the breakdown of gendered distinctions between public and private spaces (and activities) that are already implicit in the narrative performance of a journal/diary as a novel. That "Louisiana" is not just a place identifiable on a map but an intercalary place created by the merging of two characters' names – Louisa and Anna – calls attention to processes of feminization within language, within narrative itself. It suggests that narrative functions like a body might, or as an alternative to what a body might do: especially as an alternative to reproduction. Here, femininity does not mean reproduction; nor is the female body reduced to biological function as allegory of creativity. Brodber's communities are not created by way of physical reproduction, and it is conspicuous that Ella has no biological children. The model for community in this novel is not the family; blood relations are not privileged over other forms of kinship, such as writing itself, as a way of creating communities for the living and the dead. Like a "streak of lightning," or an elaborate root system that "subterraneously" connects the living with the dead, the Caribbean archipelago, which was once connected to the American continental land mass, functions in this novel as a gateway into an "anthropology of the dead? Celestial ethnography? Crazy" (Brodber 1994: 61). Not so crazy, really, because what else is cultural memory but an "anthropology of the dead"?

To say that, in *Louisiana*, it is the Caribbean that "rides" the US mainland is to claim that national boundaries are as permeable as the borders that separate the living from the dead. The dead must speak, and speak they do; it may be that we just don't know how to listen. If, at the numinous moment of possession, the point at which conversations between the dead and the living most challenge the body's assumed integrity, both human and textual bodies are "magically" invested, then national bodies can likewise turn into animate effigies and surrender their consolidated fictions of unity to the openness of memory play. Reading a text like *Louisiana*, then, means participating in the performance of a memory play, in which we, much like the characters, are made to remember experiences other than our own and, in the process, relinquish aspirations to purity and to mastery – of literary texts as much as of others. If such performances remind us that we have limited control over processes of history and of memory, we must nonetheless find ways to take responsibility for them, and for the strangers that live in our own country's regions. Acknowledging their existence is the first step in that direction.

NOTES

1   There are also recent Caribbean novels, notably Condé's *Moi, Tituba* (1986) and Cliff's *Free Enterprise* (1994), that extend their reach to other parts of the United States.

2   Glissant, following Toni Morrison's *Playing in the Dark*, has noted that "Faulkner's œuvre will be complete when it is revisited and made vital by African-Americans . . . And this completion will be achieved by a radically 'other' reading . . ." (1996: 55). My own argument resists Glissant's notion of completion, or completeness, which implies an endpoint to a process of reading that should be ongoing.

3   The commentators I have in mind here reach from those who discuss the trans-Atlantic theme in Henry James to the more recent, differently inflected, accounts of transatlantic cosmospolitanism (in Posnock's *Culture and Color* [1998]) and of the Black Atlantic (in Paul Gilroy's work). In a 1967 essay entitled "History, Myth and Fable in the Caribbean and the Guianas" (Harris 1999: 52–66), Wilson Harris lays the imaginative foundations of the work of both Gilroy and Joseph Roach in his prosthetic trope of the "phantom limb," which articulates the inescapable imbrication of literary trans-Americanisms with trans- or circum-Atlantic (and ultimately transoceanic diasporic) cultural perspectives and performances. Related here is Snead's description of Miss Rosa's abstractions as "mental prostheses that abut severed stumps. Like phantom limbs, they only recall an itch that cannot be satisfied" (1986: 105).

4   The United States suspended importation of slaves from Africa and the Caribbean soon after the Louisiana Purchase in 1803, but illegal traffic persisted.

5   Faulkner and Métraux were contemporaries, and *Intruder in the Dust* and *Voodoo in Haiti* were published only a decade apart. Métraux had been a student of Marcel Mauss' at the Institut d'Ethnologie during the 1920s and, despite his empiricist's distrust in the literary, specifically surrealist, use of ethnographic material, always remained in close touch with the French literary avant-garde through his friendship with Georges Bataille. It would not be amiss to suggest that *Intruder in the Dust* contains instances of what James Clifford calls ethnographic collage, the most salient

of which is Gowrie's corpse (see Clifford 1988: 125–6).

6   Glissant notes that, in the American South, the scandalous is associated with the French (1996: 238). If Godden is correct in asserting that Faulkner "knows that Haitian soil is a cemetery on the grandest scale," this awareness would resonate with, and validate, Harris's reading of *Intruder* as well as connect it with my reading of the bodies of both Sutpen and Charles Bon (see Godden 1994a: 490).

7   Harris implicitly cautions against perceptions of New World African-American religions as unequivocally subversive of oppressive social institutions. After all, religious practices can be appropriated and deployed by political regimes to keep in line and in place the Lucas Beauchamps and their anonymous kin. It is a matter of historical record that there is nothing inherently subversive about the "business" of Haitian vodou, which has been used to maintain dictatorial regimes in Haiti for the better part of the twentieth century (Murphy 1994: 14).

8   "Though historical in scope, *Absalom, Absalom!* is also informed by American imperialism in the Caribbean in the decades preceding the novel – as the United States occupied Cuba, Puerto Rico, the Dominican Republic and Haiti" (Stanchich 1996: 604).

9   Ladd notes that a white man could be a black man in the Deep South of the 1920s and 1930s through illegitimacy (1996: 164). We know from Harriet Wilson's *Our Nig* (1859) and other nineteenth-century texts that poverty accomplished the same thing.

10 Godden explains that "To be older than Virginia is to be located outside the slave-holding South; to be unquiet is to be Haiti" (1993: 34).

11 Porter calls attention to the fact that "It seems as if not only do poor whites father only girls (see Wash Jones), but their very ambition is female as well" (1995: 174).

12 The Conspiracy of La Escalera did not happen until 1844, but there was widespread fear of slave unrests in Cuba since the success of the revolution in Haiti. Many planters from Santo Domingo fled to Cuba, especially Santiago de Cuba, during and after the Haitian Revolution, and many Cubans ended up in New Orleans. On New Orleans see Roach 1996; and Gruesz 2001.

13 Ladd is convinced that "Faulkner wrote *Absalom, Absalom!* out of a deep familiarity with the political and cultural situation in New Orleans and Haiti, especially as it was perceived by and important to nineteenth- and early twentieth-century southerners like the ones Jason and Quentin Compson were modeled on" (1996: 142). Faulkner stayed in the French Quarter in New Orleans for six months in 1925 on his way to Europe.

14 See Robert Tallant's sensationalistic journalistic account of Marie Laveau in her three incarnations in his *Voodoo in New Orleans* (1962), part II.

15 Less obviously perhaps, Ella is also a version of Faulkner's deaf Linda Snopes Kohl, a character from *The Mansion* and *The Town* with whom she shares her married name and whom Snead has aptly described as "pure yet impure, native yet foreign, wrapped in silence yet grotesquely verbal, a flawed yet magnificent urn" (1986: 226). Residue of Faulknernian paternalism still clings to Brodber's Reuben Kohl.

16 On the Africanization of Louisiana see Roach, who notes that, in contrast to Haitian practice, women dominated spirit-world religion in Louisiana (1996: 59).

References and Further Reading

Bhabha, Homi K. (1994). *The Location of Culture*. London: Routledge.

Blake, Nancy (1985). "Creation and Procreation: The Voice and the Name, or Biblical Intertextuality in *Absalom, Absalom!*" In Michel Gresset and Noel Polk (eds.), *Intertextuality in Faulkner*, 128–43. Jackson: University Press of Mississippi.

Brodber, Erna (1994). *Louisiana*. London and Oxford, Miss.: New Beacon Books and University Press of Mississippi.

Burton, Richard D. E. (1997). *Afro-Creole: Power, Opposition, and Play in the Caribbean*. Ithaca: Cornell University Press.

Clifford, James (1988). *The Predicament of Culture: Twentieth-Century Ethnography, Literature, and Art*. Cambridge, Mass.: Harvard University Press.

Dash, J. Michael (1998). *The Other America: Caribbean Literature in a New World Context*. Charlottesville: University Press of Virginia.

Deren, Maya (1970). *Divine Horseman: The Living Gods of Haiti*. New York: McPerson. (First publ. 1953.)

Faulkner, William (1990). *Absalom, Absalom!* New York: Random House. (First publ. 1936.)

Ferrer, Daniel (1989). "Editorial Changes in the Chronology of *Absalom, Absalom!*: A Matter of Life and Death?" *Faulkner Journal* 5: 1, 45–8.

Glissant, Edouard (1996). *Faulkner, Mississippi*, trans. Barbara Lewis and Thomas C. Spear. New York: Farrar Straus Giroux.

Godden, Richard (1993). "*Absalom, Absalom!* and Rosa Coldfield." *Faulkner Journal* 8: 2, 31–66.

Godden, Richard (1994a). "*Absalom, Absalom!* and Faulkner's Erroneous Dating of the Haitian Revolution." *Mississippi Quarterly* 47: 3, 489–95.

Godden, Richard (1994b). "*Absalom, Absalom!*, Haiti and Labor History: Reading Unreadable Revolutions." *ELH* 61: 3, 685–720.

Gruesz, Kirsten Silva (2001). *Ambassadors of Culture: Transamerican Literary Contacts and the Origins of Latino Identity, 1823–1989*. Princeton: Princeton University Press.

Handley, George B. (2000). *Postslavery Literatures in the Americas: Family Portraits in Black and White*. Charlottesville: University Press of Virginia.

Harris, Wilson (1983). *The Womb of Space: The Cross-Cultural Imagination*. Westport: Greenwood.

Harris, Wilson (1999). *Selected Essays of Wilson Harris: The Unfinished Genesis of the Imagination*, ed. A. J. M. Bundy. London: Routledge.

Hemenway, Robert E. (1977). *Zora Neale Hurston: A Literary Biography*. Urbana: University of Illinois Press.

Hogan, Patrick Colm (2000). *Colonialism and Cultural Identity: Crises of Tradition in the Anglophone Literatures of India, Africa, and the Caribbean*. Albany: SUNY Press.

Hurston, Zora Neale (1990a). *Mules and Men*. New York: Harper & Row. (First publ. 1935.)

Hurston, Zora Neale (1990b). *Tell My Horse: Voodoo and Life in Haiti and Jamaica*. New York: Harper & Row. (First publ. 1938.)

Kutzinski, Vera M. (1987). *Against the American Grain: Myth and History in William Carlos Williams, Jay Wright, and Nicolás Guillén*. Baltimore: John Hopkins University Press.

Kuyk, Dirk (1990). *Sutpen's Design: Interpreting Faulkner's "Absalom, Absalom!"* Charlottesville: University Press of Virginia.

Ladd, Barbara (1996). *Nationalism and the Color Line in George W. Cable, Mark Twain, and William Faulkner*. Baton Rouge: LSU Press.

Lamming, George (1992). *The Pleasures of Exile*. Ann Arbor: University of Michigan Press. (First publ. 1960.)

Mariani, Paul (1999). *The Broken Tower: A Life of Hart Crane*. New York: Norton.

Métraux, Alfred (1959). *Voodoo in Haiti*, trans. Hugo Charteris. London: Deutsch. (First publ. 1958.)

Michaels, Walter Benn (1995). *Our America: Nativism, Modernism, and Pluralism*. Durham: Duke University Press.

Murphy, Joseph M. (1994). *Working the Spirit: Ceremonies of the African Diaspora*. Boston: Beacon.

Nichols, Peter (1995). *Modernisms: A Literary Guide*. Berkeley: University of California Press.

Niessen de Abruña, Laura (1989). "The 'Incredible Indigo Sea' within Anglo-American Fiction." In Temma F. Berg et al. (eds.), *Engendering the Word: Feminist Essays in Psychosexual Poetics*, 125–50. Urbana: University of Illinois Press.

Parkinson Zamora, Lois (1997). *The Usable Past: The Imagination of History in Recent Fiction of the Americas*. New York: Cambridge University Press.

Porter, Carolyn (1995). "*Absalom, Absalom!*: (Un)making the Father." In Philip M. Weinstein (ed.), *The Cambridge Companion to William Faulkner*, 168–96. New York: Cambridge University Press.

Reichardt, Ulfried (1997). "Perceiving and Representing Slavery and 'Race' *through* Time: William Faulkner's *Absalom, Absalom!*" *Amerikastudien/American Studies* 42: 4, 613–24.

Roach, Joseph (1996). *Cities of the Dead: Circum-Atlantic Performance*. New York: Columbia University Press.

Sánchez-Eppler, Benigno (1992). "Telling Anthropology: Zora Neale Hurston and Gilberto Freyre Disciplined in their Field-Home-Work." *American Literary History* 4: 3, 64–88.

Snead, James A. (1986). *Figures of Division: William Faulkner's Major Novels*. New York: Methuen.

Stanchich, Maritza (1996). "The Hidden Caribbean 'Other' in William Faulkner's *Absalom, Absalom!*: An Ideological Ancestry of US Imperialism." *Mississippi Quarterly* 49: 3, 603–17.

Tallant, Robert (1962). *Voodoo in New Orleans*. New York: Collier Macmillan. (First publ. 1946.)

PART II
Mapping Regions

12

New England Literature and Regional Identity

Kent C. Ryden

From shortly after the arrival of the first colonists, New England has been a prominent site of literary production. A relatively high rate of literacy and education, a word- and text-oriented church, the early presence in New England cities of printing presses, a transatlantic trade network which brought printed matter along with other goods to New England ports – these and other factors ensured that there was a constant appetite in colonial New England for psalm books, primers, almanacs, printed sermons, and political tracts, as well as imported English bibles and chapbooks. Survey textbooks of American literature are becoming more geographically and socially diverse with every new edition, but even today a glance at any of them suggests that early American literature was largely coextensive with early New England literature. The writers of the New England Renaissance, poets from Emily Dickinson to Robert Frost, and so-called "local color" writers like Sarah Orne Jewett remain canonical American literary figures, while in the nineteenth and early twentieth centuries Boston-based publishing houses like Houghton Mifflin and Ticknor and Fields, along with periodicals like the *Atlantic Monthly*, played an important role in making prose literature available to a national audience. Even today, one of America's best-selling authors, Stephen King, sets most of his novels and stories in rural and small-town Maine, and continues to make his home in Bangor. For almost 400 years, New England has housed so many writers, generated so many words, and been the focus of so much literary attention that it almost seems futile to speak briefly and meaningfully about any such thing as New England regional literature.

And yet, to think of New England as a simple geographical container for writers and their words, and of New England literature as comprising all works produced over time within the six northeasternmost United States, is one thing; to think of New England as a *cultural* region with a specific (if shifting) identity, and of New England literature as those writings which have selfconsciously addressed and reflected on that identity over time, is something else altogether, and provides a way of approaching the notion of New England regional literature with a greater degree of meaning and conceptual coherence. The physical landscape of the six New England states is a natural given, and upon that geographical surface has played out a long and complex history of aboriginal inhabitance, colonial conquest, settlement, and dispersion, revolutionary warfare, economic development and evolution, landscape change, immigration and urbanization, plus the myriad mundane details of the lives of millions of New Englanders past and present. As with the multiplicity and complexity of the literature produced within and about New England, it seems difficult to trace a coherent regional story through these braided narratives and episodes. Even today, industrial Rhode Island is very different – physically, culturally, and historically – from rural Vermont; visitors to South Providence and the Green Mountains might find it difficult if not impossible to hold both places together under the same conceptual umbrella. Over time, though, people both within and outside the region have done just that; they have continued to agree that there is such a thing as "New England," a label which implies some uniformity and consistency of meaning over the extent of the lands to which it is applied. In an ongoing act of implicit agreement and cultural collusion, Americans have selected certain qualities and characteristics, historic episodes, prominent personages, folk ways, and fragments of landscape and built environment to stand, not for the complex, multifarious, historical New England on the ground, but for the simplified and purified New England of the mind. As a physical region, to be sure, New England has an independent presence; as a cultural region, however, New England is an emphatically human invention.

Literature has played perhaps the most important role in this ongoing act of cultural construction and revision. New England was argued into being by explorers, clerics, and academics. Its presumed identifying qualities were exemplified and debated in the pages of nineteenth-century New England fiction and popular drama. As the region began to change economically and demographically in the late nineteenth century, New England writers abetted the cultural work of the colonial revival in keeping alive an image of the region as fundamentally rural, preindustrial, and Anglo-Saxon; at the same time, other writers began to look more critically at the emerging ideal of the white-steepled Yankee village, suggesting that it was not as exempt from the world's troubles as its partisans would have readers believe. This tension continued to structure New England writing in the twentieth century: some authors, particularly in the 1930s under the twin influences of the Depression and the so-called "regional revival," continued to depict and champion New England as a restorative imaginative refuge from the ravages of history, while in more recent years a younger generation of New England writers has mounted a strong critique of the regional image, restoring to literary attention those residents of New England who have historically been excluded from the region's popularly recognized identity. To think of a meaningful New England regional literature, then, is to focus on those writers and works that have engaged in the ongoing historical invention, revision, celebration, and critique of New England construed as a coherent cultural region. After briefly outlining the contours of that literature, the remainder of this essay will, equally briefly, attempt to flesh out this regional literary history with representative examples; the goal here is not to be comprehensive and exhaustive, but rather to focus on exemplars of prominent regional themes and cultural arguments.

New England began as a physical space, but that space was soon filled with cultural meaning by those who had the power to wield the pen and the press – first on a sacred basis, and later on a secular basis, as notions of the New Englander as Puritan gradually transformed into notions of the New Englander as Yankee. The term "New England" was coined and popularized by Captain John Smith in 1616, following a voyage he made along what is now the region's northeastern coast. Works like Smith's *Description of New England* (1616) and William Wood's *New England's Prospect* (1634) described and catalogued the region's climate, landscape, natural resources, and Indian populations, and laid out the case for further colonization. These and other promotional works, though, were primarily aimed at an English audience, designed to lure settlers over to New England rather than to tell New Englanders who they were. A particular literary and cultural identity for the place called "New England" – an identity developed from within rather than imposed from without – had to be worked out and written into existence in the new colonies themselves.

The first versions of a specifically New England identity were heavily religious in tone and substance, but it was an identity that was somewhat slow to develop. The first generation of New England Puritans saw themselves more as English exiles than as the kernel of a new society that would eventually grow to become a New World. They were attempting to purify their church and society while also pursuing and extending the cultural patterns of their old homes – that is, to literally create a new and better *England* – and works from Governor John Winthrop's sermon "A Model of Christian Charity" (orally delivered in 1630 but not published until the nineteenth century), with its famous "city on a hill" imagery, to countless other published sermons by Puritan divines, to poet Anne Bradstreet's 1650 "A Dialogue between Old England and New," while fully acknowledging the religious mission of the Puritan enterprise, cast the New English settlement in that particularly Old English light. The second generation of New England Puritans, however, having had a chance to acclimatize to their distance from England and to embrace their colonies as home rather than as a site of exile, re-interpreted the experience of the founding generation, identifying their migratory impulse in terms of separation rather than continuity – emphasizing the "New," that is, rather than the "England" – and outlining for the first time the lineaments of a particularly local identity. While they may not seem like "regional" literature at first, histories from Edward Johnson's 1654 *Wonder-Working Providence of Sions Savior in New England* to Cotton Mather's 1702 *Magnalia Christi Americana* recast the Puritan mission in a heroic light, mythologizing it as the "Great Migration," as an ideological errand into the wilderness, thereby ensuring that the earliest public versions of a specifically New England identity were linked primarily with religious idealism, not with the lived textures of everyday colonial life. And this, of course, is the version of colonial New England that has largely survived in subsequent histories and in the popular imagination;

given that the production of published writing in early New England was largely in the hands of a literate and ideologically motivated few, the regional identity that literature makes available to project onto the New England past is that which Puritan clerics and historians have left for us.

After the Revolution, and with the growing secularization of New England society, a new version of regional identity began to be worked out on the pages of the region's authors. Part of this identity was political in origin: upon breaking loose from British rule, New Englanders embraced republicanism as the ideal form of government, a government which not only located power and authority in the people, but depended on the virtue of those people for its strength and legitimacy. The ideal New Englander thus became someone who was religious (a legacy from the region's Puritan past), industrious, frugal, and simple; political ideology, that is, influenced the development of an idealized social type that New Englanders were encouraged to strive toward. And while political culture provided one strand of a developing regional identity, popular culture provided another in the figure of the Yankee. The song "Yankee Doodle" was originally sung by British troops to satirize what they saw as their rustic, ignorant, uncouth, ill-clad opponents from Connecticut and parts north. Once the war began going the colonists' way, though, New Englanders began adopting the song themselves as an ironic badge of pride and defiance, and the rough-hewn soldier described in the song soon began to emerge as a regional character type. Sometimes appearing as a clever traveling peddler, sometimes as a simple but shrewd farmer, the Yankee put a patriotic, comic gloss on republican virtue, and toward the mid-nineteenth century the virtuous, rural New England Yankee, by now shorn of many of his comic attributes, came to popularly represent the region for readers both within and outside New England.

The first full-blown Yankee appeared in Royall Tyler's 1787 play *The Contrast* in the form of Jonathan, the "waiter" (he refuses to be called "servant") to the strong and virtuous revolutionary hero Colonel Manly. A Massachusetts farm boy, Jonathan is awkward, foolish, gullible, and dressed in patched and outgrown clothes, and yet he also demonstrates the strengths Americans associated with their new nation: he is intensely patriotic, he resists the fleshpots of New York, and in the end he helps Colonel Manly to quash the amorous double-dealing of Manly's rival, the anglophile Billy Dimple. In broad comic strokes, the virtuous new nation provides an admirable contrast to the decadent old world, and much of that virtue and national character is located in the regionally representative Yankee. This comic character became nationally popular in the first half of the nineteenth century. Tyler's work spawned a genre of "Yankee plays" which maintained the theme of national and cultural contrast while placing the Jonathan figure in the starring role; the regional representative had become a national spokesman. In fact, it has been argued that the stage Yankee and his stereotypical costume of tall hat and blue coat eventually transmogrified into the American emblem of Uncle Sam. Other, less burlesque Yankees appeared in newspaper sketches and collections of popular tales, such as Seba Smith's "Letters of Col. Jack Downing from Downingville, Maine." Jack Downing had numerous congeners in the popular press; their stock-in-trade was to offer shrewd commentary on national events from the vantage point of their New England villages, or perhaps to travel to Washington to straighten out the government with their good republican horse sense (Smith had Downing, for instance, become a valued advisor to Andrew Jackson). Here too the regional figure was pressed into national service; embodying in comic form a version of what New Englanders saw as their idealized selves, these Yankee figures reached both a regional and a national audience on stage and in the popular press, providing those audiences with a means for thinking about the emerging and evolving nature of their regional and national identities.

Harriet Beecher Stowe is the mid-nineteenth-century author who perhaps best demonstrates the emerging New England ideal, merging landscape and character to emphasize and popularize a version of regional identity that remains recognizable today. Stowe is of course best known for *Uncle Tom's Cabin* (1852), but even that novel contains commentary on New England: its central villain, the heartless Simon Legree, is essentially a Yankee gone bad, having abandoned the tidy and virtuous Vermont village of his birth for a ruthless slaveholding life in the South. And in works from her early 1834 "A New England Sketch" through her 1869 collection *Oldtown Folks* and her 1878 fictionalized autobiography *Poganuc People*, Stowe idealized that New England village landscape, populating it with strong Yankee embodiments of republican virtue and elevating it to stand for the region as a whole. Stowe's is a sentimental, pastoral vision of a changeless world, and it is, of course, a selective vision as well. The popular Stowe, along with visual artists like the engraver John Barber, played a large part in the conversion of the white-painted New England village into a cultural icon, and her pastoral portrayals conveniently obscure the fact that those clusters of white Georgian homes were most often the product of commercial and not agricultural activity, the abodes of merchants and not farmers. Stowe's sketches contain no hint of commercial activity, nor does the increasing presence of Irish immigrants in the region warrant any portrayal in her pages. Still, Stowe's was one of the most prominent nineteenth-century voices establishing a popular sense of who "real" New Englanders were and where they lived, and in her whitewashing of New England history and the New England landscape she established a practice and a political stance that other writers after her would follow.

Throughout the nineteenth century, and particularly in the years after the Civil War, an industrial presence loomed larger and larger in the New England landscape. Water-powered factories lined the region's many rivers, and entire new industrial cities like Lowell and Lawrence, Massachusetts, and Manchester, New Hampshire, were founded and built by Boston entrepreneurs. With the advent of steam power, factories were freed from remote river valleys, and additional manufacturing centers, like Fall River, Massachusetts, grew along the New England coast. At the same time, the region experienced extensive rural depopulation over the latter half of the century as New England farms found it increasingly difficult to compete with the produce being shipped east on railroads and canals from the more fertile and easily farmed states of the American Midwest. Early New England factories tended to be staffed by

Figure 12.1   Actor Joshua Silsbee as the Yankee character Jonathan Ploughboy in Samuel Woodworth's *The Forest Rose*.

Figure 12.2 John Barber engraving of Traunton, Massachusetts, from his 1839 book *Historical Collections of Massachusetts*.

members of displaced farm families, and Lowell was famous in mid-century for its "mill girl" system of employing teenaged Yankee girls under paternalistic supervision; over time, however, the mills were increasingly dominated by immigrants from Quebec and southern Europe. New England was changing from a region of farms and small towns to one dominated more and more by industry; in the process, it was becoming increasingly diverse ethnically.

The colonial revival in America was in large part a response to these changing regional conditions, receiving additional impetus from the nation's centennial celebrations in 1876. This period saw the elevation of the Pilgrim story to the status of national icon, the architectural rediscovery and popularity of clean-lined, white-painted Georgian-style houses (still recognized as "colonials" in today's suburban neighborhoods), the refurbishment of village centers to fit the colonial ideal, and a new interest in historic preservation within New England, with particular attention paid to the surviving farmhouses of the earliest colonial period. Much of this cultural work was driven by members of the old New England elite, whereupon it became embraced more popularly. In its origins, though, it amounted to a selection and public reinforcement of a certain partial version of the New England past, one populated exclusively by hard-working English settlers and Anglo-Saxon farmers. In the face of rapidly changing circumstances, elite New Englanders tried as best they could to stake a physical, historical, and imaginative claim to conceptual ownership of the region, defining its identity on their own terms and inscribing that identity insistently on the landscape, essentially repopulating the landscape with those vanished Yankee farmers.

New England's writers played an important role in this literary repopulation and this construction of a wished-for regional past, a vision they communicated to both a regional and a national audience. Lucy Larcom's 1889 memoir *A New England Girlhood* provides a good example of the literary re-imagining of the New England past that was underway. Larcom's title is suggestive, implying that there is something regionally representative about the contours of her life. And Larcom was a Lowell mill girl as a young woman, thereby participating directly in the region's industrial transformation. Yet her achievement in the book is to make New England's industrial present seem continuous with its virtuous Yankee past; while life and economy seem to have changed on the surface, the "real" New England, in Larcom's view, remained fundamentally unscathed. The first part of the book focuses on Larcom's childhood in the old Massachusetts seaport of Beverly, a world as yet untouched by the railroad and the modern world. Larcom presents Beverly in idyllic terms: it is a place of natural beauty and outdoor enjoyment, dour yet earnest religious observance, sturdy republican Yankee virtue, and warm, sustaining family and neighborly relationships. After Larcom's father died, her mother moved the family to Lowell and managed a company boarding-house, whereupon Lucy and some of her sisters went to work in the mills. In many ways, though, Lowell emerges as an extension into the industrial Merrimack valley of the old world of Beverly. Larcom's memories focus, not on the unfamiliar regimen of industrial time or the

rigors and dangers of working around the mills' machinery – some of the fundamental changes that were affecting New England life and landscape in her lifetime –
but on the joys of working side by side with other Yankee girls, the high morals
and religious paternalism of mill management, the remaining beauties of the river
valley as seen from the factory window, and the opportunities she seized to further
her interests in literature and writing. Larcom looks back on her life through the
lens provided by the cultural needs of the late nineteenth century, providing her
readers with a reassuring sense that the vast changes sweeping through New England
did not change the region's fundamental character.

While Larcom plumbed memory to shore up a particular version of New England
identity as seen retrospectively from the present, other writers chose to bypass the
present altogether, revealing to their readers an idealized vision of the New England
past, similar in its outlines to that portrayed by Harriet Beecher Stowe, that stood
in implicit and damning contrast to the region as it existed in the late nineteenth
century. Many of these authors have been referred to, somewhat condescendingly, as
"local color" writers, focusing as they did on small-scale, closely drawn scenes of
village life, often paying close attention to regional folk ways and patterns of dialect.
The work of Rowland Robinson provides a good example of this kind of writing. His
"Danvis Tales," focusing on the fictional village of Danvis, Vermont, in the 1830s,
originally appeared in popular magazines in the 1890s, and were later collected in
several story collections. Usually centering on gatherings in the cobbler's shop of
"Uncle Lisha" Peggs or on the activities of noble outdoorsman Sam Lovel, the Danvis
tales collectively present a lovingly rendered portrait of a prelapsarian Yankee New
England. Speaking in a heavy Vermont dialect (rendered in a difficult-to-decipher
phonetic spelling), Robinson's characters are uniformly morally upright, always
willing to help a neighbor in need – to find a lost child, to help out in the face of
financial loss, even to shelter an escaped slave. The only ethnic tension is added by
the recurring character of Antoine the French Canadian, who is teased unmercifully
by Lisha and the others for his perceived uncouth ways – but at the same time is
clearly welcomed by the Danvis brotherhood; while immigration may be troubling,
it's nothing that Yankee New England can't accommodate on its own terms. When
trouble does occur in Danvis, it is usually brought by morally dubious characters
from the outside world – by slave hunters, by a land speculator who tries to cheat
Sam out of some valuable property, or by a flirtatious girl who breaks the heart of
young Peletiah Gove, only to die later in tragic circumstances after a life of sin.
Robinson's characters occupy an Edenic landscape of great natural beauty, where fish
and game are always readily available to Sam's rod and gun. By setting his tales in
the 1830s, though, Robinson makes clear that his idealized New England is emphatically a part of the lost past. Still, his Danvis tales provided readers with a
comforting New England of the mind that they could travel to in imagination – one
that was also a clear reminder of how much New England had changed.

Sarah Orne Jewett's *The Country of the Pointed Firs*, first published in book form
in 1896, is perhaps the best-known example of the village-centered New England

literature of the late nineteenth century, yet this work also suggests a degree of ambiguity in the portrayal of an idealized New England, an ambiguity that would increasingly come to characterize New England regional literature in the twentieth century. The book's unnamed female narrator first comes to the coastal Maine village of Dunnet Landing intending to write a book in splendid isolation, yet she is soon drawn into the social life of the village through the good-humored influence of her landlord, Almira Todd. Mrs. Todd is a warm and admirable figure: a herbalist, she deeply understands the natural rhythms of her native patch of earth; a gregarious sort, she is loved and admired by the entire village and provides the narrator with an entrée into the community; a member of one of the town's first families, she takes the narrator to the offshore Green Island to meet her mother and brother, who live there in an idyll of domestic contentment. Mrs. Todd seems representative of Dunnet Landing as a whole; it is a world occupied by good-hearted Yankees of the sort that also inhabit Robinson's Danvis. Set on the geographical margins of New England, seeming rooted in a static and changeless past rather than a kaleidoscopically shifting present, vanishing mistily from sight as the narrator sails away from it one last time, Dunnet Landing seems not of the world in which Jewett's readers lived, and that was likely the point. The vignettes that make up *The Country of the Pointed Firs* first appeared in William Dean Howells's *Atlantic Monthly*, and thus primarily reached a sophisticated urban audience in New England and elsewhere. Sunk deep in the new world of modernity, these readers found in Dunnet Landing and other such fictional villages a valued glimpse into what seemed to be a stable, reassuring New England past.

And yet, despite its surface appeal, Dunnet Landing is far from a perfect place. It represents a dying, moribund, unsustainable world, one dwindling through its own sterility. Once a bustling seaport connected to the markets of the world, Dunnet Landing is now a husk of its former self, with trade having long since dried up. It contains very few young people; lacking local economic opportunities, they have evidently moved on to other parts of New England and the world. The characters whom the narrator meets, Mrs. Todd included, are childless, implying a sort of barrenness in their lives and world. Moreover, Dunnet Landing contains a great deal of pain and pathos; far from being an Edenic refuge from the world's miseries, it participates in them fully. Mrs. Todd has never gotten over the early loss of her spouse. Nor has Elijah Tilley, who seems on the surface to be a stereotypically crusty and salty New England fisherman but who is deeply shattered by his recent widowerhood; when the narrator accepts his invitation to visit his house, all he can do is talk brokenly about his lost "poor dear." Captain Littlepage, a name suggesting diminution, sits alone in his house, obsessively rehearsing tales of mysterious Arctic voyages. The book's most touching vignette recounts the tale of "poor Joanna," who exiled herself to Shellheap Island after being jilted by her lover. While much of Jewett's book seems to venerate an idealized New England, at the same time it also realistically assesses the historical decline of the region's villages and rural areas. *The Country of the Pointed Firs*, then, both reinforces the sense of regional identity argued for by the colonial revival and contains within its pages the seeds of a critique of that same identity. As such, it exemplifies the literary debate over New England as a cultural region that has characterized the hundred-plus years since its publication.

Other works of nineteenth-century New England village fiction, such as Mary E. Wilkins Freeman's short stories "The Revolt of 'Mother'" (1890) and "A New England Nun" (1891), explored the tensions hidden beneath the popularly accepted façade of New England village life, offering a harsh critique of the social, imaginative, and emotional stresses and limitations placed upon small-town residents, particularly women. As such, stories like these prefigured the social criticism later mounted in other places by writers like Sherwood Anderson in *Winesburg, Ohio* (1919), Edgar Lee Masters in *Spoon River Anthology* (1915), or Sinclair Lewis in *Main Street* (1920). At the same time, there was a particularly New England context for this critique of rural and small-town life, one rooted in the ongoing decline of agriculture in the region and the accompanying loss of population in its villages and farming communities. Both within and outside its borders, New England was seen as a region in decline by many observers even as its history was being sanitized and idealized by the pens of authors and in the imaginations of readers. Regional and national commentators fretted that New England, seen as the cultural hearth of the nation and the repository of national strength and virtue, was losing its vitality and going to seed. The states of New Hampshire and Vermont began aggressively marketing abandoned farms to would-be farmers or second-home seekers, and New Hampshire instituted "Old Home Week" celebrations to lure departed residents home again for brief visits, the goal being to tempt them to move back or at least invest in the local economy. The remnant rural population came increasingly to be seen as shiftless, inbred, and morally bankrupt, their continued residence in shabby villages now seen as a sign of fecklessness rather then incorruptibility; in the 1920s, the state of Vermont went so far as to contemplate instituting a eugenics program to "improve" its rural population, to restore them to some idealized, Rowland Robinson-style version of the Vermont Yankee. These strands of thought and concern also made their way into New England regional literature in the twentieth century, as New England began to be portrayed and criticized as a region in decline alongside its earlier portrayal as a place uniquely virtuous and exempt from history.

In a fashion not unlike Anderson and Masters, Edwin Arlington Robinson, in his poems about the fictional village of Tilbury Town, Maine, offered a series of sketches of New England characters whose lives are sometimes pathetic, sometimes tragic, but hardly the stuff of celebration or emulation. Such well-known poems as "Richard Cory," "Miniver Cheevy," and "Mr. Flood's Party," along with additional poetic portraits like "Reuben Bright" or "Aaron Stark," provide glimpses beneath the seemingly unremarkable surfaces of small-town Yankee life and character to reveal lives marked and warped by loss, despair, disappointment, grief, and loneliness. Far from offering a vision of a world where existence is untroubled and days are rich and satisfying, life in Robinson's Tilbury Town (a fictionalized version of his own home town of Gardiner, Maine) rarely if ever lives up to its residents' hopes, expectations, and emotional needs. And while Robinson offered a poetic critique of regional life and character, Edith Wharton, a part-time resident of the Berkshire Mountains in Massachusetts, wrote some of the best-known prose evaluations of a decadent rural New England. Her place names give her away: North Dormer, for example, the setting of her novel *Summer* (1917), is a somnolent, marginal place (not even central to its own world, but north of it), where moral corruption and violence hide behind a static surface and where the hill folk who live above the town are barely civilized. *Ethan Frome* (1911) is set in Starkfield, a town that is cold and barren not only physically but spiritually and emotionally as well. The character of Ethan exemplifies Wharton's critique of New England life: trapped in his home town, unhappily married, unfulfilled in every way possible – indeed, suggesting the impossibility of fulfillment in such a place – Ethan attempts, with his lover, to commit suicide by sledding into a tree. They are crippled and disfigured but not killed in the attempt, and the rest of their lives – with Ethan, wife, and lover all living miserably in the same house – is a tragedy that, in its cultural and historical context, emerges as deeply regional as well as more universally human in its resonance.

Robert Frost is the twentieth-century writer most strongly associated with New England. Over the course of his career, he carved out a popular public persona as the Yankee farmer-poet, deeply rooted in the lands and ways of life of New England, a celebrant of and spokesman for the region, his craggy face both physically and metaphorically reflecting the granite features of New Hampshire's Old Man of the Mountains. And yet, taken as a whole, Frost's career and his evolving portrayal of New England exemplify the full range of ambiguity emerging in the region's literary image; while at times a celebrant and partisan, at other times he is a clear-eyed critic as well. Frost first came to literary prominence with the publication of his 1915 collection *North of Boston*, a work whose title suggests the geographical and cultural marginality of the places and people he writes about. The book is a collection of dramatic monologues and dialogues, and contains several of Frost's best-known and most often anthologized poems: "Mending Wall," "The Death of the Hired Man," and "Home Burial," to name three. And far from being a celebration of happy simple rural life, depicting the idealized New England of the colonial revival, the book amounts to a sober critique of the social and emotional costs of living in a poor and declining part of the country. The abandoned title structure of "The Black Cottage" is an emblem of the book's New England as a whole: a slowly decaying thing that the rest of the world has passed by. Some characters, particularly female characters, suffer from loneliness and overwork – the narrator of "A Servant to Servants," for instance, who pours out her heart to a visiting botanist and reveals a life both defeated and driven near madness by the endless demands of working for her husband and his hired hands, a life trapped in the kitchen with only the view through the window over the sink for relief. Other poems speak of pain and frustration, showing that New Englanders are not exempt from such things and may in fact be particularly prone to them: "Home Burial," for instance, or "The Fear." Far from being a solid rural community, Frost's New England is characterized by social isolation, by lack of communication and understanding, as in "Mending Wall," "The Code," or "The Housekeeper." The two distantly related speakers in "The Generations of Men" most firmly locate Frost's New England within the context of contemporary concerns about the region. Meeting during Old Home Week over the abandoned cellar hole of the old Stark family home, the boy and girl strike up a flirtatious friendship; if anything is to come of it, though, it will happen elsewhere, not in the played-out hills of New Hampshire.

In its way, *North of Boston* inaugurated a shift in the way Frost wrote about New England. Early reviewers and promoters of the book, including such prominent and influential figures as Ezra Pound and Amy Lowell, began crediting Frost with being a sort of rustic savant, a New Hampshire countryman and farmer who happened to also be a fine and talented poet. Frost had done some indifferent farming in Derry, New Hampshire, for about ten years, and had worked on poems there; but he had spent his childhood in San Francisco and in Lawrence, Massachusetts, had received some college education and done some schoolteaching, had moved his family to England in 1910 to set about writing in earnest, had published his first two books (*A Boy's Will* and *North of Boston*) in England, and was altogether a more complex and sophisticated figure than such a rustic persona would suggest. Frost soon embraced this image for himself, though; it resonated with the more popular, benign version of New England regional identity that coexisted with the more critical view he had aligned himself with in *North of Boston*, and by publicly taking on the role of Yankee sage he ensured a great measure of popularity and success. His poetry thus began to reinforce rather than challenge conventional views of New England, with the long title poem of his 1923 collection *New Hampshire* perhaps best exemplifying Frost's self-assigned role as regional mouthpiece and apologist. The poem begins by humor-ously establishing the state's marginality to the concerns and trends of the modern world. It doesn't have wealth, it doesn't have ambition, it doesn't have much of anything except tiny towns with odd, endearing names. But this is a virtue in Frost's eyes, a virtue matched only by that found in the hearts of the state's people, whom he proclaims the best he has ever met. New Hampshire and Vermont are identified as the two best states in the Union, in fact, and Frost wryly laments that it's hard to create literature from New England life because there is so little tragedy to be found there (a statement that would likely surprise many of the speakers in *North of Boston*). Frost continued in this largely noncritical vein for the remainder of his career, while also becoming less and less of a selfconsciously regional poet. In the public mind, though, with his many visiting professorships and speaking engagements, Frost remained the personification of New England. Even today, the line "Good fences make good neighbors" is commonly attributed to Frost himself as a good commonsense Yankee aphorism; its original ambiguous utterance by a character in "Mending Wall" as part of a complex poetic consideration of relationships between human beings is largely forgotten.

Events of the 1920s, 1930s, and 1940s help explain the shift in Frost's emphasis and public perception. The onset of the Great Depression and World War II shook many Americans' faith in modernity and history, and so many areas of cultural activity and production turned to regional themes and topics for their perceived authenticity and stability, for the imaginative bulwarks they offered against the depredations of time's passing. The "regional," in this case, was largely construed as the "rural," as those places most distant from and uncontaminated by cosmopolitan urban centers; as such, it implied changelessness and premodernity as well. The Works Progress Administration of Franklin Roosevelt's government sent writers and folklorists into the American countryside to document and preserve traditions and ways of life, the sort of cultural work echoed by James Agee and Walker Percy, say, in their 1941 book *Let Us Now Praise Famous Men*. Folklorist Benjamin Botkin began publishing his compendious treasuries of American folklore. Given this historical and cultural atmosphere, the persistent notion of New England as representing an earlier, better time and place had particular resonance, as exemplified by the publication in 1935 of the first issue of *Yankee* magazine: not only a magazine in tune with its times but one that can be seen as a latter-day extension of the colonial revival urge to edit and rewrite New England's past and present. In its dedication to the rural, rustic, and Anglo-Saxon, an emphasis sought to a large extent by its readership even today, *Yankee* offered within its pages a refuge from the world in which its readers actually lived.

This same function was also fulfilled by many writers of the time who deliberately took New England as their focus – or, more accurately, the thematic and imaginative possibilities that the enduring *idea* of New England offered in a time of social, economic, and geopolitical upheaval. E. B. White provides a good example of one such author. Born and raised just outside New York City, educated at Cornell, White was associated throughout his career with the sophisticated *New Yorker* magazine, yet he also spent much of his time at his coastal farm in North Brooklin, Maine, living there from 1938 to 1943, and then again from 1957 until his death in 1985. During his first period of year-round residency, White wrote a monthly column for *Harper's* magazine under the title "One Man's Meat"; these columns were later collected and published as a book of the same name. In this book, White uses his farm as a vantage point from which to contemplate and comment on the dark world events of the day, particularly the rise of Nazi Germany and the advent and conduct of World War II. The columns alternate between pointed political commentary and lovingly detailed vignettes of life on White's farm, where he raised sheep and chickens and produced eggs for market. To White, the course of twentieth-century history is one of spiraling decline, to the point where the fate of the world seems questionable. By contrast, his farm is presented as standing outside history to some extent, its temporal flow marked not by the downward arrow of history but by the perpetually renewing cycles of life, as exemplified by the lambs that he raises and the eggs that he collects daily. White presents a carefully crafted vision of a life that is solid, grounded, authentic, and reassuring, valued imaginative fodder for the wartime readership of *Harper's*. To be sure, he hides as much about his life as he reveals, presenting himself as a sort of Yankee farmer-essayist not unlike Robert Frost; but in so doing he reinforces and perpetuates New England's cultural usefulness as an imaginative counterbalance to an imperfect world. As such, the New England that he and others have created and recreated is a region whose identity has been defined as much negatively as positively, as much through what it does *not* contain as through what it does.

This is, of course, the New England that tourists today come to the region to consume. They want to see stone walls and picturesque white villages, Plymouth and Concord, Sturbridge Village and the Berkshires; only recently has "historic New England" been expanded to include such sites as the Lowell National Historic Park and the Blackstone Valley Industrial Heritage Corridor, the very sorts of sites that authors and colonial revivalists so actively tried to obscure in past years. In 1938, Thornton Wilder labeled his fictional Grover's Corners, New Hampshire, as *Our Town*, the imaginative property of the entire nation, the perfect place from which to contemplate the fundamental issues of life. In the 1960s and 1970s, under the influence of Scott and Helen Nearing, the back-to-the-land movement focused on rural northern New England as the perfect place to escape a corrupt and decadent modern existence and live with Thoreauvian deliberateness, fronting only the essentials of life. In these and other ways, popular conceptions and definitions of New England have demonstrated their endurance and their power. Yet these definitions are, of course, partial and selective, excluding much more than they include. The New Englander has remained predominantly the Yankee: white, Anglo-Saxon, rural, and premodern. If he has been poor, his poverty has been a blessing, a proof of his incorruptibility and authenticity. In more recent years, in keeping with broader artistic, academic, and cultural efforts to better represent the previously underrepresented in American life, New England authors have begun producing a more deliberately inclusive regional fiction, challenging conventional notions of regional identity and arguing not only that New England has historically included many more kinds of people than have conventionally shown up on the printed page, but that those people are just as much New Englanders – if not more so – as any quaint old Yankee farmer. Their fiction is perhaps more explicitly political than earlier New England writing; recognizing the exclusive nature of that writing, they posit a counter-region of sorts, producing an often grimly realistic fiction that focuses on those shadowy lands beyond the village green.

The more prominent of these "neorealists" include Russell Banks, Cathie Pelletier, Carolyn Chute, and Ernest Hebert. Hebert's 1979 novel *The Dogs of March*, the first of his series of novels about the fictional New Hampshire town of Darby, best exemplifies this trend in New England fiction. The novel's protagonist is Howard Elman, a middle-aged foreman at a textile mill who loses his job when the company he works for is bought by an outfit from South Carolina. Howard is a sort of anti-Yankee: profane and given to drinking, a factory worker who deliberately refuses to farm the fields that he owns, an imperfect father and husband, he is now cut loose in a New England in economic decline, forced to reorder his life as best he can. The novel is more than simply a story of Howard's travails, though: it focuses on competing visions of New England identity, on the struggle over who gets to define the region and on what terms. Howard's antagonist in the novel, Zoe Cutter, is a rich New Yorker who has bought the house up the hill with the goal of renovating it and opening a boutique in the barn to cater to tourists. Zoe is motivated by the New England ideal: as an unhappy young girl in Kansas City, she seized upon a *National Geographic* photograph of a New England village as her ideal place of refuge and order, and now she does everything she can to make Darby correspond to the perfect vision that she carries in her head. This means removing Howard from her line of sight, of course, along with his ramshackle house and barn and the junked cars and appliances littering his yard. Howard may be *in* New England, in Zoe's view, but he is not *of* New England. Howard's view is exactly the opposite. "New England" as an abstraction or a concept has little meaning for him; he lives in a landscape of experience, not a landscape of his mind, and it is a world in which he finds a particular beauty and utility. He is in his place regardless of what Zoe thinks: as an orphan foster child, he chose his own last name of Elman in honor of the elm tree, suggesting the extent to which he is rooted in the region. Zoe's actions and desires embody the social ideologies and power differentials that have historically been active in constructions of New England identity, and through engaging her, Howard both exposes the hidden arguments and cultural work of the seemingly benign regional image and implicitly argues that he, and others who have been similarly excluded from that image over time, should have their place acknowledged in both the New England on the ground and the New England of the mind. In the end, Zoe largely gets her way, although Howard retains enough land to defiantly erect a house trailer squarely in her line of vision. While this resolution may be Hebert's grudging acknowledgment of the power of the New England image, at the same time he raises important political questions about the larger social and cultural issues involved in questions of regional identity and representation.

The public reaction to Carolyn Chute's 1985 novel *The Beans of Egypt, Maine* provides some indication of the continuing power of the conventional New England regional image. A fierce partisan of and self-appointed spokesman for the rural New England working class, Chute sets her Bean clan in implicit contrast to the idyllic, leisured, outdoorsy, middle-class vision of regional life marketed and promoted by the L. L. Bean company of Freeport, Maine. Chute's tale is an updated example of American literary naturalism, with the members of the Bean family trapped by the influence of heredity and social environment in an inescapable cycle of poverty, accompanied in their case by despair, domestic violence, crime, and promiscuity. Even more than Howard Elman, Chute's Beans are presented as victims of the social and economic circumstances of life in modern New England. At the same time, though, Chute attempts to invest them with a certain pride and dignity as well as a strong and sustaining sense of family solidarity; one character, Beal Bean, even comes to take on ironic Christ-like overtones, dying in a symbolic crucifixion at the hands of police while angrily shooting out the windows of the fancy house of a family of wealthy newcomers from Massachusetts. Many readers, however, chose to focus on what they saw as the gritty and lurid details of the novel, focusing on how the characters behaved rather than on the social and political questions they embodied and enacted. The novel became something of a *cause célèbre* because it accomplished in a particularly provocative fashion precisely what Chute intended it to: it presented an image of an anti-New England, writing into the literary record a group of people who have always been present in the landscape but whom dominant discourses of regional identity had rendered largely invisible.

New England has always been a complicated place, of course. It has been characterized by immigration from the beginning, from the earliest English settlers to today's Southeast Asians, South Americans, and East Europeans. Its social, cultural, political, and economic histories have been as complex and changeable as its demographics. Yet throughout its history, New Englanders have examined their region through the filters of their social and cultural needs, priorities, and ideologies, filters which have let certain aspects of regional life through into their minds and imaginations and refused to admit others into the regional image. And New England's regional literature has been a central part of this perpetual process, providing a site for versions of regional identity to be formed and reformed, confirmed and critiqued. If there is anything that holds New England regional literature together as a conceptually coherent whole, it is this enduring role it has played as a vital means through which New England writers and readers have debated just exactly who they are.

REFERENCES AND FURTHER READING

Bradstreet, Anne (1650). "A Dialogue between Old England and New." In *The Tenth Muse Lately Sprung Up in America*. London: Stephen Bowtell.

Brown, Dona (1995). *Inventing New England: Regional Tourism in the Nineteenth Century*. Washington DC: Smithsonian Institution Press.

Buell, Lawrence (1986). *New England Literary Culture: From Revolution through Renaissance*. Cambridge: Cambridge University Press.

Chute, Carolyn (1985). *The Beans of Egypt, Maine*. Boston: Ticknor & Fields.

Conforti, Joseph A. (2001). *Imagining New England: Explorations of Regional Identity from the Pilgrims to the Mid-Twentieth Century*. Chapel Hill: University of North Carolina Press.

Freeman, Mary E. Wilkins (1891). *A New England Nun and Other Stories*. New York: Harper.

Frost, Robert (1915). *North of Boston*. New York: Henry Holt.

Frost, Robert (1923). *New Hampshire*. New York: Henry Holt.

Hebert, Ernest (1979). *The Dogs of March*. New York: Viking.

Jewett, Sarah Orne (1896). *The Country of the Pointed Firs*. Boston: Houghton Mifflin.

Johnson, Edward (1654). *Wonder-Working Providence of Sions Savior in New England, 1628–1651*. London.

Kemp, John (1979). *Robert Frost and New England: The Poet as Regionalist*. Princeton: Princeton University Press.

Larcom, Lucy (1889). *A New England Girlhood, Outlined from Memory*. Boston: Houghton Mifflin.

Mather, Cotton (1702). *Magnalia Christi Americana, or The Ecclesiastical History of New England*, 7 vols. London.

Robinson, Edwin Arlington (1921). *Collected Poems*. New York: Macmillan.

Robinson, Rowland (1995). *Danvis Tales*, ed. David Budbill. Hanover: University Press of New England.

Smith, John (1616). *A Description of New England*. London.

Smith, Seba (1834). *The Life and Writings of Major Jack Downing of Downingville*. Boston: Lilly, Wait, Colman, & Holman.

Steiner, Michael (1983). "Regionalism in the Great Depression." *Geographical Review* 73, 430–46.

Stowe, Harriet Beecher (1852). *Uncle Tom's Cabin*. Boston: John P. Jewett.

Stowe, Harriet Beecher (1869). *Oldtown Folks*. Boston: Fields, Osgood.

Stowe, Harriet Beecher (1878). *Poganuc People*. New York: Fords, Howard & Hulbert.

Tyler, Royall (1790). *The Contrast*. Philadelphia: Thomas Wignall. (First perf. 1787.)

Wharton, Edith (1911). *Ethan Frome*. New York: Charles Scribner's Sons.

Wharton, Edith (1917). *Summer*. New York: D. Appleton.

White, E. B. (1944). *One Man's Meat*. New York: Harper.

Wilder, Thornton (1938). *Our Town*. New York: Coward-McCann.

Winthrop, John (1963). "A Modell of Christian Charity." In Perry Miller and Thomas H. Johnson (eds.), *The Puritans: A Sourcebook of their Writings*, 195–9. New York: Harper. (First publ. 1630.)

Wood, William (1634). *New England's Prospect*. London.

13

The Great Plains

Diane D. Quantic

The Great Plains is not simply a region in the local color sense, a rural or isolated place where eccentric people and unfamiliar geography combine to create a unique scene. Where so many travelers, settlers, and writers have asserted that there is nothing to see, men and women who know that there is indeed something to see on the plains have had to create a language adequate to contain their accounts of an apparently unmarked space, a sea of grass. They know that how we define what we see determines how we respond to the place that is being viewed. For example, in O. E. Rølvaag's *Giants in the Earth* (1927), the Norwegian immigrant Per Hansa sees before him a land without boundaries where he can dream possibilities into reality, but his wife Beret does not have her husband's power of imagination and so she sees only empty space.

To become a region in the literary sense of the word, the Great Plains had to become a landscape consciously observed by native tribes, travelers, newcomers and residents, and that landscape had to be absorbed into the region's collective experience. *Place* needs a history, a time continuum, to become a context for literature. Descriptions of the Great Plains landscape repeat familiar features that have become a kind of mythic shorthand readers recognize: the buffalo hunting grounds, the sea of grass, the great American desert, the Garden of the World. These images and expectations became the symbols that underlie much Great Plains literature (Smith 1970; Quantic 1995). White settlers, spurred by the offer of "free" land and their faith in the imperialistic myth of Manifest Destiny, believed that on the Great Plains they would find the democratic utopia, the safety valve. Instead, drought and economic depression forced many to conform their myths and expectations to the climate and economy of a cash crop monoculture. The myth of the yeoman farmer and the family cow has been displaced by thousand-acre wheat farms and vertically integrated corporate feed lots. Various populations have added their own accumulated cultural baggage to the values and community expectations that the region's residents embrace or resist. Works identified as Great Plains literature reflect this landscape of climate extremes and diverse cultures. Nevertheless, the persistence of the garden/ desert dichotomy in Great Plains literature as a given or an ironic counterpoint attests to the power of myth to frame our vision of the region.

The Great Plains region spreads across the center of the northern hemisphere, vast grasslands that are subdivided into the tallgrass prairie and the short-grass region of the high plains – but just where the Great Plains begin and end will always be a matter of opinion: much depends upon one's criteria. Politically, the region is bounded in the United States by the state lines of Kansas, Nebraska, South Dakota and North Dakota, (usually) Oklahoma and (sometimes) west Texas. It extends north into the prairies of south-central Canada, but the character of the region is not really determined by the politics inside the box-like state and provincial lines. Great Plains topography impacts the region's character more directly. Its climate is determined by the distance from the oceans' moisture, the lack of physical barriers to the north and south that would moderate the storms that sweep down the region, and the gradual increase in altitude that culminates in the Rocky Mountain barrier to the west. These geographical factors affect the region's ecology and, ultimately, its economy. At the eastern rim, where grasslands fade into forest, there is usually adequate rain, and rich prairie soils grow wheat and corn. The gridded fields are interrupted by the rock-hard Flint Hills, impervious to the plow, where remnants of the tallgrass prairie pastures crease eastern Kansas and Oklahoma like a backbone. The one hundredth meridian that divides the eastern two-thirds of the states from the western regions is the accustomed boundary between the prairies and drier high plains. An almost visible line, it marks the point where the prairie's tall grasses and rolling pasturelands give way to the long views of the high plains where cattle spread across the short grass pastures and deep aquifers provide the water needed to sustain the crops that fatten the cattle.

When one considers the region's history and economy, slightly different boundaries become apparent. White settlers came onto the Great Plains with the intention of transforming the region. Throughout the nineteenth century, politics and economics determined that the line of settlement would move steadily west from the Mississippi to the Rocky Mountains. The Civil War and radical political changes in Europe and Russia in the late nineteenth century conspired to send thousands of home-seekers to the American West just as the Great Plains, cleared of Indian resistance, were opening to settlement.

These settlers were not coming into an empty region: it has always been changing. Native tribes left evidence of their earthen houses, cultivated fields, and great bison hunts. Scientists know that there have always been fluctuating periods of rain and drought in the region; that fire from lightning or fires Indians set to trap the bison herds helped sustain the open savannas; that winds constantly redistribute the soils. But American and European settlers realized the greatest transformation of the region. They plowed under the grasses in order to plant the cash crops they needed to purchase what they could not grow. A few wet years lured hopeful settlers onto the high plains, where many struggled in the inevitable dry years to farm in country best suited to grazing. Thousands failed and backtrailed to the east. One hundred years later, the rural population on the high plains continues to decline, a reality reflected in the literature's stories of struggle and dogged determination.

For the plains Indians, the horse, left behind by the Spanish explorers, brought them the ability to range over wider hunting grounds, but this meant that more people and animals had to be fed and therefore even more bison had to be found. As white settlement pushed eastern Indians onto the plains, competition for space and game increased intertribal warfare. Thus the stage was set for the violent transformation of plains Indians' societies as the United States government abandoned treaties and promises in its effort to "remove" the Native Americans from the prairie and plains. Ironically, a century later Native populations on the Great Plains are steadily increasing.

The first Europeans and white Americans to come onto the plains were explorers. The Spaniard Coronado reached Kansas in the 1540s. After the explorers came traders and trappers. Many of these early sojourners left records that add a rich historical and scientific record to any consideration of Great Plains literature (Barclay et al. 1994; Thacker 1989). The expedition led by Meriwether Lewis and William Clark, from May 1804 to October 1806, up the Missouri river and across the northern Great Plains to the Oregon coast and back to St. Louis justified the nation's purchase of the Louisiana territory. Lewis and Clark carefully mapped the region. They recorded descriptions and collected specimens of hundreds of animals and plants unknown to Americans and Europeans, and they made contact with the various Indian tribes, informing them that they were part of a new nation. Their vivid account of a remarkable journey is an important document of American and Great Plains literature.[1]

In the first decades of the nineteenth century, the US government commissioned other expeditions to explore the Great Plains. The parties, which included scientists and often artists, had instructions to record their observations of the region and evaluate its usefulness; to identify navigable rivers and land appropriate for future settlement; and to report on the region's usefulness as a barrier to prevent the diffusion of the United States population. Their reports influenced American policy for years. Edwin James wrote the account of Stephen Long's 1820 expedition. The party crossed the central plains in August, the hottest, driest part of the year: James wrote across the expedition's map "Great Desert," an image that persists even now.

By the 1820s, faint trails were crisscrossing the Great Plains. One of the most important early trails went from what is now Kansas City to Santa Fe. By the time Josiah Gregg began his years as a trader (1831–40), the trail was well established. He wrote *Commerce of the Prairies* (1844) as a guidebook for other travelers, and especially for other businessmen. Another traveler on the Santa Fe Trail was Susan Shelby Magoffin, the young bride of an established Santa Fe trader. Her letters, entitled *Down the Santa Fe and into Mexico*, were not published until 1927, but they offer a lively complement to Gregg's account. In recent years, the publication of countless journals and diaries of the men and women who traveled along the Oregon, California, and Mormon trails has added immeasurably to our historical understanding of the Great Plains (Faragher 1979; Myres 1982; Schlissel 1982; Unruh 1979).

Travel narratives were immensely popular in England and America in the nineteenth century; readers looked for adventure and the "picturesque," and the Great Plains met the necessary criteria. Works by Washington Irving and Mark Twain are representative of the Great Plains travel accounts. Irving traveled across a portion of present-day Oklahoma in 1832, soon after he returned from 17 years in Europe. His account of that adventure, *A Tour on the Prairies*, appeared in 1832 (McDermott 1944). Irving's party is itself a part of the picturesque. It includes trail hands whose uncivilized habits appall the sophisticated Irving, but whose tall tales and backwoods boasts he carefully and colorfully records. The inexperience of a young count and his English tutor provide more entertainment. By the end of his tour, Irving has abandoned elaborate comparisons to the romantic European landscape. He has been faced with an arduous trek through the cross timbers, a tangled maze of scrub oak that presents real hazards, and with the duty of putting a wounded bison out of its misery, an incident that sobers him considerably. In *Roughing It* (1872), Mark Twain recounts his adventures traveling by stage coach across the Great Plains on his way to Nevada with his brother Orion. Already gaining a reputation as a humorist and chronicler of the American scene when *Roughing It* appeared, Twain is not above embellishing his experiences for the sake of a good story. Although most of the book recounts his Nevada adventures, Twain describes the harrowing stage-coach ride and the passengers' encounters with unsavory characters along the trail; and, in the voice of his fellow-traveler Bemis, narrates his companion's encounter with a buffalo in his familiar laconic tall-tale style.

The earliest Great Plains work included in the traditional American literary canon comes from a writer who never saw the region. When he wrote *The Prairie* (1827), James Fenimore Cooper relied on James's account of the Long expedition as the source for his descriptions of the prairie landscape, but he set his story even earlier, at the time of the Lewis and Clark expedition, to emphasize his theme: that the appearance on the open "uncivilized" plains of white Americans, both the noble Natty Bumppo and the destructive Ishmael Bush, symbolizes the profound changes confronting the young republic. While Bumppo prefers the company of his Pawnee friends and represents for Cooper the best qualities of human beings, Bush represents the destructive intentions of those who claim a law and a society of their own creation (Motley 1987).

Great Plains literature includes a notable body of nonfiction that, in its attention to the region's natural history, represents a continuation of the explorers' reports. For example, the ornithologist Paul Johnsgard, whose books include *Crane Music: A Natural History of Cranes* (1991), writes observant and readable accounts of these remarkable birds that crowd the Great Plains skies in spring and fall. John Janovy, a biologist, records his observations of nature and people in Nebraska's Sandhills in *Keith County* (1978) and *Back in Keith County* (1981). These works examine the landscape that Great Plains residents have come to value for itself, not only for its economic potential.

Wallace Stegner's *Wolf Willow*, with its long subtitle, *A History, A Story and A Memory of the Last Plains Frontier* (1962), defies categorization but deserves mention. Known for his novels, essays, and environmental writings focused on the inland West, Stegner nevertheless earns a place in Great Plains literature with this account of his childhood on a wheat ranch that straddled the Saskatchewan–Montana border. The opening chapter, "The Question Mark in the Circle," remains one of the most vivid evocations of the Great Plains' "character":

> The drama of this landscape is in the sky, pouring with light and always moving. The earth is passive. And yet the beauty I am struck by, both as present fact and as revived memory, is a fusion: this sky would not be so spectacular without this earth to change and glow and darken under it. And whatever the sky may do, however the earth is shaken or darkened, the Euclidian perfection abides. The very scale, the hugeness of simple forms, emphasizes stability. It is not hills and mountains which we call eternal. Nature abhors an elevation as much as it abhors a vacuum; a hill is no sooner elevated than the forces of erosion begin tearing it down. These prairies are quiescent, close to static; looked at for any length of time, they begin to impose their awful perfection on the observer's mind. Eternity is a peneplain. (Stegner 1962: 7)

A number of other writers, among them William Least Heat-Moon in *PrairyErth: A Deep Map* (1991), Canadian Sharon Butala in *The Perfection of the Morning: An Apprenticeship in Nature* (1994), and Kathleen Norris in *Dakota: A Spiritual Geography* (1993), extend the nature commentary and write more impressionistic accounts of their encounters with the surface landscape and their deeper spiritual and emotional connections to the places they are writing about (Price, in WLA 1997: 701–10). Heat-Moon's work is an encyclopedic portrait of Chase County, Kansas in the heart of the tallgrass Flint Hills. His catalog of the landscape – places, people, the past, animals, plants, ephemera – provides the reader with a deep map: in-depth knowledge of an almost square place in the center of the Great Plains. Butala, who married a rancher and moved to southwest Saskatchewan in middle age, records her initiation into ranch life and her growing awareness of the physical and spiritual qualities of the land. Norris's work is an account of her decision to move to her maternal grandmother's home town, Lemmon, South Dakota, after years in New York City. Like Butala, Norris is surprised by her response to the land. For Norris, landscape is intimately related to the change she experiences as she becomes involved in the close-knit community. Gradually, she is drawn to the more spiritual aspects of the ascetic life she encounters in the isolated small town on the high plains. It is clear that Norris would not have discovered this part of herself if she had not moved to the Great Plains, a place that has required countless people to come to terms with themselves and what they are about.

Another variant in the natural histories of the Great Plains is represented by South Dakota rancher Linda Hasselstrom who chronicles her life in a series of works that mix poetry, essays, and accounts of ranch routine.[2] In works such as *Land Circle: Stories from the Land* (1991) and *Feels Like Far* (1999), Hasselstrom blends vivid accounts of the sheer energy it takes to handle the routine chores on an ordinary ranch with her chronicle of her own family history: the deaths of her husband and her father; her own efforts to be a writer and a rancher in the same time and space; her determination to hold onto the land.

A great many poets have recorded their impressions of the plains. Few have gained a national audience or had reputations that lasted beyond their own lifetimes; sadly, their volumes go out of print and their works are forgotten. Although William Stafford spent most of his adult life and established his career in the Pacific Northwest, he grew up on the plains of Kansas, and the Great Plains permeates his poetry. John Neihardt is a well-known Great Plains poet, but his reputation rests primarily on his relationship with Black Elk, an Oglala Sioux elder whose stories Neihardt transcribed in *Black Elk Speaks* (1932), still one of the most-read Great Plains works. A number of poets have solid reputations within their own states. Although his scope is the Midwest and the works are dated, the volumes *Heartland: Poets of the Midwest* (1967) and *Heartland II: Poets of the Midwest* (1975) edited by Lucien Stryk provide good representations of poets from the Great Plains region.[3]

Indian writers have, in the last few years, gained widespread recognition as an integral component in Great Plains literature (Hafen, in WLA 1997: 711–17). Some of the earliest Great Plains texts were written by men and women who left their tribes to be educated in far-away boarding schools. As adults they wrote autobiographies in their new language, English, to explain to white readers why their "education" was such a radical change. For example, in *American Indian Stories* (1921), Zitkala-Ša (Gertrude Simmons Bonnin) (Sioux) relates her early childhood and the trauma she experienced when plunged into a world of strange and insulting customs and a language that she could not negotiate. In volumes such as *Indian Boyhood* (1902), *Old Indian Days* (1907), and *The Soul of the Indian* (1911), Charles Eastman (Ohiyesha) (Dakota) relates his own story and his Dakota oral tradition for white audiences, a task taken on by several other writers including Luther Standing Bear (Dakota) and Ella Deloria (Dakota).[4]

N. Scott Momaday (Kiowa Cherokee) established the contemporary Indian presence in American literature with *House Made of Dawn* (1968), which won a Pulitzer Prize. In *The Way to Rainy Mountain* (1976), Momaday tracks his own story into his grandparents' tribal past. Many contemporary writers have followed Momaday's example. For example, Linda Hogan (Chickasaw), in her novel, *Mean Spirit* (1990), chronicles the complex lives of Oklahoma Indians in the 1920s and 1930s when oil was discovered under Indian lands. Hogan balances the Indians' apparent victimization by whites who will use any means necessary to control the oil-rich lands with the efforts of a medicine man and the elusive hill people to protect the Indians' lives and the things they truly value.

In her steady output of novels over the last fifteen years, Louise Erdrich has become a major figure in American literature. Writing from her perspective as an

Ojibwa and German American who grew up on the Turtle Mountain reservation in North Dakota, she has woven the same characters and sometimes the same situations from different points of view in and out of her novels. A growing body of scholarly commentary is one indication of the interest in her varied techniques and the layers of interpretations her work elicits. In *Love Medicine* (1984, revised in 1993), *Tracks* (1988), *The Beet Queen* (1986), *The Bingo Palace* (1993), *Tales of Burning Love* (1996), and *The Last Report on the Miracles at Little No Horse* (2001), Erdrich creates complex stories of extended families, connected by blood and nurturing and separated by old enmities, who live on the North Dakota reservation. Erdrich references Ojibwa legends and tales, assigning to contemporary characters in her stories the qualities of figures such as the trickster Nanabozho. In *The Antelope Wife* (1998) and *The Crown of Columbus* (1991, with Michael Dorris), Erdrich abandons her usual cast of characters to deal with other aspects of the Indian–white continuum that stretches from the time of Columbus and encompasses complex Indian and white myths and experiences that persistently if subtly influence our collective narrative of the Great Plains.

The story most often identified with the Great Plains is the story of settlement by whites and the transformation of the grasslands into neat squares of cash crops and arrow-straight roads. Willa Cather's classic accounts of this period in *O Pioneers!* (1913) and *My Ántonia* (1918) have become, for many Americans, the quintessential version of Great Plains literature.[5] Cather supports a scholarly industry that shows no sign of diminishing (Murphy, in WLA 1997: 658–69). Recently, Cather criticism has been caught up in the discussions of homosexuality in her works and her life (Anders 1999; Acocella 2000). Although some scholars continue a sometimes raucous public debate over this issue, many others continue to examine the novels themselves, focusing on Cather's artistry: how she uses and transforms her sources and how her works reflect the historical times of the stories' settings and her own contemporary world.

For a discussion of almost any aspect of the Great Plains experience, one can draw illustrations from Cather's works. *O Pioneers!* focuses on the first settlers' transformation of the rich prairie soils into prosperous farms. Cather's farmer is Alexandra Bergson, who studies the latest farming methods when her more conservative brothers resist innovation (Conlogue 2001). For them, conformity to the narrow conservatism of Black Hawk governs their decisions. As in almost all Great Plains novels, success comes at a cost. For Alexandra, the cost is the tragic triangle that entangles her ebullient friend Marie, Marie's morose husband Frank Shabata and Alexandra's brother Emil, the sibling for whom she works so that he can realize success beyond the necessary work of the farm. Marie and Emil surrender to their passion in Marie's fecund orchard, where the peace is shattered by Frank's shots that end both their lives. In the aftermath of these deaths, Alexandra, like other Cather characters, must learn to live a diminished life. She marries her friend Carl Linstrum for companionship, not romantic love – a familiar motif in Great Plains literature, where a successful marriage is a working partnership.

The story in *My Ántonia* is told by Jim Burden, one of Cather's surrogate narrators. Based on the life of Cather's friend from Red Cloud, Nebraska, Annie Pavelka, the story follows the story of the Bohemian immigrant Ántonia Shimerda. During their first impoverished winter on the Divide, her father commits suicide, despairing of his family's isolation on the high plains, living in a dugout little better than an animal's burrow. At first Ántonia works in the fields with her brother, but soon after Jim and his grandparents move to Black Hawk, Ántonia moves into town to be a hired girl for their neighbors the Harlings. Ántonia learns much about managing a household from Mrs. Harling, but she resists Mr. Harling's insistence that she conform to the family's values and not go to the town's dances. Valuing her brief period of freedom from family obligations, Ántonia leaves the Harlings and finds employment in the household of the predatory Wick Cutter, but she flees when she rightly suspects he is plotting to rape her. Jim Burden leaves Black Hawk, returning only occasionally to follow Ántonia's story. Anticipating marriage, Ántonia goes to Denver but returns unmarried and pregnant to take up life on her family's farm. Jim hears pitiful rumors of her life, but when he sees her, he begins to realize Ántonia's resiliency. In a last visit, Jim finds Ántonia surrounded by her children, a steady husband and a prosperous farm, and Cather's reader realizes that Ántonia is meant to embody a triumphant figure.

These two novels, full of pastoral allusions and heroic women, are often cited as models of Great Plains literature. The anticipated themes are here: the hardships and sacrifices of the early years; the transformation of people's lives and the land itself into ordered prosperity; the triumph over adversity; the celebration of family and community. Evidence from historical and other literary sources confirms that Cather has rendered an accurate account of the years of white settlement; and, at the same time, she has created in Alexandra and Ántonia archetypal figures of heroic women: the far-sighted homesteader, the earth mother. In many Great Plains novels, however, the grim hardships overshadow the pastoral romance that is Cather's governing theme in these two works.

Cather's other Great Plains novels are more problematic. In *A Lost Lady* (1923) and *One of Ours* (1922), Cather centers her stories on, respectively, Marian Forrester and Claude Wheeler. Just how Marian, viewed by the young Niel Herbert, is a lost lady has been a subject of much scholarly commentary. She is lost to Niel as an ideal when he realizes that she is not faithful to her husband. As her husband's health declines and they are confined to their home in Sweet Water, she is lost to the wider world that nurtures her need for society. After her husband's death she leaves Sweet Water and Niel literally loses track of her. In another sense, Marian is not lost at all. Years later, Niel learns that she has survived, doing what she must to continue to live the kind of life she thrives on: like Marie and Ántonia, Marian does not abandon passion or accept a diminished life.

Cather sets Marian's story against a broader theme of loss (Quantic 1995: 129–33). Her husband, Captain Forrester, is one of the men who has the imagination to build the railroads that transform the grasslands into a landscape of ordered fields and sharp, narrow little towns. He even builds his Sweet Water home on an old Indian camping site, an appropriation at the most basic level. His gradual decline in health, power, and wealth parallels changes in the region. Profit, not the nation's progress, governs the acts of the opportunists who replace the railroad builders. Ivy Peters, a Sweet Water shyster, embodies the rising generation of unprincipled entrepreneurs. He gains control of both Marian and her property. Marian acquiesces in his advances because, as she tells Niel, rascality "succeeds [in earning money] faster than anything else" (p. 124).

Claude Wheeler, in *One of Ours*, is perhaps Cather's most discouraged plains dweller. Written at a time when Cather was feeling the effects of rapid change and loss in her life and in the nation, the novel centers on Claude, a young man determined not to succumb to the dull, small-town commercialism of his brother, Bayliss. He marries Enid, a barren, empty woman incapable of any real romance. She insists on removing all signs of raw nature from their farmyard and transforms their house into sterile space. When Enid sails for China to join her missionary sister, Claude goes to Europe and World War I. In France he finds some of the culture and true society he missed on the plains; but before he can relish his new life, he is killed in battle.

Cather's belief in the power of the landscape to nurture those attuned to its power, and to balance the narrow conservatism of plains society is most evident in *The Song of the Lark* (1915), written between *O Pioneers!* and *My Ántonia*. In Thea Kronborg, Cather embodies the artistic ideals that are central to much of her work. Music, more especially opera, is Thea's artistic vehicle, and Cather makes it clear that Thea's early life in Moonstone, Colorado has nurtured her talent.[6] Various Moonstone residents recognize Thea's gifts and reveal parts of their own worlds to her – books, music, the landscape: all necessary to counteract the conservative townspeople who expect her to stay within the limits that small towns establish for a preacher's daughter. Later, Thea retreats to the Southwest where she experiences a coming together of all of these influences that provide the emotional force necessary, Cather feels, for the full realization of life as an artist.

Cather's works, written in the first half of the twentieth century, establish a high bar for Great Plains literature. She identifies and validates the canonical themes: struggle with and against the land, its fertility and its fierce unpredictability; the transformation of the grasslands into farms and attendant communities; the narrow conformity of people isolated from other, richer veins of American culture; and, at the same time, the power of the landscape to transform and inspire the perceptive resident.

Other major Great Plains authors include O. E. Rølvaag and Mari Sandoz. Rølvaag arrived in Minnesota from Norway when he was in his late teens. He spent his career as a faculty member at St. Olaf College in Northfield, Minnesota. *Giants in the Earth* (1927) is his best-known work, although he continued the story of Per Hansa's family in *Peder Victorious* (1929) and *Their Father's God* (1931).[7] Rølvaag integrates the immigrant story of cultural adjustment with the other classic Great Plains story, the transformation of the land. To Per Hansa, released from a preordained life as a

Norwegian peasant fisherman, the sea of grass means opportunity to one who learns to navigate it. He creates out of sod, the ground itself, an innovative combination house and barn; but to his fearful wife, Beret, the snug sod dwelling is no better than an animal's burrow. The landscape that Per Hansa imagines as a gleaming fairy king-dom means nothing to Beret: there is nothing to see, nothing to hide behind, nothing to hear. She feels psychologically erased. The usual hardships – illness, blizzards, and locust plagues – Per Hansa regards as challenges to conquer. Beret reads them as signs of doom and God's displeasure: the giants are *in* the earth, resisting their efforts to transform the grasslands into ordered farms. Rølvaag's novel, with its stark con-trasts between strength and weakness, humans and nature, hope and despair, is in some ways a more representative Great Plains work than Cather's more subtle, pastoral representations of the risks and rewards of settlement and change. If "reality" is the touchstone, then Rølvaag's novel, with all of its grim disasters, is closer than Cather's novels to the experiences recorded in biographies, diaries, and other nonfiction works. Together, the works of Cather and Rølvaag set the standard for classic Great Plains stories of settlement.

Mari Sandoz's biography of her father, *Old Jules* (1935), brought the Nebraska writer the recognition and a $5,000 prize that enabled her to leave Lincoln, where she had been working, and move to New York City, where she lived and wrote about the high plains for thirty years – a total of 22 volumes. One issue explored by Sandoz scholars centers on attempts to categorize her work. Her fiction is based on facts that she researched scrupulously, and her histories contain much that is her own inven-tion. Sandoz herself saw her role as chronicler of the plains (Stauffer 1982). She wrote only a few novels, most notably *Slogum House* (1937). As her writing career developed, she methodically set out to record the whole sweep of Great Plains history in works such as *The Beaver Men: Spearheads of Empire* (1964), *The Buffalo Hunters: The Story of the Hide Men* (1954), and *The Cattlemen: From the Rio Grande across the Far Marias* (1958). *Crazy Horse, the Strange Man of the Oglalas* (1942) is still regarded as an im-portant biography of one of the greatest Sioux chiefs. *Cheyenne Autumn* (1953) is a classic account of the Cheyennes' trek from their Oklahoma exile back to their South Dakota home.

Based on historical figures and events, Sandoz's novel *Slogum House* is one of the most violent Great Plains works. Gulla Slogum, Sandoz's portrait of an avaricious rancher in the lawless Sandhills, lurks in the shadows of her roadhouse, and sets her sons Hab and Cash and her twin daughters Annette and Cellie to work destroying, incapacitating, or seducing anyone who interferes with her land grabs. Her husband, Ruedy, with the help of their more sympathetic daughter, Libby, balances Gulla's greed. He cultivates a true Great Plains garden and provides sanctuary for the victims of Gulla's greed and violence.

In *Old Jules*, Sandoz embodies in her father various traits often at odds with one another but, according to her observations, necessary in a hard, lawless country. Jules is strong-willed, often physically abusive to his wife Mary and children, and indiffer-ent to the farm routine that becomes the responsibility of his family. But he works tirelessly to establish a true community among the isolated Sandhills homesteaders. The orchards he cultivates flourish in the sandy soils and gain statewide recognition for the Swiss immigrant. He stands up to the ranchers who illegally run cattle on open range and resort to any means at hand to intimidate the settlers.

These events, and dozens of similar ones in *Old Jules* and Sandoz's other novels and memoirs of the Great Plains, underline the contradictory mix of rewards and failures, successes and defeats that characterize the plots in much Great Plains literature. Without *Old Jules*, *Crazy Horse*, *Cheyenne Autumn*, and *Slogum House*, Great Plains literature would be significantly different and diminished.

Cather, Rølvaag, and Sandoz were not, of course, the first Great Plains writers to chronicle the years of white settlement on the Great Plains. Beginning in the 1890s, Hamlin Garland wrote about rural Wisconsin and Iowa, where he grew up, and Dakota Territory, where his parents homesteaded after he left to pursue his education in the east (McCullough 1978). On a visit to Dakota territory, Garland, appalled at the circumstances of his mother's life, determined to write about her grueling experiences. The resulting six stories make up the first edition of *Main Travelled Roads* (1891). Until 1922, Garland added stories to subsequent editions. Often identified with the local color movement in the late nineteenth century, Garland's stories have remained among the most-read works in Great Plains literature. "A Day's Pleasure" is the story of a town wife who alleviates a weary farm wife's day in town. "Among the Corn Rows," another story from the same collection, offers some balance. A Dakota homesteader, Rob, returns to Wisconsin to fetch a bride. Instead of a socially acceptable Yankee girl, he settles on Julie, a hard-working immigrant girl who is glad to exchange the dull fieldwork with no pay that her father expects of her for Rob's offer of a working partnership. These early stories signal a persistent theme in Great Plains literature: one can hope for only brief relief from the necessity of work.

Garland was part of the lively literary scene in Chicago at the turn of the century. He left behind a long shelf of books, including *Boy Life on the Prairie* (1899), *Son of the Middle Border* (1917), *Daughter of the Middle Border* (1921), and the novel *Rose of Dutcher's Coolly* (1895). The realistic effect of his two grim Great Plains novels, *Jason Edwards* (1892) and *Moccasin Ranch* (1909), is undermined by sentimental endings. Garland wrote half a dozen novels set in the Rocky Mountain West (Gish 1976). Garland was an advocate of the single tax theory of Henry George, most effectively applied in the story "Under the Lion's Paw," one of the original stories in *Main Travelled Roads*. An accomplished orator, Garland used his writing and speaking opportunities to call for reform in national farm policy, and he urged changes in America's Indian policy long before most Americans realized the Indians' precarious circumstances (Underhill and Littlefield 1976). *Main Travelled Roads*, however, remains the work that established him as an important chronicler of the Great Plains experience and an important figure in the study of realism and local color in American literature.

Garland's contemporary William Allen White published *The Real Issue: A Book of Kansas Stories* in 1897. Best known for his journalism, White spent his career as owner and editor of the Emporia (Kansas) *Gazette* (Griffith 1989; Jernigan 1983). His family still owns and edits the paper. White established himself as a folksy small-town editor, a staunch advocate for the amenities of life in a prairie town; however, through his numerous books and widely reprinted editorials, he enjoyed a national reputation.[8] Through his Republican party connections White knew almost everyone of political importance in the first half of the twentieth century. Two of White's works have remained in print fairly consistently: the novel *A Certain Rich Man* (1909) and *The Autobiography of William Allen White* (1946), which won for White, posthumously, one of his two Pulitzer Prizes (the other was for editorial writing). *A Certain Rich Man* is interesting for its examination of the corrupting influences of capitalism and monopolies on American society, even in a folksy small town. His *Autobiography* is still a good read.

Another Kansas author, John Ise, a professor of agricultural economics at the University of Kansas, chronicled his parents' homesteading years in *Sod and Stubble* (1936). Ise records the myriad disasters his parents overcame in their effort to raise 12 children on their high plains homestead in western Kansas. Since the University of Nebraska Press published *Sod and Stubble* in 1968, it has remained in print – a minor, but typical, tale of the homestead era (Rothenberger 1996).

Laura Ingalls Wilder's books that chronicle her family's many moves across the Great Plains have long been considered children's classics. In recent years, the books have received increasing critical attention by scholars interested in the history of Indian–white relations, the depiction of women, and the sources of authorial voice (Romines 1997; Miller 1998).[9] Extant manuscripts reveal the close collaboration of Wilder and her daughter, Rose Wilder Lane, a journalist and novelist in her own right. *Little House on the Prairie* (1935) and *The Long Winter* (1940) are Wilder's most important Great Plains stories.[10] The first relates the family's brief stay in Indian territory (now southeastern Kansas), on the farthest edge of advancing white settlement (Linsenmayer 2001). The second is an account of a stark winter spent in DeSmet, South Dakota, where Wilder's family finally settled, when it was merely a supply point at the end of the westbound railroad. Readers of Wilder's works who are attuned to the themes of Great Plains literature will recognize the mix of storms, economic uncertainty, and illnesses that conspire to keep the family on the margins of economic stability, and the equally strong determination of the family to endure hardship. Pa's restlessness, that results in so many of the family's moves, and Ma's shepherdess and corner shelf, that go up first in every "house" they settle into, embody the tension between movement and stability evident in so much Great Plains literature.

Other writers have chronicled the homesteading and early years of white settlement on the Great Plains. Their stories also recount the disasters and near disasters of storms (dust, blizzard, hail, drought), economic depressions, and the tyranny of merchants, railroads, and far-away brokers who determine the price of crops and, consequently, the farmers' – and the towns' – success or failure. The title of Fred Manfred's *This Is the Year* (1947) makes the plot self-evident: this *might* be *the* good year. His novel *The Golden Bowl* (1944) is a grimly realistic account of the struggle of a farm family and the drifter they take in to hold on to their South Dakota farm that is literally blowing away in the Dust Bowl. Lois Phillips Hudson's accounts of dust and failure are found in her novel, *The Bones of Plenty* (1966), and her story collection, *Reapers in the Dust* (1965).

The novels of Nebraskan Bess Streeter Aldrich, while realistic and often grim, present a more balanced and slightly more optimistic picture of settlement in novels such as *The Rim of the Prairie* (1925). Hope Williams Syke's novel *Second Hoeing* (1935) recounts the narrow lives of immigrant beet-field workers and their children in eastern Colorado. Sophus Keith Winther chronicles the despairing lives of Danish immigrants, too late to claim a homestead, who become tenant farmers in *Take All to Nebraska* (1936) and *Mortgage Your Heart* (1937). In *Shukar Balan: The White Lamb. The Story of Evaliz* (1976) Mela Meisner Lindsay recounts her German-Russian family's migration from Russia to the high plains of western Kansas at the turn of the century. These novels accumulate meaning, adding details to familiar stories until they coalesce into a recognizable body of work we call Great Plains literature.

Langston Hughes, Oscar Micheaux, Gordon Parks, and Era Bell Thompson have left accounts of the African-American experience on the Great Plains. Best known as a pioneer African-American film-maker, Oscar Micheaux wrote two autobiographical novels, *The Conquerors* (1913) and *The Homesteaders* (1917), that give accounts of the efforts of African Americans to find their places on the farms and in the small towns on the Great Plains. Era Bell Thompson's autobiography, *American Daughter* (1946), tells of her family's efforts to farm and to fit into the white communities in North Dakota. Langston Hughes's novel *Not Without Laughter* (1930) is a fictionalized account of his boyhood in Lawrence, Kansas. Hughes's story of Sonny is set in an average-sized town where the boy lives with his grandmother, his mother, and sometimes his father. His family is part of a vibrant African-American community that is largely invisible to the town's white population. They are held together through the efforts of the women who care for their children and grandchildren. Family members in Hughes's novel represent various options open to African Americans in the small prairie towns in the early twentieth century: domestic service, itinerancy, odd jobs, entertainment, imitation of the white middle class, and flight to urban centers. Gordon Parks's autobiographical novel, *The Learning Tree* (1963), is set in southeastern Kansas, a region that shares a closer history and culture with the South than with the Great Plains; nevertheless, Parks's novel and his autobiographies, *A Choice of Weapons* (1986) and *Voices in the Mirror: An Autobiography* (1992), complement the other stories of African Americans growing up in the towns of the Great Plains.

Wright Morris wrote some 20 novels between 1942, when he published *My Uncle Dudley*, and 1980, when *Plains Song for Female Voices* appeared. His three autobiographical memoirs, *Will's Boy: A Memoir*, (1981), *Solo: An American Dreamer in Europe* (1983), and *A Cloak of Light: My Writing Life* (1985) recount his remarkable life as a writer and photographer. Other works, including essays on the writer's craft and the complex relationships of the visual in both writing and photography, have established him as an important figure in twentieth-century American literature (Wydeven, in WLA 1997: 685–92). Morris is an inveterate experimenter. His novel *Field of Vision*, published in 1956, uses multiple points of view on a chronological continuum. He published *The Home Place* (1948) with text on one page and a photo on the facing page. Morris reuses phrases and images until they become clichés and then metaphors, a kind of shorthand that signals his tongue-in-cheek observation that we've been over this ground before and we are going over it again because it must be thoroughly examined to be understood. Mirrors, opaque glass, curtains, and windows proliferate in both his photos and his texts, signaling our inability to *see* the landscape in front of us, obscured as it is by the past or our own imagination. When his characters encounter these barriers they ignore them or impose on the reflections their own memories and realities.

Although some of his novels are set in other places, Morris's reputation rests on his Great Plains works, especially *The Home Place, The World in the Attic* (1949), *The Works of Love* (1949), *Field of Vision*, and *Ceremony in Lone Tree* (1959). *Plains Song for Female Voices* chronicles the range of women's responses to the Great Plains found in one intergenerational family. This novel, *The Home Place*, and *Ceremony in Lone Tree* are Morris's best-known Great Plains works. *Ceremony in Lone Tree* is an account of the ninetieth birthday celebration for Tom Scanlon, who sleeps behind the stove of Lone Tree's deserted hotel while his daughter Lois McKee, her husband, and assorted in-laws, children, and grandchildren play out a series of parodies of the Wild West. Scanlon is roused by a shot, only to fall over dead. The exploding gun is set off by Lois McKee, who thereby puts a halt to the Western scenario and restores some domestic control to the Wild West. Despite its carnivalesque tone, *Ceremony in Lone Tree* is Morris's serious commentary on the destructive and persistent power of the Wild West myth in American contemporary society. *The Home Place* chronicles the attempt of Clyde Muncy to find a place for his family to fit in. With a New York City wife and children, Clyde arrives at the farm of his Aunt Clara and Uncle Harry, typically reticent Morris plains dwellers. Significantly, although he is searching for his own boyhood, the farm is not Clyde's own home place. He is hoping, however, to finally identify some place, even the house across the road that belongs to his soon-to-be-dead Uncle Ed, as his family's home. Clyde discovers, however, that he cannot graft his family or even himself onto a not entirely accurately remembered past.

Morris's stories often foreground children or adults searching for a home. This motif no doubt reflects Morris's own migratory childhood, but it also echoes the fear that we are at the mercy of forces we cannot control: the sense of insecurity, the very real possibility of disaster and failure, that permeates Great Plains literature. By drawing on his own experiences and on the familiar motifs of Great Plains literature, which he often parodies and updates, Morris uses Great Plains settings and themes to examine late twentieth-century American insecurities.

Writers in Manitoba, Saskatchewan, and Alberta have been creating stories about their prairie region almost as long as their American neighbors. Canadian prairie works include Robert Stead's *The Homesteaders* (1916) and *Grain* (1926); Martha

Ostenso's *Wild Geese* (1925); Frederick Philip Grove's *Settlers of the Marsh* (1925) and *Fruits of the Earth* (1933); and W. O. Mitchell's *Who Has Seen the Wind* (1947).

Regarded by most Canadians as major writers, Sinclair Ross and Margaret Laurence left accounts of life in the small prairie towns of Saskatchewan and Manitoba: Ross's novel *As for Me and My House* (1941) established his reputation, while Laurence is known for her novels set in Manawaka, her version of Cather's Black Hawk or Hanover. In his novel, Ross lets the minister's wife tell her own story of isolation, the indifference of her husband, and the narrow-minded people in the small town they serve. This unreliable narrator enriches the story's possible readings. Ross's story collection, *The Lamp at Noon and Other Stories* (1968), is as unrelenting in its stories of diminished and destroyed lives and people who are victims of nature's capricious fury as any in Great Plains literature. Like Erdrich and Morris, Laurence returns to a recurring cast of characters in her novels. Like Morris, Laurence's characters are displaced nomads, searching for home. In *A Bird in the House* (1970), *The Stone Angel* (1964), and *The Diviners* (1974), Laurence explores the roots and persistence of isolation and alienation that her characters experience.[11]

In addition to *The Perfection of the Morning*, Sharon Butala's work includes novels and short-story collections that explore the issues of preservation of the grassland's fragile ecology and the need to balance the psychological and economic survival of men and women who try to survive in an often unforgiving landscape.[12] Other contemporary Canadian writers, Robert Kroetsch and Rudy Wiebe, have chronicled the Canadian experience on the plains, Kroetsch in works such as *Badlands* (1975) and *The Studhorse Man* (1969), and Wiebe in *Peace Shall Destroy Many* (1962) and in his historical novels about Indians (First Nations) and Métis on the Canadian prairies.

A surprising array of writers keep rewriting the Great Plains experience (Quantic, in WLA 1997: 720–7). Larry Woiwode, Dan O'Brien, and Kent Haruf are representative. Woiwode chronicles the lives of the Neumiller family in *Beyond the Bedroom Wall* (1975), *Born Brothers* (1988), and *The Neumiller Stories* (1989). As Woiwode's family drifts further east from the family's North Dakota homestead (the death of the family patriarch opens the first novel), they come apart as a family and as individuals. Without firm connections to *a* place they can identify as home, they become rootless migrants. The mother, Alma, like Rølvaag's Beret, can find nothing predictable or permanent to connect to. The houses they live in have already been inhabited. The children drift away into vague careers and, in one case, suicide. Despite these failings, Woiwode's characters expend prodigious energy trying to find the center, struggling to live meaningful lives even as they seem to be drifting backwards, towards the East.

An environmentalist, rancher, and writer, South Dakotan Dan O'Brien weaves his observations and concerns about people and wild things on the high plains into his work. The novels *In the Center of the Nation* (1991) and *Brendan Prairie* (1996) center on threats to the land perpetrated by developers and opportunists and opposed by ordinary people who value the land as it is. *The Rites of Autumn: A Falconer's Journey across America* (1988) is O'Brien's account of his trip down the central flyway with Dolly, a peregrine falcon he is training to return to the wild. *Buffalo for a Broken Heart: Restoring Life to a Black Hills Ranch* (2001) is an account of his own experiences as a buffalo rancher.[13]

Kent Haruf's setting is the plains of eastern Colorado, where people have to struggle to remain solvent and sane. *The Tie that Binds* (1984) shares with Sandoz's *Slogum House* the award for the grimmest Great Plains novel with the cruelest character. Roy Goodnough, whose anger causes him to miscalculate and cut off his fingers in the sharp blades of a grain-cutting header, cuts off his remaining fingers when his son threatens to leave. His son and daughter, trapped on the farm until they are old, senile, and insane, end their lives in an incestuous relationship that reveals the cruel irony of the title. Haruf's *Plainsong* (1999) is a much more balanced tale set in the same fictional region. Two bachelor farmers take in Victoria Robideaux, a pregnant high-school girl. Around this unlikely trio, Haruf creates a community of people who try to help each other and themselves to survive in a small town where, as Haruf has said, people perform acts of surprising cruelty and kindness.

Other novelists have produced one or two remarkable Great Plains works. Ron Hansen's *Nebraska: Stories* (1989) demonstrates an impressive range in time, style, and tone. Some of his stories are straightforward in style, while others use the fractured narratives of postmodernism. Philip Kimball has written *Harvesting Ballads* (1984), the story of another wanderer searching for a family in the Oklahoma and Kansas wheat fields. His novel *Liar's Moon: A Long Story* (1999) is a multilayered work, with shifts in both time and point of view, that centers on the consequences of the loss of two children who are bumped from a crowded covered wagon and raised by coyotes. Douglas Unger's novel *Leaving the Land* (1985) is an ironic study of corporate monopolies and the struggle of people on the small farms and in the small towns of western South Dakota to survive the monopoly's economic pressure as well as the usual exigencies of weather and economic uncertainty.

All of these works attest to the healthy state of Great Plains literature at the beginning of the twenty-first century. Some of them will prove to be ephemeral, but other writers will write other stories that will continue to pay attention to the landscape and to the ways that men and women, Indians and immigrants, sojourners and lifelong residents learn to live on the land. Great Plains writers have been aware, over the years, of the threats to attempts to sustain meaningful lives on the prairies and high plains: the vulnerability inherent in reliance on the cash crops required by a capitalist economic system that leaves farmers and small-town merchants at the mercy of far-away markets; storms that even today can wipe out a crop or a town in a matter of minutes; the decline in population in small towns and rural areas that diminishes the quality of life for those who remain; the social and economic barriers that continue to prevent Indians from living full lives on the Great Plains. Since these factors that create the motifs for much Great Plains literature persist, it seems certain that the literature will continue to be written as well.

NOTES

1   *The Journals of Lewis and Clark* first appeared in a paraphrased edition edited by Thomas Biddle in 1815. A 1904 edition by Reuben Thwaites is the basis for most editions now in print. The journals, including all of the writings from the expedition, an atlas, and an herbarium, are now published in a 12-volume edition by the University of Nebraska Press (1986–99).

2   Hasselstrom's other works include *Going Over East: Reflections of a Woman Rancher* (1987); *Windbreak: A Woman Rancher on the Northern Plains* (1987); *Caught by One Wing*, (1993); and *Between Grass and Sky: Where I Live and Work* (2002). With Gaydell Collier and Nancy Curtis she has edited two volumes of writing by Western women: *Leaning in the Wind* (1999) and *Woven on the Wind* (2001).

3   Indian women have added to the poetic expression of the Great Plains experience. See Louise Erdrich, *Jacklight* (1984); Linda Hogan (Chickasaw) *Red Clay* (1991), *The Book of Medicines* (1993), and *Dwellings: A Spiritual History of the Living World* (1995); Joy Harjo (Muskogee Creek), *In Mad Love and War* (1990), *A Map to the Next World: Poetry and Tales* (2000): Diane Glancy (Cherokee), *Claiming Breath* (1991), *Boomtown* (1997), and *Cold-and-Hunger Dance* (1998).

4   Luther Standing Bear's works include *Stories of the Sioux* (1930), *My Indian Boyhood* (1959), and *My People the Sioux* (1928). Ella Deloria (Dakota), a trained ethnologist, wrote her novel of precontact tribal life, *Waterlily*, in the 1940s but it was not published until 1988.

5   Scholarly editions of *O Pioneers!* (ed. Charles Mignon and Susan Rosowski; Lincoln: University of Nebraska Press, 1992) and *My Ántonia* (ed. Charles Mignon and Kari Ronning; Lincoln: University of Nebraska Press, 1994) have added considerable material to the historical and textual background of these novels. Quotes and other textual references are to these editions.

6   Although she invents names for them, the small plains towns in Cather's works are always her home town of Red Cloud, Nebraska.

7   The Swedish writer Vilhelm Moberg, in his four-volume work *The Emigrants* (1949–59) and Norway's Johan Bojer, in his one-volume *The Emigrants* (1925), also chronicle the immigration to the Great Plains from Scandinavia in the late nineteenth century. Bojer's novel retains the European view of emigration and the loss of affinity with the homeland that Rølvaag embodies in Beret.

8   White wrote a number of short-story collections, including *The Court of Boyville* (1899) and *In Our Town* (1906). He is particularly adept at chronicling the early twentieth-century political scene in *Masks in a Pageant* (1928), a series of biographical sketches of political figures. His editorials are collected in *The Editor and his People* (1924) and *Forty Years on Main Street* (1937).

9   For many years before she began writing her autobiographical Little House series, Wilder wrote articles for women readers in rural publications.

10 Wilder's other works include *By the Shores of Silver Lake* (1939); the biography of her husband Almanzo, *Farmer Boy* (1933); an account of the Wilders' early married life, *The First Four Years* (1971); *Little House in the Big Woods* (1932); *Little Town on the Prairie* (1941); *On the Banks of Plum Creek* (1937); and *These Happy Golden Years* (1971).

11 Margaret Laurence's other Manawaka novels include *A Jest of God* (1966) and *The Fire Dwellers* (1969).

12 *Wild Stone Heart: An Apprentice in the Fields* (2000) presents Butala's further observations of people and the land. Butala's fiction includes the novels *Luna* (1988), *The Gates of the Sun* (1986), *The Fourth Archangel* (1992), and *The Garden of Eden* (1998), and story collections *Queen of the Headaches* (1989), *Fever* (1990), and *Real Life* (2002).

13 O'Brien's works also include the story collection *Eminent Domain* (1987), the novels *Spirit of the Hills* (1988) and *The Contract Surgeon* (1999), the story of the doctor who treated the dying Sioux Chief Crazy Horse.

REFERENCES

Acocella, Joan (2000). *Willa Cather and the Politics of Criticism.* Lincoln: University of Nebraska Press.

Anders, John P. (1999). *Willa Cather's Sexual Aesthetics and the Male Homosexual Literary Tradition.* Lincoln: University of Nebraska Press.

Barclay, Donald A., Maguire, James, and Wild, Peter, eds. (1994). *Into the Wilderness Dream: Exploration Narratives of the American West 1500–1805.* Salt Lake: University of Utah Press.

Bojer, Johan (1978). *The Emigrants* 1925. rpt. Lincoln: University of Nebraska Press.

Conlogue, William (2001). "Managing the Farm, Educating the Farmer: *O Pioneers!* and the New Agriculture." *Great Plains Quarterly* 21, 3–15.

Faragher, John Mack (1979). *Women and Men on the Overland Trail.* New Haven: Yale University Press.

Gish, Robert (1976). *Hamlin Garland: The Far West.* (Western Writers Series.) Boise: Boise State University Press.

Griffith, Sally Foreman (1989). *Home Town News: William Allen White and the Emporia Gazette.* Lawrence: University Press of Kansas.

Jernigan, Jay (1983). *William Allen White.* Boston: Twayne.

Linsenmayer, Penny T. (2001). "Kansas Settlers on the Osage Diminished reserve: A Study of Laura Ingalls Wilder's *Little House on the Prairie.*" *Kansas History* 24: 3 (Autumn), 168–85.

McCullough, Joseph B. (1978). *Hamlin Garland.* Boston: Twayne.

McDermott, John Francis (1944). "Washington Irving as Western Traveler: Editor's Introduction." In *The Western Journals of Washington Irving,* ed. John Francis McDermott, 3–66. Norman: University of Oklahoma Press.

Miller, John E. (1998). *Becoming Laura Ingalls Wilder: The Woman behind the Legend.* Columbia: University of Missouri Press.

Moberg, Wilhelm (1949–59). *The Emigrant Novels*: *The Emigrants* (1949); *Unto a Good Land* (1952); *The Settlers* (1956); *The Last Letter Home* (1959). St. Paul: Minnesota Historical Society Press.

Motley, Warren (1987). *The American Abraham: James Fenimore Cooper and the Frontier Patriarch.* New York: Cambridge University Press.

Myres, Sandra (1982). *Westering Women and the Frontier Experience 1800–1915.* Albuquerque: University of New Mexico Press.

Quantic, Diane Dufva (1995). *The Nature of the Place: A Study of Great Plains Fiction.* Lincoln: University of Nebraska Press.

Romines, Ann (1997). *Constructing the Little House: Gender, Culture and Laura Ingalls Wilder.* Amherst: University of Massachusetts Press.

Rosowski, Susan (1986). *The Voyage Perilous: Willa Cather's Romanticism.* Lincoln: University of Nebraska Press.

Rothenberger, Von (1996). *Sod and Stubble: The Unabridged and Annotated Edition.* Lawrence: University Press of Kansas.

Schlissel, Lillian (1982). *Women's Diaries of the Westward Journey.* New York: Schocken.

Smith, Henry Nash (1970). *Virgin Land: The American West as Symbol and Myth.* Cambridge: Harvard University Press. (First publ. 1950.)

Stauffer, Helen (1982). *Mari Sandoz: Storycatcher of the Plains.* Lincoln: University of Nebraska Press.

Stegner, Wallace (1962). *Wolf Willow: A History, A Story, and A Memory of the Last Plains Frontier.* New York: Viking.

Thacker, Robert (1989). *The Great Prairie Fact and Literary Imagination.* Albuquerque: University of New Mexico Press.

Underhill, Lonnie E., and Littlefield, Daniel E., Jr., eds. (1976). *Hamlin Garland's Observations on the American Indian 1895–1905.* Tucson: University of Arizona Press.

Unruh, John D. (1979). *The Plains Across: The Overland Emigrants and the TransMississippi West.* Urbana: University of Illinois Press.

WLA (1997) *Updating the Literary West.* Sponsored by the Western Literature Association. Fort Worth: Texas Christian University Press. http://www2.tcu.edu/depts/prs/amwest.

Woodress, James C. (1987). *Willa Cather: A Literary Life.* Lincoln: University of Nebraska Press.

14

Forgotten Frontier: Literature of the Old Northwest

Bev Hogue

"[A]lmost every distinguished Ohioan of the past generations seems to have begun life in a log cabin, and to have found his way out of the dark of ignorance by the light of its great hearth fire," wrote William Dean Howells in his 1897 children's history book *Stories of Ohio* (164). As the author of a campaign biography of Abraham Lincoln, Howells understood the American public's infatuation with the romance of the log cabin, but he also knew first-hand the reality of log-cabin life. In a vain attempt to establish a utopian community after the example of Robert Owen, Howells's father in 1850 moved his family to a rustic cabin in Eureka Mills, Ohio; the experiment was a dismal failure and the family returned to city life after only a year. Howells later recalled that log-cabin year as a time of pure pastoral delight for a young boy infatuated with nature and romantic poetry – but he also recalled his family's back-breaking labor, his father's inability to interest any of the earlier settlers in his utopian scheme, and his mother's dispiriting loneliness and hardships. He wrote *Stories of Ohio* when time and distance had endowed log-cabin life with pastoral romance. While he indulged in nostalgia for the log cabin's "great hearth fire," Howells also emphasized the dark side of frontier life – the ignorance and hardship that compelled distinguished Ohioans to seek a way out.

Howells's simple summary of Ohio history provides a helpful heuristic toward understanding the literature of the Old Northwest. Three currents – the romance of the frontier, the harsh realities of settlement, and the rejection of provincial life and values – intermingle throughout this literature, each becoming the dominant stream for a time before slipping below the surface. Early accounts recognized the romance of the frontier but emphasized its harsh realities; later, urban growth and industrialization led to literature that either embraced sentimental nostalgia for a pastoral existence or rejected the narrow provincialism of agrarian life.

Beginnings and Borders

Unlike some other American regions, the Old Northwest is not particularly difficult to define. The Northwest Ordinance of 1787 established the Northwest Territory in the region north and west of the Ohio River later subdivided into Ohio, Indiana, Illinois, Michigan, and Wisconsin. Disputes with the British and Native Americans over control of the region had long limited European settlement to a few military outposts and missions, but easterners eager for new frontiers viewed the area as virgin land abounding with natural resources and ripe for settlement. The Land Ordinance of 1785 set into motion the survey that would divide the territory into square townships and sections – the Grid that guided settlement and still dominates maps of the region.

The Northwest Ordinance of 1787 called for peaceful coexistence with the Native Americans inhabiting the area, an ideal largely ignored under the pressure of settlement. A series of bloody conflicts resulted in the forced removal of most Native Americans to remote areas of the region or points farther west. Drawn by the promise of inexpensive fertile land and abundant natural resources, settlers entered the region by the hundreds of thousands, only to find that reality did not always live up to expectations. Dense forests covered much of the region, and large swaths of land were rendered nearly impassable by immense swamps and sloughs, inhospitable to all except outcasts. Many settlers kept jars of quinine on the table to battle repetitive bouts of malaria, the debilitating "ague" that dominates settlers' tales. Settlement occurred so quickly, though, that by the middle of the nineteenth century the bulk of the forests had been felled and many of the swamps drained to create fertile farmland and make room for the many small towns that dot the region.

In 1893 Frederick Jackson Turner delivered his influential lecture, "The Significance of the Frontier in American History," at the World's Columbian Exposition in Chicago, the premier city of the Old Northwest. Roughly one hundred years after the Northwest Territory had been opened for settlement, Turner declared that the end of the frontier era did not mean the end of the idea of the frontier. His words were prescient, for the 1890s and early 1900s saw a spurt of literature expressing nostalgia for the lost frontier or revolt against the cultural detritus of frontier life. Today, the term "Old Northwest" has fallen out of common parlance, preserved primarily by historians and scholars of the region; popular conceptions of the region merge it with the larger Midwest. This decline of regional identity is a relatively recent development, however; early literature presented a vivid and distinctive picture of life in the Old Northwest.

Log Cabins and Lost Souls

In the preface to *The Circuit Rider: A Tale of the Heroic Age* (1874), Edward Eggleston described the stark contrasts characteristic of frontier life in the Old Northwest: "this

mélange of picturesque simplicity, grotesque humor and savage ferocity, of abandoned wickedness and austere piety, can hardly seem real to those who know the
country now" (Eggleston 1965: v). His earlier novel, *The Hoosier School-Master* (1871),
portrayed frontier Indiana as a dark, mysterious wilderness full of ignorant, barely
human characters who could be civilized only by the light of education carried by the
schoolmaster. Eggleston's prose is itself an uneven mélange of realistic incident,
comical dialect, and sentimental description reminiscent of Dickens's death of Little
Nell, but his novels gained a wide readership and informed the popular conception of
the Old Northwest as a dark, uncivilized realm full of unknown dangers that could
nevertheless be reformed into a new Eden by the light of education.

Some earlier accounts were less optimistic. In 1803, the year Ohio achieved statehood, Thaddeus Mason Harris visited friends in southeastern Ohio; on his return to
Boston, he wrote *The Journal of a Tour into the Territory Northwest of the Alleghany [sic]
Mountains* (1805), an account of his arduous journey into Ohio's earliest settlements.
Harris noted a sharp distinction between the villagers who pursued settled agriculture and the back-settlers who pursued a more nomadic existence based on hunting;
he claimed that neglecting the cultivation of land led to lack of cultivation of hearts
and minds. Thirty years later, Caroline Kirkland found similar contrasts on the
southern Michigan frontier. In *A New Home – Who'll Follow?* (1839) and *Forest Life*
(1842), Kirkland painted a winsome but largely realistic picture of the difficulties of
frontier life, admitting that her initial attempts to view the dense forests and swamps
through a lens of romance had been crushed by the harsh realities of the region.

Eliza W. Farnham followed Kirkland's lead. *Life in Prairie Land* (1846) describes
Farnham's experience settling on the Illinois prairie in the 1830s; like Kirkland and
Harris, Farnham indulged in lush lyrical passages describing the beauty of the countryside, but she also expressed contempt for the benighted backwardness of many
settlers. Thirty years later Eggleston would claim that the schoolmaster and the
circuit-riding preacher offered the only hope for the redemption of the dark wilderness, but in Farnham's opinion, the responsibility for civilizing the frontier lay solely
in the hands of housewives. In *Life in Prairie Land*, men are mostly dim background
figures who keep busy earning a living, bilking helpless travelers, or drinking themselves into early graves. Farnham derided one frontier farmer's method of choosing a
wife: "I reckon women are some like horses and oxen, the biggest can do the most
work, and that's what I want one for" (1988: 20). Farnham asserted that frontier life
in such a situation would be "slavery," primarily because the woman had not strength
of character to remedy her situation: "There was no hope for her but to settle into her
slavery, and wear the shackles, if possible, without chafing under them. She had not
character enough to redeem herself, and the brutal treatment to which she was
doomed would tend every day to diminish the little that she had, and reduce her to
the condition of a mere machine" (Farnham 1988: 23).

Farnham blamed slovenly housewives for frontier filth and ignorance, contrasting
these women's wretched surroundings with the dainty neatness of Nature, whom she
personified as an industrious woman: "Nature, like a notable dame, has cleaned house

in proper season, got her furniture and ornaments arranged, and now seated complacently in her easy chair, challenges the admiration of beholders" (1988: 47). Her
closing apostrophe to the prairie envisions a future free of ignorance and darkness:
"Thy free plains and far-reaching streams shall be the theatre of a power and intelligence never yet witnessed! Thy countless acres shall glow with checkered beauty and
hum with busy life, when the generations of those who love thee now, sleep in thy
peaceful bosom! Land of the silent past and stirring future, farewell!" (Farnham
1988: 269).

Land of the Silent Past

Farnham's reference to the "silent past" of the Old Northwest emphasizes the absence
of voices that might provide a more complete understanding of the region. Thaddeus
Harris's benighted back-settlers, Caroline Kirkland's comically ignorant neighbors,
and Eliza Farnham's slovenly domestic slaves did not write books; their stories come
to light only through the mediating presence of educated Easterners. Similarly, the
thousands of ceremonial earthworks and mounds left behind by Native Americans
tell no tales, though they sparked intense controversy throughout the nineteenth
century. William Cullen Bryant's "The Prairies" (1833) imagined a noble life for the
Mound Builders, but the poem was based on fanciful conjecture by a poet who had
not seen the territory he described so lovingly.

   Also rare are African-American voices of the Old Northwest, at least until after
the Civil War. The Northwest Ordinance outlawed slavery in the territory but
called for escaped slaves to be returned to their Southern masters; for many Southern
slaves, crossing the Ohio River became a first step on the road to freedom, as the Old
Northwest provided many way stations on the Underground Railroad. Abolitionist
sentiment was strong in the region; in fact, Harriet Beecher Stowe researched the
lives of slaves while living in Cincinnati, later putting that information to use in
Uncle Tom's Cabin (1852).

   An interesting early treatment of racial tensions among settlers in the Old Northwest is Paul Laurence Dunbar's novel *The Fanatics* (1901). Dunbar, the son of ex-
slaves living in Dayton, Ohio, published two small volumes of poetry before William
Dean Howells brought him to the attention of the reading public by writing an
introduction to Dunbar's *Lyrics of Lowly Life* (1896). Howells boosted the young
poet's career but also angered Dunbar by insisting that poems in dialect (rather than
standard English) represented his true voice, an assertion that continues to arouse
controversy more than a century later. Dunbar's complex relationship to his region is
apparent in the poem he read before the Western Association of Writers in Dayton
in 1892. His "Welcome Address to the Western Association of Writers" opens by
evoking frontier romance in the words of Bishop Berkeley ("Westward the course of
empire takes its way"), and the poem envisions the Old Northwest falling inevitably
into the possession of "you who trace on history's page / The footprints of each

passing age" (Dunbar 1993: 307). Though the poet seems to speak for the region, Dunbar's syntax excludes him from the ranks of those who inherit the land; this subtle sense of dispossession appears in his other poems and novels, particularly *The Fanatics*.

Set in Ohio during and immediately after the Civil War, *The Fanatics* portrays the Old Northwest as contested terrain. Though it deals with the horrors of slavery and the tragic divisions caused by the war, the novel also details the everyday harassment encountered by African Americans even in the emancipated North. The novel's small-town whites, descendants of hardy frontiersmen, see themselves as the only true Americans and struggle to cope with the changes that come with Reconstruction. Even those who had loudly condemned slavery fear that a "black invasion" will destroy their quiet pastoral existence; this widespread fear erupts in violence until it becomes "an act of patriotism to push a black woman from the sidewalks" (Dunbar 1993: 184–5). In the end, though, the community chooses unity over racial division, suggesting that it might be possible for North and South, white and black to coexist on contested ground.

For many, this hope proved overly optimistic. While former slaves swelled the populations of cities like Chicago, Cleveland, and Detroit after the Civil War, the region's small towns were less welcoming. Casual racism and a growing isolationism following the First World War resulted in a rise in Ku Klux Klan activity in the region in the early decades of the twentieth century; in fact, the Klan dominated state politics in Indiana throughout the 1920s. It is hardly surprising, then, that many frontier romances published in the early decades of the century, most notably the best-selling novels of Gene Stratton-Porter, portray lily-white descendants of Anglo-Saxon settlers as the rightful possessors of the region while silencing other voices.

Late in the twentieth century, the Old Northwest's silent past found a new voice in the fiction of Toni Morrison, recipient of the 1993 Nobel Prize for Literature. Several of her novels attempt to reclaim the lost voices of the region; for instance, *Song of Solomon* (1977) imagines the blank spots in black history as a bag of silent bones the characters carry around; they cannot reconnect with the songs and stories of their silent past until they bury the bones and discover their true names. *Beloved* (1987) revisits territory earlier explored by Paul Laurence Dunbar and Harriet Beecher Stowe, re-imagining the region's role as a refuge for former slaves and exploring the difficulties facing African Americans, both fettered and free.

The Light of the Hearth Fire

William Dean Howells began giving a voice to his own silent past around 1890. Throughout his long and illustrious career, Howells was a great benefactor of Western writers, fleeing his Ohio heritage only to tirelessly open the pages of Eastern publications to Western authors such as Mark Twain and Paul Laurence Dunbar. Born in 1837, Howells had fed his youthful spirit on romantic poetry, but later championed realism in fiction and promoted the work of naturalist authors such as Steven Crane and Hamlin Garland. In more than 30 novels and nonfiction works, Howells frequently characterized his native region as the place from which provincial people escaped to seek richer lives in New England, New York, or Europe – until about 1890, when nostalgia for the lost wilderness led him to start mining his past for material. This nostalgia is evident in a cluster of late novels and nonfiction works: *A Boy's Town* (1890), *My Year in a Log Cabin* (1891), *Stories of Ohio* (1897), *The Kentons* (1902), *New Leaf Mills* (1913), *The Leatherwood God* (1916), and *The Years of My Youth* (1916).

For young boys free of adult responsibility, the frontier could be paradise; Howells's memoirs of his log-cabin year are dotted with idyllic descriptions of boyhood games and excursions into the forests, which seemed to exist solely to nourish the needs of boys. A more complex account of frontier life appears in *The Kentons* and *The Leatherwood God*, in which Howells depicts the Old Northwest as a garden that produces its own destroyers. In *The Kentons*, the innocents must resign themselves to sharing their carefully tended Ohio garden home with the clan of Bittridge, the tormentor who tempts them toward progress and a rejection of homely frontier values. In *The Leatherwood God*, his final finished novel, Howells suggests that settlers import their own snakes into the garden and then loose them on the world. The novel rejects the Puritan idea of wilderness as inherently evil, but it also demonstrates how the dim light of the forest assisted settlers in deceiving themselves. By the time he wrote *The Leatherwood God*, Howells had lost many of his family members and friends to death; his popularity was in decline, and, after the great floods of 1913, his childhood refuge was unrecognizable. Beginning with a pastoral wilderness designed for human use, he was left in the end with a landscape of loss on which to build tales of a forgotten frontier.

Nostalgia for the lost frontier was a common theme of late nineteenth- and early twentieth-century popular fiction of the Old Northwest. Maurice Thompson's *Alice of Old Vincennes*, a bestseller in 1900, is unique in focusing on the influence of early French explorers on the region. Set in the time of George Rogers Clark's capture of Fort Sackville from the British in 1779, the novel tells of innocent young Alice, an angel of the hearth equally at home in a log cabin or in the dark, dangerous forests and swamps of Indiana. Eliza Farnham would surely have approved of Alice's industriousness and ability to remain unspotted by the evils ever present in the wilderness; the novel presents the difficulties of frontier life through a lens of romance, its lyrical descriptions of frontier life suffusing the whole with a sense of nostalgia for an age "when women lightly braved what the strongest men would shrink from now" (Thompson 1900: 8).

Locating fiction in the dim and distant past was not the only way to elicit frontier nostalgia, however; Gene Stratton-Porter's popular novels situated a heroic frontier ethos in her own time. Although Stratton-Porter is remembered today primarily as an influential nature writer, her novels were far more popular during the first two decades of the twentieth century; in fact, four of them sold more than 1.5 million copies each: *Freckles* (1904), *The Girl of the Limberlost* (1909), *The Harvester* (1911), and *Laddie* (1913). Her most popular fictions are set near northeastern Indiana's impenetrable Limberlost Swamp, which was being drained as Stratton-Porter began her writing career. In Stratton-Porter's fiction, the swamp functions simultaneously as an evil morass of decay and doom, and an Eden offering bounty to the faithful steward. Stratton-Porter's morally (and racially) pure protagonists are natural aristocrats nurtured by loving nature, but the very virtues bestowed by nature lead these characters to forsake or transform the swamp. Elnora Comstock, the girl of the Limberlost, is sometimes viewed as a proto-feminist who transcends gender roles by rejecting domestic confinement, but the ultimate effect of her incursions into the wild is to extend the domestic sphere into all outdoors and thus subsume the wild within the domestic. Stratton-Porter's fictions suggest that the natural beauty of the Old Northwest should be preserved not as wilderness but as safe, sanitized, domesticated space.

Rise of the Provincial Wits

As nostalgia caused some authors to color frontier difficulties with a brush of romance, others were busy transforming those benighted back-settlers into treasuries of wit and wisdom. Caroline Kirkland, Eliza Farnham, and Edward Eggleston had found some comedy in the backwardness of their provincial neighbors, but the ascendancy of the Provincial Wits began late in the nineteenth century and continued well into the twentieth. Eccentric characters spouted homely tales, often in dialect, in newspapers, magazines, and books throughout the country, promoting an image of the Old Northwest as a refuge for simple people whose unsophisticated language belied their appreciable wisdom. This was the golden age of the Provincial Wits, of whom James Whitcomb Riley was certainly the most influential.

Riley was hardly alone in celebrating the foibles and whimsies, tragedies and triumphs of provincial life; the Old Northwest was rich in versifiers such as the prolific Julia A. Moore, the Sweet Singer of Michigan, who published pious sentimental lyrics to popular acclaim offset by biting criticism. In *The Sentimental Songbook* (1876) and *A Few Choice Words to the Public, with New and Original Poems* (1878), Moore commemorated local events, disasters, deaths, and the events of her own life in a style reminiscent of Mark Twain's Emmeline Grangerford. A minor figure now justifiably forgotten, Moore wrote some of the least felicitous lines ever to find publication in the English language; James Whitcomb Riley, on the other hand, was perhaps the most well-known poet of his age. In 14 volumes beginning with *"The Old Swimmin' Hole" and 'Leven More Poems* (1883), Riley reveled in nostalgia for the simplicity of childhood and provincial life. His winsome narrative poems provided many thousands of schoolchildren with recitation pieces, and his popularity was enhanced after he hit the lecture circuit to read his poems all over the United States. "An Old Sweet-heart of Mine" epitomizes Riley's verse:

> O Childhood-days enchanted! O the magic of the Spring! –
> With all green boughs to blossom white, and all bluebirds to sing!
> When all the air, to toss and quaff, made life a jubilee
> And changed the children's song and laughs to shrieks of ecstasy.
> (Riley 1982: 23)

Dialect poems like "The Little Town o' Tailholt" reject the bustle of city life and yearn for provincial simplicity:

> You kin boast about yer cities, and their stiddy growth and size,
> And brag about yer County-seats, and business enterprise,
> And railroads, and factories, and all sich foolery –
> But the little Town o' Tailholt is big enough fer me!
> (Riley 1982: 53)

Today Riley's verse is largely dismissed as quaint and unsophisticated, but it popularized an image of the Old Northwest as the home of charmingly backward characters leading simple lives unsullied by the stresses of modernity. This image informed a variety of works focusing on the wit and wisdom of both rustic rubes and denizens of the urban underclass, such as Zona Gale's *Friendship Village* sketches (1905), George Ade's *Fables in Slang* (1899), Finley Peter Dunne's Mr. Dooley stories (1898), and Kin Hubbard's Abe Martin dialect tales (1905–30). Even James Thurber's more nuanced and sophisticated Ohio eccentrics in *My Life and Hard Times* (1933) owe a debt to these earlier authors.

While the Provincial Wits' whimsical tales rely on unsophisticated dialect to satirize the values of the age, to evoke nostalgia for a simpler time, and to suggest that even the backward and benighted can be founts of wisdom and wit, they also demonstrate the staying power of the "picturesque simplicity [and] grotesque humor" Eggleston found among the frontier settlers of the Old Northwest. Meredith Nicholson's forgettable novel *A Hoosier Chronicle* (1912) insisted that the days of Eggleston were long past, that "those poor yaps Eggleston wrote about in 'The Hoosier Schoolmaster' were all dead and buried," but Nicholson gave the last word to the estimable Mrs. Owen, whose outlook rivaled Riley's: "It's all pretty comfortable and cheerful and busy in Indiana, with lots of old-fashioned human kindness flowing round; and it's getting better all the time. And I guess it's always got to be that way, out here in God's country" (Nicholson 1912: 606).

Godforsaken Country

God's country looks godforsaken in the works generally characterized under the "Revolt from the Village" rubric. Even while popular literature of the Old Northwest was stirring up nostalgia for a simpler time, other authors were rejecting the residue of provincialism – or obeying the urge to get away from the Old Northwest.

Booth Tarkington was a transitional figure, reflecting the whimsy of the provincial wits but also recognizing the necessity of a new type of literature that sought material for art not in nostalgia for the past but in the bustle of modern life. Many of his more than 40 novels, such as *The Gentleman from Indiana* (1899) and *Penrod* (1914), resemble Riley's nostalgic evocations of provincial simplicity; however, in three linked novels exploring the complex impact of urban sprawl, Tarkington celebrates the city as a living, growing thing, sometimes a rank weed but always a source of material for art. In *The Turmoil* (1915), the infant city grows like a cancer on the landscape of the Old Northwest but also offers healing and hope. Gene Stratton-Porter's city-sick characters find healing only by immersing themselves in rural life, but Tarkington's sick protagonist leaves a sanatorium to find healing in the bustle of a booming metropolis, where even the thick, dingy air becomes the raw material for art. Tarkington continued this theme in *The Magnificent Ambersons* (1918) and *The Midlander* (1924), in which the automobile is a major factor transforming the face of the Old Northwest by minimizing both distance and difference between urban and rural areas. Eggleston had promoted education and religion as the forces enlightening the dark spaces on the map, but Tarkington placed the automobile in that position, dramatizing how car travel demystifies the unknown and domesticates the wilderness.

Other authors' attempts to demystify the unknown paint a picture far less optimistic than Tarkington's. Earlier, Edgar Watson Howe's *Story of a Country Town* (1883) had portrayed the Indiana frontier as a bleak site of unremitting labor suited only for those not equipped to survive elsewhere. Upton Sinclair's *The Jungle* (1904) exposed the plight of immigrant workers in Chicago's meat-packing industry, while Floyd Dell's *Moon-Calf* (1920) explored the limited options available to a young man eager to escape provincial life in southern Illinois. Dell's feckless Felix Fay absorbs wisdom from his provincial environment, but in the end he realizes that for the creative man living in the Old Northwest, all roads lead to Chicago. Dell was among the Chicago Renaissance writers who saw the Old Northwest as forcing its talented young artists and thinkers to either submit to narrow provincialism or find a way out.

This tendency is most apparent in the poetry of Edgar Lee Masters and the fiction of Sherwood Anderson, who popularized an image of the Old Northwest sharply contrasting with that of sentimentalists like Stratton-Porter and Riley. Masters' *Spoon River Anthology* (1915) consists of free-verse epitaphs of residents of the fictional town of Spoon River, Illinois, where a bleak hardscrabble existence deadens the spirit, destroys hope, and stifles creativity. The town is full of hypocrites who can tell their true stories only after they are safely planted in the ground, become a part of the landscape of the Old Northwest. Griffy the Cooper tells his neighbors that they are imprisoned within barrels that limit their horizons, saying, "You are submerged in the tub of yourself" (Masters 1962: 89). Images of submersion, confinement, and burial abound in the poems; for instance, Archibald Higbie proclaims that in life he had been "all covered over / And weighted down with western soil," but in death he prays for a new birth "with all of Spoon River / Rooted out" (Masters 1962: 204). Freedom for his spirit requires the removal of Spoon River and all it represents.

Masters' occasionally lugubrious poetry represented a sharp rejection of the sing-song sentimental verse popular in his time; Sherwood Anderson's spare prose like-wise rejects the values of the village, but with a tenderness rarely glimpsed in Masters' bitter epitaphs. In *Mid-American Chants* (1918) Anderson described the writer's dif-ficult task of making art out of his native mud; his fiction is full of grotesque little men with twisted faces and uncontrollable fingers, but they nevertheless find some measure of transcendent meaning even while trapped within limited lives. His imagined past is not so much golden as brutal, his heroes not so much innocent as desperate and confused, fumbling toward meaningful action without understanding their own failures. Anderson's first published novel, *Windy McPherson's Son* (1916), closes with a meditation on the forgotten frontier: "In our fathers' day, at night in the forests of Michigan, Ohio, Kentucky, and on the wide prairies, wolves howled. There was fear in our fathers and mothers, pushing their way forward, making the new land. When the land was conquered fear remained, the fear of failure. Deep in our American souls the wolves still howl" (Anderson 1965: 325).

The wolves of failure still howl in *Poor White* (1920), in which a giant named Industry awakens and tramples over the Old Northwest, spreading wealth in its wake but irretrievably changing the face of the land. In Anderson's fiction, agricul-ture turns people into unthinking beasts but progress makes them machines. *Winesburg, Ohio* (1919), Anderson's most influential book, is a series of interconnected stories about the coming of age of young George Willard in a small Ohio town based on Anderson's childhood home. George encounters local characters like Wing Biddle-baum, whose hands reach out for connection but encounter only alienation; Doc Reefy, who ceaselessly builds up "[l]ittle pyramids of truth" only to knock them down again (Anderson 1958: 35); and Kate Swift, whose attempt to reveal the passionate truth buried beneath the calm surface of life ends in failure. Anderson compassion-ately explores the narrow lives of his characters, but in the end Winesburg, like Howells' log cabin, is a place best left behind.

Dawn Powell explored similar terrain in several novels published in the 1930s and 1940s. *Dance Night* (1930) clearly shows the influence of *Winesburg, Ohio*: two young people experience the pains of adolescence in a small town where everyone seems trapped in meaningless lives. The ending echoes *Winesburg* as well, with a young man moving away from the village of his youth: "Now the evening fast train roared through Lamptown, its triumphant whistle soared over the factory siren, in its vanishing echoes the beginning of a song trembled, a song that belonged to the far-off and tomorrow. Yes, yes, he would come away, Morry's heart answered, now he was ready" (Powell 2001: 204).

In *Come Back to Sorrento* (1932), Powell examined the difficulty of finding any song, art, or truth in a small town, but her later urban novels suggest that the problem is not regional but universal. For instance, in Powell's biting satire *A Time to be Born* (1942), Amanda Keeler (based loosely on Clare Boothe Luce) reshapes her bleak Ohio childhood to suggest the type of provincial romance promoted by James Whitcomb Riley and Gene Stratton Porter, but the novel reveals that the vacuity of Amanda's sophisticated urban life is no less soul-killing than the small-town existence Keeler had so eagerly rejected.

Glenway Wescott adopts a more elegiac mode in the stories collected in *Good-Bye Wisconsin* (1928), in which characters lead shrunken, shriveled lives of mindless labor and disillusionment in a placid landscape that disguises violence. Later, William Gass painted a similar picture in the novel *Omensetter's Luck* (1966) and his short-story collection *In the Heart of the Heart of the Country* (1968). The latter work is set in a bleak land where a man cannot know his neighbor because "there's simply no way of knowing how lonely and empty he is or whether he's as vacant and barren and loveless as the rest of us are here – here in the heart of the country" (Gass 1968: 180).

In Gass's vision of the Old Northwest, human relationships are so rare and parched that in *Omensetter's Luck* it is Brackett Omensetter's talent for connecting that makes him appear different. In an Ohio river town struggling to emerge from the darkness of the frontier era into the light of civilization, Omensetter is a throwback to Eden, a natural man whose hands "held out his nature to you like an offering of fruit; and added themselves to what they touched, enlarging them, as rivers meet and magnify their streams" (Gass 1966: 45). As a walking representation of frontier romance, Omensetter transforms his dingy existence to a riverside paradise, but the community finally thrusts out the spirit of the frontier in favor of a more stable and stale civilization.

As urban sprawl changed the face of the Old Northwest, the region frequently appeared in fiction not as virgin wilderness but as exhausted terrain. In Ernest Hemingway's Michigan stories, written between 1921 and 1938, Nick Adams seeks a pastoral paradise but finds instead a haunted garden irretrievably altered by the demands of industrialization. No longer the dark domain of ignorance so common in frontier tales, the devastated wilderness is a place of education, where the city boy can learn secrets and explore his identity. Theodore Dreiser's young city-dwellers, on the other hand, are educated in the urban jungles of the Old Northwest. In novels such as *Sister Carrie* (1900), *Jennie Gerhardt* (1911), and *An American Tragedy* (1925), Dreiser exults in the energy of cities like Cleveland and Chicago but depicts them as grinding down the wills of weak characters and strengthening the ruthless; Dreiser may create hidden refuges of pastoral delight within the hearts of his urban wastelands, but the pastoral is squeezed into insignificance by the city's irrepressible growth.

Nevertheless, the urge to revisit a lost pastoral paradise continued well into the twentieth century. In the bestselling novel *Raintree County* (1948), Ross Lockridge combined imagery from ancient myth and American history to create a character devoted to "looking for the mystic shape of a life upon the land, the legend of a face of stone, a happy valley, an extinct republic" (Lockridge 1948: 8). Unfortunately, Lockridge's suicide at age 33 prevented his unique vision of the Old Northwest from finding further expression. Meanwhile, Louis Bromfield pursued his own vision of a happy valley in rural northern Ohio. Having gained great acclaim as the author of novels dramatizing conflicts between agrarian and industrial lifestyles, such as *The Green Bay Tree* (1924), *Early Autumn* (which won the Pulitzer Prize in 1926), and *The Farm* (1933), Bromfield moved his family to France to enjoy the fruits of his success; however, the outbreak of World War II drove him back to Ohio, where he purchased several adjacent farms and turned his agrarian dreams into reality. Bromfield's Malabar Farm became an experiment in sustainable agriculture; in his nonfiction account of the experiment, *Pleasant Valley* (1945), Bromfield wrote that by returning to his happy valley and promoting agrarian reform, he hoped "to regain [his] strength by touching earth once more" (Bromfield 1997: 25).

Renaissance and Beyond

While Bromfield touched the earth, cities of the Old Northwest touched the sky and nurtured a crop of writers concerned more with progress than nostalgia. In 1912 in Chicago Harriet Monroe founded *Poetry* magazine, the first flowering of the Chicago Renaissance. Emerging writers like Edgar Lee Masters, Sherwood Anderson, Hamlin Garland, Floyd Dell, and Henry Blake Fuller labored to produce a new literature based on the tenets of modernism, the ascendancy of the machine, and the energy of urban life. The poet most closely associated with the Chicago Renaissance is Carl Sandburg, whose influential poem "Chicago" was published in *Poetry* in 1914. Sandburg's breathless and brutal poetry envisions the city as a young man working feverishly to build something new, proud of his sweat and raw physical strength. Sandburg's *Chicago Poems* (1916) demonstrate the influence of Whitman in both style and substance, celebrating the working class in variable incantatory lines built on active verbs and exalting strength, growth, and progress.

Chicago continued to play an important role in poetry of the Old Northwest throughout the twentieth century. Beginning with *A Street in Bronzeville* (1945), Gwendolyn Brooks has published 14 volumes of poetry characterizing the city as a place whose residents wear metaphorical armor to protect themselves from every-day violence and despair. In "Strong Men, Riding Horses" (1960), the American Dream of success through westward expansion has been reduced to clichés on the silver screen while the inner-city narrator admits, "I am not like that. I pay rent, am addled / By illegible landlords, run, if robbers call" (Brooks 1963: 71). Similarly, Stuart Dybek's poems and short stories explore a gritty working-class Chicago suffused by sex, violence, and ethnic conflict. In *Brass Knuckles* (1979), "My Neighborhood" describes a place where "Shadows become familiar, / recognizable dangers" (Dybek 1979: 67), but "Vivaldi" finds beauty in the urban jungle: "A meager music hovers everywhere: / at mouths of drains, echoing stairwells / where girls in muslin disappear / whispering 'allegro'" (Dybek 1979: 3).

Meanwhile, poet Philip Levine finds beauty rising from the ashes of inner-city Detroit. Levine's poems frequently tackle ethnic and racial conflicts, often giving voice to the ghosts of his immigrant forebears. Like Tarkington's weedy city, Levine's Detroit is polluted and yet purifying; for instance, "Belle Isle, 1949" (1976) recalls a childhood swimming hole:

> We stripped in the first warm spring night
> and ran down into the Detroit River
> to baptize ourselves in the brine
> of car parts, dead fish, stolen bicycles,
> melted snow.
>
> (Levine 1976: 30)

This sacramental immersion in the pollution of the city bears little resemblance to James Whitcomb Riley's "Old Swimmin' Hole," but Levine's boys seem no less innocent. Like Sandburg, Levine portrays his city as irrepressibly *alive* and outlying areas as deadly dull; for instance, in "Ode for Mrs. William Settle" (1994), he characterizes the suburbs as "a deathless / darkness with no more perfume / than cellophane" (Levine 1994: 6).

Although cities provide inspiration for many twentieth-century poets of the region, others have continued to explore the world beyond the urban wilderness. Premier among these was Hart Crane. Born in Garrettsville, Ohio, in 1899, Crane published only two small volumes of poetry – *White Buildings* (1926) and *The Bridge* (1930) – before committing suicide in 1932. Crane did not focus primarily on regional concerns but instead sought to place the region within the vast panoply of American history, myth, and culture. Influenced by both Walt Whitman and T. S. Eliot, Crane's *The Bridge* examines myths of origin and exploration. "The River" places the reader on a railroad rushing west, following the footsteps of early settlers through landscapes where the advance of progress has left billboards and rotting factories in its wake. Crane revels in the romance of the road and the American dream of happy valleys; but in the end, the road consumes the dream. The wilderness is paved and littered, and the dream that drew so many settlers to the Old Northwest has been diminished through the very act of movement, for "[t]he River, spreading, flows – and spends your dream" (Crane 1986: 61).

Theodore Roethke also characterized the Old Northwest as a place travelers pass through while frantically seeking their dreams; "Highway: Michigan" (1941) considers the impact of the automobile industry on the region, describing travelers as "prisoners of speed / Who flee in what their hands have made" (Roethke 1975: 31). The young Roethke had labored in his father's greenhouse in Michigan, and his poems burst with images of growth and decay; for instance, "The Root Cellar" (1948) takes readers into a dank domain where "Shoots dangled and drooped, / Lolling obscenely from mildewed crates, / Hung down long yellow evil necks, like tropical snakes" (Roethke 1975: 36). Similarly, Roethke's "Long Live the Weeds" (1941) celebrates

> The bitter rock, the barren soil
> That force the son of man to toil;
> All things unholy, marred by curse,
> The ugly of the universe.
> The rough, the wicked, and the wild
> That keep the spirit undefiled.
>   (Roethke 1975: 17)

This recalls Philip Levine's sacramental immersion in the polluted river; like Sherwood Anderson, Roethke recognized that undefiled art could be created from his native mud.

James Wright, a student of Roethke's, also immersed himself in his native mud, portraying Ohio's villages as dark mineshafts inclosing inhabitants in bleak hopeless lives. Wright viewed writing as a way to escape from the factory work that consumed his father and many of his friends; characterizing the Old Northwest as a place of narrow lives and minds, he also mined for treasure there. Just as Roethke's "Root Cellar" takes readers into a dank satanic realm, Wright's "In Ohio" (1963) hints at secrets that linger in cellars; the secret remains hidden, however, because residents of Wright's Ohio are mostly silent, deprived of meaningful lives and language. In "Autumn begins in Martins Ferry, Ohio" (1963), for instance, a high-school football game becomes a mythic battle of young gods, the only hope of stone-faced factory workers and their bitter wives who "cluck like starved pullets, / dying for love" (Wright 1990: 121).

Sampling the Soil

James Wright grew up in Martins Ferry, Ohio, the birthplace of William Dean Howells, but the two authors shared more than a home town. Wright's desperate factory workers and their desiccated wives may not reside in log cabins, but they bear a distinct resemblance to Howells' frontier settlers who followed a dream to the Old Northwest only to find the darkness of ignorance and eternal toil; and, also like Howells, Wright saw poetry as his ticket out of the Old Northwest. However, writers still wrestle with regional identity. In *Alive and Dead in Indiana* (1984), Michael Martone considers the challenges of pursuing a poetic vocation in a region that is already overwritten with beloved stories, insisting that "[a] real poet knows how to bomb his own city" (Martone 1984: 105). More recently, Becky Bradway's essays in *Pink Houses and Family Taverns* (2002) offer a tender and occasionally humorous look at life in Illinois towns where insularity and regional pride are the rule. Bradway transforms Riley's provincial wits into scrappy factory workers who embrace the " 'I know I'm a hick but screw you' attitude" (Bradway 2002: 139). Bradway sees education as a light in her twenty-first-century wilderness; but instead of a ticket out, education is her ticket into willing submersion in her home region. Similarly, Scott Russell Sanders explores the meaning of the region in more than a dozen works of fiction and nonfiction, including *Wilderness Plots* (1983), *The Paradise of Bombs* (1987),

Figure 14.1 Photograph of cornfield and power plant in southeast Ohio, by Bev Hogue.

Secrets of the Universe (1991), and *Writing from the Center* (1995); describing the Old Northwest as a palimpsest, Sanders tries to read the varied stories superimposed on the land. In his preface to *Staying Put* (1993), he describes the origin of his urgent need to immerse himself in his region: "On coming to a new place, my father would take a pinch of dirt, sprinkle it into his palm, sniff it, stir it with a blunt finger, squeeze it, then take it on his tongue, tasting. When I first saw him do this, I was puzzled. Why eat dirt? 'Just trying to figure out where I am,' he explained" (Sanders 1993: xiii).

If he sampled the soil of the Old Northwest today, would he find a distinctive flavor? In David Citino's poem "Depressed by a Review, I Walk toward the Mall" (1999), regional flavors are buried beneath bland mass-produced Happy Meals. Citino, who has so far published 11 volumes of poetry, compares the "vatic mouth" of Tennyson with his own voice of "pure Cleveland" and describes urban Ohio as a trash-littered parking lot that could be Anywhere USA; however, beauty is possible even within this littered wasteland: "Still, seeking solace in beauty, / I step toward the thonged, gartered / mannequins of Victoria's Secret, / mourning the ungrandeur of my days." Lost beneath Citino's littered parking lot is the wilderness that shaped so much literature of the Old Northwest, the grandeur of the forgotten frontier. No matter how much he exalted log-cabin life, William Dean Howells was happy to write his way out of it; he was followed by other authors until the log cabin that once provided the key to regional identity is now a quaint tale of a forgotten frontier. Today, as Citino's poem demonstrates, the Old Northwest's edges blur into the vague borders of Middle America, but the region still produces writers who create art from their native mud.

REFERENCES

Anderson, Sherwood (1958). *Winesburg, Ohio*. New York: Viking. (First publ. 1919.)

Anderson, Sherwood (1965). *Windy McPherson's Son*. Chicago: University of Chicago Press. (First publ. 1916.)

Bradway, Becky (2002). *Pink Houses and Family Taverns*. Bloomington: Indiana University Press.

Bromfield, Louis (1997). *Pleasant Valley*. Wooster, Ohio: Wooster Book Co. (First publ. 1945.)

Brooks, Gwendolyn (1963). *Selected Poems*. New York: Harper.

Citino, David (1999). "Depressed by a Review, I Walk toward the Mall." *Cortland Review* 7 (May). http://www.cortlandreview.com/issue/7/citino7.htm.

Citino, David (2002). *The News and Other Poems*. Notre Dame, Ind.: University of Notre Dame Press.

Crane, Hart (1986). *Complete Poems of Hart Crane*, ed. Marc Simon. New York: Liveright.

Dunbar, Paul Laurence (1969). *The Fanatics*. New York: Negro Universities Press 1969. (First publ. 1901.)

Dunbar, Paul Laurence (1993). *The Collected Poetry of Paul Laurence Dunbar*, ed. Joanne M. Braxton. Charlottesville: University Press of Virginia.

Dybek, Stuart (1979). *Brass Knuckles*. Pittsburgh: University of Pittsburgh Press.

Eggleston, Edward (1965). *The Circuit Rider: A Tale of the Heroic Age*. Gloucester, Mass.: Peter Smith. (First publ. 1874.)

Farnham, Eliza (1988). *Life in Prairie Land*, ed. John Hallwas. Chicago: University of Illinois Press. (First publ. 1846.)

Gass, William (1966). *Omensetter's Luck*. New York: New American Library.

Gass, William (1968). *In the Heart of the Heart of the Country, and Other Stories*. New York: Harper.

Howells, William Dean (1897). *Stories of Ohio*. New York: American Book Co.

Levine, Philip (1976). *The Names of the Lost*. New York: Atheneum.

Levine, Philip (1994). *The Simple Truth*. New York: Knopf.

Lockridge, Ross, Jr. (1948). *Raintree County*. Boston: Houghton Mifflin.

Martone, Michael (1984). *Alive and Dead in Indiana: Stories*. New York: Knopf.

Masters, Edgar Lee (1962). *Spoon River Anthology*. New York: MacMillan. (First publ. 1915.)

Nicholson, Meredith (1912). *A Hoosier Chronicle*. Boston: Houghton Mifflin.

Powell, Dawn (2001). *Novels 1930–1942*. New York: Library of America.

Riley, James Whitcomb (1982). *The Best of James Whitcomb Riley*, ed. Donald C. Manlove. Bloomington: Indiana University Press.

Roethke, Theodore (1975). *The Collected Poems of Theodore Roethke*. New York: Anchor Doubleday.

Sanders, Scott Russell (1993). *Staying Put: Making a Home in a Restless World*. Boston: Beacon Press.

Thompson, Maurice (1900). *Alice of Old Vincennes*. Indianapolis: Bowen-Merrill.

Wright, James (1990). *Above the River: The Complete Poems*. New York: Farrar, Straus & Giroux.

15

The Old Southwest: Humor, Tall Tales, and the Grotesque

Rosemary D. Cox

Toward a View of Humor of the Old Southwest

In "The Gander Pulling," Augustus Baldwin Longstreet comments on the prediction that his "writings will be read with increased interest a hundred years to come" by noting that "I can see no good reason, if this be true, why they should not be read a thousand years hence, with more interest." He thus takes "the liberty of dropping a word here, to the curious reader, of the year 2833" (Longstreet 1998: 75). Longstreet's wry observation is more prophetic than perhaps even he realized at the time, for even though the movement he ushered in has often been discounted as a subgenre, humor of the Old Southwest is a significant regional literature in its own right. Its unvarnished portrayal of frontier life is the first expression of American literary realism and provides a singular record of a unique period in the history of the United States. Its unabashed rendering of indigenous character and scene frequently achieves distinction in such remarkable personalities as Simon Suggs, "Big Bear" Jim Doggett, and Sut Lovingood. Its frequent affinity with fantasy and distortion provides an alternate medium for interpreting life experiences. Most notable is its pervasive influence on later writers: Samuel Clemens (Mark Twain), William Faulkner, and Erskine Caldwell, to name just three. From a twenty-first-century perspective, it can be racist, sexist, and coarse; yet through humor, tall tale, and the grotesque, the writings of the Old Southwest expose the foibles of common men and women not only to entertain but also to reveal the complexity of human nature – capable of incredible acts of cruelty and benevolence, resilient enough to overcome any adversity.

Boundaries: The Antebellum South

To avoid the confusion of terminology and locale, some scholars prefer to call this body of literature "Antebellum Southern Humor" rather than "Humor of the Old

Southwest" because the term "Southwest" is usually associated with places like Arizona, New Mexico, and Colorado, which constitute the Southwest today. But in the early nineteenth century, when this humor was written, the Southwest was defined much more in relation to settlements on the Atlantic coast. In 1783 the western boundary of the young nation was the Mississippi river. The territories beyond it were vast and largely unexplored, many still under the dominion of France and Spain. Thus, the region known as the Old Southwest began on the east coast in North Carolina, South Carolina and Georgia and expanded westward, following the rapidly moving line of the frontier through Kentucky, Tennessee, Alabama and Mississippi, then on to Missouri, Arkansas and Louisiana – the region now known as the South.

Old Southwestern humor falls within clearly definable limits. The publication in 1835 of Longstreet's *Georgia Scenes, Characters, Incidents, &c. in the First Half Century of the Republic* traditionally marks the beginning of the genre; George Washington Harris's *Sut Lovingood. Yarns Spun by a "Nat'ral Born Durn'd Fool." Warped and Wove for Public Wear*, collected and published in 1867, is usually considered the last and most accomplished work in the field. The majority of sketches in Southwestern humor appeared before 1861 because, by then, not only had the Southern frontier vanished, but the Civil War precipitated social and economic changes, particularly the suspension of periodical publication in both the North and the South (Wimsatt and Phillips 1985: 153), which dramatically affected this humor. The later comic works of William Gilmore Simms, particularly "Bald-Head Bill Bauldy" (1870), "How Sharp Snaffles Got His Capital and Wife" (1870), and *Paddy McGann; or The Demon of the Stump* (1863) can be considered part of the Old Southwestern school because they use the same traditions and techniques. Numerous works published before 1835 are also typically classified as Southwestern humor, notably the comic anecdotes of Mason Locke Weems; the Southern works of James Kirke Paulding, especially his play *The Lion of the West* (1830), featuring Colonel Nimrod Wildfire, a character with obvious parallels to Congressman David Crockett; and the writings of David Crockett himself (original and commissioned). The Crockett *Almanacs* were also published between 1835 and 1856 and include not only the usual calendars, weather forecasts, and features, but also anecdotes and fantastic tales of Crockett's exploits, further mythologizing the man and establishing the legend.

Humor of the Old Southwest had its genesis in the periodicals of the day. Longstreet's sketches, for example, appeared in his own newspaper, the *Augusta State Rights' Sentinel*, and in the *Milledgeville Southern Recorder*, before he collected and published them in book form. The *Delta* and the *Picayune* in New Orleans, the St. Louis *Reveille*, the Cincinnati *News*, the *Louisville Courier*, and the Montgomery *Mail* all became well known for their humor, but it was a New York journal, *The Spirit of the Times – A Chronicle of the Turf, Agriculture, Field Sports, Literature, and the Stage*, edited by William Trotter Porter from 1831 to 1856, that provided the pre-eminent forum for the development of Southwestern humor by publishing the majority of sketches, introducing new writers to its readership (which Porter boasted reached

40,000 by 1856, including international circulation [Cohen and Dillingham 1994: xviii]), and establishing the standards of the genre.

Besides *Georgia Scenes* and *Sut Lovingood*, some of the best-known works in Southwestern humor include William Tappan Thompson's *Major Jones's Courtship* (1843), Johnson Jones Hooper's *Some Adventures of Captain Simon Suggs, Late of the Tallapoosa Volunteers; together with "Taking the Census" and Other Alabama Sketches* (1845), Thomas Bangs Thorpe's *The Mysteries of the Backwoods; Or, Sketches of the Southwest, Including Character, Scenery and Rural Sports* (1846), John S. Robb's *Streaks of Squatter Life* (1847), Joseph M. Field's *The Drama in Pokerville* (1847), Henry Clay Lewis's *Odd Leaves from the Life of a Louisiana "Swamp Doctor"* (1850), Joseph Glover Baldwin's *The Flush Times of Alabama and Mississippi; A Series of Sketches* (1853), and Hardin E. Taliaferro's *Fisher's River (North Carolina) Scenes and Characters* (1859). That collections of humorous tales like these were enormously popular on a national scale is evident from the number of editions that were printed. *Georgia Scenes*, for example, went through five editions with dozens of reprints by 1897; *Simon Suggs* reached eleven editions by 1856. Porter's collections, taken primarily from the *Spirit* – *The Big Bear of Arkansas and Other Sketches, Illustrative of Characters and Incidents in the South and South-West* (1843) and *A Quarter Race in Kentucky and Other Sketches Illustrative of Scenes, Characters and Incidents Throughout "The Universal Yankee Nation"* (1846) – also enjoyed a wide and profitable circulation.

Authorship: The Gentleman Narrator

Humor of the Old Southwest is essentially masculine in content, focus, and appeal. In the February 18, 1837 edition of the *Spirit*, Porter maintains: "we are addressing ourselves to gentlemen of standing, wealth and intelligence – the very corinthian columns of the community" (quoted in Fienberg 1992: 241). The ideal gentlemen Porter refers to are representative of the men who wrote antebellum Southern humor. They were professional men, usually lawyers, judges, or newspaper editors, but also physicians, planters, actors, artists, state legislators, and congressmen; they were well educated, sometimes self-taught; they expressed a defensive love for the South, even though many of them had been born in the North; and they were politically conservative, supporting the Whig party, in opposition to the policies of President Andrew Jackson.

Kenneth Lynn makes a convincing argument that the "Self-controlled gentleman" wrote humorous sketches as a reaction against Jacksonian democracy, which he believed threatened Southern plantation culture. Lynn further suggests that the humorists exploited the figure of the poor white in their sketches to counter fears that the unscrupulous lower classes would usurp control of society (Lynn 1959: 61, 53, 56). Taking issue with Lynn's theories, James H. Justus proposes that the Southwestern humorists thought of themselves "more as Moderns than as partisan Whigs." Justus maintains that because the humorists have "cast their lot with the future," the personalities "who dominate their writing are unambitious yeomen and marginal settlers, whose quirky, complacent individualism resists the progressive program of the time: Manifest Destiny, economic enterprise, order, civilization" (Justus 2001: 7). Political and social satire underlie Southwestern humor to some degree, as is evident in Hooper's *Simon Suggs*, which burlesques a campaign biography, and in sketches like "Sut Lovingood Travels with Old Abe," where Harris attacks Abraham Lincoln, or "The Early Life of Sut Lovengood [*sic*], written by his Dad," which parodies "The Early Life of Grant, by his Father" published in the New York *Ledger* in March 1868. But the factors that contributed to the development of antebellum Southern humor are too complex to be confined to a single attribute. Readers should keep in mind the words of Thompson's Major Joseph Jones: "this little sketch of my perrygrinations among the big cities of the northern states, was rit with no higher aim than to amuse the idle hours of my frends, and if it fails to do that, its a spilt job" (Thompson 1880: 5).

The "Self-controlled gentleman" humorist emphasized the contrast between social classes and created comic incongruity in part through the frame structure. This technique allows the literate, articulate narrator to open the story and set up the scene which is then dramatized in the voices and actions of the common characters. The erudite narrator then closes the tale, creating a "picture-frame" effect. While writers have employed this device for centuries (examples abound in, for example, Chaucer, Boccaccio, and the *Arabian Nights*), the Southwestern humorists most likely inherited the form from oral storytelling, though there is also a precedent in the tales of Irving's *Sketch Book*. The frame device allowed the humorists to retain a respectable distance from their characters and the often offensive situations in the tales. As gentlemen of repute, unwilling to offend the sensibilities of their genteel readers, many humorists were so anxious to dissociate themselves from their earthy characters that they wrote under pseudonyms (such as "The Turkey Runner," "Skitt," "Madison Tensas, M.D.," or "N. of Arkansas") to preserve their anonymity. The frame also allows readers to form their own judgments about these plain folks, who can be respected for their virtues or condemned for their vices. Furthermore, because it distances readers from the direct action of the sketch, the frame renders violent or disturbing scenes comic, safely under the control of the sensible narrator.

Walter Blair suggests that the frame technique helps to create incongruity, which is in itself humorous. Blair lists three types of incongruity: the difference between the rhetorical language of the narrator and the coarse dialect of the characters; the distance created by the separation of the situation in the story from that of the yarn; and the disparity between the realism of the narration and the fantastic elements of the tale (1937: 92). To this list Hennig Cohen and William B. Dillingham add two other elements: the tension created between knowledge and ignorance; and the contrast of illiterate language and commonsense philosophy, as exemplified in a character like Sut Lovingood whose broad East Tennessee mountain dialect sometimes embodies remarkable wisdom (Cohen and Dillingham 1994: xxxiv).

In its early phases, Southwestern humor demonstrated very sharp distinctions between narration and scene. Longstreet's sketches in *Georgia Scenes*, for example, clearly juxtapose the Addisonian narrators, Lyman Hall and Abraham Baldwin, against the cadaverous Rancy Sniffle or exuberant *Yallow* Blossom. Nevertheless, by the time Harris was writing the Lovingood sketches, the formal frame had all but disappeared, perhaps reflecting the humorists' sense of social disintegration after the Civil War, but also ushering in a style that would be perfected by later writers.

Realism: A Frontier Perspective

One of the most important contributions of Southwestern humor to the broader American literary tradition is its realistic expression of regional elements, imparting a fresh vigor to traditional forms. Porter begins the preface to *The Big Bear of Arkansas* by claiming that "A new vein of literature, as original as it is inexhaustible in its source, has been opened in this country within a very few years, with the most marked success" (1845: 7). Despite Porter's enthusiastic assertion, antebellum Southern humor was not a nineteenth-century innovation: its antecedents include the oral tradition; classical myth; the concepts of the epic boast, the picaresque hero, and the eighteenth-century sublime; the Bible; *The Travels of Baron Munchausen*; and the work of earlier writers, notably Joseph Addison, William Byrd, Washington Irving, James Fenimore Cooper, and Sir Walter Scott. From this rich heritage, however, the Southwestern humorists created something novel: in their sketches they recorded life as they saw it, using language which, with its vivid metaphors and representational dialogue, was innovative and set a precedent for later American writers to emulate. In his preface to *The Chronicles of Pineville* (1848), Thompson states that his purpose in collecting and publishing stories of the Georgia backwoodsmen is "to present to the public a few more interesting specimens of the genus '*Cracker*'"(1880: 19). Thompson mirrors the realistic aims of his colleague and mentor, Longstreet, who in his preface to the first edition of *Georgia Scenes* gives what must be the first description of creative nonfiction: "It [*Georgia Scenes*] consists of nothing more than fanciful *combinations* of *real* incidents and characters . . ." (Longstreet 1998: 3). Longstreet thus laid the foundation for the hundreds of sketches that followed.

While they may not always present unbiased, unelaborated facts, as Clement Eaton observes, the humorists "present through their imagination and firsthand knowledge of the plain people a kind of truth that eludes the researcher in documents" (1964: 102). Even more important, according to Eaton, "they observed Southern life from within" (Eaton 1964: 103), in contrast to the travel writings of European visitors and Northern observers like Frederick Law Olmsted. Cohen and Dillingham underscore the humorists' realistic depiction of frontier life by providing a list of 22 typical subjects, including hunts, fights, horse races, courtships and weddings, camp meetings, pranks, trades and swindles, odd characters, and the naïve country boy in the city (1994: xxiv).

The humorists' desire to chronicle frontier life was further inspired by the sense of a vanishing culture. Many wanted to capture their recent past in order to preserve it for future generations. Longstreet defends just such a purpose: "the aim of the author was to supply a chasm in history which has always been overlooked – the manners, customs, amusements, wit, dialect, as they appear in all grades of society to an ear and eye witness of them" (quoted in Fitzgerald 1891: 164).

Other humorists reveal a like motive. Joseph M. Field's comment on a steamboat race at the end of "Stopping to Wood" is typical: "such a scene is not likely to be witnessed *now*, but the writer will not soon forget that such he bore a part in, some ten years ago . . ." (Field 1858: 176). As Cohen and Dillingham state, because the humorists "were among the Southern privileged, the literate and educated, who bore a burden of responsibility," they "stepped in . . . to capture a cultural phenomenon that interested, often amused, and sometimes even displeased (or, on occasion, disgusted) them" (1994: xxiv).

The Humor of Character: A Kaleidoscope of Personalities

Almost all comedy and satire in humor of the Old Southwest turn on the idiosyncrasies of character. The inexhaustible array of figures who parade through the pages of this literature are as diverse and colorful as the real people on whom they were modeled. A host of intriguing and repulsive individuals inhabit Longstreet's Georgia, for example. In "The Character of a Native Georgian," Ned Brace perplexes the occupants of a Savannah boarding house and endears himself to his hostess by feigning special dietary requirements. His pranks transcend the bounds of decency, however, when he throws the end of a funeral procession into a paroxysm of laughter. "The Fight" features Rancy Sniffle, a victim of poverty and malaria and the classic example of the Southern poor white, who delights in instigating fights where the opponents bite off each other's ears, noses, and fingers. Longstreet's ring-tailed roarer is the inimitable *Yallow* Blossom, from "The Horse Swap," who boasts, "I am perhaps a *leetle*, jist a *leetle*, of the best man at a horse swap, that ever stole *cracklins* out of his mammy's fat gourd" (Longstreet 1998: 14). For all his talk, Blossom's skill does not spare him the humiliation of being duped in the trade of a horse with a horrifying saddle sore for one that is both blind and deaf: the biter gets bit. These horses – Bullet and Kit – are just two of the many animal characters whose colorful personalities rival those of their human counterparts in Longstreet's tales.

One of the most charming characters in Southwestern humor is Thompson's Major Joseph Jones. Royall Tyler's Jonathan and Seba Smith's Major Jack Downing were models for Thompson's character, a major in the Pineville, Georgia, militia. Thompson's most famous collection of Major Jones's sketches is *Major Jones's Courtship*, written as a series of letters over a period of two years from the Major to Mr. Thompson, who, like the real author, is the editor of a popular ladies' magazine. These sketches chronicle the joys and sorrows of young Jones's courtship and marriage to Miss Mary Stallions and the tribulations of raising their infant son, Henry Clay. Unlike many stories in Old Southwestern humor that delight in the exploits of rogues and half-men-half-alligator types and emphasize the rigors of living on an untamed frontier, these stories depict, in local dialect, domestic life on a typical small plantation in Middle Georgia. Thompson demonstrates his talent for creating humorous situations particularly well in the episode where one Christmas Eve the Major hangs all night in a cloth sack suspended from a ceiling joist on the Stallions's porch so that in the morning he can become the gift that Mary will keep for the rest of her life – for better or worse. *Major Jones's Sketches of Travel* (1848) continues the account of the Major's adventures in the cities and tourist attractions of the North: he visits the nation's capitol and Niagara Falls, for instance. However, in contrast to the *Courtship* which centers on character, the *Sketches* addresses political and social issues. Thus, to some degree the Major becomes a spokesperson for Thompson's Confederate agenda.

"IT IS GOOD TO BE SHIFTY IN A NEW COUNTRY": this is the motto of Hooper's Simon Suggs, the most reprehensible – but likeable – rogue in Southwestern humor, perhaps in American literature (Hooper 1993: 12). He is a confidence man, "a central but covert culture hero," as William Lenz notes (1985: 22). *Some Adventures of Captain Simon Suggs* is written in the tradition of the picaresque novel and as a burlesque of the campaign biographies of Andrew Jackson, whom Hooper describes as "a faithful representation of the Evil One" (1993: 9). Political satire aside, Satan easily becomes a prototype for Suggs, whose physical disfigurement is matched only by his ethical distortion. Like Satan in Milton's *Paradise Lost*, Suggs has a dual appeal: he is simultaneously attractive and repulsive. From the very beginning of *Simon Suggs*, Hooper describes Suggs in heroic terms, replete with images of bestiality. Hooper notes that nature "sent him into the world a sort of he-Pallas, ready to cope with his kind, from his infancy, in all the arts by which men '*get along*' in the world." But he is god-like only in a negative sense, for, Hooper continues, "if she made him, in respect to his moral conformation, a beast of prey, she did not refine the cruelty by denying him the fangs and the claws" (1993: 13). From beating his father at cards and swindling Indians out of their land, to deceiving religious converts out of their money and blackmailing John Pullum, the "Widow Rugby's husband," out of his honest earnings, Suggs's achievements are outstanding, but they serve only his own subversive ends. Unquestionably, Suggs is an antihero, but he is also comic. His ultimate appeal is universal, as Johanna Nicol Shields notes: in laughing at and with Hooper's "vulgar character," readers were laughing "at the perils of their own freedom, at the wonders of their own ingenuity, and at the spectacle of their own greed"; even today, "We laugh at the Suggs in us" (Shields 1993: viii).

More than Suggs, Harris's Sut Lovingood resonates with the elemental impulses of human nature. In the title of the *Yarns*, Sut proclaims himself a "Nat'ral born durn'd fool," but his brutal pranks, blatant sensuality, and coarse vulgarity justify Edmund Wilson's assessment that the *Yarns* is "by far the most repellent book of any real literary merit in American literature" (Wilson 1962: 509). For all his faults, though, Sut values freedom and deplores hypocrisy, as is evident from the people he chooses

Figure 15.1   "Major Jones's Courtship."

to target. For example, when he looses lizards up Parson Bullen's trousers during a sermon, creating pandemonium as Bullen strips naked and runs through the stunned congregation to escape the "Hell-sarpints" (Harris 1966: 54), Sut is exposing the parson's lechery. In another episode, Sut is totally remorseless over Mrs. Yardley's death, even though he has indirectly caused it by frightening a horse which runs over the old woman as it charges through her prize quilts hung on a clothesline. Sut believes that Mrs. Yardley, with her polished spectacles, deserves what she gets because she is a prude and, according to Sut, "wer a great noticer ove littil things, that nobody else ever seed" (Harris 1966: 114). M. Thomas Inge observes that "Since nearly all of the victims of Sut's pranks are either hypocritical, falsely self-righteous, sinful, or down-right criminal, Sut . . . may be considered an unintentional reformer or divine scourge – of sorts" ("Introduction," in Harris 1966: 21).

Whatever his moral function, Sut represents the typical East Tennessee mountaineer, especially in his language. The dialect of the *Yarns* presents a formidable obstacle to some individuals who find it unreadable, but when read aloud, Sut's speech is a remarkably accurate rendition of the local idiom. More striking than Sut's vernacular is his use of original metaphor, a trait he shares with other characters in Southwestern humor. Sut's sexual imagery is infamous. He goes into ecstasy over Sicily Burns's breasts: "Jis' think ove two snow balls wif a strawberry stuck butainded intu bof on em" (Harris 1966: 69). And his preference for widows prompts a unique analogy: "Gin me a willin wider, the yeath over: what they don't know, haint worth larnin. They hes all been tu Jamakey an' larnt how sugar's made, an' knows how tu sweeten wif hit; an' by golly, they is always ready tu use hit." For Sut, only women of experience are worth a man's time, as his figure of speech illustrates: "Widders am a speshul means . . . fur ripenin green men, killin off weak ones, an making 'ternally happy the soun ones" (Harris 1966: 118, 119).

Even though the majority of characters in humor of the Old Southwest are men, engaged in masculine pursuits (like drinking, fighting, or hunting), a surprising number of sketches concern women. When Lenz surveyed two popular anthologies, Porter's *Big Bear* and *Quarter Race*, he discovered that women are featured in approximately 20 percent of the stories, playing central roles in 11 of the 54 sketches (Lenz 1993: 592). A wider reading in the genre reveals that Lenz's findings are representative. In a literature written *by* men, *for* men, which is as likely to ridicule the narrator, the author, and even the reader as it is the ignorant frontiersman, one would expect women characters to be the victims of male dominance and cultural assumptions. And indeed they are, in sketches like William C. Hall's "How Sally Hooter Got Snake Bit," where the vain protagonist is terrified by a sausage that she has tied around her waist for a bustle when it comes loose and dangles down to her ankles underneath her skirt. But, as Lenz and Edward Piacentino demonstrate, more often than not women actually occupy a position equal or superior to their male counterparts. The shemales of the Crockett *Almanacs* rival the men in strength, courage, and bravado. Mike Fink's daughter Sal, for example, ties the feet of about 50 Indian would-be assassins together, then pulls them into their own campfire with a "suddenachous jerk, that made the intire woods tremble" (Lauter et al., eds. 1994: 1466). Harris's Sicily Burns is another unvanquished female. In "Blown Up with Soda" she convinces Sut Lovingood that she has a powerful love potion to give him "a new sensashun." Drinking down the concoction in anticipation of winning her affection, Sut becomes the butt of a vicious joke. His stomach erupts in foam, and he flees in humiliation, taunted by Sicily's exhortation: "Hole hit down, Mister Lovingood! Hole hit down! Hits a cure fur puppy luv; hole hit *down*!" (Harris 1966: 72, 73).

Humor and character are inextricably linked. Originating as a medical term referring to one of the four liquids of the human body, "humour" evolved to mean "eccentric." The characters in Southwestern humor are certainly eccentric, and even though they may be peculiar to a specific time and region, their quirks, fears, joys, and sorrows reveal their basic humanity.

Tall Tales: Surviving an Untamed Land

When the *Mayflower* arrived on the shores of Cape Cod, a squirrel could run from the Atlantic coast to the Mississippi river, tree-limb to tree-limb, without touching the ground. The "Big Woods," as it was called, was an alien and formidable place, full of savage beasts and wild men who, according to William Bradford in his history of the Plymouth colony, "were readier to fill their sides full of arrows than otherwise" (Lauter et al., eds., 1994: 249). This frontier was one of the most important factors in the development of Southwestern humor and, if one subscribes to the theories of Frederick Jackson Turner, America itself. In his famous paper, "The Significance of the Frontier in American History," Turner suggests that because it was "the meeting point between savagery and civilization," the frontier was a vital force in shaping American life. He states: "American social development has been continually beginning over again on the frontier." Turner continues: "this expansion westward with its new opportunities, its continuous touch with the simplicity of primitive society, furnish the forces dominating American character" (1894: 200). While Turner's thesis may be too simplistic to adequately explain the complexities of the American experience, it does account for much of the deprivation and incongruity that form the wellspring of antebellum Southern humor.

By the 1830s, large cities had developed in the East, but the frontier remained essentially a vast land of inaccessible mountains and malarial swamps, unbounded rivers and expansive forests – magnificent and annihilative. Humor became a survival tool, for "Under the almost savage conditions of a wild new land," as Cohen and Dillingham explain, "laughter was one of the means by which the frontiersman could for a time forget his hardship, preserve his courage, and retain his balance and his humanity" (1994: xxxviii). If the horrors of the world can be exaggerated and vanquished in the imagination, the actual confrontation with them is not so daunting. In the words of Jesse Bier, a "land where Crockett could make the sun and earth move when they were frozen stuck and could put a piece of sunrise in his pocket was not so awesome anymore" (1968: 40–1). For the frontiersman, the tall tale became a "self-imposed mask," as Cohen and Dillingham term it, allowing him to laugh at himself, knowing that "he was playing a role, that his civilized self remained intact beneath the half-man, half-alligator comic façade he created" (1994: xxxviii).

A peculiarly American form, the tall tale employs a realistic framework, especially common language used in a very straightforward manner, to relate a story of fantastic proportions and impossible feats. It usually assumes the guise of personal narrative or anecdote and stretches the reader's (or listener's) credulity with its bizarre humor. Often the central focus of the tale is the superhuman character who accomplishes incredible deeds, a hero typically modeled on someone who actually lived. Frontier figures like Mike Fink ("King of the Mississippi Keelboatmen"), Paul Bunyan, and John Henry (the incomparable Negro "Steel-drivin' Man") are legendary, but of all these backwoods demigods the most famous is Davy Crockett, whose real-life maxim was "Be sure you are right, then go ahead" (1973: n. 1). Even excluding the Crockett *Almanacs* and the multitude of fantastic stories that have perpetuated the myth of Crockett the comet catcher, Crockett still stands larger than life. His official autobiography, *A Narrative of the Life of David Crockett of the State of Tennessee* (1834), seems more fantastic than real in its praise of Crockett's prowess. It claims, for instance, that Crockett killed 105 bears in less than 12 months (Crockett 1973: 194). The narrator of the spurious *Sketches and Eccentricities of Col. David Crockett of West Tennessee* (1833) is even more laudatory, declaring that Crockett can "slip down a honey-locust without a scratch" (Crockett 1974: 14), strip the bark off a tree by grinning at it, and kill a bear just by challenging it.

When it comes to killing bears, however, Thorpe's Jim Doggett has no equal. The hero of "The Big Bear of Arkansas" (the finest tall tale in Southwestern humor because it achieves mythic levels and is the story that gave its name to this type of humor, "The Big Bear School"), Doggett is the indomitable hunter. He brags that "in bar hunts *I am numerous*"; he frightens the bears in his region of the country so badly that they grow lean, and "the old black rascals know the crack of my gun as well as they know a pig's squealing" (Thorpe 1989: 117, 115). His gun (like the magical weapon of the epic hero) is a "perfect *epidemic among bar*," and his dog, Bowie-knife, "know[s] a bar's way as well as a horse-jockey knows a woman's" (p. 115). But the adversary in this tale is no ordinary bear: it is the "greatest bear . . . that ever lived, none excepted" (p. 118). When the bear foils Doggett's attempts to hunt it, he believes he confronts the baffling power of the demonic: "it reduced me in flesh faster than an ager. . . . *he hunted me*, and that, too, like a devil, which I began to think he was" (p. 119). Even if the bear is not the Devil, it certainly embodies the obscure omnipotence of the Deity, evident in Doggett's observation that the bear "loomed up like a *black mist*" and "*walked through the fence*" like a falling tree would through a cobweb" (p. 122). Echoing Crockett, Doggett vows "to catch that bar, go to Texas, or die" (p. 121), but in the final encounter, he is caught off guard, with his "inexpressibles" (p. 122) around his ankles. Though he fails to deliver the mortal wound, the bear dies: it is, after all, "an *unhuntable bar, and died when his time come*"

(p. 122). Doggett admits his human failings, but he is not defeated. His reputation as a hunter is still intact despite the curious circumstances surrounding this hunt. The "grave silence" (p. 122) at the end of the tale suggests that Doggett and his auditors recognize the existence of a force greater than themselves but of which they are, at the same time, an inextricable part.

While "The Big Bear of Arkansas" lends itself to a more symbolic interpretation than the average tall tale in Southwestern humor, most tall tales reflect the imaginative attempt to come to terms with an unpredictable environment that could be simultaneously wondrous and hostile. What Creath S. Thorne says of the Crockett *Almanacs* applies equally well to all tall tales in the Southwestern tradition: "What this world of terrifying storms and earthquakes, gargantuan flora and fauna, and engulfing rivers and cataracts provides for is the essential confrontation" (Thorne 1980: 95).

No region better illustrates this "essential confrontation" than Doggett's Arkansas. It is the "creation State," and, as Doggett declares, Arkansas is no ordinary place: "her varmints ar large, her trees ar large, her rivers ar large, and a small mosquitoe would be of no more use in Arkansaw than preaching in a cane-brake" (Thorpe 1989: 114). When Doggett plants a crop of beets and potatoes on his farm, they grow so large a man hoping to purchase the land mistakes them for cedar stumps and Indian mounds. Doggett's theory is justified: *planting in Arkansaw is dangerous.* . . . natur intended Arkansaw for a hunting ground, and I go according to natur" (p. 117). Living according to the laws of nature (which must be quite astonishing in a land as strange as this Arkansas) gives Doggett the special knowledge he needs to survive.

The distortion of realistic natural landscape into the fantastic locale of the tall tale thus serves a distinct purpose, as Bier maintains: "conditions of frontier life [were grossly exaggerated] in order to diminish them, upon actual contact, to what they simply were, large enough but confrontable when reduced from what was preternaturally imagined." "We heightened and supernaturalized dangers and powers," Bier continues, "in order to deflate apprehensions" (Bier 1968: 40, 41).

For tall-tale heroes in humor of the Old Southwest, boasting is an effective means of allaying these "apprehensions." Men equate themselves to dreadful natural phenomena (such as tornadoes and hurricanes), to terrifying animals (like wildcats and alligators), or to manmade wonders (like steamboats) because bragging allows them to pump up their egos to intimidate their opponents or to conceal their own feelings of inadequacy. Mike Fink's boast exemplifies the type:

> I'm a Salt River roarer! I'm a ring-tailed squealor! I'm a reg'lar screamer from the ol' Massassip'! WHOOP! . . . I'm half wild horse and half cock-eyed alligator and the rest o' me is crooked snags an' red-hot snappin' turtle . . . I ain't had a fight for two days an' I'm spilein' for exercise. Cock-a-doddle do! (Lauter et al., eds. 1994: 1465)

On a practical level, frontiersmen boasted to preserve themselves from the annihilative forces of the wilderness. By metaphorically assuming the might of what they feared, they could overcome it. Lynn expands on the concept: tall talk "was a way of beating the wilderness at its own game, of converting terror into *joie de vivre* and helplessness into an exhilarating sense of power" (1959: 27–8). Thus, the exaggerated and fantastic rendering of reality becomes one way of surviving it.

The Grotesque: Unregenerate Human Nature

Life on the Old Southwestern frontier was characterized by diversity and constant flux. This "halcyon period," as humorist Joseph Glover Baldwin christens it in *Flush Times*, was a time when "all the departments of the *crimen falsi*, held riotous carnival" (1987: 1, 185). Baldwin asks, "What country could boast more largely of its crimes?" He continues: "What more splendid rôle of felonies! What more terrific murders! What more gorgeous bank robberies! What more magnificent operations in the land offices!" Then, with a consciousness more characteristic of the twenty-first century than of his own, Baldwin condemns the mistreatment of the Native Americans: "And in INDIAN affairs! – the very mention is suggestive of the poetry of theft – the romance of a wild and weird larceny! What sublime conceptions of super-Spartan roguery! Swindling Indians by the nation!" (1987: 238).

If there is any humor at all in this spectacle, it is in the sense of the carnival which, particularly when it celebrates excess and freaks of nature, is an expression of the grotesque, a relationship introduced by Russian theorist Mikhail Bakhtin in his work *Rabelais and his World* (1965).

A curious manifestation of the grotesque in Southwestern humor is the cult of the Ugly Man. Richard M. Dorson states, "Pride in ugliness, or in the ability to depict ugliness, was a favorite tradition of the frontier." Dorson notes that "the more misshapen, cadaverous, leperlike, or generally hideous the individual under discussion, the more accomplished the raconteur. No macabre detail was overlooked in presenting these monsters" (1939: xviii). Frontier heroes like Daniel Boone and Davy Crockett celebrated their fantastic ugliness, but many Southwestern writers also took delight in their own physical peculiarities. Longstreet was "notoriously ugly," though he "possessed great charm" according to Jennette Tandy (1925: 75). Hooper, known as "alias Simon Suggs," was a physical likeness of his character, prompting a writer for the *Alabama Journal* to remark: "Hooper is ugly – theoretically, practically, decidedly ugly" (*Spirit* 1850: 52). Thorpe did not escape the barbs of ridicule for his ugly face, either, as fellow humorist Joseph M. Field writes: "[Thorpe] looked like an animated embodiment, in semi-human form, of a thick fog on the Mississippi, at half past three in the morning, to a man who has just lost his last dollar at poker" (*Spirit* 1844: 546).

Without a doubt, the ugliest character in Southwestern humor is Bill Wallis, the Ugly Man himself from Hooper's story "A Night at the Ugly Man's." Wallis is so ugly he claims that even as a child, "*a fly wouldn't light on my face*" (Hooper 1851: 45), and on first seeing himself in the spring where he had gone to wash his face, he ran back, screaming, to his mother. Wallis grows more grotesque with age. His wife has to practice kissing a cow before she can kiss him. And on one occasion he (quite profitably) frightens a steamboat away from his flatboat by revealing his face and shouting oaths to the crowd on the deck who respond by throwing a peck of buck-horn handled knives at him. Wallis's windfall is a variation on the popular frontier prank of presenting a horn-handled knife or some other physical object to the ugliest man in a community; the recipient would then pass the knife on to the next man he met uglier than himself (Anderson 1964: 203). The ultimate proof of Wallis's ugliness is when his face deflects lightning.

The grotesque functions at several levels in this story. There is the sense of the carnival freak – Wallis is, after all, pre-eminent in the community for his ugliness, and strangers (including the narrator of this tale) make special journeys to visit him. There is also the sense that this tale is a distorted boast. Wallis prides himself on his special gift, making himself like every other hero of the Old Southwest by boasting of his ugliness just as the others compare themselves to formidable creatures like wildcats, alligators, and snapping turtles.

Wallis's ugliness represents the lighter side of the grotesque in Southwestern humor; there is another, much darker aspect embodied in the horror which underlies many sketches, of which Lewis's *Odd Leaves* presents some singular instances. In "The Day of Judgment," the apprentice doctor Madison Tensas describes an incident where he and several of his acquaintances terrify the religious converts at a camp meeting near the Loosa Chitta swamp by setting fire to a stray mule they have soaked with turpentine and tar. The scene is a vision from hell: "With a scream of terror and anguish it darted off up the lane in the direction of the camp, whilst we mounted, with our long mantles floating behind us, yelling like incarnate fiends, sounding our horns, and, our many torches flashing like meteors through the night, pressed on after it in hot and close pursuit" (Lewis 1997: 63).

The ensuing chaos at the camp meeting adds yet another grotesque element to the haunting picture of torment: "Supplications for mercy, screams of anguish, prayers and blasphemies, horror-stricken moans of the converts, the maniacal shouts of the conscience-stricken sinners, and the calm collected songs of the really righteous swelled on the wind and mingled with the roaring of the flames, our piercing yells, discordant horns, and the horrible cries of the consuming animal."

The surrounding swamp echoes the sound, intensifying the horror: "the wildwood if filled with screaming devils, could not have given back a more hideous outcry" (Lewis 1997: 64). While the tragic mule never reaches the cooling waters of the Loosa Chitta in time to quench the flames, it does find peace in death. Yet from the way this story is told, it is clear that the doctor finds no solace, for he secretly agonizes over the barbarity of his actions and the more poignant question of why the human psyche can revel in such monstrosities.

Another illustration of the grotesque in Lewis's *Odd Leaves* is the sight of a cadaver's face used as the vehicle for a practical joke in "The Curious Widow." Doctor Tensas describes the terrifying features of the specimen for dissection, an albino (white Negro): his visage is completely "deformed and unnatural; a horrible hare-lip, the cleft extending half way up his nose externally, and a pair of tushes projecting from his upper jaw, completed his bill of horrors" (Lewis 1997: 76–7). The face is so awful that even after Tensas slices it off the skull and carefully wraps it up for his prying landlady's discovery, it still gives him nightmares: "I endeavoured to sleep," he says, "but that hideous face . . . locked securely in a trunk, kept staring at me through its many envelopes" (p. 77). The old lady's response to finding the face is unpredictable – she is initially transfixed then breaks into maniacal laughter, telling the perpetrators of the prank: "I was just *smiling aloud* to think what fools these students made of themselves when they tried to scare me with a dead nigger's face when I had slept with a drunken husband for twenty years!" (p. 81).

Nevertheless, her reaction does not diminish the ghastly appeal of the repulsive visage. Pointing out that Lewis is writing from the tradition of "grotesque medical comedy in which the body is dehumanized, objectified, often reduced to parts to separate it further from the once healthy or living person whose being animated it," Edwin T. Arnold states that "Such humor is intentionally offensive, a deliberate sacrilege, a carnival counterattack against the inevitability of death and corruption" (1997: xx). Arnold further notes that Lewis utilizes the "controlling metaphor of medicine and disease" not only to expose "the foibles of man, which render him ridiculous" but also to reveal "the hidden pestilences that infect and corrupt and finally destroy" (p. xiv).

From the corpse of a baby stolen from a hospital morgue to a demonic dwarf slave who attempts to murder the doctor, images of horror, particularly those relating to death and deformity, occur throughout *Odd Leaves*. But grotesque elements are not exclusive to Lewis's work, for they pervade Southwestern humor. Even Longstreet, the most decorous humorist in the tradition, describes a gruesome saddle sore in "The Horse Swap." With its demented humor in tortured dogs, mutilated body parts, and reconfigured corpses, Harris's *Yarns* abounds with grisly detail, prompting Inge to remark, "To see Sut as totally sadistic is to refuse to recognize within ourselves Conrad's 'heart of darkness,' our own tendency towards innate depravity" ("Introduction," in Harris 1966: 21). The fascination with the morbid in Southwestern humor is just another indicator of what Sut recognizes as "univarsal onregenerit human nater" (Harris 1966: 186).

The Literary Legacy

The influence of the Southwestern humorists reaches beyond their own region and time, even into the twenty-first century. Certainly Southwestern humor was different from mainstream contemporary literature of its day. Readers are apt to forget that Emerson's *Nature* was published only one year after *Georgia Scenes*; the first of the Sut Lovingood sketches ("Sut Lovingood's Daddy 'Acting Horse'") appeared the same year as Thoreau's *Walden*; and the same decade that saw the publication of *The Scarlet Letter*, *Moby Dick*, and *Leaves of Grass* also heralded *Odd Leaves*, *Flush Times*, and

Fisher's River. In contrast to most national literature, however, the work of fellow Southerner Edgar Allan Poe has much in common with the grotesque tales in Southwestern humor. That Poe knew and appreciated Southwestern humor is evident from his review of *Georgia Scenes* for the *Southern Literary Messenger*, where he applauds Longstreet's book. But writers since the Civil War have best embraced the legacy of the Old Southwest, borrowing the subjects and techniques of frontier humor, refashioning them to fit their own time and taste.

Modern critical tradition generally acknowledges that Southwestern humor reaches its pinnacle in the work of Samuel Clemens (Mark Twain). Twain was steeped in the Southwestern tradition: he owned copies of works by most of the prominent Southwestern humorists, and he shamelessly borrowed their material. The camp meeting scene in chapter 20 of *Huckleberry Finn*, for example, where the king dupes the Pokeville congregation out of their money, is modeled on Hooper's "The Captain Attends a Camp-meeting," where Simon Suggs absconds with the collection plate. Other elements in *Huckleberry Finn* also show the influence of Southwestern humor, specifically the portrayal of the duke and the king as confidence men, as well as the Royal Nonesuch and circus episodes. Twain's earlier works, particularly stories like "Jim Blaine and his Grandfather's Old Ram" (from *Roughing It*) and "The Celebrated Jumping Frog of Calaveras County" are even more clearly in the Southwestern tradition, utilizing the frame technique to spotlight a vernacular character. Yet even though his material, techniques, and realistic outlook have their roots in Southwestern humor, Twain transcends his forbears. Pascal Covici points out that "Mark Twain's fictional world is different from that of his immediate regional predecessors because it is organized around a real, and not a contrived, discrepancy between reality and appearance" (1962: 14). Leland Krauth concurs and adds, "Writing as a Victorian, Twain reformed Southwestern humor" (2001: 223).

Another major American writer to use the material and techniques of Old Southwestern humor in an original way is William Faulkner. How extensively Southwestern humor actually influenced Faulkner is unclear. He was familiar with Harris's *Yarns*, because in 1956 he mentioned Sut Lovingood in response to an interviewer's question about his favorite fictional characters (Lynn 1959: 137). But, as Inge suggests, Faulkner may simply have observed the same regional features and figures that the Southwestern humorists had encountered a century earlier (Inge 1962: 47–8). Whatever the origin of its characteristics, Faulkner's fiction shows a remarkable kinship to humor of the Old Southwest. There is an almost carnival quality to a story like "Mule in the Yard," for instance, where Mrs. Hait and Old Het chase I. O. Snopes's mules in and out of a thick fog. *The Hamlet*, the first of three novels focusing on the poor white Snopes family, is infused with Southwestern elements, as is the story "The Bear." And the journey of the Bundren family, in *As I Lay Dying*, to carry the body of the wife and mother, Addie, to her grave in Jefferson is grotesquely comic in the manner of the Old Southwest.

Like Faulkner, Erskine Caldwell demonstrates an affinity for characters and situations that echo the Old Southwest. The scene in *Tobacco Road* where Jeeter Lester climbs a ladder to peer in the window of the bedroom where his son Dude is having sex with Sister Bessie could just have easily come from Sut Lovingood's *Yarns*, as could the passage where Dude backs his car over Grandmother Lester, leaving her crushed to death in the dust. R. J. Gray remarks that the theme of Caldwell's fiction is simply "one of degeneracy – the reduction of the human being to the lowest possible levels of his experience" (1981: 298). In this sense Jeeter Lester and Ty Ty Walden (from *God's Little Acre*) are not that far removed from Rancy Sniffle, Simon Suggs, or Sut Lovingood. And like Sut, as Gray further notes, Lester and Walden "are presented as the *victims* of evil, whose strange behavior demonstrates the response of the innocent to circumstances he cannot control" (1981: 305).

Attentive readers can find traces of the Southwestern tradition in a host of twentieth-century authors – from the realism of the local colorists to the Southern gothic of Flannery O'Connor and the myth of Eudora Welty. With contemporary Southern writers like Bailey White and Fred Chappell, the Old Southwest has found a twenty-first-century voice. Who can forget White's eccentric Georgians: Red the Rat Man (from *Sleeping at the Starlite Motel*), who nurtures the pack rats he is hired to exterminate, or Louise (in *Quite a Year for Plums*), who plants messages in grass to attract space aliens to her garden? And what better than a tall tale for a new generation – Chappell's Uncle Gurton with his miraculous beard (*I Am One of You Forever*), or a metaphorical space odyssey aboard the starship *Isambard* (*Look Back All the Green Valley*)? The readers of 2833 have much to look forward to.

References

Anderson, J. Q. (1964). "For the Ugliest Man: An Example of Folk Humor." *Southern Folklore Quarterly* 28, 199–209.

Arnold, E. T. (1997). "Introduction." In H. C. Lewis, *Odd Leaves from the Life of a Louisiana Swamp Doctor*, xi–xliv. Baton Rouge: Louisiana State University Press. (First publ. 1850.)

Bakhtin, M. (1968). *Rabelais and his World*, trans. H. Iswolsky. Cambridge: MIT Press. (First publ. 1965.)

Baldwin, J. G. (1987). *The Flush Times of Alabama and Mississippi, a Series of Sketches*, intr. and ann. J. H. Justus. Baton Rouge: Louisiana State University Press. (First publ. 1853.)

Bier, J. (1968). *The Rise and Fall of American Humor*. New York: Holt.

Blair, W. (1937). *Native American Humor (1800–1900)*. New York: American Book Company.

Cohen, H., and Dillingham, W. B. (1994). Introduction. In H. Cohen and W. B. Dillingham (eds.), *Humor of the Old Southwest*, 3rd edn., xv–xl. Athens, Ga: University of Georgia Press.

Covici, P., Jr. (1962). *Mark Twain's Humor: The Image of a World*. Dallas: Southern Methodist University Press.

Crockett, D. (1973). *A Narrative of the Life of David Crockett of the State of Tennessee*, intr. and ann. J. A. Shackford and S. J. Folmsbee. Facsim. repr. Knoxville: University of Tennessee Press. (First publ. 1834.)

Crockett, D. (1974). "Introduction." In D. Crockett, *Sketches and Eccentricities of Col. David Crockett, of West Tennessee*. Facsim. rpt. New York: Arno. (First publ. 1833.)

Dorson, R. M. (1939). "Frontier Humor and Legend." In R. M. Dorson (ed.), *Davy Crockett: American Comic Legend*, xv–xxvi. New York: Spiral.

Eaton, C. (1964). *The Mind of the Old South*. Baton Rouge: Louisiana State University Press.

Field, J. M. (1858). "Stopping to Wood." Repr. in *Colonel Thorpe's Scenes in Arkansaw*, 173–6. Philadelphia: Peterson. (First publ. 1847 in *The Drama in Pokerville; the Bench and Bar of Jurytown, and Other Stories*.)

Fienberg, L. (1992). "Colonel Noland of the *Spirit*: The Voices of a Gentleman in Southwest Humor." In L. J. Budd and E. H. Cady (eds.), *On Humor: The Best from American Literature*, 240–53. Durham: Duke University Press.

Fitzgerald, O. P. (1891). *Judge Longstreet: A Life Sketch*. Nashville: Methodist Episcopal Church, South.

Gray, R. J. (1981). "Southwestern Humor, Erskine Caldwell, and the Comedy of Frustration." In S. MacDonald (ed.), *Critical Essays on Erskine Caldwell*, 298–314. Boston: Hall.

Harris, G. W. (1966). *Sut Lovingood's Yarns*, ed. M. T. Inge. New Haven: College and University Press. (First publ. 1867.)

Hooper, J. J. (1851). "A Night at the Ugly Man's." In *The Widow Rugby's Husband, a Night at the Ugly Man's, and Other Tales of Alabama*, 41–51. Philadelphia: Hart.

Hooper, J. J. (1993). *Adventures of Captain Simon Suggs, Late of the Tallapoosa Volunteers; together with "Taking the Census" and Other Alabama Sketches*, intr. J. N. Shields. Facsim. repr. Tuscaloosa: University of Alabama Press. (First publ. 1845.)

Inge, M. T. (1962). "William Faulkner and George Washington Harris: In the Tradition of Southwestern Humor." *Tennessee Studies in Literature* 7, 47–59.

Inge, M. T. (1966). Introduction. In G. W. Harris. *Sut Lovingood's Yarns*, ed. M. T. Inge, 9–24. New Haven: College and University Press.

Justus, J. H. (2001). "Introduction." In M. T. Inge and E. J. Piacentino (eds.), *The Humor of the Old South*, 1–10. Lexington: University Press of Kentucky.

Krauth, L. (2001). "Mark Twain: The Victorian of Southwestern Humor." In M. T. Inge and E. J. Piacentino (eds.), *The Humor of the Old South*, 222–35. Lexington: University Press of Kentucky.

Lauter, P., et al., eds. (1994). *The Heath Anthology of American Literature*, 2nd edn., vol. I. Lexington: Heath.

Lenz, W. E. (1985). *Fast Talk and Flush Times: The Confidence Man as a Literary Convention*. Columbia: University of Missouri Press.

Lenz, W. E. (1993). "The Function of Women in Old Southwestern Humor: Re-reading Porter's *Big Bear* and *Quarter Race* Collections." *Mississippi Quarterly* 46: 4, 589–600.

Lewis, H. C. (1997). *Odd Leaves from the Life of a Louisiana Swamp Doctor*, intr. E. T. Arnold. Baton Rouge: Louisiana State University Press. (First publ. 1850.)

Longstreet, A. B. (1998). *Georgia Scenes, Characters, Incidents, &c. in the First Half Century of the Republic*. In *Augustus Baldwin Longstreet's Georgia Scenes Completed*, ed. D. Rachels, 1–148. Athens, Ga: University of Georgia Press. (First publ. 1835.)

Lynn, K. (1959). *Mark Twain and Southwestern Humor*. Boston: Little, Brown.

Piacentino, E. J. (2000). "Contesting the Boundaries of Race and Gender in Old Southwestern Humor." *Southern Literary Journal* 32: 2, 116–40.

Porter, W. T. (1845). Preface. In W. T. Porter (ed.), *The Big Bear of Arkansas and Other Sketches, Illustrative of Characters and Incidents in the South and South-West*, vii–xii. Philadelphia: Carey & Hart. (First publ. 1843.) Special Collections and Archives, Robrt W. Woodruff Library, Emory University.

Shields, J. N. (1993). Introduction. In *Adventures of Captain Simon Suggs, Late of the Tallapoosa Volunteers; together with "Taking the Census" and Other Alabama Sketches*, intr. J. N. Shields. Facsim. repr. Tuscaloosa: University of Alabama Press, vii–lxix.

Spirit (1844). "The Rival 'Saws' of Thorpe and Field." *Spirit of the Times*, 13 Jan., 546.

Spirit (1850). "Johnson J. Hooper, esq." *Spirit of the Times*, 23 Mar., 52.

Taliaferro, Harden E. (1977). *Fisher's River (North Carolina): Scenes and Characters*. New York: Arno Press. (First publ. 1859.)

Tandy, J. (1925). *Crackerbox Philosophers in American Humor and Satire*. New York: Columbia University Press.

Thompson, W. T. (1848). Preface. In *Major Jones's Sketches of Travel. Comprising the Scenes, Incidents, and Adventures, in His Tour from Georgia to Canada*, 5–6. Philadelphia: Peterson.

Thompson, W. T. (1880). Preface. In *Major Jones's Georgia Scenes. Comprising His Celebrated Sketches of Scenes in Georgia. With Their Incidents and Characters*, 19–21. Philadelphia: Peterson.

Thorne, C. (1980). "The Crockett Almanacs: What Makes a Tall Tale Tall?" *Southern Folklore Quarterly* 44, 93–104.

Thorpe, T. B. (1989). "The Big Bear of Arkansas." In *A New Collection of Thomas Bangs Thorpe's Sketches of the Old Southwest*, ed. D. C. Estes, 112–22. Baton Rouge: Louisiana State University Press.

Turner, Frederick Jackson (1894). "XVIII – The Significance of the Frontier in American History." *Annual Report of the American Historical Association for the Year 1893*, 197–227. Washington: US Government Printing Office, 1894.

Wilson, E. (1962). *Patriotic Gore: Studies in the Literature of the American Civil War*. New York: Oxford University Press.

Wimsatt, M. A., and Phillips, R. L. (1985). Antebellum Humor. In L. D. Rubin, Jr., et al. (eds.), *The History of Southern Literature*, 136–56. Baton Rouge: Louisiana State University Press.

16

The Plantation School:
Dissenters and Countermyths

Sarah E. Gardner

Reflecting back on a long literary career, Virginia novelist Ellen Glasgow assessed her contributions to Southern letters. She recognized that she largely failed in her early attempts to counter the dominant theme in late nineteenth- and early twentieth-century Southern literature, namely sentimentalism, which she believed had eroded civilization. She nevertheless argued that her early novels offered some measure of relief to a Southern literary tradition that suffered from a "stranglehold on the intellect." In a celebrated passage, Glasgow prescribed "blood and irony" to cure a rotting Southern culture. The South needed blood because "it had grown thin and pale: it was satisfied to exist on borrowed ideas; to copy instead of create. And irony," Glasgow continued, "is an indispensable ingredient of the critical vision; it is the safest antidote to sentimental decay" (Glasgow 1943: 143). Other writers, including George Washington Cable, Charles Chesnutt, Frances Ellen Watkins Harper, and Mary Murfree, concurred with Glasgow's prescription for Southern literature. Together, they offered a critical vision of the plantation South that sharply diverged from the interpretation of the past offered by popular writers of the late nineteenth century. Their writings bear out Carl Degler's observation that "the American South is not and never has been a monolith. Always," Degler noted, "there have been diversities and divergences within its history and among its people" (2000: 3). Degler began his influential 1974 study on the "other South" by declaring "This book is about losers" (2000: 1). The subjects of his study were unable to threaten seriously the institution of slavery or to overturn white Democratic rule in the postwar South. Similarly, the literary dissenters under consideration in this essay were unable to counter the popularity and longevity of the Plantation School. Nevertheless, their works suggest that dissent in the late nineteenth- and early twentieth-century South was not "idiosyncratic, isolated . . . [or] irrelevant" (Degler 2000: ix). Rather, they point to the presence of a sustained effort on the part of Southerners, black and white, male and female, to counter "the Southern way," and comment on the forms of Southern dissent and the reasons for its failure.

Although the literary tradition against which Glasgow and her cohorts dissented was established in the 1830s with the plantation novels of John Pendleton Kennedy, it reached its fullest expression with the writings of the lost cause mythologizers of the late nineteenth century. Virginia author Thomas Nelson Page, one of the most prolific of the postbellum plantation romancers, gave the plantation legend its clearest voice. The Old South, Page asserted in 1892, "was as unique as it was distinct. It combined elements of the three great civilizations, which since the dawn of history have enlightened the world. It partook of the philosophic tone of the Grecian, of the dominant spirit of the Roman, and of the guardfulness of individual rights of the Saxon civilization. And over all, brooded a softness and beauty," he concluded, "the joint product of Chivalry and Christianity" (Page 1892: 5). In many respects, then, the plantation legend was born out of a postwar South. As literary critic Lucinda MacKethan has explained in an essay that appeared in a text on the history of Southern literature, "it was solely the newness" of the New South "that encouraged postbellum admirers of the plantation to turn a defeated way of life into a substantial legend. The design of images for a popular literature stocked with belles and cavaliers, courtships and duels, mansions and cotton blossoms, and, at the heart of the scene, wistfully reminiscing darkies," MacKethan has noted, "had to await the actual demise of the plantation world" (1985: 209). The outcome of the Civil War ensured that the South no longer posed a political or ideological threat to the rest of the nation, allowing Northern readers to embrace a mythic view of the Old South. In the spirit of reconciliation, Northern readers embraced a Southern literature that romanticized a lost civilization. Page took full advantage of the Northern postwar reading audience's desire for nostalgic literature, making extravagant claims for the antebellum South. To be sure, he was familiar with postwar critics of the South who charged the region with "sterility, with attempting to perpetuate human slavery, and with rebellion" (Page 1892: 5). He maintained, however, that the standards against which critics viewed the South were narrowly defined. "There is another standard," Page suggested, by which the South "measured the fullest stature: the sudden supremacy of the American people to-day is largely due to the Old South, and to its contemned civilization" (1892: 6).

The Plantation

At the center of the plantation legend was the plantation itself, with the big house figuring prominently. In an early article, Lucinda MacKethan has observed that most of Page's stories, novels, and essays on Southern culture "contain, near their beginning, a fairly thorough account of the home occupied by the hero or heroine" (MacKethan 1978: 317). Page opened his essay "Social Life in Old Virginia before the War," for example, by feigning a lapse in his descriptive powers. "Let me see if I can describe an old Virginia home," Page mused, "recalled from a memory stamped with it when it was a virgin page." He quickly regained his narrative prowess, outlining the simple virtues of his childhood home, Oakland. "The house was a plain 'weather-board' building, one story and a half above the half-basement ground floor," recalled Page, "set on a hill in a grove of primeval oaks and hickories filled in with ash, maples, and feathery-leafed locusts without number" (1892: 143). MacKethan has commented that Oakland "is notable for its plainness of construction; there is a quaintness in its design, a 'manliness' about its offices and quarters, a special dignity in the way it is set among historic oaks, and an ineffable grace showing through the orchards and gardens that flourish on the grounds" (1978: 318). Oakland exemplifies, in other words, all that Page admired about the plantation South.

Page employed similar tactics in his works of fiction. His 1898 novel *Red Rock: A Chronicle of Reconstruction* opens, for example, with a few lines about "the old Gray plantation, 'Red Rock'" (Page 1906a: 1). Elphinstone, the Keith's plantation in Page's 1903 novel *Gordon Keith*, "was, indeed, a world to itself: a long, rambling house, set on a hill, with white-pillared verandahs, closed on the side toward the evening sun by green Venetian blinds, and on the other side looking away through the lawn trees over wide fields, brown with fallow, or green with cattle-dotted pasture land and waving grain, to the dark rim of woods beyond" (Page 1906b: 2). In Page's first collection of short stories, *In Ole Virginia*, the plantations are, according to MacKethan, "outward and visible signs of the people who settled the Southern region and created an aristocratic utopia in the wilderness" (1978: 318). The stranger in Page's first short story, "Marse Chan," for example, comes across the "once splendid mansions," and although they were "now fast falling to decay," he inferred immediately the character of the people who built them. "Distance was nothing to these people," he concluded; "time was of no consequence to them. They desired but a level path in life, and that they had, though the way was longer, and the outer world strode by them as they dreamed" (Page 1895: 10). In "Meh Lady," the young belle and her faithful slaves fight to stave off the onslaught of Yankee soldiers and carpetbaggers, battling mightily to protect the plantation home and all that it represented.

The theme of loss, of inevitable doom to the plantation, resonates throughout much of Page's writings. Dr. Cary, the patrician hero of Page's novel *Red Rock*, for example, recognized in the heady days "before the great explosion in the beginning of the Sixties" that the impending war threatened the world of the plantation South with imminent collapse. "War is the most terrible of all disasters, except Dishonor," he warned a group of secessionists. "I do not speak of the dangers. For every brave man must face danger as it comes, and should court glory; and death for one's Country is glorious. I speak merely of the change that War inevitably brings. War is the destruction of everything that exists," Dr. Cary proclaimed confidently. "You may fail or you may win, but what exists passes, and something different takes its place." The slaveholding South will assuredly suffer because of war. "No people who enter a war wealthy and content ever come out of war so," he observed. The righteousness of the Confederate cause may compel white Southerners to fight, he reasoned, but the Old South's defenders should recognize the costs that war would surely bring (Page

1906a: 17–19). Page allowed Dr. Cary to survive the war, MacKethan argues, "in order to show the great disparity between the Old and New Souths and to emphasize how much has been lost" (1978: 323).

For Page, Reconstruction bore out Dr. Cary's fears. Indeed, Page's interpretation of Reconstruction, seen most clearly in *Red Rock*, suggests that the era represented the worst abuses heaped upon a righteous civilization. White Southerners had been "subjected to the greatest humiliation of modern times," he wrote in his preface. "Their slaves were put over them." Redemption signaled, however, the ultimate triumph of white Southerners. "They reconquered their section and preserved the civilization of the Anglo-Saxon" (Page 1906a: viii). As Fred Hobson has noted, "the year of *Red Rock*'s publication, 1898, was a time of great racial unrest and social upheaval in the South" (1983: 149). The 1898 Wilmington Race Riot destroyed the possibility of an interracial political union, under the auspices of the Populist Party, once imagined by Tom Watson.[1] Historians David S. Cecelski and Timothy B. Tyson have observed that "Few communities escaped racial terrorism – if only one city became an enduring reminder of the dangers of democratic politics and interracial cooperation." No one, they continue, "black or white, could deny that the racial massacre signaled a sea change in how white Americans would regard civil rights for African Americans." The message was clear. "White people in Wilmington had violently seized their government, and no one had acted to stop them." The aftermath of the riot ensured the emergence of "the Jim Crow social order, the end of black voting rights, and the rise of a one-party political system in the South that strangled the aspirations of generations of blacks and whites" (Cecelski and Tyson 1998: 5–6). The appearance of Page's novel, then, at the moment white supremacists violently regained control of politics in Wilmington, North Carolina, shored up the ideology of the Jim Crow South. Not surprisingly, many Southern readers praised Page's interpretation of Reconstruction. "I honestly believe you have done more to set the South right in the eyes of the world and to correct the misrepresentation of fanatics, fools & scoundrels," one reader wrote Page, "than all the other stories put together" (quoted in Hobson 1983: 150).

Despite the immediate and immense popularity of Page's writings, dissenters of the plantation legend quickly made their voices heard. Many challenged Page's vision of the idyllic plantation, sustainer of all that was "civilizing" about the Old South. In 1884, the year that the *Century* published Page's story first short story, "Marse Chan," the noted local color novelist Mary Noailles Murfree published (under the pseudonym Charles Egbert Craddock) her bleak novel *Where the Battle was Fought*. The novel made clear that some Southern writers never identified with the plantation past. Although she employs the theme of loss, she does not romanticize or idealize the plantation past. The lives of Murfree's characters were as desolate as the war-ravaged landscape. "The pulses of life throbbed languidly," Murfree observed (Craddock 1884: 96). Little interested her characters save the tragic and hopeless events of the late war. "They looked upon the future as only capable of furnishing a series of meagre and supplemental episodes," she observed (p. 174). Murfree's characters were left without a future on which they could pin their hopes and without a past to sustain them.

The home of General Vayne occupies a central place in Murfree's novel. The Vayne house overlooked the barren plain "where the battle was fought," and from its windows the General could see the ruins of Fort Despair, the place where he had lost his arm fighting the federal army. Confronted with the physical reality of his loss as well as his memories of the battle, General Vayne would, at times, surrender to "those distraught questions . . . which involved the righteousness of the Lost Cause." As he reviewed his life "doubts thickened about him. Doubts! And his right arm was gone, and his future lay waste, and his children's lot was blighted. And he had flung away the rich treasure of his blood, and the exaltation of his courage, and his potent enthusiasms, and the lives of his noble comrades, who had followed him till they could no longer." Indeed, his memories of the Confederacy so plagued General Vayne that "he was glad when the screws of the usurers came down again, and the present bore so heavily upon him that he grew dulled in the suffering of the past" (Craddock 1884: 107–8). For the General, the only guarantee fulfilled by the post-Reconstruction South was that the pain of the present could surpass that of the past.

The past did not haunt only General Vayne, however. It literally haunted the land "where the battle was fought." Murfree's characters believed that the ghosts of dead soldiers roamed the now ravaged battlefield. The shattered mirror in Vayne's home faced the world outside and offered "bizarre reflections" and "distorted glimpses," casting an eerie pall over the household. Coupled with the weird sights was the fantastic noise that emanated from the field. "It came with a hollow roar through the vastness of the night and the plain," explained Murfree (Craddock 1884: 89). To the inhabitants of the Vayne household, the noise resembled the sound of a battle fought in the distant past. "The tramp of feet, that long ago finished their marches, rose and fell in dull iteration in the distance." The wind itself contributed to the unearthly noise. "The gusts were hurled through the bomb-riven cupola, which swayed and groaned and crashed as it had done on the day when even more impetuous forces tore through its walls. Far – far and faint – a bugle was fitfully sounding the recall" (p. 96). The war, indeed the entire Southern Confederacy, had substantively little to offer the Vayne family, or the town of Chattalla. The hollow, ghost-like memories were fleeting, distant, and disembodied – wholly incapable of providing for the residents in the post-Reconstruction South.

Not even the Vayne home was capable of sustaining the family. From the parapet at Fort Despair "the shattered old house was visible in the distance, its upper windows still aflame with the sunset, as with some great inward conflagration." It certainly fit in with the surrounding ruin, but "the whole place was grimly incongruous with the idea of home" (Craddock 1884: 123–4). Here, as in other local color fiction of the late nineteenth century, "home" is a realized and fixed, yet infertile and uncreative place. Unlike the sentimental writers who conceived of the home as a metaphor for woman's nurturing influence, Murfree represented the home as an existential, concrete spot that was not only destroyed by the war, but itself a source of decay and death. Although the scene takes place before the action of the novel begins, federal raiders destroyed the Vayne home. But Murfree's image of the "inward conflagration" suggests that the forces of destruction came from inside. The family itself, still living within the ransacked house, was incapable of guaranteeing its own survival. Living with the old, crippled General Vayne were his widowed sister, Mrs. Kirby, and his daughter, Marcia, who had become hardened by the war. "She derived a commensurate idea of the grim tragedies of existence from the sight of the same crack troops before the sun went down," Murfree wrote, "decimated and demoralized, mangled and rooted" (p. 113). Unable to protect Marcia from the harsh realities of war or from its radical changes to the surrounding countryside, the Vayne home could not offer Marcia, or her dying family, any solace for the future.

Given the gloomy prediction for the South's future offered by Murfree, it is not surprising that her publisher, James R. Osgood, expressed reservations about its success. Although the novel was published during a period of tremendous growth in Civil War literature, Osgood feared for his company's financial return; and while some publishers hoped to ride the wave of popularity that Civil War narratives were enjoying in the late nineteenth century, Osgood delayed the publication of *Where the Battle was Fought*, pleading a "prevailing dulness [sic] in business, and general lack of interest in things literary," to explain the changes in the novel's production schedule. The publication of Civil War literature waxed in the post-Reconstruction years, however. James Osgood never explicitly expressed a lack of confidence in Murfree's writing. Yet his hesitancy to release *Where the Battle was Fought* suggests his doubts about the ability of Murfree's reading public to accept her bleak picture of the South.[2]

Ellen Glasgow also offered a vision of the plantation home that differed from Page's elegiac descriptions. For Glasgow, the confusion that followed in the wake of the Civil War mocked the apparent stability of the Old South; indeed, the war had exposed the antebellum South's false sense of security and forced Southerners to acknowledge that their region had been "condemned to stand alone because it had been forsaken by time" (Glasgow 1943: 13). In her novel *The Deliverance: A Romance of the Virginia Tobacco Fields*, Glasgow constructed an inversion plot of aristocratic decline. In this respect, as literary critic Richard Gray has noted, Glasgow's work does not diverge significantly from Page's novels of Reconstruction, *Red Rock* and *Gordon Keith*. But whereas Page emphasized the tragic plight of the fallen aristocracy, Glasgow used her novel to criticize the mythic version of the Old South (Gray 2000: 71). At the center of *The Deliverance* stood Blake Hall, the once gracious 200-year-old planter's mansion, with its Doric columns and its "cheerful spaciousness," which had now been claimed by the vulgar overseer and his family. "What remained was but the outer husk," Glasgow explained, "the disfigured frame, upon which the newer imprint seemed only a passing insult" (1904: 15–16). A reversal of fortune caused by the war forced the once aristocratic, now impecunious, Blake family to move to the overseer's shack, while the brutish overseer and his family now lived in Blake Hall. As Christopher Blake remarks to his sister, "it's a muck of a world" (Glasgow 1904: 50).

Through this reversal of fortunes Ellen Glasgow condemned the notion of inherited gentility, at once debunking claims to both white superiority and, implicitly, black inferiority.

The Chivalric Hero

Equally central to Page's vision of the antebellum past was the image of the chivalric hero. As Lucinda MacKethan has observed, the plantation was, for Page, "the breeding ground for heroes." Page's plantations, she continued, "provided much more than mere scenery; they supply the motivation and meaning for the works as a whole and are at the center of Page's design" (MacKethan 1978: 322). In "Social Life in Virginia before the War," Page followed a lengthy description of Oakland with an equally long caricature of the plantation master. "As to the master himself," Page wrote, "it is hard to generalize. Yet there were indeed certain generic characteristics, whether he was quiet and severe, or jovial and easy," he continued. "There was the foundation of a certain pride based on self-respect and consciousness of power." The Southern planter "believed in God," Page observed, "he believed in his wife, he believed in his blood. He was chivalrous, he was generous, he was usually incapable of fear or meanness. To be a Virginia gentleman was the first duty; it embraced being a Christian and all the virtues." The master understood fully the honors and responsibilities that came with his position. "He believed in democracy, but understood that the absence of a titled aristocracy had to be supplied by a class more virtuous than he believed them to be. This class was, of course," Page added, "that to which he belonged." To his children, the Southern master left his worldview as their heritage (Page 1892: 157–8).

Page translated his ideas on plantation gentlemen to his works of fiction. His 1903 novel of post-Civil War America *Gordon Keith* featured General McDowell Keith, "a gentleman of the old kind, a type so old-fashioned that it is hardly accepted these days as having existed. He knew the Past and lived in it; the Present he did not understand, and the Future he did not know." General Keith had survived the Civil War and the downfall of the slaveholding South "unchanged, unmoved, unmarred, an antique memorial of the life of which he was a relic. His one standard," Page noted, "was that of a gentleman" (1906b: 2). The general's son, Gordon Keith, had inherited the gentlemanly virtues of his father, despite the demise of the antebellum civilization that had nurtured them. As Lucinda MacKethan has observed, "Page's young aristocrats differ from their elders in breadth of experience but not in substance. From Marse Chan to Gordon Keith, they form a neat chain of similar young heroes waiting to put the code they have been taught to the tests that will prove them true Virginia gentlemen" (MacKethan 1978: 324). Of Gordon Keith, Page noted simply that he "was the son of a gentleman. And this fact . . . was his only patrimony." His legacy served him well, Page noted, helping "him over many rough places. He carried it with him as a devoted Romanist wears a sacred scapulary next to the heart." The plantation was Gordon's world; "the woods that rimmed it were his horizon, as they had been that of the Keiths for generations." The collapse of his world, however, had failed to divest Gordon from his "patrimony." Gordon, too, was a Southern gentleman (Page 1906b: 4).

Ellen Glasgow challenged Page's assumption that the plantation bred and sustained chivalric heroes. In *The Deliverance*, for example, she rejects Page's notion of inherited chivalry and gentility. Through Christopher Blake, a central character in the novel, Glasgow tested "the strength of hereditary fibre when it has long been subjected to the power of malignant circumstances" (Glasgow 1943: 34). Although Christopher is descended from aristocratic stock, the war has destroyed any sense of humanity in him, reducing him to the basest elements. Christopher himself acknowledges that environment, not inheritance, has determined his character. Early in the novel he recognizes "that about himself there was a coarseness, a brutality even, that made him shrink from contact with . . . others" (Glasgow 1904: 199). Bent on revenge against the overseer, Christopher spent his days conspiring to bring down the overseer's son, Will Fletcher, seducing the boy into drinking, gambling, and murder. Blake felt absolutely no compassion toward his enemy. "His god was a pagan god," explained Glasgow, "terrible rather than tender, and there had always been within him the old pagan scorn of everlasting mercy." Convinced he and his family were victims of "heroic crimes," Blake devised "heroic tortures," and would often imagine the overseer amid the flames of a lighted stake (Glasgow 1904: 92). For Glasgow, then, this tale of the lost cause would be one of hatred, not love. "The tone would be harsh," she admitted, "the illumination would never be softened or diffused" (1943: 33).

In Glasgow's novel, it is not the lusty former slave from whom the heroine needs protection, but the white son of the former plantation owner. Maria Fletcher left the Virginia tobacco fields to escape Christopher Blake, not some caricature of the African beast. For Glasgow, the Civil War did not emancipate millions of base and rapacious animals, incapable of self-rule, but rather reduced the Southern aristocrats' stock to uncivilized thugs. Here, Glasgow offered a stunning challenge to a Southern literary convention whose most notable proponent, Thomas Dixon, had published *The Leopard's Spots* in 1902 and *The Clansman* in 1905. According to Dixon, both white women and white voting rights needed protection by Southern white men from freed slaves. In a note to the reader which prefaces *The Clansman*, Dixon wrote "in the darkest hour of the life of the South, when her wounded people lay helpless amid rags and ashes under the beak and talon of the Vulture, suddenly from the mists of the mountains appeared a white cloud the size of a man's hand. It grew until its mantle of mystery enfolded the stricken earth and sky. An 'Invisible Empire' had risen from the field of Death and challenged the Visible to mortal combat" (Dixon 1905: 2). Like Page, Dixon saw the white South's vindication with "Redemption" and the Supreme Court's decisions to uphold racial segregation and disfranchisement in the South, despite guarantees in the 14th and 15th amendments to the Constitution equality and inclusion in the polity. Not surprisingly, Dixon's work fared well with readers. Within a few months of publication, *The Clansman* sold more than one million copies (Williamson 1986: 113).

Given the reception of Dixon's earlier work, Ellen Glasgow was acutely aware of her novel's potential unpopularity with readers and critics. She nevertheless persevered with untiring determination, feeling compelled to counter the prevailing narrative of the white South and the war. "I could no more help writing it than I could live and not breathe the air about me," she informed Walter Hines Page as she began penning *The Deliverance*. There will always be "happy souls who will turn out popular romances," she asserted. But there will also be others, like her, "who have never been able to forget our Gethsemane and our cross, will continue to inflict upon our publishers the books that go down into the heart of things and appeal to those few that have been there before us." Her newest novel, she believed, was "another, big, deep, human document which no one will understand because it is wrung from life itself – and not from sugared romance."[3] Despite uncertainty over its reception, Glasgow boldly put forth her most critical novel of the South and the legacy of the Confederacy.

Charles W. Chesnutt also challenged Page's vision of the plantation past. As Richard Yarborough has noted, *The Marrow of Tradition*, Chesnutt's fictional account of the 1898 Wilmington Race Riot, represented his attempt to "depict Wilmington blacks sympathetically while reporting with historical accuracy the horrifying events that rocked the North Carolina community" (Yarborough 1998: 226). Chesnutt intended *The Marrow of Tradition* to be "'both a novel and a political and sociological tract.'" Moreover, he had hoped that his novel would "expose the collective hysteria behind this 'outbreak of pure, malignant and altogether indefensible race prejudice'" (quoted in Wagner 2001: 311–12.) As Christopher C. De Santis has observed, however, *The Marrow of Tradition* represents more than a fictionalized version of the events in Wilmington. Rather, the novel "points to the lingering caste system of the antebellum poison that defeated the promises of the Reconstruction era and threatens to prevent a new and vital South from being realized" (2000: 80–1).

Mr. Delamere, the patrician gentleman of Chesnutt's novel, believes that his antebellum values of benevolent paternalism still matter in the postbellum world. His grandson, Tom, had inherited none of his grandfather's gentlemanly virtues, however. Indeed, Tom bore no physical resemblance to a Southern gentleman. He was handsome, to be sure, but "no discriminating observer would have characterized his beauty as manly. It conveyed no impression of strength, but did possess a certain element, feline rather than feminine, which subtly negatived the idea of manliness" (Chesnutt 1990: 16). Tom Delamere represented, according to De Santis, the "parasitic descendent . . . of the slaveholding aristocracy." He "feed[s] on Old South wealth, yet . . . fail[s] to retain the sense of southern honor exhibited by old Mr. Delamere" (De Santis 2000: 81). In a most un-gentlemanly act, Tom cheats at cards. "When a man of good position, of whom much is expected, takes to evil courses," Chesnutt opined, "his progress is apt to resemble than of a well-bred woman who has started on the downward path, – the pace is all the swifter because of the distance which must be traversed to reach the bottom. Delamere had made rapid headway," Chesnutt informed his readers (1990: 165).

Tom's gambling debts compel him to rob Polly Ochiltree, the shock of which kills her. He frames his grandfather's servant, Sandy Campbell, for the robbery and apparent murder. As De Santis has noted, "The framing of a black man by a parasitic descendant of the Old South wealth is the impetus that compels whites into immediate reaction against blacks" in the novel. The town's leading citizens orchestrated a lynch mob, outraging Mr. Delamere, who had defended Sandy. Mr. Delamere is, however, "finally blind to the ineffectualness of white paternalism against violent racism" (De Santis 2000: 81). An exasperated Mr. Delamere tells Major Carteret, one of the instigators of the mob, "Time was, sir, when the word of a Delamere was held as good as his bond, and those who questioned it were forced to maintain their skepticism upon the field of honor. Time was, sir, when the law was enforced in this state in a manner to command the respect of the world! Our lawyers, our judges, our courts, were a credit to humanity and civilization. I fear I have outlasted my epoch," he laments. "I have lived to hear of white men, the most favored of races, the heirs of civilization, the conservators of liberty, howling like red Indians around a human being slowly roasting at the stake" (Chesnutt 1990: 211). Of course, Mr. Delamere fails to recognize what Eric Sundquist has identified as a critical paradox in the novel. Major Carteret explained this paradox to Mr. Delamere: Sandy is no longer Mr. Delamere's property. "The negroes are no longer under our control," he said calmly (Chesnutt 1990: 212). As Sundquist explained, Sandy's freedom "places him at the mercy of lynch law" (Sundquist 1993: 432). Sandy's life is spared, De Santis observes, "not because of the protection of his white benefactor whose argument for the black servant's innocence is taken little more seriously than Sandy's own pleas that he is guiltless, but rather because the real perpetrator of the crime is eventually discovered" (De Santis 2000: 82). Mr. Delamere's absolute faith in a code that no longer governs social relations exposes the hollowness of the plantation legend espoused by Page. Time, as well as his code of honor, has forsaken Mr. Delamere. He is a relic in a world that has turned increasingly foreign and hostile to his worldview.

Slavery

A final crucial aspect to Thomas Nelson Page's plantation writings was his particular understanding of race and slavery. Although Page did not argue for the return of slavery, he did tout its civilizing aspects. "Slavery," he argued in his essay "The Negro Problem," whatever its demerits, "was not in its time the unmitigated evil it is fancied to have been. Its time has passed. No power could compel the South to have it back. But," he continued, "to the negro it was a salvation. It found him a savage and a cannibal and in two hundred years gave seven millions of his race a civilization, the only civilization it has had since the dawn of history" (Page 1892: 344). Page frequently employed former slaves to serve as spokespeople for the abolished institution. As Lucinda MacKethan has observed, Page's stories "became in fact his most effective tool for displaying what he felt was the true case concerning the relationship between whites and blacks which had once existed and could again exist in the South" (1978: 327). In one of the most oft-quoted passages from Page's first short story, "Marse Chan," Sam wistfully reminisces about his days in bondage. "Dem wuz good ole times, marster – de bes' Sam ever see! Niggers didn' hed nothin' 't all to do," he informed the stranger to the South, "jus' hed to ten' to de feedin' an cleanin' de hosses, en' doin' what de marster tell 'em to do." Echoing proslavery ideologues who derided advocates of free labor, Sam extolled the benefits of the Old South's "peculiar institution." When slaves were sick, he explained to the stranger, "dey had things sont 'em out de house, an' de same doctor come to see 'em whar ten' to de white folks when dey wuz po'ly. Dyar warn' no trouble nor nothing'" (Page 1895: 10). As Matthew R. Martin explains, Sam describes "a world of perfect order, in which both sin and labor are non-existent. Sickness is present but only as a way to show the nurturing and security this world provides. Above all it is a place of belonging," Martin notes. "Sam insists again and again on the familial nature of the plantation, on protection and inclusion as its supreme values" (Martin 1998: 22). In Page's view, Sam enjoyed a mutually beneficial relationship with his master and, as MacKethan has pointed out, his "gratitude" was "unbounded" (1978: 327).

The Plantation School's insistence that slavery was a benevolent, civilizing institution outraged many African Americans, including Frances Ellen Watkins Harper, the noted poet and social advocate. Late in her literary career, Harper determined to pen a novel that would turn the Plantation School on its head. As literary scholar Frances Smith Foster has noted, the African-American community had immediately understood the critical need to offer fictional accounts of the Old South that would "refute [the] . . . insidious stereotypes" advanced by Page and his cohorts. "Although autobiographies, biographies, and essays by Afro-Americans directly contradicted those ideas," argued Foster, "they did not necessarily reach the same level as did the fiction of the Plantation School." A novel, unlike the various forms of non-fiction, could present "facts" in "ways that would appeal to the aesthetics of the nineteenth century." Frances E. W. Harper, long an advocate for a "diversified Afro-American literature," seemed well placed to counter the writings of Page (Harper 1988: xxx–xxxi, xxxiii).

In 1892 Harper published *Iola Leroy; or Shadows Uplifted*, which served as her vehicle to dismantle the Plantation School's rendering of the institution of slavery. The novel opens with two slaves in the market, ostensibly discussing the freshness of the fish. Readers quickly learn, however, that their discussion was part of an elaborate code designed to transmit information on the state of the political crisis between the North and the South. "During the dark days of the Rebellion," Harper explained, "when the bondman was turning his eyes to the American flag, and learning to hail it as an ensign of deliverance, some of the shrewder slaves, coming in contact with their masters and overhearing their conversations, invented a phraseology to convey in the most unsuspected manner news to each other from the battle-field." Some slaves escaped to join the Union army. Others, however, "remained at home, slept in their cabins by night and attended to their work by day; but under this apparently careless exterior there was an undercurrent of thought which escaped the cognizance of their masters" (Harper 1988: 8–9). Harper's slaves have no desire to remain in bondage. Even those who had "kindly masters" desire freedom. Replying to a comment about the relative liberty that Bob enjoys on his plantation, Bob responds, "It isn't so good, but it might be better. I ain't got nothing 'gainst my ole Miss, except she sold my mother away from me. And a boy ain't nothin' without his mother. I forgive her, but I never forget her, and never expect to. But if she were the best woman on earth I would rather have my freedom than belong to her" (Harper 1988: 17–18). Similarly, Aunt Linda, when asked if she wished "those good old days" would return, replied "No, chile; neber! neber! Wat fer you take me? I'd ruther lib in a corn-crib" (Harper 1988: 162).

The novel affords Harper ample opportunity to expose the worst abuses of the institution of slavery and to debunk the portrait of it painted by the Plantation School. A conversation between Marie, a light-skinned mulatto, and her husband Eugene Leroy, a wealthy planter who defied social custom and risked enormous loss to marry Marie, conveys the distance between Harper's vision of slavery and that of Page and his cohorts. Marie finds the practice of plantation masters enslaving the offspring of their illicit affairs with their female slaves particularly barbaric. "I could never understand how a cultured white man could have his own children enslaved," she told Eugene. "I can understand how savages, fighting with each other, could doom their vanquished foes to slavery, but it has always been a puzzle to me how a civilized man could drag his own children, bone of his bone, flesh of his flesh, down to the position of social outcasts, abject slaves, and political pariahs." When Marie encourages Eugene to free his slaves, Eugene confesses that he has "neither the courage of a martyr, nor the faith of a saint; and so I drift along, trying to make the condition of our slaves as comfortable as I possibly can. I believe there are slaves on this plantation whom the most flattering offers of freedom would not entice away." Marie immediately recognizes the absurdity of Eugene's conviction. "The more intelligent" slaves, Marie explains to her naïve husband, "have so learned to veil their feelings that you do not see the undercurrent of discontent beneath their apparent good humor and jollity. The more discontented they are, the more I respect them. To me," she declares, "a contented slave is an abject creature." When Eugene questioned Marie's concern, noting that her future seemed secure, she countered by stating, "I love liberty, not only for myself but for every human being" (Harper 1988: 77, 79, 80). Once again, Harper establishes the degree to which African Americans desired freedom.

Charles Chesnutt, too, used his fiction to counter the effects of Page's vision of the institution of slavery. His first collection of short stories, *The Conjure Woman*, can in many ways be read against Page's collection, *In Ole Virginia*. Chesnutt understood his task to debunk the vision of the idyllic plantation South quite clearly. "I shall not record stale negro minstrel jokes," he reported his journal, "or worn out newspaper squibs on the 'man and brother.' I shall leave the realm of fiction, where most of this stuff is manufactured, and come down to hard facts. There are many things about the Colored people which are peculiar," he continued, "and which are interesting to any thoughtful observer, and would be doubly interesting to people who know little about them" (Brodhead, ed. 1993: 26). He later mused, "I think I must write a book. I am almost afraid to undertake a book so early and with so little experience in composition. But it has been my cherished dream, and I feel an influence that I cannot resist calling me to the task . . . If I do write," he added, "I shall write with a purpose, a high and holy purpose, and this will inspire me to greater effort." Chesnutt stated that he would write for a white audience. "The object of my writings would be not so much the elevation of the colored people as the elevation of the whites, – for I consider the unjust spirit of caste which is so insidious as to pervade a whole nation, and so powerful as to subject a whole race and all connected with it to scorn and social ostracism." Chesnutt believed that he "would be one of the first to head a determined, organized crusade" against "the barrier to the moral progress of the American people" (Brodhead, ed. 1993: 139–40).

Matthew R. Martin has noted that a comparison of Chesnutt's first story, "The Goophered Grapevine" and Page's "Marse Chan" demonstrates "how carefully Chesnutt places himself in the genre of the plantation tale and how cautiously his 'literary crusade' begins" (Martin 1998: 18). Indeed, according to Martin, Chesnutt's story seems more like a "reworking of New South propaganda" rather than an effort to "undermine the flowering cult of the plantation myth" (Martin 1998: 25). Nonetheless, Chesnutt's story differs from Page's writings in significant ways. Julius, the former slave and teller of tales, is intelligent and shrewd, rather than obsequious and wistful. His accounts of slavery emphasize "lack and labor as opposed to the plantation myth's account of ease and security." But Chesnutt renders Julius "in a manner wholly consistent with accepted racial stereotypes." His strategy kept his reading audience "entertained, while subtly undermining their expectations about plantation life" (Martin 1998: 26–7). Moreover, it ensured favorable reviews from the Northern press.[4]

The "Negro Problem" of the New South

Not surprisingly, Page used his position as a popular writer of plantation romances to enter into explicit commentary on the politics of race in the late nineteenth century. The "race question" so divided the country that "even the terminology for it in the two sections varies irreconcilably. The North terms it simply the question of the civil equality of all citizens before the law," Page observed. "The South denominates it the question of negro domination." Regardless of terminology, however, "it is to-day the most portentous and the most dangerous problem which confronts the American people." Page had no patience for those who claimed that white Southerners purposefully defied the Reconstruction amendments and federal legislation designed to bolster them. Page could not refute those charges. Instead, he charged that written law "is so subverted only in obedience to a higher law founded on the instinct of self-protection and self-preservation" (1892: 280–1). Contrary to the opinion of the Northern press, which "charges of injuries to the negro," the "real injury is suffered by the white man" (p. 283). The solution, according to Page, was to strip black men of their 15th amendment rights. "Let us establish such a proper qualification as a condition to the possession of the elective franchise," Page advised, "as shall leave the ballot only to those who have intelligence enough to use it as an instrument to secure good government rather than to destroy it." The South has done its duty well "by the negro," according to Page. "We have educated him; we have aided him; we have sustained him in all right directions. We are ready to continue our aid," he noted, "but we will not be dominated by him. When we shall be, it is our settled conviction that we shall deserve the degradation into which we shall have sunk" (1892: 343–4).

A number of other Southern authors entered into the discussion on the "negro problem" in the Jim Crow era. Not all agreed with Page's reasoning, however. George Washington Cable, for example, published a series of essays in the 1880s on the position of African Americans in the reconstructed union. As a Confederate soldier, Cable did not "question slavery as an institution," Daniel Aaron has noted, "and believed in a 'White Man's Government'" (1973: 274). Two decades of social unrest, however, caused him to rethink his position. By the mid-1880s, then, Cable was championing the civil and political rights of the freedmen. Cable believed he spoke for the "silent South," and hoped his political essays would convince Southerners to "settle" the "Negro Problem" without outside intervention (Cable 1968: 274).[5] In 1885, one year after Page published "Marse Chan," Cable published "The Freedman's Case in Equity," in the *Century*. Cable quickly detailed the fate of the newly freed slaves in the 20 years since emancipation. Although legislation and constitutional amendments had afforded African Americans certain protections, Cable noted, recent decisions by the Supreme Court, most probably the Civil Rights cases of 1883, which gutted the Civil Rights Act of 1875 and the 14th amendment, made those achievements "void." Moreover, "the popular mind in the old free states, weary of strife at arm's length, bewildered by its complications, vexed by many a blunder, eager to turn to the cure of other evils, and even tinctured by that race feeling whose grosser excesses it would so gladly see suppressed, has retreated from its uncomfortable dictational attitude and thrown the whole matter over to the states of the South" (Cable 1968: 51–2). The North's abandonment of African Americans, then, afforded the South an unprecedented opportunity to ensure justice for the newly freed men and women. Cable argued that the source of continued oppression stemmed from "the surviving sentiments of an extinct and now universally execrated institution; sentiments which no intelligent or moral people should harbor," he added, "a moment after the admission that slavery was a moral mistake." The South must act swiftly, Cable warned. It "stands on her honor before the clean equities of the issue." Defying the Constitution, "the withholding of simple rights" is expensive, Cable noted; "it has cost much blood." Concessions, he argued, "have never cost a drop."

More to the point, morality and justice cannot be deferred, he suggested, perhaps a bit naïvely. It is "every people's duty before God to seek" universal justice and equity "until the whole people of every once slaveholding state can stand up as one man, saying 'Is the Freedman a free man?' and the whole world shall answer, 'Yes'" (Cable 1968: 73–4).

Not surprisingly, the *Century* received a flurry of angry letters in response to Cable's article. As Arlin Turner explains in his edition of Cable's essays, the editors at the *Century* decided to have Henry Grady, champion of the New South and editor of the Atlanta *Constitution*, summarize the opposition rather than printing excerpts of letters. Grady's essay, "In Plain Black and White," argued for the continuation of white supremacy, noting that the whites must rule because they have "'intelligence, character, and property.'" Turner observed that the distance between Cable's and Grady's positions is most acutely realized in Grady's declaration: "'Nowhere on earth is there kindlier feeling, closer sympathy, or less friction between two classes of society than between the whites and the blacks of the South today'" (quoted in Cable 1968: 76).

Cable's rebuttal, a 17-page article titled "The Silent South," appeared in the September issue of the *Century*. In this article, perhaps more so than in "The Freedman's Case in Equity," Cable stressed the urgency with which the South must act. "We occupy a ground . . . on which we cannot remain," he wrote. Nor could the South "go backward." Cable believed that "the best men of the South are coming daily into convictions that condemn their own beliefs of yesterday as the antiquated artillery of an outgrown past" (Cable 1969: 116, 118). As Daniel Aaron has noted, Cable "badly misjudged the audience, or at least underestimated the durability of time-tested Southern dogmas immune to logic and unaffected by even his brand of tactful argumentation." If Cable spoke for the "silent South," Aaron has written, then surely the "silent contingent must have held their tongues after the public outcry proved by Cable's published lectures and articles." Few came to defend him publicly (Aaron 1973: 277). Indeed, Louisiana author Grace King believed that Cable, through his writings, especially his fiction about New Orleans, had "'stabbed the city in the back . . . to please the Northern press,' proclaiming 'his preference for colored people over white' and 'quadroons over the Creoles'" (quoted in Rubin 1969: 203). King set out to write a story, later published as "Monsieur Motte," as a corrective to Cable's writings.

Social activist Anna Julia Cooper also entered into the discussion. In 1892, the year in which Page published his essay "The Negro Question," Cooper published *A Voice from the South*, a series of essays that advocated racial uplift and the politics of respectability. Her essay "Has America a Race Problem?" ably summarizes the argument for white supremacy. "America for the Americans," she wrote scornfully. "This is the white man's country! The Chinese must go, shrieks the exclusionist. Exclude the Italians! Colonize the blacks in Mexico or deport them from Africa. Lynch, suppress, drive out, kill out! America for Americans!" (Lemert and Bhan, eds. 1998: 127). Cooper saw no particular reason to diminish the nation's race problem, however.

Cooper believed that it "is guaranty of the perpetuity and progress of . . . [America's] institutions and ensures the breadth of her culture and the symmetry of her development." She advised her readers to remain calm and maintain their convictions. "And be ready for the charge," she suggested. "The day is coming, and now is, when America must ask each citizen not "who was your grand-father and what was the color of his cuticle," but "*What can you do?*" (Lemert and Bhan, eds. 1998: 132).

Although Cooper did not change the substance of her message, she became increasingly more scathing as the nation entered the twentieth century. In "Ethics of the Negro Question," an address she delivered before a meeting of the Society of Friends in Asbury, New Jersey, Cooper noted that the "negro question" was particularly vexing to a nation still heady from the excesses of the Gilded Age. "The American conscience would like a rest from the black man's ghost," she averred. "It was always an unpalatable subject but preeminently now i[n] the era of good feeling, and self complacency, of commercial omnipotence and military glorification." Echoing George Washington Cable, Cooper argued that "The Negro is being ground to powder between the upper and the nether-millstones. The South, intolerant of interference from either outside or inside, the North too polite or too busy or too gleeful over the promised handshaking to manifest the most distant concern." Despite the persistence of "the Negro problem," she assured her audience, "our citizenship is beyond question. We have owned no other allegiance, have bowed before no other sovereign. Never has [a] hand of ours been raised either in open rebellion or secret treachery" (Lemert and Bhan, eds. 1998: 209). Once again, however, she preached patience. "When the wound is festering and the heart is so sore we can only suffer and be silent, praying God to change the hearts of our misguided countrymen and help them to see the things that make for righteousness" (p. 215).

Finally, Frances Ellen Watkins Harper used her novel *Iola Leroy* to counter the virulent rhetoric of Page and other conservative white Southerners on the "negro problem" of the New South. The argument that disfranchisement will stem the violence of the Reconstruction era prompts a Northern supporter of political and civil equality to ask, "As disfranchisement is a punishment for crime, is it just to punish a man before he transgresses the law?" Echoing Anna Julia Cooper, his friend adds calmly, "the negro is not plotting in beer-saloons against the peace and order of society. His fingers are not dripping with dynamite, neither is he spitting upon your flag, nor flaunting the red banner of anarchy in your face" (Harper 1988: 222–3). Rather than pose the kind of danger to Southern society that Thomas Nelson Page and Thomas Dixon imagined, the newly freed slaves in Harper's novels are models of decorum and propriety. Robert Leroy, Iola's uncle, proudly declares, for example, "I am a temperance man, and never take anything which has alcohol in it" (Harper 1988: 185). Iola and her brother Harry are pillars of the Methodist conference. The central characters expend a great deal of time and energy trying to reconstitute their families, which had been separated during slavery, demonstrating that "the peculiar institution" may have destroyed individual families but it did not weaken the bonds of familial love. The freed slaves in Harper's novel did not threaten the Union with

"Negro domination," but rather demonstrated their ability to participate in the polity. As Dr. Gresham remarked, "The problem of the nation . . . is not what men will do with the negro, but what will they do with the reckless, lawless, white men who murder, lynch, and burn their fellow citizens" (Harper 1988: 217).

When Carl Degler wrote *The Other South: Southern Dissenters in the Nineteenth Century* in 1974, he examined only the works and lives of white men. Degler's focus centered almost exclusively on political dissent. "In exploring a world where politics defined a man's character and demanded public acts of speaking and voting," explained historians Stanley Harrold and Randall M. Miller in the foreword to a new edition of Degler's classic text, "finding public expressions of dissent promised to reveal a good measure of the extent and nature of dissent." Degler's approach, then, left out blacks and women, because he believed their forms of dissent were "largely, although not wholly, private." Indeed, of those authors under consideration in this essay, only George Washington Cable warranted attention from Degler. For Degler, the key to understanding the "'other southerner' was not to look for him where one already knew he existed . . . but to find those white men who did not blindly march arm-in-arm with the ruling race and class" (Degler 2000: x). Degler's narrow definition of "political action" prevented him from recognizing that dissent often took a literary form. The stories, essays, and novels of Murfree, Glasgow, Harper, Cooper, and Chesnutt belie Degler's claims that "minority" dissent in the late nineteenth-century South was "largely private." Their voices were as critical of the "Southern way" as were the voices of the Readjusters and the Populists who attempted to dismantle white rule. Although the Populist movement failed, its legacy continued to influence political activists in the twentieth century. Similarly, the literary dissenters who failed to overturn the Plantation School shaped future generations of Southern authors. "The story of the Other South has no end so long as there is a South," Degler concluded in 1974, "and that, too, promises to endure for a long time" (2000: 371).

NOTES

1 Tom Watson, in arguing for the establishment of a third political party, wrote in 1892 that "the future happiness of the two races will never be assured until the political motives which drive them asunder, into two distinct and hostile factions, can be removed. There must be a new policy inaugurated," he continued, "whose purpose is to ally the passions and prejudices of race conflict, and which makes its appeal to the sober sense and honest judgment of the citizen regardless of color." See Thomas E. Watson, "The Negro Question in the South," *Arena* 6 (1892), 548.

2 James R. Osgood to M. N. Murfree, Esq., n.p., July 9, 1884, in the Mary Noailles Murfree Papers, Special Collections Department, Robert W. Woodruff Library, Emory University, Atlanta, Georgia. Sales and earnings figures for the novel while it was published by Osgood's firm are unavailable. Houghton Mifflin Co., however, picked up the reprint rights by 1889, and although their records indicate that *Where the Battle was Fought* certainly was not a runaway bestseller, it sold steadily from 1889 through at least 1915. During that period, it sold almost 2,500 copies and earned Mary Noailles Murfree over $1,000. See the firm's

book sales and book earnings records in the Houghton Mifflin Company Records, MS Am 2030, Houghton Library, Harvard University, Cambridge, Massachusetts. For a breakdown by decades of the publication of Civil War literature see Robert A. Lively, *Fiction Fights the Civil War: An Unfinished Chapter in the Literary History of the American People* (Chapel Hill: University of North Carolina Press, 1957), 22.

3 Ellen Glasgow to Walter Hines Page, Dec. 26, 1902, in Rouse, ed. (1958: 40–1).

4 See e.g. "Books of the Day," *Boston Evening Transcript*, March 22, 1899, part 2, 10; "Literature," *Washington DC Times*, April 9, 1899, 2; Florence A. H. Morgan, "Novel Notes," *Bookman* 9 (June 1899), 372–3, all repr. in Joseph R. McElrath, Jr., ed., *Critical Essays on Charles W. Chesnutt* (New York: G. K. Hall & Co., 1999).

5 Joel Williamson explains that Cable's orthodox position on race was shattered "when a mob of white men invaded the Girls' High School [in New Orleans] and forcibly expelled every girl suspected of African descent, some of whom were visibly indistinguishable from other students who were undeniably white." Cable "was outraged. He simply could not accept a racial system in which people who were perfectly white in appearance were designated black." See Williamson (1986: 77).

REFERENCES AND FURTHER READING

Aaron, Daniel (1973). *The Unwritten War: American Writers and the Civil War*. New York: Knopf.

Alexander, Elizabeth (1997). " 'We must be about our father's business': Anna Julia Cooper and the In-corporation of the Nineteenth Century African-American Woman Intellectual." In Sherry Lee Linkon (ed.), *In Her Own Voice: Nineteenth-Century American Essayists*, 61–80. New York: Garland.

Andrews, William L. (1980). *The Literary Career of Charles W. Chesnutt*. Baton Rouge: Louisiana State University Press.

Atterberry, Philip D. (1985). "Ellen Glasgow and the Sentimental Novel of Virginia." *Southern Quarterly* 23, 5–14.

Brodhead, Richard, ed. (1993). *The Journals of Charles W. Chesnutt*. Durham: Duke University Press.

Byerman, Keith (1999). "Black Voices, White Stories: An Intertextual Analysis of Thomas Nelson Page and Charles Waddell Chesnutt." *North Carolina Literary Review* 8, 98–105.

Cable, George Washington (1968). *The Negro Question: A Selection of Writings on Civil Rights in the South*, edited by Arlin Turner. New York: Norton. (First publ. 1889.)

Cable, George Washington (1969). *The Silent South*. Monclair: Patterson Smith. (First publ. 1885.)

Carby, Hazel V. (1997). " 'On the threshold of women's era': Lynching, Empire, and Sexuality in Black Feminist Theory." In Anne McClintock, Aamir Mufti, and Ella Shohat (eds.), *Dangerous Liaisons: Gender, Nation, and Postcolonial Perspectives*, 330–43. Minneapolis: University of Minnesota Press.

Cecelski, David S. and Tyson, Timothy B., eds. (1998). *Democracy Betrayed: The Wilmington Race Riot of 1898 and its Legacy*. Chapel Hill: University of North Carolina Press.

Chesnutt, Charles W. (1969). *The Conjure Woman*, intr. Robert M. Farnsworth. Ann Arbor: University of Michigan Press. (First publ. 1899.)

Chesnutt, Charles W. (1990). *The Marrow of Tradition*, intr. Robert M. Farnsworth. Ann Arbor: University of Michigan Press. (First publ. 1901.)

Craddock, Charles Egbert [Mary Noailles Murfree] (1884). *Where the Battle Was Fought*. Boston: James R. Osgood & Co.

Degler, Carl N. (2000). *The Other South: Southern Dissenters in the Nineteenth Century*, ed. Stanley Harrold and Randall M. Miller. Gainesville: University Press of Florida. (First publ. 1974.)

De Santis, Christopher C. (2000). "The Dangerous Marrow of Southern Tradition: Charles W. Chesnutt and Paul Lawrence Dunbar and the Paternalist Ethos at the Turn of the Century." *Southern Quarterly* 38, 79–97.

Dixon, Thomas, Jr. (1902). *The Leopard's Spots: A Romance of the White Man's Burden*. New York: Doubleday & Page, Co.

Dixon, Thomas, Jr. (1905). *The Clansman: A Historical Romance of the Ku Klux Klan*. New York: Doubleday, Page & Co.

Dunning, William A. (1907). *Reconstruction, Political and Economic, 1865–1877*. New York: Harper & Bros.

Finseth, Ian (1999). "How Shall the Truth Be Told? Language and Race in *The Marrow of Tradition*." *American Literary Realism* 31, 1–20.

Foster, Frances Smith (1993). *Written by Herself: Literary Production by African American Women, 1746–1892*. Bloomington: Indiana University Press.

Foster, Gaines M. (1987). *The Ghosts of the Confederacy: Defeat, the Lost Cause, and the Emergence of the New South, 1865–1913*. New York: Oxford University Press.

Gaston, Paul (1970). *The New South Creed: A Study in Southern Mythmaking*. Baton Rouge: Louisiana State University Press.

Gebhard, Caroline (1998). "Reconstructing Southern Manhood: Race, Sentimentality, and Camp in the Plantation Myth." In Anne Goodwyn Jones and Susan V. Donaldson (eds.), *Haunted Bodies: Gender and Southern Texts*, 132–55. Charlottesville: University Press of Virginia.

Gilmer, Glenda E. (1996). *Gender and Jim Crow: Women and the Politics of White Supremacy in North Carolina, 1896–1920*. Chapel Hill: University of North Carolina Press.

Glasgow, Ellen (1904). *The Deliverance: A Romance of the Virginia Tobacco Fields*. New York: Doubleday, Page, & Co.

Glasgow, Ellen (1943). *A Certain Measure: An Interpretation of Prose Fiction*. New York: Harcourt, Brace, & Co.

Gray, Richard (2000). *Southern Aberrations: Writers of the American South and the Problems of Regionalism*. Baton Rouge: Louisiana State University Press.

Greene, J. Lee (1996). *Blacks in Eden: The African American Novel's First Century*. Charlottesville: University Press of Virginia.

Harper, Frances Ellen Watkins (1988). *Iola Leroy; or Shadows Uplifted*, intr. Frances Smith Foster. New York: Oxford University Press. (First publ. 1892.)

Harrison, Beth (1990). "Ellen Glasgow's Revision of the Southern Pastoral." *South Atlantic Review* 55, 47–70.

Hobson, Fred (1983). *Tell About the South: The Southern Rage to Explain*. Baton Rouge: Louisiana State University Press.

Ladd, Barbara (1996). *Nationalism and the Color Line in George W. Cable, Mark Twain, and William Faulkner*. Baton Rouge: Louisiana State University Press.

Lemert, Charles, and Bhan, Esme, eds. (1998). *The Voice of Anna Julia Cooper: Including* A Voice from the South *and Other Important Essays, Papers, and Letters*. New York: Rowman & Littlefield.

Lively, Robert A. (1957). *Fiction Fights the Civil War: An Unfinished Chapter in the Literary History of the American People*. Chapel Hill: University of North Carolina Press.

McElrath, Joseph R., Jr., ed. (1999). *Critical Essays on Charles W. Chesnutt*. New York: G. K. Hall & Co.

MacKethan, Lucinda H. (1978). "Thomas Nelson Page: The Plantation as Arcady." *Virginia Quarterly Review* 54, 314–32.

MacKethan, Lucinda H. (1980). *The Dream of Arcady: Place and Time in Southern Literature*. Baton Rouge: Louisiana State University Press.

MacKethan, Lucinda H. (1985). "Plantation Fiction, 1865–1900." In Louis D. Rubin et al. (eds.), *The History of Southern Literature*, 209–19. Baton Rouge: Louisiana State University Press.

Martin, Matthew R. (1998). "The Two-faced New South: The Plantation Tales of Thomas Nelson Page and Charles W. Chesnutt." *Southern Literary Journal* 30, 17–36.

Nowatzki, Robert C. (1995). " 'Passing' in a White Genre: Charles W. Chesnutt's Negotiations of the Plantation Tradition in *The Conjure Woman*." *American Literary Realism* 27, 20–36.

Page, Thomas Nelson (1892). *The Old South*. New York: Charles Scribner's Sons.

Page, Thomas Nelson (1895). *In Ole Virginia, or Marse Chan and Other Stories*. New York: Charles Scribner's Sons. (First publ. 1887.)

Page, Thomas Nelson (1906a). *Red Rock: A Chronicle of Reconstruction*. New York: Charles Scribner's Sons. (First publ. 1898.)

Page, Thomas Nelson (1906b). *Gordon Keith*. New York: Charles Scribner's Sons. (First publ. 1903.)

Pettis, Joyce (1994). "*The Marrow of Tradition*: Charles Chesnutt's novel of the South." *North Carolina Literary Review* 2, 108–18.

Rainwater, Catherine (1996). "'That much abused word modern' and Ellen Glasgow's 'literature of revolt.'" *Mississippi Quarterly* 49, 345–60.

Roe, Jae H. (1999). "Keeping an 'old wound' Live: *The Marrow of Tradition* and the Legacy of Wilmington." *African American Review* 33, 231–43.

Rouse, Blair, ed. (1958). *Letters of Ellen Glasgow.* New York: Harcourt, Brace & Co.

Rubin, Louis D. (1969). *George W. Cable: The Life and Times of a Southern Heretic.* New York: Pegasus.

Silber, Nina (1993). *The Romance of the Reunion: Northerners and the South, 1865–1900.* Chapel Hill: University of North Carolina Press.

Sundquist, Eric J. (1993). *To Wake the Nations: Race and the Making of American Literature.* Cambridge, Mass.: Harvard University Press.

Wagner, Bryan (2001). "Charles Chesnutt and the Epistemology of Racial Violence." *American Literature* 73, 311–37.

Williamson, Joel (1986). *A Rage for Order: Black–White Relations in the American South since Emancipation.* New York: Oxford University Press.

Wonham, Henry B. (1997–8). "'The Curious Psychological Spectacle of a Mind Enslaved': Charles W. Chesnutt and dialect fiction." *Mississippi Quarterly* 51, 55–69.

Yarborough, Richard (1998). "Violence, Manhood, and Black Heroism: The Wilmington Race Riot in Two Turn-of-the-century Novels." In David S. Cecelski and Timothy B. Tyson (eds.), *Democracy Betrayed: The Wilmington Race Riot of 1898 and its Legacy*, 225–51. Chapel Hill: University of North Carolina Press.

17

The Fugitive-Agrarians and the Twentieth-Century Southern Canon

Farrell O'Gorman

When Vanderbilt poet–professors John Crowe Ransom and Donald Davidson – along with precocious undergraduate Allen Tate – launched a literary magazine called *The Fugitive* in 1922, it was not their intent to start a new regional movement in American letters. In fact, the group (soon to include the younger Robert Penn Warren) that would come to be known as the Fugitives largely sought to define itself against advocates of a "Southern" literature and confined their private discussions to aesthetic questions, concerning themselves not with regional identity but with the nature and proper practice of poetry. Rather than praise or criticize Southern culture, they debated the merits of American expatriate T. S. Eliot's *The Waste Land* (1922) and the question of literary modernism. By the end of the decade, however, they had – to varying degrees – become more conscious of and defensive about their regional identity, spurred by both a deeper sense of the South's alienation from the rest of the United States and a growing skepticism about the values of modern Western culture. Accordingly, the three elder writers led Warren and eight other Southern intellectuals (the "Twelve Southerners") in penning *I'll Take My Stand: The South and the Agrarian Tradition* (1930) and henceforth were also associated with the cultural rather than literary criticism of the group that became known as the Agrarians.

By virtue of their long and varied individual achievements as men of letters, as well as their success in fostering other like-minded writers and defining the critical terms in which the literature of the American South has been most exhaustively defined and interpreted, the Fugitive-Agrarians are the single most important literary group of the twentieth-century South. Indeed, it is largely to them that the credit belongs for the critical perception and interpretation of the Southern Renascence that the region enjoyed between the world wars and continues to be conscious of in its literature; in its wake, they have been both lauded and vilified for creating the very understanding of "Southern" literature that has dominated twentieth-century criticism. Though their own achievements (except those of Warren) waned after the midcentury, their legacy for Southern creative writers and critics was and remains immeasurable. To be sure, the voices decrying that legacy and its perceived exclusiveness proliferated in the last quarter of the century and into the new millennium. But in the very act of defining themselves against the older tradition, dissenting critics perpetuate its influence: differing strands of concern and value in Southern literature can now be more clearly distinguished precisely because of the clarity and depth of the dominant strand that the Nashville poet–critics eventually molded. Furthermore, there remain recent voices that have sought to expand the Southern canon not by jettisoning the critical standards and definitions that ultimately have the roots of their articulation in 1922 Nashville, but rather by applying them more broadly. For all these reasons, an understanding of the Fugitive-Agrarians is crucial to any understanding of Southern literature in the century that began with its greatest flourishing and has ended with questions about the final passing of a Southern regional identity – questions that had been articulately raised by the Agrarians themselves – being voiced as loudly as ever.

The Fugitive

In his mature essay "A Southern Mode of the Imagination" (1959), Allen Tate drew on an epigram of W. B. Yeats – "out of the quarrel with others we make rhetoric; out of the quarrel with ourselves, poetry" – in attributing the flowering of his native region's modern literature to a shift in the Southern mind "from melodramatic rhetoric to the dialectic of tragedy." Tate himself would observe that this shift was evident in embryonic form as early as *The Adventures of Huckleberry Finn* (1884), but could not take full effect until after World War I, when the South finally "looked round and saw for the first time since 1830 that the Yankees were not to blame for everything" (Tate 1968: 592). The work of writers other than Twain – including Ellen Glasgow, who hailed from the same Virginia upper class as Tate's mother and who had published fine works of social realism in the first two decades of the century – might have suggested otherwise, but most critics have traditionally agreed with Tate in crediting the European war and accompanying American social changes with catapulting the heretofore benighted South to new levels of literary excellence and, indeed, to a central place in national letters.

Tate's definition is more immediately appropriate to consideration of the Fugitive group itself, which had its origins in dialectic of the most fundamental sort – in the extended dialogues that took place at a gentlemanly Nashville *agora* hosted in the years just before the war by Sidney Mttron Hirsch, a Jewish raconteur, self-professed orientalist, linguist, and dabbler in the occult. Though Davidson had first met Ransom as an undergraduate in his Shakespeare class a few years earlier, it was at Hirsch's salon that the two men cemented their friendship, enthusiastically joining like-minded participants in turning its wide-ranging philosophical discussions toward literature. Their efforts were interrupted, however, by the American entry into the war, in which both briefly served. When the group reassembled, Ransom had published a first book,

Poems about God (1919), and Davidson had worked at writing poetry for some time; but the direction they now took was galvanized not so much by these efforts as by the 1921 addition to their number of a gifted and temperamental undergraduate whose commitment to literature was already complete. Allen Tate's precocious and enthusiastic embrace of modernism jarred the instinctively traditional Ransom and Davidson and has rightly been given credit for creating the ferment of interest in poetry that led to the establishment of the little magazine its creators named *The Fugitive*.

Beginning in April 1922, the magazine would ultimately publish work by numerous poets in 19 issues over a three-year period – work of necessarily diverse nature and quality. But under the editorial leadership of Ransom, Tate, Davidson, and (after 1924) Warren, the larger implications of its title were consistently maintained. Ransom had suggested those implications in the first issue's foreword:

> Official exception having been taken by the sovereign people to the mint julep, a literary phase known rather euphemistically as Southern Literature has expired, like any other source whose stream is stopped up. The demise was not untimely: among other advantages THE FUGITIVE is enabled to come to birth in Nashville, Tennessee, under a star not entirely unsympathetic. THE FUGITIVE flees from nothing faster than from the high-caste Brahmins of the Old South. (quoted in Cowan 1959: 48)

The magazine would in fact "flee" not only from the conventions of local color writing and the nostalgic plantation myth, but also from progressive New South ideals that favored rapid industrialization of the region. The former were carried on in the Fugitives' own time by the Poetry Society of South Carolina, while the latter were held sacred by many prominent journalists of the day as well as Edward Mims, chair of the Vanderbilt English Department and author of *The Advancing South* (1926). Rather than fall victim to either of the twin obsessions that had divided Southern letters along polemical lines since Reconstruction, *The Fugitive* sought to ignore the question of region altogether and concern itself with that sphere which it deemed the true provenance of the poet – the aesthetic.

In doing so its creators largely adopted the critical standards they had already formulated at their face-to-face meetings: they believed that "primarily poetry must not be sentimental; it must not be obvious; . . . it must be intellectual as well as emotional," and it should favor imagery over exposition (Cowan 1959: 45). Already they esteemed the ambiguity, irony, and internal tension – dialectic as opposed to rhetoric – that would gain favor under the New Criticism as later articulated by Ransom, Warren, Tate, and their disciples. A common commitment to these characteristics and to a stringent formalism generally (an aspect of their aesthetic not inconsistent with the classical curriculum at Vanderbilt) nonetheless left much room for disagreement among the poet–critics. Tate was the high priest of modernism among the group and was lavish in his praise of Eliot in particular, often to the consternation of Ransom, who could not at first reconcile a commitment to form with any admiration of *The Waste Land*, as the dispute he carried on with Tate in William

Rose Benet's *The Literary Review* made clear (Cowan 1959: 123–5). Such debates helped make known the seriousness and sophistication of the editors of *The Fugitive*, which – though largely ignored by the Vanderbilt administration and only sparsely admired in the South – won both national and international recognition, numbering among its admirers Robert Graves and Eliot himself.

Ransom's own poetry was, beneath its often deceptively archaic diction, consistently modernist in its devotion to wit, irony, and paradox; almost all of his best verse, including "Bells for John Whiteside's Daughter," "Philomela," and "The Equilibrists," was written during 1922–5, and most of it was published in *The Fugitive* (Ransom's best-known poem with a clearly Southern concern, "Antique Harvesters," was not published until 1927). Davidson, though personally closer to Tate than was Ransom, was farthest from him in literary bent: the true conservative of the group, he had a strong interest in traditional forms, early working at short lyrics in the mode of the young Yeats and developing a lifelong interest in the English ballad tradition. His worthiest Fugitive lyrics were collected in *An Outland Piper* (1924), but his own métier was the long and more polemical verse that would come with his commitment to the Agrarian movement. Tate's best work was ahead of him as well, as was that of Warren – as much of a prodigy as Tate, if not more; and one whom Tate himself credited with having the greatest "power" of them all soon after he joined the group in 1923.

Long financially tenuous, its contributors distracted by personal concerns, *The Fugitive* ceased publication in 1925, but its legacy in Southern letters would continue to grow throughout the century. Ransom's foreword – though less earnest in tone, and though its author would likely regret the comparison – was somewhat similar to the preface to the 1855 edition of *Leaves of Grass* in that it had presented the first issue of *The Fugitive* as a sort of literary Declaration of Independence. And, like Whitman's work, it would, ironically, become the cornerstone of a new tradition. That its publication took place not on the Fourth of July but instead in April, the month of the Confederate attack on Fort Sumter, went unremarked by its editors at the time. When those editors became Agrarians and laid claim to their region, however, the date seemed more appropriate. Before they had sought to be good poets who happened to work in – even in spite of – the South; now they would become, quite consciously, Southern writers, although for at least some of them the South became as much metaphor as place.

The Rise of the Agrarians

The immediate impetus for the shift of the former Fugitives' concerns from the aesthetic to the social has generally been identified as the Scopes Trial of 1925. The Christian fundamentalists who resisted the teaching of Darwin's theory of evolution in Dayton, Tennessee, brought national ridicule upon the South for its apparent refusal to join the modern world, and although the most important writers who had

been associated with *The Fugitive* felt little immediate affinity with uneducated religious enthusiasts, they sensed in the crisis a manifestation of larger regional tensions
they had previously sought to ignore. The former Fugitives had themselves scattered
geographically, but in the closing years of the decade these literary modernists found
themselves united in their sense that their native region's broader cultural antimodernism in fact had a certain merit that only lacked appropriate articulation. They would
attempt that articulation in *I'll Take My Stand: The South and the Agrarian Tradition*,
a collection of essays by "Twelve Southerners," published in 1930, that asserted both
the South's distinctiveness as an American region and the significance of its besieged
values within the larger context of Western civilization itself. While each of the
12 essays had its own focus – some, for example, were by social scientists directly
concerned with the enduring value of a primarily agricultural economy in the region
– the book in the broadest sense argued for the humane values of a traditional society
such as the authors saw embodied in the passing rural South. It also argued for the
value of regionalism generally in its opposition to the crushing conformity of modern
mass society.

    Davidson, Ransom, Tate, and Warren each followed his own path to – and beyond
– the movement that was dubbed Agrarianism. At home in Nashville, Davidson
made the first and simplest conversion from poet to cultural critic. In many ways the
least complicated thinker of the group, he instinctively rose in defense of his homeland in the wake of Scopes. Thereafter his essays would steadfastly defend the region,
in part by arguing that an agricultural society was more suited to fostering the arts
than an industrial one. His essay for *I'll Take My Stand*, "A Mirror for Artists," makes
this case and finally argues that the artist in turn has a duty to support such a society;
accordingly, his own verse would shift from a lyric to a hortatory mode in its celebration of the South, beginning with *The Tall Men* (1927), his epic of the Tennessee
pioneers. Ransom, too, remained in Nashville (and was, like his colleagues, a native
of the Upper South), but his attraction to Agrarianism remained perhaps the most
complicated of the group. In his 1927 essay "The South – Old or New," which was
later seen as a sort of prelude to the Agrarian manifesto itself, he claimed that the
region had been built on "European principles" that ran counter to the rapacious
pioneer spirit generally associated with the United States (Conkin 1980: 48). Though
he would in the early 1930s immerse himself in the study of economics in an effort
to justify the practical value of agrarianism, Ransom's initial and deepest attraction
to the movement was in relation to his abiding interest in the larger philosophical
questions that also shaped his *God Without Thunder* (1930). That the Agrarian manifesto's introductory "Statement of Principles" belongs primarily to him is evident in
its claim that "art depends, in general, like religion, in a right attitude to nature";
it can only decay in an "industrial" society wherein "we receive the illusion of having
power over nature, and lose the sense of nature as something mysterious and contingent" (Twelve Southerners 1977: xlii–xliii). Such statements suggest the degree to
which Ransom's concerns with social order – and with the South itself – were ultimately subordinate to his concerns with religion and, above all, with art.

For him and for Tate (both of whom posited a more aristocratic model of Southern society than did Davidson), the South defended in *I'll Take My Stand* was at least as much a metaphor for a traditionally envisioned "good society" as it was a particular region of the United States. Tate's thoughts in this regard began developing about 1927, when he – now living and writing in New York City – abandoned his not infrequently negative assessments of his native region to write a laudatory review of *The Tall Men* and begin a biography of Confederate general Stonewall Jackson. More attracted to the apparent virtues of his region now that he had departed it, he wrote to Davidson: "I've attacked the South for the last time, except insofar as it may be necessary to point out that the chief defect the Old South had was that in it which produced . . . the New South" (Fain and Young, eds., 1974: 191). Shortly thereafter he proposed the book of prose essays in defense of the South that was to become *I'll Take My Stand* (Davidson and, to a lesser degree, Ransom would finally do most of the work of editing it). Before that project came to fruition, however, Tate would spend a year in Europe on a Guggenheim fellowship, meeting many of the expatriate American writers of the period and deepening his emulation of Eliot. Even as he intensified his engagement with the South and perfected his poetic style – his first volume of poetry was published in 1928 – he became further convinced of the dissociation of sensibility and detachment from tradition that he saw as the inevitable fate of the modern. Hence "Ode to the Confederate Dead" (1936), begun in 1926 and set in a Southern graveyard, is not a celebration of a past heroic age:

> Turn your eyes to the immoderate past,
> Turn to the inscrutable infantry rising
> Demons out of the earth – they will not last.
> Stonewall, Stonewall, and the sunken fields of hemp,
> Shiloh, Antietam, Malvern Hill, Bull Run.
> Lost in that orient of the thick-and-fast
> You will curse the setting sun.

Rather, in Tate's own analysis, the poem renders the experience of modern "solipsism" or "narcissism" – "the failure of the human personality to function objectively in nature and society," a failure necessarily bound up with that personality's detachment from the past ("Narcissus as Narcissus" [1938], in Tate 1968: 596).

As such the poem underscores the true depth of Tate's dissatisfaction with modernity and suggests that even in the late 1920s, at the height of his enthusiasm about the South, his primary concerns remained aesthetic and religious. Under the influence of Eliot in both regards, he wrote to Davidson in 1929 that "Philosophically we [the Agrarians] must go the whole hog of reaction, and base our movement less upon the actual old South than upon its prototype – the historical social and religious scheme of Europe. We must be the last Europeans – there being no Europeans in Europe at present" (Fain and Young, eds., 1974: 230). Accordingly, the essay he contributed to *I'll Take My Stand* claimed that the Old South's great virtue was that it was a feudal society; its great flaw, that it lacked a feudal religion. Tate's "Remarks on the Southern Religion" was therefore finally not a celebration of the region's religiosity but a tormented indictment of its inadequacy (and clearly reveals Tate's increasing attraction to Catholicism, to which he would finally convert in 1950).

Tate's sentiments regarding religion were mildly distressing to Davidson, but not as much as were Warren's regarding race. The youngest Fugitive had since 1925 undertaken graduate work at Berkeley, Yale, and Oxford – writing a critical biography of abolitionist John Brown while in England – and had remained in close touch with only Tate. Nonetheless, the native of Guthrie, Kentucky, retained a familiarity with the realities of rural Southern culture that was perhaps the most immediate of all the former Fugitives. When his old companions solicited an essay on race for the symposium, Warren submitted "The Briar Patch," a conservative enough piece by later standards but one that Davidson and at least one other contributor – historian F. L. Owsley – found to be too generous to "the Negro" and even subtly progressive in its attitude toward segregation. Warren, whose enthusiasm for the entire project was only lukewarm, had unintentionally sparked discord over one unspoken but crucial problem that Southern Agrarianism never directly addressed: the South's racial code. Most of the contributors clearly conceived of "the South" as the white South, complacently accepted the Jim Crow arrangements of their time, and believed in the intellectual inferiority of blacks. But Davidson and Owsley were actively committed to the defense of segregation and second-class citizenship for blacks, while H. C. Nixon, a historian and economist who contributed to the book, was even more open than Warren in his desire for equality and integration.

Such tensions were only implicit in the book itself. The peculiar racial factors that were vital to agricultural arrangements in much of the South – particularly the sharecropping system that followed in the wake of chattel slavery and Reconstruction – were directly addressed in only a few essays other than Warren's, and there from somewhat discordant perspectives. Finally, this was only one of the many aspects in which the book failed to function as a unified vision of and argument for the value of agricultural life in the region and the nation as a whole (though other regions of the country obviously maintained predominantly agricultural economies at the time, the book was clearly not written so much to appeal to, for example, Midwesterners as it was to affront Northeastern intellectuals). Despite its monolithic title, *I'll Take My Stand* was finally shaped by diverse intellects and was patently impractical as a manifesto; but the book succeeded in other respects. The men of letters who made up the "Twelve Southerners," as Paul Conkin has noted, ultimately shared and promulgated a view of Southern history as having been defined since the Civil War by the subjugation of the region's agricultural interests – those of the small yeoman farmer as well as the large planter – to an exploitative industrial oligarchy based in the North. They also convincingly depicted their region's besieged culture as having an exceptionally strong sense of the value of "family, place, leisure, and religion." And in their eloquent prose they had, perhaps not in spite of but because of the diversity of their views, finally succeeded in writing what would in the long run become not just a book for Southerners but "one of the most influential documents of cultural dissent in American history" (Conkin 1980: 86–8). In later decades it would be seen both inside and outside the South as a valuable assertion of a quasi-religious humanism and as an important native critique of consumer capitalism that was particularly prescient in its environmental concerns.[1]

Such influence would be a long time in developing, however. Initial reviews were widespread but generally mixed or negative, and Southern newspapers – most of them under the sway of a progressive New South ideology – tended to be harshest in their criticism of what they often saw as a dangerously romantic view of the region's socioeconomic problems. Many Northern reviewers could not take the book seriously as a direct call to political action, occasionally lampooning what they saw as its neo-Confederatism, but often were surprising in their admiration of the book as a literary artifact. Their judgments would prove apt enough in the long run, though at the time – as the nation sank into the depths of economic depression – many of the Agrarians themselves became increasingly serious about the real political relevance of their views and began to consider further how they might not merely develop their critique of industrialism but instead recommend positive action. Ransom and Tate would devote a good deal of time in the first half of the new decade to investigating the real potential of Agrarianism as a social movement, establishing contact with Hilaire Belloc and publishing a second symposium, *Who Owns America?* (1936), in conjunction with the English Distributists (a small political and economic reform movement associated with Belloc and G. K. Chesterton). But by the end of the 1930s almost all of the original contributors had fallen into disarray, apathy, or disagreement, and moved on to new concerns.

Ransom, Tate, and above all Warren – who, despite contributing to *I'll Take My Stand*, had never fully identified himself with the movement – still had long and productive roles to play in American letters after 1940. Of the original four, only Davidson would steadfastly continue to identify himself as an "Agrarian" of any sort (Owsley and Andrew Lytle, a younger Vanderbilt graduate and an enthusiastic contributor to *I'll Take My Stand* who would later become an accomplished fiction writer, joined him in this regard). Davidson devoted the rest of his life to arguing for the value of regionalism in America, and not only in the South; he spent his summers teaching in Vermont, where he came to admire rural New England and embraced Robert Frost as a Yankee embodiment of his poetic ideal – chthonic, traditional, rooted in a place and a folk culture. But his own verse became increasingly polemical and his essays more strident in their claims that American regions were being threatened by an intrusive federal government. His call for a renewed sectional politics in the United States and his notion of regionalism itself – which was in large part developed in a longstanding debate with sociologist Howard W. Odum, one of the leaders of the progressive Regionalist movement at the University of North Carolina that emerged contemporaneously with Agrarianism – were outlined in such later works as *The Attack on Leviathan: Regionalism and Nationalism* (1938).[2] Davidson continued to demonstrate at this point in his career, as always, a familiarity with and admiration of the small farmers and folk culture of the upland South – aspects of the region that Tate and Ransom often tended to ignore while praising the culture they imagined at least possible for (if not actually characteristic of) its leisured aristocrats. But his comparatively democratic views in this regard, his very understanding of at least some elements of the poorer and middle-class white Southern mind, were to some degree bound up with the virulent racism that increasingly characterized his late career. The South Davidson praised from *The Tall Men* on had been that of the Anglo-Celtic yeoman and had been predicated on folk ways that maintained the supposed racial purity of that culture. He voiced his despair vehemently as he saw that South – or at least the states' rights legislation which sought to preserve it – increasingly threatened after the midcentury, and when he died in 1968 he had written a great deal that would eventually taint not only his own name but also the name of the Agrarian project itself. His later work alone makes a strong case for applying to Agrarianism the racist label that it deserves only in part.

But such charges against the Fugitive-Agrarians would not dominate the Southern literary scene in the half-century following the publication of *I'll Take My Stand*. Rather, critics such as Louis D. Rubin, Jr., who would shape the study of Southern literature from the 1950s on, almost invariably looked back with admiration upon the broader cultural aspirations that sparked the project. In the introduction to the edition of *I'll Take My Stand* published in 1977 – a year when a desegregated and increasingly prosperous South seemed to have at last fully rejoined the United States, itself now under the guidance of a president from Georgia, and the Agrarian project seemed to many quixotic at best – Rubin affirmed that "the book's real [and still relevant] importance" lay in "its assertion of the values of humanism and its rebuke of materialism" (Twelve Southerners 1977: xxi). In this regard he embraced Tate and Ransom's vision of the Old South as a metaphor (one Tate had furthered in the 1930s with poems such as "The Mediterranean" and "Aeneas at Washington") embodying nothing less than the highest religious and humanistic ideals of Western culture. Hence, for Rubin and his generation of critics, the Agrarians had primarily presented the Southern tradition – whatever its flaws – as still somehow offering to a deracinated modern world a picture of "the good society, the community of individuals, the security and definition that come when men cease to wage an unrelenting war with nature and enjoy their leisure and human dignity" (Twelve Southerners 1977: xx).

Furthermore, this generation of critics accepted many of the specific characteristics of Southern culture emphasized by the Agrarians and adopted them as hallmark themes of the region's literature. If the Fugitives had begun to establish aesthetic criteria for judging the merits of the literature of the modern South, the Agrarians had highlighted certain aspects of the Southern experience that provided a cultural and historical grounding for defining the distinctiveness of the region's literature in years to come. Unlike most Americans, the Southerner had a strong historical consciousness and a tragic sense of history; an awareness of human limitations and a particular suspicion of the Utopian promise of modern science. Less distinctively, perhaps, the Southerner had a traditional sense of the value of community and family, an exceptionally strong religiosity and sense of place, and both a closeness to and an awed reverence for nature. But such is the beginning of another story – that of the long-established but now contentious legacy of the Fugitive-Agrarians in Southern letters.

The Expanding Legacy: The New Criticism and the Southern Renascence

After the late 1930s, the Fugitive-Agrarians remained scattered across the country (only Davidson would remain in the South for good) and would never again work together as closely as they had before. Nonetheless, they remained friends and allies in their literary milieu. And that milieu was increasingly not only regional: after 1940 especially, Ransom, Tate, and Warren became major forces in the shaping of twentieth-century American letters. Unlike their old teacher, Tate and Warren remained active as poets, with the younger Warren especially emerging in his own voice (and as an accomplished writer of fiction as well: *All the King's Men* [1946], which drew upon the career of Governor Huey Long in the years leading up to Warren's 1934 arrival at Louisiana State University, is one of the masterpieces of twentieth-century American fiction). But these three became perhaps even more influential as critics and editors. When Ransom left Vanderbilt for Ohio's Kenyon College in 1937, he abandoned amateurish politics to concentrate on writing literary criticism and editing the new *Kenyon Review*. Allen Tate would briefly follow a similar path at the *Sewanee Review* in eastern Tennessee in the mid-1940s, as would Warren, together with Vanderbilt graduate and Fugitive-Agrarian protégé Cleanth Brooks, at the *Southern Review* in Baton Rouge. Though these journals claimed no necessarily regional bias, they both shored up the South's growing reputation for literary excellence and nurtured promising young writers from the region whose form and themes appealed to the editors. They also provided a base for refining and promulgating the principles of literary criticism that had been implicit in the Fugitive aesthetic, principles that had been bandied about and developed piecemeal by various writers on both sides of the Atlantic in the previous decades but began their ascendancy at about the time Ransom's eponymous *The New Criticism* (1941) was published.

The legacy they left in twentieth-century American letters is immense. Though other works have broken necessary ground, only Charlotte H. Beck's *The Fugitive Legacy: A Critical History* (2001) provides a comprehensive study of this vast and vital topic. Tracing the influence of the Fugitive-Agrarians and their associates, she claims that "the Fugitives' most vital contribution" to Southern letters was "their sponsorship of those writers who, in their own way, have continued what began in Nashville, Tennessee, in the 1920s" (Beck 2001: 11). Beck examines that sponsorship as it was developed in the classroom, in personal friendships, in critical advocacy, in publishing, and even in channels for financial support such as the Kenyon Review Fellowships that helped fund the young Flannery O'Connor and Elizabeth Spencer. She convincingly establishes the substantial extent to which writers such as O'Connor, Randall Jarrell, Caroline Gordon, Katherine Anne Porter, Eudora Welty, Peter Taylor, and James Dickey ultimately benefited from their association with, and shared many of the aesthetic standards of, the Fugitive-Agrarian circle. She also devotes substantial attention to the New Criticism and its American formulation not so much by Ransom as by his disciple, Brooks. From the midcentury until his death near its close – in critical works such as *The Well-Wrought Urn* (1947) and in pedagogy, especially in the vastly influential textbook *Understanding Poetry* (1938) which he co-edited with Warren – Brooks would become the primary exponent of the principles the Fugitives had begun tentatively formulating to themselves after the century's first great war.

Beck's statement that the Fugitive achievement must not be "confused with the narrow politics of Agrarianism and relegated to a reactionary piety for regionalism and dead tradition" (2001: 11) is perhaps more problematic than her other claims. A central tenet of the New Criticism is that literature is not to be understood primarily in terms of its political intent or the historical circumstances in which it was created. But there is a clear tension between this tenet and at least some of the criticism written by the Fugitive-Agrarian circle, a tension that would have consequences for the understanding of Southern literature that developed under their aegis in the second half of the century. Contemporary critics such as Michael Kreyling are apt to see the supposedly ahistorical aesthetic of the Fugitives and the traditionalist social views of the Agrarians as two sides of the same coin, and the principles of the New Criticism as a willed diversion from the ways in which literature might address (or fail to address) real and pressing social problems in the region.

But one does not necessarily have to go even this far to see an apparent contradiction in some of Brooks' and Tate's interests. Even as they preached the New Criticism, they speculated substantially upon how the Southern historical experience had shaped the region's literature. Brooks (one of the most prolific and influential critics of Faulkner in the decades following his acceptance into the American canon) sounded very much like an Agrarian in at least certain of his essays – for example, "William Faulkner's Criticism of Modern America," "The Crisis of Culture as Reflected in Southern Literature," and others collected in *Community, Religion, and Literature* (1995). And even as Tate, together with his wife Caroline Gordon, was editing anthologies such as *The House of Fiction* (1950) that featured rigorously technical New Critical commentary on short stories by modern writers from Ernest Hemingway to Elizabeth Bowen, he was also writing "historicized" essays on the distinctiveness of Southern literature. In "The New Provincialism" (1945) he accounted for the contemporary flourishing of his region's literature in clearly historical terms: "With the war of 1914–1918, the South reentered the world – but gave a backward glance as it slipped over the border: that backward glance gave us the Southern renascence, a literature conscious of the past in the present" (Brooks 1995: 545).

This not necessarily New Critical understanding of what Tate was the first to deem the "Southern Renascence" had been articulated at greater length in "The Profession of Letters in the South" (1935), in which Tate identified the "peculiarly historical consciousness" of the Southern writer as a product of its time – a time which "has made possible the curious burst of intelligence that we get at a crossing of the ways, not unlike, on an infinitesimal scale, the outburst of poetic genius at the end of the sixteenth century when commercial England had already begun to crush feudal England" (Tate 1968: 533). The analogy Tate employs here clearly echoes *I'll Take My Stand*, implying that the ultimate cause for the emergence of the Fugitives and other significant modern Southern writers was not World War I or the Scopes Trial but the Civil War itself – or rather, the clash of a waning agrarian and an ascendant industrial society that had precipitated it.[3] Tate's work in these essays at least partly explains why so many of the Southern writers favored by the New Critics were those whose views of the region's history – or at least whose dominant concerns – seemed consistent with those of the Agrarians; it provides the most articulate link between Fugitive–New Critical aesthetics and Agrarian themes. Such work is significant not only in itself but also in its pervasive influence on the one crucial legatee Beck fails to consider at any length: Louis D. Rubin, Jr., almost certainly the single most influential critic of Southern literature in the second half of the twentieth century.

Rubin's *Southern Renascence: The Literature of the Modern South* (1953) was – as Rubin and co-editor Robert D. Jacobs noted retrospectively in its fifth printing – "the first attempt at an inclusive examination of the literature of the modern South" (1968: ix), and it was to become a cornerstone in the education of what has been deemed the "Rubin generation" of critics of Southern literature. *Southern Renascence* clearly reveals that from the beginning Rubin's conception of the region's literature largely paralleled that of the Nashville group: nine of its twenty-nine essays (including four of the six essays on poetry) were either by or about individual Fugitive-Agrarians, and if close associates such as Gordon, Brooks, and younger students of the Fugitive-Agrarians – for example, critic Walter Sullivan, intellectual historian Richard Weaver – and writers such as Welty and Porter are included in the circle, very few "outsiders" were considered at all. Chief among these was William Faulkner, who, after finally winning acclaim among American critics in the late 1940s and receiving the Nobel Prize in 1950, had almost singlehandedly made the literature of the South an intellectually respectable field of study. He was the subject of four essays here, but nonetheless Rubin felt compelled to justify even his merit partly by claiming that he had an unconscious and organic relation to the Vanderbilt group: "certainly," he claimed, "the political, social, and aesthetic principles of Ransom, Tate, Warren, and Davidson have been abundantly put into effect by William Faulkner" (Rubin and Jacobs, eds., 1968: 291). Similarly, Rubin's argument for the achievement of Thomas Wolfe – whose *Look Homeward, Angel* (1929) and later works had actually been dismissed by the Fugitive-Agrarians for their apparent formlessness and verbosity – was couched in terms that echoed those of the Vanderbilt school. According to Rubin, one significant "Southern characteristic" found in Wolfe's work is "a sense and awareness of time . . . a deep and omnipresent feeling for the historical and tribal memory, for tradition and continuity" (Rubin and Jacobs, eds., 1968: 292). When he cites Tate's remarks on the region's "peculiarly historical consciousness" and then goes on to discuss Wolfe's sense of the "timelessness of the earth," it becomes abundantly clear that, to Rubin, Southern literature is primarily literature characterized by those hallmark themes highlighted in the work of the Agrarians.

It is also, at its best, characterized by the rigorous attention to form so valued by the New Critics. In aesthetic matters, Rubin revered the high modernism of Eliot and Joyce – as numerous comments in his influential anthology *The Literary South* (1979) and critical works make clear – but he was also a literary historian of the sort the New Critics quarreled with when they held sway in American letters at the midcentury. As an academic trained in the new field of American Studies, he was inclined to view literature in terms of its historical context, but paradoxically he placed the Fugitive-Agrarians and their aesthetic formalism at the center of the regional canon he shaped in such works as the magisterial *History of Southern Literature* (1985). Furthermore, the Southern literary history that he most preferred finally shared a great deal with Tate's essays in that it was "historical" primarily in its engagement with the history of ideas.

In writing that literary history – and shaping the Southern canon – Rubin would ultimately include a number of writers who had generally not been looked upon with favor by the New Critics, particularly white progressives such as Kate Chopin and Erskine Caldwell and African Americans such as Charles Chesnutt and Richard Wright. He would do so because their work clearly reflected a significant portion of the Southern experience, though he still tended to interpret that experience in light of Agrarian themes. At least some of those themes, however, had after the midcentury been given a new direction, depth, and specificity by the mature Warren. In his long dramatic poem *Brother to Dragons* (1953) and nonfiction such as *Segregation: The Inner Conflict in the South* (1957), Warren – along with historian C. Vann Woodward, whose *Southern Renascence* essay "The Irony of Southern History" foreshadowed *The Burden of Southern History* (1960) – gave a twist to the old theme of the South's intense and tragic historical consciousness. Warren and Woodward joined Faulkner's implicit campaign to wed inextricably the burden of guilt for wrongs committed against African Americans to the general historical sense that *I'll Take My Stand* had asserted as characteristic of the region's (white) writers. Rubin acknowledged this unforeseen metamorphosis of the Agrarian legacy in his shaping of the modern canon of Southern literature, not only by considering how it had informed the work of white writers – how racial guilt had affected the white writer's experience and depiction of "the human heart in conflict with itself," as Faulkner in his Nobel speech (and in the character of Quentin Compson) had foreshadowed Tate's dictum on the dialectic imagination – but also by expanding consideration of those black writers for whom the legacy of slavery had long been present in unavoidably concrete form.

Such inclusion was, to some latter-day critics, not enough. Kreyling has faulted such apparent liberalism on the grounds that it was ultimately "reconciled" with its "elder and more conservative [Agrarian] source" (1998: 32). He levels at Rubin's work a particularly regional form of the charge that has long marred the New Criticism generally: that a willed (Fugitive) inattention to historical reality on aesthetic grounds is bound up with an essentialist and implicitly conservative vision of the (Agrarian) South. And so the story of the integration of the Southern canon leads us to the beginning of the most recent chapter of the Fugitive-Agrarian legacy – the mounting assaults it has faced as the region moves into the new century.

The Embattled Legacy: The Fugitive-Agrarians and Southern Letters Now

The sudden arrival of a modernity slow in coming to the South has already been cited as a cause of the Fugitive-Agrarian movement; now, nearly a century later, we are told that the region once again lags behind. Fred Hobson noted in 1991 that, with a few exceptions, the Southern writer in the postmodern world remains a modern "*writer*," one who may "experiment with time sequence or point of view" but does not constantly question the fundamental "narrative order, structure, and meaning" underlying his or her work (Hobson 1991: 9). Now, a decade later, Michael Guinn proclaims gladly in *After Southern Modernism* that true postmodernity has finally arrived – albeit a bit "late" – in the region's literature (Guinn 2000: ix). Or at least it has for creative writers; he claims that the South's critics generally remain bound by the modernist terms of the old regime. If his work calls for rethinking the terms in which contemporary Southern literature is interpreted, Kreyling's *Inventing Southern Literature* (1998) calls for completely recasting the terms in which the entire canon established by the Fugitive-Agrarians and their legatees has been conceived – though the usefulness and relevance of those terms continue to be defended, albeit with significant qualifications, by Hobson and other critics.

In fact, the region's canonical writers have been transforming and moving beyond the Fugitive-Agrarian–New Critical model of Southern literature ever since it became established (and, of course, even the archetypal "Southern writer" in this model – Faulkner – has always produced viable and fluid interpretations by critics outside it). Some of the most prominent members of what has been dubbed the second generation of modern Southern writers broke subtly from the tenets of the modernist school even as it was being established in *Southern Renascence* and elsewhere. Flannery O'Connor, who rose to prominence in the 1950s, won the admiration of the Fugitive-Agrarian circle with her portraits of a fading rural South, but her intense theological interests – largely shaped by the revival in European Catholicism at the midcentury – finally marked her ultimate concerns as quite distinct from theirs. For O'Connor as for Walker Percy, a Catholic convert who immersed himself in the work of neo-Thomist Jacques Maritain along with Kierkegaard and more contemporary existentialists, the critique of modernity put forth in such works as *A Good Man Is Hard to Find* (1955) and *The Moviegoer* (1961) finally owed more to an internationalist Roman Catholicism than to Southern heritage. Indeed, in their fictions, traditional regional mores and reverence for the past ultimately present only flawed and futile counterpoints to the encroaching consumer society of the larger United States. Neither displayed the nostalgia for a feudal social order that had finally led Tate to Catholicism, and their choices of form – O'Connor's superficially naturalistic grotesques, Percy's satirical and sometimes disjointed first-person narratives – suggested a new sort of aesthetic vision. Though "traditionalists" of a sort, these two writers were not descendants of the Fugitive-Agrarians; as Lewis P. Simpson has observed, they practiced an "aesthetic of revelation" consistent with a Christian existentialism that in fact ran counter to the Agrarian "aesthetic of memory" (1980: 244–54). Morally they demonstrated that the Agrarians could be questioned not only from a secular and progressive but also from a profoundly Christian perspective: both satirized that which intellectual historian Mark Malvasi has more recently critiqued in the Nashville group, a tendency in "southern conservative thought . . . to divinize the secular, to replace the piety for God with a piety for history, society, and tradition" (1997: xiii).

O'Connor's and Percy's styles and character types – if not necessarily their religious orthodoxy – have made them among the more prominent influences on contemporary Southern fiction. But the leading writer in that regard, according to Hobson, is Eudora Welty (Hobson 1991: 9). Though her work was long embraced by the Fugitive-Agrarian circle and is in many ways quite consistent with traditional themes (as essays such as "Place in Fiction" suggest), Welty also participated in a different tradition in her depiction of Southern female experience. In works such as *Delta Wedding* (1946) and *The Optimist's Daughter* (1972), she explored and chronicled the South with an eye to the everyday, the domestic, in a manner that made her historical vision more original than that of those post-Renascence male writers – William Styron, Shelby Foote – who tended to idolize Faulkner. She also captured the region's language in exuberant comic style in stories such as "Why I Live at the P.O." (1941), which Hobson and Tony Earley have identified as particularly important for understanding much of the literature coming out of the region today.

Hobson notes the degree to which the story contains the references to "celebrities and brand names" that would come to mark a literature (like the region around it) increasingly engaged with national popular culture; hence, it prefigures the derogatorily classified "K-mart realism" of the late twentieth century. During that time Southern literature of a certain sort itself became a hot-selling commodity in the region, but all too often degenerated into an unintentionally parodic "Grit lit" which dealt primarily in clichés and stereotypes. Earley, though he sees "Why I Live at the P.O." itself as a "work of genius," believes that shallow readings of the story (those which fail to discern the narrator's circumstances and motives) have provided a sort of "template" for such fiction. A sort of generalized misreading of one story so "rife with caricature, overstated eccentricity, and broadly drawn humor . . . has come to represent Southern writing and, through that representation, the South itself." Earley

– himself one of the most promising young writers to emerge from the region in recent years – calls not for further pandering to commercial tastes with characters who are little more than "the prototypical Southern names that . . . have come to promise colorful Southern doings," but instead for writers who portray the people of the region "in all their complexity and diversity and Christ-hauntedness and moral ambiguity" (Earley 1999: 14–16).

There have been a number of such writers in the time since the integrated South fully re-entered the Union – and began a long turn toward greater economic prosperity – in the wake of the tumultuous 1960s. The generation of writers that rose to prominence in the latter decades of the twentieth century has indeed borne witness to a share of "complexity and diversity" such as had not been generally recognized in the region previously. Poets such as Maya Angelou and writers of fiction such as Alice Walker and Randall Kenan often write with a clear knowledge and appreciation of Faulkner and O'Connor, but even more so of the African-American tradition that they participate in and extend: Kenan's forthright concern with homosexuality links him to Harlem's James Baldwin, while Walker was largely responsible for the rediscovery of the work of long-neglected Floridian Zora Neale Hurston. Female writers of fiction have emerged across the region in force and wonderful variety: writers such as Anne Tyler, Doris Betts, Lee Smith, Jill McCorkle, Kaye Gibbons, and Josephine Humphreys, all of whom are conscious of and respond to different aspects of the tradition of modern Southern literature. And, of course, male fiction writers such as Cormac McCarthy, Barry Hannah, Reynolds Price, Padgett Powell, Richard Ford, and Clyde Edgerton have emerged from the region – as have poets who seem to owe little or no debt to the Fugitive-Agrarians, such as A. R. Ammons, and those who in some sense do, such as Wendell Berry and Fred Chappell.

Berry is the living Southern writer most aptly described as agrarian, if not wholly Agrarian, in outlook: a working farmer and advocate for an environmentalism conceived in terms of Christian stewardship, he has written in praise of the Nashville group but is (despite such recent poems as "The mad farmer, flying the flag of Rough Branch, secedes from the Union" [1994]) perhaps more aptly described as a sort of "Kentucky Thoreau" (Bryant 1997: 247). Chappell has in a number of essays reflected thoughtfully on what he sees as the rich legacy of the Fugitive-Agrarians for contemporary Southern poets.[4] And his tetralogy of his native North Carolina mountains that begins with the novel *I Am One of You Forever* (1985) has won praise from Hobson for its unselfconscious embodiment of the "enduring southern concerns of place, nature, community, and the endurance of the past in the present" (Hobson 1991: 82).

Though such themes of the sort valued by the Fugitive-Agrarians clearly apply to it, Chappell's Appalachia is in fact a subregion of the South that the Nashville group had generally ignored. But they – and Davidson in particular, who was more receptive to literature which had its origins in the impoverished mountain folk culture than were Ransom and Tate (Beck 2001: 122) – would likely have been less surprised at Chappell's claim to a piece of their legacy than they would at Ernest Gaines'.

Gaines is certainly one of the best African-American novelists to emerge from the region in the second half of the century. But he has also been praised by Hobson for writing, within the parameters of his own tradition, a fiction that plays the same role within contemporary Southern literature that "white Southern fiction" once played on the American scene – that of "a powerful, folk-based, past-conscious, often mythic expression of a storytelling culture within a larger literature" (Hobson 1991: 93). Like Chappell's tetralogy, works such as *The Autobiography of Miss Jane Pittman* (1971) and *A Gathering of Old Men* (1983) take place in a very specific community within a Southern subregion (in this case, Louisiana's Cajun country) that is marked by its own distinctive folk culture. Hobson – in part building on Woodward's claim that the African-American writer can, given his historical roots and intense experience of defeat and poverty, in some ways be seen as the "quintessential Southerner" – demonstrates convincingly that Gaines' rendering of his community can be read as the fulfillment of the best in the tradition of Southern literature that the Fugitive-Agrarians mapped out, though they themselves could never have foreseen such a development.

This is exactly the sort of claim to which Kreyling objects in *Inventing Southern Literature*, and which marks the great critical debate over the value and relevance of the Fugitive-Agrarian legacy today. While Hobson and others continue to modify and qualify that legacy, Kreyling rejects it vehemently, arguing that

> The Agrarian project was and must be seen as a willed campaign on the part of one elite to establish and control "the South" during a period of intense cultural maneuvering. The principal organizers of *I'll Take My Stand* knew full well that there were other "Souths" than the one they touted; they deliberately presented a fabricated South as the one and only real thing. (Kreyling 1998: xii)

Despite the interest in history professed by its proponents, Kreyling maintains, the Agrarian "South" was in fact only an idealized entity seen through the eyes of upper-class white males. Accordingly, the Agrarians in defining their region in terms of past, place, and community deliberately ignored the real and troubling divisions of race, class, and gender that marked the region. They were supported in doing so by Fugitive aesthetic values that led to a valuing of belletristic texts as opposed to those works of social criticism that were generally dismissed by the New Critics as propaganda rather than art (e.g. Lillian Smith's *Strange Fruit* [1944]; Wright's *Black Boy* [1945]). Kreyling indicts critics who try to subsume the more liberal sentiments of Warren and Woodward into the older and "essentially conservative" Agrarian paradigm for subtly carrying on a tradition of elitist denial rather than engaging the real complexities of the region. Hence he portrays any attempt to understand a writer such as Gaines in traditional "Southern" rather than "African-American" terms as misguided and misleading.

Such claims are provocative and add to the vitality of criticism in the region, but they are finally overstated. Little is made in *Inventing Southern Literature* of the Fugitive-

Agrarians' warm reception and support of female writers such as Gordon, Porter, Welty, and O'Connor. Rubin is criticized for favoring the aesthetic complexity of Ralph Ellison's *Invisible Man* (1952) over the more readily apparent social critique of Wright, but he is given little credit for expanding his vision of the Southern canon to include both of them – or for forthrightly pronouncing Jean Toomer's *Cane* (1923), a modernist exploration of African-American life in rural Georgia by a black Washingtonian, to be "the first fully mature work of the Southern Literary Renascence" (Rubin, ed., 1986: 429).[5] Indeed, *The Literary South* and *The History of Southern Literature* do give relatively substantial treatment not only to African-American writers but also to a number of those more liberal and polemical white writers – Glasgow, Caldwell, T. S. Stribling, Lillian Smith, James Agee – who had not won favor with the New Critics. But such inclusion goes largely unmentioned in *Inventing Southern Literature*, as does Rubin's personal support of such younger female writers and critics as Lee Smith, Annie Dillard, and Lucinda H. MacKethan. Similarly, while Hobson's attempt to find common ground in discussing African-American literature and Southern literature is lambasted, his extensive explication of the region's liberal tradition – the work of writers such as Walter Hines Page, Odum, and Lillian Smith – and his appreciation of recent Southern ironists such as Humphreys and Ford is unjustifiably ignored. In his efforts to dismantle completely the tradition established by the Fugitive-Agrarians, Kreyling portrays even those critics who have been most effective in expanding and diversifying the regional canon as somehow tainted.

Carried to its extreme, Kreyling's call for the final categorization of writers along lines of race, class, and gender effectively undermines any notion of a regional literature, and he does not call for a new Southern canon so much as the problematization of the old. But nonetheless he – at a time when continuing Southern distinctiveness seems less assured than ever – is less worried than the Agrarians themselves had been about the final passing of the region. He ends with a rousing call to dialogue: depicting the South as more a collection of contending ideas than a region, he goes on to assert its significance as no less than "the richest site yet discovered in the U.S. cultural terrain for the study of and participation in the reinvention of culture" (Kreyling 1998: 182). Some of his convictions are shared by Michael Guinn – who is similarly wary of creating a counter-canon that necessarily defines itself in reaction to the old – as he, too, derides the Fugitive-Agrarian legacy in *After Southern Modernism* (2000). But Guinn is primarily concerned with the inadequacy of modernist critical approaches in explaining the literature of the contemporary South. He provides compelling readings of specific texts as he makes his case that the region's contemporary literature is marked partly by "a resurgence in literary naturalism" written by "newly educated poor southerners" – for example, Harry Crews, Larry Brown, and Dorothy Allison – whose class experience runs counter to any pastoral Agrarian vision of the South (Guinn 2000: xii). Even more hostile to traditional readings are the works of those "mythoclasts" – Ford, Kenan, McCarthy, Hannah – who use postmodern techniques to undermine and parody "the modernist and racialized structures of the past" (Guinn 2000: 185).

Guinn is certainly correct in stating that individual "post-Renascence writers have achieved their own vision on their own terms" and that the contemporary critic must seek to recognize and understand those terms. Whatever the continuity of the region itself, the best writers to emerge from the South have always met the task of seeing it anew – usually by entering into dialectic, intentionally or not, with their predecessors. And achieving such vision has always meant stretching boundaries, often geographical as well as artistic. So it is for McCarthy and Ford, who have long lived and set much of their fiction in the West and Northeast. So it was for Oklahoma's Ralph Ellison, whose invisible narrator, from his New York cellar, made such a strong case for at least some conflation of the African-American and Southern canons: "I've sometimes been overcome with a passion to return into that 'heart of darkness' across the Mason-Dixon line . . . Sometimes I feel the need to reaffirm all of it, the whole unhappy territory and all the things lovable and unlovable in it, for all of it is part of me" (Ellison 1995: 579).

So it was for Allen Tate over seven decades ago – living among expatriate modernists in Paris, dreaming of Old Virginia, sending letters westward to Tennessee.

NOTES

1 For praise of the Agrarian critique of American capitalism by a historian whose views of the South have been shaped by Marxism, see Genovese (1994).
2 For a detailed account of the relationship between Davidson and Odum, see Hobson (1983).
3 Daniel Joseph Singal has argued that Tate's thesis – and in a sense the underpinning of the Agrarian movement itself – has little basis in historical reality because "the South did not industrialize significantly in the two decades between the wars. . . . Not until well after the Second World War did a majority of Southerners take industrial jobs and begin to live in places that could plausibly be described as

urban" (Singal 1982: xii). He argues that the underpinnings of the region's intellectual renaissance lay instead in the individual sensibilities of writers torn between Victorian and Modernist cultures – a battle that raged throughout Western society but can nowhere "be seen with greater clarity than in the American South" (Singal 1982: 8).
4 See especially Chappell (1997, 1993).
5 For that matter, Tate himself in the heyday of *The Fugitive* wrote to Toomer praising *Cane* for its use of modernist technique to break with "the caricatured pathos of Harris and others of the southern school of sentimental humors." Allen Tate to Jean Toomer, Nov. 7, 1923 (Toomer 1988: 161).

REFERENCES AND FURTHER READING

Agar, Herbert, and Tate, Allen, eds. (1936). *Who Owns America? A New Literary Declaration of Independence*. Boston: Houghton Mifflin.
Beck, Charlotte H. (2001). *The Fugitive Legacy: A Critical History*. Baton Rouge: Louisiana State University Press.
Bové, Paul (1992). "Agriculture and Academe: America's Southern Question." In *Mastering Discourse: The Politics of Intellectual Culture*, 113–42. Durham: Duke University Press.
Brooks, Cleanth (1995). *Community, Religion, and Literature*. Columbia: University of Missouri Press.

Bryant, J. A., Jr. (1997). *Twentieth-Century Southern Literature*. Lexington: University of Kentucky Press.

Chappell, Fred (1993). *Plow Naked: Selected Writings on Poetry*. Ann Arbor: University of Michigan Press.

Chappell, Fred (1997). "'Not as a leaf': Southern Poetry and the Innovation of Tradition." *Georgia Review* 51, 477–89.

Conkin, Paul (1980). *The Southern Agrarians*. Knoxville: University of Tennessee Press.

Cowan, Louise (1959). *The Fugitive Group: A Literary History*. Baton Rouge: Louisiana State University Press.

Donaldson, Susan V. (1997). "Gender, Race, and Allen Tate's Profession of Letters in the South." In Anne Goodwyn Jones and Susan V. Donaldson (eds.), *Haunted Bodies: Gender and Southern Texts*, 402–518. Charlottesville: University Press of Virginia.

Earley, Tony (1999). "Letter from Sister: What We Learned at the P.O." *Oxford American* 25, 14–16.

Ellison, Ralph (1995). *Invisible Man*. New York: Vintage. (First publ. 1952.)

Fain, John T., and Young, Thomas Daniel, eds. (1974). *The Literary Correspondence of Donald Davidson and Allen Tate*. Athens, Ga: University of Georgia Press.

Fante, John (1980). *Ask the Dust*. Santa Rosa: Black Sparrow. (First publ. 1939.)

Genovese, Eugene D. (1994). *The Southern Tradition: The Achievements and Limitations of an American Conservatism*. Cambridge, Mass.: Harvard University Press.

Guinn, Michael (2000). *After Southern Modernism: Fiction of the Contemporary South*. Jackson: University Press of Mississippi.

Hobson, Fred (1983). *Tell About the South: The Southern Rage to Explain*. Baton Rouge: Louisiana State University Press.

Hobson, Fred (1991). *The Southern Writer in the Postmodern World*. Athens, Ga: University of Georgia Press.

Humphries, Jefferson, and Lowe, John, eds. (1996). *The Future of Southern Letters*. New York: Oxford University Press.

King, Richard (1980). *A Southern Renaissance: The Cultural Awakening of the American South, 1930–1955*. New York: Oxford University Press.

Kreyling, Michael (1998). *Inventing Southern Literature*. Jackson: University Press of Mississippi.

Lawson, Lewis A. (1984). *Another Generation: Southern Fiction since World War II*. Jackson: University Press of Mississippi.

Malvasi, Mark G. (1997). *The Unregenerate South: The Agrarian Thought of John Crowe Ransom, Allen Tate, and Donald Davidson*. Baton Rouge: Louisiana State University Press.

Manning, Carol S., ed. (1993). *The Female Tradition in Southern Literature*. Urbana: University of Illinois Press.

Rubin, Louis D., Jr. (1978). *The Wary Fugitives: Four Poets and the South*. Baton Rouge: Louisiana State University Press.

Rubin, Louis D., Jr., gen. ed. (1985). *The History of Southern Literature*. Baton Rouge: Louisiana State University Press.

Rubin, Louis D., Jr., ed. (1986). *The Literary South*. Baton Rouge: Louisiana State University Press. (First publ. 1979.)

Rubin, Louis D., Jr., and Robert Jacobs, eds. (1968). *Southern Renascence: The Literature of the Modern South*. Baltimore: Johns Hopkins University Press. (First publ. 1953.)

Simpson, Lewis P. (1980). *The Brazen Face of History: Studies in the Literary Consciousness in America*. Baton Rouge: Louisiana State University Press.

Simpson, Lewis P. (1994). *The Fable of the Southern Writer*. Baton Rouge: Louisiana State University Press.

Singal, Daniel Joseph (1982). *The War Within: From Victorian to Modernist Thought in the South*. Chapel Hill: University of North Carolina Press.

Tate, Allen (1968). *Essays of Four Decades*. Chicago: Swallow.

Toomer, Jean (1988). *Cane: A Norton Critical Edition*, ed. Darwin T. Turner. New York: Norton. (First publ. 1923.)

Twelve Southerners (1977). *I'll Take My Stand: The South and the Agrarian Tradition* (1930). Baton Rouge: Louisiana State University Press.

18

Romanticizing a Different Lost Cause: Regional Identities in Louisiana and the Bayou Country

Suzanne Disheroon-Green

Louisiana has long been considered a strange and mysterious place, home to gumbo, voodoo, bayous, and French Creoles: in many ways a region as foreign to the Southern culture with which it is most closely associated as the South is to the larger United States. Readers and writers alike find themselves inexplicably seduced by this swampy region, reveling in the romance inherent in the stereotypes of sultry nights, dark, passionate women, hot-blooded men, and forbidden pleasures. But why has Louisiana proven such a hotbed of distinctive regional writing? What makes the literary tradition which has developed in Louisiana differ from that of the deep South, or from the American literary tradition as a whole?

As a part of the deep South, an area romanticized because of its plantation homes, lush green landscapes, and generous hospitality, Louisiana has developed a "peculiar brand of southernness" that is "singularly romantic even among southern states" (Brown and Ewell 1992: 3). Significant cultural differences distinguish Louisiana from the larger Southern identity:

> Primary among the state's anomalies are the strong French and Catholic strains in its character, manifest in its Napoleonic civil code, its festivals of Mardi Gras and All Saints', its devotion to the culinary arts, and its general tolerance of liquor, languor, and lewdness – within limits. Such peculiarities have redefined in Louisiana – sometimes subtly and sometimes sharply – the cultural and geographic places out of which the South has constructed its prevailing mythologies. (Brown and Ewell 1992: 10)

Richard Gray has also noted that "the fact of the South as a distinct and homogeneous region has increasingly been called into question, but the idea of the South as an identifiable structuring of culture remains intact" (1985: xxi). The mythologies of the South, and of Louisiana specifically, derive from a cultural tendency to romanticize the South and the Lost Cause.

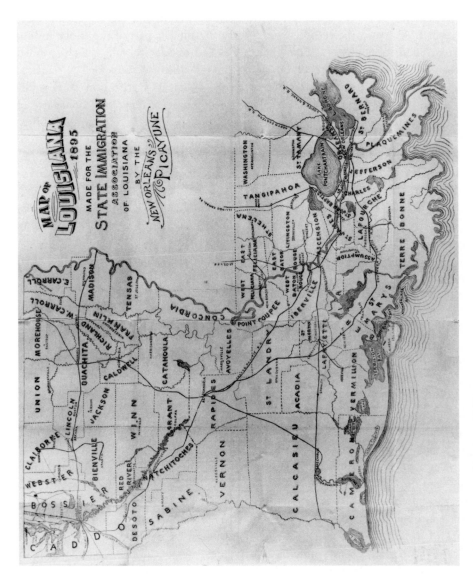

Figure 18.1 Map of Louisiana, 1895.

Despite its geographical link to the American South, and hence the Southern literary tradition, Louisiana maintains a regional identity that is unique among Southern states. This regional identity developed, initially, because of a colonial experience that diverged from that of other early settlers in North America. Rather than acculturating to continued British rule, as was the case with most other American settlements prior to the late eighteenth century, Louisiana was a French possession until 1763, when the territory was ceded to Spain as a part of the treaty ending the French and Indian War. Under the brief period of Spanish rule, which spanned less than 40 years, most aspects of day-to-day life remained the same for Louisianians. It was not until the United States purchased the Louisiana territory in 1803 – following the return of the region to the control of Emperor Napoleon Bonaparte of France just long enough for the sale to be accomplished – that the cultural differences between the American way of life and those of the French and Spanish began to come into conflict.

The impact of French culture on Louisiana and its literature cannot be overemphasized. After the Louisiana Purchase of 1803, United States law gradually became the law of the land in the region, but the French influence continued and remains, in fact, strongly evident today. As historian Daniel Boorstin has argued, "remnants of French . . . culture in Louisiana . . . and the survival of Roman Law in Louisiana were stronger, more widespread, and more durable alien elements than were then found elsewhere in the eastern United States" (1965: 170). The French version of Roman law, which came to be called the Napoleonic Code, provided the basis for the Louisiana judicial system.

Further, French continues to be the primary language of many homes in Louisiana and is a far more common second language throughout the state than any other (Johnson 1989: 428). In 1980, slightly more than 10 percent of Louisiana residents reported French as their native language, and Louisiana contains the "largest concentration of French-speaking natives with an indigenous ethnic tradition in the United States" (Johnson 1989: 428). All of these native French-speakers, with rare exceptions, are descendants of "one or some combination of [the] French-speaking groups that largely made up Louisiana's colonial and antebellum population" (Johnson 1989: 428). The French influence is still strongly felt in the Creole and Acadian communities,[1] and throughout the state as a whole, in its dialects, religion, and folk customs.

Because of the influence of its rich French heritage, Louisiana diverges from the larger Southern region in three areas: the Creole and Acadian communities that undergird the intellectual climate, artistic and literary statement, and overall social fabric of the region; the atypical racial attitudes present in the region, which in turn influenced the place of women in Louisiana culture; and the influence of the Catholic Church, as opposed to the predominantly Protestant influence throughout the remaining Southern states.

The immigration and settlement patterns of Louisiana were further complicated by the influx of French Acadians who had been exiled first from France and then from Canada. These immigrants were displaced from Nova Scotia by the British as early as 1755, and began arriving in Louisiana between 1760 and 1763, settling along the Mississippi and various bayous throughout Louisiana. A larger-scale immigration by the Acadians, often called Cajuns, to Louisiana constituted the "greatest single movement of colonists from Europe to America in colonial history" (Wilds 1996: 27). This involved a group of Acadians who had returned to their homeland and then, after subsisting in France for nearly thirty years, accepted the offer of the Spanish king to transport them to Louisiana. The Cajun community in south Louisiana still thrives and is characterized by its close-knit communal relationships, its music and food, and other folk traditions which are reflected in its storytelling and literature.

Perhaps the most significant deviation from American culture was found in the racial codes enforced in Louisiana. During the antebellum period, the United States operated under a binary racial system, in which an individual was either white, and thereby entitled to the relevant privileges of citizenship, or non-white, and relegated to the status of slave. Even in the rare cases in which a person of color was free, such freedom was a precarious possession. The presumption was that a person of color was enslaved unless they could prove otherwise, and even demonstrable freedom could be revoked on the flimsiest of grounds. Slaves were not afforded any protection under the law and could be abused physically and sexually by their owners, who often engaged in such abuse with impunity.

In Louisiana, racial politics were a bit more complicated. While slavery was practiced throughout the region, strict laws governing the care and working conditions of slaves were enforced by the French, laws which were later explicitly retained by the Spanish. For example, slaves were allowed the right to marry individuals of their own choosing, children were not separated from their mothers at the young ages at which such separations occurred in the United States, and slaveholders were admonished to teach their charges Catholicism and to prohibit them from working on holy days. Failure to fulfill these responsibilities could lead to, among other things, the loss of the slaves. Further, slaves were afforded some protection from physical and sexual abuse under the law and could offer evidence in court against whites if the situation warranted it.

Equally influential on the development of Louisiana culture was the development of an intermediate racial caste. In addition to the privileged whites and the enslaved African Americans, a sizeable third group, called the *gens de couleur libre* or free people of color, completed the racial landscape. A large portion of this population were the descendants of the emancipated Marie Thereze or Coincoin. Coincoin was the slave of the aristocratic St. Denis family, who had been instrumental in the settling of Natchitoches, the oldest city in the Louisiana territory. Coincoin was granted her freedom after she saved the life of her mistress. Mme. St. Denis was suffering from a terminal illness from which her doctors despaired of curing her. Coincoin begged for the opportunity to try folk healing methods on her beloved mistress, and upon Mme. St. Denis's recovery, the grateful family granted Coincoin her freedom and a parcel of land on Cane River in central Louisiana. Coincoin worked tirelessly to purchase each of her enslaved children and gradually increased her landholdings, establishing a sizeable and profitable plantation. At the time of her death, her land holdings were divided among her children, and the colony of *gens de couleur libre* was established.

Unlike other Southern states, Louisiana recognized these people *de couleur* – people of Creole, Native American, or other mixed racial heritage – as belonging to a higher class than their darker-skinned counterparts. As historian Gary Mills has pointed out,

> under the title of gens de couleur libre, free part-white Creoles were accorded special privileges, opportunities, and citizenship not granted to part-Negroes in other states. Preservation of this third racial class in Louisiana society was contingent upon strict adherence to the caste system by its members [who often possessed] more white blood than black, and [were] quite often on good terms with and publicly recognized by their white relatives . . . into this complex caste system still another factor injected itself: economic status. Louisiana's legal code provided a wider berth of economic opportunities to free people of color than could be found in any of the other states . . . the extent to which individual members of this third class utilized their opportunities often determined their degree of social acceptability in society as a whole. (1977: xiv)

Historians have demonstrated that "race relations in . . . Louisiana evolved in a pattern borrowed from the West Indies, one that tended to treat free mulattoes as a social group with special privileges and status." The free black population of Louisiana was perceived as "an intermediate element between the races. This more sophisticated system of race relations, with its keener awareness of the complexities of color, encouraged the development of a more porous racial boundary than elsewhere in the South, at least until the intensifying racism of the late antebellum era pushed free mulattoes downward toward the lower caste" (Bardaglio 1995: 60).

The *gens de couleur libre* shared some rights with their white counterparts during the French and Spanish colonial era. They owned property, and this property frequently included slaves. Free people of color entered into business arrangements – often with their white counterparts – married at their discretion, and bore children who carried their fathers' names, regardless of race. After the Louisiana Purchase, however, American law gradually took effect in Louisiana. The "one-drop rule" and, later, Jim Crow laws became the de facto standard for the rights – or lack thereof – of people of color, effectively eliminating many of the rights that had been taken for granted prior to the Louisiana Purchase. American law destroyed the caste system in Louisiana, clearing the way for the longstanding colonial caste system to devolve into one of the most viciously enforced biracial hierarchies of any Southern state. Following the Civil War, the white aristocracy held the highest status, and former slaves held the lowest – in this way, there was little difference from the rest of the Southern region. The Creole community, however, held a nebulous place in the middle of this hierarchy. They were not fully accepted into white society during the best of times because they had some non-white blood in their background – and their lack of whiteness became more of an issue as the nineteenth century wore on – but they felt that they were

superior to their black counterparts, and so held themselves apart from the communities of former slaves.

Exclusively Creole communities, such as the Iberville colony on Cane River, did
not wholly escape the strictures of the caste system because of their prosperity,
however. The free people of color in Louisiana possessed what H. E. Sterkx has called
"quasi-citizenship" during the era leading up to the Louisiana Purchase, enjoying "a
better legal position than any of their counterparts in other states of the South"
(1972: 171). Yet free people of color could not vote, and "at no time were . . . ever
deemed wholly equal; they were generally recognized by law as second class citizens"
(Sterkx 1972: 160). Laura Foner has also pointed out that "although free people of
color shared the same class position of many Whites as planters, they were socially
excluded from membership in that class and were forced to form a separate and
subordinate caste" (1970: 420). Even within Creole societies, the "many generations
of intermarriage by blacks with whites and Native Americans produced an intricate
internal caste system within black Creole society based on skin tone, dialect, and
family history" (Ancelet 1989: 422). While far from ideal, the position of the *gens de
couleur libre* in Louisiana society implicitly held more freedom, in terms of both
economic issues and personal relationships, than was available to non-whites in any
other Southern state of the era.

Ironically, following the transfer of Louisiana to the United States, the territory
which had previously been the most permissive in its treatment of people of color
became the most virulently oppressive. Being "sold down the river" to Louisiana
rapidly became the fear of most slaves, who learned of the sweltering humidity, the
subhuman working conditions, and the high death rate among slaves. In fact, conditions for slaves living in Louisiana following the American takeover were so harsh
that they invited comparison to the setting of the scenes of gruesome cruelty in
Harriet Beecher Stowe's *Uncle Tom's Cabin*. Local legend goes so far as to identify the
model for Stowe's Simon Legree as a central Louisiana resident, Robert McAlpin,
who owned a plantation in Natchitoches Parish which adjoined the family lands of
Kate Chopin's husband, Oscar. McAlpin was reputed to be extremely cruel to his
slaves. The story, the validity of which is supported by numerous extant affidavits,
relates that Stowe and some traveling companions were guests in McAlpin's home on
an extended visit. McAlpin returned from an engagement one afternoon to find
Stowe talking at length with some of his slaves about their lives and working
conditions and became enraged. McAlpin summarily dismissed Stowe and her party
from his home and, in retaliation, Stowe ostensibly modeled Legree after her former
friend.[2] Whether the legend is fact or fiction, it is indicative of the quality of life that
slaves could expect on many Louisiana plantations, a life that was frequently depicted
in the literature of the region.

The tripartite racial system of Louisiana to a large extent structured the place
afforded to women. As Barbara Ewell has suggested, "place in the South also defines
social stratification, particularly for African-Americans, but also for women, who,
like blacks, need to 'know their place' as the subordinates of white men in an

intensely patriarchal culture" (Brown and Ewell 1992: 4). Accordingly, women's social and domestic roles are clearly defined in Louisiana culture. The positions that women were expected to occupy fell into a hierarchy, much like that dictated to people of color. In the larger Southern region, several distinct categories existed: white women of privilege; poor white women who were not esteemed by society, and who had little hope of overcoming their outcast status even if they overcame their economic disadvantages; and women of mixed race, who did not clearly fit into either category. Those women who were born into the Southern aristocracy, despite their reputation as pampered girls, had a rigidly defined future ahead of them from which they could not honorably escape. In their youth, young aristocratic women "had few tasks other than to be obedient, to ride, to sew, and perhaps to learn reading and writing . . . a girl was to stay home until such time as a suitable – that is, lucrative – marriage was arranged for her" (Seidel 1985: 6). Following her successful launch into womanhood, the belle began a life that was not what she had been brought up to expect, given that "her cluster of attributes of appearance and purity belied the reality of her situation" (Seidel 1985: 7). Although raised to believe that she possessed magical powers that enchanted the men around her, upon her marriage she was met with reality: "often disappointed by the gentleman who turned out not to be the cavalier, who married her because her 'magic' attraction was her dowry, often distressed by her change in status from a pampered, sought-after belle to a hardworking but anonymous wife, the belle-turned-matron was herself a laborer on the plantation" (Seidel 1985: 7). Throughout the South, both before and after the Civil War, a woman of privilege, who was "supposed to embody the ideals of her culture" but whose "scope of . . . activities was severely limited" (Westling 1985: 8), enjoyed little more freedom than any other group outside of the white male aristocracy.

In Louisiana, however, the tripartite system influenced women as stringently as it did people of color. While those at the ends of the spectrum – full-blooded black or white, the haves and the have-nots – were well schooled in the expectations that society held for them, an ethereal middle ground existed for some women of mixed heritage; and along with this middle ground came a sliding scale of morality. For example, a Creole woman could bear the child of a white man out of wedlock, and though she might endure harsh words from her family and snubs from some friends, she could still be considered marriageable, as is suggested by Lyle Saxon's *Children of Strangers* (1937). While the community was certainly not happy with the tainting of its young women, it accepted their shortcomings as a matter of course because of the perceived desirability of acquiring whiteness, even through children. Should the same young woman bear the child of a black man, however, she would immediately "lose caste," and could never re-enter that middle segment of the population that allowed her some privileges not available to the slave population and, later, to the free black community.

The trope of the tragic mulatto, as exemplified by Saxon's novel, represented an enduring element in the fiction of Louisiana writers. During the antebellum period, and even stretching into the Civil War years themselves, "reading or retelling the standard story of the woman of ambiguous race had been considered a betrayal of Southern loyalties" (Elfenbein 1989: 13). Writers of the post-Civil War period, however, defied this convention, seemingly adopting the "Northern view that interracial sex in the South had caused God to forsake [the South's] cause" (Elfenbein 1989: 13), and accordingly typified the archetypal tragic mulatto not only by her amazing beauty but also by her brushes with threats to her innocence – threats which all too often came to fruition. Her beauty attracted the unwanted attentions of unscrupulous men who wanted to possess her physically, but who paid no heed to the consequences of such attentions to the woman. As Barbara Ladd has pointed out, the woman of mixed racial heritage in literature is portrayed as "a tragic kind of American geisha" (1996: 1). Further, the tragic mulatto, both in "the literature of abolition, as well as in historical novels written long after emancipation" possesses "connections to 'aristocracy' through her white father, and sometimes through her African mother as well. [She is] virtually indistinguishable from the idealized white heroines" (Ladd 1996: 2), except insofar as her "taint" of blackness excludes her from unequivocal acceptance by either the white aristocracy or the African-American culture. Despite the seeming advantages of beauty and desirability, the tragic mulatto is "wretched because of the 'single drop of midnight in her veins,'" wishing for "a white lover above all else. For this she 'must go down to a tragic end'" (Zanger 1966: 63; Brown 1966: 144). Literary examples of the trope abound, including pieces such as Kate Chopin's "Désirée's Baby" and "La Belle Zoraïde," stories in which the mixed-race woman meets a tragic end because of assumptions about her race, assumptions that do not prove to be true in either case; George Washington Cable's *Madame Delphine*; and Grace King's "Little Convent Girl." Each of these writers demonstrates the pathetic fate dealt to women of mixed heritage who dare to overreach that which society deigns to allow them.

These literary depictions of the tragic mulatto are, in fact, rather misleading. Whereas the literati tended to portray mixed-race women as victims of circumstance who had no control over their destinies, their relatives, in fact, had a significant hand in their barter. An attractive woman of mixed heritage could form a "permanent or semipermanent [*sic*] alliance with a wealthy white man. . . . For this reason, these women strove to please" (Elfenbein 1989: 17). Elaborate balls were hosted by shrewd mothers who, realizing that their daughters faced futures marked by financial uncertainty, would place them on display before wealthy white men. They "bargained for extramarital alliances with white men who would become their daughters' *maris*. These alliances, which were called *plaçages*, in many instances became lifetime quasi-marriages, with the white man devising a means for his children to be educated as ladies and gentlemen in Paris and for their inheritance of his wealth" (Elfenbein 1989: 17).

Despite the fiscal advantages of such arrangements, however, the *plaçage* system was degrading to its core, as women of mixed heritage were "forced to barter for an advantageous arrangement" (Elfenbein 1989: 17), in which they assumed "as a merit and a distinction what is universally considered in the civilized world a shame and a disgrace" (King 1904: 348). In the final analysis, women of mixed racial heritage were "as enslaved as their slave sisters and as their truly white sisters, who were coerced to maintain their chastity both before and after marriage by a standard of conduct that applied only to them" (Elfenbein 1989: 18). The options available to women of mixed ancestry frequently left them with little choice but to submit to the type of concubinage so prevalent during this era.

Louisiana, then, possessed a delicately balanced system of racial and gender roles. The key to balancing such a system was strict adherence to that system by members of all castes. Because of this three-caste system, which allowed some legal rights and personal autonomy to those in the middle, Louisiana's attitudes toward race and gender are to a large extent inconsistent with those prevailing in the rest of the South. As the United States drew closer to the Civil War, these incompatibilities caused Louisiana law to become less tolerant of those in the middle caste, but the differences are significant enough still to be felt today and continue to be reflected in the literature of the state.

Race and gender do not constitute the only sources of Louisiana's unique regional identity. The Southern region has traditionally been a Protestant stronghold, with clear tendencies toward the fundamentalist and the charismatic. While this is not to say that the South is exclusively Protestant, the religious attitudes and influences of the region have a markedly Protestant flavor. However, Catholicism has been widely practiced in Louisiana since the arrival of the first European explorers and had become an integral part of the religious and social landscape by the early seventeenth century. Catholics "constitute nearly three-fifths of total church membership in Louisiana" (Shortridge 1989: 558), following the consolidation of Catholic influence in Louisiana that accompanied the influx of French Canadians after their deportation from Nova Scotia.

Louisiana draws much of its religious heritage from the teachings of the Catholic Church, and these differences are reflected in the literature of the region. The confessional aspects of Catholicism, combined with the associated guilt feelings, and the patriarchal system that the Catholic church supports, lend a sense of self-doubt to the works of many Louisiana writers, Andre Dubus and Rebecca Wells notably among them. Numerous Louisiana writers also demonstrate a tendency to explore the roots of Catholicism found in paganism and its rituals, perhaps as part of a search for outlets from the guilt often associated with Catholicism by those who feel that they are not satisfactorily following the church's behavioral directives. While alcohol, sexual experimentation – often with both genders – and depression are associated with the literature of the Southern region at large, paganism, voodoo, and hoodoo offer to Louisiana writers additional paths that the fallen may pursue.

Given the substantial influence of continental Europe on Louisiana, it would be surprising if the cultural identity of the state had emerged in any kind of unified form. Even within itself, Louisiana consists of several divergent subcultures: the northern portion of the state, presently touted as the "Sportsman's Paradise;" the Cane River region of central Louisiana; the Cajun country in the southwestern part of the state; and the French Creole city of New Orleans, which even today holds mythic status.

Specific writers of these subregions, and the influence which Louisiana's cultural history has exerted on their writing, will form the basis for the remainder of this discussion.

The Louisiana literary tradition began, not surprisingly, with historical writings recording the development of the region and the adventures of those who were instrumental in its exploration. Literary works written during the period leading up to and immediately following the Louisiana Purchase largely fall into two categories: documentary materials, such as histories, letters, and travel narratives; and creative works, such as poetry and novels. Until the late 1700s, narrative forms which recorded exploratory expeditions, the resulting colonial settlements, and associated personal experiences were the dominant literary genre. Much of the literature produced during this era was written in French, with many of the literary artists spending at least some of their time studying and/or writing in France. In addition, the oral narrative tradition that was already firmly entrenched, especially among members of indigenous Native American communities, continued to flourish.

The earliest writing from the colonial era of Louisiana came from the pens of diarists such as Henry de Tonti and Jacques de la Metairie, each of whom recorded his perceptions of events during Robert Cavelier de La Salle's exploratory expeditions. Travel narratives were written by missionaries such as Father Paul du Ru and Father François-Xavier Charlevoix; Henry de Joutel penned a historical journal of La Salle's second expedition. André Pénicault produced a history of the Iberville colony spanning 22 years, and this work continues to provide scholars with a substantial portion of the primary source material available concerning Louisiana's early history. Further contributions were made by Ursuline nuns Mare de Saint-Augustin Tranchepain and Marie Madeline Hachard. Tranchepain kept a journal describing her voyage to colonial Louisiana, and Hachard's letters to her family in France were later published, in part for the information they contained and in part because, as John Wilds (1996) points out, contemporary readers were charmed by their tone.

The first comprehensive history of Louisiana was written by Antoine Simon Le Page du Pratz in 1758. Du Pratz lived in Louisiana for a time, but, finding colonial life not to his liking, he returned to France. Charles Gayarré also wrote a comprehensive discussion of the development of the territory, titled *History of Louisiana: The French Domination*. Gayarré's three-volume *History* is still considered by many to be an authoritative history of the colonial period in Louisiana.

The first truly literary figure in Louisiana, Julien Poydras, a French poet and plantation owner, did not emerge until the late 1770s. Originally written in French, two of Poydras' three lengthy poems praised Governor Bernardo de Gálvez (1777). His masterpiece, "The God of the Mississippi," is especially noteworthy for its praise of both black and white soldiers during Gálvez's campaigns, and his treatments of people of color as equals to their white compatriots were unusual for this era. His third poem, titled "A Prise du Morne du Baton Rouge" was written to commemorate the liberation of Baton Rouge from British control, and demonstrates the suspicion with which intruders were viewed.

Following the cession of Louisiana to the United States through the period leading to the Civil War, much of the literature written in Louisiana continued to be composed in French. Literary writers of this era included Creole poets and brothers Dominique and Adrien Rouquette. The Rouquettes were both greatly influenced by the French romanticism of Hugo and Chateaubriand, with whom the poets were acquainted. Dominique published pieces such as *Meschacébéenes* (1839), and *Fleurs d'Amérique* (1857). Adrien published *Les Savanes* (1841) and *L'Antoniade* (1860), which served as precursors to his masterpiece, a narrative poem reflecting on the Native American, titled *La Nouvelle Atala* (1879). According to John Wilds, this piece likely was derived from his experiences as a missionary to the Choctaw Indians in St. Tammany Parish. Further, Charles Testut Mercier's autobiographical novel, *L'Habitation Saint-Ybars*, details his experiences on an antebellum plantation.

Literary contributions were not limited to the white community, however, even during this era of racial inequality. *Les Cenelles* (1845), an anthology of poetry by free people of color living in the Louisiana territory, has been called by Rayburn S. Moore the "most curious of all the volumes of antebellum Southern verse," in part because most of the contributors to it were "all near-white, free New Orleanians" (1985: 120). The volume contained 82 poems by 17 poets and is considered the first anthology of African-American poetry published in the United States (Bryan 1998: 84). Contributors to the volume included Victor Séjour, Nelson Debrosses, and Armand Lanusse, all of whom wrote in French. Victor Séjour, a free person of color born in New Orleans who later migrated to Paris, also became a successful playwright. His most important works include *Richard III: Drame en cinq actes, en prose* and *La Tireuse de Cartes*, both of which were published in Paris.

The writers whose work appeared during the Civil War era and its aftermath – along with the cultural milieu which surrounded them – have continued to be influential upon later Louisiana writers and their works. Figures such as Grace King, Ruth McEnery Stuart, and George Washington Cable wrote of life in New Orleans during the pre- and post-Civil War era, and their choice of subject-matter and use of vernacular dialects led to their categorization as "local colorists." For many years, the designation of a writer as a producer of local color was tantamount to calling him or her a minor writer rather than one who penned significant literary works. Despite this designation, George Washington Cable became one of the most respected voices of this era and has been credited with "discovering New Orleans as a literary subject" (Cleman 1996). His most significant work, *The Grandissimes*, provides an illuminating snapshot of postbellum Louisiana, seemingly with the intent of demonstrating the treachery of blacks that most white readers took for granted and upholding the tradition of white superiority. In reality, Cable's work often criticizes the racial caste system, pointing out the flaws in its construction and its effects on community and interpersonal relationships. Toward that end, Cable's New Orleans Creoles are clever, often overcoming adversity, as in "Mme. Délicieuse" and "Belles Demoiselle Plantation" from *Old Creole Days*. Conversely, fellow New Orleanian Grace King, who began her own literary career because of her opposition to Cable's depictions of New

Orleans, painted lovely verbal portraits of Creole New Orleans, but espoused a more traditional view concerning racial issues. For example, in her story "The Little Convent Girl," published in the collection *Balcony Stories*, King relates the effects upon a young girl of learning the truth about her ethnicity after leading a sheltered life which has shielded her from knowledge of her racial heritage. Upon learning, cruelly, of her black ancestry, the girl chooses suicide over the discrimination and oppression that await her as a woman of mixed racial heritage. King's fiction frequently reaffirms her position to her readers: that blackness is an undesirable state, and that death is perhaps preferable to blackness.

Writers such as Ruth McEnery Stuart, Kate Chopin, and Sallie Rhett Roman each depict the lives of women in Louisiana and the struggles which ensue when they aspire to nontraditional roles. Of this group, Kate Chopin is something of an enigma among her late nineteenth-century comrades, in large part because she does not tacitly accept the Louisiana status quo for women and people of color. While she does portray women and people of color in traditional, oppressed roles in some cases, she just as often defies social convention. As early as her first novel, *At Fault*, Chopin shows a widow assuming the responsibility of running her deceased husband's sizeable plantation, and even after winning her second husband, she does not relinquish the care of the plantation to him. Chopin's women often chafe within the confines of marriage, leading them to engage in adulterous relationships without consequence, to celebrate privately the death of a husband because of the freedom the death represents, or to choose suicide over the continuation of an unfulfilling relationship. In "The Storm," Chopin shows adultery to be a desirable outcome for two individuals who have spent years longing for each other; the one-time sexual relationship serves to strengthen their respective marriages, rather than to harm them as Chopin's readers would have expected. "The Story of an Hour" at first demonstrates the growing joy of a woman upon learning that her husband's death has set her free, despite the fact that she loved him. When she discovers that news of his death was erroneous, Mrs. Mallard dies, not from the shock of the happy news, but from the disappointing loss of freedom so newly gained. In *The Awakening*, Edna Pontellier follows numerous whims in her search for a satisfactory alternative to the demands of her marriage and family, but her attempts prove fruitless, leading her to choose death by drowning over a troubled and unfulfilling existence. Similarly, Chopin stirs up the race question, showing African-American characters such as LaFolle in "Beyond the Bayou" defying traditional behavioral rules by approaching the front door of the "big house" and politely declining to leave before her wishes are fulfilled. Chopin's writing is also notable not only because she strikes a delicate balance between stories of the rural Cane River region and those set in urban New Orleans, but because, even before Faulkner, she created an entire fictional community, replete with recurring characters, events, and settings, in which to place her stories.

Members of the white aristocracy were not the only writers telling stories of Louisiana, however. Writers such as Arna Bontemps, Zora Neale Hurston, and Alice Dunbar-Nelson draw upon the rich tradition of narrative and folk traditions inherent in Louisiana, elements which provide the foundation for their works. Perhaps more significantly, their works, not surprisingly, reflect the complicated social fabric of the region, describing life in the bayou state from the perspective of the perpetually disenfranchised. Through the choices their characters make, these writers demonstrate that they will continue to struggle to make their voices heard, even if they must take extreme steps to do so. For example, Hurston spent several months studying New Orleans hoodoo and Haitian voodoo. Her studies and her own journey toward ordination as a voodoo priestess led Hurston to create some of her best work, work that is not often recognized as bearing the influence of one of the major alternative religions of New Orleans. Despite its Florida setting, *Their Eyes Were Watching God*, according to Pamela Glenn Menke, demonstrates Hurston's "subversive imagination" and must be viewed as an "integral companion" (2001: 123) to works more obviously influenced by the extensive study of voodoo which she undertook in both Louisiana and Haiti, *Jonah's Gourd Vine* and *Tell My Horse*. Arna Bontemps's "A Summer Tragedy" illustrates the hopeless plight of African Americans in the South when they become old and infirm. Rather than slowly dying a humiliating death by inches, Jeff and Jennie Patton choose suicide while they still have the strength to make their own choice. The tragedy is not so much the death of a loving elderly couple as the type of society which would make such a choice seem the only logical one to individuals who had devoted their lives to scratching out a meager living for themselves. Alice Dunbar-Nelson demonstrates local color attributes of the lives of Creoles of color living in New Orleans, showing the fervent belief in Catholicism sprinkled liberally with voodoo, the genteel dialects and manners of the members of the Creole community, and the inescapable racial and gender categories that restricted the potential of so many members of that community.

As the twentieth century advanced and American attentions turned toward international warfare, Louisiana writers continued with their prolific and well-received literary output. Writers such as Walker Percy, Tennessee Williams, Lyle Saxon, James Aswell, John Kennedy Toole, and Robert Penn Warren described the cultural landscape of the bayou country. Huey Long, Louisiana's favorite son, wrote fictionalized political autobiographies such as *Every Man a King* and *My First Days in the White House*, which detail not only his own exploits but the cultural landscape of the region which he called home. Their writing dealt, in many cases, with what have come to be considered "traditional" Southern topics: family, honor, place, race, caste, and religion; yet they also provide insight into the subregion of Louisiana which is depicted in their writing. For example, the eccentricities and alienation of Percy's, Williams's, and Toole's characters are further highlighted by the oddities of New Orleans itself. New Orleans has long held a special place in the hearts of Louisianians, a place it owes to the same seductive aura that "one perceives and welcomes in certain European centers . . . Here one finds the midday languor, the appreciation of the good things of life: food and drink are taken seriously, ease is valued, hustle is absent, the warm Mediterranean climate is absorbed" (Kennedy, ed., 1989: xiv). Despite such romantic descriptions, however, the city possesses its dark side:

New Orleans predictably acquired a celebrity for entertainments other than the refined and picturesque. Grog shops, card rooms, and brothels were common in the wharf areas, along with high levels of violence and crime. Also, restrictive trade and tariff laws in Louisiana under both the French and Spanish administrations had made smuggling, pirating, and other forms of disregard for authority both a condition of survival and an accepted custom, even patriotic practice, evidenced most notably by the social standing of the Creole pirate Jean Lafitte. New Orleans's reputation as the "Big Easy," a wide-open sin city, was longstanding and multifaceted, going well beyond the refined exotica of the quadroon balls and river/port-city debaucheries to include various forms of governmental corruption and the mysterious practices of the African-Caribbean religion known as voodoo . . . The recurrent note in nearly every description of New Orleans is striking contrasts – of Old World refinements and frontier coarseness, of rigid exclusiveness and unparalleled openness and tolerance, of languorous decay and vigorous growth and progress, of exotic allure and unmistakable danger. (Cleman: 1996)

Tennessee Williams makes use of the New Orleans sensibilities, both by living in the city and by making use of it as a setting on more than one occasion. He portrays some of his most disturbed characters as (non)survivors of the Southern belle myth, and also offers glimpses into the sufferings of individuals with alternate sexualities, a topic made tolerable to his readers because of the presumption that New Orleans, Williams's home during most of his active writing years, was a decadent and exotic, if morally bankrupt, city. Readers found it unsurprising, even understandable, that such a city should spawn the stories that Williams spun. Blanche Dubois, of *A Streetcar Named Desire*, as well as Amanda and Laura Wingfield of *The Glass Menagerie*, each suffer as a result of the expectations placed on women. Blanche is the woman left behind at the old family plantation home in Mississippi to care for aged, dying, and destitute relatives. Her desperate attempts to make the traditional, appropriate match lead her to choose a homosexual as her husband. She is left feeling undesirable and rejected – and ultimately responsible for her young husband's suicide. Consequently, her subsequent violations of propriety and decency in her hapless attempts to connect emotionally with another human being lead her to dementia and resulting commitment to a mental facility. Amanda Wingfield is another Williams character who suffers under the delusions imparted to Southern women: one must have numerous gentlemen callers, choose an appropriate husband, and make a comfortable home at all costs. Her misplaced priorities, coupled with her cloying, demanding nature, serve to drive away first her husband, and later her son. Her daughter, Laura, suffers from a physical disability which constitutes her identity. Laura sees herself as physically crippled, an identity which is inadvertently encouraged by Amanda, and her identification with her disability causes her to become emotionally paralyzed as well. Much like Blanche, Laura is unsuccessful in establishing a lasting connection with another person in the real world, so she seeks comfort in fantasy, in the form of her collection of glass figurines.

Other writers who place their work in New Orleans, capturing the allure of the city for readers of regional fiction, include John Kennedy Toole and Walker Percy. John

Kennedy Toole creates, in Ignatius J. Reilly, the personification of New Orleans and its idiosyncrasies. Ignatius considers himself the intellectual superior to his contemporaries, consistently making pronouncements as to the moral virtue – or lack thereof – of the people surrounding him. His unusual interactions with others, often while he is dressed in a pirate costume selling Lucky Dogs in the French Quarter, personify the numerous communities of social misfits who found themselves attracted to New Orleans, a place where individuals could follow their own inclinations largely undisturbed. Walker Percy's *tour de force* similarly makes use of aspects of New Orleans's personality, focusing on a peripheral member of a wealthy and well-established local family. Percy's *The Moviegoer* struggles with the intersections between religion and philosophy and speculates as to the causes and possible sources of relief for emotional ennui. Percy presents a protagonist who is a well-to-do young man living his life vicariously through a stream of B-movies and young women because of his inability to find either an emotional anchor or a lasting passion for anything. He becomes involved with, and ultimately marries, his mentally ill cousin. The works of these writers embody the spirit of New Orleans, in part because they are touched by the "sad ironies of dehumanized commerce and violence . . . as Walker Percy's Moviegoer or John Kennedy Toole's Ignatius Reilly amply prove" (Codrescu 1992: vii).

Similarly, the thematic issues at work in the novels of Saxon and Aswell demonstrate the realities of life in rural central Louisiana. Writers of the Cane River region also recorded the cultural milieu that they observed during the early twentieth century. Lyle Saxon addresses the traditionally Southern issue of race relations in his only novel, *Children of Strangers*, which relates the story of a young woman of mixed racial ancestry. Famie Vidal becomes involved with a white convict and bears his child out of wedlock. Rather than finding herself cast out of proper society, however, she and her child are accepted because she has borne the child of a white man. She goes on to marry, but loses her caste status in the end because she begins consorting with an African-American man, a man whom her Creole relatives consider beneath her. Saxon was also an avid collector of Louisiana folk stories, and despite recent criticism that his collection methods were unreliable, his work contributed to what we know of oral folk narratives from Louisiana. James Aswell, the son of a longstanding Louisiana congressman, set most of his fiction in Natchitoches, focusing much of his attention on the foibles and hypocrisies of what he viewed as a prototypical small Louisiana town. In *There's One in Every Town*, Aswell ostensibly tells the story of a young woman of questionable moral virtue, but close reading reveals that he is in fact criticizing the racial views of the townspeople, who ostracize the girl and her family not merely because of her sexual activity, but because the family is of mixed race, yet attempting to pass for white. Aswell's greatest commercial success, *The Midsummer Fires*, offers a frank look at the sexual dysfunction of a middle-aged painter who returns to Natchitoches hoping to regain both his fortune and his ability to perform sexually. Gael Ring travels to New Orleans in search of his manhood, ultimately finding both his muse and his potency through his interactions with an underaged girl. Residents of Natchitoches were scandalized by much of Aswell's writing, both because of its frankness and because of its overt criticism of Natchitoches and some of its oldest families; at one point *The Midsummer Fires* was burned in the town square by a local Baptist minister. Writers from Cane River, Natchitoches, and central Louisiana such as Chopin, Aswell, and Saxon demonstrated their awareness of, and to some extent their distaste for, the attitudes of the provincial people around whom they lived.

More recently, the fiction of writers from different parts of Louisiana has continued to tell the stories of groups long silenced. John Dufresne and Michael Lee West describe the lives of poor white trash in northern Louisiana, while Rebecca Wells tells of the suffocating influences of Catholicism and alcoholism on upper-middle-class women in central Louisiana. Popular writer James Lee Burke captures the cadences of Cajun speech patterns in his Dave Robichaeux mysteries, while Ernest Gaines describes the struggles of African Americans in southern Louisiana against the tough Cajuns who would take their land – and thus their livelihoods – away. Gaines presents the continuing struggle against prejudice, both externally, from the white community, and internally, as people within the black community accept a hierarchy which bases the value of individuals on the lightness of their skin.

Contemporary New Orleans writers, ranging from Moira Crone, Ellen Gilchrist, and Pulitzer Prize winner Robert Olen Butler to popular sensations Anne Rice and Andre Dubus show the issues plaguing those still living in the Big Easy. Gilchrist tells stories of clueless, privileged women who never miss an appointment at the beauty parlor, but have no idea that their children are drug dealers. She describes honor tarnished in the name of saving face before an outsider. Gilchrist's LaGrande counters a Yankee invasion of her space – the local country club where she is the undisputed tennis champion – with a lie, a lie which is tacitly approved by the men of the old guard. Gilchrist shows that traditional Southern honor exists on a sliding moral scale in the modern era; as long as no one catches LaGrande in the lie, the behavior is acceptable because it puts the upstart Yankee in her place. Robert Olen Butler addresses the development of immigrant communities in southern Louisiana, telling the stories of Asian populations in a strange and somewhat unaccepting land. *A Good Scent from a Strange Mountain* describes the intersection between the ways of the homeland and the American way. The title story of the collection aptly demonstrates the conflict that arises when the younger generation turns to American ways of solving problems while the family patriarch lies dying, dreaming philosophical conversations with the friend of his youth, Hô Chí Minh. Andre Dubus demonstrates the negative effects of Catholic guilt in motivating behavior, while Anne Rice draws upon the mystique of New Orleans to tell stories, not only of vampires, but of the women who suffered under the system of *plaçage*. Their stories attract readers because their settings are simultaneously incredible and real, and the voices of the residents authentic.

An intriguing region in part because of its "peculiar brand of southernness," Louisiana has consistently elicited the creative powers of some of America's best writers. Whether relating stories of the rural or the urban, of the enslaved or the free, of privileged white men or oppressed black women, Louisiana writers give expression to the unique voices which tell the stories of this romantic and mysterious region, voices which continue to resonate for us for generations after their speakers have passed on.

NOTES

1   The term "Creole" has been defined in many ways since its introduction in Louisiana, and should not be confused with the linguistic use of the term, which applies specifically to emergent languages. Spanish colonials used the term Creole to refer to individuals born in the New World who were of European – specifically Spanish – heritage. As time passed, the term came to mean anything or anyone born in Louisiana. The term was applied to produce as in Creole tomatoes, and livestock, as in Creole ponies, and as recently as the late nineteenth century was most closely associated with that which was indigenous to the region. When used to refer to people, the term Creole implied the aforementioned definition: anyone of European (specifically Spanish) lineage born in Louisiana. Today, the term is more often defined as any person who is of French colonial or Spanish colonial ancestry, who may or may not be of two or more races. Even within the state of Louisiana, people have difficulty agreeing on an accurate definition of the term. For example, in New Orleans, until the early twentieth century, the term Creole was used to describe descendants of French aristocracy, while the term Creole of Color was used to describe individuals of a mixed racial heritage that included some African-American or Native American blood. The designation "of color" was gradually dropped, and the term Creole came to mean biracial people living in New Orleans. The term *gens de couleur libre* (free people of color) was used in the Cane River region of central Louisiana from the colonial era until the mid-twentieth century, at which point this group also laid claim to the term

Creole as a descriptor of their ethnicity. In other parts of Louisiana, whites of colonial French descent also continue to self-identify as Creoles. In short, this term has become highly politicized, leading to some confusion as to its "correct" use.

2   In fairness to Robert McAlpin and his legacy, I should mention here that, despite the documentary evidence supporting the claim that McAlpin was indeed the model for Legree, several other legends circulate which attribute the heinous slaveowner's characteristics to other Southerners. For example, a South Carolina resident, James Mathewes Legare, is also mentioned as a possible source. While attending St. Mary's College in Baltimore:

> Legare found time to fabricate an elaborate spoof on his ancestral line in the form of a "genealogy" which he buried in an iron casket in a Charleston garden. When unearthed later, it caused a sufficient stir in the newspapers as far away as Boston as to suggest that the hoax may have influenced Harriet Beecher Stowe when she tagged her low-born villain in Uncle Tom's Cabin (1852) with the aristocratic Carolina surname, pronounced "luh-gree." (Davis 1979)

Other possible culprits from states ranging from Kentucky to Georgia have been suggested as well. A more detailed discussion of the source material for Simon Legree is forthcoming in the article titled "Seeking the Source of Evil: Harriet Beecher Stowe's Simon Legree."

REFERENCES

Ancelet, Barry Jean (1989). "Cajuns and Creoles." In Charles Reagan Wilson and William Ferris (eds.), *Encyclopedia of Southern Culture*. Chapel Hill: University of North Carolina Press.

Bardaglio, Peter W. (1995). *Reconstructing the Household: Families, Sex and the Law in the Nineteenth-Century South*. Chapel Hill: University of North Carolina Press.

Boorstin, Daniel J. (1965). *The Americans: The National Experience*. New York: Vintage/Random House.

Brown, Dorothy H., and Barbara C. Ewell (1992). *Louisiana Women Writers: New Essays and a Comprehensive Bibliography*. Baton Rouge: Louisiana State University Press.

Brown, Sterling (1966). *The Negro in American Fiction*. Washington: n.p. (First publ. 1937.)

Bryan, Violet Harrington (1998). "Shared Traditions and Common Concerns: The African-American Literary Community in Twentieth-Century New Orleans." In Richard S. Kennedy (ed.), *Literary New Orleans in the Modern World*. Baton Rouge: Louisiana State University Press.

Cleman, John (1996). *George Washington Cable*. New York: G. K. Hall.

Codrescu, Andrei (1992). "Introduction," in John Miller and Genevieve Anderson (eds.), *New Orleans Stories: Great Writers on the City*. San Francisco: Chronicle.

Davis, Curtis Carroll (1979). "James Mathewes Legare." *Dictionary of Literary Biography*, vol. 3: *Antebellum Writers in New York and the South*, ed. Joel Myerson, 199–201. Detroit: Gale Group.

Elfenbein, Anna Shannon (1989). *Women on the Color Line: Evolving Stereotypes and the Writings of George Washington Cable, Grace King, Kate Chopin*. Charlottesville: University Press of Virginia.

Foner, Laura (1970). "The Free People of Color in Louisiana and St. Domingue: A Comparative Portrait of Two Three-Caste Slave Societies." *Journal of Social History* 3, 406–30.

Gayarré, Charles (1885). *History of Louisiana*, 3rd edn. New Orleans: Armand Hawkins.

Gray, Richard (1985). *Writing the South: Ideas of an American Region*. Baton Rouge: Louisiana State University Press.

Hurston, Zora Neale (1990). *Mules and Men*. New York: Perennial. (First publ. 1935.)

Johnson, Jerah (1989). "French." In Charles Reagan Wilson and William Ferris (eds.), *Encyclopedia of Southern Culture*. Chapel Hill: University of North Carolina Press.

Kennedy, Richard S., ed. (1989). *Literary New Orleans in the Modern World*. Baton Rouge: Louisiana State University Press.

King, Grace (1904). *New Orleans: The Place and the People*. New York: Macmillan.

Ladd, Barbara (1996). *Nationalism and the Color Line in George W. Cable, Mark Twain, and William Faulkner*. Baton Rouge: Louisiana State University Press.

Mell, Milfred (1938). "Poor Whites of the South." *Social Forces* (Dec.), 153–67.

Menke, Pamela Glenn (2001). "'Black Cat Bone and Snake Wisdom': New Orleanian Hoodoo, Haitian Voodoo, and Rereading Hurston's *Their Eyes Were Watching God*." In Suzanne Disheroon-Green and Lisa Abney (eds.), *Songs of the New South: Writing Contemporary Louisiana*. Westport: Greenwood.

Mills, Gary B. (1977). *The Forgotten People: Cane River's Creoles of Color*. Baton Rouge: Louisiana State University Press.

Moore, Rayburn S. (1985). "Antebellum Poetry." In Louis D. Rubin, Jr. (ed.), *The History of Southern Literature*, 118–26. Baton Rouge: Louisiana State University Press.

Rubin, Louis D., Jr., gen. ed. (1985). *The History of Southern Literature*. Baton Rouge: Louisiana State University Press.

Saxon, Lyle (1989). *Children of Strangers*. Gretna, LA: Pelican. (First publ. 1937.)

Seidel, Kathryn Lee (1985). *The Southern Belle in the American Novel*. Tampa: University of South Florida Press.

Shortridge, James R. (1989). "Religious Regions." In Charles Reagan Wilson and William Ferris (eds.), *Encyclopedia of Southern Culture*. Chapel Hill: University of North Carolina Press.

Sterkx, H. E. (1972). *The Free Negro in Ante-Bellum Louisiana*. Rutherford: Fairleigh Dickinson University Press.

Wall, Bennett H. (1997). *Louisiana: A History*. Wheeling, Ill.: Harlan Davidson.

Westling, Louise (1985). *Sacred Groves and Ravaged Gardens: The Fiction of Eudora Welty, Carson McCullers, and Flannery O'Connor*. Athens, Ga: University of Georgia Press.

Wilds, John (1996). *Louisiana Yesterday and Today*. Baton Rouge: Louisiana State University Press.

Zanger, Jules (1966). "The tragic Octoroon in Pre-Civil War Fiction." *American Quarterly* 18, 63.

19

The Sagebrush School Revived

Lawrence I. Berkove

If the Sagebrush School had yielded no other result than Mark Twain, it would be worth investigation on that account. This recently rediscovered movement, however, deserves study for its own merits as well. The Sagebrush School was named after the hardy bushes that thrive in the high and arid country east of the Sierra Nevada mountains, and its authors were principally Nevadans, especially those from the Comstock Lode, the extraordinarily rich vein of mixed silver and gold ores in western Nevada.[1] The jocular name refers to a group of loosely connected but impressively talented authors who worthily recorded a unique facet of the epic conquest of the West in the late nineteenth century. Although they were literally frontiersmen, the sophistication they acquired autodidactically should not be underestimated: they read Shakespeare, Milton, Homer, and Dante, as well as the classics of English and European literature, and took an active interest in the scientific and political affairs of their time. They were Renaissance men: vigorous, multitalented, involved and active in their communities, surprisingly productive, and artistically significant in the approximately 50 years of their existence. The Sagebrush School was a broad-based movement that included fiction, humor, essays, poetry, drama, journalism, memoirs, and history among its genres. It especially excelled in humor; and it raised the literary hoax to the level of high art. No overview of Western literature, indeed of American literature, can be complete that does not take it into account, for it left a legacy that is truly distinguished.

The Character of Sagebrush Literature

Drawn to Nevada by the discoveries and mining, beginning around 1859, of extraordinarily rich deposits of silver and gold, most members of the Sagebrush School were strong and independent personalities, and versatile authors. They were responsible for some of the most talented writing of nineteenth-century Western literature.

Widely known and respected in its own time but lost and neglected for a century, the Sagebrush movement has been largely overlooked until recently because most of its writers were transient residents of Nevada, and the majority of their writings were never collected. Almost all of the writers associated with the movement were journalists who worked on newspapers in the communities that sprung up near the sites of mines that supported them for only a few decades. When the mines were no longer profitable, they were closed and the population of the communities moved on. As a result, the short lifespans of these communities, and consequently, of their newspapers, were not conducive to the establishment of a continuous culture which preserved the records or the literary traditions of its writers. The writers dispersed to other parts of the country, and the newspapers and magazines in which they published were either lost or relegated in broken runs to a few scattered archives.

As these remnants have been found and connected, however, it has become apparent that the Sagebrush movement was far more than an isolated and inconsequential regional phenomenon of unsophisticated local talent. Quite to the contrary, all of the writers associated with it came from other, more developed, parts of the country, attracted to the Nevada Territory by the high wages and opportunities that brought not only prospectors but also outstanding entrepreneurs, engineers, financiers, lawyers, and theatrical personalities. By the same token, the population of the Nevada Territory was cosmopolitan as well as vigorous, coming from all over the world: British, Irish, Cornish, German, French, Jewish, Chinese, Mexican, Chilean, whites and African Americans from all parts of the United States, as well as Native Americans from Nevada. This unusual mix of immigrant ethnic backgrounds had in common the self-selected quality of risk-taking. It was the last wave of frontiersmen and is distinguished from the earlier waves of hunters, farmers, and lumbermen by its members being more technologically inclined and more oriented toward profit rather than settlement. Many of them were skilled miners or tradesmen, and the newspapers and journalists serving them reflected their sophistication and daring. The mining communities wanted more than just the necessaries of life. They craved culture. Most communities of any size built "opera houses"; imported first-rate acting troupes, singers, and lecturers; and supported several newspapers. The talented journalists on those newspapers, over and above their regular duties, gave rein to their creative impulses and contributed material of literary merit to the feature columns of their newspapers.

Although much of the subject matter of Sagebrush literature is about the West, and Western vernacular often appears in it, these are not characterizing features, for they were used in other parts of the West as well. Most of the Sagebrush writers prided themselves on their cosmopolitanism and their ability at writing formal English, and some of the best Sagebrush literature deals very slightly, or even not at all, with Western situations or personalities. What does distinguish the movement is its blend of such intangible qualities as manliness, forthrightness, wit, and sensitivity to moral and psychological subtleties. Not all its writers, of course, have all these qualities, nor in the same proportion, but there is enough of an overlapping to establish a mutual relationship.

The Sagebrush ideal of manliness had more to do with honor than with *machismo* or being law-abiding. Because law and justice were so tenuous in the Comstock region, and so inconsistently maintained, the Sagebrush writers were often skeptical of both the legal system and institutionalized religion, and did not place much reliance on them. But they did expect a lot from individual men and, as a consequence, they supported fair play and equity more than legality. They inclined to the position that if a man had bedrock principles that were admirable and consistently upheld, he would be "justified" in upholding his rights, even if it meant going against the system.

Among the component parts of manliness, the Sagebrush writers included sensitivity. They were psychologically acute in their depiction, analysis, and appreciation of character; they valued intellect, and especially admired wit, even when it was mischievous. While they recognized the need, sometimes, for men to respond to violence with violence, they shunned bullying, brutality, and meanness. The writers themselves typically displayed, unashamedly, aesthetic proclivities. While they were scornful of hypocrisy and artificial elegance, they were sympathetic toward what they perceived as sincere expressions of beauty, passion, and sentiment, and most of their poetry – and there was a good deal of poetic activity in the movement – was frankly sentimental. There was no corresponding Sagebrush standard for women. Although its writers, like most elsewhere in the country at that time, were inclined toward the ideal of "feminine" women, Sagebrush writers tended to be more egalitarian and liberal, and less committed to a double standard.

The best Sagebrush writers were strongly moral. This may seem surprising in a region notorious for its lawlessness, corruption, and tolerance of gambling, drinking, and prostitution, and Sagebrush authors were not always in full agreement with each other. Nevertheless, if they did not have much regard for Sunday-school standards of public decorum, they did share a high regard for such personal virtues in individuals as integrity, resourcefulness, courage, and loyalty.

The Hoax

The most interesting manifestation of this emphasis on morality is the way it is demonstrated in the most distinctive and accomplished Sagebrush contribution to literature: the hoax. With so much wealth at stake in the mines, mine-owners and financiers often bought off – or intimidated – the agents of the justice system: police, judges, and juries. At voting time, wealthy owners and investors literally paid cash for votes, and thus earned for Nevada the sobriquet of "the rotten borough." Journalists were bribed to hype mining properties, and mining company boards of directors often lied to stockholders about the value of properties and of the ore that was mined, assessed stockholders for imaginary projects, and manipulated the stock market.

Swindles and hoaxes were therefore an everyday occurrence on the Comstock. *Caveat emptor* might have been the unofficial standard in the area, and if a man was foolish enough to allow himself to be taken in, he had little hope of having his wrongs redressed by the courts. It was perhaps inevitable that Sagebrush writers would describe hoaxes in their writings, and also incorporate them into their styles. With real-life hoaxes occurring so frequently, the reading population of Nevada recognized literary hoaxes as representing familiar aspects of life, and the more ingenious, audacious, or subtle they were, the more they resembled reality.

The literary hoax deliberately misrepresents something at odds with fact – because it is untrue, impossible, or highly improbable – with the use of details intended to make it seem plausible. It also implicates the reader, who falls victim to the deceit by not reading carefully and thoughtfully. The hoax occupies the middle ground between a lie and a tall tale. Unlike the tall tale, which entertains by its obvious exaggeration, the literary hoax attempts to outwit its audience; but, unlike a real hoax, it is not quite a lie because it contains subtle clues that can be found, and if found, expose it. Failure to detect a hoax results in a misreading of a text. Conversely, the discovery of the nature, range, and depth of a literary hoax can be an effective learning experience. Unlike the real-life hoax, moreover, the literary hoax does no harm. It is intended to delight and instruct. At worst, it may embarrass the gullible and naïve, but it also may inoculate them with skepticism by making them more alert to dangerous hoaxes, and thus more likely to detect them.

The general qualities of Sagebrush literature are best explained by reference to the specific works of individual authors. Mark Twain, especially in *Roughing It*, is an excellent exemplar of Sagebrush ideals and techniques, but he is treated separately in this volume and discussions of him elsewhere are abundant. It is appropriate, therefore, to examine the works of the more typical members of the School, or other authors influenced by it. These include Dan De Quille, Samuel Post Davis, Joseph Thompson Goodman, Rollin Mallory Daggett, Charles Carroll Goodwin, James W. E. Townsend, Alfred Doten, James Gally, Fred H. Hart, Henry Rust Mighels, and Arthur McEwen. Associated with the Sagebrushers, though not precisely one of them, is Ambrose Bierce.

Sagebrush Journalists

The most evident aspect of Sagebrush literature is journalism. Most newspapers were dependent upon the mine-owners and local governments for business and patronage, and took the side of the strong against the weak. Only a few editors, notably Henry Rust Mighels and Samuel Post Davis of Carson City, and Joseph Thompson Goodman of Virginia City, were independent enough to write hard-hitting editorials attacking the abuses and corruption that abounded in the area. Inasmuch as journalists were expected to be manly and personally stand behind what they wrote, and irate targets of their attacks occasionally sought satisfaction from writers with fists or guns,

Sagebrush journalism could be a character-building – or reputation-breaking – experience. Mark Twain's sketch, "Journalism in Tennessee" (1869), and Joe Goodman's later "The *Trumpet* Comes to Pickeye!" are both reflections of Comstock journalism in which there is less exaggeration in the vigorous humor than most readers might guess.[2]

The most eminent Sagebrush journalist is Joe (Joseph Thompson) Goodman. Best known for being the editor and publisher of the *Virginia City Territorial Enterprise*, and the man responsible for hiring Twain and starting him on his writing career, he was a friend and advisor to Mark Twain for the rest of Twain's life. But from his achievements during the rest of his life, as well as those arising from his editorial responsibilities, it is obvious that Goodman was not only multitalented, but also distinguished in those talents. Once he became an owner of the newspaper in 1861, Goodman set its tone and established its editorial policy, which was to be accurate, independent, and fearless. Among his early accomplishments, for example, was the exposure of the corruption of the entire bench of the Nevada Territory Supreme Court, which forced the resignation of all its justices. In 1872, Goodman denounced the proposal of a company to mine diamonds in Arizona as a swindle, and stood fast against blustering threats of lawsuits until an independent geologist investigated the site and found it to be barren of diamonds except some planted imported ones. An even more notable editorial achievement was his opposition to the candidacy of William Sharon for US senator. Sharon was one of the wealthiest and most powerful and ruthless financiers on the Comstock and had his heart set on being elected. A scorching editorial Goodman wrote denounced Sharon with brutal frankness and famously destroyed his hope of winning the 1872 election (Berkove 1999e).

Naturally, such a bold attitude toward controversy was inevitably challenged by opponents, and Comstock mores dictated that a journalist who wished to be respected had to be prepared to personally defend what he wrote. Goodman on more than one occasion settled challenges with fists. The most revealing incident that demonstrated his character, however, arose over an article the *Enterprise* published in 1863 that insulted editor Tom Fitch of the *Virginia Daily Union*. Fitch impetuously challenged Goodman to a duel. Although Goodman had not written the article, he took responsibility for it as editor and accepted the challenge. At the duel site, Goodman, a crack shot, learned that Fitch was inept with pistols, so he determined to only wound Fitch. At the first exchange, Fitch missed Goodman but Goodman felled Fitch with a shot to the knee. Instantly, Goodman ran over to Fitch, apologized to him, explained what had happened, and insisted on personally caring for Fitch until he recovered. Fitch, grateful for having had his life spared, thenceforth became Goodman's friend.

Goodman thus passed the test of ability as well as honor and was not challenged again, but the incident probably had an unexpected consequence in the career of Mark Twain, who looked up to Goodman. Not long after the Fitch duel, the Nevada legislature outlawed dueling. When Goodman later left town for a few days, he appointed Twain to take charge of the paper in his absence. Twain soon got involved in an acrimonious dispute in print with another editor that rapidly escalated to the

Figure 19.1 Photograph of Joseph Thompson Goodman (1838–1917).

point that Twain foolishly challenged the editor to a duel. Some friends of Twain notified him that the authorities were about to arrest him for flouting the law, so Twain immediately fled to California. Goodman kept Twain on the payroll as the paper's California correspondent, but the move was a fateful one for Twain as it launched him on the next phase of his career.

Goodman served the *Enterprise* not only as editor but as a theater critic, a role in which he displayed enlightened aesthetic standards as well as his characteristic independence and feistiness. One of his most important stands, which was far ahead of its time, was a spirited and serious defense in 1864 of Adah Isaacs Menken's simulation of nudity in the play *Mazeppa*. Although she was clothed in tights, most reviewers found the illusion of nudity scandalous and were highly critical of her. Goodman, very much in the minority, strongly praised her artistry and compared her act to "painting and sculpture, and the other arts which have developed their most beautiful and divine conceptions in ideal likenesses of the human form" (quoted in Fatout 1964: 163–4; Berkove 1997: 12–13). This was not a facetious position taken for the love of controversy, but a thoughtful one that few, if any, reviewers in any other part of the country would have taken. Goodman was a highly ethical individual, and even in his critical standards he would not allow prudery to dictate to him.

In addition to his principled editorials and theater reviews, Goodman deserves a reputation for being an outstanding writer of journalism. In 1870, while on an extended visit to Europe, Goodman sent back to the *Enterprise* a series of nine long but pithy travel letters from France and England. Published as coming from "an irregular correspondent," the letters are a fascinating and perceptive account, written in a virile but sensitive style, of the encounter of an editor from America's Old West with European culture and society. The series invites comparison to Twain's *Innocents Abroad* (1869), which Goodman had obviously read, and to the letters that Henry James wrote from Italy in 1869. Goodman studied Europe carefully and he deeply appreciated it, but ultimately remained proudly and unawedly American.

When Goodman left the Comstock in 1875, one of his subsequent activities was to found and edit a literary journal, the *San Franciscan*, in 1884. Although Goodman sold it after six months, he solicited manuscripts from many of his friends, and the journal while he edited it became a valuable anthology of Californian and Comstock writers. He also developed an interest in the mysterious Mayan hieroglyphics which had been recently discovered. From his home in California, Goodman devoted several years to studying this material, which baffled the best Meso-American archaeologists in the world. He discovered how to decipher the glyphs, and published his results in 1897. His approach was the key that unlocked otherwise inaccessible secrets about Mayan culture, and his work is still used by archeologists (Berkove 1999e).

In 1908 and 1909, Goodman contributed a number of Comstock memoirs to a series entitled "By-the-Bye" that the trade weekly *Nevada Mining News* published. Despite the relative obscurity of the newspaper, the series is the most extensive, accurately detailed, and revealing account of the Comstock that has ever come to light. Goodman's contributions were outstanding for accuracy and literary ability in that remarkable series, whose contributors were the best surviving Comstock writers. Just recently rediscovered and republished after a century as *The Devil's in the Details* (Berkove, ed., 2003), the series by itself would justify the importance of Comstock literature, and is a major source of information about a unique episode in American history.

Alfred Doten is another notable Sagebrush author. He is best known not for his lifetime of journalism but for his diaries and several historical essays he wrote toward the end of his career. Like other Comstock newsmen, Doten worked for a variety of newspapers until he owned and edited his own, the *Gold Hill News*. His journalism was competent but not otherwise remarkable; however, once the Comstock began to decline, after 1880, Doten utilized his encyclopedic knowledge of the region in writing several memoirs, the most important of which is "Early journalism in Nevada" (1899), which contains anecdotal information about his colleagues, including Mark Twain, not otherwise available.

Doten came to public attention in 1973, when his recently discovered journals were published in a three-volume edition by the Western scholar Walter Van Tilburg Clark. In their factual way, they are eye-opening revelations of the full play of human nature that occurred on the Comstock, and are bound to be surprising to anyone who conceives that life in the full can only be experienced in a metropolitan center of high culture. Niel Herbert, in Willa Cather's *A Lost Lady* (1923), enjoyed reading Ovid's *Heroides* because it made him feel that he "was eavesdropping upon the past, being let into the great world that had plunged and glittered and sumptuously sinned long before little Western towns were dreamed of" (Cather 1972: 81–2). Niel never realized that the same things he read about in the classics were happening all the time right in front of his eyes (Berkove 1991b). Just as "By-the-Bye" takes us behind the scenes and below the surface of the plunging, glittering, and sumptuously sinning in the little Western towns of the Comstock, Doten's journals afford us valuable glimpses of details too mundane or intimate for newspapers but nevertheless useful for the insights they may lead to. Begun in 1849, when he boarded ship in Plymouth, Massachusetts, for California, and added to continuously until the last night of his life in 1903, the journals establish Doten as the Pepys of the Comstock. He probably never suspected that his journaling, a hobby rather than a project intended for public consumption, would have significance for anyone else but himself. But precisely because the journals are unedited records of the quotidian events of the mining communities of California from 1849 to 1863, when Doten moved to Nevada; of the Comstock from 1863 to 1903; and of the private as well as public doings of its personalities – including himself – during all those years, they immediately became an indispensable source of information for historians and biographers (Berkove 1999c).

Little of the journalism of Henry Mighels has been collected, and his one book, *Sage Brush Leaves* (1879), consisting of literary essays composed in his last year of life, is not typical of his newspaper style. Compared in his lifetime to Ambrose Bierce, and like him a wounded veteran of the Civil War, he was known for his integrity, his scorn of imposture and deceit, and for his fierce attacks on those he considered malefactors. He refused to pander to either the classes or the masses, but his newspaper, the *Carson Appeal*, was read because his forthright reporting commanded respect. When Mighels died of cancer at 49, Sam Davis was hired to replace him, and carried on his tradition of fearlessness and integrity. Detractors began to disparage Mighels almost immediately after his death, upon which Davis promptly established his credentials by announcing his readiness to defend Mighels *in any way* against his detractors. This was correctly understood to mean with fists or guns. His challenge was not taken up.

Davis subsequently went on to make his own mark in Nevada. Convinced – correctly – that US Senator and Comstock magnate James Fair was directly implicated in at least one murder, Davis was the only editor who dared to accuse this most unscrupulous of the Comstock "Silver Kings." In 1892, Davis went to jail for refusing to name a source, and in 1895 he again openly used a secret source to criticize an investigation of the Carson City Mint. Davis was also active in politics and was elected in 1902 as state controller. In that position he additionally served as *ex officio* state insurance commissioner – a post that most people would have regarded as a safe sinecure: but Davis carried his ideals with him. In 1905 he revoked the license of a New York insurance company for misusing its funds for political purposes and for attempting to bribe him, forcing the president of the company to resign and the company to restore the funds. In 1906, when an earthquake devastated San Francisco, many insurance companies attempted to reduce their losses by pressuring policy-holders to settle for less than the sums to which they were entitled. Davis, without consulting anybody, unilaterally announced that any insurance company which did not pay one hundred cents on the dollar in San Francisco would lose its license to do business in Nevada. When other states began to follow Davis's lead, the insurance companies backed down and paid claims in full (Berkove 1999f).

Before he arrived on the Comstock, Rollin Mallory Daggett distinguished himself in Western journalism by being one of the founders of the *Golden Era*, an outstanding San Francisco literary periodical that published most of the best authors of Western literature. He later served as an editor of the *Enterprise* under Goodman and also for a time after Goodman sold it in 1875. He was known for his pugnacious style, for he loved a fight, and also for his wit (Berkove, 1999b).

Charles Carroll Goodwin began his Comstock career as a judge, but took over the editorship of the *Enterprise* after 1875 when Daggett was away. In 1885 he became owner and publisher of the *Salt Lake City Tribune*, and made it a respected and forceful newspaper. With characteristic Comstock audacity, Goodwin took up several journalistic crusades: free silver,[3] opposition to the influence of the Mormon church, and support for the wealthy entrepreneurs of the West. The first cause was a common one for Comstockers, because Nevada was mainly a silver-mining state, but Goodwin's editorial stance on the subject was ferociously one-sided. The second cause was remarkable for a major paper in Utah, but Goodwin was convinced of its justness. As for the third, it constitutes the majority of his book of memoir sketches, *As I Remember Them* (1913). Today his defense of men whom history tends to regard as robber barons seems benighted, but his stands stemmed from sincere convictions, were based for the most part on personal experiences, and arose from Comstock mores that emphasized loyalty to friends (Berkove 1999d).

Arthur McEwen is better known in American journalism for being an influential editor of the *San Francisco Examiner* and the *New York Journal*, and the chief editor of Philadelphia's *North American* (Doten 1973a: 2238) but he got his start on the

Comstock and absorbed some of its independence and fearlessness. He became intellectually committed to political reform, support of labor, and opposition to unregulated capitalism, and while in San Francisco in 1894 and 1895 found it desirable to push his agenda by publishing his own newspaper, *Arthur McEwen's Letter*. The stridency of his arguments angered Ambrose Bierce, a journalistic lion on the *San Francisco Examiner* with opinions of his own, and the two openly traded insults to the credit of neither and the dismay of many of their common friends.

Although this brief scan of Sagebrush journalism testifies to its colorful and pungent quality, the main case for the Sagebrush School must ride on the literature its authors produced. This record, although only recently uncovered and relatively undeveloped, is exciting and impressive in its prospect. Often infused with humor, it embraces fiction, poetry, drama, and memoirs and history.

Sagebrush Humorists

The Comstock loved humor, particularly the witty kind. It received warmly Fred H. Hart's *The Sazerac Lying Club: A Nevada Book* (1878), compiled from items he had earlier published as editor of the Nevada newspaper, the *Austin Reveille*. It consists mostly of tall tales and "stretchers," and the introduction openly announces its character: "This purports to be a book on lies and lying, but it does not treat of the lies of politicians, stock-brokers, newspaper men, authors, and others, who lie for money; neither does it touch on the untruths of scandal, mischief, or malice, but only on those lies which amuse, instruct and elevate, without harm." The book was popular, quickly going to a fifth edition.

Particularly prized were the delightfully outrageous lies of James William Ellery Townsend, the original of Bret Harte's "Truthful James" (but better known as "Lying Jim"), who uttered them spontaneously or as he set type. Nevada newspapers passed them around as quickly as they came out. For example, he once made light of the severity of a heatwave by claiming that when he was a correspondent for the *New York World* in Madrid (a total fabrication), "it was so warm there that I had to carry my mouth full of ice to keep my teeth from sweating." Another time, while serving as a witness at a trial, he gave testimony as to the date that mining began at a certain site. Still under oath, he later asked to correct his testimony. He got the date right, he said, but "I used the wrong word when I said 'mining.' I meant to say 'quarrying.' They were lifting the gold out in blocks, sir." The courtroom exploded in laughter and Townsend was excused as a witness.[4] Only a fraction of Townsend's writing (and lies) has been collected (Dwyer and Lingenfelter 1984), but even more incredible than the lies he told is a real-life hoax in which he participated. Some swindlers went to Europe to sell potential investors shares in what they knew to be a worthless mining property. To gain credibility they hired Townsend to publish a weekly newspaper from a deserted mining town near the property. Townsend set up a hand press and produced the paper single-handedly. For content, he made up fictitious figures for the non-existent's mine's production, conjured up local businesses that placed ads in the paper, and peopled the town with imaginary citizens who engaged in activities that never happened and were even sometimes caught in fanciful scandals. For well over a year, Townsend regularly sent copies of the paper to his conspirators in Europe. Eventually the scam was discovered and the conspirators were brought to trial in California. Amazingly, Townsend was not convicted, but his exposure did not diminish in any way the Comstock's appreciation of his creative wit. One can only conjecture what American literature lost when Townsend did not live to write his autobiography, whose title he proposed to be *Truth, with Variations*.

Sagebrush Writers of Fiction

Without a doubt, the most beloved Sagebrush author, and the most broadly talented, intrinsically important, and generally respected after Mark Twain, is William Wright, better known by his pen name of Dan De Quille. In his lifetime, De Quille had both a national and an international reputation, and he has remained, with Sam Davis, one of only two Comstock authors in addition to Mark Twain whose work has been frequently reprinted. Indeed, the comparison to Twain is not gratuitous, for Twain and De Quille were not only colleagues together on the *Enterprise*, but also close friends and room-mates (Berkove 1999a). It has been established that they influenced each other significantly, and what appear to be borrowings from various of De Quille's writings can be seen in such of Twain's books as *Roughing It, Life on the Mississippi*, and *Huckleberry Finn*.[5]

None of the major Western authors – Twain, Bret Harte, Ambrose Bierce – knew the West as extensively and deeply as De Quille. He left his home in Iowa in 1857 for California, moved to the Comstock in 1860, and remained there until shortly before his death in 1898. De Quille started off as a prospector, but had more success with placing his writings in newspapers and magazines than with finding profitable ore. In 1861 he joined the *Enterprise* as a full-time reporter, and remained intermittently associated with it until it suspended publication in 1893. Although De Quille enjoyed the reputation of being the most competent and trustworthy mining journalist on the Comstock, he was most famous even in his early years for the humorous writings he composed in his spare time. For most of his life, De Quille apparently maintained two careers: one as a professional journalist with specific duties, and the other as a freelance creative writer. De Quille was extremely prolific. Although his journalism remains mostly ungathered and unstudied, a good deal of his fiction has now been collected and reprinted.

While still a prospector, De Quille earned a reputation for being both interesting and humorous from the pieces he contributed to various West Coast periodicals – especially the *Golden Era*, which published few issues between 1860 and 1865 that did not include some item, generally humorous, by De Quille. Among the most ambitious was a series of travel letters called "Washoe Rambles," based on an 1861 prospecting trip he took with several companions in western Nevada, then known generally as "Washoe," and eastern California. Most of the series was readably descriptive, but for entertainment value De Quille slyly slipped in humorous fabrications without giving the reader any indication, thus creating a seamless work of fact and fancy. It has been suggested that the "Washoe Rambles" series quite possibly served Twain as one of his models for *Roughing It* (De Quille 1963: 11).

The humorous hoaxes De Quille called "quaints" are certainly the best-known and most beloved of his works, and are central to an appreciation of the genre of the Comstock hoax, of which he was a master. Many of these hoaxes, although written with tongue in cheek, are scientific in nature, and are capable of deceiving even modern readers. His "Solar Armor" (1874) quaint, for example, was originally printed as a straightforward news story about an invention, something like a diving suit with a portable air-conditioner, that would enable its wearer to survive in the hottest environment. Its inventor supposedly tested it out by attempting to cross Death Valley in summer. A rescue party found him dead in the desert several days later. He had apparently been unable to turn off his refrigeration unit and was frozen stiff, an icicle hanging from his nose!

The hoax is told so artfully that most readers overlook the one detail that gives it away: the extravagant last item of a body (with an icicle) remaining frozen after several days in Death Valley in the summertime. The story spread around the country – even the *Scientific American* noted it – and also to England, where an editor of the London *Daily Telegraph* expressed a desire for more information. De Quille, learning of this wish from a Comstock subscriber to the *Telegraph*, promptly wrote a sequel, supplying more "details" (De Quille 1990a: 14–19). This is an example of the hoax *par excellence*: an account that challenges or exceeds credulity being plausibly related as fact, but with a tell-tale hint that can give it away to an alert reader. Sometimes an in-group is alert to the hoax. In "the Great Land-Slide Case" episode of chapter 34 in Twain's *Roughing It*, everyone in the Comstock court room knew what was happening except the target, General Buncombe. In the "Solar Armor" instance, only exceptionally wary readers would have detected the first hoax, but the whole Comstock community was probably in on the second stage.

Throughout his career, De Quille wrote additional quaints in the same manner: hoaxes about eyeless fish that lived in hot water in the depths of mines and that died of exposure when transferred to cool surface water; about mountain alligators; and about petrified birds that sang in petrified forests. His hoax about "A Silver Man" (1865) was clearly inspired by Twain's 1862 hoax "The Petrified Man," and used the same subject – the impossibility of petrifying flesh – to fool the same people who fell for the earlier one (De Quille 1990a: 3–8). Both hoaxes were successful, but De Quille's is the more polished and entertaining. He deserves the record for the longest-running hoax, his famous quaint about "the traveling stones of Pahranagat," rocks which were mutually attracted to travel to each other. The first stage of this hoax was published in 1865 or 1866, the second – an open admission of the hoax – in 1879, and the third, a revitalization of the hoax, in 1892 (De Quille 1990a: 9–13).

De Quille's fictional range is far wider than these quaints, and even his later humorous stories are seldom only humorous. He wrote almost every conceivable kind of story, from adventure to ghost to parable, and demonstrated psychological acuity and ethical sensitivity in many of them. "A Dietetic Don Quixote" (1885) skillfully and sympathetically details the process by which a man subordinates his rational faculty to an irrational end in starving himself to death for health reasons (De Quille 1990a: 93–9). "The Fighting Horse of the Stanislaus" (1874) is a daring and seemingly humorous retelling of a true story in a way that subtly criticizes the brutality of a powerful and living politician who used animals to fight each other (De Quille 1990a: 163–9). "Lorenzo Dow's Miracle" (1893) is a delightfully written tale of how the great preacher cannily recognized and brilliantly ended an adulterous affair (De Quille 1990a: 123–8). "The Eagles' Nest" (1891), one of De Quille's most powerful and affecting tales, subtly criticizes how men foolishly risk their lives for money (De Quille 1990a: 209–22).

The antimaterialistic theme of this last story makes De Quille a rarity in the mining West. The theme recurs throughout his oeuvre, especially in two of his most important works, the novellas *The Gnomes of the Dead Rivers* (1880; 1990) and *Dives and Lazarus* (1988). (The later dates reflect posthumous publication.) *Gnomes* is a beautiful and sophisticated parable of how the desire for wealth perverts even good intentions. *Dives and Lazarus* is the longest and most imaginative work of fiction De Quille ever wrote, one of a small number of such works by Americans that address the free silver controversy of the 1890s, and a remarkable book for the end of the nineteenth century. Based on Dante's *Divine Comedy* and the New Testament, and influenced by a number of famous works of classical and familiar literature and legend, De Quille's book narrates the fascinating adventures of the souls of two recently deceased men who are lost in the underworld on their way to their ultimate (and separate) destinations. One is Lazarus, a poor but honest Comstock miner, and the other is Magnificus Auriferous Dives, a wealthy US senator who voted for the gold standard. Reading the book in conjunction with Mark Twain's "The Man That Corrupted Hadleyburg" (1898) and *Extract from Captain Stormfield's Visit to Heaven* (1900) will reveal surprising similarities as well as differences in the final beliefs of the two Comstock friends, and expand the reader's appreciation of the range of American literature at the end of the century.

Sam Davis is second only to De Quille in his literary range and ability outside journalism. The possessor of a bold and exuberant sense of humor, he made some influential friends in Californian literary circles when he emigrated there from the East in 1872, but found his spiritual home on moving to the Comstock in 1875. He took root immediately, and began publishing works of humor, fiction, and poetry in various Western newspapers and magazines. In 1886, encouraged by Ambrose Bierce, he published some of them in a collection inadequately titled *Short Stories*. Their quality is attested to by the fact that some of the pieces have been frequently reprinted. "The Typographical Howitzer" (1880), for example, is a choice item of humor that purports to be an account of what happened when Twain and De Quille, driving a wagon filled with forms of set type, were surrounded by hostile Indians. Having, by chance, a small cannon and some gunpowder with them but no shells, they loaded the type into the cannon and fired it. Each load of type is a work of some contemporary author, including Twain, and thus the devastation that is caused appears to be a direct commentary on the quality of the writing (Davis 1886: 127–31). The satire is witty but good-humored. Dan De Quille is complimented as the focus of "A Sagebrush Chief," which relates how he outhoaxes some fellow journalists (Davis 1886: 100–9). The poem "Binley and '46" is an audacious hoax, a convincing imitation of Bret Harte's style, to which Davis signed Harte's name (Davis 1886: 187–9). It circulated around the country – most notably in *Frank Leslie's Illustrated Magazine*, which gave it a full-page publication and an illustration (2 May 1874) – before Davis finally confessed that it was a "literary forgery."

Other tales in the book reveal Davis to have depth as well as artistry. "The Reporter's Revenge" (1884) is a critical analysis of a religious hypocrite, but its main value might be in its speculation of what happens in the mind of a man being hanged in the instant before his death (Davis 1886: 91–9). Similarities to the tale – which Bierce almost certainly read – in Ambrose Bierce's most famous story, "An Occurrence at Owl Creek Bridge" (1890), qualify it as a probable source (Berkove 2002: ch. 6). "A Christmas Carol," (first published in the *Argonaut*, c.1875) later better known as "The First Piano in Camp," incorporates a hoax, but it is one that Davis uses to deftly raise the theological question of whether it is better to have faith and be subject to deceit, or to be without feeling but protected against trickery (Davis 1886: 3–9).

Davis continued to write fiction for the rest of his life. Although most of it is presently uncollected, individual works reflect a growing interest in both moral and theological issues – which is not surprising inasmuch as he was the son of an Episcopal priest. "My Friend the Editor" (Davis 1889) is a fictional retelling of Jim Townsend's scam of publishing a phony newspaper, and a balanced analysis of the protagonist as both good and bad. "The Loco Weed" (Davis 1899) exhibits naturalistic elements in its use of a hallucinogenic weed to reveal men and animals equal before nature's indifference. "The Mystery of the Savage Sump" (1901?), based in part on De Quille's hoax of the eyeless fish that lived in hot water, and in part on Davis's knowledge of the crimes of Senator James Fair, studies the terrible effect that greed can have on a ruthless individual, and is probably Davis's most subtle but powerful work of social criticism. In a presently unpublished story, "The Conversion of Champagne Lil," Davis probes the theological issue of individual salvation by faith or works. Stories as good as these would be ornaments in the oeuvres of better-known authors. Davis also participated in the "By-the-Bye" series of the *Nevada Mining News* and contributed many of its most moving, witty, and gripping columns.

De Quille and Davis are the major Sagebrush authors of fiction, but other Comstock writers contributed memorably to this genre. Joe Goodman's "The *Trumpet* Comes to Pickeye!" has already been mentioned as a minor classic. He also wrote other, presently uncollected stories, which were published in the *Argonaut* of 1881. Rollin

Daggett published *Braxton's Bar* (1882), a novel about California gold-mining, and several short stories in the 1890s. One of them, "My French Friend," appeared in the *Overland Monthly* (1895) and is quite possibly a precursor of Willa Cather's 1905 "Paul's Case." C. C. Goodwin's best work of fiction is "Sister Celeste"(1884), a delicate and moving story about a nun's response to a miner who fell in love with her. Goodwin later incorporated it into his novel about Comstock miners, *The Comstock Club* (1891). Arthur McEwen ventured into fiction with stories published in the *Argonaut*, the *San Franciscan*, and the *San Francisco Examiner*. James W. Gally began his writing career in Nevada as a regular contributor to the *Enterprise*. In 1875 he moved to California and became more prolific, publishing stories and essays in a variety of West Coast periodicals. His best-known works are the story "Big Jack Small" (1875) and the novel *Sand* (1879). Both enlarge on facets of the manliness that was associated with Nevada and the West Coast: good-heartedness beneath a rough and profane exterior in the first, and courage ("sand") in the second. John Franklin Swift's novel *Robert Greathouse* (1870) was praised in its day not so much for its plot as for basing its characters on real-life and recognizable personages of the early Comstock.

Like Mark Twain, Ambrose Bierce does not fit neatly into the mold of Sagebrusher, but it now appears for biographical and stylistic reasons that the influence on him of Sagebrush writers and literature is substantial. Bierce was on very friendly terms with Sam Davis over a number of years, and he also knew Mark Twain and Joe Goodman. Bierce, furthermore, stated several times that he had visited the mining regions of Nevada. He possibly visited with Davis on one or more of those occasions. It is certain that Bierce at least read the works of De Quille, not only because both men published in the same issues of San Francisco magazines and newspapers but also because, as an editor, Bierce accepted some of De Quille's submissions. Bierce, moreover, is the only important California author to have cultivated the art of the hoax. As Carey McWilliams observed, it is impossible to discuss Bierce apart from the hoax, for there are many examples of it in his oeuvre (Hall 1934: iii–vi). The outstanding example is his best story, "An Occurrence at Owl Creek Bridge." The argument for giving it this status has been detailed elsewhere, where a case has been made for comparing its amazing mastery of the hoax with the best of Twain (Berkove 2002: ch. 6). While Bierce cannot be designated a Sagebrusher, it is clear that he must have assimilated important lessons from the movement, most particularly the hoax techniques that were being used by nearby Sagebrush authors whom he knew and whose works he read.

Sagebrush Poets and Dramatists

Poetry was a standard component of Western literary periodicals, and a few Comstock authors took it seriously. Goodman and Daggett competed with each other for local poetic honors. Many of their poems tend to be artificially lofty, written for some occasion, and neither writer composed anything that would challenge Whitman or Dickinson, but both did write some very competent and memorable poetry, particularly in their latter years. Two elegiac poems, Goodman's frequently reprinted "Virginia City" (see e.g. Berkove 1991a: 27) and Daggett's tender "My New Year's Guests" (1881) are their best known, but other very good ones remain unknown only because they have not been collected. Sam Davis also wrote poetry from the beginning of his career to the end of his life. It is varied and talented, and more of it deserves recognition.

All three of these authors also wrote some plays. In Goodman's plays, only two of which have survived, he showed a penchant for bold innovations. A review of one of his early efforts compared its opening scenes to the nineteenth-century classic *Richelieu*, with Roman senators, magnificent language, and lofty sentiments. But the last scene turned the play into a burlesque. Some actors came out with kegs of beer and sprayed the other actors, the orchestra, and the audience with the brew. The result was pandemonium, but the audience loved it (Davis 1880: 227–8).

This kind of boisterousness, however, is totally absent from Goodman's most important surviving play, *The Psychoscope* (1872). Co-authored with Rollin Mallory Daggett, *The Psychoscope* is an important event in American theater history. It was called a "sensational" play because it featured unusual stage effects. Although it is not a work of great literary merit, it is outstanding from the perspective of literary history. Innovative in its use of science fiction, psychology, and detective motifs, it was probably two generations ahead of its time in its use of realism. For example, two scenes in the play are set in a brothel, and one of them shows prostitutes luring, drugging, and robbing an unsuspecting victim. The prostitutes also curse, and are not repentant at the end. The play's stark realism shocked Virginia City and even the acting troupe which contracted to produce it. Some of the troupe's leading actors, reluctant to give themselves a bad reputation by playing such scandalous roles, sabotaged the first night's performance by deleting some lines and altering others. Goodman and Daggett turned the critical guns of the *Enterprise* on the cast, and forced them to improve their performance. The leader of the troupe subsequently offered Goodman and Daggett $10,000 (approximately $140,000 in 2002 dollars) for the rights to the play but they refused to sell, knowing that their work would be emasculated. Although the play was long remembered on the Comstock it was not produced again. It was, in fact, lost until 2001, when its rediscovered text was published.

Another one of the play's most important features is its pre-Howellsian defense of realism, put into the mouth of one of its characters, a playwright. Criticized for writing a play that failed to reward virtue and punish vice, the character argues that the morality of his play stems from its being true to life. "Is the story of the crucifixion less instructive because the curtain rings down with Christ upon the cross and his enemies exultant? To pervert the scene would rob it of its moral force. The spectacle of flagrant injustice is the best of moral teachers." It is regrettable that *The Psychoscope* was not given the chance to influence contemporary American drama, but the fact remains that it is a remarkable example of the advanced intellectual and cultural vitality of the Sagebrush movement.

Toward the end of his life, Sam Davis wrote *The Prince of Timbuctoo*, a comic opera in the tradition of Gilbert and Sullivan, and of Gay's *Beggar's Opera*. Textual references to South Africa's Boer War, Roosevelt's "big stick" policy, the growth of trusts, and American economic imperialism date it as having been written no earlier than 1902 and give it a dimension of social criticism. The sparkling libretto and the musical quality of its songs are delightful. It is far too good to remain unknown.

Sagebrush Historians

Sagebrush writers excelled in one additional literary genre: history. The outstanding example of this is Dan De Quille's *The Big Bonanza* (1876), the classic account of the Comstock Lode. It has been frequently reprinted and it is largely responsible up to now for having kept his reputation alive. It is occasionally enlivened with De Quille's sly humor, as when he slips in among some factual remarks the observation that Comstock children tend to grow tall, probably because there is less atmospheric pressure at its altitude to stunt their growth, and Blair traces three episodes in *Huckleberry Finn* to a possible origin in it.[6] De Quille, who knew the Comstock better than anyone else, intended the book to promote the Comstock, so he played down or suppressed negative information that he had (Berkove 1999a: 28–30). But *The Big Bonanza* remains so generally informative and highly readable that although it requires augmentation, it will never be superseded. Sam Davis also edited, and partly wrote, a two-volume *History of Nevada* in 1913. It is based on Myron Angel's 1881 *History of Nevada* but includes material that Angel missed, as well as covering events that occurred subsequently. Not as literary as *The Big Bonanza*, it is thorough and respected as a standard source.

Toward the end of their lives, a surprising number of former Sagebrushers wrote memoir essays, or series of essays, for newspapers. Dan De Quille, Joe Goodman, Rollin Daggett, C. C. Goodwin, Jim Townsend, and Alf Doten, are among the most prominent of the literary figures, Thomas Fitch among the political personalities, and David Belasco among the dramatists. Wells Drury, a later Comstock journalist, and Goodwin additionally wrote books about their recollections, as did former US Senator William M. Stewart. The "By-the-Bye" series of the *Nevada Mining News* in 1908 and 1909 enlisted the best surviving Sagebrush authors, especially Davis and Goodman, and also Goodwin, giving them an opportunity at the end of their lives to be frank but anonymous. As a consequence, whereas their earlier newspaper memoirs might have withheld some potentially explosive material, what they wrote for this series was almost uninhibited. The literary quality of these memoirs is exceptional. All the authors were superb raconteurs. Nevertheless, what is so striking about all Sagebrush memoirs or histories, apart from their excellent styles and interesting subject matter, is the common conviction of every single author that the Comstock experience was extraordinary and exhilarating, the most remarkable time of their lives. For more than a century, Sagebrush literature was all but forgotten. Now that it is being made available once again, it is apparent that it is an extraordinary and precious part of the American heritage.

NOTES

1. Among the earliest mentions of the Sagebrush School is Ella Sterling Cummins's *The Story of the Files* (Cummins 1893: 102–18). I have herein somewhat expanded her selections because some authors she assigned to other categories (e.g. James Gally, Joseph Goodman, and Arthur McEwen) began their writing careers in Nevada and retained some influences from the experience. Edgar M. Branch's *The Literary Apprenticeship of Mark Twain* is an important early assessment of what Twain learned from his contemporaries, including Sagebrush colleagues.

2. That editorial accountability was not a joking matter on the Comstock is attested to in the memoir of Wells Drury, another Comstock journalist:

> It was not absolutely necessary for an editor to fight as well as write, but at least he must show a willingness to defend himself in a manly way and stand on his rights, or else his usefulness in journalism would be impaired to the verge of nothingness. In other words, he might as well walk the grade [i.e. leave town], first as last, since his days were likely to be few and full of trouble (Drury 1984: 169).

The failure of Comstock editor Conrad Wiegand to respond to pressure "in a manly way" was, at face value, the reason why Mark Twain devoted Appendix C of *Roughing It* to ridiculing him. The fuller story behind the appendix, and one in which Twain does not come off nobly himself, is told in my article, "'Assaying in Nevada': Twain's Wrong Turn in the Right Direction" (Berkove 1995).

3. The free silver movement tried to end the monometallic gold standard and and begin the free (i.e. unrestricted) coining of silver dollars at the rate of 16 units of silver to one of gold. Western states produced silver, and silver dollars would make money more plentiful.

4. *Nevada Mining News*, Aug. 27, 1908. This newspaper published a weekly series of Comstock memoirs, titled "By-the-Bye," between April 30, 1908 and May 27, 1909. The entire series has been collected and edited in *The Devil's in the Details* (Berkove, ed., 2003). Where authorship of anonymous items has been determined, the attribution occurs in the end notes.

   Some of Townsend's lies (e.g. the ones just quoted) are cited, with variations of context, in different sources. Either Townsend re-used his lies, altering them to fit different circumstances, or else those who reported them made a few "creative" changes of their own.

5. The most complete listings of mutual influence of De Quille and Twain can be found in my Western Writers Series pamphlet *Dan De Quille* (Berkove 1999a: 33–9). Edgar Branch cites two possible De Quille influences on *Roughing It* (1966: 285 n.44). In "Dan De Quille and 'Old Times on the Mississippi'" and "More Information on Dan De Quille and 'Old Times on the Mississippi'" I establish two influences of De Quille on *Life on the Mississippi* (Berkove 1986, 1988). In "Dan De Quille and *Roughing It*: Borrowings and Influences" I supplement and expand to three Branch's examples and additionally note a striking resemblance of Colonel Sherburn's murder of Boggs in the second half of chapter 21 of *Huckleberry Finn* to the new passage (Berkove 1994: 55).

6. Walter Blair determines that "significant parallels" to episodes in *The Big Bonanza* occur in chapters 1, 8, and 15 of *Huckleberry Finn* (Blair 1960: 121–7).

Belasco, David (1991). *Gala Days of Piper's Opera House and the California Theater*. Sparks, NV: Falcon Hill.

Berkove, Lawrence I. (1986). "Dan De Quille and 'Old Times on the Mississippi.'" *Mark Twain Journal* 24: 2 (Fall), 28–35.

Berkove, Lawrence I. (1988). "New Information on Dan De Quille and 'Old Times on the Mississippi.'" *Mark Twain Journal* 26: 2 (Fall), 15–20.

Berkove, Lawrence I. (1991a). "Life after Twain: The Later Careers of the *Enterprise* Staff." *Mark Twain Journal* 29: 1 (Spring): 22–8.

Berkove, Lawrence I. (1991b). "Willa Cather's *A Lost Lady*: The Portrait of a Survivor." *Willa Cather Yearbook 1* (The Mildred Bennett Festschrift), 55–68. Lewiston, NY: Mellen.

Berkove, Lawrence I. (1994). "Dan De Quille and *Roughing It*: Borrowings and Influence." *Nevada Historical Society Quarterly* 37: 1 (Spring), 52–7.

Berkove, Lawrence I. (1995). "'Assaying in Nevada': Twain's Wrong Turn in the Right Direction." *American Literary Realism* 27: 3 (Spring), 64–79.

Berkove, Lawrence I. (1997). "*The Psychoscope:* Frontier Realism." *ATQ* 11: 1 (March), 7–18.

Berkove, Lawrence I. (1999a). *Dan De Quille*. (Boise State University Western Writers Series, no. 136.) Boise: Boise State University.

Berkove, Lawrence I. (1999b). "Daggett, Rollin Mallory." *American National Biography*, vol. VI, 3–4. New York: Oxford University Press.

Berkove, Lawrence I. (1999c). "Doten, Alfred." *American National Biography*, vol. VI, 778–9. New York: Oxford University Press.

Berkove, Lawrence I. (1999d). "Goodwin, Charles Carroll." *American National Biography*, vol. IX, 268–9. New York: Oxford University Press.

Berkove, Lawrence I. (1999e). "Goodman, Joseph Thompson." *American National Biography*, vol. IX, 244–6. New York: Oxford University Press.

Berkove, Lawrence I. (1999f). "Samuel Post Davis." In Kent P. Ljungquist (ed.), *Dictionary of Literary Biography*, vol. 202: *Nineteenth-Century American Fiction Writers*, 92–9. Detroit: Gale Research.

Berkove, Lawrence I. (2001). "Joe Goodman, In His Own Write." *Nevada Magazine* 61: 1 (Jan.–Feb.), 16–19.

Berkove, Lawrence I. (2002). *A Prescription for Adversity: The Moral Art of Ambrose Bierce*. Columbus: Ohio State University Press.

Berkove, Lawrence I., ed. (2003). *The Devil's in the Details*. Reno: University of Nevada Press.

Blair, Walter (1960). *Mark Twain and Huck Finn*. Berkeley: University of California Press.

Branch, Edgar Marquess (1966). *The Literary Apprenticeship of Mark Twain* (1950). New York: Russell & Russell.

Cather, Willa (1972). *A Lost Lady*. New York: Vintage. (First publ. 1923.)

Cummins, Ella Sterling (1893). *The Story of the Files: A Review of Californian Writers and Literature*. [San Francisco]: World's Fair Commission of California.

Daggett, Rollin Mallory (1882). *Braxton's Bar*. NY: Carleton.

Daggett, Rollin Mallory (1895). "My French Friend." *Overland Monthly* 25: 145 (Jan.), 62–8.

Daggett, Rollin Mallory, and Goodman, Joseph Thompson (2003). *The Psychoscope*, ed. and intr. Lawrence I. Berkove. Reno, NV: Great Basin.

Davis, Samuel Post (1880). "Dramatic Recollections." *Nevada Monthly* 1: 3 (May), 226–30.

Davis, Samuel Post (1886). *Short Stories*. San Francisco: Golden Era.

Davis, Samuel Post (1889). "My Friend the Editor." *San Francisco Examiner*, 21 July.

Davis, Samuel Post (1899). "The Loco Weed." *Nevada Magazine* 1: 3 (Oct.), 166–70.

Davis, Samuel Post (1913). *History of Nevada*, 2 vols. Las Vegas: Nevada Publications.

De Quille, Dan [William Wright] (1947). *The Big Bonanza*, intr. Oscar Lewis. New York: Crowell. (First publ. 1876.)

De Quille, Dan [William Wright] (1963). *Washoe Rambles*, intr. Richard E. Lingenfelter. Los Angeles: Westernlore.

De Quille, Dan [William Wright] (1988). *Dives and Lazarus: Their Wanderings and Adventures in the Infernal Regions*, ed. and intr. Lawrence I. Berkove. Ann Arbor: Ardis.

De Quille, Dan [William Wright] (1990a). *The Fighting Horse of the Stanislaus*, ed. and intr. Lawrence I. Berkove. Iowa City: Univ of Iowa Press.

De Quille, Dan [William Wright] (1990b). *The Gnomes of the Dead Rivers*, ed. and intr. Lawrence I. Berkove. Sparks, NV: Falcon Hill, 1990.

Doten, Alfred (1973a). "Early Journalism in Nevada." *The Journals of Alfred Doten, 1849–1903*, 3 vols., ed. Walter Van Tilburg Clark, vol. III, 2225–56. Reno: University of Nevada Press.

Doten, Alfred (1973b). *The Journals of Alfred Doten, 1849–1903*, 3 vols., ed. Walter Van Tilburg Clark. Reno: University of Nevada Press.

Drury, Wells (1984). *An Editor on the Comstock Lode* (1936). Reno: University of Nevada Press.

Dwyer, Richard A., and Lingenfelter, Richard E. (1984). *Lying on the Eastern Slope: James Townsend's Comic Journalism on the Mining Frontier*. Miami: Florida International University Press.

Fatout, Paul (1964). *Mark Twain in Virginia City*. Bloomington: Indiana University Press.

Fitch, Thomas (1978). *Western Carpetbagger: The Extraordinary Memoirs of "Senator" Thomas Fitch*, ed. Eric N. Moody. Reno: University of Nevada Press.

Gally, James W. (1880). *Sand, and Big Jack Small*. Chicago: Belford Clarke.

Goodman, Joseph Thompson (1897). *The Archaic Maya Inscriptions*. London: Taylor & Francis.

Goodman, Joseph Thompson (1939). "The *Trumpet* Comes to Pickeye!" San Francisco: Book Club of California.

Goodman, Joseph Thompson (1977). *Heroes, Badmen and Honest Miners: Joe Goodman's Tales of the Comstock Lode*, ed. Phillip I. Earl. Reno: Great Basin.

Goodman, Joseph Thompson (1997). "'An Irregular Correspondent': *The European Travel Letters of Mark Twain's Editor and Friend Joe Goodman*," ed. and intr. Lawrence I. Berkove. *Mark Twain Journal* 35: 2 (Fall), 1–44.

Goodwin, Charles Carroll (1891). *The Comstock Club*. Salt Lake City: Salt Lake Commercial Club.

Goodwin, Charles Carroll (1913). *As I Remember Them*. Salt Lake City: Salt Lake Commercial Club.

Hall, Carroll D. (1934). *Bierce and the Poe Hoax*, intro. Carey McWilliams. San Francisco: Book Club of California.

Hart, Fred H. (1878). *The Sazerac Lying Club: A Nevada Book*. San Francisco: Keller.

Mighels, Henry Rust (1879). *Sage Brush Leaves*. San Francisco: Bosqui.

Stewart, William M. (1908). *Reminiscences of Senator William M. Stewart of Nevada*, ed. George Rothwell Brown. New York: Neale.

Swift, John Franklin (1870). *Robert Greathouse*. New York: Carleton.

Twain, Mark (1993). *Roughing It*, ed. Harriet Elinor Smith and Edgar Marquess Branch. San Francisco: University of California Press. (First publ. 1872.)

20

Re-envisioning the Big Sky: Regional Identity, Spatial Logics, and the Literature of Montana

Susan Kollin

In *The Big Sky*, A. B. Guthrie's classic tale chronicling the end of the mountain man era in the northern Rockies, Zeb Calloway meets up with his wayward Kentucky nephew Boone Caudill and alerts the younger man that he has arrived in Montana ten years too late to enjoy the frontier adventures the region once offered. According to him, the fur trade has brought such extensive changes to the land that the very elements which made the region a wild and intriguing space have now vanished. When Uncle Zeb laments despairingly to his nephew, "She's gone, goddam it! Gone! ... The whole shitareee. Gone, by God," he speaks what might very well be the most famous lines in Montana literary history (Guthrie 1974: 150). Published in 1947 with a setting located in the previous century, A. B. Guthrie's novel captures a structure of feeling that continues to shape Euro-American attitudes about Montana and the American West in general. An anxiety of belatedness – the fear that the "real" West has somehow passed away and that the region is now destined to go the way of other American regions – has not only long informed popular sentiments about the West, but also promises to be a rather difficult belief to dislodge.

The irreverent Montana poet, playwright, and artist Greg Keeler has made a living for over 20 years offering no-holds-barred critiques of whatever regional clichés seem in need of deflating. Keeler has kept himself busy producing satirical comment-aries on everything from the vagaries of cowboy living to the state's environmental shortsightedness, and from all indications, such work is likely to occupy him for some time to come. In a recent essay that examines the power of A. B. Guthrie's popular novel, he addresses how modern residents of Montana are still implicated in what Ken Egan calls an "apocalyptic" way of thinking. Keeler goes on to confess that even he has not escaped the seductions of such beliefs, explaining that when he first encountered *The Big Sky* as a young boy in Oklahoma, he felt a "huge sense of triviality" in his own life, "as if all the importance and excitement in human endeavor had happened long ago and far away." After moving to Montana in the 1970s and witnessing even more changes taking place across the state, Keeler began

Figure 20.1   "Callin' Ahead," by Greg Keeler.

to recognize the irony of the situation. "It wasn't until a few years ago that I realized Uncle Zeb might have been full of the stuff he thought was all gone," Keeler writes, "just like the young entrepreneur I overheard last week on Main Street here in Bozeman, Montana. He said something to the effect of, 'I remember when there was just one McDonald's here in Bozeman; now there are two plus a whole shit-load of other fast food joints. Man, has this place gone all to hell.'" For Keeler, such responses to the passing of time and changes in the region need to be exposed for the narrow forms of thinking they endorse. The attitudes are most problematic, he argues, because they encourage us to avoid taking responsibility for these developments. As he explains, not only do we avoid culpability for these problems, but we also "doom our ideals" when we insist on claiming that "someone else has sold out the West" (Keeler 2000: 8).

Greg Keeler is not the only Montana resident to note the ironies entailed in this line of thinking. Literary critic Ken Egan warns about what he calls the "mythology of failure" expressed in Guthrie's novel, a sense of resignation and fatalism that still holds currency in the state with often dire consequences for the region (Egan 2001: 9). Egan points to some of the state's more famous residents, including the Militia of Montana, the Freemen, the Unabomber, and Earth First! as signs that "the disease of self-pity originating in an irreparable break from past greatness" may not be waning in any perceivable way in the near future (Egan 2001: 10). Writer Mary Clearman Blew concurs with this assessment, addressing the problems that arise in Guthrie's novel at the moment when the Euro-American characters, figuring themselves as somehow "reeling out of paradise," respond to their dilemma by projecting blame onto outsiders, developing in turn a misguided and xenophobic fear of invasion. "In reinventing our past out of the wealth of stories and diaries and accounts from the preceding periods," she writes, "how could we ever have believed in so much innocence to be lost?" (Blew 1988: 633).

Even as residents in present-day Montana continue to understand their state as "Big Sky country" or "the Last Best Place" – both geographical slogans adopted from celebrated books about Montana – the state nevertheless faces perennial problems in its self-image. A recent newspaper article in the "Big Sky" section of the *Bozeman Daily Chronicle*, for instance, cautions residents about new developments arising out of fast-paced growth which are rapidly altering the quality of life in the region. " 'Last Best Place' Urged to Control Sprawl," the headline reads. Pointing to the emergence of new subdivisions and commercial strips along the edges of towns like Bozeman and Billings, the article warns that many Montana cities are threatening to become indistinguishable from places such as "Dallas and Cleveland." Smart-growth initiatives appear to be the only solution to the problems of runaway development, whereby "[e]very place winds up looking like no place" (Gevock 2001). Hollywood's recent interest in Montana as a site for film settings and second homes; the influx of class-privileged amenity seekers from other states; and the arrival of gourmet coffee houses, sushi bars, upscale boutiques, and even large chain stores such as The Gap and Wal-Mart all indicate that new forms of regional identity may in fact be needed in the state.

Such developments also encourage us to consider the factors that enabled Montana to become positioned as a national refuge or site of retreat in the spatial logics of the United States. From the nineteenth century on, Montana has figured as a sanctuary from the problems of urban industrialism in the eastern half of the nation. The state thus functions much like other western American places, serving imaginatively as a safe haven from all that is wrong with the rest of the country, a site supposedly able to shrug off changes that are taking place elsewhere while remaining resolutely anti-modern. The discursive production of this "Last Best Place" operates as a counter-modern response that is a decidedly modern one after all, a reaction fully ensconced within modern sensibilities and feelings. As such, the various forms of cultural production that position "the Big Sky" as oppositional space do so within the very logic they set out to critique. The most recent local complaint, emerging in the 1990s – that Montana is in decline now that it has been "discovered" by outsiders hoping to cash in on its picturesque landscapes and quality of life – functions as both a reaction to and a symptom of a larger regional design shaping both local and national spaces. It becomes important to re-examine A. B. Guthrie's novel *The Big Sky*, the ur-text for much of white Montana's literary self-understanding, for the ways its sentiments continue to shape and inform Euro-American definitions of the region.

Even as we examine the concerns arising from the novel, however, a danger emerges in dwelling on the text's sensibilities without ever moving beyond them. Ken Egan suggests, for instance, that we should grant Guthrie's novel "less canonical priority," dislodging the narrative from its position in the literary imagination of Montana in order to emphasize other regional issues and concerns (2001: 15). While there may be some merit to this argument, in a state whose license plates advertise the region as "the Big Sky" and whose self-promotion is tied up with ideas about its redemptive possibilities, we may still need to come to terms with the power of these ideas and what they entail for regional identity in the West. This essay examines the cultural work Guthrie's text has performed in the state's literary tradition and in the structures of everyday life across Montana. In particular, I am interested in assessing how the novel offers explanations and solutions that often mislead us about the nature of the problems we face in the region. Taking Mary Clearman Blew's advice that we investigate the other side of "the Big Sky tradition" (1988: 636), I turn to other narratives that counter this portrait, examining how Montana has been re-imagined by groups with different regional visions and environmental sensibilities.

*

After more than a half century since its publication, A. B. Guthrie's popular Western tale continues to hold a central place in the literary history of Montana. Widely taught in high-school and college classrooms across the state, *The Big Sky* was adapted for the screen in 1952 in a film directed by Howard Hawkes. The text still serves as a perennial favorite of scholarly criticism, with a recently published anthology celebrating the fiftieth anniversary of its first publication. Much of *The Big Sky*'s popularity may be tied to the ways it addresses problems associated with what William Bevis calls the "Daniel Boone paradox": the notion that those who try to escape to the wild are doomed to destroy that very space by bringing changes to the land (Bevis 1996: 34). This belief in the inevitability of regional destruction poses problems in that it situates Euro-Americans as both the victims of change and somehow ill-suited to or misplaced in nature. Both of these notions leave Euro-Americans with no basis for building an environmental ethic in the land, as the two positions suggest that there are no options available for avoiding the region's destruction.[1]

In *The Big Sky*, the interplay between insight and blindness operates as a central theme and means through which Guthrie launches his critique of the main character, Boone Caudill, a figure clearly linked to a previous American frontier hero, Daniel Boone. What the protagonist in *The Big Sky* can and cannot see in the region – what he foregrounds and what he places at the margins – are important elements that delineate his shortcomings as an environmental actor in the land (Bryant 1996). Although he cherishes the wildness of the region he encounters, Boone remains unable to see the ways his fur-trading practices and economic exploitation wreak havoc in the land. Vision and the lack of insight emerge as crucial concerns at another point when the child of Boone and Teal Eyes is born blind, the result of his untreated venereal disease and a sign that Boone's actions will have strong and long-ranging consequences in the region. Yet even as Guthrie offers a critique of his main character for his brutality, lack of vision, and inability to understand how his actions toward the land and its people are ultimately destructive, the author remains unaware of the ways in which he, too, is subject to the very critique he is launching.

While Guthrie is clearly interested in re-examining the ecologies and politics shaping the fur-trading West and remains critical of Boone Caudill as a figure complicit with the loss of the world he prizes, the novel nevertheless participates in the very sensibilities it seeks to dismantle. Guthrie begins the text by tracing Boone's journey away from the violence of his alcoholic father and the restrictions of his home life in Kentucky, through St. Louis and up into Blackfeet country in the Rocky Mountain West. The author takes care to explore the competing sentiments shaping his protagonist, the love that Boone expresses toward the land as well as the violence that marks his relationship to this world. Thus even though he flees from the brutality of his family life, Boone proves to be very much his father's son by engaging in violence on various levels. Early in the novel, for instance, he expresses a desire to be an "Indian killer" just like his father, a compulsion for brutality that continues throughout the text as he manages to physically harm nearly every person who is close to him. Boone's violence operates on another level as well. For him, the construction of a Euro-American masculine self requires the existence of various Others against which he defines his identity. In this ongoing construction of an Other, Boone engages in what Gayatri Spivak calls "epistemic violence," a by-product of imperial relations in which the constitution of the colonial subject as Other emerges as a form of violence in its own right (Spivak 1990: 77). Boone's actions and attitudes toward the black, Indian, and female characters he encounters prove to be violent on both a physical and an epistemic level as he constructs these groups as inferior Others, figures that enable him to experience a certain kind of freedom and independence in the region but who are not given a full humanity.

Guthrie becomes implicated in the concerns plaguing his main character primarily through his romantic portrayals of the land as a sublime nature and his depictions of the region as a "Big Sky" offering untold adventures. At one point, for instance, the main character stands on the banks of the Missouri River and scans the terrain.

> From the top Boone could see forever and ever, nearly any way he looked. It was open country, bald and open, without an end. It spread away, flat now and then rolling, going on clear to the sky. A man wouldn't think the whole world was so much. It made the heart come up. It made a man little and still big, like a king looking out. (Guthrie 1974: 103)

This idealized nature, vast and unpopulated, allows certain kinds of men to imagine themselves as monarchs, as kings overseeing their vast domain. The "Big Sky" motif that appears here figures the West as an expansive, promising terrain. This view of the land as a vast, empty space waiting to be claimed is repeated in another section after the characters make their way further west. Guthrie describes the region they encounter as a "raw, vast, lonesome land, too big, too empty. It made the mind small and the heart tight and the belly drawn, lying wild and lost under such a reach of sky as put a man in fear of heaven" (1974: 156). Using a possessive ideology that idealizes the region as a grand and unclaimed space there for the taking, Guthrie ends up participating in the very colonizing gestures he criticizes in Boone. The text's ambivalence about the process of claiming land has also vexed critics, who have often launched their own criticisms of these actions only to become caught up in a similar logic. Even Wallace Stegner, often considered the dean of Western American literary criticism, provides a commentary on the novel that is implicated in this line of thinking.[2] As he explains in his 1965 foreword to the text, "The West of *The Big Sky* is Innocence, anti-civilization, savage and beautiful and doomed, a dream that most Americans, however briefly or vainly, have dreamed, and that some have briefly captured" (Guthrie 1974: x). The problem with such assessments is that they falsely universalize a particularized experience of landscape. While Stegner suggests that the vision of the West offered by the novel is a dream shared by "most Americans," Guthrie himself specifies this spatial longing for a "Big Sky" as an aspect of Anglo masculinity, a sentiment that is not necessarily shared by the rest of the characters in the novel.

The limitations in Guthrie's environmental and social vision have been addressed over the years by various writers who have recast both the motif of vision and the geographical trope of the "Big Sky." Salish author D'Arcy McNickle, for instance, published two novels about the environmental and political struggles of Montana Indians that offer quite different understandings of regional identity and provide alternative solutions to the problems facing its inhabitants. McNickle's first book, *The Surrounded*, published in 1936, appeared ten years before *The Big Sky*. Offering a different understanding of the issues addressed in Guthrie's text, *The Surrounded* tells the story of Archilde Leon, a Salish mixed-blood who struggles to reconnect with his community upon his return from a federal Indian boarding school. After the publication of *The Surrounded*, McNickle began writing his second novel, *Wind from an Enemy Sky*, which tells of the struggles of the residents on the Little Elk Reservation in actively resisting the building of a dam on sacred tribal lands. Written over a span of 30 years, the book was published in 1978, one year after McNickle's death.

In his first novel, McNickle traces understandings of the land from the point of view of those colonized by white settlement. In *The Surrounded*, the protagonist Archilde Leon recalls a moment at boarding school involving a vision of the sky that contrasts quite visibly with the portrait Guthrie provided in his novel.

He remembered the day clearly, for apparently it had a profound effect on him. The students were playing in the school yard late one afternoon, just before the supper hour. The sky was clear except for a single cloud, resembling at first a puff of smoke, which had drifted directly above the yard. Its contour changed, becoming elongated and flattened, and finally, by curious coincidence, it assumed the form of a cross – in the reflection of the setting sun, a flaming cross. (McNickle 1978a: 101–2)

At first Archilde reads the sky as a Christian sign of the second coming of Christ and announces his vision to the prefect, who tells the other schoolboys to kneel and pray for what it signifies. Later, however, Archilde's understanding of the sign shifts as he watches a bird fly overhead through the cross, only to return several times before disappearing. What seizes his imagination this time is the bird's "unconcernedness," its failure to recognize the cross as a sign emanating from the Christian God. With the realization that there might be other interpretations of nature's signs, Archilde begins to understand the possibility that multiple points of view exist in the world. McNickle writes that later, Archilde "felt himself fly with the bird. When he looked at the priest again he saw in him only darkness and heaviness of spirit. He would never feel at ease around the prefect after that; and he would never fear him. There would be something of scorn in his thoughts" (McNickle 1978a: 103).

Appearing a decade before Guthrie's novel was published, *The Surrounded* offers a different spatial logic and understanding of regional identity. Highlighting themes of vision and insight, McNickle links these ideas to a vastly different reading of the "Big Sky." Here geographical signs are shown to be culturally specific entities. The sky that Archilde reads and interprets differs quite markedly from the sky encountered by the priest and other white characters. In the novel, vision and insight are linked to and shaped by one's social location. That Archilde experiences two divided understandings of the sign indicates that human relations to the natural world are not universally determined but may differ according to the cultural position one occupies. This distinction is important in the novel as various characters map different meanings onto the land. Archilde himself undergoes transformations in his interpretations of the land and of human relations to the nonhuman world. Upon his return to the Flathead Indian Reservation after being educated at the boarding school, for instance, Archilde initially feels distanced from the community's beliefs. Later Modeste, the blind chief of the community, offers tribal visions to the young man, helping draw him back into the community through stories and ceremonies. In contrast to the sightless child in Guthrie's novel, who functions as a sign of Boone's brutality and the imminent destruction of the land, Modeste's blindness serves constructive purposes. Enlisting Archilde to serve as his walking guide, Modeste uses his blindness to help the young man develop connections to the tribal world, an act that helps ensure a better future for both Archilde and the community.

Meanwhile, the Euro-American trader George Moser in *The Surrounded* expresses a view of the land that differs somewhat from the tribal view expressed by Modeste. Like the mountain men in Guthrie's novel who encounter Montana in the 1830s and 1840s only to bemoan their late arrival in the region, George Moser settles in Montana on the Flathead Reservation in the late nineteenth century and soon begins to lament his own belatedness in the land:

> The fact was that he had turned to Indian trading because he had heard that fortunes were being made at it, but he had come too late. The fur trade was gone when he arrived and the Salish Indians were a starving lot, once their game was killed off. The

only money they had was what the Government advanced them, and somebody else got that. (McNickle 1978a: 29)

Rather than figuring himself as a victim of these changes, however, Moser understands his own complicity with the problem. After tribal lands are thrown open to Euro-American homesteaders following the Dawes Act, he witnesses the dire effects of the land rush on his own livelihood.

> Everyone went slightly crazy. Mr. Moser now knew this and rued his own touch of insanity. Land prices shot skyward, and he bought up a good deal all the way up, some at the top. He lent money on the basis of those fabulous valuations, and few such loans were repaid . . . A decade had passed since then and the bottom had fallen out of everything. (McNickle 1978a: 31)

Here, Moser takes responsibility for the changes he has witnessed across the region. Noting the ways his own greed contributed to grossly inflated land prices, the character holds himself accountable in part for the disastrous consequences of uncurbed development on the reservation.

D'Arcy McNickle's second novel, *Wind from an Enemy Sky*, published over 30 years after *The Big Sky* was written, also traces regional concerns from the point of view of the indigenous inhabitants of the land. Telling the story of tribal resistance to commercial development of reservation lands, *Wind from an Enemy Sky* also uses the theme of vision and insight, doing so in a manner that foregrounds tribal ways of seeing. Like Modeste in *The Surrounded*, Bull, the tribal elder in *Wind from an Enemy Sky*, discovers that he has to teach his grandson Antoine how to encounter the world with new eyes. Like Archilde in *The Surrounded*, Antoine has just returned from a federal boarding school where he has been taught to reject tribal ways. Surveying the damage done to the land after a concrete dam was driven into a canyon on Indian lands, his grandfather reacts with anger to these developments. "[W]hen a man goes anyplace, whether to hunt or to visit relatives, he should think about the things he sees, or maybe the words somebody speaks to him. He asks himself, What did I learn from this? What should I remember? Now I will ask, What did you see today?" Antoine is surprised by the question, explaining that he saw the mountains, rocks, and big trees. Bull then suggests gently to the young man, "I could tell you some things maybe you didn't see" (McNickle 1978b: 8–9). What Antoine perhaps didn't notice, and what the government officials responsible for building the dam likewise overlooked, are the sacred qualities of the canyon and the river, both of which are being killed by development. McNickle thus plays on ideas of sight and vision, emphasizing the fact that government officials and tribal peoples often view the natural world in vastly different ways. Antoine remembers the lesson his grandfather taught him about seeing and ponders his remarks at various moments throughout the novel. "What did you see? What did you learn? What will you remember?" (McNickle 1978b: 116).

McNickle also refigures the "Big Sky" motif in the novel. The characters turn to the sky numerous times, reflecting on it as a powerful sign of the sacred world. At one point, the narrator addresses the shifting historical meanings that the people have assigned to this big sky:

> The old people could remember when the Little Elk valley, like the sky above it, had been free and open – a country of low rolling hills, wooded stream courses, meandering wagon roads, and game trails leading to watering places. Then surveying parties came and drove wooden stakes in the ground. After that, strangers from across the mountains came. And after that, wire was stretched between posts and the open country was gone. Now the soft rolling hills and gentle swales were cut into squares, and the traveler could only go where roads or lanes allowed passage between fences. (McNickle 1978b: 222)

The sky also serves as an important element in the novel when the Indian characters struggle to reclaim a sacred medicine bundle that was taken from the tribe and given to a museum several years before. After a group sent from the tribe seeks to petition government officials for the medicine bundle's return, the women who remain at the reservation turn their attention to the sky. "They watched the sky and argued about the signs." Trying to determine whether the mission would be successful, they decide that the sky is bringing something new. "The air smelled of change" they conclude, in a reading that proves accurate (McNickle 1978b: 59). Unfortunately, however, the changes that the federal government brings to the region are largely detrimental to tribal life. Questioning the wisdom of killing the river in order to build a concrete dam, one character ponders what other violations are likely to come next. "Will they open the earth and drop us in it? Will they take the sun out of the sky?" (p. 14). Later, when the government officials fail to stop the dam and return the medicine bundle, their actions leave the tribe in a dire situation. As the narrator explains, it is as if the government "has pulled the sky down on all of them" (p. 247). The novel ends by suggesting that the tribe's success in turning back the "enemy sky," a closing image in the text, lies in the next generation. It is thus up to Antoine and other young people on the reservation to have a vision of the future. "A people needed young ones who would put the sun back in the sky" (p. 204).

McNickle's revisions of the "Big Sky" tradition made popular by A. B. Guthrie have been extended by other Montana writers. Missoula writer and critic William Kittredge, for instance, launched a critique that recasts popular romantic sentiments about Montana and the West in his memoirs and essay collections. Taking on one particular narrative – the anxieties of belatedness resulting from rapid changes occurring across the region – Kittredge points to fears about recent waves of newcomers moving into Montana and the West. In a marked departure from *The Big Sky*, which provides a largely despairing view of change from an Anglo point of view, Kittredge tries to envision a profoundly different way for Euro-Americans to respond to new developments in the region. In his collection of essays *Who Owns the West?*, Kittredge offers a reading of the dilemma facing contemporary Montanans.

Popular mythology, trying to name our circumstances, has it that we are overrun with tourists, computer companies, and good Thai restaurants . . . These new settlers are not just well-to-do citizens making a getaway from the overpopulated insanities of our cities but also refugees out of Mexico and Southeast Asia bringing the enormous energies of the dispossessed. The West is being resettled, again, by people seeking sanctuary and opportunity. Some Native Americans smile and shake their heads. "Now," they say, "It's happening to you." (Kittredge 1996: 4–5)

As Kittredge points out, the irony about growth in the West is that many Euro-Americans are suddenly amazed to now find themselves positioned in a space very similar to that which Indians have occupied since the beginning of contact. Such displacement is often a disconcertingly new experience for those groups who have long considered themselves entitled to the region. "People whose forefathers took the land from the Indians now confront the same fate," Kittredge notes wryly. "They are furious, thinking everything their people fought and suffered for, over generations, will be taken away" (Kittredge 1996: 112).

Even though he addresses the irony appearing in expressions of belatedness emerging from newcomers in the state, Kittredge also acknowledges that certain recent developments have proven to be rather disastrous for the region. He thus joins other geographers, historians, and literary critics who have pointed out the ways developments across the West since the 1990s have rapidly transformed the region to the extent that the Old West of the ranching, mining, and logging era has now been transformed into a New West fueled largely by a postindustrial service-sector economy. Among the particular targets of Kittredge's scorn are projects that aim to recapture the nostalgic Old West of a previous era but that end up positioning the region as an "out-West theme park" or "Disneyland West" (Kittredge 1996: 136). In Bozeman, Montana, for instance, a town that has experienced both the advantages and disadvantages associated with rapid growth occurring over the last 15 years of the twentieth century, a popular T-shirt with the caption "A Tourist Runs Through It" responds to recent transformations that are reshaping the state. Playing off the title of Robert Redford's popular filmic adaptation of Norman Maclean's *A River Runs Through It*, the T-shirt protests new levels of commercial development and exploitation arising out of a new surge of interest in things Western.

For many residents in Montana and the West, such changes often mean that workers face a dire future employed in low-paying McJobs, while more affluent outsiders are able to enjoy the amenities offered by the region. As the editors of the recent *Atlas of the New West* point out, objections about the transformation of the West into a land of "sprawling cities, greenlawn suburbs, and ranchette estates" are worthy economic complaints, even if they also echo similar concerns voiced by folks across the region a hundred years ago (Riebsame 1997: 12). After all, the Old West that many white Americans pine for today served as the New West for the Indians who originally occupied the land, a point that is made quite lucidly in the novels of D'Arcy McNickle and other Indian writers. Addressing the sense of despair among

Euro-Americans, Kittredge suggests, "As anywhere, in the West people – out-of-work redneck timber-fallers and stockbrockers and lady veterinarians, laughing boys, dancing ladies, all of us – have no choice but to reimagine and embrace the future" (1996: 7).

For Kittredge, part of the solution to the problem of disenfranchisement lies in moving beyond a narrative of defeat toward a more complicated understanding of change that allows for the creation of a different spatial logic. "Despair, the music tells me, is a useless way of connecting to the world. Slow down, it tells me, and love what there is" (Kittredge 1996: 6). Kittredge is not advocating an alternative story of decline, nor is he suggesting that all regional changes should be embraced or are somehow inevitable. Instead, he argues that Montana and the West should adopt a responsible environmental ethic and forge new Western identities that refuse to seek refuge in fatalism and that recognize the ways we are responsible for changes we bring to the land. "What we need in our West is another kind of story," he explains, "in which we can see ourselves for what we mostly are, decent people striving to form and continually reform a just society in which we can find some continuity, taking care in the midst of useful and significant lives" (Kittredge 1996: 76).[3]

*

If figures such as D'Arcy McNickle and William Kittredge are eager to move beyond the "Big Sky" tradition in imagining a more useful regional identity for Montana, some women writers have also sought to re-envision the spatial logics that define the state. Countering popular understandings of what they call "Big Guy" country and employing a playful revision of Guthrie's novel, many Montana women writers have sought to redirect narratives about the state in order to incorporate the stories and experiences of its female residents. Using family oral tales, her great-grandfather's personal letters, newspaper reports, and photographs, Blew's narrative *All But the Waltz: Essays on a Montana Family*, is particularly successful in laying bare the underside of the "Big Sky" tradition, the masculinist Anglo dream of Montana and the West as a vast, rugged terrain in which to test one's power, strength, and stamina. Rather than trace changes through a narrative of doom and despair or position the white settler community as victims unfairly displaced from the land, Blew recasts the framework through which Montana has traditionally been imagined. In attempting to redirect the "Big Sky" tradition that positions the geography as an untrammeled paradise offering adventure and intrigue for the American Adam, she finds that the region's gender conventions are likewise in need of re-examination. The mythology of the "Big Sky" is far from being a gender-neutral concept, Blew indicates; just as the myth specifically encodes racialized views of the land, so it also captures masculinist fantasies about expansive nations and selves.

Blew argues that, by positing the white male adventurer as the ideal subject of narrative, "Big Sky" myths necessarily exclude American Indians and women from its pleasures. In *All But the Waltz* Blew takes care to document the costs of this exclusion, showing that Euro-American men also pay a price for this dream. One strand of the "Big Sky" tradition that particularly concerns her may be found in stories of the various male figures in her family and community who suffer tremendous losses as they try to achieve what ultimately proves to be an impossibility. These romantic, stoic men of the West criss-cross her life, encapsulated in the form of a husband who offers opportunities for excitement and risk but who ultimately chooses detachment and solitude as his fate. The son of a Kansas cattleman, this romantic daredevil exchanges the life of the ranch for the experiences of oil-rigging, taking Blew on a roller-coaster ride with periods of tremendous economic boom followed by the inevitable bust. After being diagnosed with lung disease, he withdraws from social life, choosing isolation and retreat in a pattern determined by the myth. Her father accepts a similar fate as well, one day leaving the ranch and his family, never to be seen alive again. Rather than face the defeat of a life he so valued, he decides instead to turn his back on these problems, removing himself from familial and communal ties in order to end his life in solitude. For Blew, "Big Sky" myths are not just dangerous beliefs but often prove deadly to those who take them too seriously. At one point in her narrative, she expresses disappointment and anger at the paths these Western men follow:

> My rage was at my father's acquiescence to that romantic and despairing mythology which has racked and scarred the lives of so many men and women in the West. The design by which he perceived his life can be traced clearly in his favorite books. During his last years he read and reread those old favorites – Louis L'Amour, Zane Grey, A. B. Guthrie . . . I often wondered whether his fiction reading offered a pattern for his sense of himself, or a mirror. But so strongly did he believe in a mythic Montana of the past, of inarticulate strength and honor and courage irrevocably lost, that I cannot escape the conviction that a conscious choice shaped the way he died. (Blew 1991: 45)

Much of Blew's anger is directed at narratives that suggest that once change hits the region, life really isn't worth living anymore. According to this convention, with nothing worthwhile to take its place and no adaptation possible, the end of the frontier dream spells the demise of the true West and real living. Written by a daughter of the West, *All But the Waltz* seeks to replace this dire take on contemporary Western living. The collection offers a counter-view of the deadly West, showing the tragic consequences its dominant narrative conventions often hold for residents.

Krista Comer provides a reading of Blew's text that is particularly useful for discussions of regional identity and the spatial logics of "Big Sky" narratives. As she points out, the stories Blew recounts in *All But the Waltz* are typically fragmented and incomplete, tales that ultimately capture the impossibility of any narrative mastering all reality (Comer 1999: 226–7). Blew's decision to narrate her family story in this manner corrects the larger tradition of writing the region as a single, unified history. Erasing the authority of different stories, these dominant narratives of Montana have usually stressed romance, intrigue, and heroism. In her writings, however, Blew opts for a postmodern narrative approach that enables her to incorporate forms of know-ledge found in dreams and allows her to speculate about the past rather than assert a claim on some "real" West. The text, for instance, opens with a memory Blew recalls about a sow and her piglets stranded on dry ground in the middle of a river during a particularly treacherous storm. As Comer explains, the event is recalled by the adult author who recognizes the animals' predicament as her own and as an event that pro-vides structure and meaning to her own life experiences as a Westerner. Blew con-cedes the unstable nature of memory, writing that recollections of the past "seem to me as treacherous as the river . . . How can I trust memory, which slips and wobbles and grinds its erratic furrows like a bald-tired truck fighting for traction on a wet gumbo road?" (Blew 1991: 3–4). Understanding her specific location in the region, Blew is unwilling to allow her version of the story to stand for everyone's truth. She is later confronted by a disbelieving father who asserts the impossibility of her regional memories. Blew, however, holds on to this moment of the pigs as a story that gives insight and vision into her life, and in doing so, asserts her right to dispute official explanations and authoritative stories of the West (Comer 1999: 227).

As a result, even the most cherished and enduring regional beliefs are not left to rest in *All But the Waltz*. Taking on the history of white settlement in Montana, Blew addresses the Euro-American practice of mapping and surveying the land, a project necessary to claiming space as territory and an act that ultimately transforms the world "from a place to be alive in to a place to own" (1991: 9). She begins by pondering the lives of the Indian inhabitants in the region and the experiences they must have had living in a land that eventually underwent numerous acts of remapping. Examining the writings of Lewis and Clark, Blew addresses a landmark the explorers renamed the Judith river. "In recording it, they altered it," she writes.

> However indifferent to the historical record, those who see this river and hear its name, Judith, see it in a slightly different way because Lewis and Clark saw it and wrote about it. In naming the river, Lewis and Clark claimed it for a system of governance that required a wrenching of the fundamental connections between landscape and its inhabitants. (Blew 1991: 9)

If the government surveys added to the land, they also took something away, a realization she extends to stories she recounts about her great-grandfather, Abraham, whose life in many ways serves as the center of the narrative. Carrying on in the tradition of Lewis and Clark, her great-grandfather

> controlled the space that stretched beyond his imagination by measuring and mapping it for settlement. As he wrote about that external world he was pinning down and mapping and limiting, he seems not to have been aware how much he was concealing in the telling, or how much, in the process of his mapping, he was erasing of a landscape and a way of life. (Blew 1991: 34)

Such is the case of the lone, romantic white settlers like Guthrie's Boone Caudill, who fail to understand the consequences of their regional visions. Is there a way to narrate place that does not engage in similar acts of control, mapping, and discursive limiting? In allowing certain geographical visions to take imaginative hold of a region, how do we ensure that other views are not in turn hidden, subsumed, or erased? These are the questions Blew considers as she struggles to recast the narrative conventions shaping regional understandings of Montana and the West.

Mary Clearman Blew had other important female precursors who also intervened in myths of Montana as the "Big Sky," only two of whom I have space to discuss here.[4] The celebrated journalist and author Dorothy Johnson is perhaps Montana's most famous writer of short stories; many of her pieces have been adapted for the screen, including *The Hanging Tree* (1959), *The Man Who Shot Liberty Valance* (1962), and *The Man Called Horse* (1970). Born in 1905, Johnson lived until 1984. Most of her short stories appeared in the 1940s and 1950s, making her a contemporary of A. B. Guthrie. What is intriguing for a discussion of "Big Sky" myths and sensibilities is how Johnson interrogates the codes and conventions of the popular Western, a cultural form that has wielded great power in defining how Montana and the West are understood in the dominant national imagination. Her writings meditate on popular elements of the formula, re-envisioning in particular Indian–white relations by reworking the conventions of the captivity narrative.

In "Lost Sister," a story published in *The Hanging Tree*, Johnson encourages readers to reconsider what constitutes frontier savagery and civilization, and to interrogate the racial politics of whiteness as its unfolds under the "Big Sky." Told from the point of view of a nine-year-old boy whose father was killed by Indians, the story initially unfolds within a white settler sensibility. In the beginning of the narrative, the boy's views of the region are shaped by racial assumptions: whites are superior, Indians need to be subordinated. He thus speaks the racial discourses of the era, or rather they speak him. When his Aunt Bessie, who has been held captive by Indians for 40 years, is finally reunited with her family, the boy's understanding of his place in the world is suddenly unsettled. Believing she has undergone a "terrible experience" living with Indians, her relatives are astonished to discover that their lost sister never loses her sense of being out of place in white society (Johnson 1995a: 5). Working against the expectations of popular Western stories, Johnson portrays these well-meaning family members as the real captors. Such reversals continue in the story as the young boy begins to see the world through the eyes of Aunt Bessie.

> she looked at me sometimes, thoughtfully, as if measuring my worth. By performing athletic feats, such as walking on my hands, I could get her attention. For some reason, I valued it. She didn't often change expression, but twice I saw her scowl with disapproval. Once was when one of the aunts slapped me in a casual way. I had earned the slap, but the Indians did not punish children with blows. Aunt Bessie was shocked, I think, to see that white people did. The other time was when I talked back to someone with spoiled, small-boy insolence – and that time the scowl was for me. (Johnson 1995a: 9)

Aunt Bessie thus teaches the boy a lesson about race and regional identity that questions white assumptions about the frontier. By evaluating how the region has been codified in popular literature, Johnson helped lay the groundwork for rewriting the West. Her narratives indicate how the racial ecologies of the West operate to extend both physical and epistemic forms of violence which are needed to keep Indians subordinate throughout the region, and in turn counter certain forms of epistemic violence that emerged as the region became codified as a promised land and space of intrigue for Euro-Americans.

In addition to recasting narrative conventions shaping Indian–white relations, Johnson's stories also made efforts to examine certain forms of masculine identity that were crucial to the foundations of the mythic West. Many of her stories thus present white male identity as a precarious and unstable entity in constant need of being shored up. In "The Man Who Shot Liberty Valance," a story published in *Indian Country* (Johnson 1995b), Western masculinity – the basis of the popular Western – is rendered something of a farce. When Senator Ransome Foster turns up at the funeral of an old acquaintance, Bert Barricune, he finally has the chance to confront the forces that made him the successful figure that he is. Told in flashbacks, the story reveals how "Ranse" Foster's identity as a respected man of the community was won through a gunfight with the town outlaw, Liberty Valance. Previously bullied and abused by Valance, Foster decides at one point to stage a showdown in which he will finally put an end to his arch-rival. He thus positions himself as bait for the outlaw, appearing as a meek and grovelling man whose frequent sneers and cringes make him an object of male derision in the town. When the showdown finally takes place, Johnson uses the moment as an occasion to reflect on the Western codes and conventions that established regional expectations and identities.

> This is the classic situation, Ranse realized. Two enemies walking to meet each other along the dusty, waiting street of a western town. What reasons other men have had, I will never know. There are so many things I have never learned! And now there is no time left. He was an actor who knew the end of the scene but had forgotten the lines and never knew the cue for them. (Johnson 1995b: 102)

Suddenly finding himself in the script of the classic Western, Foster realizes that he does not fit well into this narrative framework. His misplacement in the story, we learn, is tied to his inability to properly embody the dominant form of Western masculinity required by such narratives. Liberty Valance is shot and killed in the shoot-out, not by Foster but by his romantic rival, Bert Barricune. The legend becomes truth for the rest of the community, however, as Foster eventually wins a seat in the Senate, a victory predicated on his ill-won reputation. What Johnson succeeds in showing readers in her stories, then, are the ways Western legends come to be established and perpetuated by codes and conventions of the myth that regulate race and gender identities throughout the region.

Although her writings aimed at recasting "Big Guy" myths of Montana and the West, critics have argued that at times Johnson came perhaps a bit too close to replicating the frontier stereotypes of her era. In a few of her stories, for instance, the critique she offers is buried or only partially implied. Sometimes, too, these narratives are marked by forms of nostalgia that have had negative consequences for the region (Blew 1988: 634). In other stories, the critique Johnson provides is undercut somewhat by her insistence on adopting a white point of view that threatens to further marginalize Indians, even if that view is later dismissed in the story. In spite of these problems, however, Johnson's writings are noteworthy for the ways they helped open the door for later revisionist Westerns, particularly the pro-Indian and counterculture Westerns that took off in the 1960s and 1970s and upset the race and gender codes of the region's classic narratives. Her stories are important for the ways in which they challenge the myth of Montana and the West as "Big Sky" country, a vast, empty terrain awaiting the arrival of American Adams who will ensure that the romance of conquest is a central aspect of the region.

*

It seems fitting to conclude an essay that seeks to recast the "Big Sky" tradition with the life accounts of the Crow medicine woman Pretty-shield, whose narrative was recorded and published by Euro-American interpreter Frank Linderman in 1932. Pretty-shield's text serves as an important corrective to the vision A. B. Guthrie later popularized in his novel because it is marked by a refusal to discuss Indian life after the contact period. While this refusal may resemble forms of nostalgia for an idealized past that have been dismissed by critics, we might better consider this response a kind of "radical" or "critical" nostalgia – what Maria Damon describes as a "proactive creation of collective experience" that allows other kinds of memory to take imaginative hold of a region (1993: 113). Elizabeth Blackmar offers insights into these forms of counter-memory; as she explains, rather than serving as a "veil of distorting sentiment, a longing that can never be transformed into active motive or critical insight," critical forms of nostalgia often allow us "to see more clearly what is before us and thus become a stance for analysis or dissent" (Blackmar 2001: 324–5). For these critics, Pretty-shield's refusal to recount life in the postcontact period might operate as an active form of resistance and should thus be regarded as a type of nostalgia fundamentally different from that posited by A. B. Guthrie and others.

The radical or critical vision that Pretty-shield deploys in her narrative refuses to allow Euro-Americans to define Montana or the West. Instead, Pretty-shield's memories of the precontact period enable her to produce a counter-narrative to the wild West myth of Montana as the site of heroic cowboys, stoic Indians, and majestic buffalo. At one point, she explains:

> The happiest days of my life were spent following the buffalo herds over our beautiful country. My mother and father and Goes-ahead, my man, were all kind, and we were so happy. Then, when my children came I believed I had everything that was good on this world. There were so many, many buffalo, plenty of good fat meat for everybody. (Linderman 1974: 248–9)

In contrast to the conventional visions of Montana as rugged, romantic space, Pretty-shield offers scenes that rarely figure in popular Western literature. She provides tales of Crow women participating in battle and engaged in action. She emphasizes the humor of tribal people, an element typically denied the stoic Indian of classic stereo-types. Pretty-shield also counters the epistemic violence involved in colonial efforts that create subordinate and dehumanized Others. Turning the tables on this tradition, she largely remains silent about the forward march of the frontier, the heroic encroach-ment of an invading white culture. Yet these silences speak volumes. As Lisa Aldred suggests, Pretty-shield's refusal to read postcontact Montana renders it as negative space in her account of the region. Pretty-shield's insistence on not highlighting these aspects of Montana history thus signifies a resistance to the conquest of Indian lands.[5] As such, the text provides an alternative regional identity and offers a differ-ent spatial logic that positions Indians at the center of Montana literature and refuses to allow the Anglo West to serve as the only version remembered or recorded.

A lesson to be learned from Pretty-shield's narrative, then, might be that Montanans and other Westerners alike need to develop a historical consciousness that under-stands how landscapes have been lost and gained, made and remade across the region for quite some time and for vastly different groups. If we understand regional iden-tity as a rhetorically constituted entity rather than naturally given, we may be able to regard even the most enduring forms of self-understanding as open to contestation and revision. In the case of Montana, a state whose identity was determined in large part from populations in the Eastern United States and beyond, forms of regional self-understanding need to be understood as intimately linked to developments taking place elsewhere in the world. That maverick theorist of frontier literature Leslie Fiedler insisted long ago that we understand Montana as an invention of the Romantic movement, a by-product of European letters, rather than a unique or self-sustaining development. A professor of English at the University of Montana from 1941 to 1964, Fiedler had something to say about Montana's self-image. The popular vision of the state, he argued, is

> torn between an idolatrous regard for its refurbished past (the naïve culture it holds up
> defiantly against the sophistication of the East, not realizing that the East requires of it
> precisely such a contemporary role), and a vague feeling of guilt at the confrontation of
> the legend of its past with the real history that keeps breaking through. (Fiedler 1988:
> 746)

In many ways, Fiedler anticipated the debates about the "New West" which emerged in the 1990s. Some 50 years before these conversations took hold of the region, Fiedler recognized the problems plaguing those who are "deliberately cut off from history and myth, immune even to the implications of their own landscape" (1988: 745). In making Montanans and other Westerners more aware of their own legitimat-ing mythologies, Fiedler restored to memory histories of the region as an invented landscape. Fiedler's comments suggest that in order to shift popular understandings that define the region, it is also necessary to rethink the histories informing Montana's place in the national imaginary as well as the manner in which the United States as a whole understands itself through places such as Montana. If, as the new Regional Studies tells us, spatial identities are not geographically determined but socially and discursively constituted, perhaps Montanans and other Westerners alike will recognize that some aspects of the region's past are not desirable to hold onto, but deserve to be relinquished after all, and that alternative configurations of the logics of space might well be worth pursuing.

NOTES

1 William Bevis suggests that the problems of *The Big Sky* are actually the problems of the West as a whole. The novel has thus become a classic for many readers because it captures this "western sense of tragedy, of an inevitable and awful end." Despair, however, "is supposed to be foreign to the frontier" and operates as a decidedly "unAmerican" idea. For further discussion of these points, see Bevis (1990: 4–8).

2 For an overview of Wallace Stegner's contributions to the field of Western American literary criticism, see Comer (1999: 39–49). See also chapter 31 by Richard Cracroft in this volume.

3 Although his interest in moving beyond a defeatist sentiment or exceptionalist argument is well recorded in his later writings, as co-editor of the popular Montana anthology, *The Last Best Place*, William Kittredge has been implicated somewhat in the tradition of

thinking he critiques here. A vast improvement over the title of a 1943 collection edited by Joseph Kinsey Howard – *Montana, High, Wide, and Handsome* – the title of the more recent collection unfortunately captures aspects of the siege-like mentality of many in the state who are fighting to safeguard the Montana they love best. If the case of *The Last Best Place* is any indication, the struggle to rethink Montana's regional identity and its place in the spatial logics of the West may persist for some time to come.

4 As female literary precursors to Mary Clearman Blew, B. M. Bower and Mildred Walker also produced narratives that intervened in different ways in the dominant Euro-American understanding of Montana.

5 Conversations with Lisa Aldred helped me understand more fully the narrative strategies Pretty-shield employs in the text.

REFERENCES

Bevis, William (1990). *Ten Tough Trips: Montana Writers and the West*. Seattle: University of Washington Press.

Bevis, William (1996). "Region, Power, Place." In Michael Kowalewski (ed.), *Reading the West: New Essays on the Literature of the American West*, 21–43. New York and Cambridge: Cambridge University Press.

Blackmar, Elizabeth (2001). "Modernist Ruins." *American Quarterly* 53, 324–39.

Blew, Mary Clearman (1988). "Frontier Dreams." In William Kittredge and Annick Smith

(eds.), *The Last Best Place: A Montana Anthology*, 633–7. Seattle: University of Washington Press.

Blew, Mary Clearman (1991). *All But the Waltz: Essays on a Montana Family*. New York: Viking.

Bryant, Paul T. (1996). "External Characterization in *The Big Sky*." *Western American Literature* 31, 195–210.

Comer, Krista (1999). *Landscapes of the New West: Gender and Geography in Contemporary Women's Writing*. Chapel Hill: University of North Carolina Press.

Damon, Maria (1993). *The Dark End of the Street: Margins in American Vanguard Poetry*. Minneapolis: University of Minnesota Press.

Egan, Jr., Ken (2001). *"The Big Sky* and the Siren Song of Apocalypse." In William E. Farr and William W. Bevis (eds.), *Fifty Years after* The Big Sky: *New Perspectives on the Fiction and Film of A. B. Guthrie Jr.*, 9–19. Helena: Montana Historical Society Press.

Farr, William E. and William W. Beavis, eds. (2001). *Fifty Years after* The Big Sky: *New Perspectives on the Fiction and Films of A. B. Guthrie, Jr.* Helena: Montana Historical Society Press.

Fiedler, Leslie (1988). "The Montana Face." In William Kittredge and Annick Smith (eds.), *The Last Best Place: A Montana Anthology*, 744–52. Seattle: University of Washington Press.

Gevock, Nick (2001). " 'Last Best Place' Urged To Control Sprawl." *Bozeman Daily Chronicle*, June 8, 2001, p. A3.

Guthrie, A. B., Jr., (1974). *The Big Sky*, with foreword by Wallace Stegner. Boston: Houghton Mifflin. (First publ. 1947.)

Howard, Joseph Kinsey (1943). *Montana, High, Wide, and Handsome*. New Haven: Yale University Press.

Johnson, Dorothy M. (1995a). *The Hanging Tree*. Lincoln: Bison Books/University of Nebraska Press. (First publ. 1959.)

Johnson, Dorothy M. (1995b). *Indian Country*. Lincoln: Bison Books/University of Nebraska Press. (First publ. 1953.)

Keeler, Greg (2000). "She's All Gone." *Connections: A Regional Resource for Readers and Writers* 1 (Winter), 8–9.

Kittredge, William (1996). *Who Owns the West?* San Francisco: Mercury House.

Kittredge, William, and Smith, Annick, eds. (1988). *The Last Best Place: A Montana Anthology*. Seattle: University of Washington Press.

Kowalewski, Michael, ed. (1996). *Reading the West: New Essays on the Literature of the American West*. Cambridge: Cambridge University Press.

Linderman, Frank B. (1974). *Pretty-shield, Medicine Woman of the Crows* (1932). Lincoln: Bison Books/University of Nebraska Press.

McNickle, D'Arcy (1978a). *The Surrounded* (1936). Albuquerque: University of New Mexico Press.

McNickle, D'Arcy (1978b). *Wind from an Enemy Sky*. San Francisco: Harper & Row.

Riebsame, William (1997). "Preface." In William Riesbame et al. (eds.), *Atlas of the New West: Portrait of a Changing Region*, 12–13. New York: Norton.

Spivak, Gayatri Chakravorty (1990). *The Postcolonial Critic: Interviews, Strategies, Dialogues*, ed. Sarah Harasym. New York: Routledge.

21

Regions of California: Mountains and Deserts

Nicolas Witschi

When the Joad family in John Steinbeck's *The Grapes of Wrath* finally crosses into California by driving over the Colorado River at Topock, Arizona, its members experience a touch of uncertainty, disorientation, and even fear. Expecting to see the oft-mythologized agricultural promised land of milk and honey, what they find instead is an unforgiving desert beneath their feet and a wall of seemingly insurmountable mountains to the west. When Pa and, two pages later, Uncle John opine separately, "This here's California," Tom cautions them both that they have yet to cross this desert before them, a place he ominously calls "a murder country." Tom's reminder even has the effect of prompting Pa to revise his assertion to the point of saying, "wait till we get to California. You'll see nice country then." Tom, ever the realist, responds, "Jesus Christ, Pa! This here *is* California" (Steinbeck 1976: 260–3). At the heart of this sequence in chapter 18, which takes place as the Joads pause to bathe in the Colorado's waters, stands the difference between the idealized promise that "California" represents and the "broken rock wilderness" (p. 260) with which the travelers find themselves confronted. On one level simply a destination for migrant farm workers, California is fully revealed in this moment as also being a powerful idea largely removed from any consideration of political boundaries such as state lines. Across the river from Topock, the Joads may have been standing on Californian soil, but they did not yet think of themselves as being fully in California. Indeed, once they have made their perilous night-time trek through the Mojave Desert and up to the top of the Tehachapi Mountains, where "suddenly they [see] the great valley below" with its "vineyards, the orchards, the great flat valley, green and beautiful, the trees set in rows, and the farm houses," one of them again whispers with a touch of awe, "It's California" (pp. 292–3). This time, the sight of rich agricultural land criss-crossed with verdant, fruit-bearing trees confirms the Joads' expectations; they are now, they believe, in the California they had hoped to find. The desert and mountains through which they have just struggled turn out merely to have been challenging, peripheral obstacles they had to suffer in order to realize and attain the supposedly real thing.

Places that stand at and define the edges of the California region, places such as the Mojave Desert and Death Valley, the Owens Valley, the Tehachapis, the Sierra Nevada, the Coast Ranges, and the Siskiyous, have a long history of inspiring such awe and confusion. However, not all travelers through these spaces have felt as compelled as the Joads to dismiss them as antithetical to the California definition. Indeed, the mountains and deserts of the far western reaches of the continent have inspired an extensive record of literary appreciation that reaches not only as far back as the diaries of seventeenth-century Spanish priests and soldiers who traveled north from Mexico but well beyond to the innumerable myths and tales of Native American oral traditions. However, the questions implicitly raised by Steinbeck about how one defines the "real" spaces of California and how they are to be represented in words begin to play a significant role in the literature that emerges in the middle of the nineteenth century, when the California region assumes its contemporary prominence in the popular cultural imagination of the United States. Bret Harte, for one, reported in 1867 to the Boston *Christian Register* that the extraordinary-seeming accounts of California weather were in fact true, that "April shower[s] of great violence, lasting some two or three days" and "snow thirty to forty feet deep" were no more than "common yearly meteorological" occurrences in the mountains. He assured his readers, "You will say you have read something like this in Munchausen, but these are the facts. . . . Imagine what ought to be the fiction of such a people" (Harte 1990: 122). Remarkably few writers of California regionalism have approached the state's mountains and deserts as places for fiction, in that the majority of notable writings about California's more remote wilderness areas assume a documentary mode (even as a plenitude of fictionalizing, inventiveness, and outright falsehood is often found in such works).[1] A rhetoric of empirical observation and truthful description sets the dominant tone for a literary regionalism that, through the conventions of travel reportage and personal adventure, continually seeks to understand, define, and ultimately inhabit these powerful landscapes. This formal feature is as true for California's most recent explorer-essayists, such as John McPhee and David Rains Wallace, as it is for the very first chroniclers of the 1849 Gold Rush, which serves both literally and figuratively as the event that, for most Americans, first put California's mountains and deserts on the map.

The traveler to California's gold fields in 1849 had a rather limited set of options for getting there. A journey by ship from New York around Cape Horn and finally into San Francisco Bay could take anywhere from five to eight months. Those who elected to disembark at the Isthmus of Panama, trek through the rainforest, and hop aboard another steamer headed for San Francisco could significantly reduce their time at sea, especially once the advent of regular steamship service into and out of Panama cut the trip to a duration of only six weeks. The vast majority of gold-seekers, however, lacking the funds or the time for an ocean voyage and wary of an isthmus jungle crossing, opted for the overland route. The already well-traveled California–Oregon Trail proved by far to be the most popular means of reaching the West – roughly 32,000 emigrants came by this route in 1849 alone – and every single person who chose this path was guaranteed to encounter the mountain and desert spaces of the American interior. The Joads were thus hardly the first to feel daunted by the final obstacles to their goal presented by the landforms on California's eastern edges. Indeed, published accounts of forty-niner cross-country journeys are replete with descriptions and discussions of the fearsome deserts that gold-seekers were required to cross before achieving the Mother Lode country in the western foothills of the Sierra Nevada (see Fender 1981).

One such account, William Lewis Manly's *Death Valley in '49*, testifies to the way in which a now-famous stretch of the Mojave Desert got its name (naming is, of course, a crucial function of regional literature). More importantly, it also speaks to the dangers posed to travelers by uncertain or incomplete information, an uncertainty that was more often than not further complicated by the landscape itself. A lead miner from Wisconsin, Manly joined a group of California-bound emigrants camped near Salt Lake City who called themselves the Sand Walking Company. As Patricia Nelson Limerick has noted, "the logic of the straight line" (1989: 45), the unshakable feeling that blank spots on a map might best be traversed by taking the shortest route between two points, had led more than a few overland parties into danger and ruin in and around California's mountains (including, before the Gold Rush, the infamous Donner Party of 1846 [see Starr 1973: 126–8]). Seeing such a blank spot on their map, several families in Manly's group decided to forgo the lengthy Santa Fe trail that wound down through Tucson and then Los Angeles (Manly 1894: 109–11). As Manly tells it, he felt an obligation to these people and so went along as they departed from the main trail.

Eventually, however, they found themselves in trouble, encamped at the eastern edge of a "long, narrow valley" that "seemed the most God-forsaken country in the world" (Manly 1894: 145). With the wagons stuck, the oxen dying, and water and provisions desperately low, Manly and one other company member volunteered to continue westward in search of aid. As they climbed out of the far end of the valley, Manly and his companion paused to reflect on what still lay before them:

> From this was the grandest sight we ever beheld. Looking east we could see the country we had been crawling over since November 4th. "Just look at the cursed country we have come over!" said Rogers as he pointed over it. To the north was the biggest mountain we ever saw, peaks on peaks and towering far above our heads, and covered with snow which was apparently everlasting.

> This mountain seemed to have very few trees on it, and in extent, as it reached away to the north seemed interminable. South was a nearly level plain, and to the west I thought I could dimly see a range of mountains that held a little snow upon their summits, but on the main range to the south there was none. It seemed to me the dim snowy mountains must be as far as 200 miles away, but of course I could not judge accurately. After looking at this grand, but worthless landscape long enough to take in its principal features we asked each other what we supposed the people we left behind would think to see mountains so far ahead. We knew that they had an idea that the

coast range was not very far ahead, but we saw at once to go over all these mountains
and return within the limits of fifteen days which had been agreed upon between us,
would probably be impossible. (Manly 1894: 154)

A key phrase in Manly's recollection is "worthless landscape," which appears at first
glance to conflict directly with the sublimity implied by the phrase "grandest sight." As
a reminiscence of what took place in 1849, Manly's comment on Death Valley's lack
of value fairly represents early and mid-nineteenth-century attitudes about such desert
spaces: they were to be avoided at all costs. However, "grandest sight" hails from the
time of the book's publication in 1894, in that it comes from a moment in cultural history when the American tourist class was beginning to appreciate the beautiful and
the sublime in its native deserts.[2] By virtue of this juxtaposition, Manly's description
manages to capture both the terror of a stranded overland traveler and the awe that
someone in a more contemplative mood and secure position might experience.

A further notable feature of *Death Valley in '49* is that Manly's account of his trek
in search of provisions (he and Rogers do eventually make their way to "civilization"
and return in time to rescue the party members they had left behind) is finished less
than halfway through the book. In addition to recounting some of his experiences in
the goldfields proper, Manly fills out the remainder of his book by returning to the
stories of other Sand Walking Company survivors, detailing the adventures that each
family had had in traveling through the Utah Territory and how they subsequently
spent their Death Valley days and nights while awaiting rescue. As Limerick elegantly
puts it, "In 1849, he saved eight people from thirst and starvation in the desert. In
1894, publishing *Death Valley in '49*, he tried to save them from anonymity" (Limerick
1989: 46). Thus there stands a certain collective impulse to Manly's assertion that
"Many accounts have been given to the world as to the origin of the name [of Death
Valley] and by whom it was thus designated but ours were the first visible footsteps,
and we the party which named it the saddest and most dreadful name that came to
us first from its memories" (Manly 1894: 217). A product of the rush for gold,
Manly's narrative succeeds by reminding its readers that human communities bear
ineradicable ties to the regions they pass through and inhabit.

The physical and emotional trauma experienced by most people connected with
the Gold Rush did not end with the completion of the journey through the final
desert stretches before the mountains, for there was plenty to be found in the goldfields themselves. Again, as is the case in Manly's memoir, the documentary motive,
the impulse to tell it as it really was, predominates in narratives from the foothills of
the Sierra Nevada. Among the many who recounted in print their successes and
failures in the search for gold, two writers in particular, Louise Clappe and Alonzo
Delano, deserve attention as significant contributors to the literary history of California's mountain regions. Clappe came west from Massachusetts with her husband
in late 1849 and, under the pen-name Dame Shirley, published in 1854–5 a series
of letters in a new San Francisco literary magazine called *The Pioneer* that vividly
depicted the 14 months she had spent living and working in the diggings. Ostensibly

addressed to Clappe's sister back home, the so-called Shirley Letters are unmistakably written for a wider readership (recent evidence suggests that, before her departure for the mines proper, Clappe had made arrangements to send her writing to a newspaper in Marysville, California). Clappe's 23 epistles touch on virtually all aspects of the mining life, and they benefit from the added perspective of Clappe's being one of the relatively few women to participate in the daily life of an early placer mine.

In a rhetorical gesture she uses frequently to signal the documentary motive underlying her work, Clappe (writing as Dame Shirley) admits, "I know how deeply you are interested in everything relating to California, and therefore I take pains to describe things exactly as I *see* them, hoping that thus you will obtain an idea of life in the mines, *as it is*" (Clappe 1998: 35). In this respect, Dame Shirley stands as an early proponent of the sort of realism that would come to dominate the literature of the American West, a realism marked by an emphasis on the visual and framed in relation to a scene of nature or natural resources (see Witschi 2002). But more importantly, she asks key questions about what counts as real in the mountains and as realism in literary expression, for in her letters Dame Shirley tracks the ways in which the mountains are fundamentally changed by the sudden incursion of a gold-fevered crowd. Consider, for example, her reflections on the attraction of an irrigation canal used to bring water to a mine:

> I wish that you could see this ditch. I never beheld a NATURAL streamlet more exquisitely beautiful. It undulates over the mossy roots and the gray, old rocks like a capricious snake, singing all the time a low song with the "liquidest murmur," and one might almost fancy it the airy and coquettish Undine herself. When it reaches the top of the hill, the sparkling thing is divided into five or six branches, each one of which supplies one, two, or three "long-toms." There is an extra one, called the "waste-ditch," leading to the river, into which the water is shut off at night and on Sundays. (Clappe 1998: 112)

The idea of natural beauty is here briefly suspended in a conventional Romantic language that deftly returns to a more prosaic discussion of mining technology (a long-tom is used to shake gold dust free from its matrix of dirt and gravel). This language, which has so much more behind it than plain documentary reportage, has the effect of questioning the premise that beauty inheres only in nature. Even if taken ironically, Clappe's observation about the "natural" ditch suggests that more is being done to the mountains than simply the excavation of a valuable metal. The very terms by which they are to be appreciated are also being altered.

Alonzo Delano, who had already passed through the more northerly Humboldt desert and into California near Mt. Lassen by the time Manly's Sand Walking Company was organizing itself, did what quite a few gold-seekers did during and immediately after the initial rush in '49: he published the journals he had written during his overland journey, first as newspaper dispatches back in Ottawa, Illinois, and then, in 1854, with a New York press, as a book entitled *Life on the Plains and among the*

Diggings (which, true to form, includes a diary account of a harrowing desert passage along the Lassen Cut-Off). Even in the relatively separate career he was carving out as a Sacramento-based humorist under the name Old Block, Delano still favored the documentary stance. His 1853 collection of satiric tales, *Pen-Knife Sketches, or, Chips of the Old Block*, begins with an introductory note that explains how no writer had yet written about

> a miner's disappointments; the weariness of his toil, his suffering from hunger and thirst; his isolation among the hills; the yearning of his heart for home and the loved ones there; of his painfully climbing stupendous hills, or diving into deep gulches, sweltering under a burning sun, in search of the object of his honest ambition, or, as it after proved, of diggings that might afford him at least the means of obtaining sufficient to support life. (Delano 1853: 3–4)

Delano, in turn, promises to document this "other side" of the story, which his fellow miners have told him still remains to be revealed. The stories in *Pen-Knife Sketches* thus provide humorous takes on such figures as the greenhorn, the experienced prospector, postal service in the mines (such as it was), the gambler, and San Francisco – even a painfully funny account of Delano's miserable crossing of the Isthmus of Panama, which he had made after having returned home for a short time in 1852.

Delano was one of the Gold Rush's best and most widely read contemporary authors, in part because he actively published both in the East and in California. In this regard, he provides a particularly useful case study of the relationship between region and its reproduction in literary terms. Consider, for example, the overlaps evident in the books he published separately as Old Block and Alonzo Delano. One particular passage of note, which appears in only slightly varying form in both *Pen-Knife Sketches* and *Life on the Plains*, concludes a section on the hardships faced by miners by pointing to a "disposition 'to laugh at all sorrow when it comes'" (Delano 1853: 28). The next example, which Old Block/Delano offers to demonstrate this tendency, begins with the description of an "effigy of a man" that some frustrated miner, perhaps having lost everything but his sense of humor, had propped against the side of an abandoned shanty. This "caricature of humanity" was found

> standing upright, rigged out in an old shirt, a very ragged pair of pants, boots which looked as if they had been climbing rocks since leather was invented; in short, the image represented a lean, worn-out, meagre, woe-begone miner, such as might daily be seen at almost every point in the upper mines. On the shirt was inserted "My claim failed – will you pay the tax?" alluding to the tax on foreigners. Appended to the figure was a paper bearing the following scroll, written in good business hand:–
>
> "Californians! O! Californians! Look at me. Once as fat and saucy as a privateersman; but now – look ye – a miserable skeleton. In a word, a used up man. Never mind, I can sing away, notwithstanding:–

> 'O, Californy! this is the land for me,
>   A pick and a shovel, and lots of bones,
> Who would not come the sight to see?
>   The golden land of dross and stones!
> Oh, Susannah, don't you cry for me,
>   I'm *living dead* in Califor-nee!' "
>   (Delano 1853: 28–9)

A spoof of the fabled song that forty-niners chanted as they disembarked in San Francisco, this excerpt represents for Old Block "a subject of jest." But when this passage, with very little modification, is published in *Life on the Plains*, Alonzo Delano frames it as a sorrowful example of "failure" (1854: 348). A further gloss from *Pen-Knife Sketches* that contrasts this "doggerel rhapsody" with "the chaste tone and beauty of sentiment of that charming celebration ode written by Mrs. Wills" (1853: 29) is modified in *Life on the Plains* to say the following: "Ludicrous as it may appear, it was a truthful commentary on the efforts of hundreds of poor fellows in the 'golden land' " (1854: 349). In the first instance, the target of ridicule is the sentimental verse of one Mrs. Wills, employed to set off the effigy's status as humor. In the second, however, the adjective "ludicrous" signifies the effigy's verses themselves, thereby highlighting the more earnest tone of the narrator's assertion about the broader "moral" accuracy of the effigy. Although the effigy is in both instances positioned as humorous, in the Old Block version, written for a California readership, it serves as an example of humor alone, while in Delano's *Life on the Plains* it represents a pathetic statement of hardship endured.

Delano's dismissal of the sentimental in *Pen-Knife Sketches* (in the case of Mrs. Wills's verse) is more a tactic of the moment than it is a recourse to the pejorative meaning that "sentimental" would eventually assume. Even a quick reading of Old Block's satiric sketches reveals an extensive reliance on the mode. Indeed, the one formal feature that can be found in abundance in both types of texts – Old Block's California humor and Alonzo Delano's travel reportage – is sentimentalism, a mode of writing heavily inflected with affect and sympathy. For example, a sketch by Old Block describing the typical miner recounts how, in the face of excruciating physical labor, "the poor miner cries oftener than the child, cleaning out the black sand, broiling under the scorching sun at noon, shivering with cold at night. . . . I am an old miner, and if I don't change that subject, I shall cry myself" (Delano 1853: 12).

The story of "Peter the Hunter" and his heroic daughters is given the relatively basic treatment of an adventure tale in *Pen-Knife Sketches* (Delano 1853: 48–50), whereas readers of *Life on the Plains* are treated to the added detail that "Peter's lip quivered, his eyes filled with tears, and he could not go on" recounting the deeds of his girls (1854: 323). The sentimental mode is arguably Delano's strongest appeal, directed both at miners in the West who have shared his experiences (he very often addresses them directly in his narrations) and at East Coast readers hoping for information about that faraway event that may or may not have swallowed up their sons and brothers and husbands.

Alonzo Delano contributed to a number of different textual renditions of the California Gold Rush, mixing a sentimental tone with the largely satiric sketches he wrote for Californians and also with the more earnest, heart-stopping adventure tales published in the East. Very much dependent on the readerly expectations of a variety of regions, such writings, when considered more fully than they have been thus far, have the potential to complicate any interpretation of literary regionalism that relies exclusively on presumptions about either gender or a Boston-based publishing machine as the sole originators of mid-nineteenth-century regional literature. More to the point, Delano and also Clappe are vital to the history of literary regionalism in the United States as a whole for more than the interest their texts generate as historical records. Their achievements in populating the mountains of California with the characters and, perhaps more importantly, with the particular blend of satire, realism, and senti-mentalism that would prove so successful for Bret Harte, Mark Twain, and many other local colorists to come, definitely merit more careful consideration.

Even as Harte was, in the late 1860s and early 1870s, bringing his career up to full speed with a series of brilliantly satiric sketches about life "in the diggings," another post-Gold Rush generation of writers was already beginning to re-envision the mountains not as minescapes filled with humor-tinged hardship but rather as unspoiled, visually pleasing adventure playlands where the vigorous body could bask in the sublime and reaffirm itself (and its self). Approaching the mountains from the east, Clarence King, a field geologist and graduate of Yale who could count Henry Adams and W. D. Howells as friends and admirers, begins his 1872 account *Moun-taineering in the Sierra Nevada* with the by-now familiar desert crossing formula.[3] However, while the first chapter relies on mirage and disorientation as dominant tropes in conveying the awesome uncertainty of the mountains to come, King largely divests the desert-crossing narrative of its burden of profound suffering and adapts it instead into a tale of mountain adventure and appreciation. Thus, King begins his story with an almost bemused account of the "bewildering effect" (1872: 15) of desert heat and light in order to emphasize the ostensibly more solid nature of the observations he will later make from various points in the high Sierra. The questions that King poses of the Yosemite Valley are crucial to the book as a whole. He asks: "what sentiment, what idea, does this wonder-valley leave upon the earnest observer? what impression does it leave upon his heart?" (King 1872: 184). King places at the center of his narrative the perceiving self, using himself as the exemplary observer of mountains. His are the impressions that count.

King articulates the visual aspect of the mountains by repeatedly referring to the effect that mountain light has on his mind. Indeed, at one point he assures his readers, "I was delighted to . . . expose myself, as one uncovers a sensitized photo-graphic plate, to be influenced" (1872: 126). In the descriptions of King's climbs on Mt. Tyndall, Mt. Shasta, and Mt. Whitney, as well as in his discussions of the Yosemite Valley and other such areas in the Sierra Nevada, time and again one comes across passages that wax poetic about the quality of mountain light. And, as noted above, the desert crossing of the opening chapter provides the foil, insofar as in the desert, light has the potential to mislead, whereas up high it is "of a purity and refinement quite different from the strong glare of the plains" (p. 48). One particular thirst-induced mirage offers King a vision wherein "The dreamy richness of the tropics, the serene sapphire sky of the desert, and the cool, purple distance of mountains, were grouped as if by miracle." This tantalizing "illusion" of unity is, however, soon enough replaced by the sight of "the white desert unrelieved by a shadow; a blaze of white light falling full on the plain." By contrast, a view of these same deserts obtained from the summit of Mt. Tyndall betrays no such "bewildering effect of this natural magic" (p. 15). Rather, looking down from the top of the Sierras, King sees "plains clouded with the ashen hues of death; stark, wind-swept floors of white, and hill-ranges, rigidly formal, monotonously low, all lying under an unfeeling brilliance of light" (p. 77). Granted, in the first instance King retains a full awareness of the illusory quality of desert light. However, his choice of language in describing the mountains refuses even to speculate on the unreliability of impressions. His sight in the mountains is crystal clear, his descriptions detailed, precise, and above all compelling. Ironically enough, several readers of the first edition rightly pointed out that in his penultimate chapter, King mistakenly thinks himself to be standing atop a fogbound Mt. Whitney when in fact he is on the next mountain over. However, this revelation does not alter the fact of King's confidence, however wrong it may have been at that one moment, in his ability to gauge the mountains with geologic and metaphoric accuracy. As *Mountaineering in the Sierra Nevada* recounts a series of thrilling climbs, adventurous travels, and encounters with less-than-savory characters, King goes from being unsure of scenery and self in the desert to being – pun intended – on more solid footing in the mountains. And in getting there, he and his climbing partner confidently assume figurative possession of "our new Alps" (p. 93).

In the practice of looking down on the desert with self-assurance and of claiming the mountains as one's own, Clarence King is hardly alone, for what King does from the summit of Mt. Tyndall, his more famous contemporary, John Muir, does from the summit of Mt. Ritter. Describing a similarly hair-raising ascent of another never-before-climbed Sierra peak, Muir also notes with some satisfaction "a land of desolation covered with beautiful light" and spread "map-like" beneath him (Muir 1894: 66). To be sure, the two men did have their differences. For one, they had each come to California for different reasons: King as a Yale-educated scientist intent on joining the crew of Josiah Whitney's official State Geologic Survey, Muir as a day-laborer with a predilection for wandering. They also differed greatly in their interpretations of California's geologic history. King favored a catastrophic explanation for the origin of such places as Yosemite Valley – the Valley floor simply subsided in one cataclysmic event – whereas Muir favored the relatively new theory of gradual, uniform glacial erosion (subsequent scientific inquiry has, of course, borne out Muir's version). Finally, King's tenure as a popularizer of geologic exploration effectively ended after the publication of his first book, for he would write nothing about his leading the Survey of the 40th Parallel, his directorship of the US Geological Survey, or his many years as a mining entrepreneur. Muir, on the other hand, sustained a long and highly fruitful career writing in advocacy of wilderness preservation.

Yet, taken together, these two men have probably done more to shape California's mountains in the popular imagination than did all other writer–explorers from the late nineteenth century, the heyday of far Western exploration literature. With respect to the Sierra Nevada, King's *Mountaineering* and Muir's *The Mountains of California* are the classics in the field, and as such they share a number of distinctive and telling traits. For one, each book is largely a compilation of essays previously published in magazines such as the *Atlantic Monthly*, *Harper's*, the *Overland Monthly*, and *Scribner's*. Through these channels, both writers had already reached a widespread, well-to-do, and relatively sophisticated audience, guaranteeing that each man's first book would be received as the product of an established expert. As noted above, both books present thrilling accounts of first-time ascents in the high Sierra, and when not concerned with climbing, both dwell for some time on the flora, fauna, and occasional human remnants that dot the valleys found between the range's granite massifs. Both King and Muir exhibit a tendency to juxtapose their empirically obtained, complex knowledge of the natural world with the almost willful (or so it seems) ignorance of local workers and herdsmen. King's sense of self in light of the Newty family (1872: 94–111) compares quite directly with Muir's treatment of the miners in *Mountains* (1894: 325–37) and also of the shepherd Billy in *My First Summer in the Sierra* (1911: 172–3). Thus do these keenly observant and robust devotees of nature supplant the local laborers and natives as the true experts on everything mountain-related. Finally, both King and Muir subtly shift the terms of appreciation away from the narrative of hardship established by the published journals and letters of the Gold Rush, replacing it with a rhetoric that emphasizes the visual dimension of the mountains. The narratives of the Gold Rush were fundamentally concerned with communities of people. Muir and King each travel so far into the unpopulated reaches of the Sierra Nevada (according to them, Native Americans were never seen in the highest regions), and describe these journeys in such rhapsodically picturesque terms, that despite their occasionally lingering on figures such as Billy or the Newtys, their mountains of California are successfully re-interpreted as being virtually uninhabited and wild. According to their respective books, the only ones who genuinely inhabit these spaces, both physically and spiritually, are King and Muir.

But Muir, for his own part, accomplishes much more than the mere imbrication of his ego within the landscape, despite the fact that, in a twist of cultural irony, his name may now be found all over the Sierra Nevada. A John Muir Trail (which includes a stop at the Muir Hut on top of Muir Pass) runs along the Sierra crest from Yosemite Valley to Mt. Whitney; a John Muir Wilderness area covers the hills just east of Sequoia National Park; and a number of physical features, from mountain lakes and peaks to redwood groves to a gorge in Tuolumne Canyon, bear the name of this founding member of the Sierra Club and progenitor of the American wilderness preservation movement (for the record, there is also a Mt. Clarence King). This large-scale inscription of the name Muir on the California landscape derives primarily from the fact that in scores of articles and more than half a dozen books, Muir successfully conveyed to late nineteenth- and early twentieth-century readers the idea that wilderness was inherently valuable. That is, he taught Americans how to recognize, revere, and fight for the preservation of natural spaces. Consider, for instance, the following passage from *The Mountains of California* in which Muir, standing atop Mt. Ritter, muses on how one develops an intimacy with a sublime landscape:

> [T]he inexperienced observer is oppressed by the incomprehensible grandeur, variety, and abundance of the mountains rising shoulder to shoulder beyond the reach of vision; and it is only after they have been studied one by one, long and lovingly, that their far-reaching harmonies become manifest. Then, penetrate the wilderness where you may, the main telling features, to which all the surrounding topography is subordinate, are quickly perceived, and the most complicated clusters of peaks stand revealed harmoniously correlated and fashioned like works of art. (Muir 1894: 68–9)

Seeing is the crucial activity in this passage, and Muir's self-professed expert way of seeing the art-like aspect of the Sierra Nevada maintains, to this very day, a terrific influence on environmentalist attitudes. Moreover, Muir's own personal experiences in the mountains, presented most keenly in *My First Summer in the Sierra*, reflect a spiritual awakening to the interconnectedness of the natural world, of which humans are an essential part. Thus, Muir deftly uses the mountains of California to create a wilderness aesthetic that has had lasting implications for American culture and politics.[4]

Muir spoke for an ecological vision founded on the interdependence of all things, an idea that most readers have found concisely summarized in his oft-quoted observation, "When we try to pick out anything by itself, we find it hitched to everything else in the universe" (Muir 1911: 211). As an abstraction, though, such a quip does little to typify the specific quality of Muir's writerly relationship with the region. Published in 1911, *My First Summer in the Sierra Nevada* offers the diary account of Muir's 1869 life-changing encounter with California's mountains (as such, it bears a slight resemblance in form to Manly's *Death Valley in '49*, in that the voice is at times that of an enthusiastic young Muir and at other times clearly that of the more deliberative elder statesman of the environmental preservation movement), and among its pages may be found plenty of much more nuanced examples of Muir's sense of the world and of how sense is made of the world. The entry for July 20, for instance, finds the writer mulling over the frustration he feels in trying to draw an accurate picture in his sketchbook of the Yosemite Valley:

> I would fain draw everything in sight, – rock, tree, and leaf. But little can I do beyond mere outlines, – marks with meanings like words, readable only to myself, – yet I sharpen my pencils and work on as if others might possibly be benefited. Whether these picture-sheets are to vanish like fallen leaves or go to friends like letters, matters

not much; for little can they tell to those who have not themselves seen similar wildness, and like a language have learned it. (Muir 1911: 174)

In this one passage alone Muir deploys a number of his favorite devices, not the least of which is the metaphoric conflation of book leaves with tree leaves. Building on this idea, Muir treats the very wilderness itself as a visual language to be learned, one that presumably cannot be communicated through pencil marks on a page but rather must be interpreted through the unmediated marks of "rock, tree, and leaf." But what to make of a writer who gives not the picture in his sketchbook but rather words about that supposed sketch? Relying on the rhetorical trick of preterition (that is, he writes about something by saying he cannot write about it), Muir expresses the essential hope he has of *seeing* his way to an understanding of how the universe is hitched together. However, such seeing is nevertheless intimately tied to the equally eye-dependent act of reading that both he and his audience must perform, and so Muir invokes the traditional notion of a book of nature not only to assert his ability to read this book but also to assure his readers that by reading him, that is, by reading the word sketch he has drawn, they too may come close to reading nature itself.

The writings of John C. Van Dyke, who traveled extensively in the American West from the 1890s through the 1920s, provide further confirmation of the extent to which a language of visual appreciation was setting the terms by which California's marginal spaces were to be understood. Thanks in part to the example set by the mountain writers who preceded Van Dyke, even the once-formidable desert was becoming something of a valuable visual commodity (the advent of safe, comfortable, and speedy rail service through the desert also had a lot to do with this shift). A professor of art history at Rutgers, Van Dyke was at the time one of the nation's most widely known proponents of the "art for art's sake" movement, and in books such as *The Desert: Further Studies in Natural Appearances*, Van Dyke applied these aesthetic principles to the genre of landscape appreciation. Often hailed as a "prose poem" about southern California's arid regions, *The Desert* mixes carefully observant discussions of rock forms, sand patterns, and the heartiness of desert plants with rhapsodically lyrical passages about the effect of the desert on human perception. And once again the key ingredient is light, evident in Van Dyke's central premise: the desert rewards the attentive viewer with "that beauty in landscape which lies not in the lines of mountain valley and plain, but in the almost formless masses of color and light" (Van Dyke 1903: 127). Published in 1901 and revised only slightly for a second edition in 1903, *The Desert* is credited with having inaugurated a decade's worth of excellent and compelling California desert books, among them Mary Austin's *The Land of Little Rain* and George Wharton James's *The Wonders of the Colorado Desert*. Of these three, Van Dyke's book is most deliberately focused on an exclusively aesthetic approach to the scenery. With respect to its fidelity to the autobiographical motive still very much active in California regionalist writing, *The Desert* also challenges one's sense of how strictly "true" an experientially founded narrative must be. Recent criticism suggests that instead of enduring the days and weeks of dangerous trekking depicted in his book, Van Dyke in fact did little more than look at the desert from the porch of a lodge or the back deck of a Pullman car (Teague 1997: 142). However one judges such handling of a narrative convention, Van Dyke's work provides vital evidence of a significant cultural shift in the perception of desert value.

As the twentieth century began to mature in its first few decades, California's deserts and mountains had achieved widespread definition and cultural recognition largely through the textual productions of the Gold Rush, including Bret Harte's stories; of John Muir and Clarence King; and of John C. Van Dyke and Mary Austin. However, as the century progressed further, a visual language increasingly set the terms of understanding and appreciation. That is, by the midcentury, the practice of looking was the primary means by which the popular imagination assimilated California, a phenomenon generally true of the American West as a whole (see Dorst 1999). Hollywood, for one, could famously use its nearby mountain and desert spaces to represent everything from the Crimea to India to Korea (the settings, respectively, of the films *The Charge of the Light Brigade*, *Gunga Din*, and *M*A*S*H*), and viewers on some level understood this. However, the one artist who perhaps more than anyone else recreated California's extraordinary landscapes as quintessentially Californian was Mary Austin's friend and occasional collaborator Ansel Adams. With notable images such as "Winter Sunrise, Sierra Nevada, from Lone Pine, California," created in 1944 from a site in the semi-arid Owens Valley not far from where Austin had once lived, as well as with a great many breathtaking black-and-white images of Yosemite Valley in all seasons, Adams provided what have come to stand as the definitive documents of the California wilderness sublime. Adams, in short, signifies the lasting legacy of the turn to the idealized, almost exclusively visual aesthetic first put forward by the likes of John C. Van Dyke.

The basis for such an assertion becomes clearer when one considers the production history of "Winter Sunrise" that Adams himself provides in his book *Examples: The Making of 40 Photographs*. In writing of the darkened hills that span the middle of the image and which stand between the silhouetted horse in the foreground and the distant, craggy peaks of Mt. Whitney, Adams laments:

> The enterprising youth of the Lone Pine High School had climbed the rocky slopes of the Alabama Hills and whitewashed a huge white L P for the world to see. It is a hideous and insulting scar on one of the great vistas of our land, and shows in every photograph made of the area. I ruthlessly removed what I could of the L P from the negative (in the left-hand hill), and have always spotted out any remaining trace in the print. I have been criticized by some for doing this, but I am not enough of a purist to perpetuate the scar and thereby destroy – for me, at least – the extraordinary beauty and perfection of the scene.

> . . . This photograph suggests a more agreeable past and may remind us that, with a revived dignity and reverence for the earth, more of the world might look like this again. (Adams 1983: 164–5)

Figure 21.1 "Winter Sunrise in the Sierra," by Ansel Adams.

Adams may wish for his photograph to remind viewers of a landscape long gone and, perhaps, inspire them to seek to reinstate it. However, the lyrical yet unmistakably documentary quality of the image also evokes a feeling that is very much in the present tense. No doubt countless viewers of "Winter Sunrise" have taken it to be an accurate impression of what the eastern edge of the Sierra Nevada really looks like, for such is the power of black-and-white photography in the popular imagination. Unlike Clappe, who wrote of seeing a certain beauty in the meanderings of an irrigation ditch, Adams has no desire (at least in this particular instance) to reproduce any aspect of a scene which does not conform to his idea of a wilderness's being anything but completely natural. He may be no purist in a photo-documentary sense, but he clearly is one in terms of mountain and desert imagery.

We now live in an age when such an image as Adams's is easily taken as ocular proof of California's natural beauty and bounty. Yet it too is just a fantasy that further signifies the rift, keenly felt by the Joads, that can still open up between perceptions and landforms, between assumptions about California's exceptionalism and the supposedly "real" thing. Perhaps one antidote to this rift may be found in the poetry of Gary Snyder. Combining a lifelong study of Buddhism with his interests in ecology and myth, and doing so with a touch of playful anarchism, Snyder is not one to approach the mountains of California in the boundary-oriented, overtly realist methods elucidated thus far. To be sure, he is deeply interested in the material world. However, the crucial factor in Snyder's mountains, that which separates his representations from the many products of Western practices that have come before, is his insistence that people live in them too. A central tenet in much of Snyder's work, poetry as well as prose, is the potentially rewarding relationship that people may have with their local environments, or bioregions. In a poetry largely devoid of metrics but greatly influenced by Chinese and Japanese forms, the accomplishments of fellow San Francisco Renaissance poets Kenneth Rexroth and Allen Ginsburg, and the principles of field composition, Snyder strives continually to focus his readers' attentions onto the ethical responsibilities inherent in the practice of daily life, wherever such living may ultimately occur. In Snyder's transplantation of Buddhist practice to the mountains of California there is no rift, or, as the title of a recent collection of his poetry suggests, *No Nature* – only an everyday life that is very much worth attending to.

NOTES

1　This is not to say that there exists no regionalist fiction about California's mountains and deserts. In addition to that of Bret Harte and Mary Austin, one should also keep in mind the work of Mary Hallock Foote, who wrote and sketched (for publications such as *Scribner's* and the *Century*) largely autobiographical renditions based on her time as a mining engineer's wife in the Coast Range south of San Francisco. However, the documentary motive also drives such generally fictional works as Mark Twain's *Roughing It*, which employs the conventions of factual reportage and personal experience as the base of its humor, and Wallace Stegner's *Angle of Repose*, wherein the author makes ample, albeit controversial, use of Foote's letters and autobiographical writings to craft the character of Susan Burling Ward. Even *The Grapes of Wrath* derives to some extent from documentary material, in that while composing the novel Steinbeck relied extensively on the research into Depression-era migrant workers' lives he had conducted for his "Harvest Gypsies" report.

2　See Limerick (1989) and Teague (1997) for further examinations of how American perceptions of and attitudes towards deserts evolved over the course of the nineteenth century.

3　The tendency to establish a California narrative by passing first through the deserts and mountains before arriving at the emotional heart of both the region and the story persists to this day. For a recent example see Philip Fradkin's *The Seven States of California* (1995), which begins with the author's recounting his arrival in 1960 via a Volkswagen Bug driven across Death Valley. The opening of John McPhee's *Assembling California* (1993) also hints at this manner of entry. A century earlier, Frank Norris had already noticed the ubiquity of this structuring device: his 1899 novel *McTeague* notoriously reverses the pattern by having the title character leave San Francisco, work for a time in the mines near Colfax, and finally encounter both his nemesis and his eventual death on the salt flats of, once again, Death Valley.

4　Muir's accomplishments are largely in the arena known as wilderness preservation, a movement that as often as not found itself at odds with those in favor of shepherding and managing resources, namely conservationists. For an excellent example of Teddy Roosevelt-style conservationist prose set in California's mountains, see Stewart Edward White's 1911 book *The Cabin*. A popular writer of adventure tales and genre satires, White (a friend of Roosevelt's) also published several collections of his essays on hunting, fishing, trekking, and, eventually, building a summer home in the high Sierra just east of Fresno.

References and Further Reading

Adams, Ansel (1983). *Examples: The Making of 40 Photographs*. Boston: Little, Brown.

Clappe, Louise Amelia Knapp Smith (1998). *The Shirley Letters from the California Mines, 1851–1852*, ed. Marlene Smith-Baranzini. Berkeley, CA: Heyday Books. (First publ. 1854–5.)

Delano, Alonzo (1853). *Pen-Knife Sketches, or, Chips of the Old Block, a series of original illustrated letters*. Sacramento: published at the Union Office.

Delano, Alonzo (1854). *Life on the Plains and Among the Diggings: being scenes and adventures of an overland journey to California; with particular incidents of the route, mistakes and sufferings of the emigrants, the Indian tribes, the present and the future of the great West*. Auburn, NY: Miller, Orton, & Mulligan.

Dorst, John D. (1999). *Looking West*. Philadelphia: University of Pennsylvania Press.

Fender, Stephen (1981). *Plotting the Golden West: American Literature and the Rhetoric of the California Trail*. Cambridge: Cambridge University Press.

Foote, Mary Hallock (1899). "How the Pump Stopped at the Morning Watch." *Century* 58, 469–72.

Fradkin, Philip (1995). *The Seven States of California: A Natural and Human History*. New York: Henry Holt & Co.

Harte, Bret (1990). *Bret Harte's California: Letters to the* Springfield Republican *and* Christian Register, *1866–67*, ed. Gary Scharnhorst. Albuquerque: University of New Mexico Press.

James, George Wharton (1906). *The Wonders of the Colorado Desert*. Boston: Houghton Mifflin.

King, Clarence (1872). *Mountaineering in the Sierra Nevada*. Boston: James R. Osgood & Co.

Limerick, Patricia Nelson (1989). *Desert Passages: Encounters with the American Deserts*. Niwot, Colo: University Press of Colorado.

McPhee, John (1993). *Assembling California*. New York: Farrar, Straus & Giroux.

Manly, William Lewis (1894). *Death Valley in '49: Important chapter of California pioneer history, the autobiography of a pioneer, detailing his life from a humble home in the Green Mountains to the gold mines of California; and particularly reciting the sufferings of the band of men, women and children who gave "Death Valley" its name*. San Jose: Pacific Tree and Vine Co.

Muir, John (1894). *The Mountains of California*. New York: Century.

Muir, John (1911). *My First Summer in the Sierra*. Boston: Houghton Mifflin.

Snyder, Gary (1995). *No Nature: New and Selected Poems*. New York: Pantheon.

Starr, Kevin (1973). *Americans and the California Dream, 1850–1915*. New York: Oxford University Press.

Steinbeck, John (1976). *The Grapes of Wrath*. New York: Penguin USA. (First publ. 1939.)

Teague, David W. (1997). *The Southwest in American Literature and Art: The Rise of a Desert Aesthetic*. Tucson: University of Arizona Press.

Van Dyke, John C. (1903). *The Desert: Further Studies in Natural Appearances*. New York: Charles Scribner's Sons. (First publ. 1901.)

Wallace, David Rains (1983). *The Klamath Knot: Explorations of Myth and Evolution*. San Francisco: Sierra Club Books.

White, Stewart Edward (1911). *The Cabin*. New York: Grosset & Dunlap.

Witschi, Nicolas (2002). *Traces of Gold: California's Natural Resources and the Claim to Realism in Western American Literature*. Tuscaloosa: University of Alabama Press.

Wyatt, David (1986). *The Fall into Eden: Landscape and Imagination in California*. Cambridge: Cambridge University Press.

22

Regions of California:
The Great Central Valley

Charles L. Crow

California's Great Central Valley, comprising the Sacramento and San Joaquin water-sheds, is a geological wonder, and one of the most productive farming areas on the planet. In many ways, in its appearance and its culture, it is not like the rest of California. Set apart by mountain ranges, flat, punishingly hot in summer, foggy in winter, it has neither the photogenic landscape nor the gentle Mediterranean climate evoked by California in the popular imagination. On a relief map or globe it is im-mediately recognizable, and nearly unique on the Earth's surface: a huge, flat, elongated oval surrounded by mountains. The Valley's farms supply food to the nation and the world. Its highways and pipelines and canals are the bones and arteries of the nation's richest economy. The California Aqueduct, running down the valley's west side, is, we are told, one of three man-made structures (with the Great Wall of China and London's Millennium Dome) easily identifiable from space.

Yet today, as for the last 300 years, most travelers who see the Central Valley are on their way to somewhere else. People who remain in the Valley have come to work; they are not seeking glamor or fame or recreation. The Valley's farming commu-nities, small towns, and cities have little fashionable buzz, with the possible exception of Sacramento, California's capital.

The literature of this region always has reflected these superlatives and negatives. The themes of the Valley are potentially epic; yet the lives of most of its residents are gritty and ordinary. There is a social consciousness in Valley literature, and often a defiant strain of working-class populism. Central Valley writers recall a complex and often disturbing history of immigration and settlement, and frequently of exploita-tion and racial and class conflict. Episodes of Central Valley history such as the Gold Rush (which used the Valley as its staging area), the Mussel Slough Tragedy, the arrival of Dust Bowl refugees, and its continuing farm labor unrest, have echoed in national politics and have provided background for the Valley's literature. Like the literature of California generally, the writings of the Great Central Valley often pre-sent an urgent restatement of the American Dream, a longing for renewal, upward mobility, and a true home place. Like American literature at large, Valley literature records both fulfillment and disillusion. As Carey McWilliams, the state's great activist-historian, wrote long ago, the bland appearance of California's agricultural interior conceals "many secrets from a casual inspection," and has "a melodramatic history" (McWilliams 1939: 5, 7). Thus the writers of this apparently featureless flatland have much to reveal, and have produced a compelling body of literature in consequence.

Unparalleled Invasions

Before European contact, California had the greatest concentration of Indians north of Mexico. The Central Valley had perhaps 160,000 of the state's 310,000 native inhabitants (Heizer and Elsasser 1980: 27). (Indeed, as figures for the precontact population of the Americas recently have been revised upward, this estimate may prove to be too low.) Their largely peaceful Central Valley communities were concentrated along the wooded borders of the principal rivers, in the foothills of the Sierra, and around the lakes and marshes at the southern end of the Valley, and enjoyed an ample diet of salmon, acorns, waterfowl, elk, deer, and antelope, supplemented by grass seeds, tubers, and edible grubs and insects. These peoples may have occupied their territories for as long as 10,000 years, and thus were one of the most stable and enduring populations of the New World. This stability offers an ironic contrast to the subsequent tumultuous history of the state, with its rapid series of human and environmental changes, begun by Spanish explorers and continuing today.

Translations exist of some songs and myths of the Valley Indians, owing in part to the efforts of early anthropologists like Alfred Kroeber. Everyone knows the story told by Kroeber's widow Theodora of Ishi, who was found near Oroville in 1911, the last survivor of the Yana tribe, which had occupied a territory at the eastern edge of the Valley and in the Sierra foothills above. It is a mistake, however, to regard the Indians of the Central Valley entirely as lost peoples. Descendants of the original population still survive; some assimilated into other communities, others in small reservations, in some cases within their historic territories. Inevitably, in time, voices will appear to articulate the experience of these groups, as has begun already elsewhere in California.

Description of the Central Valley in European languages begins in 1772, when Franciscan priest Fray Juan Crespi, traveling with explorer Captain Pedro Fages, climbed a spur of a mountain east of San Francisco Bay, and saw "a great plain as level as the palm of the hand, the valley opening about half the quadrant, sixteen quarters from northwest to southeast, all level land as far as the eye could reach" (Haslam and Houston, eds., 1978: 19).

The mountain on whose slope Crespi stood is now called Mt. Diablo, and it is believed that more of the Earth's surface can be seen from its summit than from any other point on the planet; yes, more even than from Mt. Everest, because of the unrestricted lines of sight. This mighty prospect would be described again in 1862 by William Henry Brewer, a member of Josiah Whitney's US Government surveying team:

> *The* great features of the view lie to the east of the meridian passing through the peak. First, the great central valley of California, as level as the sea, stretches to the horizon both on the north and the southeast. It lies beneath us in all its great expanse for near or *quite three hundred miles of its length!* But there is nothing cheering in it – all things seem blended soon in the great, vast expanse. Multitudes of streams and bayous wind and ramify through the hundreds of square miles – yes, I should say *thousands* of square miles – about the mouths of the San Joaquin and Sacramento rivers, and then away up both of these rivers in opposite directions, until nothing can be seen but the straight line on the horizon. On the north are the Marysville Buttes, rising like black masses from the plain over a hundred miles distant; while still beyond, rising in sharp clear outline against the sky, stand the snow-covered Lassen's Buttes, *over two hundred miles in air line distant from us* – the longest distance I have ever seen. (Brewer 1930: 264–5)

This intelligent writer's panoramic description is worth pausing over, for it anticipates many similar passages in Valley literature. From the viewpoint of someone walking on the Valley floor, or riding on horseback or in a vehicle, it is very difficult actually to *see* this landscape, to have any sense of its shape or scope, or, in modern times, its fields or crops. Thus writers of the Valley often create what might be called "perspective moments": views from hills or mountains, in which the Valley reveals its impressive strength and power – and when it makes sense. As California-born philosopher Josiah Royce put it, "viewed from any commanding summit, the noble frankness of nature shows one at a glance the vast plan of the country" (Haslam and Houston, eds., 1978: 16). Such scenes often contrast the ordinary struggling lives of people in the Valley with the insight gained from the commanding summit.

In the 90 years between the panoramic descriptions of Crespi and Brewer, unparalleled invasions had transformed the Valley. Its very appearance changed, as the native prairie grasses, which had sustained herds of deer, elk, and antelope for thousands of years, were replaced by "immigrant species" – foxtails, tumbleweed, perennial grasses of several kinds – in just a few decades. "This successful invasion is one of the most striking examples of its kind to be found anywhere" (Bakker 1984: 168). The radical alteration of the landscape was being completed in the 1860s by a combination of drought and overgrazing by cattle and sheep, witnessed by Brewer in his excursions up and down California.

The influx of plants, of course, had its human counterpart. During the age of the missions, when settlement clung to the coast, changes in the interior began slowly. By the 1840s, "the splendid idle forties," as Gertrude Atherton later styled them, which saw the twilight of Mexican rule in California, a visitor to the Central Valley would have found some large cattle ranches, a few squatters and trappers, and a changing Indian population in which diminished local tribes mixed with coastal peoples who had fled the missions. Mary Austin's novel *Isidro* (1905), set in the Central Valley, the coastal mountains, and Monterey, recaptures something of this era. At the same time, the early 1840s saw small groups of settlers find their way across the imposing Sierras into the Valley. The Stevens Party in 1844 was the first to bring wagons across the mountains, and was followed soon by other groups, including the Donner Party of 1846, whose ordeal by cold, hunger, and cannibalism cast a dark shadow over the period.

The exception to the "idleness" of the forties was the very energetic emigrant John Augustus Sutter (1803–80) who, during this decade, built a Mexican land grant of over 48,000 acres into an inland barony around the junction of the American and Sacramento rivers (site of the present state capital). His Nueva Helvetica may be seen as the first of many attempts to control great sections of the Valley and to organize its economic potential. He employed Indian labor to build a fort and plant wheat, orchards, and vineyards: a forecast of agricultural innovations later in the nineteenth century, and of the pattern of white owners exploiting dark-skinned farm labor. He was able to maintain his holdings during the transition from Mexican to American rule, but his fledgling empire was swept away when his partner in a sawmill project, James Marshall, discovered gold on the American River in 1848. The following year the slow trickle of emigrants became a mighty torrent.

The Gold Rush, a demographic shift unrivaled in modern peacetime history, changed the nation and the Valley. The title of J. S. Holliday's history is accurate: *The World Rushed In*. Tens of thousands of men from around the world – ultimately *hundreds* of thousands – stormed the foothills and mountains above the Valley floor. The towns of Stockton and Sacramento, soon to be the capital of the new state, served as base camps for men and equipment, and built fortunes that would dominate the economy and politics of the West for decades.

The literature of the Gold Rush inevitably is more concerned with perilous journeys to California, by sea or across the plains and over the Sierras, and with life in the mountains, than with life on the Valley floor. Nevertheless, diaries and memoirs of the period provide glimpses of the developing region. Most valuable is the memoir of the English-born Sarah Royce (1819–91), the mother of the philosopher and historian Josiah Royce, who, in her old age, rewrote her diaries into a lively and articulate narrative. In *A Frontier Lady*, published in 1932, Sarah Royce provides a stirring account of her journey west in 1849 and her subsequent life in Grass Valley, in the foothills east of Sacramento.

Sarah Royce and her fellow well-known Gold Rush memoirist, "Dame Shirley" (Louise Amelia Knapp Smith Clappe, 1819–1906), experienced no discourtesy from the miners, though both understood the menacing side of this era. The collision of different groups of nearly lawless and rapacious men spawned acts of violence, vigilantism, and racial conflict that set unfortunate precedents for California's future. One victim of racially motivated violence, Joaquin Murietta (c.1832–53), vowed vengeance for the death of his brother, the rape of his wife, and the loss of his claims, and spread terror up and down the Sierra foothills and eastern Valley. The details of the adventures and death of this "Mexican Robin Hood" are obscure, and largely folkloric; but the legends and scraps of fact were transformed by John Rollin Ridge into his melodramatic novel, *Life and Adventures of Joaquin Murietta* (1854). Ridge, who also used the pen name Yellow Bird, was a San Francisco journalist and the son of a murdered Cherokee Nation leader. His own life had its melodrama and mysteries: he was said to have tracked down and killed his father's murderers in the Oklahoma Indian Territories. His novel about Joaquin Murietta occupies a strange position as both the first novel by an American Indian and the first novel of California Mexican-American experience.

The lawlessness of Murietta's day had not disappeared in the 1860s, when the Whitney survey parties were trekking up and down California. Geologist Clarence King, who had been hired by Brewer, tells of fleeing in the night, his horse's hooves muffled, from suspicious wayfarers at an inn in Visalia, and being pursued by the mounted bandits through the following day, until he reached safety in Mariposa. This episode is the "Kaweah's Run" chapter in his splendid and only book, *Mountaineering in the Sierra Nevada* (1872). Perhaps, later readers have suspected, the episode is fictional; but it does capture the scruffy and dangerous character of life in the remote reaches of the Valley at that time.

In the years after the Civil War, the land began another transformation. While cattle and sheep ranching continued on a large scale, the Valley also became one of the world's great producers of wheat – a dry-weather crop requiring no irrigation. Vast cattle ranches and wheat ranches were formed, usually by colorfully unscrupulous land grabs, into which the last of the Mexican ranchos disappeared. To give a single and notorious example, Henry Miller (originally Heinrich Alfred Kreiser, 1827–1916), a butcher turned cattle rancher, once had himself towed around the valley in a boat drawn by horses, in order to claim that a tract was swampland eligible for reclamation under federal law. By such practices he amassed 1.4 million acres of land. At the same time, the railroad network was extended through the valley by the Central Pacific: an immensely powerful corporation controlled by the "big four" (Huntington, Crocker, Stanford, and Hopkins), whose wealth came originally from supplying Forty-Niners. Fat with government land grants (alternating sections along the right of way offered as incentives to build the system), the railroad became one of the biggest landlords of the valley, as well as controlling the only transport to market. Thus a pattern of subsequent Valley history was set: huge agricultural and corporate interests essentially colonizing the region, competing with one another, vying for control of governments and courts in back-room deals.

A resulting clash between economic interests produced one of the most notorious events in California history, and one of the classic gunfights of the old West: the Mussel Slough Tragedy of May 11, 1880. The broad outlines of the conflict are clear enough. The railroad invited ranchers to lease land cheaply along its routes, with a promise to sell at reasonable prices after improvements were made. However, the land was eventually offered at greatly inflated prices. Cary McWilliams would later write, "There is no more shameful chapter in the history of corporate swindling in the United States than this story" (1939: 17). The ranchers formed a league to lobby and protest. In the gun battle that erupted during an attempt to evict some of the original settlers, seven people were killed.

The details of the event are much murkier. While the episode involved the interests of big money, the battle was fought by ordinary people, some of whom had been friends. Other agendas, only dimly visible from this distance, may have been involved, including the historic Western opposition between farmers and cattlemen. Of the events of that day, the only undisputed facts are that two men, Mills Hart and Walter Crow, accompanied by a US marshal, arrived to take possession of property once leased by members of the league. A crowd of armed league members, perhaps as many as 30, rushed to the scene to prevent this. Crow and Hart may or may not have been deputies, or pawns in the pay of the railroad, or simply frontiersmen in search of a good land deal. The fight may have begun with an accidental discharge of a weapon. The US marshal did not intervene in the resulting intense exchange of gunfire. Hart was mortally wounded with the first shots, while Crow, a cattle rancher and a locally famous marksman, apparently killed five of his opponents, faced down the rest with his probably empty pistol and shotgun, and escaped the scene of the fight on foot, only to be ambushed and shot down later in the day. His back-shooting killer was doubtless known to many, but his identity, like many other details of that early summer day, disappeared into the secret lore and family memories of the Valley. No one was ever charged for Crow's murder.

The Mussel Slough Tragedy can be seen as an archetypical Valley story: ambiguous and melodramatic, woven with layers of conflicting narrative, involving ordinary lives disrupted by large historical events and big-money interests. Not surprisingly, it has cast a long shadow over the region's literature. Mussel Slough is in the background of works from Jack London's *The Star Rover* (1915) to Oakley Hall's recent detective novel, *Ambrose Bierce and the Queen of Spades* (1998). Philosopher Josiah Royce used it as the basis for his only novel, *The Feud of Oakfield Creek* (1887); and Frank Norris used a version of the shoot-out as the climax of *The Octopus* (1901), the first great novel of the Central Valley.

In the opening chapter of *The Octopus*, Presley, a visiting Eastern writer, rides his bicycle through the Valley and meets many characters, providing us with an introduction to the novel's people and setting. At day's end, he climbs a hill and looks across the vast wheatlands:

> The whole gigantic sweep of the San Joaquin expanded, Titanic, before the eye of the mind, flagellated with heat, quivering and shimmering under the sun's red eye. At long intervals, a faint breath of wind out of the south passed slowly over the levels of the baked and empty earth, accentuating the silence, marking off the stillness. It seemed to exhale from the land itself, a prolonged sigh as of deep fatigue. It was the season after the harvest, and the great earth, the mother, after its period of reproduction, its pains of labor, delivered of the fruit of the loins, slept the sleep of exhaustion, the infinite repose of the colossus, benignant, eternal, strong, the nourisher of nations, the feeder of an entire world.

Ha! there it was, his epic, his inspiration, his West, his thundering progression of hexameters. . . . As from a point high above the world, he seemed to dominate a universe, a whole order of things. (Norris 1986: 613–14)

The inspiration gained from this perspective moment is shattered, however, when Presley descends to the Valley floor to find a scene of horror: the mangled and bloody bodies of a flock of sheep through which a locomotive has run at high speed. On one level the novel that follows is an attempt by Norris, Presley, his mystical alter ego Vanamee the shepherd, and us, the readers, to reconcile the contradictory visions of this first chapter. After hundreds of pages the lives of many characters are destroyed by the conflict of ranchers and the railroad, as presaged by the slaughter of sheep. Yet at the end Presley has another perspective moment when he surveys the Valley (from a pinnacle in imagination; he is physically on a ship in the Pacific), and recognizes that if the individual dies, the life force represented by the wheat endures, works for the ultimate good, and flows from the Valley outward to a hungry humanity.

The Octopus is an ambitious novel by a young writer whose considerable powers were not always fully under control. The book is often overwritten to the point of self-parody (as the quoted passage shows), and is flawed by racist stereotypes that should not be explained away. Norris also took some liberties with the history and geography of the region. Nonetheless, he largely got it right. He was the first to capture the agricultural and economic themes of the Valley, the first to see this landscape as a *center*, not a place marginal to the larger world, and he anticipated most of the issues that other writers about the Valley would explore for the next hundred years.

A Canal Runs Through It

An incomplete irrigation ditch transverses the landscape of *The Octopus*, and it is there that the armed ranchers await the marshal and his posse sent to evict them. This excavation also forecasts the next wave of dramatic changes for the Central Valley.

Increasingly elaborate dams and canals would grow, in the twentieth century, into one of the great technical achievements of the human race. Taking a long view, however, this turning of California, and especially the Central Valley, into what historian Donald Worster (1992) calls a "hydraulic society" is a doomed enterprise. Artificial irrigation in time inevitably results in the ruin of farmland by concentrating salts in the soil. Hydraulic societies always fail in the long run, though the short run may last for many decades.

So dry-weather crops in the Central Valley were replaced with even more profitable grape vineyards and orchards of fruit and nut trees: peaches, figs, olives, pomegranates, plums, almonds, walnuts, and more recently citrus – a cornucopia of specialty crops shipped around the world. Another crop, cotton, which had been grown in a small way earlier, was reintroduced on a large scale in the early years of the twentieth century.

Thus the appearance of the Valley changed, becoming a vast green patchwork of irrigated orchards, vineyards, and fields. This transformation had immense social consequences. Cotton, orchard fruits, and grapes are labor-intensive crops, especially at harvest time, requiring teams of laborers to move swiftly from one area to another, picking each in turn as it ripens. This agricultural imperative – the need for cheap migrant labor to pick fruit and cotton – determined much of the demographics of the Central Valley in the twentieth century. Successive waves of migrants from Japan, the Philippines, the Dust Bowl regions of the Great Plains, and Mexico were drawn to the Valley, often by bogus descriptions of opportunity there, and have stayed, over time, to mix with other population groups such as Armenians, Basques, Volga Germans, Portuguese, Dutch, and Chinese, each with its own particular history in the Valley, along with westward-drifting Americans of all backgrounds, to give the region its particular ethnic mix. The Central Valley is now, in fact, one of the most ethnically diverse regions in the country.

At the eve of World War II, Kevin Starr asserts, California "had reached a long-lasting plateau of completion" (1996: 339). That is, its government and companies had built modern cities and an infrastructure of highways and bridges and utilities to support them – work that had continued through the Great Depression. The completeness of the Central Valley, applying Starr's observation, could be seen in its transformed farmlands, watered by an ever-expanding system of dams and canals. Children had grown to adulthood amid mature orchards and carefully graded fields, tended at harvest time by gangs of migrant workers; the land had been ever so, it would have seemed to them.

In 1939 three classics of Central Valley literature were published, in different genres, portraying Valley life in this phase of its evolution: William Everson's *San Joaquin*, Cary McWilliams's *Factories in the Field*, and John Steinbeck's *The Grapes of Wrath*.

William Everson (1912–94) was born in Sacramento and raised in Selma, just south of Fresno. Like many Valley writers after him, he attended Fresno State College. His *San Joaquin* is the first collection of verse about Valley farmland by a writer of real talent, and captures the landscape through the eyes of someone native to the place. No one before Everson had written poems describing the quiet somber light of the foggy winter landscape, the pruning of grapevines, or the ghost towns of the Sierra foothills (now haunted by the memory of rowdy miners and of Joaquin Murietta). Everson would continue writing through a long career, including a middle phase when he used the name Brother Antoninus.

Cary McWilliams (1905–80), historian and political activist, documented in *Factories in the Field* the history of the exploited, nearly invisible farm laborers who had been an essential component of the Valley since the early twentieth century. *Factories in the Field* is a thorough, factual, angry book. McWilliams's account of the Wheatland riot (August 13, 1913) must be read by anyone concerned with California's farm labor history. Little changed between Wheatland and the 1930s, McWilliams shows, except the ethnic origins of the immigrant groups. At the time he wrote – and for long after – the struggle of farm labor for decent conditions continued with little success.

The most famous description of immigrant labor in the Central Valley is, of course, *The Grapes of Wrath* by John Steinbeck (1902–68). Steinbeck's own heritage lay in the Salinas Valley, another of California's agricultural regions; though not a native of the Central Valley (any more than Norris had been), he understood the issues of migrant labor, and brought his considerable talent and passion to the story of the "Okies:" dispossessed farm families from Oklahoma and neighboring states fleeing the drought of the Dust Bowl.

When, halfway through *The Grapes of Wrath*, the Joad family looks down on the floor of the southern San Joaquin Valley from the Tehachapi Pass, they see "the vineyards, the orchards, the great flat valley, green and beautiful, the trees set in rows, and the farm houses" (Steinbeck 1939: 309–10). This is the California they had imagined and sought during their hard crossing of the desert, and the vision is so powerful that they must pull their battered truck to the side of the road and gaze in reverence. As they descend to the Valley floor, they find something different: a system of near-peonage that mocks the aspirations of the disenfranchised. *The Grapes of Wrath* has been bitterly resented in the Valley, both by established farmers and even by the Okies themselves and their descendants, who were embarrassed by what they found to be undignified, patronizing, and inaccurate descriptions of their lives. To many readers then and now, however, *The Grapes of Wrath* is a compassionate and honest account of conditions one would have found everywhere in the Valley. The Joads' experiences up and down Highway 99 mirrored those of thousands of émigrés from the Dust Bowl, many of whom Steinbeck had met and interviewed.

To the above three books of the 1930s by Everson, McWilliams, and Steinbeck, one might add a fourth: Carlos Bulosan's *America is in the Heart*. Though not published until 1946, Bulosan's memoir is a description of the author's life before the war as a laborer up and down the West Coast, including the Valley. Bulosan (1911?–56) lived the exploited life described by Steinbeck and McWilliams before becoming a labor organizer and a writer. (McWillliams, in fact, would later write an introduction to a reprint of Bulosan's book.) Bulosan enjoyed a brief vogue from his poetry and from a book of stories based on Philippine folklore, *The Laughter of My Father*, but he died in his forties, broken in health and in poverty.

After World War II, the Dust Bowl Okies and other groups were largely replaced by Mexicans in the fields of the Valley. Protests organized by Cesar Chavez in Delano in 1965 against conditions little changed since the days of the Wheatland riots brought renewed national attention to the conditions of farm labor, helped to spark a national Chicano political and cultural movement, and summoned a new generation of Mexican American authors. Among those joining Chavez's boycott against grape growers in 1965 was Luis Valdez, who left a mime company in San Francisco for Delano, and created El Teatro Campesino (The Farm Worker's Theater). For several years Valdez's group used amateur players to perform "actos," collaboratively developed motivational plays, for farm workers in the fields of the San Joaquin. Eventually the group broadened its goals and moved to San Juan Bautista on the coast. Valdez's best-known play is *Zoot Suit* (1978), based on anti-Mexican riots in Los Angeles during World War II.

The arrival of political and cultural self-awareness among Mexican Americans in the Valley may be seen as the cumulation of forces set in motion when water first began to flow through irrigation ditches and transformed the landscape.

A Drive Down Highway 99

The spine of the Valley is Highway 99, one of the nation's storied roadways, first made visible in fiction in *The Grapes of Wrath*. The Joads drove up and down 99 in search of work, as have generations of farm laborers and other wayfarers before and since. Strung along Highway 99 are the Valley's towns, to the traveler mere exit signs on the highway, but each with its history and its stories; and many have found authors to give them voice.

Sacramento and Stockton are the oldest of the Valley's cities, and the closest to the urban center of San Francisco Bay. Sacramento, of course, has special prominence as the state capital. Joan Didion (b. 1935) is a native of Sacramento, a fifth-generation Californian, daughter of a Valley land developer, though her writing career has been pursued in Hollywood and New York. Her first novel, *Run River* (1963) portrays a decadent landed gentry of the Sacramento Valley in the period from the 1930s to the 1950s. The culture is insulated, semi-incestuous, conscious of its own passing; the plot tinged with Gothic shadows. Didion's essays, collected in *Slouching toward Bethlehem* (1968) and *The White Album* (1979), and several later volumes, present an insider's view of the California establishment. She writes knowledgeably of politics, the movie studio system, California's water supply. Her voice is distinctive, minimalist, and ironic. Writing from what is essentially a California version of a Tory sensibility, she expresses skepticism about social change, and a somewhat qualified nostalgia for an earlier California life. In *Run River* her description of the social scale descends no lower than the manager of the family-owned hops ranch.

For Richard Rodriguez (b. 1944), who grew up in an immigrant family that had fought its way into the lower middle class, Joan Didion's Sacramento had "nothing to do with me" (1992: 217). In two excellent books, *Hunger of Memory* (1982) and *Days of Obligation* (1992), Rodriguez describes his own childhood in the Valley, his university days and his engagement with the political, ethnic, and gender issues of his times. The last chapter of *Days of Obligation* is a historical meditation weaving together memories of growing up in Sacramento with his parents' memories of Mexico, and the history of Sacramento, including the story of John Sutter. Recently, autobiographical sections in *Brown: The Last Discovery of America* (2002) continue the chronicle of this best-known Mexican American intellectual.

Robert Roper's 1973 novel *Royo County* is set in a countryside apparently south of Sacramento. The name of the county is imaginary, but the valley land and themes are portrayed with great accuracy and power. The novel opens with a description of the flat landscape and an account of the vigilante-style killing of a Mexican suspected of a crime. Several deliberately murky plot-lines propel the narrative, one involving a young man fleeing the vengeance of gangsters from "The City." By the end of the novel we know that the fugitive boy and his girlfriend have fled the Valley too late to escape murderous pursuers, but we do not see their fate. Various secrets of the community are revealed, and over the whole setting, as in so much California literature, broods a sense of a conspiracy involving real estate development, certain to bring unwelcome change. The novel's last image is that of a sexually brutalized child, standing in a field, pretending to be a flower – an image vaguely recalling the allegorical subplot about the raped Angèle in *The Octopus*.

Stockton, the next large town south of Sacramento, is an important shipping center, a railroad junction and seaport, for ships can sail to it though a deep-water channel from San Francisco Bay. The Stockton roots of Maxine Hong Kingston (b. 1940), one of the nation's most widely read authors, are underappreciated, though Kingston has stressed her Valley heritage in interviews. *The Woman Warrior* (1970) and *China Men* (1980) are eclectic postmodern works, mixing novelistic techniques with personal memoir and history, ranging from ancient to modern China, through the Chinese immigrant experience in early California and Hawaii and New York, to the author's childhood and maturity. While Stockton was not named in *The Woman Warrior* (and some Eastern critics assumed that San Francisco was being described), the two books provide, in a series of episodes, a detailed view of Stockton's Chinese American community in the 1940s and 1950s. The brilliant opening of *The Woman Warrior*, "You must never tell anyone what I am about to tell you, my mother said," presages the lifting of the lid on a closed Valley community. (These lines are echoed by Rodriguez in *Hunger of Memory*: "I am writing about those very things my mother has asked me not to reveal" [1982: 175].) Near the end of *China Men*, describing the funeral procession of her great-uncle the river pirate, Kingston takes us on a tour of the Skid Row and Chinatown sections of Stockton she has memorably evoked in the two books – the house she grew up in, the shuttered building where her father once ran a gambling den, the Chinese school, the benevolent association, the laundry on El Dorado Street – and out into the countryside to the Chinese cemetery.

Kingston's Stockton schoolmate, Leonard Gardner, describes the same Skid Row cityscape in *Fat City* (1969), which was made into a movie (1972) directed by John Huston and shot on location in Stockton. Though set in the 1950s, Gardner's *Fat City* has the feel of Steinbeck's Great Depression or the writings of Beat writers like Kerouac and Snyder. Its two main characters, Billy Tully and Ernie Munger, are boxers struggling on the lowest edges of their profession. Both men are drifters, with little clear future or hope of success. Gardner convincingly portrays the world of the down-and-out: the cheap hotels, boxing gyms, and stoop labor in the fields of the surrounding countryside (fields where Maxine Hong Kingston's mother occasionally worked).

South of Stockton is the town of Modesto, portrayed in Stephen Varni's *The Inland Sea* (2000). Varni's autobiographical bildungsroman depicts the difficult relationship of the protagonist with his father, a liquor wholesaler, his work as an adolescent in Stockton, his college years in the Midwest, and his return to his home town. Like most recent descriptions of the Valley, Varni's novel records the passing of the orchard era of his city, as walnut and almond groves give way to sprawling malls and housing developments.

Fresno, at the center of the Valley and the state, had no boost from the Gold Rush, and was described by Brewer as a dusty and depressing crossroads. It began to develop after the coming of the railroad as an agricultural and shipping center, and now is the largest city of the San Joaquin, the seat of the wealthiest agricultural county in the nation. It has an unusual ethnic amalgam, and is the home of a state university that has played an important role in the region's literature.

Fresno's Armenian community was begun in the nineteenth century by immigrants who found the nearby farmland suitable for crops like those of their homeland, and was augmented by refugees from Turkish persecution during World War I. The most famous son of this community, William Saroyan (1908–81), made Fresno during the Depression a place of freedom and adventure for boys, like the St. Petersburg of *Tom Sawyer*. In stories collected in *My Name is Aram* (1940), *The Man with the Heart in the Highlands* (1968), and *Madness in the Family* (1988), Saroyan embellishes his own childhood (omitting a bleak three-year sojourn in an Oakland orphanage following his father's death), and celebrates his protagonist's wanderings though the community and neighboring fields, swimming in irrigation ditches and playing hooky, encountering colorful characters of many backgrounds, and enjoying the eccentricities of his large extended family. He wrote in his introduction to *My Name is Aram* that Fresno was "as good a town as any in the world for a writer to be born into" (Saroyan 1940: viii). Yet Saroyan's generally sunny outlook does not mask entirely what he called elsewhere "the universe of ice." The Gargoglians of *My Name is Aram* share with other émigrés not only poverty but a continuous ache for a lost homeland. This is the point of "The Poor and Burning Arab": Uncle Cosgrove understands the alienation of Khalil, the Arab, though they have almost no language in common, and he can scarcely bear to explain his emotions to his American-born nephew. In "The Pomegranate Trees," Aram's uncle Melik pursues his dream of an orchard, and it need not be explained that he is trying to recreate the landscape of his childhood. The bank's foreclosure on the land, and the death of the trees when they are not irrigated, are examples of the universe of ice at work – the harshness of reality against which Saroyan and his characters can pit only their life-affirming imagination.

The lost orchard would return as a potent symbol in Valley literature later in the twentieth century, and continues so today (for example, in Varni's novel) as farmland retreats before urban sprawl, and smog increasingly obscures the Sierras.

Mark Arax is a younger member of the same Fresno Armenian community, and his family knew Saroyan's. (There may be a reference to a market owned by Arax's father and uncle in *The Human Comedy* [Saroyan 1943].) Mark Arax was a reporter for the *Los Angeles Times* when he decided to return to his home town to investigate and write about a crime that occurred when he was a boy: the murder of his own father. Though Arax admires Saroyan, and describes a meeting with the elderly writer, *In My Father's Name: A Family, A Town, A Murder* (1996) is intended as a corrective to the general exuberance and celebration of Saroyan's view of Fresno. Arax's father became a nightclub owner after leaving the grocery business, and was a popular and respected figure. Apparently resisting a web of bribery and protection into which he was being drawn, the senior Arax was shot down by two gunmen in the office of his nightclub. As in most Central Valley tales, the shadows do not part entirely. Arax seems on the verge of locating his father's assassins when the narrative ends, leaving the reader wondering if all has been told. Though evasive about the investigation's outcome, the book is a convincing exposé of the longstanding corruption, with the complicity of its police department, of this apparently placid community.

Another Fresno native is Gary Soto, probably the most distinguished living poet of the Valley. Soto writes of growing up in a working-class family in a series of memoirs, beginning with *Living up the Street* (1985). Soto's essays, here as elsewhere, resemble short stories, and often recall Saroyan's cheerful anarchy: "Perhaps the most enjoyable summer day," writes Soto in "Being Mean," "was when Rick, Debra, and I decided to burn down our house" (1985: 12). The young Gary is recalled as a bad good boy (like Tom Sawyer), who alternated between being "sweet" and being "your basic kid with a rock in his hand" (Soto 1985: 36). Unlike Saroyan's stories about Aram, however, Soto confronts more directly the shadow that both writers shared: the childhood loss of a father. This searing event appears again and again in both his poems and his prose memoirs. His childhood was lived on the edge of poverty and in part with a stepfather the boy detested. Like other members of the family, Soto worked in the surrounding farmlands during summer vacations. Later, Soto studied creative writing at Fresno State under Philip Levine, a poet and gifted teacher who nurtured talent from the region for many years. (Other Valley writers to study under Levine include Lawson Inada, Shirley Ann Williams, and Louis Omar Salinas.)

Soto's first book of poetry, *The Elements of San Joaquin* (1977) whose title perhaps deliberately invokes Everson's, is an important milestone, bringing a distinguished voice to Mexican American experience of this region. Soto's verse probes the painful childhood memories of his autobiographical essays, and also evokes the landscape and his experience laboring during the summers in Valley fields. Soto's subsequent career has been prolific, producing novels, adolescent fiction, and other collections of poetry and essays.

Southeast of Fresno, David Mas Masumoto reveals another generally silent community, that of Japanese American farmers. Emigrants from Japan had played an essential role in developing the agriculture of the Central Valley (and the West generally), but many farm families of this group lost their land because of internment during World War II, and the decline continued after the war as young members of the community, often college graduates, pursued careers in the cities. The highly educated Masumoto resisted this trend, taking over his parents' farm near the small town of Del Ray. *Country Voices* (1987), a collection of essays, interviews, and photographs, chronicles the history of his community. Two collections of essays, *Epitaph for a Peach* (1995) and *Harvest Son* (1998), record his struggle to preserve his family's ties to the land and the traditional varieties of peaches they raised. Masumoto provides a wholesome reminder that family farms do exist in the Valley; it is not all giant corporate farming. Nowhere else can one find such an accurate account of the seasonal changes and the life of ordinary farmers living close to the land in this region.

Driving south from Fresno toward Bakersfield, the landscape seems endless and unchanging. However, the extreme southern end of the central valley is, in two geographic ways, distinct from the rest of the region. Technically, it is not even the San Joaquin. The southernmost four rivers emerging from the Sierras into the Valley once flowed into a vast complex of wetlands and lakes including the extensive, if shallow, Tulare Lake. This waterland did not connect with the northward-flowing San Joaquin river except in times of overflow. The four rivers now are dammed, however, and the former wetlands, drained and graded into level fields, are scarcely even a memory for the farmers and townspeople of the region. Except in flood, the south end is visually coextensive with the rest of the Valley floor.

The other distinguishing factor is the presence of oil. Beneath the southern end of the Valley lies one of the nation's major oil reserves. Because of its oil industry, Bakersfield, the southernmost of the Valley cities along Highway 99, with its satellite communities Oildale and Taft, has a hardscrabble, blue-collar atmosphere, and seems in many ways more like a town in Texas or Oklahoma than California. This end of the Valley is the only part of California where "Okie" still signifies a recognizable social group. It was here, after all, that the Joads first dropped from the Tehachapi Pass, east of Bakersfield, and looked for work. Many of their real-life descendants still work here as oilfield roughnecks. It is not surprising, then, that Bakersfield is the West Coast center of country and western music. One of its biggest stars, Merle Haggard, was raised here. Country music will be judged by many to be the true artistic expression of the Valley's southern end. The Bakersfield mix of Valley themes – oil, country music, farming, and (as always) a land-development conspiracy – is captured admirably in the recent detective novel *Blackheart Highway* (1999) by Richard Barre, in which a private eye from Santa Barbara enters the case of a country singer bearing some resemblance to Merle Haggard.

The essential literary figure of the Valley's southern end is Gerald Haslam (b. 1937). Haslam is a protean man of letters, a scholar, anthologist, essayist, and fiction writer, and he has done more than anyone to give voice to the Central Valley generally, and to his home town of Oildale. His anthologies, *California Heartland* (1978), *Many Californias* (1992), and *The Great Central Valley: California's Heartland* (1993), and his collection of essays *The Other California: The Great Central Valley in Life and Letters* (1994), are the best points of departure for any study of Valley literature. The bilingual child of a Mexican mother and an Okie father (the once-offensive term proudly claimed), Haslam has deep roots in the region's working-class heritage. His essays, perhaps his finest work, collected in *Voices of a Place* (1987) and *Coming of Age in California* (1990) are worthy of comparison with the more celebrated personal essays of Didion. His subjects include his community and family, his work on farms and in oilfields, and his complex interaction with his father. Other essays present a memorable diverse gallery of southern Valley characters, including his childhood schoolmate, Merle Haggard. Haslam is also a novelist (*Masks*, 1976) and writer of some six collections of short stories set in the Valley, beginning with *Okies* (1975). He has recently published the definitive study of California Western music, *Workin' Man Blues* (1999).

Highway 99 exits the Valley south of Bakersfield, climbing up the Grapevine Canyon toward the Tejon pass, following, approximately, the route of the Butterfield Stage line in the late nineteenth century. Over this pass in 1888 came the Hunter family: a woman, her son, and a daughter, recently graduated from college, who would be known to us as Mary Austin. The family settled at the edge of the Valley floor near the mouth of Grapevine Canyon on a hot, dusty, and waterless landscape – an oppressive place to a young woman from the green fields of Illinois. (It is still depressing to many people.) In *Earth Horizon* Austin would describe how she sank into depression and anorexia, nearly starving before reviving her health by walking in the hills and eating wild grapes. An equivalent spiritual healing began as a result of her meeting with Edward Fitzgerald Beale, former Surveyor General of California and Nevada under the Lincoln administration, and proprietor of the vast Tejon Ranch. Beale taught Mary about the countryside and its history, thus beginning her intellectual and emotional engagement with the region. This was a transition for Mary Austin comparable to young Willa Cather's first winter on the Divide, when she "fought it out" with the countryside and came to love it.

General Beale, Mary's mentor, was a living compendium of nineteenth-century California history. He came to California as a naval officer in 1846, had fought alongside Kit Carson in the battle of San Pasqual in the south, and was the bearer of dispatches to Washington in 1848 announcing the discovery of gold at Sutter's Mill. Later he settled in the hills near the Tejon Pass and founded a ranch. The Tejon Ranch would continue under Beale family ownership into the twentieth century, when it passed into other hands, and it still exists. According to historian Kevin Starr, Beale's Tejon Ranch achieved, for a time, an alternative vision of California – representing what the whole state might have become if it had been allowed to mature slowly; that is, if the world had not rushed in (see Starr 1985: 22–30). The ranch hired surviving California Indians as respected employees, along with a mixture of hands from Basque, Mexican, Portuguese, and other backgrounds. For decades a kind of middle landscape was realized, a working and prosperous ranch in harmony with the place and among its peoples. One of the Tejon hands, Arnold R. Rojas (1899–1988), of mixed Sephardic, Spanish, and Indian heritage, would write in detail of cowboy life on Beale's ranch in sketches he collected and published himself in *Those Were the Vaqueros* (1974) and *Vaqueros and Buckaroos* (1979); he was interviewed by Gerald Haslam, who wrote an essay about him (1987: 65–71).

Though most of Mary Austin's California sketches and stories are set in the Owens Valley region and the Mojave Desert to the east, some of the pieces in *Land of Little Rain* (1903) and *The Flock* (1906) provide a glimpse of the lost period of Beale's ranch. *The Flock*, like many of the best Central Valley books, mixes history and landscape description with autobiography. The life of shepherds in the Central Valley, the mountains, and the Mojave deeply engaged Austin's imagination. In a fragmentary poem, written during her last few days of life, she named her shepherd friends of long before, and imagined joining them again around their campfire. A true regionalist in the best sense, Austin strove for a solid knowledge of the ecology and the people of her chosen landscape, and, the first to write of it, knew it better than almost anyone since.

Highway 99 passes the site of Fort Tejon, where Beale served as a young officer, and rises toward the Tejon Pass, first explored in 1772 by the indefatigable Spaniard Pedro Fages (whose chaplain Juan Crespi viewed the Valley from Mt. Diablo the same year). The approach to the pass provides one of the best views of the Valley floor as it marches away northward in green checkerboard squares toward the horizon. Continuing across the pass, one descends toward Los Angeles – and another California altogether.

Conclusion

Every region is part of a larger human and ecological web or network, and is in some sense both a margin and a center. As its name suggests, and a glimpse at a map will prove, the Great Central Valley is California's center, its core; the rest of the state is its margin, a rind or shell around this interior heartland. Yet the Great Central Valley, though richer and larger than many entire countries, is also a margin: it is an economically colonized space, and has been since the state's founding. It exports most of the wealth it produces. It is both essential and nearly invisible to the cultural and financial centers of the coast. It plays little part in the image of California projected by popular culture around the world. Yet – and therefore – the Central Valley has produced a distinctive and important literature, recording the lives of this diverse and ever-changing land.

References and Further Reading

Arax, Mark (1996). *In My Father's Name: A Family, A Town, A Murder*. New York: Simon & Schuster.

Austin, Mary (1903). *Land of Little Rain*. Boston and New York: Houghton Mifflin.

Austin, Mary (1905). *Isidro*. Boston and New York: Houghton Mifflin.

Austin, Mary (1932). *Earth Horizon: The Autobiography of Mary Austin*. New York: Literary Guild.

Austin, Mary (2001). *The Flock*. Reno: University of Nevada Press. (First publ. 1906.)

Bakker, Elna (1984). *An Island Called California: An Introduction to Its Natural Communities*, 2nd edn. Berkeley and Los Angeles: University of California Press.

Barre, Richard (1999). *Blackheart Highway*. New York: Berkley Prime Crime.

Brewer, William Henry (1930). *Up and Down California in 1860–1864: The Journal of William H. Brewer*. New Haven: Yale University Press.

Bulosan, Carlos (1944). *The Laughter of My Father*. New York: Harcourt, Brace & Co.

Bulosan, Carlos (1946). *America is in the Heart: A Personal History*. New York: Harcourt, Brace & Co.

Clappe, Louise Amelia Knapp Smith (1949). *The Shirley Letters from the California Mines, 1851–1852*. New York: Knopf. (First publ. 1854–5.)

Crow, Charles L. (1990). "Norris, Crow, and the Mussel Slough Tragedy." *California English* 26, 20–1, 30–1.

Didion, Joan (1963). *Run River*. New York: I. Obolensky.

Didion, Joan (1968). *Slouching towards Bethlehem*. New York: Farrar, Straus & Giroux.

Didion, Joan (1979). *The White Album*. New York: Simon & Schuster.

Everson, William (1939). *San Joaquin*. Los Angeles: Ward Ritchie.

Gardner, Leonard (1969). *Fat City*. New York: Popular Library.

Hall, Oakley (1998). *Ambrose Bierce and the Queen of Spades*. Berkeley: University of California Press.

Hart, James D. (1978). *A Companion to California*. New York: Oxford University Press.

Haslam, Gerald (1975). *Okies: Selected Stories*. Santa Barbara and Salt Lake City: Peregrine Smith.

Haslam, Gerald (1976). *Masks: A Novel*. Penngrove, Calif.: Old Adobe.

Haslam, Gerald (1987). *Voices of a Place: Social and Literary Essays from the Other California*. Walnut Creek: Devil Mountain.

Haslam, Gerald (1990). *Coming of Age in California: Personal Essays*. Walnut Creek: Devil Mountain.

Haslam, Gerald (1992). *Many Californias: Literature from the Golden State*. Reno: University of Nevada Press.

Haslam, Gerald (1993). *The Great Central Valley: California's Heartland*, with photographers Robert Dawson and Stephen Johnson. Berkeley and Los Angeles: University of California Press.

Haslam, Gerald (1994). *The Other California: The Great Central Valley in Life and Letters*. Reno and Las Vegas: University of Nevada Press.

Haslam, Gerald (1999). *Workin' Man Blues: Country Music in California*, with Alexandra Haslam Russell and Richard Chon. Berkeley: University of California Press.

Haslam, Gerald and James D. Houston, eds. (1978). *California Heartland: Writing from the Great Central Valley*. Santa Barbara: Capra.

Heizer, Robert F. and Albert B. Elsasser (1980). *The Natural World of the California Indians*. Berkeley and Los Angeles: University of California Press.

Holliday, J. S. (1981). *The World Rushed In: The California Gold Rush Experience*. New York: Simon & Schuster.

King, Clarence (1872). *Mountaineering in the Sierra Nevada*. Boston: J. R. Osgood & Co.

Kingston, Maxine Hong (1976). *The Woman Warrior: Memoirs of a Girlhood among Ghosts*. New York: Knopf.

Kingston, Maxine Hong (1980). *China Men*. New York: Knopf.

Kroeber, Theodora (1961). *Ishi in Two Worlds*. Berkeley and Los Angeles: University of California Press.

London, Jack (1915). *The Star Rover*. New York: Macmillan.

McWilliams, Carey (1939). *Factories in the Field: The Story of Migratory Farm Labor in California*. Boston: Little, Brown.

Masumoto, David Mas (1987). *Country Voices: The Oral History of a Japanese American Family Farm Community*. Del Ray, Calif.: Inaka Countryside Publications.

Masumoto, David Mas (1995). *Epitaph for a Peach: Four Seasons on my Family Farm*. San Francisco: HarperSanFrancisco.

Masumoto, David Mas (1998). *Harvest Son: Planting Roots in American Soil*. New York: Norton.

Norris, Frank (1986). *The Octopus: A Story of California* (1901). In *Frank Norris: Novels and Essays*. New York: Library of America.

Ridge, John Rollin (Yellow Bird) (1955). *Life and Adventures of Joaquin Murietta, The Celebrated California Bandit*. Norman: University of Oklahoma Press. (First publ. 1854.)

Rodriguez, Richard (1982). *Hunger of Memory: The Education of Richard Rodriguez: An Autobiography*. Boston: D. R. Godine.

Rodriguez, Richard (1992). *Days of Obligation: An Argument with my Mexican Father*. New York: Viking.

Rodriguez, Richard (2002). *Brown: The Last Discovery of America*. New York: Viking.

Rojas, Arnold R. (1974). *Those Were the Vaqueros*. Shafter, Calif. (self-published).

Rojas, Arnold R. (1979). *Vaqueros and Buckaroos* (self-published).

Roper, Robert (1973). *Royo County*. New York: Morrow.

Royce, Josiah (1887). *The Feud of Oakfield Creek*. Boston: Houghton Mifflin.

Royce, Sarah (1932). *A Frontier Lady: Recollections of the Gold Rush and Early California*. New Haven: Yale University Press.

Saroyan, William (1940). *My Name is Aram*. New York: Harcourt, Brace.

Saroyan, William (1943). *The Human Comedy*. New York: Harcourt, Brace.

Saroyan, William (1968). *The Man with the Heart in the Highlands and Other Stories*. New York: Dell.

Saroyan, William (1988). *Madness in the Family*. New York: Dell.

Soto, Gary (1977). *The Elements of San Joaquin*. Pittsburgh: University of Pittsburgh Press.

Soto, Gary (1985). *Living up the Street*. San Franciso: Strawberry Hill.

Starr, Kevin (1985). *Inventing the Dream: California through the Progressive Era*. New York: Oxford University Press.

Starr, Kevin (1996). *Endangered Dreams: The Great Depression in California*. New York: Oxford University Press.

Steinbeck, John (1939). *The Grapes of Wrath*. New York: Viking.

Valdez, Louis (1978). *Actos y El Teatro Campesino*. San Juan Bautista, Calif.: Menyah Productions.

Valdez, Louis (1992). Zoot Suit *and Other Plays*. Houston: Arte Publico.

Varni, Stephen (2000). *The Inland Sea*. New York: Morrow.

WLA (1997) *Updating the Literary West*. Sponsored by the Western Literature Association. Fort Worth: Texas Christian University Press.

Worster, Donald (1992). "Hydraulic Society in California." In *Under Western Skies: Nature and History in the American West*. New York: Oxford University Press. (First publ. 1982.)

23

Los Angeles as a
Literary Region

David Fine

In a 1955 television interview, Flannery O'Connor remarked, "I think to know yourself is to know your region and that is to know the world, and in a sense, paradoxically, it's also to be in exile from that world. So that you have a great deal of detachment" (Magee, ed. 1987: 8). In a later (1963) piece in *Atlantic Monthly*, she expressed again the "double consciousness" (to borrow W. E. DuBois' term) of the regional writer, who is simultaneously inside and outside the territory: "The Georgia writer's true country is not Georgia, but Georgia is an entrance to it. One uses the region to suggest what transcends it" (Magee, ed. 1987: 110). Regions confer identity, a sense of place – of being "in place" – and in doing so also carry the awareness of relationship to, and separation from, the larger world, the "other" that lies beyond the particular place.

Regions are thus contested territory; boundaries between region and nation are porous and ambiguous. Regions have been represented in literature both as autonomous and cohesive places, distinct from other places, and as slices, or subdivisions, of larger places, never wholly distinct from them. As constructed landscapes shaped and defined by human intervention, by cultural mapping and appropriation, regions negotiate the path between the local and the national (or global). This negotiation of geographies is particularly relevant to a discussion of Los Angeles regional fiction – a migrant fiction constructed almost wholly, until the most recent few decades, by outsiders to the region.

The conventional wisdom has it that regional writing is the product of writers born in, nurtured by, and strongly attached to the regions about which they write. The region is what Eudora Welty has called on different occasions "the heart's field." Regional writing is not the act of the tourist, but of the man or woman who belongs to the region, who has a strong and abiding love for, and cultural knowledge of, the territory. A corollary assumption, particularly in earlier regionalist criticism, has it that regional writing represents a form of geographic determinism: the land shapes the writer, shapes identity and character. Absent from such an assumption is the fact that the writer is not only shaped by, but shapes, the land about which he or she writes – shapes our way of seeing it.

The regional fiction of Los Angeles (or "Greater Los Angeles," meaning the vast basin known colloquially as "The Southland"), poses clear and distinct exceptions to these assumptions, foregrounding that sense of exile about which O'Connor spoke. From its beginnings (from, that is, its founding piece, Helen Hunt Jackson's 1884 romance, *Ramona*), fiction about the Los Angeles/southern California region has been the construct of outsiders, men and women not born to the manor, but newcomers to this place at the edge of the West – most conspicuously as screenwriters in the 1930s (with the advent of sound movies) and over the next few decades.[1] Any discussion of Los Angeles fiction must begin with the fact that the men and women who first conferred a literary identity on the city were newcomers, migrants, and visitors, whose sense of displacement, of dislocation, gives the fiction its distinctive qualities. It wasn't the outside world (the East, the Midwest, the South, even Europe) that was "other," but Los Angeles itself. It was the place of exile, of removal.

The distanced perspective of the writer as outsider, his or her detachment, alienation, and sometimes utter confusion (rendered in tones ranging from fascination to derision) conferred on the region its identity as a placeless place, an unreal Oz-like landscape.[2] When the writers arrived, the city, despite the Depression, was still in the midst of an explosive population and building boom that had begun in the 1880s, following the completion of two rail lines into the region, and would continue for the next 50 years. To the freshly arrived writers in the 1930s the city appeared as a sprawling, seemingly chaotic, improvised semi-urban landscape (historian Carey McWilliams called it "rurban"). Gauging it against the places they left behind, the writers felt they had arrived at a place with no clearly discernible center (and, without center, no periphery), no identifiable reigning architectural style (and in its place an "anything goes" attitude toward the built landscape), and no sense of a regional past that, despite the mission and Spanish-derived buildings cropping up everywhere, could exert any local aesthetic authority or convince them that they had, in fact, arrived in a place.

The consequence was a regional fiction that played, at times obsessively, on themes of unreality, improvisation, and masquerade, eliciting these themes in image patterns that took in the extended city's landscape, both natural and architectural. I can think of no other regional literature that so pervasively appropriates the vast landscape – the eclectic and bizarre architecture (mimicking every style in architectural history); the centerless sprawl; the preponderance of roads, highways, and cars; and the proliferation of cults, healers, and medical quacks (who followed in the wake of the health-seekers drawn to the place by booster claims of the miraculous healing power of the climate). The look of the land offered the writers, as outsiders, metaphors for instability, fragility, and deception – contrasts to the places they left behind, the remembered places.

As the work of the migrant writer, Los Angeles fiction offers a sense not only of spatial, but of temporal dislocation. Much regional writing carries the dimension of time – the passage of time, that is – expressed either explicitly or implicitly. A region's past is played off against its present. One thinks of Edith Wharton's old and new New York, Sherwood Anderson's pre- and postindustrial Ohio Valley, or William Faulkner's ante- and postbellum Mississippi as places notated in the context of change, places situated in the transformative historical process of modernization, urbanization, and the shifting demographics of race, class, and power. In Los Angeles fiction, by contrast, the opposition, the tension, is not between the region's present and its past, but between the local present and a past carried from some other place. History is not so much absent as it is displaced; it exists as a different region, carried in memory. History is geography; the past is a remembered elsewhere.

Immigrant fiction – both the turn-of-the-century fiction written by European immigrants (Ole Rolvaag, Abraham Cahan, Anzia Yezierska, and others) and the more recent fiction (set in Los Angeles and elsewhere) of Asian and Latin American immigrants – centers on the disjunction of Old and New Worlds, lands left behind and lands found. The past is dismembered geographically from the present but never far away in memory. Immigrant (and migrant) fiction is the literature of crossings, of uprooting and transplantation. New settlers seek fresh starts, but bring selves nurtured elsewhere. If regions confer identity, the identity of the immigrant is never fixed, but always floating between two realms. One is both inside and outside the region. Immigrants and migrants try to graft old ways on to the new land, but the graft doesn't always take. Nathanael West, who came to Hollywood as part of the vast migration of writers in the 1930s, has his Yale-trained artist-spokesman Tod Hackett muse ruefully in *The Day of the Locust* (1939) that "he would never again paint a fat old Nantucket barn, old stone wall, or sturdy Nantucket fisherman" (West 1962: 60). His contemporary, James M. Cain, two years after his 1931 arrival, wrote home (to H. L. Mencken's *American Mercury*), in a piece ironically called "Paradise," about a southern Californian architectural landscape in which gas stations were built to look like the Taj Mahal and structures resembling giant oranges, windmills, mosques, and tea-kettles were to be found everywhere. "There is no reward for aesthetic virtue here, no punishment for aesthetic crime," he wrote (J. Cain 1985: 166). The Los Angeles of the newly arrived writers was, more often than not, rendered as an "aesthetic crime," an anarchic landscape set down in a basin that sprawled from mountain to ocean and lacked any governing architectural control or authority. All this became the raw material for constructing a fiction preoccupied with conferring a sense of insubstantiality and unreality.

This way of seeing (or not seeing) the place, established by the 1930s migrant writers, has persisted to the present day. In Alison Lurie's *The Nowhere City* (1965), Paul and Katherine Cattleman move from New England to Los Angeles, where they live in a bungalow in a neighborhood called Vista Garden – with no vista and no garden. The stucco bungalows come in "ice cream colors," and the whole neighborhood, in which houses are continually being razed, moved, or rebuilt, has the appearance of a movie set. Houses look like pagodas and gas stations look like lighthouses. A giant plaster cow towers over a drive-in milk bar. Katherine tells a friend that coming in from the airport she passed a 20-foot-high revolving cement donut; like the enormous hole in the donut, Los Angeles is for her a huge advertisement for nothing. For Lurie, as East Coast writer, decoding Los Angeles entails the piling of one image of urban disarray on to another, agglomerating a mountain of chaos. She does this largely through comic incongruities: smog against palm trees, flowers so big as to appear artificial, a French chateau crawling along the street on the back of a truck, beach crowds almost naked against Merry Christmas signs, sun-worshippers lounging beside empty swimming pools. More recently, Robert Parker, the Boston-based writer who created the Spencer series of detective novels (and completed Chandler's unfinished *Poodle Springs* in 1989, as well as writing a sequel to *The Big Sleep* called *Perchance to Dream*), brings Spencer to Los Angeles in *A Savage Place* (1981), giving Parker a chance to respond to the chaotic sprawl of the city:

> I didn't know any place like it for sprawl, for the apparent idiosyncratic mix of homes and businesses and shopping malls. There was no fixed point for taking bearings. It ambled and sprawled and disarrayed all over the peculiar landscape – garish and fascinating and imprecise and silly, smelling richly of bougainvillea and engine emissions, full of trees and grass and neon and flowers and pretense. (Parker 1981: 143)

Novels about the West Coast city are, thus, also novels about other places. More precisely, they are about the ambiguous interaction of places lost and found. Los Angeles regional fiction is, in this sense, biregional or bicoastal – and, in the case of British expatriates to Hollywood (Evelyn Waugh, Christopher Isherwood, Aldous Huxley, and others) – binational.

Joan Didion, in an essay titled "Some Dreamers of the Golden Dream," noted that "the future always looks good in the golden land" because "no one remembers the past" (Didion 1981: 20). It is perhaps equally true to say that no one entirely forgets the past – or is allowed to forget it. This is particularly the case in the tough-guy crime novel that found a home in southern California in the 1930s. What makes the detective stories of Raymond Chandler and, later, Ross Macdonald, Joseph Hansen, John Gregory Dunne, James Ellroy, Michael Connelly, and Walter Mosley so central to the local tradition is that they focus, most frequently, on crimes committed, and buried, in past time; crimes that the private eye or police detective forces into present consciousness. Skeletons in the closet – or buried underground or encased in concrete – are not allowed to remain hidden. In the resurrection of Los Angeles *noir* fiction (and film) since the 1970s, the focus is often on historic crime – as in the fiction of James Ellroy and John Gregory Dunne (who have both written novels centered on the Black Dahlia murder of 1947), or in such screenplays as Robert Towne's *Chinatown* (which takes its starting point from the Owens Valley water theft). Such works reconstruct actual crimes, fictionalizing and sometimes out-sensationalizing the already sensational crime stories drawn from the headlined past. The local detective story is about excavating the past, recovering memory and historic time. The American West has, conventionally and mythologically, been associated with timelessness, with the escape or release from history. To go west is to escape the burden of history. Los Angeles fiction says otherwise.

Writing against the booster vision of southern California as the locus of the fresh start, the new beginning, the writers who came in the 1930s and after – whether they were writing hardboiled crime stories, Hollywood novels, or novels about the urban, ethnic underclass – have been preoccupied with the representation of an insubstantial and unsettled land, filled with unsettled migrants and exiles and lying precariously at the very edge of the continent: what poet Robinson Jeffers called "the drop off place." This sense of being at the very edge of the continent, smack up against the Pacific, runs through the fiction as geographic equivalent for reaching the end of the dream. It's the place where both land and hope run out, where there is no place left to go. The California highway becomes a cul-de-sac carrying one back to the past, to beginnings, or downward to exhaustion or death.

Parallel to the cultural instability elicited in the writers' Los Angeles is the instability of the land itself. Natural as well as man-made disasters have provided the plotlines for much of the region's fiction, as they have for much of the region's history. The sun-drenched land that drew the migrants is also the land of destructive earthquakes, brush fires, floods, droughts, and mudslides. In John Fante's *Ask the Dust* (1939) and F. Scott Fitzgerald's Hollywood novel *The Last Tycoon* (1941), the 1933 earthquake centered on Long Beach marks a profound shift in the protagonists' consciousness and identity. In Fitzgerald's work it marks the beginning of his producer-hero Monroe Stahr's downward spiraling from studio power and authority to impotence and exhaustion. In other works, like Myron Brinig's fantasy *The Flutter of an Eyelid* (1933) and Curt Gentry's quasi-documentary work *The Last Days of the Late, Great State of California* (1968), the "big one" brings the apocalypse, causing the whole coast to slide into the ocean. Atomic or nuclear destruction appears in fictions ranging from Aldous Huxley's futuristic *Ape and Essence* (1948) to Carolyn See's *Golden Days* (1987), Cynthia Kadohata's *In the Heart of the Valley of Love* (1992), and several novels of Steve Erickson.

Other kinds of disaster, man-made and natural, have provided material for the writers. Every year, the hot, dry Santa Ana winds (the kind of weather in which, Raymond Chandler tells us, meek housewives sharpen kitchen knives while eying their husbands' necks) race from the desert through mountain passes on the way to the ocean, firing not only tempers but also the dry mountain and canyon chaparral. The burned hills, no longer covered by protective brush, erode and become rivers of mud when winter rains come. Cliffs give way, dumping tons of mud onto houses and coastal highways. The title story of Gavin Lambert's *The Slide Area* gives some sense of the encounter between cliff and ocean:

> High lurching cliffs confront the oceans, and are just beginning to fall apart. Signs have been posted along the highway. DRIVE CAREFULLY and SLIDE AREA. Lumps of earth and stone fall down. The land is restless here, restless and sliding. . . . The land is falling. Rocks fall down all over. The cliffs called Pacific Palisades are crumbling slowly down to the ocean. (Lambert 1951: 8)

The place where the ocean meets the land – the very site of the houses of those who have made it big – recurs in the fiction as the setting for disastrous endings, for the calamitous encounter of an upwardly mobile population with a vulnerable coastline. Ross Macdonald's crime fiction, much of which is set along the coast from Santa Monica to Santa Barbara, gives this theme particular significance. Tidal waves, oil spills, and forest fires – the kind that denude the hillsides and precipitate landslides – are linked by Macdonald with crimes committed and hidden on the land by the rich, who live luxuriously in the hills and canyons along the coast, having gained their wealth by exploiting both laborers (largely Mexican Americans) and the land itself. Ecological disasters are offered as responses to human greed – responses of an angry God to the kind of rapacity that allowed a vast coastal basin lying on unsettled land to be heedlessly exploited for profit, a process of relentless commodification that has been going on since the building boom of the 1880s. In Macdonald's novels, present disturbances are the consequences of brutal acts committed in the past (acts motivated by greed, jealousy, egoism, or hate), sometimes just a generation or two earlier; past acts are hauntings, ghosts in the family attic that Archer, Macdonald's detective, brings down into present consciousness, linking generations.

Macdonald, whose Lew Archer first appeared in 1949 (in *The Moving Target*), is the literary heir to Raymond Chandler, whose private eye Philip Marlowe first appeared in *The Big Sleep* in 1939 and reappeared in a series of novels to 1958. In the brand of tough-guy detective stories pioneered by Dashiell Hammett and the hard-hitting stories in the popular pulp magazine *Black Mask*, and anchored in Los Angeles by Raymond Chandler, crime is not an aberrant act – the act of a single, often a deranged individual, as it was in the more genteel detective stories of, say, an Agatha Christie or Dorothy L. Sayers – but a pervasive feature on the landscape, a network that crosses neighborhoods, class, and racial divisions. The city itself is corrupt, and the detective, far from the rational problem-solver, is the streetwise, hard-hitting tough guy who digs for answers in the muck, mixes it with people from all classes – and across the entire basin – and gets beaten, shot at, and drugged for his trouble, often coming away without really "solving" anything. For Chandler, who likened the solution of the crime to the olive in the martini, the city was always more interesting and book-worthy than the solution to the puzzle.

Chandler arrived in Los Angeles in 1912, earlier than most of the migrant writers, although he did not begin writing fiction until the 1930s. Throughout that decade he served his apprenticeship writing stories for *Black Mask*, which he later "cannibal-ized" for his novels, beginning with *The Big Sleep*. With an eye to the growth and change the city underwent from the time of his arrival, Chandler invested its physical and architectural landscape in novel after novel with moral and symbolic meaning. In Chandler's geography – as in Macdonald's – the criminals are generally the rich, who have moved high up into the hills, into large, pretentious houses (done up in a variety of historical, mostly Mediterranean, styles) surrounded by high walls that isolate and insulate them from crimes committed in the past and on the flatland below.

The Big Sleep establishes the pattern. General Guy Sternwood, not a criminal himself, has nonetheless made millions by exploiting the city's oil reserves and then moved into the hills, above the site and source of his wealth. The "primal" crime, the event that sets off everything else in the novel, is his wayward daughter Carmen's murder of the man who jilted her, whose corpse lies in the oilfield below the house, amid the deep gouges in the city's bedrock, the covered-over wounds made by the oil derricks. In his next novel, *Farewell My Lovely* (1940), this kind of geographic dislocation and relocation recurs. Velma Valenti, ex-torch singer and gangster's moll, has committed a crime in the city's flatland, framed a man for it, married a rich judge, moved up into the hills, and taken a new name and identity, barricading herself "in one of those great silent estates with twelve-foot walls and wrought iron gates and ornamental hedges".

Such movement is consistent with the demographics of the city. In the sprawling landscape of Los Angeles, status and respectability are achieved not by movement to a higher floor in the same apartment building (as in, say, Paris) or even to a better house or better street in the same neighborhood, but by movement to a different neighborhood, which in Los Angeles' terms means up into the hills or against the ocean. To "move up" carries both social and geographic meaning. In Chandler's fiction, to be more precise, it is to move away from, and above, the scene of the crime. The job of Marlowe, as detective, is to drag the criminal rich down to the flatland, carry them back to their histories, their crimes. He destroys their views, their prospects, their anonymity. He makes them remember past crimes, sometimes, as in *The Big Sleep*, by forcing them to re-enact those crimes. His task is to cure them of their amnesia. This is what places Chandler, as well as Macdonald, so squarely in the regional tradition. In the land dedicated to the proposition of the fresh migrant start, the detective is there as the reminder that the past is inescapable. One carries one's past into the present, and however successful he or she is in burying that past for a time, it resurfaces. There are always blackmailers and detectives.

While the booster version of Los Angeles, constructed by a downtown/Pasadena coterie of business interests beginning in the 1880s and 1890s, oriented the city to its eastern border, to the regenerative qualities of the desert and the Spanish/Mexican/Indian Southwest, the generation of writers who came in the 1930s and after positioned it to the West, reflecting the westward shift in the city's power and population (one result of the movie industry's incursion). Los Angeles, in its twentieth-century literary construction, faces the ocean, not the desert, and in the city's iconography the oceanfront is the site of both new beginnings and sudden endings. In the 1930s proletarian hardboiled crime novel that came to Los Angeles, like the detective story, by way of *Black Mask*, the ocean is the setting for the final act of a good number of protagonists. Before the fiction of his better-known contemporaries James M. Cain, Horace McCoy, and Raymond Chandler, Paul Cain [George Sims] established the hardboiled crime tradition with its fast-paced action, slangy, racy (at times racist) narration and dialogue, and sensational, violent plotlines. His novel *Fast One* (1933) is the real progenitor and the most relentlessly brutal of the 1930s hardboiled crime stories, a bloodbath rivaling Hammett's *Red Harvest* and W. R. Burnett's *Little Caesar*. In introducing it to its *Black Mask* audience (where it was serialized in 1931), editor Joseph Shaw used the term "New Wild West" to announce the migration of hardboiled crime fiction to southern California. Kells, its gangster hero, is a migrant who has arrived in a city already sodden with corruption, a place in which he has to stake out his territory and stake out his enemies. The rapid, clipped narrative deals with the manipulation of power, pitting, like Hammett's Continental Op, crooked politicians, rival mobsters, and competing gangs against one another in a war to control gambling, alcohol, drugs, prostitution, and the protection racket. By the mid-1920s the private auto had altered the notion of space and distance in Los Angeles, and, appropriately, much of the novel takes place on the road. Anticipating James M. Cain's protagonists, who equate fast driving with freedom, Kells speeds across the vast terrain of Los Angeles chasing power and control: "They went out Sunset at about seventy miles an hour, went on through Beverly Hills, out Beverly Boulevard. At the ocean they turned north. The road was being repaired for a half-mile or so. Kells slowed to thirty-five" (P. Cain 1978: 299). But, as in so much Los Angeles crime fiction, the road that points to new beginnings reaches a dead end at the edge of the ocean; Kells and his female companion are killed in a car crash in the rain and fog along the coast near Ventura.

Since Los Angeles emerged in the 1920s and 1930s as a city on wheels, the automobile has offered itself to novelists as either death instrument or metaphor for the illusory promise of mobility. In much of the fiction the speeding car on the highway represents the delusional belief that fast travel translates into freedom. The delusion is given special intensity in James M. Cain's Los Angeles novels, particularly *The Postman Always Rings Twice*, *Double Indemnity*, and *Mildred Pierce*.[3]

"They threw me off the hay truck at noon," the first of these novels begins, and its pace never slows down. Frank Chambers is a highway drifter who, having hitch-hiked up the coast from Mexico, stumbles on the Twin Oaks Tavern, "a roadside sandwich joint" with a filling station and "a half dozen shacks they call an auto court" (J. Cain 1934: 3–4). A few paragraphs later he meets the owner's wife Cora, and before the chapter ends he has taken a job at the Twin Oaks; before the second chapter ends a few pages later, the two have become lovers, and a short chapter later they plot the murder of Cora's husband. On an open stretch of land near the coast they commit the murder, and at the novel's end, Frank, in the postman's second ringing, having escaped punishment for the murder he did commit, is convicted of a murder he didn't – the accidental death of Cora, whose car goes into a culvert along the coast. The highway along the coast once again becomes the site of death; the open road leads not to escape or the fresh start but to calamity. So fast-paced is the action, so banal and clipped the language, that the novel has offered itself readily to parody – and there have been several over the years. But the novel has its potency; in presenting the male protagonist as an unencumbered drifter on the open road, Cain not only offers a resonant Depression image, but, along with Paul Cain, introduces what is to be a dominant metaphor in Los Angeles literature: the man or woman behind the wheel of a speeding car heading nowhere but to disaster. In *Mildred Pierce* (1941), the heroine's attempt to elevate her status and lifestyle is represented spatially as the attempt to speed along Foothill Boulevard from her middle-class house in Glendale to the house of her lover in upper-class Pasadena. For a character like Mildred Pierce, social mobility means geographic mobility; personal power and control over one's destiny are linked to the presence of the highway: "She gave the car the gun, exactly watching the needle swing past 30, 40, and 50. . . . The car was pumping something into her veins, something of pride, of arrogance, of restrained self-respect that no talk, no liquor, no love could possibly give" (J. Cain 1944: 77).

The Los Angeles hardboiled crime story reflects the collective desires and fears of the Depression decade. It expresses the rage and frustration of these years, as well as the desperation to succeed, against all odds, in a migrant, up-for-grabs city. One year after the 1934 publication of Cain's *Postman*, Horace McCoy, another young migrant writer who came to write screenplays, published the first of his two hardboiled Los Angeles novels, *They Shoot Horses, Don't They?*, and the two novels, each a first-person confessional account of a man condemned to death for the murder of a female partner, were almost immediately linked. In both cases the "murder" carries considerable irony and ambiguity. In Cain's novel Cora's death is an accident; in McCoy's the murder of Gloria Beatty is rendered as a mercy killing, the male's acceding to the female's urging that he "pinch hit for God" and put her out of her misery. This kind of ambiguity – a rupture of the boundary between cold-blooded murder and other kinds of violent death – runs through the local brand of hardboiled fiction. Gloria Beatty, the woman in McCoy's novel, is the most nihilistic, death-obsessed woman to appear in this fiction. She and her partner Robert Syverton, a pair of out-of-work Hollywood dream-chasers, have entered a dance marathon hoping to win prize money and a chance to be "discovered" by a talent scout. The marathon, staged not only *at* the ocean but *over* it, in a dance hall at the very end of the Santa Monica pier, functions symbolically as the highway does in the fiction of Paul Cain and James M. Cain – the site of endless movement that leads to no destination, except exhaustion and death. As they stagger on the dance floor, Gloria tells Robert that "[t]he whole thing is a merry-go-round. When we get out of here, we're right back where we started" (McCoy 1939: 76).

But they don't end up where they started; after 897 hours of futile movement, underscored by the persistent ebb and flow of the ocean pounding beneath their feet, the dance marathon, a *danse macabre*, is shut down following a shooting, and the pair move out of the claustrophobic hall onto the pier, where they look at the movie stars' houses and Robert accedes to Gloria's death wish. As in James M. Cain's coastal highway that doubles back on itself, betraying its promise of mobility and freedom, McCoy's dance marathon above the ocean represents, with its endless circularity, repetitiveness, and essential meaninglessness, the symbolic site for the betrayal of the promise of new beginnings. At the ocean there is no place left to go. That the marathon is staged as pure theater – an elaborate spectacle cynically manipulated by its criminal promoters to draw crowds of thrill-seekers – makes it a parody of the "dream factory," suggesting the novel's connection to Hollywood fiction. McCoy's next novel, *I Should Have Stayed Home*, extends – as its title indicates – this appropriation of Hollywood as site of dream's end.

Like a number of local crime stories, including George Hallas' *You Play the Black and the Red Turns Up* (a 1938 medium-boiled, parodic version of the crime tale in which a Hollywood director and a "wrong girl" murder get mixed up in a loony comic plot), Raoul Whitfield's *Death in a Bowl* (in which the title's "bowl" refers to the Hollywood Bowl, where a conductor is murdered onstage), Raymond Chandler's *Little Sister*, and James Ellroy's *L.A. Confidential*, Hollywood and the hardboiled come together. Both as place and as industry, Hollywood is represented as the locus of deception, corruption, and masquerade. From its emergence in the 1920s (most notably in the satirical novels like Harry Leon Wilson's *Merton of the Movies* [1922] and Carl Van Vechten's *Spider Boy* [1927]), the Hollywood novel has taken for its essential theme the confusion of reality and illusion, real life and reel life.

In Nathanael West's *The Day of the Locust*, the supreme fiction to come out of Hollywood, that confusion reaches a pathological or hallucinogenic level in his representation of characters – a cast of would-be starlets, ex-vaudevillians, Hollywood hangers-on, and drugstore cowboys – who seem wholly unable to distinguish between living and acting. Identity is performance, a matter of adopting screen poses, being "in character." West's people, as observed by Tod Hackett (himself not immune to the Hollywood siren call), walk the streets of Hollywood as if playing to the cameras, and the exotic houses they inhabit, aping and parodying every style in architectural history, look as if they have been constructed on the back lot by studio carpenters. Hollywood, the neighborhood, is represented, grotesquely, as an extension of the back lot. It is as if the studio lots, not large enough to contain all the constructed fantasies, spilled their excesses onto the surrounding streets.

West's real subject in this novel, which he originally titled *The Cheated*, is the pernicious effect of mass culture on individual and collective identity. With the coming of the movies, Hollywood became the epicenter of an entire culture cheated by the puerile fantasies of the industry. Fed on dreams of sex, glamor, and celebrity, the migrant crowd in the novel (the cheated masses) wander the streets of Hollywood, fully costumed and filled with frustration. Hackett comments prophetically on their capacity to turn their frustration into violence: "Their boredom becomes more and more terrible. They realize they've been tricked and burn with resentment. . . . The sun is a joke. Oranges can't titillate their jaded palates. Nothing can ever be violent enough to make taut their slack minds and bodies. They have been cheated and betrayed. They have saved and slaved for nothing" (West 1962: 178).

West's take on Hollywood has its antecedents in earlier novels – not only the more genial satires of Harry Leon Wilson and Carl Van Vechten from the 1920s, but also, and more closely, Carroll and Garrett Graham's *Queer People* (1930), a dark Hollywood novel that blends comic satire, melodrama, murder, and more than a hint of antisemitism, and Myron Brinig's *The Flutter of an Eyelid* (1933), a surrealistic rendering of Hollywood types that ends, apocalyptically, with the whole coast sliding into the ocean (not before the narrator makes his escape back to his New England). *The Day of the Locust*, though, by pursuing relentlessly the disastrous consequences of confusing life and fantasy and tracing the downward spiral that leads from movieland titillation to boredom, frustration, rage, and ultimately vengeful mob violence, goes beyond anything that came before and stands as *the* Hollywood novel, the essential source for every Hollywood novel that has come since.[4]

Because most Los Angeles regional fiction until the past few decades has been the work of migrant writers who came to the city as screenwriters, its principal settings have been Hollywood and the Westside – its beach communities, hills, and coastal canyons. These are the sites the writers knew best, the territories they could appropriate in fictions ranging from the hardboiled to Hollywood to the apocalyptic. The instability of the land at or near the ocean's edge has repeatedly been invoked, and equated with the instability of the migrant and mobile population. But however seductive coastal and hillside Los Angeles has been to the writers, the fact remains that the vast majority of its migrant population did not settle anywhere near the coast or the Hollywood Hills, but inland, in the vast, flat plain stretching in every direction from downtown: east across the Los Angeles river to the large Mexican-American barrio, south to Watts and "South Central," and south again all the way to Wilmington, San Pedro, and the harbor. This is the spread-out Los Angeles one sees from a plane coming from the East as it descends at LAX. Undeniably and historically, this is the heartland of the city, and it is the setting for a good number of novels written by ethnic minority writers – themselves frequently migrants or immigrants. A few Anglo-American writers explored inland Los Angeles in their fiction, notably Don Ryan in *Angel's Flight* (1927), a satiric view of the city's wandering population viewed from the top of Bunker Hill, and Raymond Chandler in *Farewell, My Lovely* and *The High Window*, where detective Marlowe's search takes him into the inner city and Pasadena. Essentially, though, the territory was claimed for fiction by its ethnic residents.

In the years just before, during, and after World War II, two central-city writers, both migrants, stand out: the Italian American John Fante and the African American Chester Himes – the former in several novels, most distinctively *Ask the Dust* (1939), and the latter in *If He Hollers Let Him Go* (1945) and *Lonely Crusade* (1947). Fante, a migrant from Colorado in the early 1930s, wrote compellingly about the Bunker Hill neighborhood he inhabited in his early years in the city in *Ask the Dust*. By the 1930s, with the westward expansion of the city, the once-elegant downtown neighborhood of jigsaw Victorians had deteriorated into a warren of boarding houses, flophouses, and cheap hotels. For Fante, though, the neighborhood was not an index of urban decay, but the site of both a vital community and the frustrated dreams of a migrant population that crowded into the city in the twenties and thirties. It emerges as a region of both hope and despair, embodying the California promise and its denial. It is the place his young protagonist, Arturo Bandini, lives, dreams, and hopes, where he completes his first novel and has his sexual initiation; but it is also the place where the masses of dream-seekers from the Midwest play out their last act, "doomed to die in the sun, a few dollars in the bank, enough to subscribe to the *Los Angeles Times*, enough to keep alive the illusion that this was paradise, that their little papier-mache homes were castles".

In his darker moods, Fante's vision of the doomed inhabitants of the city coincides with West's (whose Hollywood novel was published the same year); but in contrast to the detached and derisive tone of West's spokesman, Bandini's voice is full of sympathy and compassion: "The uprooted ones, the empty sad folks . . . the folks from back home. They were my countrymen, these were the new Californians." His tone, sometimes rising to ebullience, is not that of the prophet of doom, commenting sardonically, contemptuously, on the fallen land. Far darker is the tone of the narrators of Himes' two Los Angeles novels: offering painful witness to the migration of blacks into wartime Los Angeles' defense industry, their protagonists are men who are almost psychotically torn apart by the hatred and hostility they encounter in the city. The racism they face is as brutal as anything they faced before migrating from the South or Midwest. Like Richard Wright's Bigger Thomas (in *Native Son*, 1940), they are reduced to a state of alternating fear and anger, helpless panic and explosive rage.

A half-century after Himes' wartime Los Angeles novels Walter Mosley, clearly influenced by Himes (and by his own family history), looked back to black Los Angeles in the forties, fifties, and sixties in a series of crime novels set in Watts. Mosley's postwar Watts was an insular community, a bordered enclave of blacks, most of them wartime migrants from Texas and other Southern states. People knew one another, shared a language, a culture, a way of relating to one another. Cut off from the larger city, the Watts Mosley depicts has a small-town Southern atmosphere. An essential difference between the fiction of Himes and that of Mosley, in fact, is that Mosley constitutes his black Los Angeles as a community – one that is constantly threatened from without but which nonetheless has its solidarity – whereas Himes' protagonists are existential loners, men who live without community, without participation in a group to lend them support. Easy Rawlins, Mosley's reluctant detective, is a migrant from Texas, like most of his neighbors. As a man who knows the turf and has an "easy" relationship with his neighbors, he is seduced, sometimes coerced, into solving problems, most often the problems of power-wielding whites who thrust themselves into the black community seeking information or a woman who has disappeared in the black community (as in *Devil in a Blue Dress*, 1990). As cultural mediator, he negotiates the territory between loyalty to his community and the job he is paid by whites to perform. In reconstructing a time and place in history Mosley is something of a cultural historian, a role far different from that of Himes, who was writing painfully about a life he had recently lived.

Watts has changed enormously since the years Mosley chronicled in his Easy Rawlins novels. It is no longer an exclusively black community, but a mixed ethnic neighborhood of black Americans, Mexican Americans, and Asians. East of Watts lies the large Mexican American barrio. East Los Angeles, once a Jewish enclave, became in the 1920s and succeeding decades the principal Mexican American zone, although today the Mexican-American population is spread all over the basin. Despite their numbers (close to half the population of Los Angeles today), Mexican Americans have until recently figured only marginally in fiction about the city. In the latter decades of the twentieth century, however, they became more and more conspicuous, the subject of fiction written both by Anglos and by Chicanos/Chicanas. Among the novels have been Oscar Zeta Acosta's *The Revolt of the Cockroach People* (1973), about the Chicano moratorium and strike of 1970; Ron Arias' *The Road to Tamazunchale* (1975), a dream narrative about the last days of an aging East Los Angeles man; Thomas Sanchez' *Zoot Suit Murders* (1978), which, like Luis Valdez' play of the same year, *Zoot Suit*, is about the wartime Sleepy Lagoon murder case and the ensuing "zoot suit" riots; and Danny Santiago's [Dan James's] *Famous All Over Town* (1983), about a young "tagger" who leaves his spray-painted tag all over East Los Angeles. What links these novels is that all four, though grounded in the real life of the Mexican-American community, cross conventional generic boundaries: fiction and reportage (Acosta), fiction and magic realism (Arias), fiction and historical reconstruction (Valdez), and fiction and social criticism (Santiago/James). Among fictions about Mexican-American Los Angeles written by non-Mexican-Americans have been John Rechy's *The Miraculous Day of Amelia Gomez* (1991); T. Coraghessan Boyle's novel about a pair of illegal Mexican immigrants setting up housekeeping in a canyon beyond the gated white community of a liberal, affluent Anglo couple, *Tortilla Curtain* (1995); and Kate Braverman's splendid novel, bordering, like Rechy's, on magic realism, *Palm Latitudes* (1998).

Tracing the development of Los Angeles regional fiction since the 1930s leads one inescapably toward certain conclusions. First, despite the fact that more and more of the city's writers today are not migrants, but native-born, the fiction arguably remains essentially a migrant fiction, leaning heavily toward the experience of the outsider, the disenfranchised, the marginalized. Now, though – and World War II marks the watershed – the outsider is no longer typically the Anglo-Saxon migrant from the Midwest, but the black, Hispanic, or Asian who, as migrant, immigrant, or old settler, constitutes the large underclass of the multicultural city – a city in which nonwhites now make up more than half the population but hold little of its power. The diversity of postmodern Los Angeles reveals itself, too, in the recent evolution of the local crime and detective story. Today's detective is no longer played only as the single, white, unencumbered (and, often enough, misogynistic, homophobic, and racist) male. He may, in fact, be a she (as in, for example, the fiction of Sue Grafton, Jan Burke, and Wendy Hornsby), a gay male (in Joseph Hansen's Dave Brandstetter novels), an African American (the detectives of Walter Mosley, Gar Anthony Haywood, and Gary Philips), a Chicano (the novels of Michael Nava), or an orthodox Jew (Faye Kellerman). Or the detective may be not the private eye, but a police detective in the new version of the local police procedural novel that emerged with the novels of Joseph Wambaugh and has its most successful practitioners today in James Ellroy and Michael Connelly. In recent years, too, we have had more of the doomsday fiction that emerged in the 1930s and 1940s works of Nathanael West, Myron

Brinig, and Evelyn Waugh, in novels like Carolyn See's *Golden Days*, Cynthia Kadohata's *In the Heart of the Valley of Love*, and those of Steve Erickson (all of which deal with survivors in a futuristic, post-apocalyptic Los Angeles). Today's literary city may not float into the sea after "the big one," as earlier versions had it, but a sense of endings that goes back to hardboiled and Hollywood fiction of the 1930s remains as a conspicuous feature on the local literary landscape. The major difference in the most recent incarnations of the Los Angeles doomsday novel is that the focus is not on the disaster itself, but, more optimistically, on the will to survive it, the determination to go on, to begin again – and this, after all, is the impulse that has been there from the start in the city at the edge.

NOTES

1 Although I am tracing the real emergence of Los Angeles regional literature to the 1930s, there are some noteworthy novels in the preceding decade, among them Mark Lee Luther's *The Boosters*, Don Ryan's *Angel's Flight*, Carl Van Vechten's *Spider Boy*, and Upton Sinclair's *Oil!*

2 L. Frank Baum, with appropriate irony, settled in Los Angeles after the fame of *The Wizard of Oz* and wrote *Dorothy and the Wizard*, set in Los Angeles.

3 James M. Cain wrote two other novels set at least in part in Los Angeles, *The Embezzler* and *Serenade*. Neither is relevant to my treatment.

4 Both F. Scott Fitzgerald and Aldous Huxley were working on their Hollywood novels, respectively [*The Love of*] *The Last Tycoon* and *After Many a Summer Dies the Swan* (both 1939), while West was working on his, so there is no line of influence there. Budd Schulberg's *What Makes Sammy Run*, Norman Mailer's *The Deer Park*, and Leon Wurlitzer's *Slow Fade* do show West's influence in both characters and imagery. Many of the more recent Hollywood fictions are, wholly or in part, *romans a clef*, among them Peter Viertel's *White Hunter, Black Heart*, Erica Jong's *How to Save Your Own Life*, Jill Robinson's *Perdido*, Josh Greenfeld's *Mr. Hollywood*, and John Rechy's *Marilyn's Daughter* – novels that to one degree or another form part of that line of descent from West.

REFERENCES

Acosta, Oscar Zeta (1973). *The Revolt of the Cockroach People*. New York: Bantam.

Arias, Ron (1975). *The Road to Tamazunchale*. Tempe, Ariz.: Bilingual Press.

Boyle, T. Coraghessan (1995). *Tortilla Curtain*. New York: Penguin.

Braverman, Kate (1998). *Palm Latitudes*. New York: Linden.

Brinig, Myron (1933). *The Flutter of an Eyelid*. New York: Farrar & Rinehart.

Cain, James M. (1934). *The Postman Always Rings Twice*. New York; Knopf.

Cain, James M. (1944). *Mildred Pierce*. Cleveland: World Press. (First publ. 1941.)

Cain, James M. (1985). "Paradise." In *Sixty Years of American Journalism by James M Cain*, ed. Roy Hoopes. Bowling Green, Ohio: Popular Press. (First publ. 1933.)

Cain, Paul [George Sims] (1978). *Fast One*. Carbondale: University Press of Illinois. (First publ. 1933.)

Didion, Joan (1981). "Some Dreamers of the Golden Dream." In *Slouching toward Bethlehem*. New York: Simon & Schuster.

Fine, David (2000). *Imagining Los Angeles: A City in Fiction*. Albuquerque: University of New Mexico Press.

Fitzgerald, F. Scott (1941). *The Last Tycoon*. New York: Scribners.

Graham, Carroll, and Graham, Garnett (1930). *Queer People*. New York: Vanguard.

Hallas, George [Eric Knight] (1938). *You Play the Black and the Red Turns Up*. New York: Robert McBride.

Himes, Chester (1945). *If He Hollers, Let Him Go*. New York: Doubleday, Doran.

Himes, Chester (1947). *Lonely Crusade*. New York: Knopf.

Kadohata, Cynthia. *In the Heart of the Valley of Love* (1992). Berkeley: University of California Press.

Kowalewski, Michael (1994). "Writing in Place: The New American Regionalism." *American Literary History* 6, 171–83.

Lambert, Gavin (1951). *The Slide Area*. New York: Ballantine.

Lurie, Alison (1977). *The Nowhere City*. New York: Penguin. (First publ. 1965.)

McCoy, Horace (1939). *They Shoot Horses, Don't They?* New York: Knopf. (First publ. 1935.)

Madden, David, ed. (1968). *Tough Guy Writers of the Thirties*. Carbondale: University Press of Illinois.

Magee, Rosemary M., ed. (1987). *Conversations with Flannery O'Connor*. Jackson: University of Mississippi Press.

Mosley, Walter (1990). *Devil in a Blue Dress*. New York: Simon & Schuster.

Parker, Robert (1981). *A Savage Place*. New York: Dell.

Riegel, Christian and Wyile, Herb, eds. (1997). *A Sense of Place: Reevaluating Regionalism in Canadian and American Writing*. Edmonton: University of Alberta Press.

Ryan, Don (1927). *Angel's Flight*. New York: Boni & Liveright.

Sanchez, Thomas (1978). *Zoot Suit Murders*. New York: Dutton.

Santiago, Danny [Dan James] (1983). *Famous All Over Town*. New York: New American Library.

See, Carolyn (1987). *Golden Days*. New York: McGraw Hill.

Slide, Anthony (1995). *The Hollywood Novel: A Critical Guide to over 1200 Works with Film-Related Themes and Characters, 1912–1994*. Jefferson, NC: McFarland.

Sundquist, Eric (1988). "Regionalism and Realism." In Emory Elliott (ed.), *The Columbia Literary History of the United States*, 501–24. New York: Columbia University Press.

Valdez, Luis (1971). *Actos*. San Juan Bautista, Calif.: Centro Campesino Cultural.

Van Dyke, John C. (1980) *The Desert*. Salt Lake City: Peregrine Smith. (First publ. 1901.)

West, Nathanael (1962). *The Day of the Locust*. New York: New Directions. (First publ. 1939.)

24

North and Northwest: Theorizing the Regional Literatures of Alaska and the Pacific Northwest

Susan Kollin

As a theoretical framework for literary studies, regionalism has faced various critical battles over the years. Following its heyday in the 1930s and 1940s, place-based studies of American literature have experienced numerous cycles of interest and moments of decline, as each decade critics and writers debate the problems and possibilities associated with regional studies. The major criticism tends to argue that regional writing is minor work limited by a narrowly focused literary vision. Often thought to be inferior writing that may have proved popular among locals but failed to achieve larger recognition nationally or internationally, regional literature is frequently dismissed as a provincial and conservative reaction against an ever-encroaching and homogenizing modernism. In his anthology of Pacific Northwest literature, Bruce Barcott explains the problem. "Most writers cringe at the 'regionalist' label," he writes. "The tag carries the smell of failure, as if the writer got his or her specifics right but failed to translate them into universals" (Barcott 1994: xiii). Tracing the ways regional studies in literature has gone in and out of fashion over the years, it is worth noting that among American historians, regionalism has not experienced quite the same rollercoaster ride. For many US historians, the study of regional differences serves as a useful corrective to an overly generalized picture of the nation where one region's identity is typically made to stand for all others. If regionalism has had a stronger foothold among historians for this reason, it might be useful to consider what prevents it from occupying a similar place in literary studies. After all, should the development of more nuanced understandings of national specificities not be an important concern for literary scholars as well?

Perhaps regional scholarship has lagged behind in literary criticism because the field has concerned itself too much with issues of aesthetics and canonicity, with the perceived literary merit of a text or group of texts. Based on humanist understandings of artistic production and reception – that we consume "great works" of art in order to gain social capital, to edify or enlighten ourselves – scholarly concerns about the aesthetic qualities of regional literature often stifle other areas of criticism in the field. All too often, regional scholars tend to preoccupy themselves with making a case for why this or that writer deserves broader national attention, and often these arguments are based on examinations of the literary merit of their writing. At conferences and in various books and journals devoted to regional studies, literary scholars still tend to apologize for their object of study, making a case for why this text is wrongly considered minor rather than major, on the periphery rather than in the center, locally focused rather than nationally or internationally oriented. By allowing concerns about canonicity and literary value to dominate debates about regionalism, however, literary critics end up narrowing the scope of their study, overlooking other issues that deserve scholarly attention. Rather than letting humanist readings of merit and value shape regional studies, we might instead interrogate the very notion of regionalism itself, asking how American regions came to be in the first place and what function they serve in understandings of the nation as a whole.

It is interesting to note that at a time when many critics are mired in debates about the value and merits of regional writing, there are some indications that place-based literature is gaining increased public attention and a growing spotlight in the literary marketplace. The burgeoning sections of travel writing and regional literature in bookstores across the United States, for instance, say a great deal about how strongly the political economy of travel and tourism influences the production of regional literatures and identities. Historian Ann Fabian has remarked at length on these connections; as she points out, regional literature – linked as it is to a tourist economy – often contributes to the project of designating certain places as desirable attractions, reshaping the local into a national or even international object of consumption for readers as well as a highly lucrative promotional device for writers (Fabian 1992: 235). The travel industry, of course, is not alone in providing regional writing with a captive audience but has instead worked hand-in-hand with developments like the growing environmental movement, which has also created a renewed interest in the local and the regional. In an age of ecology, concerns about the environment often translate into increased attention to once maligned regions and a growing fascination with "other" geographies. From all indications, it seems there is still much critical work to be done in assessing the cultural function of regional discourses. Moving away from the vise grip of aesthetics, studies of literary regionalism can offer important insights about the role of narrative in the construction of place and nation.

The writings of various "New Americanist" scholars who have begun questioning the metanarratives shaping US literary studies are useful in situating regional studies as a tool for theorizing the formation of American identity. Amy Kaplan, for instance, examines nineteenth-century metropolitan responses to local writing, pointing out that the concept of region in this period often emerged "as the projection of a desire for a space outside of history, untouched by change" (1991: 252). Regional differences (typically represented by spaces outside the urban East) served to enhance a sense of national well-being. While some places seemed all too familiar and ordinary to writers, other spaces operated as new, distinct, and full of intrigue. As Kaplan explains, regionalism in this context functioned to help naturalize the nation by locating the "primal origins" of nationalism firmly within "prenational communities" (1991: 263). At the same time, however, these projections were often challenged by counter-stories and prior histories, as the inhabitants of a given space struggled to assert a voice and presence that disturbed the official account of place (Kaplan 1991: 252). By restoring to history these larger cultural and political uses of regionalism as well as the responses to them, Kaplan and other critics are placing regional studies firmly within larger discussions of US nation-formation. Any account that seeks to historicize literary regionalism and understand its cultural work must move beyond aesthetic discussions about the merit of a given text, taking into consideration the role narrative plays in the incorporation and designation of new regions, as well as the function it serves in the formation of the United States.

In the discussion which follows, I focus on the place-based literatures of Alaska and the Pacific Northwest, regions that have remained largely undertheorized in studies of American literary history. Rather than reading the regional literatures of these places through an aestheticizing framework that dismisses or apologizes for this writing, my aim is to examine how regional discourses about Alaska and the Pacific Northwest function culturally, politically, and nationally. As relatively new regions on the nation's maps, the Pacific Northwest and Alaska are useful subjects for analysis with a view to what they can reveal about the imperatives of nation-building in the United States. In arguing for a comparative perspective in studies of regionalism, Robin W. Winks points to the ways scholars often do not allow research on regionalism "to ask questions about the nation as a whole" (1983: 15). Yet regionalism, as most scholars would agree, makes sense only as a critical approach within a national context. Indeed, it would be very difficult to understand the form and function of literary regionalism outside a larger national history. A comparative approach such as the one Winks calls for would not eliminate discussions about the aesthetics of regionalism, but would reframe these debates by allowing critics to consider by which standards the literary value of a text is to be assessed, whose definitions bestow artistic merit on a work of literature, and what function these standards serve in the larger national project. In recasting our approach to aesthetics in this way, regional scholars would also be able to assess how literary standards in turn dictate national definitions in ways that often exclude or marginalize certain regions.

Reading the Pacific Northwest

Starbucks and grunge culture, spotted owls and logging disputes, microbreweries and gortex; majestic mountains, glaciers, forests, rivers, salmon, and the Pacific Ocean: such images often dominate understandings of the cultural and natural landscapes that comprise the Pacific Northwest of the United States. Popular as they are, however, these images do not adequately capture the diversity of spaces encompassing the region, which for many critics includes Washington, Oregon, Idaho, parts of northern California, and the northwest corner of Montana, spaces that are varying and distinct and that often fall out of the geographical stereotype of rainforests and salmon. A region composed of disparate landscapes, the Pacific Northwest tends to resist clear demarcations. Some scholars suggest, for instance, that the Pacific Northwest refers to the land drained by the Columbia River, a definition that would include parts of British Columbia as well. Meanwhile, other critics argue that the Pacific Northwest is best understood as the land located between Mount Hood in Oregon and Mount St. Elias in southeast Alaska. Often used interchangeably throughout the region, the terms Pacific Northwest and Northwest themselves cause confusion. The United States, after all, has witnessed various "northwests" throughout its history, so that the region we consider northwest today serves as only one of several spaces to receive this geographical designation. Culturally and politically too, the Pacific Northwest is divided quite strongly. In various urban centers, for instance, progressive social movements thrive well, while certain rural areas in the region serve as home to some of the nation's most conservative antigovernment activities. All of this is to say that any attempt to pin down the region either geographically or culturally is necessarily fraught with problems.

In a thoughtful article that examines constructions of regional identity, historian John Findlay traces how understandings of place in the Pacific Northwest have shifted dramatically throughout the nineteenth and twentieth centuries. In an attempt to denaturalize perceptions of the region, Findlay points to the ways in which many writers and critics associate elements of nature with the Northwest, situating aspects such as the mountains, ocean, and (especially) salmon as the "heart and soul" of the region (1997: 37). He notes, however, that this sentiment is not actually a "timeless formation" of Pacific Northwest identity, but a relatively new development, an attachment that seems to increase as the region's natural environment appears to diminish (Findlay 1997: 37–8). Although nature itself shifts and changes as do our ideas of it, the Pacific Northwest is able to appear as an authentic and enduring space because its identity has been linked to an unaltered natural environment. In making sense of how the region is understood today, Findlay argues, it is important to assess the ways in which ideas of nature often function as a powerful way of fixing in place what is in fact a "contingent and constructed" spatial identity (1997: 38).

The work of Washington writer Timothy Egan is useful to examine in assessing constructions of Pacific Northwest identity and recasting the region as a place closely connected to the natural world. As the Seattle correspondent for the *New York Times*, Egan has devoted himself to chronicling the vast changes that have shaped the region in recent years, describing in particular how debates and struggles over the environment might more aptly define the region. His book, *The Good Rain: Across Time and Terrain in the Pacific Northwest*, appeared in 1990 during a period when the Northwest was receiving increased attention from a variety of sources. The growing popularity of the West as a tourist destination and the renewed national interest in outdoors recreation of all sorts, the rise of Bill Gates and the new-tech economy based in part in the Pacific Northwest, the emergence of a hip music scene, and the popularity of prime-time television shows such as *Twin Peaks* and *Northern Exposure* – both of which were filmed in Washington State, although the latter was set in a fictional town in Alaska – helped redirect the country's attention toward the Pacific Northwest. Egan's text traces many of these developments while examining the emergence of a distinct regional response to all this newfound fashionableness. He begins his book describing a popular Northwest bumper sticker that announces to outsiders, "We Ain't Quaint," remarking wryly that there seems to be "some kind of revolt under way" across the region (Egan 1990: 23). In the wake of a growing awareness of this relatively belated American region, locals often responded much like the rural folks "discovered" by the Eastern metropolis in Amy Kaplan's study of nineteenth-century regionalism. In both cases, a refusal to serve as the nation's quaint Other functions as a means of resisting larger national definitions of identity. Egan's book devotes itself to countering the quaintness label, showing readers another side of the region's development. Instead of locating a space whose occupants have special ties to the natural world, he finds a region where land disputes, resource wars, and other environmental struggles reign.

While the Pacific Northwest gained increased national attention in part because of its image as a youthful and undeveloped space, the region, as Egan notes, is in many ways no different from other American spaces in that it too faces many of the same developments that have already plagued the rest of the United States. Rather than regarding the Northwest as a unique environment set off from other American regions, Egan points out that we should understand its close relationship to the rest of the nation. He thus recounts the history of the Northwest's development in the early nineteenth century, which began in part with the aid of Eastern capitalists such as John Jacob Astor. He tells of the place names originating in the eastern United States that define various landmarks across the region. The map of Oregon, for instance, is graced with cities named Salem, Medford, Springfield, and Portland. Meanwhile, Seattle was first known as "New York-Alki," the last word deriving from Chinook jargon meaning "eventually," an apt name for a city in which many boosterists placed their greatest hopes (Egan 1990: 26). Egan continues through the twentieth century, describing how one timber company, Weyerhauser, which previously had logged out Midwestern states such as Wisconsin and Minnesota, moved further west, forever changing the history and landscape of the Pacific Northwest. Far from being a refuge from the rest of the nation, then, the Pacific Northwest might be better regarded as a place undergoing forces of development similar to those that have already shaped and reshaped other American regions.

Throughout his book, Egan examines in particular the notion that a relationship to the natural environment accounts for Pacific Northwest identity. Although he falls into this trap himself at times and argues that nature defines the regional character ("Forget the boundary of Canada and America at the 49th Parallel . . . the Northwest is united by landscape, not divided by latitude lines. The regional icons – salmon and trees and mountains and water – spring from the elements. If people here become too far removed from those basic sources of life, then they lose the bond to a better world"), Egan also addresses the ways in which the history of white settlement across the region might testify otherwise (1990: 11). Indeed, by defining the regional identity of the Pacific Northwest through particular understandings of nature, scholars risk engaging in a kind of crude geographical determinism that overlooks how human cultures themselves have shaped the land. Historian Richard White suggests that perhaps we have gotten it all wrong; by focusing on the ways geography has shaped regional cultures, we often neglect to make sense of how cultures themselves play a role in remaking nature (White 1983: 109). Like White and other scholars, Egan points to the ways in which ideas of nature have shifted over time across the region. In the nineteenth century, for instance, industrial development in the Northwest was often spurred by ideologies that were markedly less reverent toward the environment and presented nature as little more than "a disease awaiting the cure that had yet to cross the Rockies" (Egan 1990: 40). This legacy continues to shape the region's identity today as the Northwest still fights its status as a national "resource colony" (Egan 1990: 174).

Egan thus devotes much time to addressing the ways the timber industry, previously and for decades an economic mainstay in the region, increasingly faces a dire future as once vast forests now house vast clearcuts. At one point he asks, with a slightly mock-elegiac tone, "[W]here have all the jobs gone? In the last decade, more timber was cleared from the Northwest than ever before, by the fewest amount of loggers ever employed for such volume. Like the big trees themselves, romance and heroism are fast fading from the lumberjack trade." Even the organizations established to manage and protect the land turn out to be complicit with the environment's demise. "A curious paradox is at work on the forests of the Olympic Peninsula," he explains. "[W]hile the American government scolds Brazil for cutting and burning its tropical rain forest, the Forest Service is aiding and abetting the death of the American rain forest." Likewise, as he notes, across the region the Department of Natural Resources has been popularly renamed the "Department of Nothing Remaining" (Egan 1990: 23, 48, 47).

Far from being a unique space whose enduring power is linked to a timeless natural environment, the Pacific Northwest instead faces a number of transformations as industry, government, and various local populations struggle over the region's future. Egan writes of the land disputes initiated by various Northwest tribes whose ancestors signed numerous treaties that have since been ignored by the government. He tells of the clashes between members of a growing environmental movement and laborers in the timber and fishing industries. He also describes the environmental transformations that have dramatically remade the urban environments of the region in the short span of his own lifetime.

> Gridlock and cocaine gangs rule the valley in the city where I live. Once it was full of small farmers and family merchants, a long, tree-lined boulevard with views straight up to the north spine of Mount Rainier. Now the farmers are all gone, and many Seattle merchants operate from behind bullet-proof windows, and the walls are spray-painted with the slogans of young men who kill one another because somebody is

wearing the wrong-colored hat. . . . I drive through the valley to get to my home; sometimes, stuck in traffic, I daydream off Rainier's distant glaciers. Other times, I'm an urban warrior, adrenalin-primed for combat, even if the only battle is one to beat a yellow light. (Egan 1990: 34)

In Egan's descriptions of the Northwest, it becomes clear that the region's reliance on an enduring sense of nature to provide it with a strong sense of self is in need of rethinking. By adopting a particular sense of nature to give the region an identity, residents across the Northwest overlook the ways in which nature itself has a history, the ways in which ideas of nature shift and change across time and place, and the ways in which groups of people often clash with each other as they struggle to define their relationship to the natural world.

In an interesting move, Egan's book begins with a quotation from Ken Kesey's popular novel, *Sometimes a Great Notion* (1964). With an opening that is marked by as much reverence as irony, Egan pays tribute to one of the region's most celebrated literary texts, a novel that offers a passionate if somewhat confused response to the regional changes experienced during the mid-twentieth century. Telling the story of the Stampers, a long-time Oregon logging family, *Sometimes a Great Notion* chronicles the cost of expansion in ecological and personal terms. The novel traces generations of a self-reliant family who have been forced to confront various changes as the landscape that long provided them with viable livelihoods undergoes rapid transformation. When a labor union threatens to step in and alter the relationship that these independent loggers have forged with the land, figures like Hank Stamper struggle to save their jobs and regional identities. The archetypal independent Western hero, Hank battles his Oregon neighbors, vowing he'll never give an inch. He likewise battles the Northwest environment, as a logger who both loves and destroys the Oregon forests that provide him with a livelihood, and as a businessman who fights the river that serves as his last chance for economic and personal survival. Kesey sets up Hank as a misguided but sympathetic character, indicating by the end of the novel, as the hero loses everything, that stubborn, self-reliant Western figures like Hank ultimately cannot survive in this new West.

In portraying Hank's contradictory attitudes toward the landscape and in showing how survival is an impossibility for him, Kesey works to recast conventions of the classic Western, a genre to which he uneasily pays homage. As critic Elaine B. Safer points out, while Kesey uses the conventions of the quest, a central aspect of the popular Western, he also interrupts the narrative trajectory. In questing literature, the hero leaves his community, undergoes a series of adventures, and returns to his people who reward him for his heroism. In *Sometimes a Great Notion*, however, heroism and its rewards are withheld (Safer 1988: 141). Using another twist of the classic Western, Kesey restores Indian characters and concerns to a genre that is well known for marginalizing or excluding native perspectives. At one point, he describes an Indian elder who rises from his couch "to stop the roll-over in his TV set." As the narrator explains, "[h]e spends a lot of time adjusting his westerns" (Kesey 1964:

203). The image provides readers with an apt description of what American Indians face as they struggle to find themselves in a region and form that have been popularly defined by others.

At times, though, Kesey's narrative is also marked by an ambivalence toward native characters that limits the ways his narrative manages to address alternative perspectives in the genre. The character Indian Jenny, for instance, comes close to providing a counter-view to Western clichés but ultimately ends up functioning within the stereotype of the profaned modern Indian. Portrayed as broken down and often drunk, Indian Jenny serves as the town prostitute, her monthly government checks enabling her to be a frequent presence in the neighborhood bars. When the resistant loggers overhear her muttering something about the moon and the tides, Hank sets into action, devising a plan that will allow him to move timber down the river to the buyers. Although the plan seems to provide him with an answer to his dilemma, the solution turns deadly as the river takes lives and ultimately destroys Hank's chances of survival. As the narrative closes, Indian Jenny is left to the side of the action, a figure largely forgotten and abandoned. Having served as a shadowy Other in the text, her presence needed but not fully accommodated by the rest of the characters, she is considered expendable by the novel's end.

In the years since the publication of Kesey's popular Oregon novel, numerous authors have arrived on the scene who are interested in questioning myths of Northwest identity by restoring other voices and visions to the regional picture; I have room here to discuss only two of them. Both novelist Marilynne Robinson and poet, novelist, and short-story writer Sherman Alexie offer visions of the Northwest that counter popular understandings of regional identity. A former resident of the region, Marilynne Robinson grew up in Idaho, the setting of her 1980 novel, *Housekeeping*. Raised on the Spokane/Coeur d'Alene Indian reservation, Sherman Alexie has produced volumes of poetry and prose as well as a successful screenplay for the anti-Western film, *Smoke Signals* (1998), directed by Arapaho film-maker Chris Eyre. In different ways, both authors question sentimental understandings of the region. Foregrounding class and gender issues, Robinson recasts the traditional male hero of the Western, featuring instead a community of women who inscribe the region differently. Alexie addresses questions of class and regional identity, linking both to a reading of race and place in the contemporary Indian West.

In an interview, Marilynne Robinson once described an awareness she had while working on her novel *Housekeeping* that she was rewriting the West, restoring in particular women's presence in popular representations of the region (Galehouse 2000: 118). Working against the formula Western, which often consigns women of all races to the margins or else in roles that are peripheral to the real action of the story, Robinson tells the story of Ruth Stone, a young, parentless girl who leaves her sister and community in order to join her Aunt Sylvie in a life of travel. The novel examines Western rural life and the place that white women typically occupy in it. A radical departure from popular representations of white Western women, Aunt Sylvie doesn't move through the world in traditional ways. Sylvie has many odd characteristics: she collects newspapers that she never manages to throw out, sleeps on park benches in the middle of the day, wears her coat at all times, and tells stories, each of which has "to do with a train or a bus station" (Robinson 1980: 68). Having lost contact with her husband and most of her family at some point, she has spent much of her life drifting through the country, an anomaly of sorts because of her identity as a female transient.

Opting out of the world of housework and domesticity, Sylvie defies the gendered politics of mobility in order to experience the openness of a transient life, recruiting her young niece along the way. By featuring the possibilities of Sylvie's life, the novel calls attention to the ways in which the classic Western generally presents mobility as the prerogative of the Anglo male hero, a privilege largely withheld from women as a group. Although they are often presented as being closer to nature, white women are frequently depicted as removed from the natural world and are thus restricted in their movement through it. Indians, both male and female, also receive a similar fate, a point that is not directly addressed in the novel. Throughout the narrative, Robinson instead focuses on Anglo female characters who manage to establish a different relationship to place. Defying the codes of the Western that dictate more moderate lives for white women, Sylvie and Ruth set out for parts unknown. Their travels are not part of the myth of the expansive American Adam and his quest to be the first; nor are the two women interested in conquest and ownership. Instead, they venture outside the spatial configurations of white womanhood in order to achieve a different experience of region.

Sherman Alexie has also devoted himself to rewriting the spatial features of the classic Western, revising along the way aspects of Pacific Northwest regionalism that encode Euro-American definitions of place. Questioning understandings of Northwest identity that suggest the region's character is closely tied to the environment, Alexie shows that the Northwest might be better characterized by longstanding struggles over land between Indians and white settlers. In his collection of short stories, *The Lone Ranger and Tonto Fistfight in Heaven* (1993), the broken treaties of the nineteenth century exert a presence in the region as land disputes of the previous century take new form, this time characterized by indigenous struggles against utility companies, law enforcement officers, and other representatives of the state. Complete with HUD homes, diet Pepsi cans, 7–11 stores, and commodity cheese, the setting of Alexie's narrative is an irredeemably modern landscape, a space whose residents struggle for survival and sovereignty, a land marked more by poverty than pastoralism. Images of Custer, forced sterilizations, Mount Rushmore, uranium mining, white sitcom families, and the Bureau of Indian Affairs collide in the text as Alexie works to portray the region from an indigenous perspective.

During a selfconscious re-enactment of the classic Western shootout on Main Street, for instance, the narrator in one story enters a reservation 7–11 during the graveyard shift, confronting a frightened store manager who nervously keeps an eye his every move. When he finally reaches the counter with his purchases, the relieved clerk manages to maintain polite conversation. "'Will this be all?' he asked . . . in that company effort to make me do some impulse shopping. Like adding a clause onto a treaty. *We'll take Washington and Oregon and you get six pine trees and a brand-new Chrysler Cordova*" (Alexie 1993: 183–4). Alexie stages various other showdowns in the text as modern Indians still struggle to claim a rightful place in the region. When an Indian driving in a residential neighborhood in Seattle is pulled over by a white police officer, for instance, he is asked, "What are you doing out here? . . . You're making people nervous. You don't fit the profile of the neighborhood." In a comment that captures quite well the politics of space shaping the narrative as a whole, the character responds, "I wanted to tell him that I didn't really fit the profile of the country but I knew it would just get me into more trouble" (Alexie 1993: 182–3).

Throughout his collection, Alexie features various Indian characters who struggle to redefine the spatial ideologies and regional discourses that effectively remove Indian presence from the land, taking care to show how certain ways of thinking about place operate to exclude or marginalize different populations. In doing so, Alexie often parodies myths of the Northwest as a region whose citizens have forged a special tie with nature, taking on in particular the trite beliefs associated with the mainstream environmental movement. One story, for instance, opens in 1974 with a description of the US exhibit at the World's Fair in Spokane, a display featuring depoliticized and dehistoricized references to Indian culture.

All the countries have exhibitions like art from Japan and pottery from Mexico and mean-looking people talking about Germany. In one little corner there's a statue of an Indian who's supposed to be some chief or another. I press a little button and the statue talks and moves its arms over and over in the same motion. The statue tells the crowd we have to take care of the earth because it is our mother. I know that and James says he knows more. He says the earth is our grandmother and that technology is our mother and that they both hate each other. (Alexie 1993: 129)

Here Alexie calls attention to the tendency of environmentalists in the Pacific Northwest to build their arguments for nature on aspects of Indian culture, including figures such as Chief Seattle, whose famous speech, long a favorite among Euro-American nature lovers, has undergone numerous bad translations that often misrepresent Indian beliefs. Over the years, various Euro-Americans groups who have accepted such borrowings have been taken to task for profiting and even trivializing a belief-system that they fail to fully understand. The irony here is that the United States, though far from being a force that favors indigenous views of the land, nevertheless appropriates aspects of Indian culture, incorporating decontextualized slogans as a way of representing itself to the world. Even as the country portrays itself as a multicultural space, a nation that includes indigenous people in its definitions of self, Alexie demonstrates how US concerns, whether political, cultural, or environmental, actually operate in a different fashion. Recalling the ways the Pacific Northwest salmon debates and other struggles over nature often centrally impact Indian lives even though input from the tribes is usually not solicited by mainstream environmentalists, Alexie reminds readers: "Ain't no salmon left in our river. Just a school bus and a few hundred basketballs" (1993: 39).

Alexie's visions of the Pacific Northwest landscape show us the underside of dominant regional images that depict the character of the space as tied closely to concerns about nature. His writings demonstrate how, to the contrary, geographical identities, place-based identities, and regional discourses are always situated and contingent, always historically and culturally specific, and always subject to disagreement and debate. Like understandings of the nation, productions of regional identity often have negative consequences for less powerful groups whose experiences and beliefs are not taken into consideration. In Alexie's writings, the Pacific Northwest is not simply the hip, fashionable region it has come to be known as in recent years. Instead, it is a complicated and contested region whose history and future identity are still being worked out and debated.

Alaska and the Far North

As another relatively new region on the national stage, Alaska allows us to uncover aspects of nationalism and regionalism that are not frequently addressed in studies of American history, literature, and culture. Widely regarded as the nation's "Last Frontier," Alaska has often fascinated Americans because of its status as a place set off from the settled spaces of the Lower 48.[1] The region is largely considered to be wild terrain, the quintessential home of North American nature, a land that helps draw the United States' frontier past into the present era. Although it remains far from undeveloped terrain, in the dominant geographical imagination of the United States Alaska is nevertheless considered unsullied, unspoiled, and largely unmarked by culture. In this way, the region functions as "anachronistic space," Anne McClintock's term for geography figured as primitive or out of step with history, where time has somehow disappeared and where progress has long ago been halted in its tracks. Anachronistic space for McClintock is land "perpetually . . . marooned and historically abandoned." Emerging as a colonial response that places cultural and geographical Others outside the Enlightenment time of the European self, anachronistic space figures spatial difference as an historical rupture. Alaska's location *vis-à-vis* the rest of the nation, its position as a northern terrain physically unlinked to the continental United States, allows it to exist in this "permanently anterior time" (McClintock 1995: 40–1, 30). The region's appeal lies in its position as antimodern space, its apparent ability to resist change and the ravages of history, while remaining fully archaic.

Emerging out of a particular set of circumstances, such understandings of Alaska were aided by the regional literature that appeared after the US purchase of Alaska in 1867. Prior to being an American region, Alaska was the site of other nations' national projects. Russian, Spanish, French, and British voyages in the eighteenth century, for instance, made what is present-day Alaska a desired destination for various European explorers in search of seal pelts and the ever-elusive Northwest Passage. As the first voyagers to successfully make claims on the land, Russian explorers later named the region "Russian America," keeping the land under colonial administration until 1867. The native people of Alaska – the Eskimos, Aleuts, and Indians – waged several battles against their colonizers (both Russian and American), but were eventually defeated and ultimately had no say in the land transfer.

The US purchase of the region occurred for particular reasons; according to historian Walter LaFeber, after the Civil War the United States became interested in creating an overseas empire designed to address the problems of agrarian and industrial overproduction. As the primary architect of what LaFeber calls the "New Empire," Secretary of State William Henry Seward negotiated the purchase of Alaska in order to secure a strategic base for the nation's overseas markets (LaFeber 1963: 25–6, 407–17). At the time, the region was intended to be the first in a long line of territorial acquisitions the nation sought in order to create a "security perimeter" of US-owned lands in the Pacific (Crapol and Schonberger 1972: 136). Much of the early regional literature of Alaska thus appeared in the form of exploration narratives and government reports. By the end of the nineteenth century, however, this new American region attracted other uses as the tourism industry discovered the aesthetic potentials of Alaska. The California naturalist John Muir made several trips to Alaska, and his accounts of the glaciers, mountains, and forests of the region did much to popularize the land as a unique natural wonder in the nation's popular imagination. Although he would later lament the rapid growth of travel in the region, Muir's writings helped to open Alaska to other nature tourists and to reposition Alaska as a prime object of interest for the growing preservationist movement.

With the series of gold strikes in the late nineteenth century across Alaska and western Canada, and especially after gold was discovered near Bonanza Creek in the Yukon Territory, Alaska and the Canadian North captured new international attention. Figures like Rex Beach, James Oliver Curwood, and Jack London all contributed to the imaginative production of Alaska by transforming the region into a new setting for their frontier adventure narratives. As the most popular frontier writer of the region, Jack London wrote a series of short stories and novels in the late nineteenth and early twentieth century whose settings continually shift between the Yukon and Alaska to the extent that even today readers and critics misrecognize the Klondike as US terrain. For these writers, Alaska and the Yukon were places to experience outdoor adventures and to test one's strength and stamina. In an era when Anglo-Saxon males felt themselves overwhelmed by the new immigration and feared becoming emasculated by domesticated life in the cities, the Far North was viewed as a last refuge, a safe haven for beleaguered Euro-Americans in search of invigorating outdoors experiences. This understanding has held such power that today, Alaska is still regarded as a space uniquely set off from the rest of the country, a position that provides the region with much of its symbolic capital in the popular imagination.

Like the nineteenth-century writers Kaplan discussed, who looked to locales outside the eastern United States in search of spaces seemingly untouched by the encroachments of modern life, many Americans today continue to figure Alaska as a vast,

Figure 24.1   Photograph of tourists on a cruise ship in the Glacier Bay National Park, by Susan Kollin.

undeveloped land that helps recapture aspects of the nation's past. Such understandings of Alaska operate in a manner that shares much in common with what Kaplan regards as a central motivation for US regionalism. Positioned as a frontier or wilderness refuge in the national imaginary, Alaska serves as a "prenational" site for locating the "primal origins" of the nation (Kaplan 1991: 263). Yet even as the region has been understood as a uniquely wild space in the nation's geographical imagination, there are many writers who are working to recast these larger perceptions of the region. It is clear, for instance, that such visions of the land do not serve the region's indigenous populations particularly well. Tlingit Indian author, educator, and linguist Nora Dauenhauer is one figure who has sought to redirect popular understandings of the region. In her poetry, plays, and personal essays, Dauenhauer is careful to demonstrate that Alaska is not an empty space awaiting the arrival of Euro-American adventurers or an unclaimed terrain to be used for purposes of self-glorification and self-promotion. Over the years Dauenhauer and other Alaska Native writers have worked at envisioning different ways of understanding Alaska, creating new images and portraits of the land that disrupt the regional discourses serving larger Euro-American national projects.

In her poetry, for instance, Dauenhauer examines how the burgeoning tourism industry that brings nature enthusiasts to "exotic" lands has threatened the integrity of indigenous communities across the state. In recent years, for instance, travelers have been able to take chartered flights to tour Eskimo fishing camps in the Arctic, spending as little as half a day and a few hundred dollars for the opportunity. In the poem "Village Tour, Nome Airport," Dauenhauer writes of a white tour guide with a "glossy smile" who "slides" over to a Native seamstress and asks if she can touch her coat. She does so without waiting for permission, later explaining to the tour group that they "make them by hand." The poem expresses a certain degree of selfconsciousness about the tourist gaze, as the narrator is likewise positioned as an outsider and a participant in a travel industry that is disruptive to the Native community. In that sense, the poem questions certain dichotomies between colonizer and colonized. Later, the narrator watches as the seamstress, "[a]s if frozen," sits in silence (Dauenhauer 1988: 27). Here the exotic Other – in this case the Alaskan Native woman – is recontextualized, reconfigured, and revalued in the white tourist economy as a new object of interest and wonder, an object to be touched and even sampled. Although Dauenhauer does not address what the Native seamstress might be thinking, the woman's silence nevertheless says much about the indignities of having her culture and her privacy invaded by these visitors. At the end of the poem, a youth in handcuffs waiting to be transported to California also becomes incorporated into the tour as the guide knowingly tells her group, "They all go to jail" (Dauenhauer 1988: 27).

Dauenhauer also addresses the environmentalisms that shape images of Alaska as a glorified Last Frontier, the staging grounds for particular, exclusive uses of nature. Her often-anthologized poem "Genocide," for instance, tells of the conflicts between subsistence living and wilderness protection. Echoing the form of Japanese haiku, Dauenhauer writes,

> Picketing the Eskimo
> Whaling Commission,
> an over-fed English girl
> stands with a sign,
> "Let the Whales Live."
> (1988: 26)

Here the environmentalism of certain outside groups that has long shaped Alaska as a wilderness remove turns out to have quite negative consequences for the indigenous people of the region. Ultimately the poem reveals how new forms of imperialism emerge as antiwhaling campaigns and other preservationist movements become forces contributing to Alaska Native dispossession and displacement in the land. Dauenhauer, like other Alaska Native writers, is interested in questioning the goals and purposes of the mainstream environmental movement. Whose interests are valued and placed in the foreground and whose interests are overlooked and marginalized become important concerns in recasting larger visions and uses of the region.

Tlingit author Robert Davis also writes about Alaska in a way that connects with Dauenhauer's work and recasts what Kaplan argues is the cultural work of regionalism. In his poem, "The Albino Tlingit Carving Factory," Davis writes of the ideology of consumption that radically transforms Tlingit artists' relationship to their artwork, environments, and communities but also ironically provides monetary support for them. The nature tourists who yearn to own a piece of the nation's primitive past they believe they are encountering during their visits to Alaska often seek carvings whose value they do not fully understand. Davis thus describes the necessary shortcuts the Tlingit artists take in their production of tourist arts. They do not spend time searching out the "perfect grained red cedar." They do not "talk to the trees" or properly season their boards. Instead, the materials they use come from "Spenard Building Supply" in Anchorage at "$2.15 per board foot" (Davis 1986: 23). These shortcuts serve as a form of resistance, a way of countering the encroaching commodification of Tlingit culture in the tourist industry and in certain forms of New Age environmentalism. A century earlier John Muir expressed his dismay at what he witnessed during his cruises through the Inside Passage, when visitors turned away from the majestic glaciers, directing their attention to the sides of the tour ships where Tlingits sold their wares. Muir's consternation arose because he considered the natural world of Alaska's glaciers, mountains, forests, and seas more authentic than the cultural world of the Indians as presented in the tourist trade (Muir 1988: 245). Like many Euro-American travelers in this period, Muir regarded both the natural world and indigenous cultures as largely corrupted by contact with whites, and thus believed that the Tlingits he encountered on his cruises functioned as little more than a debased version of the "real thing."

This dichotomy between genuine and inauthentic Indians, between a real and a false Alaska, operates as a powerful white invention that the Tlingit carvers throw back on the tourists. If the white nature tourists feel anxiety about their encounters with the native Other and have concerns that they may in fact be duped, that what they are buying may not be the genuine goods they desire, then Davis and the other carvers he describes exploit this opportunity. They give the tourists what they expect – the inauthentic tourist fare. Davis explains:

> We do not go to the iron-rich cliffs
> for red ochre paint mixed in stone
> paintbowl with dog salmon eggs
> spit through mouthful of spruce bark.
> Nor do we try for the subdued blue-green
> of copper sulphate with virgin's urine,
> or black from the deepest charcoal.
>
> You want crude carvings?
> you want them harsh and vicious?
> Okay,
> they might be African for all you care.
> Hell, we have to make a living too.
>   (Davis 1986: 23)

Although ever-anxious to encounter authentic Native culture, white tourists in Alaska are often inadequately equipped to distinguish between the myriad cultures that they have deemed "primitive." For the visitor, in fact, a basic interchangeability exists among all so-called unmodern people. If it is a truism that the oppressed are required to know their dominators more intimately than their dominators know them, then Davis and the other Tlingit carvers he writes about may be said to have more than a strong acquaintance with white desires and yearnings. Delivering what the buyers seem to expect anyway, the Indians at the carving factory give the tourists what they want. After all, they have to earn a wage for themselves in the new cash economy.

Ultimately the presence of Raven, a trickster figure among Pacific Northwest Indians, serves to dislodge the problems imposed by these larger national ecologies, by outside visions of place that are imported to the region. In his longer poem "Saginaw Bay: I Keep Going Back," Davis envisions the world through Tlingit philosophy, writing of Raven, "[c]locksure smooth talker, good looker," and telling of how it all began. Once Raven throws the light,

> everything takes form –
> creatures flee to forest animals,
> hide in fur. Some choose the sea,
> turn to salmon, always escaping.
> Those remaining in the light
> stand as men, dumb and full of fears.
>   (Davis 1986: 14)

For Raven, the world is so remarkable that even he is amazed at its creation. It is interesting to note that in this piece human beings do not operate as the primary ecological players. Instead, Raven along with the forest animals and the salmon are central figures in the world, while men and women are thought to lack a similar knowledge and thus remain full of fear. This story of beginnings differs from the accounts associated with Euro-American origins and history in Alaska. Davis, for instance, tells of a site near Kake named Hamilton Bay, "This place some European captain named for himself / so it could exist properly. (Go and subdue the earth and / name everything in it" (1986: 22). The author remains clearly critical of the spirit of possession and dispossession, of those who, taking up the task of renaming the land, thus believe they have somehow called the world into being themselves.

Davis recounts the history of the region in the wake of cultural contact, building on traditional oral narratives to recount the arrival of whites.

> I've heard of men in black robes who came
> instructing heathen natives:
> outlaw demon shamanism,
> do away with potlatch,
> pagan ceremony,
> totem idolatry.
> Get rid of your old ways.
> The people listened.
>
> They dynamited the few Kake totems —
> mortuary poles fell with bones,
> clan identifiers lost in powder,
> storytellers blown to pieces . . .
>
> People began to move differently, tense.
> They began to talk differently, mixed.
> Acted ashamed of gunny sacks of k'ink;
> and mayonnaise jars of stink eggs,
> and no one mashed blueberries
> with salmon eggs anymore.
>   (Davis 1986: 16–17)

Davis speaks of the changes thrust upon Tlingits from outside forces and the effects these forces have on the ways his people understand themselves and each other, the ways they comprehend their history and their relationship to the natural world. Ultimately, his response to cultural upheaval involves resisting the genocidal forces that threaten to annihilate Tlingit culture.

When a logging company from Outside moves into his community, the owners bring heavy cables which they erect from the beach to the woods, and later allow bulldozers to leave deep trails in the ground. The upheaval that the Tlingits have endured under white advancement takes both a social and an environmental form here. The Tlingit community is suddenly invaded by "[r]edneck rejects, tobacco spitters" who get drunk in their bunkhouses at day's end, harass the Tlingit women, and brag about the loads they carried, "who got maimed / and did they take it like a man" (Davis 1986: 18–19). For Davis, the loggers' violence is symptomatic of the larger disease of expansion and conquest: "Some men can't help it," he explains, "they take up too much space, / and always need more" (1986: 19). The logging company, which provides only a few jobs for the Tlingits, also leaves its marks on the land, violently gnawing away at the forest

> till the sky once swimming with branches
> becomes simply sky, till there is only
> a scarred stubble of clearcut
> like a head without its scalp of hair.
>   (Davis 1986: 19)

As Native groups across Alaska continue to face difficult decisions about development and land use, many of the smaller communities such as Kake are hit especially hard. These communities, already facing a shortage of jobs, are often targeted by large corporations and multinationals as prime sources of cheap labor and raw materials. For Tlingits who are struggling to enter the cash economy, the tradeoff between tradition and economic opportunities complicates matters. In the wake of the congressional passage of the Alaska Native Claims Settlement Act (ANCSA) in 1971, whereby Native land rights across Alaska were extinguished and replaced by the establishment of landowning corporations, the struggle for economic independence and environmental sovereignty has still not been settled. Davis's collection of poetry aims to rethink popular understandings of nature that shape the region, dismantling along the way popular stereotypes that depict Alaska as a primordial wilderness region awaiting nature enthusiasts who seek to throw off a confining modernity in favor of a more authentic and primitive world. His work instead introduces the expansion of white culture and capital as central concerns for nature advocacy in Alaska, and reminds us that regional identities are often contested and in need of revision.

Recasting Regionalism

By focusing attention on local geographies and spatial particularities, regional studies enable us to assess the ways in which dominant national paradigms have failed to adequately address the specificity of US cultural regions and often overlooked important regional differences. Because regions such as Alaska and the Pacific Northwest occupy a marginal position in American cultural paradigms, our critical studies have not kept up with the United States' expansionist activities, nor come to terms with the consequences of its incorporation of new lands. While regionalism aims to rectify oversights in nationalist visions, such studies face their own problems when certain geographical areas become solidified as constant, unified, or coherent entities. Rather than thinking of American regions as a given, however, we might instead understand them as objects constructed by a whole set of cultural practices. The scrutiny with which we examine national studies must be employed when we conceptualize regional studies; instead of regarding regions as *a priori* zones into which the nation is logically carved or divided, we might examine how regional identities themselves operate as discursive formations. Rather than seek out concrete geographical entities, we might devote ourselves to analyzing what Anne Goldman calls the "multiple interruptions and breaks in the national map" (2000: 9).

In this way, we might want to take seriously the observations about regional identity made by Alan Holt, the frontier adventurer in James Oliver Curwood's novel *The Alaskan*, who argues that the case of Alaska has tremendous implications for the ways we theorize American regional studies. As Curwood's protagonist explains, Alaska offers a dramatic transformation of the nation's contours, repositioning all American regions by pushing the West further toward the Pacific. The incorporation of Alaska resituates the "West Coast," he argues, by making California the Midwest, the geographical center of the United States. Taking this observation one step further, we may also note that Alaska itself ceases to be West at the point when the Aleutian Islands cross over the International Date Line and become East. If the history of the West is the "story of how the American map came to have the boundaries it shows today," then the incorporation of places like Alaska cannot be overlooked even as the area moves outside the traditional American trajectory, encompassing not one but multiple regional identities (Cronon et al. 1992: 15).

NOTE

1   The discussion of Alaska appearing here is adapted from my book, *Nature's State:* *Imagining Alaska as the Last Frontier* (Kollin 2001).

REFERENCES

Alexie, Sherman (1993). *The Lone Ranger and Tonto Fistfight in Heaven*. New York: HarperPerennial.

Barcott, Bruce (1994). "Introduction." In Bruce Barcott (ed.), *Northwest Passages: A Literary Anthology of the Pacific Northwest from Coyote Tales to Roadside Attractions*, xi–xxii. Seattle: Sasquatch Books.

Crapol, Edward P., and Schonberger, Howard (1972). "The Shift to Global Expansion, 1865–1900." In William Appleman Williams (ed.), *From Colony to Empire: Essays in the History of American Foreign Relations*, 135–202. New York: Wiley.

Cronon, William; Miles, George; and Gitlin, Jay (1992). "Becoming West: Toward a New Meaning for American History." In William Cronon, George Miles, and Jay Gitlin (eds.), *Under an Open Sky: Rethinking America's Western Past*, 3–27. New York: Norton.

Dauenhauer, Nora Marks (1988). *The Droning Shaman*. Haines: Black Current.

Davis, Robert (1986). *Soulcatcher*. Sitka: Raven's Bones.

Egan, Timothy (1990). *The Good Rain: Across Time and Terrain in the Pacific Northwest*. New York: Knopf.

Fabian, Ann (1992). "History for the Masses: Commercializing the Western Past." In William Cronon, George Miles, and Jay Gitlin (eds.), *Under an Open Sky: Rethinking America's Western Past*, 223–38. New York: Norton.

Findlay, John M. (1997). "A Fishy Proposition: Regional Identity in the Pacific Northwest." In David M. Wrobel and Michael C. Steiner (eds.), *Many Wests: Place, Culture, and Regional Identity*, 37–70. Lawrence: University Press of Kansas.

Galehouse, Maggie (2000). "Their Own Private Idaho: Transience in Marilynne Robinson's *Housekeeping*." *Contemporary Literature* 41, 117–37.

Goldman, Anne E. (2000). *Continental Divides: Revisioning American Literature*. New York: Palgrave.

Kaplan, Amy (1991). "Nation, Region, and Empire." In Emory Elliot (ed.), *The Columbia History of the American Novel*. New York: Columbia University Press.

Kesey, Ken (1964). *Sometimes a Great Notion*. New York: Penguin.

Kollin, Susan (2001). *Nature's State: Imagining Alaska as the Last Frontier*. Chapel Hill: University of North Carolina Press.

LaFeber, Walter (1963). *The New Empire: An Interpretation of American Expansion, 1860–1898*. Ithaca: Cornell University Press.

McClintock, Anne (1995). *Imperial Leather: Race, Gender, and Sexuality in the Colonial Contest*. New York: Routledge.

Muir, John (1988). *Travels in Alaska*. San Francisco: Sierra Club.

Robinson, Marilynne (1980). *Housekeeping*. New York: Bantam.

Safer, Elaine B. (1988). *The Contemporary American Comic Epic: The Novels of Barth, Pynchon, Gaddis, and Kesey*. Detroit: Wayne State University Press.

White, Richard (1983). "The Altered Landscape: Social Change and the Land in the Pacific Northwest." In William G. Robbins, Robert J. Frank, and Richard E. Ross (eds.), *Regionalism and the Pacific Northwest*, 109–27. Corvallis: Oregon State University Press.

Winks, Robin W. (1983). "Regionalism in Comparative Perspective." In William G. Robbins, Robert J. Frank, and Richard E. Ross, eds., *Regionalism and the Pacific Northwest*, 13–36. Corvallis: Oregon State University Press.

25

Texas and the Great Southwest

Mark Busby

Every continent has its own great spirit of place. Every people is polarized in some particular locality, which is home, the homeland. Different places on the face of the earth have different vital effluence, different vibration, different chemical exhalation, different polarity with different stars: call it what you like. But the spirit of place is a great reality.

D. H. Lawrence, *Studies in Classic American Literature* (1923)

If a man couldn't escape what he came from, we would most of us still be peasants in Old World hovels. But if, having escaped or not, he wants in some way to know himself, define himself, and tries to do it without taking into account the thing he came from, he is writing without any ink in his pen. The provincial who cultivates only his roots is in peril, potato-like, of becoming more root than plant. The man who cuts his roots away and denies that they were ever connected with him withers into half a man.

John Graves, *Goodbye to a River* (1960)

A Journey through the Literary Southwest

The writers quoted above refer to the spirit of their place that they have attempted to capture in their works – the symbiotic relationship between places and writing. The geographer Yi Fu Tuan calls this feeling "topophilia," by which he means the perception of sacred place and *genii loci*, the spirits that inhabit particular places in the landscape. Texas folklorist J. Frank Dobie prefers to use the Spanish word *querencia* (from *querer*, to love) to refer to the feelings that some living things have for special places.

Although commentators have often noted the importance of place to writers, Texas and Southwestern writers have sometimes suffered from unclear identity. Is Texas Southern or Southwestern? What is the Southwest and what are its characteristics and literary qualities? In *Guide to Life and Literature of the Southwest*, J. Frank Dobie provides a generous definition: "The principal areas of the Southwest are, to have done with air-minded reservations, Arizona, New Mexico, most of Texas, some of Oklahoma, and anything else north, south, east, or west that anybody wants to bring in."

The greater Southwest is a physical region that runs from the piney woods of East Texas to the Gulf Coast, across the rolling Texas Hill Country to the dry deserts of Trans-Pecos West Texas, New Mexico, Arizona, Nevada, Utah, southern Colorado, and southern California, and includes the several states of northern Mexico. To comprehend the Southwest requires knowledge of how the various cultures in the Southwest – Native American, Mexican American, African American, and Euro-American – have been affected by and have altered the natural environment. To understand the region requires knowing a mix of cultures determined by geographical, geological, and biological forces; shaped through historical development and literature; altered by various languages. Moreover, it requires recognizing the relationship between the region and the broader national identity. The harsh Southwestern landscape has historically led Southwesterners to glorify an American individualism long celebrated in our national documents; frontier attitudes have often characterized Southwestern culture. Many of the historical and literary texts demonstrate how Anglo-American settlers entered an unknown world and saw nature as a resource for their singular use. But many minority cultures question the emphasis placed on individuality instead of community. Their response to the hot, arid land of scorpions and rattlesnakes, saguaro and sage, has been to band together in communal, supportive societies.

The region's history reflects the lives and interaction of these diverse peoples. Alvar Nuñez Cabeza de Vaca (discussed below) was the first European to travel through the region, from 1528 to 1536. When Juan Oñate settled New Mexico in 1598, he brought cattle and horses, animals that would eventually transform the natural environment through overgrazing and alter the human landscape when the Plains Indians, particularly the Comanche and Apache, discovered that they were even more powerful hunters and warriors on horseback than on foot. For the next two centuries, with no great wealth found and an inimical landscape, the Southwest developed slowly, serving primarily as a buffer for Spanish developments in Mexico. After Mexico achieved its independence from Spain in 1821, the Mexican government offered land grants in Texas to Anglo settlers such as Moses Austin and his son Stephen, and the Anglo migration into the Southwest began. That resettlement set in motion the major events that shaped the region in the nineteenth century: Texas' independence, the US war with Mexico, the discovery of gold in California, the coming of railroads, the Civil War, the Indian wars, and the growth of the cattle-ranching and mining industries. The twentieth century saw a radical change in attitudes toward the Southwest, its image transformed from a vast desert wasteland hostile to humans to a beckoning sunbelt. Cattle and ranching gave way to oil, aircraft, and space industries, then to high finance and high technology.

Literary Qualities

Historically, writers journeying across the Southwest – from explorers such as Cabeza de Vaca to twentieth-century nature writers such as John Graves and Edward Abbey – have attempted to capture their responses to the natural and cultural phenomena they encountered. Much of the writing about Texas and the Southwest emphasizes encountering and coming to terms with a rich variety of human cultures; but just as often, the literature explores the aesthetic and pragmatic challenges posed by the natural conditions of this region, where lush pine forests give way to empty plains that sometimes stretch so far that the eye yearns for even the slightest hill to lean itself against (as Roy Bedichek commented in his 1951 *Adventures with a Texas Naturalist*), where most of the indigenous vegetation is thorny and fruitless, and where often there is not enough water to sustain either cities or livestock. In 1853 and 1854 Frederick Law Olmsted, later to become known for designing New York City's Central Park, traveled by horseback across Texas and then published his experiences as *A Journey through Texas*. Traveling is a natural act in a region with long distances. Texas, for example, covers 266,807 square miles. It is 801 miles from the Panhandle in the north to Brownsville in the south, and 773 miles from the easternmost bend in the Sabine River to the westernmost point of the Rio Grande near El Paso. With all this territory, journeying continues to be a necessary reality for the region.

Much Southwestern literature has a foundation in the frontier mythology that is central to the larger American experience. Frontier mythology refers to a cluster of images, values, and archetypes that grew out of the confrontation between the uncivilized and the civilized world: what Frederick Jackson Turner called the "meeting point between savagery and civilization." Civilization is associated with the past and with Europe, with society – its institutions and laws, its demands for compromise and restriction, its cultural refinement and emphasis on manners, its industrial development, and its class distinctions. The wilderness that civilization confronts offers the possibility of personal freedom, where single individuals can test themselves against nature without the demands for social responsibility and compromises inherent in being part of a community.

Southwestern mythology draws from frontier mythology, particularly the emphasis on the Southwest as a land of freedom and opportunity, where individuals can demonstrate those values that the Anglo myth reveres – courage, determination, ingenuity, and loyalty, among others. The major indigenous American hero – the cowboy – is a product of Texas's frontier legacy. But the Southwest's frontier history and geography produce deep feelings of ambivalence. On the one hand, the vastness of its area seems to negate borders; on the other, the region's location on the edge of Southern and Western culture and along the long Rio Grande border with Mexico reinforces an awareness of borders. In fact, one of the major features of Texas fiction is ambivalence – the act of being torn, pulled in several directions at once. Early settlers who both conquered nature and felt simultaneously at one with it began the feelings of ambivalence that Larry McMurtry admitted still cut him "as deep as the bone" in his luminous essay "Take My Saddle from the Wall: A Valediction" in *In a Narrow Grave*.

The ambivalence of being drawn at the same time toward such opposing forces as civilization/wilderness, rural/urban, individual/community, past/present, aggression/ passivity, and numerous others is central to the Southwestern legend, and it grows in intensity in the contemporary Southwest as the schism between old and new tears more strongly at the human heart. Often Southwestern writers examine the sharp division between the frontier myth that lives inside and the diminished outside natural world fraught with complexity, suffering, and violence but leavened with humor, compassion, and love.

Three other important elements of the Southwestern frontier myth were identified by Larry Goodwyn in an 1971 essay titled "The Frontier Myth and Southwestern Literature." Goodwyn first concluded that the "frontier legend is pastoral," with a strong emphasis on the primitivistic belief that being outdoors leads to living moral lives. Second, "the legend is inherently masculine: women are not so much without 'courage' as missing altogether; cowgirls did not ride up the Chisholm Trail." And third, Goodwyn found that the frontier myth "is primitively racialist: it provided no mystique of triumph for Mexicans, Negroes, or Indians."

Much of the ambivalence that later writers exhibit stems from these older elements. The primitivism of the legend, with its emphasis on the positive values that living close to the land breeds, certainly contributes much to these feelings of ambivalence. Early works often demonstrate the sexism and racism of the old legends and have called forth important responses from women and minority writers who articulated their own views of the world and from others who are sensitive to these ugly legacies. They include such Southwestern women writers as Mary Austin, Sarah Bird, Willa Cather, Sandra Cisneros, Naomi Nye, Carolyn Osborn, Katherine Anne Porter, and Carmen Tafolla; other Indian and Mexican-American writers such as Rudolfo Anaya, Dagoberto Gilb, Rolando Hinojosa, Leslie Silko, and Joy Harjo; and African-American writers such as Ralph Ellison, J. California Cooper, and Reginald McKnight.

To these elements of Southwestern mythology – *journeying, ambivalence, primitivism, racism,* and *sexism* – another ambiguous element continues from the frontier past: *violence.* In an *Atlantic* essay in 1975, McMurtry excoriated Texas, noting that the frontier emphasis on violence was one of the few vestiges of the Old World still hanging on: "If frontier life has left any cultural residue at all, it is a residue of a most unfortunate sort – i.e., that tendency to romanticize violence which is evident on the front page of almost every Texas newspaper almost every day" (1975b: 35). Richard Slotkin examined the implications of the myth of violence in three books beginning with *Regeneration through Violence: The Mythology of the American Frontier, 1600–1860* (1973), in which he identified the archetypal pattern – the American hunter who journeys out into the wilderness, confronts the Indian in a violent confrontation, and regenerates himself and his people. The long history of Southwestern literature demonstrates the sad reality of this dubious legacy as many writers examine violence in varying ways. That history looks back to a long prehistory, now clearly acknowledged in American literary anthologies.

The Oral Tradition

For many years anthologies of American literature, reflecting the East Coast inclination that dominated the field in America, began with the literature of the Puritans, typically with William Bradford's journal. But the multiculturalism movement of the latter twentieth century led to a fuller definition and understanding of the literatures of America. Now most anthologies begin rightly with a discussion of the American Indian oral tradition, which acknowledges the power of narrative long before European and New World contact. While Indian bands across the country had myths and legends about their origins as a people, about the nature of the physical world, about social order and appropriate behavior, and about human nature and the problem of good and evil, because Southwestern native groups were scrutinized carefully by the new discipline of anthropology at the end of the nineteenth century and their stories fully recorded, the anthologies often include Southwestern tribal stories such as Pueblo tales about Spider Woman, Navajo stories of the Hero Twins and Changing Woman, or Hopi tales about The Coming of the Spanish and the Pueblo Revolt.

Spanish Explorers

The revised anthologies of American literature continue looking Southwest in the next major period, since many of the experiences recorded in the journals of Spanish conquistadors, missionaries, and explorers took place in the Southwest. Among these are *A Relation of the Revered Father Fray Marcos de Niza, Touching His Discovery of the Kingdom of Ceuola or Cibola* . . . (1439); Pedro de Casteneda's *The Narrative of the Expedition of Coronado* 1540; Don Antonio de Otermin's *Letter on the Pueblo Revolt of 1680*; and Don Diego de Varga's *Letter on the Reconquest of New Mexico* (1692).

    None of these is more important than Alvar Núñez Cabeza de Vaca's *Relación*, the story of his time after being shipwrecked on the coast, probably near Galveston, in 1528. When Cabeza de Vaca washed up on the shores of Texas after an ill-fated expedition with the Spanish explorer Narvaez, he labeled the place Malhado or Misfortune Island, the Island of Doom. His important book is the first to recount a confrontation and reconciliation between the European explorers and the native peoples, and it has all the elements of good literature – both structural (escape and return, journey) and thematic (mythic parallels, frontier myth, regeneration through violence, and the elemental theme of a man's survival after having been stripped of all resources but his own mind and imagination). Cabeza de Vaca was born in Jerez de la Frontera into a family that took the title Cabeza de Vaca, "head of a cow," from his mother's side of the family. In 1212 one of her ancestors – a shepherd named Martín Alhaja – had helped the Spanish Christians win an important battle against the Moors by marking an unguarded mountain pass with a cow skull. In 1527, Cabeza de Vaca was appointed the treasurer of a royal expedition of about 300 men, led by Pánfilo de Narváez, to Florida. In April 1528 the expedition sailed into Tampa Bay, began an overland march to Apalachee Bay, and then attempted to reach Mexico in makeshift boats. Separated from Narváez, Cabeza de Vaca led a small band of survivors to an island, probably Galveston, where native people captured them. Early in 1535, Cabeza de Vaca and the three other survivors of the expedition – Dorantes, Castillo, and Esteban the Moor – escaped and began a journey across what are now the southwestern United States and northern Mexico. In 1536 they reached a Spanish settlement on the Sinalo River in Mexico. In 1537 Cabeza de Vaca returned to Spain and was rewarded with an appointment as governor of Río de la Plata (now largely Paraguay). His account of the Narváez expedition, *Relación*, and his tales of the Zuñi and their villages, the legendary Seven Cities of Cíbola, encouraged other expeditions to America, particularly those of the explorers Hernando de Soto and Francisco Vásquez de Coronado in 1540.

For historians, Cabeza de Vaca's importance comes from his having been the first European to travel the Southwest and write reports that spurred increased exploration of the region. For anthropologists the significance derives from the information in his reports on his journey across the Southwest about numerous tribal bands: the Karankawas, Caddoes, Atakapans, Jumanos and Conchos, Pimas, Opatas, and the loose bands of hunter-gatherers now called Coahuiltecans. For literary scholars, Cabeza de Vaca's book serves as the prototype for much American literature that followed. As Tom Pilkington notes, the book's theme of the "physical and emotional struggle for an accommodation between races" is "a conflict that has never been very far removed from the American consciousness and one that has always been a factor in the works of our best and most vital writers" (1983: 145–6). And Frederick Turner, in *Beyond Geography: The Western Spirit against the Wilderness*, suggests that Cabeza de Vaca's story serves as the first captivity narrative, which became the most significant early American narrative and the basis for the Western from Cooper to Eastwood.

The Frontier Southwest, the Cowboy, and the Modern Southwest, 1821–1960

Cabeza de Vaca's narrative led later Spaniards to the Southwest, bringing the horses and cattle that would transform the region, even though they never found the golden cities they sought. After Mexico achieved independence from Spain in 1821 and began offering land grants to Anglo settlers, the next major era began. Southwestern literature of the nineteenth century is primarily about the various travelers to the region and the folk tales and songs that grew up with them. As I noted earlier, the

Southwestern story reflects the larger Western one of the strong influence of the frontier, often reflecting the much-discussed and powerful story of being drawn to a dream of paradise. The cowboy is one of the dominant icons produced by the power of the frontier myth and is primarily a Texas and Southwestern figure. After the Civil War, when Texas veterans discovered their homes and livelihood in disarray, with herds of wild cattle roaming the land, some enterprising vets began to round up the cattle, beginning the trail drives that are the heart of cowboy legend. That life lasted about 25 years, from 1870 to 1895, when barbed wire, the opening of the railroads, and economic downturns ended the golden days of trail driving. Still, the cowboy is internationally recognizable as an American icon – a symbol of frontier freedom and independence.

As Henry Nash Smith demonstrated in *Virgin Land*, the story of the cowboy began to be told in dime novels toward the end of the nineteenth century and also by former Pinkerton agent Charlie Siringo in his popular memoir *A Texas Cowboy* (1886). Alfred Henry Lewis, who had worked on ranches in Texas and Arizona before he became a journalist, published *Wolfville* (1897), a novel based on his experiences. The beginning of the twentieth century saw an increased interest in the cowboy as the embodiment of frontier values with Americans, led by Frederick Jackson Turner's famous 1893 address, fearing that the end of the frontier signaled the end of the traits that had defined the country. The dime novels gave way to serious literary treatments such as Owen Wister's *The Virginian* (1902), Andy Adams's trail-drive novel, *The Log of a Cowboy* (1903), much of the work of New Mexico's Eugene Manlove Rhodes, especially *Good Men and True* (1910) and his highly praised short novel, *Paso por Aqui* (1927), Emerson Hough's *North of 36* (1923), and Conrad Richter's *Sea of Grass* (1937). Texas traveler Stephen Crane wrote short stories that drew from the cowboy Southwest, such as the now classic "The bride comes to Yellow Sky" (1898), in which the train and the bride enter the frontier world and change everything irrevocably. And William Sydney Porter (O. Henry) drew from his own experiences on sheep ranches in South Texas, especially in *Hearts of the West* (1907), to create stories with distinctive surprise endings, such as "The Hiding of Black Bill" and "The Last of the Troubadours" (which J. Frank Dobie called "the best range story in American fiction"). Some early women writers also wrote about cowboys. Mollie E. Moore Davis's *The Wire-Cutters* (1899) predates the novels by Wister and Andy Adams usually pointed to as the beginning of the Western. Davis uses the fence-cutting wars, where cowboys cut fences to get access to water, as the basis for the story of ranch life and romance, which includes gunplay and murder. These works ultimately led to one of the major American genres, the Western, recognized by being set in the nineteenth century, with cattle, cowboys, horses, Indians, and outlaws.

One writer who extended the reach of the cowboy story was J. Frank "Pancho" Dobie, the man who almost singlehandedly brought Texas literature to respectability. Neither a fiction writer nor a scientific folklorist, Dobie was a raconteur, a compiler of stories. Still, most collectors of Texas literature begin with copies of Dobie's books. Dobie's correspondence with an old cowboy named John Young formed the

Figure 25.1 "J. Frank Dobie at Joe Small's BBQ, ca. 1957," by Russell Lee.

basis for his first book, *A Vaquero of the Brush Country* (1929), which told of Young's life as a cowboy. Dobie collected cowboy stories throughout his career, especially in *The Longhorns* (1942) and *The Mustangs* (1952). He also mined the Spanish Southwest with stories of searches for ancient treasure. In 1931 Dobie published *Coronado's Children*, his first book about lost mines and one of the first books by a non-Eastern writer to be selected by the Literary Guild and thereby distributed nationally. As A. C. Greene notes, in his *The Fifty Best Books on Texas*, *Coronado's Children* was "the book that made it possible for a Texas writer to stay at home and make a living" (1982: 9).

Dobie was one of the "Texas Triumvirate," the "Big Three" of Texas literature, alongside historian Walter Prescott Webb and naturalist Roy Bedichek. In fall 1994 a statue of these three famous Texans was placed at the entry of Barton Springs in

Zilker Park in Austin. Webb's book *The Texas Rangers* (1935) helped establish the Ranger myth that still appears in Texas popular culture, from former Rangers Call and McCrea in *Lonesome Dove* to the television series *Walker, Texas Ranger*. Webb glossed the racism attributed to the Rangers in border wars, and his book *The Great Plains* (1931) tends to stereotype Indians and Mexican Americans. Still, surveys of Western historians identify Webb's book as the most influential in shaping their views of Western history.

Roy Bedichek was for many years director of the University Interscholastic League and began to write only after retiring from this position, when he was nearly 70. In *Imagining Texas* Tom Pilkington noted of Bedichek:

> A lifetime of observing nature and of wide and intelligent reading had produced a truly remarkable understanding of the working of the natural order. His *Adventures With a Texas Naturalist* (1947) is a quiet statement of joy in the observation and appreciation of the state's plant and wildlife; it is at once a philosophical treatise, a celebration of life, and a minor classic in the field of natural history. *Karankaway County (1950)* and *The Sense of Smell* (1960), sequels to his first book, are on only a slightly lower level of achievement. (1981: 8)

Like Aldo Leopold and John Van Dyke, Bedichek served as forerunner to the environmental literature explosion in the 1960s, discussed below.

While Mollie E. Moore Davis wrote about the cowboy, pioneer women, Annette Kolodny concluded in *The Land Before Her: Fantasy and Experience of the American Frontiers: 1630–1860*, transformed this traditionally male frontier archetype in a fundamental way. Like the men, westering women journeyed because of the beckoning dream of economic success. But ultimately "women claimed the frontiers as a potential sanctuary for an idealized domesticity. Massive exploitation and alteration of the continent do not seem to have been part of women's fantasies. They dreamed, more modestly, of locating a home and a familial human community within a cultivated garden" (Kolodny 1984: xii–xiii).

Early twentieth-century Southwestern women writers had a marked effect on literary history. Mary Austin (1868–1934) wrote of two areas, the eastern Sierra Nevada desert region of California and the high plateau country of northwestern New Mexico. Her two important works deal with these areas. *The Land of Little Rain* (1903) serves as a model for later nonfiction treatments of the natural world and describes the people and physical features of the Sierra Nevada, and *The Land of Journey's Ending* is about New Mexico, where Austin thought the combination of Indian, Spanish, and Anglo history would produce a new civilization.

Austin lived much of her life in those two areas and drew heavily from her own experience within the region. Willa Cather, on the other hand, while widely associated with the Southwest – mainly because of the success of *Death Comes for the Archbishop* (1927) – drew from visits rather than from living in the region. Like many others, her interest in the region was piqued partially by the aggressive promotion of the Santa Fe Railroad, which drew hundreds of tourists to New Mexico and Arizona. Cather, tired of the stress of magazine editing in New York, made a long visit to Winslow, Arizona, in 1912 to visit her brother Douglass, a Santa Fe employee headquartered there. That visit ultimately led to Cather's three major Southwestern works, *The Song of the Lark*, *The Professor's House*, and *Death Comes for the Archbishop*.

On a visit to Santa Fe in 1925 Cather's interest in Jean Lamy, first Bishop of Santa Fe, increased after she found a biography of Joseph Machebeuf, first Bishop of Denver, a lifelong friend of Lamy's from their seminary days in France. Cather was particularly interested in the reaction of these well-educated, highly civilized men to the primitive frontier world in which they lived. She based her characters Jean Marie Latour and Joseph Vaillant on Lamy and Machebeuf, and demonstrated how this new environment radically transformed them.

Interest in the Southwest perhaps influenced the award of the 1930 Pulitzer Prize to Oliver LaFarge's *Laughing Boy* (1929), a novel that slipped into obscurity toward the end of the century. LaFarge was an anthropologist, and his details of Navajo life strengthened the book, but his lack of experience as a novelist led to an overly romanticized and romantic work, focusing on the love story of the title character and Slim Girl, that now seems amateurish. Still, Mary Austin served on the Pulitzer selection committee and Cather praised the novel.

Another New Mexico writer who achieved a following in the 1920s and 1930s was Harvey Fergusson, with novels about nineteenth century New Mexican history, *Wolf Song* (1927) and *In Those Days* (1929), and later with *Grant of Kingdom* (1950) and *The Conquest of Don Pedro* (1954). Fergusson was born in Albuquerque, the product of a distinguished New Mexico family. His sister, Erna Fergusson, wrote one of the notable books defining the region.

Not all Texas and Southwestern writers of the early part of the twentieth century celebrated the region as Austin, Cather, and Dobie did. One of Dobie's contemporaries was Katherine Anne Porter (1890–1980), who grew up just five miles north of San Marcos, Texas, in the small community of Kyle. Porter's stories, such as "The Grave" and "Noon Wine" are set in central Texas, and almost every major anthology of American literature taught in college classes includes a story by her. Throughout her life Porter muddied the water about her past, shaving four years off her age and claiming to have been brought up among a Southern "white pillared" crowd. Porter's Southwestern past was unhappy, and she got out of Texas "like a bat out of hell" as soon as she could. But her strong, ambivalent women, like Miss Sophia Jane Rhea of *The Old Order*, come from that past, and through these characters Porter comments on its strengths and weaknesses. Similarly, Dorothy Scarborough (1878–1935) in *The Wind* (1925) presented a less than favorable view of Texas. *The Wind*, made into a now classic silent film with Lillian Gish in 1927, presents a harsh West Texas environment with an unrelenting wind and an unsupportive community that drive its main character insane.

Notable African-American and Hispanic writers of the Southwest published during this period. Sutton E. Griggs was born in Texas and educated at Bishop College in Dallas. His works, such as *Imperium in Imperio* (1899) and *Unfettered* (1902), widely read by black readers, foreshadowed themes that dominated later African-American literature by calling for full rights for black citizens, examining the possibility of revolt, and indicating the need for an organization to champion black rights. Another Texan, J. Mason Brewer (1896–1975), achieved success primarily through his folk-lore collections, many of which appeared in the annual volume of the Texas Folklore Society edited by Dobie. Dobie also encouraged Mexican-American writers, especially Jovita Gonzalez, who wrote a master's thesis with Dobie and who served as the president of the Texas Folklore Society in 1931–2. Arguably the most important Southwestern writer of color during this period was Ralph Ellison (1914–94). Born and reared in Oklahoma, Ellison attended Tuskegee Institute in Alabama and then moved to Harlem after losing his scholarship. His early stories often deal with Oklahoma, and his major work *Invisible Man* (1952), set mainly in Harlem, clearly concerns the themes of freedom and restriction raised by Ellison's Southwestern past.

Several other Southwestern writers before 1960 achieved noteworthy successes. While poetry and drama did not begin to flourish until later, some poets, particularly New Mexican ones, achieved a degree of acclaim, including Witter Bynner, Fray Angelico Chavez, Alice Corbin Henderson, Haniel Long, Arthur Sampley, and Winfield Townley Scott. The most important early Southwestern playwright was Lynn Riggs, whose *Green Grow the Lilacs* later became the popular American musical *Oklahoma*. Other writers of note during this period are Ross Calvin, Edwin Corle, William Eastlake, Loula Grace Erdman, Fred Gipson, Tom Lea, and George Sessions Perry. Lea, who developed a reputation as both a painter and a writer, wrote a lengthy history of the King Ranch, two important novels, *The Brave Bulls* and *The Wonderful Country*, lived into the twenty-first century, and was mentioned by President George W. Bush in his acceptance speech for the Republican presidential nomination in 2000.

The Renaissance in Southwestern Literature, 1960 to the Present

In the 1960s, after some important publications at the end of the 1950s, Southwestern literature began a regional and national resurgence that continued throughout the remainder of the century. Fiction, much of it still about the cowboy and frontier past, continued to be the major genre, with writers around Texas, New Mexico, and Arizona achieving major success, but drama, poetry, and, particularly, environmental literature demonstrated a vital presence. Among the forerunners in the 1950s were several east Texas writers. Physically and historically, east Texas has strong ties with the South. The green piney woods and lush blackland soil of much of east Texas look more like the South, and many of the early settlers of east Texas brought slavery and cotton farming with them. Their influence led Texas to join the confederacy. Yet one deep east Texas town, Nacogdoches, was also one of the earliest outposts on the northern frontier of New Spain and has a strong Spanish influence that ties it to San

Antonio rather than Vicksburg or Atlanta. East Texas writers often claim the Southern heritage, especially since the shadow of William Faulkner looms heavily over American literature. Three of the most important east Texas writers are three Willams – William Humphrey, William Goyen, and William Owens. Humphrey is probably the best-known, primarily because his novel *Home from the Hill* (1958) was filmed starring Robert Mitchum. Goyen was more of a stylist, but both his novel *The House of Breath* (1950) and Owens's *Fever in the Earth* (1958) are concerned with the importance of oil in east Texas lives.

In 1961 the dominant name in Texas letters for 40 years published his first novel. Larry McMurtry grew up in the small town of Archer City, just south of Wichita Falls. McMurtry, a prolific writer, published 23 novels, five books of non-fiction, several screen and teleplays, and hundreds of book reviews between 1961 and 2001. Six of his novels have been made into movies and four into television mini-series. Some of the most important works are *Horseman, Pass By* (1961), *Leaving Cheyenne* (1963) *The Last Picture Show* (1966), *In a Narrow Grave* (1968), *Terms of Endearment* (1975), *Lonesome Dove* (1985), *Duane's Depressed* (1999), *Walter Benjamin at the Dairy Queen* (1999), *Paradise* (2001), and *Boone's Lick* (2000). In 1994 McMurtry published his first collaborative novel, *Pretty Boy Floyd*, written with Diana Ossana. Their second novel, *Zeke and Ned*, was published in 1997. The sheer quantity of work he has produced suggests that McMurtry is a compulsive writer, and he has admitted that he gets a headache if he does not complete his self-imposed task of writing at least five double-spaced pages every day – over 1,800 manuscript pages a year.

Although he is not as well-known as McMurtry, another west Texas writer of prominence who has written primarily about the cowboy Southwest is Elmer Kelton. Where McMurtry has taken a critical approach to traditional Texas literature, Kelton has taken the traditional Western genre novel and moved beyond it. He has published several important novels about Texas: *The Day the Cowboys Quit* (1971), *The Good Old Boys* (1978), *The Man Who Rode Midnight* (1987), and *The Time It Never Rained* (1973), among others. He has won the Texas Institute of Letters fiction award and is widely respected as a historical novelist. Although his work has been compared to that of Louis L'Amour, Kelton notes that where L'Amour's Western heroes are six feet two and courageous, his main characters are five feet eight and scared.

Another important west Texas writer is Robert Flynn. Until the mid-1980s Flynn's modest reputation rested on a little-known novel titled *North To Yesterday* (1967), a blackly humorous work about the Southwest. Although he had won the Western Heritage Award, in the 1970s Flynn stopped publishing, and *North to Yesterday* went out of print. But the novel's supporters continued to praise it, Flynn began to publish again in the mid-1980s, and he is now one of the most important writers in Texas, having served as the president of the Texas Institute of Letters. Flynn returned to his mythical west Texas town with *Wanderer Springs* (1988) and again in *Tie Fast Country* (2001).

More recently, the most important Southwestern writer focusing on the cowboy past is Cormac McCarthy, whose powerful novels embody a strong revision of the traditional Western story. McCarthy's enigmatic Southwestern novels, including *Blood Meridian* (1985) and the border trilogy – *All the Pretty Horses* (1992), *The Crossing* (1994), and *Cities of the Plain* (1998) – are tied together through the repetition of the powerful metaphor of border crossings, a metaphor for a complex and oxymoronic melding of nihilism and optimism, good and evil, illusion and reality, human and nature, and several similar contrasts that examine the complex intertwining of positive and negative forces to present ultimately a worldview that suggests a nihilistic optimism. McCarthy draws from a powerful tradition – from Dostoevsky to Melville, to Twain, to Crane, to Faulkner and Southern literature, to American Westerns – for his powerful works that at the center are about ontology and epistemology, being and knowing. He uses the border metaphor to create a complicated way of knowing the world that is not simply black or white, good or evil, life or death, but an oxymoronic melding, a continuing dialectic between the forces of death and life, end and beginning, and other apparent dualities. R. G. Vliet predated McCarthy with philosophical novels about the cowboy world with *Rockspring* (1974) and *Solitudes* (1977).

New Mexico has produced several writers who have achieved a national reputation. The first of John Nichols's Chamisaville trilogy – *The Milagro Beanfield War* (1974), *The Magic Journey* (1978), and *The Nirvana Blues* (1981) – was made into a major motion picture by Robert Redford. Non-Native American writer Tony Hillerman has a loyal following for his series of mystery novels featuring Navajo detectives.

Environmental Literature

In 1960, the primary inheritor of the Dobie–Bedichek–Webb mantle, now the Dean of Texas letters, John Graves, published *Goodbye to a River* (1960). What make Graves a memorable writer are his subtlety and distinctive style, an amalgamation of fiction, folklore, philosophy, history, nature, personal experience, anecdotes, and allusion presented with repeated use of sentence fragments, ellipses, dashes, parenthetical remarks, and dialogue. Graves achieves a balance of high and low, moving from a quotation by Shakespeare or Veblen to regional dialect. In his three major works, *Goodbye to a River*, *Hard Scrabble* (1974), and *Notes from a Limestone Ledge* (1980), Graves builds upon the Old Order's concern with the passing Southwest but approaches it with a complex blend of nostalgia and acceptance built from a cosmopolitan understanding of the way of the world and a powerful emphasis on the value of preserving the natural environment. Graves's concern with the natural world and the relation to it of humans is mirrored by numerous other Southwestern nonfiction writers, including Rick Bass, Charles Bowden, Stephen Harrigan, Gary Paul Nabham, Terry Tempest Williams, Ann Zwinger, and especially Ed Abbey.

Although Abbey began as a fiction writer and achieved some success with *The Brave Cowboy* (1956; filmed with Kirk Douglas as *Lonely are the Brave*, 1961), and with *The Monkey Wrench Gang*, his nonfiction, particularly *Desert Solitaire* (1968), is the bedrock of his work. An examination of wilderness and freedom, *Desert Solitaire: A Season in the Wilderness* is the clearest example of "Cactus Ed's" approach, which combines philosophy, autobiography, fiction, close observation of nature, and attitude. Abbey, like Thoreau in Walden, condensed his three seasons as a park ranger at Arches National Monument in Utah into a single year. Among his other nonfiction works are *Abbey's Road* (1979), *Good News* (1980), *Down the River* (1982), and *Beyond the Wall* (1984).

The Urban Southwest

An important Texas writer who staked out the state's urban environment was Billy Lee Brammer, whose one published work, *The Gay Place* (1961), has become the classic Texas political novel. (The title reflects its time, not ours, and refers to a happy place.) Brammer, who served as an assistant to Lyndon Johnson, attempted to imagine what Texas would have been like had Johnson been Governor of Texas. Brammer never realized his potential as a writer and died at age 48, but his novel lives, reissued by the University of Texas Press. A contemporary of Brammer, Edwin "Bud" Shrake, wrote two novels set in Texas cities, *But Not for Love* (1964) and *Strange Peaches* (1972). Shrake was a sportswriter in Dallas and an acquaintance of Jack Ruby in the days before John Kennedy was assassinated there, and his work bears the mark of that fatal day. Later, Shrake wrote two important novels about the nineteenth-century Southwest, *Blessed McGill* (1968) and *The Borderland* (2000).

Kentucky-born Barbara Kingsolver has also written about the urban Southwest, especially in *The Bean Trees* (1988), set primarily in Tucson, Arizona; *Animal Dreams* (1990); and *Pigs in Heaven*, which moves from Kentucky to Washington.

The Texas Gulf Coast stretches from the bayous of Louisiana to the salt marshes leading to Brownsville, including the oil-refining areas around Beaumont/Port Arthur, the urban port of Houston, and the tourist-rich areas of Galveston and Corpus Christi. Several Texas writers hail from the Gulf Coast of Texas, notably Horton Foote, James Lee Burke, and Stephen Harrigan. Foote, best known for his plays and scripts such as *Trip to Bountiful* and *1918*, also wrote the novel *The Chase*. James Lee Burke, whose most widely known creation is his Louisiana detective Dave Robicheaux, draws from his Texas Gulf Coast background as well. Harrigan has lived in central Texas now for 20 years, but he grew up along the coast, and his novel *Aransas* is one of the best books about the coast. His *The Gates of the Alamo* (2000) has been hailed as the definitive novel about the fated Texas mission.

Mexican American Literature

Since the mid-twentieth century, Southwestern Mexican American writers have become increasingly important, led initially by Américo Paredes, a folklorist who taught at the University of Texas for many years. Paredes collected *corridos*, Mexican folk ballads that originated along the border and usually dealt with skirmishes between Mexican Americans and Texas Rangers and celebrated the courage of Mexicans who stood up against the oppressive Rangers. Paredes concentrated on folk ballads about Gregorio Cortez, a vaquero who lived with his brother Romaldo in south Texas near El Carmen at the turn of the century. What happened in 1901 is unclear, because there are several versions of the story, but in broad terms it seems that because of a misunderstanding, Gregorio Cortez killed Sheriff W. T. Morris. When the sheriff accused Cortez of stealing a horse, Gregorio Cortez came out of his house with his pistol in his hand and shot the Sheriff, setting into motion a lengthy flight from the authorities. Ultimately he was captured, tried, and sentenced to life imprisonment, but he was pardoned after 12 years in prison. The story gave rise to a series of *corridos* along the border. Paredes eventually wrote up the legend in *With His Pistol in His Hand*, published in 1958. In 1982 the story was transformed into a film called *The Ballad of Gregorio Cortez*. Paredes' book demonstrated the power of the story and of Mexican American storytelling.

Another important south Texas Mexican American author was Tomás Rivera (1935–1984), whose one book, . . . *y no se lo tragó la tierra / And the Earth Did Not Part* (1971), was filmed by Severo Perez as *And the Earth Did Not Devour Him* in 1994. It is a loosely connected series of vignettes about a migrant family moving from Texas to Minnesota in 1952. Both the book and Rivera were highly influential, as he became chancellor of the University of California at Riverside in 1979, the first Chicano chancellor in American higher education.

Rivera's life and work were clearly significant for Rolando Hinojosa, whose several books about the South Texas Valley constitute a continuing series: *Estampas del valle y otras obras* (Sketches of the Valley and Other Works) (1973), *Klail City y sus alrededores* (Klail City and its Environs) (1976), *Mi Querida Rafa* (My dear Rafe) (1981), *Rites and Witnesses* (1982), *The Valley* (1983), and *The Useless Servants* (1993).

Probably the best-known Southwestern Chicano writer is Rudolfo Anaya, whose *Bless Me, Ultima* is the bestselling Mexican American novel. It tells the story of a youthful character, Tony Marez, as he grows up in New Mexico. Tony witnesses death in various forms before he escapes from the potential captivity of a life as a Catholic priest. He will become a shaman for the Christlike teachings of the Golden Carp as he is reintegrated into a primitivistic approach to the world through the teachings and model of Ultima, the old *curandera* or healer who uses her magic to cure Tony's uncles of the curse the *brujas*, or witches, had placed on them, and to show Tony the power of the natural world. More recently, Anaya has written a series of mystery novels set in New Mexico.

Over recent years a number of other Mexican American writers, including poets and dramatists discussed below, have published significant works. Dagoberto Gilb, who was a journeyman carpenter in El Paso with an MA in art history before he began publishing and who now teaches at Southwest Texas State University, has published two collections of stories, *The Magic of Blood* (1993) and *Woodcuts of Women*

(2001), and a novel, *The Last Known Residence of Mickey Acuna* (1994). Gilb won the PEN/Hemingway Award and was a PEN/Faulkner finalist for his first collection. In 1994 he won a prestigious Whiting Award.

Other important Mexican-American authors include Denise Chávez, author of drama, poetry, and fiction, including a collection of related stories, *The Last of the Menu Girls* (1986), and the novels *Face of an Angel* (1995) and *Loving Pedro Infante* (2001); and Sandra Cisneros, who won early fame for a book about growing up in Chicago, *The House on Mango Street* (1983). Cisneros later moved to San Antonio and turned to the Southwest in *Woman Hollering Creek and Other Stories* (1991). Cisneros is also a poet, author of *My Wicked Wicked Ways* (1992) and *Loose Woman* (1994). In 2002, she published *Caramelo; or, Puro Cuento: A Novel.*

American Indian Literature

The contemporary awakening of Southwestern American Indian literature began with N. Scott Momaday's *House Made of Dawn* (1968), winner of the Pulitzer Prize. Momaday, a Kiowa raised among the Pueblo in New Mexico, later received a Ph.D. from Stanford. His works draw from his knowledge of both Euro-American literature and the Native American oral tradition. Momaday's success inspired others, especially Leslie Marmon Silko (Laguna Pueblo), whose *Ceremony* (1977) is now a classic work. Silko has also published *Laguna Woman* (1974), *Almanac of the Dead* (1991), *Yellow Woman and a Beauty of the Spirit* (1996), and *Gardens in the Dunes* (1999).

Louis Owens, of Mississippi Choctaw, Oklahoma Cherokee, and Irish descent, wrote the novels *Wolfsong* (1991), *The Sharpest Sight* (1992), *Bone Game* (1994), and *Nightland* (1996), as well as nonfiction works *Other Destinies: Understanding the American Indian Novel* (1992) and *Mixedblood Messages: Literature, Film, Family, Place* (1998) before his suicide in 2002.

Southwestern Drama

American drama since 1960 demonstrates a variety of elements that are primarily the result of two developments – the growth of powerful regional theaters, and the emergence of Off-Broadway and Off-Off-Broadway playhouses. These changes, which in turn resulted from the Broadway clawhold on American theater, allowed several Southwestern dramatists to gain national prominence during the period. But Southwestern drama, like American drama in general, found its presence diminished after a few important years from the 1960s to the 1980s. From the 1990s, Broadway came to be dominated by big-budget musicals and revivals of classic plays; new plays declined as new playwrights turned to film and television to reach audiences. But during the preceding three decades, Southwestern playwrights like Preston Jones, Sam Shepard, Lanford Wilson, and Mark Medoff established themselves as significant

Figure 25.2   Leslie Marmon Silko, by Don Anders.

American dramatists. Minority and women Western writers, including Luis Valdez, Hanay Geiogamah, and Frank Chin, also influenced the look of contemporary South-western drama.

Preston Jones and Sam Shepard represent the extremes of Western drama since 1960. Jones's plays are generally comic examinations of small-town Southwestern life, presented realistically with stock characters speaking recognizable dialect; Shepard's magical realism is peopled with mythic figures that often float off into incantatory monologues. Jones got his start with Paul Baker at the Dallas Theater Center; Shepard began Off-Off-Broadway. Despite these differences, both Jones and Shepard wrote plays that concentrated on themes central to much Southwestern American literature. Both, for example, demonstrate a deep ambivalence toward the impermanence of the values of the mythic West and the heroic images it spawned.

Jones's three plays comprising *A Texas Trilogy* – *The Last Meeting of the Knights of the White Magnolia*, *The Oldest Living Graduate*, and *Lu Ann Hampton Laverty Oberlander* – began in 1973–4 at the Dallas Theater Center, where Jones had been an actor since 1960. After their successful Texas performances, the three plays were presented at the Eisenhower Theater at the Kennedy Center in Washington DC, in 1976, to receptive audiences, but when they opened in repertoire on Broadway, they received tepid reviews. Jones went back to Texas, continued to write plays, and died in 1979 from complications to bleeding ulcers at age 43.

Sam Shepard followed a different trail. Born in Fort Sheridan, Illinois, in 1943, he grew up in South Pasadena, California, but left for New York, heading east in 1963. First he became a waiter at the Village Gate, a popular jazz club, where he met Ralph Cook, the founder of Off-Off-Broadway's Theater Genesis. Cook encouraged Shepard to write, and in 1964 Theater Genesis presented Shepard's two one-act plays, *Cowboys* and *The Rock Garden*. Since that time Shepard has written over 40 plays, and won 10 Obie awards and a Pulitzer Prize for *Buried Child* (1979). Other important Shepard plays are *Cowboys* #2 (1967), *The Unseen Hand* (1969), *Operation Sidewinder* (1970), *Cowboy Mouth* (1971), *The Tooth of Crime* (1972), *Geography of a Horse Dreamer* (1972), and *True West* (1980). Although Shepard's face and name became better known into the 1990s, primarily because of his work in film, after 1986 he presented only a few new plays, notably *States of Shock* (1991) and *Sympatico* (1994).

Where Jones's strength was the realistic Southwestern comic language of his characters, Shepard's vitality stems from his mythic imagination. Both writers, though, have been concerned with the loss of the heroic ideals and coherent values that the American West formerly represented. In Jones's plays the contemporary Southwest is often effete, enervated, or materialistic. Old patterns embracing racism, sexism, and corrupted individualism hang on in unsympathetic ways. Shepard, often in dazzling, absurdist fashion, presents a similar world that has fallen or is falling away from something valuable. While Jones's plays concentrate on the ennui of small-town Southwestern life, Shepard's emphasize the fragmentation of a world searching for characters that can continue to embody positive mythic values in new ways.

Horton Foote, who has become one of the most acclaimed writers about small-town America, especially Wharton, Texas, his home town, influenced Jones's emphasis on small-town Texas. He has written about Wharton in a nine-play series about four generations of his Texas ancestors. Several of these plays have been made into films: *Trip to Bountiful* (1985), *1918* (1985), *On Valentine's Day* (1986), and *Convicts* (1991). Besides adapting his own work for the screen, Foote has written screen adaptations of Harper Lee (*To Kill a Mockingbird*, 1962), William Faulkner (*Tomorrow*, 1972) and John Steinbeck (*Of Mice and Men*, 1992). He won his first Oscar for Best Screenplay for *To Kill a Mockingbird* and a second for his only original feature screenplay to date, *Tender Mercies* (1982), the portrait of a country singer – a performance that won a Best Actor Oscar for Robert Duvall. The Signature Theater Company in New York City honored him by devoting its 1994–5 season to his work. One of those productions, *The Young Man from Atlanta*, won the 1995 Pulitzer Prize.

Mark Medoff, a longstanding faculty member at New Mexico State University in Las Cruces, took both the regional theater and the Off-Off-Broadway routes. The Southwest provides the setting for several of his plays, such as his first one, *Doing a Good One for the Red Man: A Red Farce* (1969), which was first produced in San Antonio, Texas, by the Dallas Theater Center. His first popular success, *When You Comin' Back, Red Ryder?* (1973), took the Off-Off-Broadway route, initially produced by the Circle Repertory Theater Company. Like Shepard, Medoff dramatizes a contemporary West where traditional heroes have vanished. In a quiet New Mexico diner, a freaky doper smuggling marijuana to California menaces the patrons and the night attendant, Stephen Ryder. Stephen cannot transform himself into the cowboy hero, Red Ryder, nor can he summon Red's faithful Indian companion, Little Beaver. To confirm his point about lost heroes, Medoff uses a Paul Simon line as an epigraph: "Where have you gone, Joe Dimaggio / A nation turns its lonely eyes to you . . ."

With *Firekeeper* (1978), Medoff resumed his relationship with the Dallas Theater Center. The play revolves around the activities of a priest, a mentally disturbed Hispanic girl, a local sheriff (played by Preston Jones at the DTC), and an old Indian. The Indian at one point recalls the legend of the firekeeper, the shaman who could determine the right path for men to follow. Neither law nor religion seems to be able to provide this information in Medoff's contemporary Southwest. Medoff's most successful play, *Children of a Lesser God* (1979), does not have a Southwestern setting.

Other Western and Southwestern playwrights began to find greater acceptance for their work in the 1970s. Jack Heifner in *Vanities* (1978) focuses on three Texas girls at various times of their lives. His two one-acters about Texas women – sisters in *Patio*, mother and daughter in *Porch* – achieved moderate success. James McLure, trained at Southern Methodist University in Dallas, received acclaim for *Laundry and Bourbon*, *Pvt. Wars*, and *Lone Star* (1980). *Lone Star*, first presented by the Actors Theater of Louisville, combines light, folksy humor with a weightier analysis of the effects of the war on a Vietnam veteran. D. L. Coburn, a Dallas friend whom Preston Jones encouraged to write, won a Pulitzer Prize for *The Gin Game*, an unsentimental play about old people in a nursing home that could be anywhere.

Texas chic aided Larry King's and Peter Masterson's *The Best Little Whorehouse in Texas* (1978). *Whorehouse* grew out of a *Playboy* article that Texas journalist King had written about the closing of the legendary Chicken Ranch, a brothel outside LaGrange, Texas. Using the traditional Western theme of individual freedom versus the constraints demanded by civilization (represented by a meddling television journalist), this musical (songs by Carol Hall) enjoyed an extended Broadway run and a less successful film version with Dolly Parton and Burt Reynolds. Buoyed by the success of his first play, King went on to write several others, including *The Night Hank Williams Died*, *The Kingfish*, *Golden Shadows Old West Museum*, and *The Dead Presidents' Club*. He also published several noteworthy nonfiction collections, especially *Confessions of a White Racist* (1972), for which he earned a National Book Award nomination.

An important Chicano playwright, probably the most prolific one, is Carlos Morton. His works include *Johnny Tenorio* (1983), *The Savior* (1986), *The Miser of Mexico* (1989), and *Pancho Diablo* (1987). Known for his humorous, satirical characters, Morton's plays include modern-day versions of Don Juan, of Molière's miser, and of the Devil himself. *El Jardín* presents a comic creation story. Denise Chávez, mentioned above, studied with Mark Medoff at New Mexico State University and began writing plays in the early 1970s, focusing on Chicano culture.

The most significant Southwestern American Indian playwright in recent years is Hanay Geiogamah, a Kiowa-Delaware who established the American Indian Theater Ensemble in the 1970s with Ellen Stewart's help. Later called the Native American Theater Ensemble, the company toured America and Europe presenting Geiogamah's plays, among others. Although oral performance is central to Indian tradition, drama is a European literary form. Geiogamah combines the two and explores Indian culture and history. Most of his plays focus on contemporary Indian life, with glimpses into the past. *Body Indian* (1972) examines the way the Indian body politic undermines itself. Bobby Lee is an alcoholic who has lost his legs to the archetypal American machine in the garden – the train. When he gets drunk in the apartment of some friends', they steal his lease money. *Foghorn* (1973) takes its title from the foghorns used to harass the Indians who occupied Alcatraz in 1969. It presents a variety of Indian stereotypes, from Pocahontas to activists at Wounded Knee, in an effort to exorcise them. In *49* (1975) the subject is an Indian celebration broken up by police.

Other notable Indian playwrights are Diane Glancy (Cherokee), author of such plays as *The Lesser Wars, Jump Kiss, The Woman Who Was a Red Deer Dressed for the Deer Dance*, and *The Best Fancy Dancer the Pushmataha Pow Wow's Ever Seen*; and LeAnne Howe (Choctaw), author of *Indian Radio Days* and, with Roxy Gordon, *Big Pow Wow*. Both Glancy and Howe have also published fiction and nonfiction.

The Chinese-American experience in the West has been explored by Frank Chin in *The Chickencoop Chinaman* (1972) and *The Year of the Dragon* (1974). Another play with a Southwestern setting was presented by Douglas Ward and the Negro Ensemble Company. Charles Fuller's *The Brownsville Raid* (1978), was based on a 1906 incident. When the town of Brownsville, Texas, was shot up, white townspeople charged that members of a black regiment were responsible. Eventually the entire regiment was dishonorably discharged. Fuller, who grew up in Philadelphia, won the Pulitzer Prize for *A Soldier's Play* (1982).

Poetry

Looking back at Southwestern poetry from the midcentury, J. Frank Dobie declared it "mediocre," but during the second half of the century poetry flourished across the diverse groups that constitute the Southwest. In Texas, the most accomplished poets include William Barney, Vassar Miller, Naomi Shihab Nye, and Walt McDonald.

Barney's work reveals the deep influence of Robert Frost applied to Texas culture in *Kneel from the Stone* (1952), *The Killdeer Crying* (1977), and *A Cowtown Chronicle* (1999). Vassar Miller's poems, collected in *If I Had Wheels of Love* (1991), are often philosophical and religious, and reflect Miller's lifelong affliction with cerebral palsy. Naomi Shihab Nye of San Antonio began to reach a national audience after a television profile by Bill Moyers. Her works include *Different Ways to Pray* (1980) and *Hugging the Juke Box* (1982). Walter McDonald of Lubbock, an air force pilot who taught at the Air Force Academy before moving to Texas Tech, has been one of the most prolific Texas poets since the 1970s. His work focuses on both Vietnam and west Texas, juxtaposing the harsh landscapes. His collections include *Caliban in Blue and Other Poems* (1976), *Rafting the Brazos* (1988), *Counting Survivors* (1995), and *Blessings the Body Gave* (1998).

Among other notable works by Texas poets are those of Dave Oliphant, who is also a critic, translator, and publisher, author of *Lines and Mounds* (1976), *Footprints* (1978), *Maria's Poems* (1987), and *Austin* (1985); Betty Adcock's *Beholdings* (1988); and Jerry Bradley's *Simple Versions of Disaster* (1981). R. S. Gwynn of Beaumont, originally from North Carolina, combines humor with a fine feeling for form in such works as *Bearing and Distance* (1977), *The Narcissiad*, a satirical poem (1982), and *No Word of Farewell: Poems 1970–2000* (2001). *The Drive-In* won the Breakthrough Award from the University of Missouri Press in 1986.

One of the major developments in Southwestern poetry in recent years has been the explosion of poetry by ethnic poets, especially Mexican-American and American Indian poets. Many of these writers, such as Sandra Cisneros, Diane Chavez, N. Scott Momaday, and Leslie Silko, discussed earlier, publish in various genres. Chicano poets draw from specific cultural experiences; many easily merge English and Spanish. Tino Villanuevo's *Scene from the Movie GIANT* (1993) is a long meditation about the effect of watching a major film that deals with ethnicity at a theater in San Marcos, Texas, Villanuevo's home, in the 1950s. Ray Gonzalez is primarily a poet, author of *The Heat of Arrivals: Poems* (1996), *Cabato Sentora: Poems* (1999), *Turtle Pictures* (2000), and *The Hawk Temple at Tierra Grande* (2002). He is also editor of *After Aztlan: Latino Poetry of the Nineties* (1998), and he has published a memoir, *Memory Fever: A Journey Beyond El Paso Del Norte* (1999), and a short-story collection, *The Ghost of John Wayne, and Other Stories* (2001).

In New Mexico, Jimmy Santiago Baca is also primarily a poet, author of *Black Mesa Poems* (1995), *In the Way of the Sun* (1997), *Set This Book on Fire* (1999), *Healing Earthquakes* (2001), and others. His memoir, *A Place to Stand* (2001), examines his years in prison, where he taught himself to become a poet. Baca is also the author of a collection of stories and essays, *Working in the Dark: Reflections of a Poet of the Barrio* (1992); a play, *Los tres hijos de Julia* (1991); and a screenplay, *Bound by Honor* (1993).

Alberto Ríos grew up in Nogales, Arizona, the subject of *Capirotada: A Nogales Memoir* (1999). His poetry includes *Whispering to Fool the Wind: Poems* (1982), winner of the Academy's Walt Whitman Award; *Five Indiscretions: A Book of Poems* (1985); *The Lime Orchard Woman: Poems* (1988); and *Teodora Luna's Two Kisses: Poems* (1990).

He is also the author of *Pig Cookies and Other Stories* (1995), *The Curtain of Trees: Stories* (1999), and *The Iguana Killer: Twelve Stories of the Heart* (1984), which won the Western States Book Award.

American Indian poets around the Southwest also derive subjects and images from their cultural experiences, often drawing from Native American myth and legend. Among the important poets are Joy Harjo, author of *She Had Some Horses* (1983), *In Mad Love and War* (1990), *The Woman Who Fell from the Sky: Poems* (1996), and *A Map to the Next World: Poems and Tales* (2001). Pueblo poet Simon Ortiz's poetry draws images from the desert and the Southwestern landscape in such works as *Out There Somewhere* (2001), *From Sand Creek: Rising in this Heart Which Is Our America* (2000), *Men on the Moon: Collected Short Stories* (1999), and *Woven Stone* (1992). Like other Indian writers, Ortiz looks to a tribal past and the ancient oral traditions of Acoma Pueblo.

Luci Tapahonso (Navajo) was born in Shiprock, New Mexico, and is the author of *One More Shiprock Night: Poems* (1981), *Seasonal Woman* (1981), *Sáanii Dahataał the Women Are Singing* (1993), and *Blue Horses Rush In* (1997). Tapahonso grew up on the largest Indian reservation in the United States and learned English as a second language after her native tongue, Diné (Navajo). Consequently, her poems and stories often include Diné. She attended the University of New Mexico and studied with Leslie Silko, who was then a faculty member there.

Ofelia Zepeda (Tohono O'odham), born and raised in Stanfield, Arizona, near the Tohono O'odham and Pima reservations, is considered the foremost authority in Tohono O'odham language and literature. Her works include *When It Rains* (1982), translations of Papago and Pima poetry; *Home Places* (1995); and *Ocean Power: Poems from the Desert* (1995).

Cultural mix is also important to some Southwestern poets such as Ai, who initially identified herself as an African-American poet. She has since described herself as "1/2 Japanese, 1/8 Choctaw, 1/4 Black, and 1/16 Irish." Born Florence Anthony in Albany, Texas, in 1947, Ai grew up in Tucson, Arizona, and later changed her name to "Ai" ("love" in Japanese). Her poetry is edgy, often confronting violent themes. *Vice* (1999) won the National Book Award for Poetry. Other books are *Killing Floor* (1979), which won the 1978 Lamont Poetry Award of the Academy of American Poets; *Sin* (1986); *Fate* (1991); and *Greed* (1993). Other notable Southwestern African-American poets include Lorenzo Thomas and Harryette Mullen.

CONCLUSION

Southwestern American literature has clearly moved out of the margins and now stands as a distinct part of the American literary scene. With the rising emphasis on Chicano, American Indian, and environmental writing around the country, Southwestern literature, where these genres flourish, demands increased emphasis in American literature anthologies and critical discussions of national literature. But even as these types gain in recognition, a counter-movement has arisen. Because the literature now recognized as Southwestern often draws from a past that reveres wild nature and romanticizes the wilderness and ethnic minorities, some critics have called for writers to recognize the reality of the urban Southwest, where ethnic divisions trouble city-dwellers and where the revered wilderness has disappeared. Writers such as Larry McMurtry have also called for Texas and Southwestern literature to move away from the "country and western literature" of the past and look to the urban Southwest for subject matter. Indeed, some writers have moved in those directions. The new trends along with the now traditional types and the population explosion in the Southwestern "sunbelt" states indicate the continuing vitality of the region's literature in the new century.

References and Further Reading

Abbey, Edward (1956). *The Brave Cowboy.* New York: Dodd, Mead.

Abbey, Edward (1968). *Desert Solitaire: A Season in the Wilderness.* New York: McGraw-Hill.

Abbey, Edward (1977). *The Journey Home: Some Words in Defense of the American West.* New York: Dutton.

Abbey, Edward (1984). *Beyond the Wall.* New York: Holt, Rinehart, & Winston.

Adams, Andy (1903). *The Log of a Cowboy.* Boston: Houghton Mifflin.

Adams, Andy (1904). *A Texas Matchmaker.* Boston: Houghton Mifflin.

Adams, Andy (1907). *Reed Anthony, Cowman: An Autobiography.* Boston: Houghton Mifflin.

Allen, Paula Gunn (1982). *Shadow Country.* (Native American Series.) Los Angeles: UCLA.

Allen, Paula Gunn (1983). *The Woman Who Owned the Shadows.* Albion, Calif.: Spinsters Ink.

Allen, Paula Gunn (1991). *Grandmothers of the Light: A Medicine Woman's Sourcebook.* Boston: Beacon Press.

Anaya, Rudolfo (1972). *Bless Me, Ultima.* Berkeley: Quinto Sol.

Anaya, Rudolfo (1989). *Aztlan: Essays on the Chicano Homeland.* Albuquerque: El Norte.

Anderson, John Q., Gaston, Jr., Edwin W., and Lee, James W. (1972). *Southwestern American Literature, A Bibliography.* Chicago: Swallow.

Barthelme, Donald (1981). *Sixty Stories.* New York: Putnam.

Bedichek, Roy (1947). *Adventures with a Texas Naturalist.* Austin: University of Texas Press.

Bedichek, Roy (1950). *Karankawa Country.* Garden City: Doubleday.

Brammer, William (1961). *The Gay Place.* Boston: Houghton Mifflin.

Brewer, J. Mason (1976). *Dog Ghosts and the Word on the Brazos.* Austin: University of Texas Press.

Busby, Mark (1983). *Preston Jones.* (Western Writers Series no. 58.) Boise: Boise State University Press.

Busby, Mark (1991). *Ralph Ellison.* New York: Twayne/Macmillan.

Busby, Mark, ed. (1993). *New Growth/2: Contemporary Short Stories by Texas Writers.* San Antonio: Corona.

Busby, Mark (1995). *Larry McMurtry and the West: An Ambivalent Relationship.* Denton: University of North Texas Press.

Busby, Mark, with Heaberlin, Dick (2001). *From Texas to the World and Back: Essays on the Journeys of Katherine Anne Porter.* Fort Worth: TCU Press.

Cabeza de Vaca, Alvar Núñez (1993). *The Account: Alvar Núñez Cabeza de Vaca's Relación,* trans. Martin A. Favata and José B. Fernández. Houston: Arte Publico Press. (First publ. 1542.)

Capps, Benjamin (1967). *The Brothers of Uterica.* New York: Meredith.

Cather, Willa (1915). *The Song of the Lark.* Boston: Houghton Mifflin.

Cather, Willa (1971). *Death Comes for the Archbishop.* New York: Vintage. (First publ. 1927.)

Cather, Willa (1972). *A Lost Lady.* New York: Vintage. (First publ. 1923.)

Cather, Willa (1973). *The Professor's House*. New York: Vintage. (First publ. 1925.)

Cervantes, Lorna Dee (1981). *Emplumada*. Pittsburgh, PA: University of Pittsburgh Press.

Chandler, Raymond (1975). *Farewell, My Lovely*. New York: Ballantine. (First publ. 1940.)

Chandler, Raymond (1977). *The Big Sleep*. New York: Ballantine. (First publ. 1939.)

Chin, Frank (1981). *The Chickencoop Chinaman, The Year of the Dragon: Two Plays*. Seattle: University of Washington Press.

Cisneros, Sandra (1983). *The House on Mango Street*. Houston: Arte Publico.

Cisneros, Sandra (2002). *Caramelo; or, Puro Cuento: A Novel*. New York: Knopf Random House.

Coburn, D. L. (1978). *The Gin Game*. New York: Samuel French.

Dobie, J. Frank (1952). *The Mustangs*. Boston: Little, Brown.

Dobie, J. Frank (1967a). *Some Part of Myself*. Boston: Little, Brown.

Dobie, J. Frank (1967b). *Tongues of the Monte*. Austin: University of Texas Press.

Dobie, J. Frank (1967c). *A Vaquero of the Brush Country*. Austin: University of Texas Press. (First publ. 1929.)

Flores, Dan (1990). *Caprock Canyonlands: Journeys into the Heart of the Southern Plains*. Austin: University of Texas Press.

Flynn, Robert (1967). *North to Yesterday*. New York: Knopf.

Garreau, Joel (1931). *The Nine Nations of North America*. Boston: Houghton Mifflin.

Geiogamah, Hanay (1980). *New Native American Drama*. Norman: University of Oklahoma Press.

Gilb, Dagoberto (1993). *The Magic of Blood*. New York: Grove.

Gilb, Dagoberto (1994). *The Last Known Residence of Mickey Acuña*. New York: Grove.

Gilb, Dagoberto (2001). *Woodcuts of Women*. New York: Grove.

Goodwyn, Larry (1971). "The Frontier Myth and Southwestern Literature." *American Libraries*, Feb., 161–7; April, 359–66. Repr. in John Gordon Burke, ed., *Regional Perspectives: An Examination of America's Literary Heritage* (Chicago: ALA, 1973), 175–206.

Goyen, William (1950). *The House of Breath*. New York: Random House.

Graves, John (1960). *Goodbye to a River, A Narrative*. New York: Knopf.

Graves, John (1974). *Hard Scrabble: Observation on a Patch of Land*. New York: Knopf.

Graves, John (1980). *From a Limestone Ledge: Some Essays and Other Ruminations about Country Life in Texas*. New York: Knopf.

Greene, A. C. (1969). *A Personal Country*. New York: Knopf.

Greene, A. C. (1982). *The Fifty Best Books on Texas*. Dallas: Pressworks Publishing.

Griggs, Sutton E. (1969). *Imperium in Imperio*. New York: Arno Press. (First publ. 1899.)

Harjo, Joy (1979). *What Moon Drove Me to This*. New York: I. Reed Books.

Harjo, Joy (1983). *She Had Some Horses*. New York: Thunder's Mouth.

Harrigan, Stephen (1980). *Aransas*. New York: Knopf.

Harrigan, Stephen (1984). *Jacob's Well*. New York: Knopf.

Harrigan, Stephen (2000). *Gates of the Alamo*. New York: Knopf.

Heifner, Jack (1978a). *Patio/Porch*. New York: Dramatists Play Service.

Heifner, Jack (1978b). *Vanities*. New York: Samuel French. (First publ. 1977.)

Hinojosa, Rolando (1982). *Rites and Witnesses*. Houston: University of Houston/Arte Publico.

Hinojosa, Rolando (1983). *The Valley*. Ypsilanti, Mich.: Bilingual Editions.

Hinojosa, Rolando (1993). *The Useless Servants*. Houston: University of Houston/Arte Publico.

Hogan, Linda (1979). *Calling Myself Home*. Greenfield Center, NY: Greenfield Review Press.

Hogan, Linda (1981). *Daughters, I Love You*. Denver: Loretto Heights College Publications.

Hough, Emerson (1923). *North of 36*. New York: Appleton.

Humphrey, William (1977). *Farther Off from Heaven*. New York: Knopf.

Jones, Preston (1976). *A Texas Trilogy*. New York: Hill & Wang.

Jones, Preston (1977). *Santa Fe Sunshine*. New York: Dramatists Play Service.

Kelton, Elmer (1973). *The Time It Never Rained*. Garden City: Doubleday.

Kelton, Elmer (1980). *The Wolf and the Buffalo*. Garden City: Doubleday.

King, Larry L. (1980). *Of Outlaws, Con Men, Whores, Politicians, and Other Artists*. New York: Viking.

King, Larry L., and Masterson, Peter (1978). *The Best Little Whorehouse in Texas*. New York: Samuel French.

Kolodny, Annette (1984). *The Land Before Her: Fantasy and Experience of the American Frontiers 1630–1860*. Chapel Hill and London: University of North Carolina Press.

Lea, Tom (1952). *The Wonderful Country*. Boston: Little, Brown.

Lea, Tom (1957). *The King Ranch*. Boston: Little, Brown.

Lewis, Alfred Henry (1897). *Wolfville*. Chicago: A. L. Burt.

Lewis, Alfred Henry (1902a). *Wolfville Days*. New York: F. A. Stokes.

Lewis, Alfred Henry (1902b). *Wolfville Nights*. New York: F. A. Stokes.

McCarthy, Cormac (1992). *All the Pretty Horses*. New York: Knopf.

McCarthy, Cormac (1994). *The Crossing*. New York: Knopf.

McCarthy, Cormac (1998). *Cities of the Plain*. New York: Knopf.

McLure, James (1980a). *Lone Star*. New York: Dramatists Play Service.

McLure, James (1980b). *Pvt. Wars*. New York: Dramatists Play Service.

McMurtry, Larry (1961). *Horseman, Pass By*. New York: Harper.

McMurtry, Larry (1963). *Leaving Cheyenne*. New York: Harper.

McMurtry, Larry (1966). *The Last Picture Show*. New York: Dial.

McMurtry, Larry (1968). *In a Narrow Grave*. Austin: Encino.

McMurtry, Larry (1972). *All My Friends Are Going to Be Strangers*. New York: Simon & Schuster.

McMurtry, Larry (1974). *When You Comin' Back, Red Ryder?* Clifton: James T. White.

McMurtry, Larry (1975a). *Terms of Endearment*. New York: Simon & Schuster.

McMurtry, Larry (1975b). "The Texas Moon and Elsewhere." *Atlantic* 235: 3 (March), pp. 29–36.

McMurtry, Larry (1985). *Lonesome Dove*. New York: Simon & Schuster.

McMurtry, Larry (1989a). *Moving On*. New York: Touchstone. (First publ. 1970.)

McMurtry, Larry (1989b). *Some Can Whistle*. New York: Simon & Schuster.

McMurtry, Larry (1991). *Buffalo Girls*. New York: Pocket Books. (First publ. 1990.)

McMurtry, Larry (1993). *The Evening Star*. New York: Pocket Books. (First publ. 1992.)

McMurtry, Larry (1994a). *The Late Child*. New York: Simon & Schuster.

McMurtry, Larry (1994b). *Streets of Laredo*. New York: Pocket Books. (First publ. 1993.)

McMurtry, Larry (1995). *Dead Man's Walk*. New York: Simon & Schuster.

McMurtry, Larry (1997). *Comanche Moon*. New York: Simon & Schuster.

McMurtry, Larry (1999a). *Duane's Depressed*. New York: Simon & Schuster.

McMurtry, Larry (1999b). *Walter Benjamin at the Dairy Queen*. New York: Simon & Schuster.

McMurtry, Larry (2000). *Boone's Lick*. New York: Simon & Schuster.

McMurtry, Larry (2001). *Paradise*. New York: Simon & Schuster.

McMurtry, Larry (2002). *Sin Killer*. New York: Simon & Schuster.

McMurtry, Larry, with Ossana, Diana (1994). *Pretty Boy Floyd*. New York: Simon & Schuster.

McMurtry, Larry, with Ossana, Diana (1997). *Zeke and Ned*. New York: Simon & Schuster.

Medoff, Mark (1975). *The Wager and Two Short Plays*. Clifton, NJ: James T. White.

Momaday, N. Scott (1968). *House Made of Dawn*. New York: Harper & Row.

Momaday, N. Scott (1975). *The Gourd Dancer*. New York: Harper & Row.

Olmsted, Frederick Law (1968). *A Journey Through Texas: or, a Saddle-trip on the Southern Frontier*. New York: Dix, Edwards. (First publ. 1857.)

Ortiz, Simon (1976). *Going for the Rain*. New York: Harper & Row.

Ortiz, Simon (1977). *A Good Journey*. Berkeley: Turtle Island.

Owens, Louis (1992). *The Sharpest Sight*. Norman: University of Oklahoma Press.

Owens, Louis (1994). *Bone Game*. Norman: University of Oklahoma Press.

Owens, Louis (1995). *Wolfsong*. Norman: University of Oklahoma Press.

Owens, Louis (1999). *Dark River*. Norman: University of Oklahoma Press.

Owens, William A. (1958). *Fever in the Earth*. New York: G. P. Putnam's Sons.

Paredes, Américo (1958). *"With his pistol in his hand"; A Border Ballad and its Hero*. Austin: University of Texas Press.

Pilkington, William T. (1973). *My Blood's Country: Studies in Southwestern Literature.* Fort Worth: Texas Christian University Press.

Pilkington, William T. (1981). *Imagining Texas: The Literature of the Lone Star State.* Boston: American Press.

Pilkington, William T. (1983). "Epilogue." In *Cabeza de Vaca's Adventures in the Unknown Interior of America*, trans and ann. Cyclone Covey. Albuquerque: University of New Mexico Press. (First publ. 1961.)

Porter, Katherine Anne (1955). *The Collected Essays and Occasional Writings of Katherine Anne Porter.* New York: Harper.

Rhodes, Eugene Manlove (1910). *Good Men and True.* New York: Henry Holt.

Rhodes, Eugene Manlove (1927). *Once in the Saddle* and *Pasó par Aquí.* Boston: Houghton Mifflin.

Rhodes, Eugene Manlove (1955). *Bransford of Arcadia, or The Little Eohippus.* New York: Henry Holt.

Richter, Conrad (1937). *The Sea of Grass.* New York: Knopf.

Rivera, Tomás (1971). *. . . y no se lo tragó la tierra / And the Earth Did Not Part.* Berkeley: Quinto Sol.

Rose, Wendy (1973a). *Hopi Roadrunner Dancing.* Greenfield Center, New York: Greenfield Review Press.

Rose, Wendy (1973b). *Academic Squaw – Report to the World from the Ivory Tower.* Marvin, S. Dak.: Blue Cloud Quarterly.

Scarborough, Dorothy (1923). *In the Land of Cotton.* New York: Macmillan.

Scarborough, Dorothy (1925). *The Wind.* New York: Harper & Bros.

Shepard, Sam (1979). *Buried Child.* New York: Urizen.

Shepard, Sam (1981). *Seven Plays.* New York: Bantam.

Silko, Leslie (1974). *Laguna Woman.* Greenfield Center, New York: Greenfield Review Press.

Silko, Leslie (1977). *Ceremony.* New York: Viking.

Tapahonso, Luci (1981). *Seasonal Woman.* Santa Fe: Tooth of Time.

Webb, Walter Prescott (1931). *The Great Plains.* New York: Grosset & Dunlap.

Williams, Terry Tempest (1995). *Desert Quartet.* New York: Pantheon.

Williams, Terry Tempest (1992). *Pieces of White Shell: A Journey to Navajoland.* Albuquerque: University of New Mexico Press. (First publ. 1984.)

Williams, Terry Tempest (1991). *Refuge: An Unnatural History of Family and Place.* New York: Pantheon.

Wister, Owen (1902). *The Virginian.* New York: Macmillan.

26

Hawai'i

Brenda Kwon

Introduction: Deconstructing "Paradise"

Say the word "Hawai'i"[1] and many people picture a tropical island paradise: fragrant flower leis, palm trees swaying gracefully in the warm breeze, the soft rush of waves kissing the shore. Vacationers sit along the beach, refreshing drinks in hand, preparing to later swim, snorkel, or surf in the clear blue waters. The sun bronzes their skin and they delight in the beauty of the islands, so different from the rhythm of their daily lives.

While certainly alluring, this image of Hawai'i has been both its livelihood and its downfall. Carefully packaged to entice visitors from around the world, the "paradise on earth" fantasy is the base upon which Hawai'i's tourist economy thrives. Without it, thousands of hotel workers have no jobs, luxury stores stand empty, and an entire industry halts.

The islands' travel industry developed shortly after World War II, when the United States, finding itself in the position of dominant world power, began to see the Pacific as pivotal in its relationship with Asia. Besides having the militaristic goal of maintaining strategic control over the Pacific islands for reasons of "national security," the United States sought to profit from emerging Asian markets. When Hawai'i's sugar industry became less lucrative because of a glut on the world market, the situation became ripe for Henry John Kaiser, who had earned a name for himself by engineering the development of roads and dams on the West Coast in the 1920s and 1930s, to step in. After visiting Hawai'i in the 1950s, Kaiser saw the potential for a major tourist economy, particularly since Florida and California had recently undergone similar metamorphoses. Investing several millions of dollars into the building of extravagant resorts, Kaiser initiated a construction boom. His vision became a reality carrying huge dollar signs on its back; even the agricultural elite, with their large landholdings, took part in investing in the new economy, building its own resorts on land previously used for sugar planting.

The economy clearly prospered from the islands' newest commodity: itself. But while the new industry did create jobs – though principally in the service sector – it also resulted in the laying off of its agricultural workers, many of whose families had been part of plantation societies for generations. These laborers, suddenly finding themselves out of work, fell upon hard times; communities were destroyed, and Hawai'i's people displaced. And herein lies the dark side of paradise: its effect on the people of Hawai'i.

Although tourism is fairly recent in Hawai'i's history, the concept of paradise is not. Early missionaries saw the islands as a place in which they could create the New World, a heaven on earth, so to speak (see Sumida 1992). While foreign influences brought some measure of benefit to the islands, it is hard to overlook the cultural and physical eradication Native Hawaiians experienced as a consequence of these interventions. Under subjugation by missionaries and merchants, all seeking to transform the islands into their particular forms of paradise, Native Hawaiians relinquished their dress, customs, dance, and language, not to mention, land, power, and, eventually, autonomy, when foreign domination culminated in the illegal overthrow of the Hawaiian nation in 1893 by a group of American annexationists. "Paradise," then, is fraught with associations of violence and colonization, which many feel continue today under the guises of the tourist industry and the military.

For non-Native islanders, most often referred to as "Locals," tourism and the concept of paradise have also been damaging insofar as they have commodified Local culture and lifestyles. Because "blending in with the Locals" nurtures a sense of belonging, Local dress, music, and food are products high in demand: perhaps the mark of a true dependent economy (see Kent 1993). Nevertheless, despite reservations and objections, islanders – Native and non-Native alike – recognize their reliance upon tourism and are forced to become complicit with the industry. And while Local culture, like Hawaiian culture, holds among its values a deep respect for the *'āina* (land), prompting objections to resort development, its relationship to the land differs from that of Native Hawaiians, and for this reason it is useful to delineate Local and Hawaiian identity in Hawai'i.

The term "Local" continues to be contested because of the difficulty in fixing the criteria by which it is to be defined. Generally, "Local" is used to refer to anyone of Asian or Pacific Islander descent who has been in the islands for longer than one generation. Although some long-time residents of European ancestry might be considered Local, historically the term has been used to distinguish itself from "white"/ *haole* ("foreigner").[2] More politicized definitions of "Local" call for a lineage that can be traced back to the plantation labor experience of the nineteenth and early twentieth centuries, and with this, a working-class background. Also encompassed by the term is language (Hawai'i Creole English or HCE), as well as a set of actions, behaviors, and codes – hence the term "Local-style."

In the era of Hawaiian sovereignty, the difference between "Hawaiian" and "Local" is strongly emphasized. Native Hawaiians fall into the category of "Local," but the reverse does not necessarily hold true. Locals do not identify as Hawaiian unless they claim indigenous blood; similarly, only those things that have a direct connection to

Native culture are deemed "Hawaiian." Furthermore, Locals and descendants of plantation workers brought to Hawai'i as cheap labor for the sugar industry were not part
of the illegally overthrown Hawaiian nation. Therefore, as much as Locals might feel
exploited by tourist industry, they cannot claim the same disenfranchisement that
Native Hawaiians do.

Herein lies the tension regarding the relationship of Locals to the islands: to what
degree are they exploited and to what degree do they exploit? On the one hand, we
must acknowledge a global economy that actively brought Asian laborers to Hawai'i
to fuel the sugar industry. Essentially contract laborers lured by promises of "the
good life," plantation workers struggled within a system that pitted racial groups
against one another through disparate pay scales, employed a strategy of debt to keep
workers from leaving the plantations, and treated them as expendable units of labor.
On the other hand, within a larger structure of colonialism, these workers and their
descendants, ultimately establishing roots and achieving some measure of power in
Hawai'i, benefited from land stolen from Native Hawaiians. This latter perspective
has given rise to a new term, "settler colonialism," which defines Locals as migrants/
settlers and *not* indigenous to the islands of Hawai'i, and therefore requires them to
evaluate their responsibility to Hawaiian sovereignty and admit their collusion with
more powerful forces of colonization in Native Hawaiian dispossession.

Further complicating the issue is the ethnic hierarchy within what we call "Local."
Many critics have observed the dominance in Local society of Japanese Americans,
whose leverage can be partially attributed to their large numbers on the plantations.
Their collective power aided several significant events resulting in changes to Hawai'i's
social, political, and economic landscape, among them the 1920 labor strike unit-
ing Japanese and Filipinos and the 1954 party shift from Republican to Democrat.
The same power has not been wielded by Filipinos, who, with Hawaiians, comprise
the majority population working in service-sector jobs, or Koreans, whose presence
and historically marginal position in Hawai'i are themselves consequences of Japan's
colonization of Korea. Charged with internal tensions, notwithstanding its precarious
relationship with Native Hawaiians, Local society can hardly sustain claims to being
a multiethnic paradise in which "everyone gets along" (see Grant and Ogawa 1993).

Those who have wanted to see Hawai'i as a paradise – multiethnic or otherwise –
do so at the expense of a true understanding of the intricate history of the islands, as
well as the continuing legacy of a colonial past, for "paradise" is not a term that
allows for racism, bloodshed, injustice, or exploitation. The exploration of "Local"
and "Hawaiian" identities is wholly integral to an understanding of Hawai'i's people,
as its absence transforms the islands into a site erased of its true history, meant
simply for enjoyment and entertainment; in short, paradise. Here we can begin to
understand the role of literature in Hawai'i: to give voice and presence to those
whose lives openly refute and have been written over by that very concept.

Unfortunately, limitations on space constrain the scope of this chapter. It is impossible to cover Hawai'i's vast body of literature, and discussions must be brief. For this
reason, readers must approach the works mentioned here as starting points only rather

than as representative texts. Within an arguably postcolonial territory, the authors in this chapter tell stories that resist a colonial mindset, and as such are mainly island-born writers, many claiming long histories in Hawai'i. This is not to exclude or devalue writers from the mainland/continent who are certainly capable of criticizing hegemonic practices. If one of the purposes of this literature is, in part, to legitimize the voices of those who have been silenced or exoticized, then space should rightly be given to those whose connection to the islands carries the weight of time and experience.

Who Writes Hawaiian Literature?

Stroll into a typical Honolulu bookstore, and you will find in the "Hawaiiana" section authors such as Wing Tek Lum, Marie Hara, Haunani-Kay Trask, and Gary Pak. You will also see books written by Jack London, James Michener, and Mark Twain, three writers whose names the general public no doubt recognizes, yet who are neither Hawaiian nor Local, nor even island-born. Why, then, do their publications constitute "Hawaiiana?" Simply enough, these distinguished literary figures spent time in Hawai'i and chose to write about the islands. But the question remains, is that enough?

Many people, when asked to name a book of "Hawaiian literature," would very likely pick James Michener's *Hawaii*. An epic tale that begins with the volcanic formation of the Hawaiian islands and ends with characters in contemporary society, Michener's book compellingly interweaves literature and history to construct the lives of Hawaiians, Asian laborers, and *haole* missionaries and businessmen. Enormously successful, *Hawaii* tightly linked Michener to the islands. Furthermore, in 1959, the year of Hawai'i's statehood, University of Hawai'i professors A. Grove Day and Carl Stroven asked him to write the introduction to their anthology entitled *A Hawaiian Reader: The Exotic Literary Heritage of the Hawaiian Islands*. In it, Michener congratulates Hawai'i for being a "maturing international society" and lauds the islands for their "advanced state of culture" (Day and Stroven, eds. 1959: xi). He also praises the editors for choosing what he sees as the "best" literary work about Hawai'i.

The notion of aesthetics has long been debunked as an apolitical measure of judgment; to read the table of contents of *A Hawaiian Reader* is to see that Michener, Day, and Stroven consider the "best" Hawaiian literature to be not that of the island-born, but that written by transplanted residents and visitors to the islands. Beginning with Captain James Cook's account of his discovery of what would later be called "The Sandwich Isles," the volume includes the works of foreign-born writers such as Mark Twain, Robert Louis Stevenson, Jack London, and W. Somerset Maugham, authors credited for generating the "literary heritage" of Hawai'i. The only island-born writer in the anthology's main section is the Revd. Abraham K. Akaka, a Hawaiian-Chinese *kahu* (shepherd) who, after earning his degree at the University of Chicago, returned to Hawai'i to pursue religious work.

Placing Akaka's selection at the end of the section suggests, at the very least, that no other Hawaiians or Locals had been writing anything "of quality."[3] The editors do include "[f]ive pieces representing ancient Hawaiian literature and lore [that] have been placed at the end of the book" (Day and Stroven, eds. 1959: vii). That these five pieces, which include the Kumulipo or Hawaiian creation chant, represent "ancient Hawaiian literature" immediately complicates the editors' statement that the selections have been arranged in chronological order by "date of incident or setting" and suggests, in the manner of discovery narratives, that Hawai'i's literary and historical origins begin with European contact. Furthermore, the pieces function as a memorial of sorts: their title, "Ancient Hawai'i," in addition to their placement, indicates native voices that have disappeared and no longer exist.

The second volume, published nine years later in 1968, fares questionably better in its selections, which include pieces by two island-born writers, Samuel Mānaiakalani Kamakau and Milton Murayama. Day and Stroven re-emphasize their concern with an historical progression that begins, in striking counterpoint to the Kumulipo, with "Michener's evocation of the volcanic formation of the Islands and [continues] with the legends of the ancient Polynesian settlers." Drawing from "logs of early voyagers, journals of the first missionaries, narratives of travelers and sojourners, and short stories and nonfiction by later writers," the anthology ultimately constructs Hawaiian history from a colonial and imaginative point of view while discounting a native one. Of Samuel Kamakau's account of Captain James Cook's experiences in the islands, the editors write, "Perhaps the chief value of Kamakau's legendary account lies in showing how the Hawaiians of his generation *preferred to recollect* the incursions of the first Europeans in their islands" (Day and Stroven, eds. 1968: 43–4, emphasis added).

The absence of native and islander voices in Day and Stroven's anthologies reinforces the perception of Hawai'i as populated by a primitive people whose experiences and perspectives have scarce historical or cultural value.[4] If the voices of Michener, Twain, Stevenson, and London constitute "Hawaiian literature," then little room is left for the indigenous and island-born to tell their own stories. Exemplifying paradise construction, the dominant ideology here is that Hawai'i's value comes from what others have made it. When Michener praises Hawai'i for its "advanced state of culture," he praises its university, its museums and art academy, its symphony, its theater, and its libraries; in other words, its ability to transcend the native state (Day and Stroven, eds. 1959: xi).

Contrary to these perceptions, Native Hawaiians *were* writing – about themselves, about their memories, and about the loss of their home. Of primal importance, then, is a discussion of the voices existing previous to and alongside *A Hawaiian Reader*; the works of those excluded in paradise.

Hawai'i's Literary Tradition

The privileging of the written word too often results in the exclusion of oral narratives from one's sense of what is "literary." Oral cultures face a number of challenges in order to prove the legitimacy of their art, and Hawai'i is no exception. Viewing history as an integral component to storytelling, unwritten works are sometimes dismissed as "record" and not "literature," where the line between the two is generally arbitrary and unfixed. The use of *mele* (song), preserved in the form of *hula*, has been and continues to be for indigenous Hawaiians a rich source of heritage and strength, far from lost or dead. Today, many *kumu hula* (*hula* teachers) and *hula hālau* (*hula* schools) who battle the commodification of *hula* strive to preserve and perpetuate Native Hawaiian culture and values, thus continuing the vital force of the oral tradition of Hawai'i.

While much of early Hawaiian literature remains oral, three Native Hawaiian men made significant contributions to establishing a written literary tradition: David Malo (1795–1853), John Papa 'I'i (1800–70), and Samuel Mānaiakalani Kamakau (1815–1876). Forming their works upon the history, beliefs, myths, and origins of Native Hawaiians, they challenged explorationist viewpoints by recounting Hawaiian life – including the impact of colonization – through the eyes of those who most felt its force.

David Malo gained his knowledge of the traditions and history of Hawai'i through his association with members of the royal court, including Queen Kaahumanu's brother, the high chief Kuakini; and 'Auwai, a favorite chief of Kamehameha I. A poet, storyteller, athlete, and *hula* practitioner, he held great authority among Hawaiian royalty for his talents, which he would later repudiate upon his conversion to Christianity in 1823. After conversion, Malo espoused Western culture and, being an avid reader, at the age of 36 enrolled as one of the first pupils of a high school established at Lāhaianāluna. He later became an ordained minister, devoting his life to Christianity and the pursuit of knowledge.

Under the encouragement of his teachers, Malo documented his knowledge of Hawai'i in three works: *Mo'olelo Hawai'i*, a compilation by several students who comprised the Hawaiian Historical Society; *Hawaiian Antiquities* (also called *Mo'olelo Hawai'i*); and *Life of Kamehameha*. Today, only *Hawaiian Antiquities* remains in print, providing a vision of old Hawai'i that ranges over the formation of the land, various traditions and religious ceremonies, and the construction of canoes and houses. Despite the fact that Malo embraced Western scholarship with ardor, he was not impervious to the pain caused by the colonization of the islands. These seemingly disparate emotions created a tension that would play out in his writing and become apparent in his tone, which often reveals the development of his Western-Christian viewpoint. At times, he clearly questions ancient convictions; discussing the varied genealogies of the formation of the islands, Malo remarks, "It is possible, however, that there has always been land here from the beginning, but we cannot be sure because the traditions of the ancients are utterly unreliable and astray in their vagaries." Yet Malo also casts doubt on Western study: "In these days certain learned men have searched into and studied up the origin of the Hawaiian Islands, but whether their views are correct no one can say, because they are but speculations" (1951: 4, 3).

The detail with which Malo writes about Hawaiian rituals and beliefs, however, belies his expressed disdain of them. In fact, Malo's intricate descriptions in *Hawaiian Antiquities* result in what could very well serve as an instruction manual. As much as he supported Christianity, he also took care to preserve specific prayers and *mele*, for instance, concerning the medical treatment of the sick by kāhuna (priests). Thus, rather than eradicate the "ancient" knowledge, Malo, in the very act of writing, enables its survival and continuation.

Although Malo's work is uneven and unfinished, *Hawaiian Antiquities* remains invaluable not only for the authoritative information it presents, but for its glimpse into the mind of a man who grew up under the Hawaiian *kapu* (taboo) system and whose perspective reflected the effect of Western religious influence. While it might be painful to hear Malo comment that "[s]ome of these miserable practices of the ancient Hawaiians were no doubt due to their devotion to worthless things (idols?)" (1951: 117), we cannot ignore the reality of the opposing worldview Christianity brought to the islands, and might perhaps feel sympathy for a man caught between two vastly different cultural visions.

If conversion prompted Malo to turn away from Native Hawaiian beliefs, values, and practices, John Papa 'I'i balanced his life as a staunch Christian with an intense reverence for ancient culture. Born five years after Malo, 'I'i also witnessed the islands in transition between the old ways and an emerging system of government. Closely tied to the royal court, 'I'i lived for ten years in the household of Liholiho, until Liholiho (by then Kamehameha II), wishing to observe the effects of Christian teaching, sent him to study under the Revd. Hiram Bingham. Over his lifetime, 'I'i occupied a number of governmental positions, including superintendent of O'ahu schools; member of the new Treasury Board under King Kamehameha III, the Board of Land Commissioners, and the House of Representatives; and associate justice of the Supreme Court of Hawai'i. His connection to the court and government provided him with an intimate view of Hawai'i's people and its political system, and *Fragments of Hawaiian History*, a compilation of writings selected from articles he had written between 1866 and 1870 for the Hawaiian language newspaper *Ka Nūpepa Kū'ōko'a*, combines personal experience with historical fact to provide a vivid account of Hawai'i's cultural changes.

In *Fragments of Hawaiian History*, 'I'i covers such diverse topics as Kamehameha's origins and ascension, Native medicinal practices, his own life, and island geography. His closeness to the subjects about which he writes is apparent in his descriptions; 'I'i focuses on real people forming history, rather than figures through which history occurs. In describing Kamehameha, 'I'i shows us the humanity of a man who desired prosperity for the people and who took an active part in their daily lives. His view of Kamehameha as far from primitive or barbaric is remarkable in that it resists the notion that Hawai'i's kingdom was in need of redemption by Western influences.

Nevertheless, 'I'i's Christian beliefs do show in his writing. In his account of the death of chiefess Kalaniakua, who committed suicide after suffering emotional torment from Liholiho's grandmother Liliha, 'I'i recites Proverbs 14: 32. Criticizing Kalaniakua's actions less than the values they reflect, 'I'i connects two ideologies that in Malo's mind were incompatible. Although 'I'i held active roles in the government of Queen Ka'ahumanu and Kamehameha II, which brought the old system to an end, his respect for the old ways and loyalty to the Nation of Hawai'i permeate his writing. Bringing to life the events of the islands during this period, 'I'i's work differs from Malo's not only in its more fluid narrative, but in its inclusion of personal experience, which allows us as readers striking access to an old Hawai'i that has frequently been misrepresented and mystified.

Generally regarded as Hawai'i's greatest historian, Samuel Mānaiakalani Kamakau undertook his Western education when, at the age of 17, he left O'ahu to study at Lāhaināluna's missionary high school on Maui. Upon completion of his studies, he became a teacher's helper, then, at age 26, began writing articles about Hawaiian culture and history, for which he had a great passion. In 1841 he helped form the Hawaiian Historical Association, whose goal it was to "obtain and preserve" as much historical data as possible. Writing in his spare time, Kamakau took employment in a number of public capacities, serving in such positions as principal, school agent, tax assessor, legislator, and district judge. Later in his life he converted to Catholicism and returned to O'ahu, where, faithful to his love, he wrote a regular column on Hawaiian history for *Ka Nūpepa Kū'ōko'a*.

What distinguishes Kamakau from his predecessors and successors, in addition to his prolific work, is the inclusion of his own fiercely honest perspectives on the events of Hawaiian history. Like Malo and 'I'i, Kamakau had converted to Christianity and ardently upheld its principles, yet this did not preclude loyalty to his Native heritage. He took issue with the inaccurate information he felt had circulated about Hawai'i and believed the preservation of the truth was crucial to the cultural survival of Native Hawaiians. Kamakau's writing is preserved today in four main works, compiled from articles written between 1866 and 1871 for the Hawaiian-language newspapers *Ka Nūpepa Kū'ōko'a* and *Ke Au 'Oko'a*. The fourth work, *Ruling Chiefs of Hawai'i*, covers the era spanning 'Umialiloa's pre-Cook reign over the island of Hawai'i, up to the death of Kamehameha III in 1854.

In *Ruling Chiefs of Hawai'i*, Kamakau's merging of Native and Christian thought is apparent. According to Kamakau, upon Cook's arrival on the island of Kauai, many debated whether he was the god Lono (the god "who had gone away promising to return") or whether he was *haole* (a foreigner). When Cook left Kauai and landed at Kealakekua on the island of Hawai'i, some of the kāhuna, believing him to be a god, led him to a *heiau* (temple) where, in prayer to him, they made sacrifices and "covered [him] with a cloak of red tapa like that about the images" (Kamakau 1992: 100). Kamakau comments upon this incident, declaring that Cook's action – entering an "idolater's place of worship" and partaking of the offering as a Christian – ultimately led to his death shortly thereafter during a fight over a stolen boat. While Kamakau could easily indict Cook for allowing himself to be worshipped – that is, to assume a superior position to Hawaiians – he instead chooses a

Christian-based evaluation of Cook's folly. Far from being anti-European, Kamakau openly values Western contact for the benefits it provided and refuses to nostalgize or idealize life under the *kapu* system, pointing out its weaknesses as well as its strengths. However, Kamakau's primary concern remains the good of the people, and thus he keeps a keen eye on the effect of cultural changes on Native Hawaiians. This perspective, prompting him to constantly scrutinize the events around him, provides him with much insight and depth into Hawai'i's history. An authoritative and well-trusted voice on the Hawai'i's past, Kamakau continues to enlighten many scholars and students of Hawaiian history today.[5]

The Voice of the Overthrow: Lili'uokalani

Malo, 'I'i, and Kamakau witnessed Hawai'i in transition; however, it was decades after their deaths that Natives experienced its overthrow. Published in 1898, *Hawaii's Story by Hawaii's Queen* was a plea for justice from Queen Lili'uokalani (1838–1917) to those who would urge the United States to re-establish the nation it had stolen.

The conflict between Western and Native culture affected Lili'uokalani deeply throughout her life. Her education by missionary teachers and her marriage to John Owen Dominis, whose mother objected to the interracial marriage despite Lili'uokalani's *ali'i* (royal) blood, caused her much pain, and as a result, Lili'uokalani turned to her people for comfort. A great love for them determined many of her actions as well as those of her brother, King Kalākaua. During an attempt to garner international support for Hawai'i's threatened monarchy, Kalākaua died in San Francisco in 1891, uttering the message, "Tell my people I tried." Lili'uokalani thus ascended to the throne with full intent to maintain the independent status of the kingdom.

Through a powerful and enduring collusion of economic and military interests, 13 American sugar planters, backed by armed soldiers who had marched onto the grounds of 'Iolani Palace, overthrew the Nation of Hawai'i, declared the vacancy of the throne, and formed a provisional government. After US minister plenipotentiary John L. Stevens officially recognized the provisional government, Lili'uokalani, fearing further loss of Native life, relinquished the throne under protest. Urging the people "'*onipa'a*," to stand firm, the Queen promised to fight for reinstatement of the Hawaiian monarchy. A formal investigation of the overthrow by US minister James H. Blount later that year determined that the provisional government had in fact been established without consent of the people of Hawai'i, leading President Cleveland to condemn US complicity in the overthrow, declare the illegality of the new government, and refuse to advance the annexation treaty to the Senate. Using the argument of interference in the internal affairs of Hawai'i, however, Sanford B. Dole ignored Cleveland's order to restore the monarchy, and in 1894 the Senate announced that the provisional government would undergo no further questioning.

Thus, on July 4, 1894, the provisional government proclaimed itself the Republic of Hawai'i, and despite the efforts of many Hawaiians to reverse the events, the United States officially annexed Hawai'i in 1898.

In 1895, the Republic of Hawai'i charged Queen Lili'uokalani with treason and imprisoned her for nine months. During her confinement, she was given the choice of either endorsing a document declaring her abdication or being executed along with six of her subjects. Signing her married name but not her ruling one, Lili'uokalani continued to protest, and in this spirit wrote *Hawaii's Story by Hawaii's Queen*. An autobiography that, like the work of John Papa 'I'i, greatly personalizes the events of history, Lili'uokalani's story speaks to the silencing of the Native voice and challenges the notion that a people and a nation are meant for the taking. Critiquing the shift from alliance with foreign influences to domination by them, the Queen articulates feelings of betrayal involved in a takeover by those considered part of a trusted nation and makes it clear that her choice not to fight was predicated not upon weakness, but upon the realization that armed conflict against the United States would only be in vain. Appealing to a fundamental sense of rightness, Lili'uokalani questions a colonial practice at odds with American ideals of justice and equality.

Equally important to her philosophical inquiry into the actions of the annexationists, Lili'uokalani's reminiscences of her childhood and upbringing allow us to see her not only as a queen, but as a woman who deeply cared for Hawai'i's past and future. Her family history, woven into memories of her education, marriage, and accession, once more illuminates the need to see the colonized as more than subjects. Allowing us to hear the story of the overthrow from the woman whose title made her an official target, Lili'uokalani continues to be an inspiration for today's historical scholars and supporters of Hawaiian sovereignty.

Continuing the Legacy: Mary Kawena Pukui and John Dominis Holt

A number of the works from the early days of Hawai'i's literary tradition have one thing in common: written in the Hawaiian language, they would not be accessible to many readers were it not for the efforts of Mary Kawena Pukui (1895–1986), one of Hawai'i's most eminent and beloved scholars of Hawaiian language, history, and culture. Born to a Native mother and a father from Massachusetts, Pukui was raised by her maternal grandmother under the Native hānai (adoption) system, which allowed her to learn and maintain Hawaiian culture and traditions. After her grandmother's death, Pukui continued with her education at various schools during a time in which speaking Hawaiian was either discouraged or prohibited, and punished. However, supported by her parents, she maintained her bilingualism, and with the encouragement of Laura C. Green, a neighbor in Honolulu, wrote stories and recollections of her Native background.

Pukui quickly earned her reputation as a skilled translator, and in 1928 began working with Bishop Museum, undertaking a number of projects preserving Hawaiian
language, stories and tales, cultural and medicinal practices, and ancient *mele*. In her
many works, Pukui, having provided "the bridge that takes us back to the original
source" (Enomoto 1997), brought together both oral and written traditions. Going
beyond the continuation of a literary heritage in Hawai'i, Pukui asserted its longstanding presence, countering the notion that Hawai'i's literature had only recently
come into being.

In the foreword to *The Water of Kane*, a collection of the different islands' legends
as retold by Caroline Curtis to Pukui, the authors uphold the belief that these stories
are "part of the heritage of the children of these islands, no matter what their racial
background" (Pukui and Curtis 1951: 5). Intended to foster an "understanding and
appreciation of the civilization that was here before [these] islands were 'discovered,'"
The Water of Kane takes Hawaiian history one step back from the Hawaiian monarchy
to the time of the gods. In a tale from O'ahu, the gods, in appreciation for the beauty
of the land, create humans to make use of and rule over the *'āina*, thus establishing the close relationship between the people, the land, and divinity, a bond that
continues today in the practice of *mālama 'āina*, or preservation of the land. Other
creation tales, such as "Why Hilu Fish Are Striped," explain natural phenomenon
and reveal such Native cultural values as reverence for the gods and respect for one's
elders.

Proving that legends are not necessarily relegated to the past, "The Sharks of Pu'uloa"
connects modern history with a mythic one, reminding us that ancient Hawai'i neither
can nor should be erased. In Pu'uloa, now known as Pearl Harbor, the chiefess Ka'ahu
and her brother became sharks after a shark god, enjoying their play in the ocean,
changed their form. Loved by the people, Ka'ahu and her descendants protected Pu'uloa,
driving out "man-eater" sharks from Maui. Because Ka'ahu's son had his home in a
cave there, when the navy later made plans to build a drydock at that spot, many old
Hawaiians urged them to choose another place for their construction, as "'[t]he spirit
who guards the cave [would] not like men to build above it.'" The navy continued
with its plans, only to have the drydock suddenly collapse upon its completion. The
roof of the cave had broken, but no one had died in the accident; because Ka'ahu
loved people, she "'wanted no one killed at Pu'uloa'" (Pukui and Curtis 1951: 157).

Mary Kawena Pukui's contributions preserved a large body of Hawaiian knowledge, but they also taught others about the land and its people who once existed,
fostering pride in those who now struggled to do so. John Dominis Holt (1919–83)
would pick up this thread, becoming a Native voice that refused to be silenced,
demanding truth and questioning injustice. As a young man, Holt, battling constraints born of a widespread reluctance to accept a Hawaiian who was intellectually
curious, eagerly left Hawai'i to study on the continent. Anxious to see the world, he
did not anticipate returning, yet the pull of his home and blood brought him back to
the islands, where he began to examine works written about Hawai'i, challenging
those that demeaned Natives and their past.

Well schooled in the classics and raised in a household deeply entrenched in both its European and indigenous roots, Holt asserted that Western culture could not claim superiority to Hawaiian culture; that Hawaiian legends and *mele* rivaled classical Greek and Roman mythology and poetry; and that *hula*'s origins were no different in nature from those of ballet. A firm believer in the power of education, he encouraged Hawaiians to pursue intellectual thought and later advocated home schooling, since he felt the educational system's social atmosphere led youth to seek status among their peers. Throughout the remainder of his life, Holt contributed tremendous support to the Hawaiian community; as a scholar and writer, he provided an eloquent and poetic example through his expressions of Hawaiian identity.

A founding member of the Homerule Movement, which sought to excavate Hawaiianness and regain power for Natives, Holt wrote *On Being Hawaiian* in 1964 and provided a voice for burgeoning sentiments on Native self-determination. The reaction to an article that appeared in a local newspaper concerning Hawaiians and Hawaiian lands, *On Being Hawaiian* delves into questions of race, representation, history, and preservation. Calling for the protection "for future generations of all the people of Hawaii the great legacy of ancient Hawaiian culture" (Holt 1995: 9), Holt contends that misrepresentations of Natives have destructive and detrimental effects on the progress of contemporary Hawaiians. Pointing out the relationship between that misrepresentation, cultural genocide, and material culture, Holt calls on Hawaiians to become active participants in self-preservation, which necessitates self-definition: "They tell us we are all kinds of things, but what do we think of ourselves?" (Holt 1995: 19).

Acknowledging that the pain of self-definition can run deep, particularly for those of multiple heritages living in an historically complex environment that is racially, generationally, and socioeconomically diverse, Holt wrote *Waimea Summer* (1976). In this novel, Holt explores the negotiation of identity through the character of Mark Hull, a 14-year-old boy of Hawaiian and European ancestry. Coming from a city environment on O'ahu, Mark spends the summer at Waimea, experiencing the *paniolo* (cowboy) culture in which his father was raised. At the house of Uncle Fred, his father's cousin, Mark feels pulled in several directions, but mainly between his Western upbringing and his Hawaiian roots. Mark's *haole* worldview causes conflict on several levels. Emotionally, he attempts to conduct himself in the manner of his European predecessors, although he is directly confronted with and affected by displays of pure and uninhibited emotion which his parents would have called "too Hawaiian." Religiously, he both suspects and gives credence to the talk of kāhuna, supernatural powers, and ghosts, a conflict highlighted with the illness of Puna, the young son of Uncle Fred.

Holt refuses to oversimplify racial and cultural difference in his novel, and his rich characterizations illustrate the intricate interworkings of Hawai'i's society. Additionally, Holt's multilayered use of Hawaiian, HCE, and English illustrates how language develops out of one's socialization. None of the characters really speaks the same as any other; even Mark's voice is distinct in his conversations with other boys his age. Beautifully written and vivid in its descriptions, *Waimea Summer* continues to be valued for its portrayal of Waimea's *paniolo* country and its presentation of the enigmatic nature of identity, and Holt for his dedication to the Hawaiian community.

Talking Story: The Local Renaissance and Bamboo Ridge

In 1978, writers from Hawai'i and the continent gathered at Mid-Pacific Institute in Mānoa to attend "TALK STORY: Our Voices in Literature and Song – Hawaii's Ethnic American Writers' Conference," a symposium intended to encourage Hawai'i and Asian American literature. Sponsored by the Hawaii Ethnic Resources Center: Talk Story, Inc., founded by Stephen Sumida, Marie Hara, and Arnold Hiura, the landmark event signaled a critical shift towards a previously unexamined field and the conscious attempt to define a Local sensibility. In her preface to the ensuing anthology, entitled *Talk Story: An Anthology of Hawaii's Local Writers*, Maxine Hong Kingston points to the shared geography of the writers, as all "have lived some time in Hawaii." The question remained, however, to what degree geography influenced the writers and their visions: "Surely, writers, who do not ignore daily life, must be somehow affected by the cadences of local speech and the shades of the local green. The fun in reading this anthology is to see whether there are such Hawaiian patterns" (Chock et al., eds. 1998: 5).

The fact that Kingston, like several of the authors in the volume, is not Native might trigger comparisons to Day and Strovens' *A Hawaiian Reader* anthologies; after all, once again we see "visitors" – albeit of predominantly Asian descent – to the islands writing the islands, recalling notions of settler colonialism. Furthermore, the association of "Local" with "Asian American" tellingly indicates the subsuming of a Native presence under an Asian one, notwithstanding the dependence of Local characteristics upon Native values. However, one difference presents itself: during a time in which many colleges began instituting ethnic studies programs, the development of Asian-American literature sought to give voice to previously marginalized writers and experiences. Thus, as Asian-American writers spoke out, Local and Native writers who had been silenced by master narratives also wrote their "view from the shore" (see Sumida 1991).

The anthology, which includes the work of several well-known island authors such as Dana Naone, Edward Sakamoto, and Eric Chock, signaled an explosion of writing by and about people in Hawai'i. The goal, as Kingston stated, was to explore tendencies that shaped the notion of Local life. Immediately discernible are the concept of tradition, particularly an ethnic one; language, in the writers' use of both "standard" and Hawai'i Creole English; and a working-class perspective, the legacy of a plantation society. However, these patterns, among others, had appeared long before "TALK STORY." Written roughly 20 years prior to the conference, Milton

Murayama's *All I Asking For Is My Body* (1959) addressed a topic rarely acknowledged or critically assessed in island literature: plantation life. Living in the Japanese
plantation camp in pre-World War II Hawai'i, Murayama's "good son" character
Kiyo feels the force of family obligations, while his brother Tosh, whose passion
is boxing, grows increasingly frustrated with his family's refusal to break out of
what he sees as a dead-end life. Portraying generational conflict, gender construction,
and the push to accept or resist assimilation, Murayama, himself born and raised in
Lāhaināluna and "Pig Pen Alley" on Maui, illustrates a tension that had been felt
among many of Hawai'i's *nisei* (second generation). Yet at a time in which Japanese
held enough collective power to resist mass internment but nevertheless had their
loyalty questioned, Murayama's characters find that they have debatable control over
their lives, a condition that Kiyo struggles to understand, especially when he
discovers that a lifetime of being "good" guarantees him no safety from the anti-
Japanese sentiments following the bombing of Pearl Harbor. In many ways, the
characters ultimately gamble with outcomes; and, literally ending the novel with
a gamble, Murayama complicates the "easy choice," suggesting that there is no
winning without losing. Murayama's novel, considered a classic, maintains its
impact through its honest and complex tale of the Japanese plantation experience in
Hawai'i.

If Murayama helped shape a direction for Local literature, Bamboo Ridge, the
foremost publisher of island writing, became its institution. Founded in the same
year as the "TALK STORY" conference, Bamboo Ridge was from the outset equated
with Local literature. Its quarterly journal established many Local authors' careers,
and continues today to be part of a strong voice in emerging literature, expanding its
reach to include continental authors in connection with island ones. Two volumes
of work published by Bamboo Ridge provide a comprehensive sampling of Local
writers: *The Best of Bamboo Ridge* (1986) and *Growing up Local: An Anthology of Poetry
and Prose from Hawai'i* (1998). At the same time as the editors speak of Hawai'i
authors as having a "distinct sensitivity to ethnicity, the environment (in particular
that valuable commodity, the land), a sense of personal lineage and family history,
and the use of sound, the languages, and the vocabulary of island people" (Chock and
Lum 1986: 5), they establish diversity as key to Local writing.

In *The Best of Bamboo Ridge*, the subjects are indeed diverse, forming a "mixed
plate" of Hawai'i's many voices. Among other explorations, the writers' treatment of
language is significant in its demand for the legitimizing of Hawai'i's linguistic
history. HCE, born out of the plantations and having working-class roots, has carried
with it class-based prejudices implying that those who speak it are uncultured,
uneducated, and incapable of complex thought. Yet Diane Kahanu's "Ho. Just cause
I speak pidgin no mean I dumb" uses HCE to delve into the nature of language
and translation, subverting dominant ideas of "literary language," a move repeated
in other HCE works such as Darrell H. Y. Lum's "Beer Can Hat" and Michael
McPherson's "Junior Got the Snakes." Winnie Terada's "Intermediate School Hapai"
and Charles M. Kong's "Pele's Own," narrated in "standard" English, employ HCE

dialogue to capture distinct tones and meaning in their characters' voices, while yet other writers, such as poets Juliet Kono, Cathy Song, and Martha Webb, recount definitive island experiences through "standard" English. As much as the collection marks a Local sensibility, Native concerns also make their appearance, for instance in Rodney Morales' "Daybreak over Haleakalā/Heartbreak Memories (A Two-sided Hit)," which speaks to issues of land preservation and self-identity, as his three main characters gain a stronger sense of their indigenous connections through a tragic event. Similarly, Frederick Wichman, who describes himself as "a haku mo'olele, telling the ancient tales of Kauai so that they will not be forgotten" (Chock and Lum 1986: 325), continues Native storytelling traditions in "Nā Keiki O Nā-'Iwi," a tale of Mū, the forest people.

While *The Best of Bamboo Ridge* introduced a varied collection of Local works, 12 years later *Growing up Local* took that diversity and located it within larger themes of childhood, adolescence, and adulthood. By compiling sometimes radically different experiences of what it means to be Local, the volume complicates the integrity of the term, even as it maintains it through the anthology's presentation. While the struggle for acceptance runs through many of the stories comprising the first section, for instance, the types of acceptance contrast with each other. Lei in Marie M. Hara's "Fourth Grade Ukus" seeks validation through language, recounting her experiences in school, where HCE was much like *'uku* (lice): something to rid the children of so that they would grow to be respectable adults. Yet in an excerpt from Nora Okja Keller's stunning novel *Comfort Woman*, Becca, of Korean and white parentage, secretly seeks acceptance from her peers, to whom she is "nothing but a stink Yobo." Likewise, in the second section, Pua in Puanani Burgess' poem "Hawai'i Pono'ī" discovers her Hawaiian heritage during a trip to 'Iolani Palace, gaining a greater sense of self, while the speaker in Stacy Chang's "Attack from within" struggles with an eating disorder and her desire to shed herself of her body. The third section, often displaying speakers looking back upon their roots, features such pieces as Gary Pak's short story "The Watcher of Waipuna" from a collection bearing the same title, in which the main character, Gilbert Sanchez, uses his childhood memories to save his family's land; and Ho'oipo DeCambra's "I Come from a Place," a poem about varying origins. In reading the collection, "Localness" becomes more and more difficult to define, yet perhaps this is the point. In constant flux, Local identity contains forces that unite and divide islanders, and requires careful consideration rather than facile generalization in its analysis.

Bamboo Ridge has sometimes been criticized for exclusionary publishing practices and for its privileging of Local over Native issues. The latter charge especially highlights the tension between the two, particularly regarding Local culture's often unacknowledged debt to Native Hawaiian cultural practices. As reassessment of the relationship persists, at times creating separate literary traditions, it is nevertheless difficult to deny the major role Bamboo Ridge, continuing to publish full-volume works as well as quarterly journals, has played in shaping what we call Local literature today.

Emerging Literature

Contemporary Hawai'i literature, an expanding field of critical and literary work, has grown tremendously, attesting to the islands' refusal to exist as a silenced and exoticized territory. Native authors sustain protest against the continuing colonization of their home, while Local authors strip away the veneer of paradise by writing stories about the pain, struggle, and sometimes violence their characters experience. The luxury of having to choose authors to discuss here does not go unappreciated, although a proper discussion of emerging island work would include writers such as Kathleen Tyau, Ty Pak, Nora Keller, Garrett Hongo, and Kiana Davenport, among others already mentioned. As Local and Native boundaries remain under scrutiny, it seems appropriate to discuss these traditions separately; although intersection certainly occurs, the differing histories ultimately beg separate treatment.

Although Hawai'i literature has retained a geographical specificity which speaks to a particular audience, a few authors have crossed over to mainstream audiences and publishing houses, the most recognizable being Lois-Ann Yamanaka. Her poetry and novels have gained widespread critical attention for their use of HCE and their portrayal of characters in gritty, sometimes disturbing situations that leave readers unable to view Hawai'i as nothing more than a vacation spot. Regional literature often demonstrates its difference, and in her first novel, *Wild Meat and the Bully Burgers*, Yamanaka does exactly this with a number of Local signifiers, including HCE terminology, the "Checkers and Pogo Show," and the song "Nightbird" by Local music group Kalapana. Yet in her coming-of-age novel about Lovey, a Local girl who longs to marry a *haole* and whose female icon is Barbie, Yamanaka points a finger at the far-reaching effects of American pop culture, demonstrating Hawai'i's intense connection to the United States. Judging whiteness as the model of perfection, Lovey's feelings of inadequacy overwhelm her. However, she also measures herself against ideals of femininity set by Local Japanese girls like the pretty and petite Lori Shigemura who, along with her friends, ostracizes Lovey for being poor and unpopular. As Lovey moves towards self-acceptance, she realizes the forces that drive her, including her love for her sometimes abusive father, and her desire to create a sense of home for herself and her family. Demonstrating that HCE can be both humorous and poignant, Yamanaka uses language, as do many Local authors, to create realities inexpressible through "standard" English; Lovey's voice, even in narration, provides us with a clear picture of her emotional and psychological outlook. Yamanaka's writing succeeds in taking the particulars of Hawai'i and retaining their integrity for mainstream audiences.

Like Yamanaka, Chris McKinney writes about an extraodinarily complex Hawai'i. With *The Tattoo*, which earned its author the Hawai'i Literary Arts Council's 2000 Cades Award, McKinney explores masculinity, racial hierarchies, and class structure through the figure of Ken Hideyoshi, a Local boy whose troubled past leads him to a life of crime and a prison term. Ken's familial and economic situations determine many of his choices, and even as he sees the destruction of those around him, he finds his street skills as profitable as they are dangerous. While in prison, Ken receives a tattoo of a Japanese character meaning "The Book of the Void," the title of the book written by Miyamoto Musashi, and it is during these tattoo sessions that he unfolds his life story, from his upbringing on the Windward side of Honolulu with his abusive father and loyal best friend Koa, to his employment with a Korean crime ring, to his love affair with Claudia Choy, the daughter of a Korean bar owner. Understanding that his family lineage provides both pride and ruin, Ken seeks ways to allow himself and others a future that does not necessitate self-destruction, although he discovers that saving others sometimes requires self-sacrifice in the manner of the samurai. Using the Pali Highway as a literal bridge between the Windward side and Honolulu, McKinney reinforces a geography that suggests distinct lines – between classes, races, and gender – that circumscribe our lives. Violence often erupts when these lines are crossed; in defiance of them, Ken remains locked away, an act of ultimate self-erasure. McKinney's book is vivid, graphic, and powerful, and he indicates a new generation of Local writers, promising a new literary tradition bringing to light Hawai'i's troubled present, a testament to the fact that all is not perfect in paradise.

However, Native authors had been asserting all along that Hawai'i was indeed troubled. As goals of sovereignty move toward realization, Native Hawaiians come together to express shared concerns for Native welfare and the Nation of Hawai'i. In the anthology *He Alo Ā He Alo*, voices including those of S. Haunani Apoliona, Kekuni Blaisdell, and Imaikalani Kalahele recount history, current problems, and visions of the future through essays, poetry, illustrations, interviews, and letters. A multidimensional treatment of Hawaiian sovereignty, the collection provides strength through its diversity; while sometimes proposing divergent models of self-determination, educators, writers, politicians, private citizens, and government employees nevertheless agree overwhelmingly on the undeniable need for it. Even the thoughts of Native children create an impact, declaring that Hawaiians' intense connection to the land and the fight for sovereignty will continue. Providing a richly textured discussion of Native self-determination, *He Alo Ā He Alo* disproves the all too prevalent perception that sovereignty is an issue that only "militant Hawaiians" pursue, and certainly, contemporary publications such as the Hawaiian literary journal *'Ōiwi* maintain Native cultural survival with a force rivaling that of the resurgence of Hawaiian arts, language, and cultural awareness in the 1970s.

Perhaps the figure most stigmatized by those opposed to or ignorant of Hawaiian sovereignty has been Haunani-Kay Trask, an outspoken and activist professor of Hawaiian Studies at the University of Hawai'i. A member of the sovereignty group Ka Lāhui Hawai'i, Trask has fought to bring the discussion of self-determination to the forefront, often suffering attack and criticism for her impassioned and truthful views. Two of her works, *From a Native Daughter: Colonialism and Sovereignty in Hawai'i* and the poetry collection *Light in the Crevice Never Seen*, present complex perspectives on the effects of colonization. The essays that form *From a Native Daughter* address a range of subjects from global politics and the "new world order" to Trask's own experiences of retaliation and exclusion for her political beliefs within the University of Hawai'i system. To read these essays is to understand that Trask, to whom the adjective "angry" is often assigned, simply demands justice for a situation that continues to cause damage to Native Hawaiians. In her poetry, Trask broaches these issues through a different lens, one whose emotional honesty makes it impossible to demonize her. In expressions of concern for her people and culture, Trask allows readers to see her connection to Hawai'i's past, one whose strength fuels her concerns for Natives today:

> O Noa, we don't
> live like you anymore
> there is nothing
> certain in this world
> except loss
> for our people
>
> and a silent grief,
> grieving
>   (Trask 1994: 10)

Battling Native invisibility and eradication, Trask, with other Hawaiian writers, upholds the literary tradition of Hawai'i and proves beyond a measure of doubt that Natives were always here, always writing, and will continue to do so.

NOTES

1   The Hawaiian language uses two diacritical marks – the macron or kahakō, and the glottal stop or 'okina – that are crucial to the pronunciation and meaning of the words. Some quoted material within this section does not use the marks; other Hawaiian words in the text of this chapter do. While "Hawai'i" is a Hawaiian language term, Anglicized words such as "Hawaiian" do not feature the 'okina, and thus the mark has been omitted there.

2   For a thorough discussion of the Massie trial, see Rosa 2000.

3   Hawaiians had an extremely high literacy rate, and a number of Hawaiian-language newspapers, written and read by Natives, had been in circulation from 1845 to 1877.

4   For further discussion of these anthologies, see Stephen Sumida, "Waiting for the Big Fish: Recent Research in the Asian American Literature of Hawaii," in Eric Chock and Darrell H. Y. Lum, eds., *The Best of Bamboo Ridge* (Honolulu: Bamboo Ridge Press, 1986), 302–21.

5   With the resurgence of the Hawaiian language, Kamakau's writings on Kamehameha I have been compiled in a new volume in their original language: *Ke Kumu Aupuni* (Honolulu: 'Ahahuui 'Olelo Hawai'i, 1997).

References and Further Reading

Chock, Eric; Harstad, James R.; Lum, Darrell H. Y.; and Teter, Bill, eds. (1998). *Growing Up Local: An Anthology of Poetry and Prose From Hawai'i*. Honolulu: Bamboo Ridge.

Chock, Eric, and Lum, Darrell H. Y., eds. (1986). *The Best of Bamboo Ridge*. Honolulu: Bamboo Ridge.

Chock, Eric; Lum, Darrell H. Y.; Miyasaki, Gail; Robb, Dave; Stewart, Frank; and Uchida, Kathy, eds. (1978). *Talk Story: An Anthology of Hawaii's Local Writers*. Honolulu: Petronium Press/Talk Story, Inc.

Day, A. Grove and Stroven, Carl, eds. (1959). *A Hawaiian Reader: The Exotic Literary Heritage of the Hawaiian Islands*, vol. I. Honolulu: Mutual Publishing.

Day, A. Grove and Stroven, Carl, eds. (1968). *A Hawaiian Reader: The Exotic Literary Heritage of the Hawaiian Islands*, vol. II. Honolulu: Mutual Publishing.

Enomoto, Catherine Kekoa (1997). "In his Mother Tongue." 9 June 1997. http://starbulletin.com/97/06/09/features/story3.html.

Fujikane, Candace, and Okamura, Jonathan, eds. (2000). *Whose Vision? Asian Settler Colonialism in Hawai'i*. Los Angeles: UCLA Asian American Studies Center Press.

Furrer, Roger MacPherson, ed. (1993). *He Alo Ā He Alo/Face To Face: Hawaiian Voices on Sovereignty*. Honolulu: American Friends Service Committee.

Grant, Glen, and Ogawa, Dennis M. (1993). "Living Proof: is Hawaii the Answer?" *ANNALS*, AAPSS, 530, 137–54.

Holt, John Dominis (1976). *Waimea Summer*. Honolulu: Topgallant.

Holt, John Dominis (1995). *On Being Hawaiian*. Honolulu: Ku Pa'a.

'I'i, John Papa (1959). *Fragments of Hawaiian History*, trans. Mary Kawena Pukui. Honolulu: Bishop Museum Press.

Kamakau, Samuel Mānaiakalani (1992). *Ruling Chiefs of Hawaii*. Honolulu: Kamehameha Schools Press.

Kent, Noel (1993). *Hawaii: Islands under the Influence*. Honolulu: University of Hawai'i Press.

Lili'uokalani (1990). *Hawaii's Story by Hawaii's Queen*. Honolulu: Mutual.

McKinney, Chris (1999). *The Tattoo*. Honolulu: Mutual.

Malo, David (1951). *Hawaiian Antiquities: Mo'olelo Hawai'i*, trans. Nathan B. Emerson. Honolulu: Bishop Museum Press.

Michener, James A. (1959). *Hawaii*. New York: Random House.

Murayama, Milton (1988). *All I Asking for is my Body*. Honolulu: University of Hawai'i Press. (First publ. 1959.)

Pukui, Mary Kawena, and Curtis, Caroline (1951). *The Water of Kane*. Honolulu: Kamehameha Schools Press.

Rosa, John P. (2000). "Local Story: The Massie Case Narrative and the Cultural Production of Local Identity in Hawai'i." In Candace Fujikane and Jonathan Y. Okamura (eds.), *Whose Vision? Asian Settler Colonialism in Hawai'i*, 93–115. Los Angeles: UCLA Asian American Studies Center Press.

Sumida, Stephen H. (1991). *And the View from the Shore: Literary Traditions of Hawai'i*. Seattle and London: University of Washington Press.

Sumida, Stephen H. (1992). "Sense of Place, History, and the Concept of the 'Local' in Hawaii's Asian/Pacific American Literatures." In Shirley Geok-lin Lim and Amy Ling (eds.), *Reading the Literatures of Asian America*, 215–37. Philadelphia: Temple University Press.

Trask, Haunani-Kay (1993). *From a Native Daughter: Colonialism and Sovereignty in Hawai'i*. Honolulu: University of Hawai'i Press.

Trask, Haunani-Kay (1994). *Light in the Crevice Never Seen*. Corvallis, Oregon: Calyx.

Yamanaka, Lois Ann (1996). *Wild Meat and the Bully Burgers*. San Diego, New York, and London: Harcourt Brace.

PART III
Some Regionalist Masters

27

Bret Harte and the Literary Construction of the American West

Gary Scharnhorst

One of the pioneers in the use of regional local color, Bret Harte was perfectly situated to tap the growing interest in the American West after the construction of the transcontinental railroad in the late 1860s. His story "The Luck of Roaring Camp," published in the *Overland Monthly* in August 1868, was "the first resounding note" in the development of a distinctive Western American literature, as Kate Chopin wrote in 1900. In it, he "reached across the continent and startled the Academists on the Atlantic Coast. . . . They opened their eyes and ears at the sound and awoke to the fact that there might some day be a literary West" (Chopin 1900: 1). No less a luminary than Mark Twain considered Harte at the time "the finest writer" in the West and turned to him for help and advice in editing *The Innocents Abroad* (Clemens 1990: 359). Harte, he admitted, "trimmed and trained and schooled me patiently until he changed me from an awkward utterer of coarse grotesquenesses to a writer of paragraphs and chapters that have found a certain favor" (Clemens 1995: 316). Harte was "our Theocritus at last, and from California, whence we least expected him," as the *North American Review* declared in 1871 (1871: 235). His astonishing success with a sheaf of poems and stories in the *Overland* between 1868 and 1870 not only challenged genteel assumptions about the bleak literary promise of the West but helped to open the pages of Eastern papers to a new school of Western writers, including Mark Twain, Joaquin Miller, Prentice Mulford, John Hay, Charles Warren Stoddard, and Ina Coolbrith. In brief, his success as a Western American regionalist earned him international renown. In 1890, Havelock Ellis ranked Harte with Hawthorne, Poe, and Mark Twain among the "imaginative writers . . . America had produced . . . of world-wide significance" (Ellis 1890: 86).

*

Ironically, Francis Brett Harte (1836–1902) was not a native Westerner, and he lived in California only between the ages of 17 and 34. Born in Albany, New York, to a struggling schoolteacher, the dispossessed son of a founder of the New York Stock Exchange, and his wife, a descendant of revolutionary war heroes, Harte was formally educated up to the age of only 13. In 1854 he followed his widowed mother to Oakland, California, and by the spring of 1857 he had settled briefly in Tuolumne County, where he spent a few weeks in placer mining. In 1860 he became a typesetter for the San Francisco *Golden Era*, one of the few literary magazines on the Pacific coast, and so began his writing career in earnest. His Western serial "The Work on Red Mountain" (1860), which he revised and published under the title "M'liss" three years later, foreshadowed the direction his career would take: he would write of things and people indigenous to California during the Gold Rush.

To be sure, he invariably depicted the West through a filtered lens and in a soft light. Though he was unskilled as a writer of Western dialect, he paid careful attention to local setting and stories centered on character types – rough miners, genteel schoolmarms, whores with hearts of gold, gruff stage drivers, dandy gamblers, inscrutable Asians – who rarely transcend the stereotypical. Predictably, all of his Western stories bear a close family resemblance. As he later explained his approach to regionalism in "The Rise of the 'Short Story'":

> The gold discovery had drawn to the Pacific slope of the continent a heterogeneous and remarkable population. The immigration of 1849 and 1850 had taken farmers from the plough, merchants from their desks, and students from their books, while every profession was represented in the motley crowd of gold-seekers. Europe and her colonies had contributed to swell these adventurers – for adventurers they were whatever their purpose; the risks were great, the journey long and difficult – the nearest came from a distance of over a thousand miles; that the men were necessarily pre-equipped with courage, faith and endurance was a foregone conclusion. They were mainly young; a grey-haired man was a curiosity in the mines in the early days, and an object of rude respect and reverence. They were consequently free from the trammels of precedent or tradition in arranging their lives and making their rude homes. There was a singular fraternity in this ideal republic into which all men entered free and equal. Distinction of previous position or advantages were unknown, even record and reputation for ill or good were of little benefit or embarrassment to the possessor; men were accepted for what they actually were, and what they could do in taking their part in the camp or settlement. The severest economy, the direst poverty, the most menial labor carried no shame nor disgrace with it; individual success brought neither envy nor jealousy. What was one man's fortune to-day might be the luck of another tomorrow. Add to this the Utopian simplicity of the people, the environment of magnificent scenery, a unique climate, and a vegetation that was marvelous in its proportions and spontaneity of growth; let it be further considered that the strongest relief was given to this picture by its setting among the crumbling ruins of early Spanish possession – whose monuments still existed in Mission and Presidio, and whose legitimate Castilian descendants still lived and moved in picturesque and dignified contrast to their energetic invaders – and it must be admitted that a condition of romantic and dramatic possibilities was created unrivalled in history. (Harte 1899: 5–6)

Figure 27.1 Bret Harte.

Harte's discovery of California as a field for fiction made almost as much a stir as the discovery of gold at Sutter's Mill.

Harte's stories and sketches for the *Golden Era* caught the eye of Jessie Benton Frémont, who in turn introduced him to Thomas Starr King, the minister of the First Unitarian Church of San Francisco. Frémont and King recommended Harte to

James T. Fields, the editor of the *Atlantic Monthly*, who published Harte's early story "The Legend of Monte del Diablo" in the October 1863 issue of the magazine alongside Ralph Waldo Emerson's poem "Voluntaries" and Henry David Thoreau's "Life without Principle." As King wrote to Fields, "I am sure there is a great deal in Harte, & an acceptance of his piece would inspirit him, & help literature on this coast where we raise bigger trees & squashes than literati & brains" (Scharnhorst 1992: 7).

Through Frémont's influence, too, Harte was appointed to a series of governmental sinecures, the last one as Secretary to the Superintendent of the US Mint. He married the former Anna Griswold, a contralto in the choir at King's church, in August 1862. Yet he had also begun to chafe at his distance from Eastern centers of culture. He lamented the subtle restraints on "intellectual life and activity" in the West (Harte 1990: 125). "The curse of California," he privately complained in February 1868, "has been its degrading, materialistic influences" (Scharnhorst 2000: 36), and he yearned to resettle in the East where, he thought, his literary ambitions were more likely to be realized.

Harte's ambivalence to things Western was never more apparent than in the 40 letters he published between January 1866 and March 1868 as the California correspondent of two Massachusetts papers: the Boston *Christian Register*, a Unitarian weekly; and the *Springfield Republican*, one of the most prestigious dailies in the country, edited by Samuel Bowles. Though he had lived in California for a dozen years, in these essays Harte adopted the voice of an Eastern expatriate. "When you meet" at "the Eastern borders of the continent," he invited his readers, think tenderly of the "unrelieved sentinels at the Western gate." Like a foreign correspondent, he tried to describe the exotic tastes and habits of Californians. They were gamblers by nature, famous for fast living. Like the Arabian Prince, they "prefer their cream tarts with pepper." They "are naturally cosmopolitan" and "innately liberal," though they could also be too materially and narrow-minded. California literature would never come of age, he predicted, so long as the state had "more writers than readers" and "more contributors than subscribers" (Harte 1990: 52, 55, 68, 73, 140). His columns in the *Springfield Republican*, more than any other publication, brought Harte to the attention of the Eastern literary establishment. In January 1867, for example, Bowles compared Harte favorably to his (then) friendly rival Mark Twain. Harte, he insisted, "is less demonstrative in his qualities," "his humor is more subjective, and his scholarship more thorough and conservative." In all, he is "the best of the California humorists after all" (Bowles 1867).

In mid-1868, Harte struck paydirt: he was invited by the founder of the *Overland Monthly* to become its first editor. His role in helping to open the American literary West as its founding editor cannot be overestimated. Whereas the publisher, Anton Roman, hoped the magazine would hew a more commercial line, Harte wanted it to be a more purely literary publication, a catalyst to the growth of a distinctive Western literary tradition no more limited in its appeal than the *Atlantic Monthly*, upon which it was modeled. "I am trying to build up a literary taste on the Pacific slope," as he explained, "and we may be short-lived. But I want to make a good fight while it lasts" (Scharnhorst 1992: 22). In the end, Harte prevailed, though not without the good fight. The first issue of the *Overland* in July 1868 contained nothing "distinctively Californian" (Harte 1899: 7), nothing "of that wild and picturesque life which had impressed him, first as a truant schoolboy, and afterwards as a youthful schoolmaster among the mining population," and so, he averred, "should no other contribution come in, he himself would supply the omission." Still, "The Luck of Roaring Camp" reached print in the August 1868 issue, as he often explained, over the objections of the printer and proofreader, who persuaded Roman that it was vulgar. This crisis borne of the provincialism Harte disdained was resolved only when he insisted the story appear without change or he would resign as editor of the magazine. Not only was it then published, but the tide turned in Harte's favor when it was hailed in the East as one of the best magazine stories of the year. Sam Bowles praised "The Luck" in the *Springfield Republican* as "a genuine California story," a tale "so true to nature and so deep-reaching in its humor, that it will move the hearts of men everywhere" (Bowles 1868). Mark Twain thought the tale "almost blemishless" and Harte's "most finished work" (Booth 1954: 493). James T. Fields offered to publish in the *Atlantic* "anything [Harte] chose to write, upon his own terms" (Harte 1997: 25). "Since Boston endorsed the story," Harte later crowed, "San Francisco was properly proud of it" (Dam 1894: 46). "I'll try to find time to send you something," he replied to Fields. "The *Overland* is still an experiment, and should it fail . . . why I dare say I may be able to do more" (Harte 1997: 24).

Far from failing, however, the magazine prospered under Harte's editorship. By the end of 1869, it enjoyed a circulation of about 3,000 copies per number, and it sold as many copies (Taylor 1870). Harte instinctively understood that in a state that had "more contributors than subscribers" he had to attract a national readership. Four years later, Harte again explained to a Chicago publisher who wished to start up a magazine that while he "always believed that the West offered an excellent field for an original, first-rate magazine," it could not be merely a local magazine "patronized by Chicago interests." To survive it would require "subscriptions outside of Chicago, by St. Louis, by Cincinnati, by Omaha, by San Francisco" (Harte 1997: 92–3).

In any event, with the critical success of "The Luck" in the second issue of the *Overland*, Harte was emboldened "to follow it with other stories of a like character" (Harte 1899: 7). Put another way, he began to tailor his stories for Eastern readers of the magazine. However regional his subject, the nine tales he published in the *Overland* during his tenure as its editor subtly condescended to the Western types he depicted. They were in every case pitched to appeal to Eastern readers who were enthralled by the romance of the Gold Rush and the exotic West. He wrote his Western tales not as a realist but in the style of a romancer on the Dickensian model. Or, as Harte explained in his preface to *The Luck of Roaring Camp and Other Sketches* (1870), he aspired simply to collect "the materials for the Iliad that is yet to be sung" in epic strains about the Gold Rush (Harte 1870). His second *Overland* tale, "The

Outcasts of Poker Flat" (January 1869), not only depicts the horror suffered by the Donner Pass emigrants but burlesques the myth of the hardy pioneers. "Tennessee's Partner" (October 1869), though often vilified for its ostensible sentimentality, is less a tale of two miners' affection than it is a story of deceit and revenge. In "The Idyl of Red Gulch" (December 1869), the Eastern schoolmarm Miss Mary flees the uncouth West for the genteel society of Boston in the final paragraphs, foreshadowing Harte's own departure for the East a few months later. Similarly, in "Brown of Calaveras" (March 1870), he has his cynical hero save the failing marriage of an Eastern beauty and her jealous husband by urging them to leave the West. In short, in his best Western writing Harte challenged the dime-novelized treatment of the frontier. His gamblers may be libertines, but they are also chivalrous; his redshirt miners may be coarse, but they are also charitable; and his fallen women may be "easy," but they are also self-sacrificial.

Harte also wrote many of these early satires of the West from what may fairly be deemed a Unitarian or liberal Christian perspective, given his friendship with T. Starr King. In them, he parodied or lampooned biblical text in order to challenge parochial beliefs, to subvert religious orthodoxy, to ridicule hypocrisy. On first reading, for example, "The Luck of Roaring Camp" may seem to be a modern retelling of the gospel accounts of the Nativity, with the Christ child renamed "Luck" and the dissolute mining camp a "city of refuge" reclaimed through his influence. However, the tale may be more fairly read as a subtle parody of the Nativity, with a mixed-blood prostitute named Cherokee Sal, an ironic Madonna indeed, and a plethora of gamblers and miners who mimic Wise Men from the East. Rather than a reincarnation of Christ on the frontier, Tommy Luck is a false Messiah. His first name recalls the Doubting Apostle and an apocryphal gospel, and his surname evokes blind Chance. In the final paragraphs of the story, the mining camp is swept away in a flood of biblical proportions. The "luck of Roaring Camp" is, in the end, all bad. Similarly, Harte's "Mr. Thompson's Prodigal" (July 1870) reverses Christ's parable of the Prodigal Son, and "Brown of Calaveras" (March 1870) revises the parable of the Good Samaritan. "Miggles" (June 1869) features a type of Mary Magdalene who atones for her sins by a life of selfless devotion to an "imbecile paralytic" named Jim (or James, according to legend the brother of Jesus). To be sure, the satirical formula Harte adopted in many of his most popular and successful Western stories disturbed some staid and conventional reviewers. *Zion's Herald*, a Methodist weekly published in Boston, for example, complained that Harte "gilded vice" and "abolished moral distinctions" in his tales. At the close of "The Outcasts of Poker Flat," indeed, "nobody can tell" which of the women who freezes to death "is pure and which corrupt" and so "they are buried in the same grave" – which, of course, is Harte's entire point (*Zion's Herald* 1870). As W. D. Howells observed, in Harte's fiction "ladies with pasts were of a present behavior so self-devoted that they could often put their unerring sisters to the blush" (Howells 1901: II, 228).

Of the 25 poems Harte contributed to the pages of the *Overland*, "Plain Language from Truthful James" (September 1870), more popularly known as "The Heathen

Chinee," was by far the most famous. A satire of anti-Chinese prejudice in California often misinterpreted as an *endorsement* of such prejudice, this dramatic monologue was as nearly an overnight sensation as possible when San Francisco was six days distant from New York by railroad. More than "The Luck" or "The Outcasts," which had appeared without signature, "Plain Language" made Bret Harte a household name across the country. Mark Twain averred in March 1871 that Harte was "the most celebrated man in America to-day," "the man whose name is on every single tongue from one end of the continent to the other," and the poem "did it for him" (Clemens 1995: 338). The publisher of the *Overland* reported that "the news agents in the East doubled their orders" for the magazine in the wake of the poem's appearance (*Overland* 1883: 12), with total circulation reaching about 10,000 per issue. Within days the poem had been reprinted in dozens of magazines and newspapers, including such stalwarts as the *New York Tribune, Boston Transcript, Portland Transcript, Providence Journal, Hartford Courant*, and the *Saturday Evening Post* (Scharnhorst 1995: 41–5). It was parodied at least 15 times – to satirize flirtatious women ("Plain Language from Truthful Jane"), the Treaty of Washington ("Plain Language from Truthful Bull"), the presidential ambitions of Horace Greeley ("The Heathen Greelee"), and so forth (Scharnhorst 1996: 392–3). Fields, Osgood & Co. of Boston issued an edition of Harte's collected *Poems* featuring "Plain language" for the 1870 Christmas season – and it became the most popular of all of Harte's books, with six printings totaling some 2,200 copies sold within its first five days in print, some 20,000 copies sold during its first two years, and another 10,000 sold over the next five years (Houghton Mifflin records). Despite the commercial success of "Plain Language," however, Harte professed to hate it. "Just think of the degradation of going down to posterity as the author of such trash as 'The Heathen Chinee,'" he said to Mary E. W. Sherwood the next summer (Sherwood 1902: 308). He wanted to write finer things than Westerns, especially after he left the West.

By the close of 1870 and at the height of his popularity, Harte's work was in demand from coast to coast, and his name had become a type of literary brand name. (He would later successfully enjoin the publication of a story falsely attributed to him on exactly these grounds.) He was offered the editorship of *Putnam's* and the *Lakeside Monthly* in Chicago, and was invited to contribute to the *New York Tribune, The Galaxy, Harper's Monthly* and *Weekly*, and *Scribner's*. In the attempt to keep him in San Francisco, he was also offered a salary of $5,000 to edit the *Overland*, plus $100 for each of his contributions to its pages, plus an interest in the magazine, plus the Professorship of Recent Literature at the new University of California in Berkeley. As Ambrose Bierce explained, he "could not afford to remain in California – where there is a conspicuous lack of the sense necessary to the appreciation of genius – unless he were bribed with a lucrative sinecure" (Scharnhorst 2000: 59).

Then came the reckoning. Finally lured East in February 1871 by the promise of literary fame and fortune (and, incidentally, the most lucrative contract to that date in the history of American letters), Harte wrote exclusively for the firm of J. R. Osgood & Co., publishers of the *Atlantic Monthly* and *Every Saturday*, over the next twelvemonth for the munificent salary of $10,000. He wrote Bierce back in San Francisco that "of the commercial value of my own stuff I really had no conception whatever," but that "for the sake of keeping my books in the one house" he had "made some pecuniary sacrifice" (Harte 1997: 46, 48). Though Harte has long been criticized for failing to fulfill his obligations under the terms of this contract – Howells, for example, later claimed that the "net result in a literary return to his publishers" was merely "one story and two or three poems" (Howells 1910: 301) – in fact Harte honored the contract by contributing *more* than the twelve articles specified as the minimum number while it was in effect, though to be sure he often submitted his material late and the quality of his writing fell off dramatically. His first story in the *Atlantic*, "The Poet of Sierra Flat" (July 1871), implicitly ridiculed the Western theme that had won him the contract. He assumed the patronizing tone of the Brahmins toward his comic frontier types. His Christmas story "How Santa Claus came to Simpson's Bar," the product of a prolonged gestation, was published three months late, in the March 1872 issue of the *Atlantic*, and Henry James thought the tale, with its false pathos, "better than anything" in Harte's "second manner – though not quite so good as his first" (James 1974: 270). Despite the timeworn critical assumptions about Harte, his career was neither brief nor punctuated by frequent failures. In fact, he probably should be credited with saving the *Atlantic Monthly*. Subscriptions to the magazine had plummeted in the wake of the controversy over Harriet Beecher Stowe's essay "Lady Byron Vindicated" in the September 1869 issue, and Harte's was the marquee name the publisher needed to shore up subscriptions and raise advertising revenue. A prototype of the man of letters as a man of business, he learned through painful experience to gauge the market for his "wares."

To no one's surprise except perhaps his own, Harte's contract with Osgood & Co. was not renewed in the spring of 1872. Hardly a year after his departure from San Francisco at the height of his fame, he was forced to try to salvage his fortunes by trading on his name and reputation. He slipped into the doldrums – between July 1872 and June 1873, when he should have been in the prime of his career, he published exactly one story and four poems – and the joke went the rounds that he had reversed the path of the sun, rising brightly in the West and setting in darkness in the East; or else he was compared to the stick that comes down in the dark after the rocket has gone up in a blaze of glory. But he was still bankable, even as his star was fading. He earned most of his income between 1872 and 1874 by lecturing on "The Argonauts of '49," by his own estimate some 150 times, from Boston and New York in the East to Omaha in the Midwest, Toronto in the North, and Atlanta in the South. Once again, the lecture was carefully crafted to exploit his renown as an exotic Western writer and California's as a foreign land. The Gold Rush "was a crusade without a cross, an exodus without a prophet," he began. "It is not a pretty story; I do not know that it is even instructive; I do not know that it is strictly true." He regaled his mostly Eastern and Southern audiences for an hour with humorous if patronizing anecdotes about "the lawless, irreligious band" who "had left families, creditors, and in some instances even officers of justice" for the goldfields. "There were husbands who had deserted their own wives, – and in some extreme cases even the wives of others, – for this haven of refuge" (Harte 1882: ix, xi, xiv). Unfortunately, Harte often disappointed his audiences not only by the near-whisper of his delivery but by his dandified appearance and his frequent intoxication at the podium. "What the people expected in me I do not know, possibly a six-foot mountaineer, with a voice and lecture in proportion," he confessed.

> They always seemed to have mentally confused me with one of my own characters.
> . . . Whenever I walked out before a strange audience there was a general sense of disappointment, a gasp of astonishment that I could feel, and it always took at least fifteen minutes before they recovered from their surprise sufficiently to listen to what I had to say. I think, even now, that if I had been more Herculean in proportions, with a red shirt and top boots, many of the audience would have felt a deeper thrill from my utterances and a deeper conviction that they had obtained the worth of their money.
> (Dam 1894: 50)

In the space of two years he went from being the highest-paid and the most popular writer in America to freelancing stories to the Sunday editions of the New York *Sun* and the *New York Times*.

Like an actor typecast as a romantic hero, it seems, Harte was expected by his audience to perform a certain role, to write a certain type of Western story, for the rest of his life. In a word, he became the writer the literary market made him. When he tried to experiment, as in a couple of poems written from and about Newport in the summer of 1871, or in a series of stories in 1893–8 in which he fictionalized his experience as the American Consul in Glasgow, he was castigated by the critics. Whenever "he travels away from California," one reviewer carped, his "stories that deal with life in other regions, whether humorous or pathetic, are commonplace" (*Athenaeum* 1879). Harte's later poems and stories were mostly written according to the same tired and tested Western formula. "My stories have always been *contracted for*, *accepted* and the *prices fixed* before I had put pen to paper," he bragged to Howells in September 1874 (Harte 1997: 100). The *New York Tribune* paid him $100 per poem; the *New York Times* paid him $600 for the story "The Rose of Tuolumne" (April 1874) and $500 for "A Passage in the Life of Mr. John Oakhurst" (June 1874). *Scribner's* paid him $1,000 for "An Episode of Fiddletown" (August–October 1873) and $500 for "A Monte Flat Pastoral" (January 1874). When Howells offered him only $300 to publish "The Fool of Five Forks" in the *Atlantic*, he withdrew the manuscript and sold it to the *New York Times* for $400, where it appeared in September 1874. By then, however, he seemed trapped in a cycle of self-parody. He contracted, partly through the intercession of Twain, to write a novel for the American Publishing Company of Hartford, a subscription house – and finally finished the manuscript in 1875, nearly three years later. The novel, *Gabriel Conroy*, was an utter disaster, a hodgepodge or grab-bag of undeveloped characters and subplots. Horace Scudder, in his review of it for the *Atlantic*, concluded that "all the dark passages through which [the reader] has been wandering" lead finally "not into the light, but into the vegetable cellar" (Scudder 1882: 266).

For better or worse, Harte had become a literary celebrity who traded on his name, who gauged the market for his writings with a calculating eye. "I do wish you lived out of a literary atmosphere which seems to exclude any vision of a broader literary world beyond," including "its methods, profits and emoluments," he chastened Howells (Harte 1997: 100). "I grind out the old tunes on the old organ and gather up the coppers," he confessed in 1879, "but I never know whether my audience behind the window blinds are wishing me to 'move on' or not" (Harte 1926: 154). He "wrote Bret Harte over and over again as long as he lived," as Howells remarked. It "was the best thing he could do" because the "cockney-syntaxed, Dickens-colored California" of his imagination appealed to "the insatiable English fancy for the wild America no longer to be found on our map" (Howells 1910: 299). "I have only one jar to dip into," as he told an interviewer in 1901 (Carew 1901). Privately, Harte disparaged these "monotonous romances" with their recurring laconic gamblers, decayed Spanish aristocrats, and rustic miners.

Undeterred by his declining fortunes, Harte contracted in the spring of 1875 to write a comic play for the actor Stuart Robson, for $6,000. In *Two Men of Sandy Bar* he would marry plot elements of two of his *Overland* stories, "Mr. Thompson's Prodigal" and "The Idyl of Red Gulch." When he finished the initial draft of the farce three months later, he estimated that it would require over four hours to perform. When it was finally produced in Chicago and New York in the summer and fall of 1876, the play was condemned by the critics. The *New York Times* declared that Harte had written not a script but a "nondescript," that the play was "the worst failure witnessed on the boards of our theatres for years" and "the most dismal mass of trash that was ever put into dramatic shape before a New York audience" (*New York Times* 1876). The *New York Herald* compared it to "one of Beadle's dime novels struck by lightning (*New York Herald* 1876). Mark Twain reminisced in 1907 that, in fact, the play "would have succeeded if anyone else had written it" (Clemens 1940: 275). Indeed, Twain so enjoyed *Two Men of Sandy Bar* that he agreed to co-author another play with Harte "& divide the swag" (Clemens and Howells 1960: I, 157). The result was perhaps the most disastrous collaboration in the history of American letters: a lame comedy of mistaken identity that awkwardly introduced the character of the Chinese laundryman in Harte's poem "Plain Language from Truthful James" into the plot of his story "A Monte Flat Pastoral." *Ah Sin* was "a most abject & incurable failure," as Twain finally admitted to Howells (Clemens and Howells 1960: I, 206). As a result of their failed collaboration, Harte and Twain fell out and would never reconcile.

Notoriously improvident, Harte had begun to run up debts even before his contract with Osgood expired in the spring of 1872. His friend Noah Brooks, the former associate editor of the *Overland*, recalled later that "he was continually involved in troubles that he might have escaped with a little more financial shrewdness" (Brooks 1902: 350). He was sued in New York City superior court in 1874 by the haberdashers Lord and Taylor for some $1,150, though Harte tried to evade payment on the grounds that he lived in New Jersey and earned royalties from a Massachusetts publisher, so how could a New York business garnish his income? (Harte 1997: 110–11). He was hounded by other creditors in the city, such as the proprietors of the Sturtevant House and the grocers Park and Tilford. "I hope to live to pay these bills, for they *ought to be paid*," as he allowed, but he added with characteristic illogic that "it would only plunge me in debt again to attempt to pay them now" (Harte 1997: 297). John Hay later remembered that he had "complained to Bret Harte of my lack of funds. 'Your own fault,' said the wise Argonaut. 'Why did you fool away your money paying your debts?'" (Thayer 1915: II, 402). As the result of his profligate spending, Harte was broke and living with his family nearly hand-to-mouth during the winter of 1877–8. The New York *World* noted at the time that "it is an open question as to what improvement in Mr. Harte's style would be wrought by his reduction to a state of abject penury; but the experiment of ruining him is worth trying." He begged William Waldorf Astor for a job, but to no avail (Harte 1997: 164). To the end of his life he recalled his despair during that hardscrabble winter: "I could not, and *would not under any circumstances*, again go through what I did in New York the last two years and particularly the last winter I spent there" (Harte 1926: 308). In April 1878, he finally landed on his feet: he was appointed the US Commercial Agent to Crefeld, Germany – where over the next two years he would rejuvenate his literary career. He was transferred to the Glasgow consulate in July 1880 and remained in that office until July 1885. Like many a redshirt miner in California who left behind a family in "the States," however, he would never return to the United States and, although he would support Anna Harte until his death, he would not see her again for over 20 years.

Unfortunately, Harte lost many of his American readers after he left for Europe. "They are not paying me well for my articles in America," he mused, "– nor do they seem to care much for them. The *Atlantic* don't want anything, and *Scribner* has only taken one" (Scharnhorst 1992: 1–2). He suspected that Houghton Mifflin was "swindling me," his royalty checks were so small – "less than I can get for the *translation*" rights in Germany (Harte 1997: 342). The New York *World* dismissed him as "a hack" whose career had "petered out." As the sales of his westerns waned in the United States, however, his popularity in Europe steadily grew, and Harte, ever sensitive to the nuances of the market, adjusted his style accordingly. He wrote his friend John Hay, the Assistant Secretary of State, in February 1880 that he had had no idea "of my tremendous popularity as a writer" in Germany. "My books are everywhere" (Harte 1997: 247). Harte's "Goldgräber Geschichten" were published in German translation more often during the 1870s than the work of any other American writer, and within 12 years of his introduction to German readers he "had become the most popular American author" in the country, with over 40 German editions of his works in print (Timpe 1965: 219). A columnist for *Critic* asserted in 1885 that "of all living Americans" Harte was "the best known and most read" in Germany (Rosenthal 1885: 85). "My German readers are still loyal to me," he wrote his friend Clara Schneider in 1887, "and they do not appear to be yet tired of translations of all I do" (Harte 1997: 343). As late as 1912, a decade after his death, Harte's books had appeared in more German editions than had Mark Twain's, and in 1914 they were still considered bestsellers (Fulton 1914: 56–7). Little wonder that Wallace Stegner once joked that Harte's popularity "was always greatest in direct proportion to the reader's distance from and ignorance of the mines" (1961: x).

Harte adapted to his new market by pandering to European readers' notions of the "Wild West" and by writing increasingly sensational and violent tales. As Henry Adams later wrote in his *Education*, Harte insisted on the power of sex in his stories "as far as the magazines would let him venture" (Adams 1961: 385). In the spring of 1880 he was invited by the Royal Academy in London to respond to the "Toast to Literature" – the first non-British writer to be so honored. In 1884, anticipating his dismissal from the Consular Service (he would be fired in July 1885 for "inattention to duty"), he hired a literary agent, A. P. Watt of London, who adroitly managed his career during the last 18 years of his life. "Until authors know a little more about business, or are less likely to feel that it interferes with that perfect freedom essential to literary composition," Harte wrote Watt in 1885, "it seems better that they should employ a *business man* to represent them with those other *business men*, the publishers" (Harte 1997: 323). His productivity increased dramatically after Watt began to represent him. He published a collection of Western fiction every year between 1883 and 1902, by far the bulk of his collected works. He credited Watt in 1886 not only with increasing his share of the literary market in England but with increasing the rate of payment he received: "I am quite convinced that *the commission I pay you has been fully returned by the appreciation of the market value of my work through your efforts*" (Scharnhorst 2000: 178). Though he often bemoaned the "terrible grind" of literary production, he wrote on average about 100,000 words per year in the late 1880s and early 1890s, and earned on average about $10,000 in each of these years – an income similar to the salary he was paid by Osgood & Co. in 1871–2. "I have never stood so well in regard to the *market value* of my works in any other countries as here [England]," he wrote in August 1885, and so he remained abroad even after he lost his consular appointment (Harte 1997: 330). "Just now in England there is no one who can fill a certain want as I can – or as the English publishers *think* I can," he wrote his wife Anna in October 1886, to justify remaining abroad rather than rejoining his family in the United States (Harte 1997: 339). He lived in London and regularly wrote for British magazines until his death, and his tales continued to be regularly translated into German, French, Italian, Russian, Swedish, and other languages.

Like Buffalo Bill Cody, Harte reinforced a popular if sensational mythology about the West in his signature brand of Western fiction. (Significantly, Harte befriended Cody in London in 1887, when Buffalo Bill brought his Wild West show to Earl's Court.) Certainly Harte was no literary realist in the Western stories he wrote late in his career, if ever he had been before. Howells reminisced after Harte's death that when he left California "the age of observation was past for him" (Howells 1910: 299). (Harte left his eye in San Francisco?) Bailey Millard, the book editor of the *San*

Francisco Chronicle, told Rudyard Kipling in 1889 that "Bret Harte claims California, but California don't claim Bret Harte" (Kipling 1989: 45). Similarly, Frank Norris, who parodied Harte's Western fiction in *McTeague*, "The Hero of Tomato Can," and elsewhere, declared his "great faith in the possibilities of San Francisco and Pacific Coast as offering a field for fiction," but not "the fiction of Bret Harte . . . for the country has long since outgrown the 'red shirt' period" (Scharnhorst 1993: 8). When Harte found his brand of local color Western writing fading in popularity, Mary Austin noted in 1902, "he did what he considered the only safe thing, and carried his young impression away to be worked out untroubled by any newer fact" (Austin 1902: 690). The Harvard philosopher Josiah Royce, the son of a Forty-Niner, observed in 1909 that, "as a Californian, I can say that not one childhood memory of mine suggests any social incident or situation that in the faintest degree gives meaning or confirmation to Bret Harte's stories" (1909: 233).

Virtually every Western tale Harte wrote, especially late in his career when he cranked up his production of them for newspaper syndication, was written according to a pat formula. Each one opens with a *mise-en-scène*, a description of the California climate and landscape he remembered through the veil of nostalgia. His so-called "warmed-Overland" stories often contained an ensemble of recurring characters, too, such as the physician Dr. Duchesne, who figures in 14 tales; the blustering lawyer Colonel Starbottle, a forerunner of W. C. Fields, who appears in 20 stories and a play; the stage driver Yuba Bill, who appears in 16 stories; and the gambler Jack Hamlin, who appears in 20. Late in his career, too, Harte began to write trilogies of Western novels with the same cast of characters, such as *A Waif of the Plains*, *Susy*, and *Clarence* in 1889–94, and *Chu Chu*, *The Devotion of Enriquez*, and *The Passing of Enriquez* in 1894–8. As for Harte's writing method, he once described it in terms reminiscent of Henry James's "The Art of Fiction": "I do not usually *begin* with a *plot*, but – having a few characters and a situation in my mind, – I let *them* work out the plot in *their* own lives and generally find they do it better than I can!" (Harte 1997: 437). In fact, of course, his plots usually ran along the same well-worn ruts.

In an attempt to escape "this perpetual grinding out of literary copy which is exhausting me" (Harte 1997: 361), he repeatedly tried his hand at writing plays with a Western setting. "Like the old California miner who works 'for grub,'" as he wrote his wife Anna, "I have always the hope of 'striking something' – in a play perhaps – that may lift me out of this drudgery" (Scharnhorst 2000: 194). Between 1882 and 1897 he wrote, always with a collaborator, 11 play scripts and two librettos, usually adapted from his own fiction. Harte harbored few illusions about the literary merit of these scripts, but he hoped a successful play would net him as much as $6,000 a year in royalties – far more than he might earn in literary piecework for the magazines. He also recognized his own limits: "I can write dialogue like an angel, draw character like a heaven-born genius, but I can't make *situations* and *plots*" (Harte 1926: 213). In 1895 he co-wrote the play *Sue*, based on his story "The Judgment of Bolinas Plain," with his friend T. Edgar Pemberton, the drama editor of the *Birmingham Post*. With the American actress Annie Russell in the title role of the *ingénue*, the melodrama was staged in New York in the fall of 1896, toured the eastern half of the United States in the fall and winter of 1896–7, and was produced in London in June–July 1898. It received mixed reviews in New York – Howells, for example, thought it "almost as bad in structure and false in motive as a play could very well be" (1896) – but it became a critical if not quite a commercial success in London. "It should have a better hearing here than in my own country," Harte figured, because "the London audiences and critics are not afraid of being thought *vulgar* if they like to hear of 'common' people or American subjects" (Harte 1997: 415). That is, Harte thought the Western melodrama would succeed in England for the same reasons his Western fiction remained popular there. And he was correct. The play was favorably reviewed in the *Academy* ("seldom has so good an all-round representation been witnessed on the London stage"), the *Athenaeum* ("admirably played"), the *Pall Mall Gazette* ("an object-lesson to our own actors and actresses"), and the *Speaker* ("delights by its very artlessness"). Clement Scott in the London *Daily Telegraph* pronounced Harte "a born dramatist" (Scharnhorst 1995: 188–9).

When Hamlin Garland visited Harte at his flat in Lancaster Gate in London in May 1899, he confided to his diary that the author was "affable and polite but looked old and burnt out, his eyes clouded, his skin red and flabby" (1968: 143). Harte was already suffering from the throat cancer that would kill him in May 1902; but he continued to write literally to the end of his life. After his health began to fail he tried desperately to provide a nest-egg for his family. He published 27 stories and earned about $17,000 during the final two years of his life. At his death, his friend Henry Adams declared he had been one of "the most brilliant men of my time" (Adams 1938: 391).

It was not an opinion that was widely shared by Harte's contemporaries. His personal and literary reputation suffered irreparably over the years as the result of his feud with his former friend Twain. When Harte was rumored to be in line for his initial diplomatic appointment to Crefeld, Twain tried to prevent it. He urged Howells, whose wife was related to Rutherford B. Hayes, to intercede with the new President and so

> prevent the disgrace of literature & the country which would be the infallible result of the appointment of Bret Harte to any responsible post. Wherever he goes his wake is tumultuous with swindled grocers, & with defrauded innocents who have loaned him money. He *never* pays a debt but by the squeezing of the law. He borrows from all new acquaintances, & repays none. His oath is worth little, his promise nothing at all. He can lie faster than he can drivel false pathos. He is always steeped in whisky & brandy; he gets up in the night to drink it cold. No man who has ever known him respects him. (Murphy 1985: 89–90)

Little wonder that, two years later, Howells would model the character of the scoundrel Bartley Hubbard on Harte (even to the initials B. H.). Yet, to his credit,

Howells also *helped* rather than hindered Harte's campaign for the appointment. He wrote Hayes that while Harte "is notorious for borrowing and *was* notorious for drinking," he "never borrowed of *me*, nor drank more than I (in my presence)." The job "would be a godsend to him," Howells added, because "he has had a terrible lesson in falling from the highest prosperity to the lowest adversity in literature" (Howells 1928: I, 251–2).

Harte received the appointment, but Twain did not temper his criticism. Interviewed in Australia as late as 1895, Twain vented his anger at Harte in a well-publicized comment:

> I detest him, because I think his work is "shoddy." His forte is pathos, but there should be no pathos which does not come out of a man's heart. He has no heart, except his name, and I consider he has produced nothing that is genuine. He is artificial. That opinion, however, must be taken with some allowance, for, as I say, I do not care for the man. (Shillingsburg 1988: 32)

Twain fulminated against Harte most famously in his autobiographical dictation in 1907, five years after Harte's death. "I think he was incapable of emotion, for I think he had nothing to feel with. I think his heart was merely a pump and had no other function. . . . He was bad, distinctly bad; he had no feeling, and he had no conscience," he declared (Clemens 1940: 265, 272). Predictably, many Twain scholars over the years have sided against Harte in depicting the Twain–Harte feud. For example, Bernard De Voto once described him as "a literary charlatan whose tales have greatly pleased the second-rate" (1932: 164). Under the circumstances, who dared to hint that Harte was more aggrieved than Twain in their dispute?

*

After his death, in short, Harte's literary reputation was up for grabs. Predictably, his passing was mourned in England more than in the United States. The London *Spectator*, for example, asserted that he had "probably exerted a greater influence on English literature than any other American author" (*Spectator* 1902); while the New York *Nation* editorialized that during his long and prolific career Harte had apparently never "received a new impression" or "made a new observation" (*Nation* 1902), the young G. K. Chesterton lamented the passing of "a genuine humorist" (1902: 179). Harte did not so much found a school of disciples as a host of imitators, including Damon Runyon and O. Henry. Julian Hawthorne and Leonard Lemmon in *American Literature: An Elementary Textbook* (1891) praised Harte as "a brilliant innovator" who spoke in "a new voice" (1891: 244, 247). Fred Lewis Pattee echoed the point in his *History of American Literature*: Harte's early stories "were work of literary art worthy to be compared with the rarest product of American genius" (1903: 398). Brander Matthews asserted that Harte "had a finer sense of form" than Dickens (1907: 253). Several successful theatrical and motion-picture adaptations of Harte's stories were produced early in the twentieth century. The play *Salomy Jane*, based on Harte's tale "Salomy Jane's Kiss," was a Broadway hit in 1907. This horse opera in turn inspired a number of feature films – a total of at least 24 movies produced between 1909 and 1955 starring such actors as Douglas Fairbanks, Mary Pickford, and Ronald Reagan.

Harte was clearly at the height of his modern popularity during the second quarter of the twentieth century. His commodification as a literary property, the appeal of his brand of regional fiction, was epitomized in the 1920s as Tuolumne and Calaveras counties came to be known as "Bret Harte country"; and with the construction of State Highway 108 the small town of Twain-Harte, near the goldfield Harte briefly worked in 1857, became a popular tourist attraction with an annual Bret Harte Pageant. "Of all the Californias that men have invented for their delight or their profit," the travel writer Mildred Adams observed in 1930, "Bret Harte's is the most charming" (Adams 1930: 11–12). Though excoriated by the New Critics in the 1940s and 1950s for his stilted dialogue, confused plots, sentimental tone, and incoherent symbolism, Harte, like a monster in a Saturday matinee, never seems to stay buried.

References and Further Reading

Adams, Henry (1938). *Letters of Henry Adams, 1892–1918*, ed. Worthington Chauncey Ford. Boston and New York: Houghton Mifflin.

Adams, Henry (1961). *The Education of Henry Adams*. Boston: Houghton Mifflin. (First publ. 1918.)

Adams, Mildred (1930). "Glamour Clings to Bret Harte's Hills." *New York Times Magazine*, 31 Aug., 12–13.

Athenaeum (London) (1879). "Novels of the Week," 22 March, 375.

Austin, Mary (1902). "Jimtown: a Bret Harte Town." *Atlantic Monthly* 90, 690–3.

Booth, Bradford (1954). "Mark Twain's Comments on Bret Harte's Stories." *American Literature* 25 (Jan.), 492–5.

Bowles, Samuel (1867). "Books, Authors, and Art." *Springfield Republican*, 16 Jan., 1.

Bowles, Samuel (1868). "Two Rising Monthlies." *Springfield Republican*, 30 Sept., 2.

Brooks, Noah (1902). "Harte's Early Days." *New York Times Saturday Review of Books*, 24 May, 350.

Carew, Kate (1901). "Kate Carew's 12-minute Interview on 12 Subjects with Bret Harte." New York *World*, 22 Dec., 5.

Chesterton, G. K. (1902). *Varied Types*. New York: Dodd, Mead.

Chopin, Kate (1900). "Development of the Literary West." *St Louis Republic*, Sunday magazine, 9 Dec., 1.

Clemens, Samuel L. [Mark Twain] (1940). *Mark Twain in Eruption*, ed. Bernard De Voto. New York and London: Harper.

Clemens, Samuel L. (1990). *Mark Twain's Letters, 1867–1868*, ed. Harriet Elinor Smith and Richard Bucci. Berkeley, Los Angeles, and London: University of California Press.

Clemens, Samuel L. (1995). *Mark Twain's Letters, 1870–1871*, ed. Victor Fischer and Michael B. Frank. Berkeley, Los Angeles, and London: University of California Press.

Clemens, Samuel L., and Howells, W. D. (1960). *Mark Twain–Howells Letters, 1872–1910.*, ed. Henry Nash Smith and William M. Gibson. Cambridge, Mass.: Belknap.

Dam, Henry J. W. (1894). "A Morning with Bret Harte." *McClure's* 4 (Dec.), 38–50.

De Voto, Bernard (1932). *Mark Twain's America*. Boston: Little, Brown.

Ellis, Havelock (1890). *The New Spirit*. London: George Bell & Sons.

Fulton, Robert (1914). "Glimpses of the Mother Lode." *Bookman* 39: iii, 49–57.

Garland, Hamlin (1968). *Hamlin Garland's Diaries*, ed. Donald Pizer. San Marino: Huntington Library.

Harte, Bret (1870). "Preface." In *The Luck of Roaring Camp and Other Sketches*. Boston: Fields, Osgood.

Harte, Bret (1882). "General Introduction." In *The Works of Bret Harte*, vol. II, ix–xxv). London: Chatto & Windus.

Harte, Bret (1899). "The Rise of the 'Short Story.'" *Cornhill*, 7 (July), 1–8.

Harte, Bret (1926). *The Letters of Bret Harte*, ed. Geoffrey Bret Harte. Boston and New York: Houghton Mifflin.

Harte, Bret (1990). *Bret Harte's California: Letters to the* Springfield Republican *and* Christian Register, *1866–67*, ed. Gary Scharnhorst. Albuquerque: University of New Mexico Press.

Harte, Bret (1997). *Selected Letters of Bret Harte*, ed. Gary Scharnhorst. Norman, Okla., and London: University of Oklahoma Press.

Harte, Bret (2001). *The Luck of Roaring Camp and Other Writings*, ed. Gary Scharnhorst. New York: Penguin.

Hawthorne, Julian, and Lemmon, Leonard (1891). *American Literature: An Elementary Text-book*. New York: Heath.

Houghton Mifflin records, Houghton Library, Harvard University.

Howells, Mildred (1928). *Life in Letters of William Dean Howells*. Garden City: Doubleday.

Howells, W. D. (1896). "Life and Letters." *Harper's Weekly*, 10 Oct., 998.

Howells, W. D. (1901). *Heroines of Literature*. New York and London: Harper.

Howells, W. D. (1910). *Literary Friends and Acquaintance*. New York and London: Harper.

James, Henry (1974). *Henry James Letters 1843–1875*, ed. Leon Edel. Cambridge, Mass.: Belknap.

Kipling, Rudyard (1989). *Kipling in California*, ed. Thomas Pinney. Berkeley: Bancroft Library.

Matthews, Brander (1907). *The Short Story*. New York: American Book Co.

Murphy, Francis (1985). "The End of a Friendship: Two Unpublished Letters from Twain to Howells about Bret Harte." *New England Quarterly* 58, 87–91.

Nation (1902). "Bret Harte," 26 June, 502–3.

New York Herald (1876). "Amusements," 29 Aug., 5.

New York Times (1876). "The Two Men of Sandy Bar," 29 Aug., 5.

North American Review (1871). "Harte's Poems." 112, 234–5.

Overland Monthly (1883). "The Overland Dinner." Supplement, 1–16.

Pattee, Fred Lewis (1903). *A History of American Literature: A Textbook*. New York: Silver, Burdett.

Rosenthal, Lewis (1885). "Bret Harte in Germany." *Critic*, 21 Feb., 85–6.

Royce, Josiah (1909). "Provincialism: Based upon a Study of Early Conditions in California." *Putnam's* 7, 233–4.

Scharnhorst, Gary (1992). *Bret Harte*. New York: Twayne.

Scharnhorst, Gary (1993). "Harte, Norris, and 'The Hero of Tomato Can.'" *Frank Norris Studies* 15, 8–10.

Scharnhorst, Gary (1995). *Bret Harte: A Bibliography*. Lanham, Md.: Scarecrow.

Scharnhorst, Gary (1996). "'Ways that are Dark': Appropriations of Bret Harte's 'Plain Language from Truthful James.'" *Nineteenth-Century Literature* 51, 377–99.

Scharnhorst, Gary (2000). *Bret Harte: Opening the American Literary West*. Norman, Okla., and London: University of Oklahoma Press.

Scudder, Horace (1882). "Harte's Sketches and Stories." *Atlantic Monthly* 3, 264–8.

Sherwood, Mary E. W. (1902). "Bret Harte." *New York Times Saturday Review of Literature*, 10 May, 308.

Shillingsburg, Miriam (1988). *At Home Abroad: Mark Twain in Australasia*. Jackson: University Press of Mississippi.

Spectator (1902). "News of the Week," 10 May, 715.

Stegner, Wallace (1961). "Introduction." In *The Outcasts of Poker Flat and Other Tales*, vii–xvi. New York: Signet.

Taylor, Bayard (1870). "Through to the Pacific." *New York Tribune*, 5 Aug., 2.

Thayer, William Roscoe (1915). *The Life and Letters of John Hay*. Boston and New York: Houghton Mifflin.

Timpe, Eugene T. (1965). "Bret Harte's German Public." *Jahrbuch für Amerikastudien* 10, 215–20.

Zion's Herald (1870). "Our Book Table," 12 May, 572.

Mark Twain: A Man for All Regions

Lawrence I. Berkove

There can be no doubt that Mark Twain qualifies as a regionalist writer; but the question is, "which region?" Almost every other regionalist writer is associated with just one specific region, but Mark Twain has an embarrassment of riches in this regard: a variety of regions can lay legitimate claim to him. He was born in Florida, Missouri, and raised in Hannibal, Missouri, and can therefore be considered either a Southern or a Midwestern author. He was a pilot on the Mississippi River, and so can again qualify as either a Southern or Mississippi valley author. He worked and wrote in Nevada and California, and may be legitimately classified as a Western, Rocky Mountain, Southwestern, or Comstock author. He visited and wrote about Hawaii, another region. He lived briefly in Buffalo, NY, and spent many productive summers in Elmira, NY, and he lived for two decades in Connecticut, and so can be claimed by New York or New England. And, like Henry James, he has impressive qualifications as an American international author. As a consequence of this unusual mobility and the growth that resulted from it, while Twain cannot be adequately comprehended and appreciated without taking regional influences into consideration, neither can he be restricted to any one region. In the final analysis he amalgamated what he learned from all of them into his own, transcendent style and into his unique philosophy.

The Matter of Hannibal

Not long ago, what Henry Nash Smith called the "Matter of Hannibal" (1967: 72) – the experiences and information he acquired as a result of growing up in his home town – was considered *the* main source of Twain's roots, and it still is and always will be *a* main source. The years of his childhood and young manhood certainly left a lasting impression on him. It is clear that he acquired a keen sense of place in Hannibal, not just of its landscape, but also of its culture, people, vernacular, and mores. *The Adventures of Tom Sawyer* (1876) and *Huckleberry Finn* (1885) immortalized

Hannibal and its vicinity in the 1840s, at least as it would have appeared to a boy. So clearly visualized is the fictional town of St. Petersburg that visitors to Hannibal today who tour the preserved buildings (including Twain's home) of its historic section, and the nearby cave described in *Tom Sawyer*, often have a feeling of *déjà vu*.

Rising up behind Tom Sawyer's house is what the novel calls Cardiff Hill, to whose summit Tom climbed. From that vantage point can be seen the Mississippi river to the east and, across the river, the flat countryside of Illinois. It is still a lovely view; but however young Sam Clemens experienced it, it was an important memory for Mark Twain, for it fed his lifelong sensitivity to the unreliability of appearances. The Missouri of the 1840s was a slave state – Twain knew people who owned slaves, and also slaves themselves – and Illinois was a free state. When one looked across the river from Cardiff Hill, therefore, it was almost like glimpsing another country, a place with very different laws.

A question often asked by readers of *Huckleberry Finn*, therefore, is why Jim didn't just cross the river and escape to friendly territory, instead of teaming up with Huck and rafting south on the Mississippi in the hope of catching a steamboat at Cairo, the town at the southern tip of Illinois, that would go to Cincinnati, an outpost of liberal politics and the underground railroad on the Ohio river. The answer is that while Illinois was legally a free state, the inhabitants of its western and southern portions were more in sympathy with slavery than was the liberal majority population of Chicago and the state's northern and central sections. If Jim had crossed the river, he would have been almost sure to be caught by bounty hunters and returned. In fact, this is made clear in chapter 11 of *Huckleberry Finn*, when Mrs. Judith Loftus tells Huck that her husband is out with friends looking for an escaped slave. Mrs. Loftus's sympathetic willingness to help Huck, whom she assumed was a runaway apprentice, was also strictly speaking illegal as well as at variance with what her husband would have done, and the novel's understated glimpse of this woman's independent mind symbolically reflects the conflict of conscience that, well before the Civil War, was already creating social turmoil in the area and would soon divide communities and even families against themselves.[1]

The freedom or security that the Illinois shore seemed to offer, therefore, was illusory. Whether or not young Sam Clemens realized this has not been determined, but without question Mark Twain was fully aware of it. It was one of many illusions of which he became aware as he reflected on the "Matter of Hannibal," and it undoubtedly contributed to the layered style of writing he cultivated and mastered, in which the surface plot and the deeper thematic levels run in different directions, often counter to each other, for appearances are often deceitful in his books and illusion is a major theme in them.

For Twain, as was the case with many "realistic" writers of the Old Southwest, romanticism was practically identified with illusion. Unlike those other writers, however, who tended to eschew romanticism entirely or to set it up as an obvious target, Twain first mastered romanticism and used it, and only then undercut it. As a result, generations of Twain readers have picked up the surface romantic level of his

Figure 28.1 Mark Twain at his childhood home, Hannibal, 1902.

books and been largely unaware that it was meant to cloak what was really happening. In *Huckleberry Finn*, for example, the theme of freedom is an illusion. Once Huck and Jim's raft passes Cairo, it thenceforth has slave territory on both sides and with every minute drifts ever more deeply south, toward New Orleans and its infamous slave market. The expectation that Jim will find freedom by going south towards the place he dreads most is unrealistic; only a romantic would write a book that requires a miracle to save its heroes, and Twain most definitely was not a romantic.[2]

Twain pessimistically regarded the hopes that manumission or emancipation could provide solutions to slavery as illusions. For one thing, he knew the mindset of slave states too well to think that those measures would work. The issue of slavery in *Huckleberry Finn*, in fact, is itself somewhat of an illusion. The Civil War had ended legal slavery; Twain did not waste novels on dead targets, and legal slavery was a dead target in 1884. What *was* happening in the South in the mid-1880s, however, was the proliferation of Jim Crow laws whose purpose was to re-impose social, political, and legal discrimination on blacks that would so circumscribe the freedoms that had been granted them by the 13th amendment to the Constitution (1865) as to practically negate them. In addition, the South had begun implementing the convict-lease system, by which blacks who were convicted, sometimes for trifling infractions, were given long prison sentences and then leased out to employers as laborers under conditions which resembled their former slavery. This process of practically reconstituting slavery through legal legerdemain is what Twain attacked in *Huckleberry Finn*. He did it circumspectly but powerfully through the novel's grim parodies of means the South was using to subvert the 13th amendment, but mostly through his use of the pre-Civil War category of "free man of color" (f.m.c.) that had applied to manumitted slaves.

The nub of the issue was that freed slaves were not "free." In all the slave states, f.m.c.s labored under a host of legal restrictions that made their freedom what Twain later called in *Connecticut Yankee* "a sarcasm of law and phrase." Generally, they could not vote, bear arms, testify in a court of law, work at certain occupations, or even travel at will (Berkove 1968: 307–8). Readers of *Huckleberry Finn* who think that because Jim has been manumitted at the conclusion of the book he is free are therefore hoaxed, as is he – and as, for that matter, are Huck and Tom. Jim becomes not a free man but an f.m.c. At its deepest level *Huckleberry Finn* has a tragic instead of a happy ending. Its tragedy is that the appearance but not the substance of a change has taken place. Jim's manumission will bring no practical improvement to him, as emancipation was proving to make almost no difference to the black freedmen of the post-Civil War South. Twain, along with the South's other two leading authors, George Washington Cable and Joel Chandler Harris, saw quite clearly what was happening, and attacked it (Berkove 1980). The subtlety and indirection of *Huckleberry Finn*'s conclusion was partly tactical, for an open indictment of the corrupt deception of the system which falsely professed to extend freedom to the freed slaves would have made the book openly polemical and so less appealing. More importantly, however, more obvious social criticism in the novel would have skewed Twain's main point, for his opposition to black slavery and to its practical restoration was a consequence of his deeper hatred of any kind of slavery, and Twain believed that *all* humans were slaves (Berkove 1993).

This belief was the consequence of Twain's theological orientation, and that theology was the second (and more powerful and far-reaching) reason why Twain was pessimistic about the possibility of freedom for any humans. Hannibal was where Sam Clemens received instruction in the religion whose doctrines he wished as an adult to reject but could not extirpate from his convictions. They remained deep within him for the rest of his life and central to his writing. The religion was frontier and fundamentalist Calvinism, a severe and gloomy creed that affirmed the corruption of human nature by sin, and predestination, usually to hell or, rarely, to heaven. Specific biographical information about this aspect of his education is presently scant, but what he absorbed is evidenced in his notes and journals, his correspondence, and some of his autobiographical pieces, but especially in his fiction. For example, a quiet and largely overlooked comment in chapter 5 of *Tom Sawyer*, describing Tom's attendance at church, gets to the core of it: "The minister gave out his text and droned along monotonously through an argument that was so prosy that many a head by and by began to nod – and yet it was an argument that dealt in limitless fire and brimstone and thinned the predestined elect down to a company so small as to be hardly worth the saving."

Tom did not pay much attention to the theology of the sermon, but Sam Clemens did, and echoes of it reverberate in almost all of Twain's works. The significance of this is simple but startling: if humans are predestined, they are not free. Since all humans, Calvinism taught, are predestined, it follows that no one is free: whites no more than blacks, rich and seemingly powerful no more than poor and weak. Human freedom, therefore, is indeed illusory. Even more, it is deceptive (Berkove 1992). Although Twain disparaged this theology early and late, he was unable to extinguish his belief in it (Wecter 1952: 88). As much as he hated it, it made sense to him, and its doctrines typically supply the themes that unify his works and drive them. No line, therefore, in all of Twain's writings is so profoundly and pessimistically ironic as Tom's ringing command regarding Jim in chapter 42: "Turn him loose! he ain't no slave, he's as free as any cretur that walks this earth!" Ironically, as Twain saw it, Jim *was* as free as any man in this world – but only because no man was free. The gloomy consequences of this belief underlie almost all of Twain's literature from at least *Roughing It* (1872) on.

Hannibal in the 1840s was close to the frontier, and Twain retained many memories of the hustling development projects and get-rich-quick schemes that attended the settling of the land. His early novel, *The Gilded Age* (1873), famously named the era in America's history during which the conspiracies of government and private enterprise resulted in the wheeling and dealing that determined where railroads and river dredges and therefore new towns would go, and which development plans got funded. In the character of Colonel Beriah Sellers Twain brilliantly memorialized the extravagant optimism of an archetypal visionary of the period, but the novel also contains biting portraits of individuals who either are unscrupulous by nature or lose their virtue when they succumb to temptation. Frontier states like Missouri (as well as Washington DC, which figures in the novel and in which Twain also lived for some months), seen this time from the perspective of adulthood rather than that of young children, show Twain to have been a sophisticated and ironic observer of how governmental policies were often determined by lobbyists representing moneyed interests which had little regard for the public weal.

Yet one more feature of the "Matter of Hannibal" that is responsible for one of Twain's monumental literary achievements is the vernacular of the region. Young Sam Clemens was perfectly at home in the language of the uncultivated townspeople, farmers, rivermen, and slaves of the region, and took pleasure in mastering its varieties and pungency. While still in his formative years, he also read the dialect humorists of New England, the Midwest, and the Old Southwest, such as Benjamin P. Shillaber, Seba Smith, David Ross Locke, George Washington Harris, Augustus Baldwin Longstreet, and Johnson Jones Hooper, and realized that vernacular had potentialities that extended beyond local color and literary realism. *Huckleberry Finn*, entirely written in the language of a poorly educated Missouri boy, established for all time that great literature could be fashioned out of vernacular; that "substandard" language could represent intelligence and complexity of character, and achieve precision and depth. Huck not only turns his own linguistic handicaps into advantages, but also replicates these achievements in the vernaculars he captures when he recounts the words of the rest of the characters of the book: Jim, Miss Watson, the raftsmen of chapter 16, the Grangerfords, the King and the Duke, Uncle Silas Phelps, and Tom Sawyer. Today, there is not a country in the world whose authors do not follow the trail that Twain broke, in that remarkable novel, away from formal literary language.

The Matter of the River

Twain's piloting years on the Mississippi River, 1857–61, took him back and forth between St. Louis and New Orleans, and gave him a sense of America's heartland, another major regional influence.[3] Comprising what is called "the Matter of the River" (Smith 1967: 72), they constitute his second formative period. During these years Twain clearly stocked up on vivid impressions of life and people that he used for the rest of his career. A brief return to the river in 1882, this time as a steamboat passenger, refreshed those impressions and added some new ones. *Life on the Mississippi* (1883), a cornucopia of vignettes, memoirs of the golden years of Mississippi river steamboating, subsequent philosophical reflections, and authorial self-revelations, is the book *par excellence* that records Twain's experiences in this region (Kruse 1981). Although a few of the book's famous passages derive from writings by another author,[4] *Life on the Mississippi* is without doubt an essential book for a knowledge of Twain.

Chapter 38, for example, "The House Beautiful," is his sarcastic description of the standardized exterior and interior decorations of the typical "best dwelling" of every town and village along the river. In chapter 17 of *Huckleberry Finn*, Huck describes the same sort of house but from the admiring perspective of a naïve boy who is seeing it all for the first time. The novel's bloody Grangerford–Shepherdson feud (chapter 18) has its origin in the Darnell–Watson feud outlined in chapter 26 of *Life on the Mississippi*. The typical Twainian theme of illusion is overtly represented at least twice in the course of the travel book: once at the end of chapter 9, where Twain unforgettably contrasts a picturesque sunset scene on the Mississippi from the opposing perspectives of one who sees it romantically, as a thing of beauty, and of a steamboat pilot, to whom all its lovely touches are ominous signs; and again in chapter 52, "A Burning Brand," where an ungrammatical but eloquent letter of repentance turns out to be a skillful swindle. Twain's skepticism about the depth of sudden moral reform, implied in that letter, is repeated in chapter 5 of *Huckleberry Finn*, where Huck's father solemnly swears to renounce liquor forever and convinces a lenient judge of his conversion – for one day. During the night, pap sneaks out of the judge's house and gets drunk again.

On the river, Twain received an education in human nature from the variety of types he encountered. When Colonel Sherburn, in chapter 22 of *Huckleberry Finn*, faces down the crowd that has come to punish him for shooting poor Boggs, and says "I was born and raised in the South, and I've lived in the North; so I know the average all around," the authority for that statement undoubtedly came from what Twain had learned on the river about his countrymen. He had seen proud and courageous men, like Sherburn, who were also heartlessly deadly, and mobs of men who, even when they had a just cause, were still cowards. In *Pudd'nhead Wilson* (1894), Twain created the small river town of Dawson's Landing, whose residents were mostly unsophisticated and not nearly as virtuous as they thought themselves to be. At a time when small towns were still being idealized, Twain recognized that they were often closed societies, too unselfcritical and complacent about their limitations, and too conducive of oppressive conformity. In his portrayals of the slave Roxy and her son, Twain created a most damning indictment of small-minded small-town environments, and of how character can be warped and injustice perpetuated by them.

Twain came to understand that human nature doesn't vary from place to place, or change over time. Sailing up and down the river, Twain observed the dynamics of small-town society and studied the characters of the profane but dedicated rivermen he worked with: he saw sincere but shallow clergymen, con artists, eminent personalities, mean-spirited and spiteful individuals posing as good citizens, and simple and trusting souls. No matter how different were the clothes, customs, and dialects of the people, places, and eras Twain later wrote about, to some degree they all had their origins in the Mississippi river communities he had earlier assimilated.

But when he said, in chapter 14 of *Life on the Mississippi*, that he loved the piloting profession "far better than any I have followed since," that avowal must be taken with a grain of salt, for he followed it with an even more extravagant claim: "a pilot . . . was the only unfettered and entirely independent human being that lived in the earth." Twain was given, both earlier and later in his life, to making such sweeping generalizations when he was satisfied (always temporarily) with his state of affairs; for at no point in his life did Twain ever believe that any human being was completely free. In the journals and diaries from his piloting days, Twain records recurrent nightmares of danger and catastrophe on the river.[5] A pilot had awesome responsibilities, and precisely because Twain was a good and responsible pilot he was not free from the pressures and stresses of his work. In addition, the theological beliefs about predestination embedded in him by his Hannibal boyhood denied freedom. It was, to him, an illusion. He loved the idea of it, but in his more sober and contemplative moods he was convinced that it was only an illusion.

The Matter of the West

With the advent of the Civil War and the closing of the Mississippi river to civilian traffic, Twain's piloting career came to an end and he entered the Western phase of his training in regionalism, what might by analogy be called "the Matter of the West." Although he later claimed he went West for a three-month vacation (*Roughing It*, ch. 1), it is more likely that he was fleeing the Civil War. In his "Private History of a Campaign that Failed" (1885), Twain recounts his brief adventures as an irregular soldier for the Confederate cause.[6] In the sketch, he claims that his loyalties vacillated between the Union and the Confederacy and that his decision to become a rebel was somewhat impulsive. If so, Twain was – like many others from the border states regions – deeply torn between loyalties to their communities and to a larger ideal. The opportunity to travel to Nevada with his brother, who was a Union man, saved him from being forced into military life. Nevada was a mining region, and its gold and silver production was so badly needed by the Union that the draft did not affect the residents of the territory. If Twain did indeed intend to be away for only three months, that period of time was probably designated because it was widely believed that the war would be over by the end of it and all matters settled. On the contrary: in three months the war was just gathering momentum; but after three months in Nevada, Twain had come to like the territory and decided to stay. It was a fateful decision.

Twain's first job was as secretary to his brother, who had been appointed Secretary of the Nevada Territory, but the work seemed tame compared to the possibilities of discovering a rich claim of gold or silver. So he tried his hand at prospecting, but found it much harder work than he had imagined, and unprofitable. When he wasn't working he wrote humorous, often ironic, articles which he sent to local papers. One of them, Virginia City's *Territorial Enterprise*, was favorably impressed by his submissions, and offered him a job. He accepted, and was launched upon the writing career that ultimately brought him fame.

As a reporter on the *Enterprise*, Twain entered fully upon the last of his three great formative periods, his Western years. As was also the case in Hannibal and the Mississippi river valley, Twain was instantly attracted to the piquantly eloquent vernacular of the region, and gloried in the literary potentialities of what most local colorists had merely treated as picturesque speech. He also had an opportunity to observe his fellow humans in action away from the regulating influences of established society, religion, and law. The West was the quintessence of the romantic attraction of the American frontier; it promised, in a sense, a new Utopia. What Twain found beyond the romance, however, was oddly in accord with what Hawthorne had earlier recognized in the opening lines of *The Scarlet Letter*: "The founders of a new colony, whatever Utopia of human virtue and happiness they might originally project, have invariably recognized it among their earliest practical necessities to allot a portion of the virgin soil as a cemetery, and another portion as the site of a prison." The influence upon Twain of the West was profound, and it additionally pulled together everything he already learned or been exposed to.

Having to write about what was going on in the mining community induced him to observe it closely and thoughtfully. What he saw was an immense commercial and industrial enterprise – the development of the silver and gold mines of the Comstock

Lode – being directed by a few visionary but sometimes ruthless men, and carried out by thousands of workers who put their lives in jeopardy for either high salaries or the hope of wealth. He saw rapidly growing towns and a new state in the Union in the process of formation, and saw that many of the legislators and public officials were not particularly well educated, bright, competent, or honest. He saw violence and even murder go unpunished and unchecked, deceit rampant, and corruption rife even among judges and sworn juries. Given his already ironic inclination, he was struck by the gap between appearance and reality, between truth and conventional wisdom. Once he saw it so clearly on the Comstock, he realized that he had seen it all along in his earlier years, and he began to reinterpret his previous experiences. It only remained for him to find some way to express it.

He was helped toward this end by the remarkable and exceptionally talented men who worked on the *Territorial Enterprise*. Under the leadership of the owner and publisher, Joseph Thompson Goodman, an individual of extraordinary integrity and courage, the *Enterprise* was respected both for the excellence and reliability of its coverage of mining news (the main item of interest on the Comstock) and for the independence of its editorial positions. Its independence derived from the fact that, almost alone among Nevada newspapers, it did not need the patronage of either the mining companies or government, and was therefore under no obligation to any outside influences (Goodman 1997: 2). The newspaper staff took their lead from Goodman and were given free rein by him to say whatever they wished, provided only that it was accurate and that they were prepared to personally stand behind what they wrote. Most of them were bold and forthright but also moral individuals, and also among the best writers west of the Mississippi; and they were fiercely pro-Union in their sentiments. They liked Twain and inspired, trained, and supported him. He needed that support, for he sometimes antagonized Nevadans by his ironies. It is hard to imagine where else he might have gone and whom else he might have met that would have been so compatible with his own emerging ideals and goals. He assimilated his environment happily, and rapidly rose to eminence in it.

His main mentor was the slightly older but much more experienced and, at that stage of his life, more accomplished colleague Dan De Quille, whom Twain found to be a kindred spirit. The two men became room-mates and engaged in friendly rivalry in the pages of the *Enterprise*, including some rather sharp bantering in which they honed their wits against each other. Like De Quille, Twain was not as bluntly confrontational as Goodman or some of the other writers; his métier was humor, particularly ironic humor. De Quille helped Twain improve the talent for humor he already had, to make it more versatile and subtle, and he also provided Twain with examples of what he himself had already written that served Twain as models and material he could use for his own work (Berkove 1999: 36–40). Twain was a very fast learner and made rapid progress toward perfecting his layered style of writing. His humor sugar-coated his observations, and his irony rendered part of what he said invisible to those not alert enough to recognize it; but beneath these stylistic wrappings Twain was a cutting critic of the coarseness, pretense, and immorality that were so common on the Comstock. Here he learned to see through the illusion of respectability and custom, to respond to it morally, and to cloak his criticisms with subtle irony and satire.

Another mentor was Artemus Ward, who visited the Comstock in late December 1863 and gave a series of enormously popular lectures. Ward, of course, was not a Westerner at all. He had been born and raised in Maine, and achieved prominence first as a writer for the Cleveland *Plain Dealer* and then as a traveling lecturer. Ward either invented or perfected an original lecture style: drolly delivered and seemingly discursive, ranging over a wide variety of topics without ever addressing its announced topic, but actually subtly focused by means of indirection. Its unity derived from the fact that Ward returned to certain themes upon which he seemed to stumble in individual sections of his discourse. Thus, although he seldom or never made his themes explicit in any separate item, he almost subliminally organized his routine by controlling his recurrences to what he intended to be his main points. This was done with consummate artistry, and Ward was enormously successful in tours both in the United States and England, leaving audiences dazzled and enchanted by his routines.

When Ward appeared on the Comstock in December 1863, he took it by storm — and was also so taken by it that he extended his stay. He got along especially well with the staff of the *Enterprise*, and he never had a more intensely attentive listener than Mark Twain. Twain, by all accounts, spent as much time as he could in Ward's presence, drinking in Ward's style, studying it, and eventually comprehending and assimilating it. Twain ultimately was able to do in prose as well as in lecture what Ward had done only in lecture: give the impression that he was rambling aimlessly while in reality he was in complete control of his material and skillfully directing it. What must have made Ward's technique especially attractive to Twain was that it was congruous with his established bent toward the hoax; it was, in fact, a species of hoax.

Indeed, probably the main lesson Twain learned on the Comstock was how to hoax his readers. The hoax, although not a Comstock monopoly, was somewhat of a Comstock specialty. Every day, in all walks of life, naïve individuals were being deceived by hoaxes that ranged from practical jokes to serious misrepresentations of commercial ventures or legal issues. The essence of any hoax is to make something improbable or impossible seem plausible, and hoaxes always depend on credulous victims who accept what they hear or see at face value. Immersed in a culture in which hoaxes were so common, it was natural that Comstock writers learned to incorporate them into their literature. De Quille was a past master at the hoax, although always either in a kindly way or for a moral purpose, and Twain first learned to match him (albeit more acerbically) and then ultimately to surpass him. Considering that almost all of Twain's major writings have hoaxes at their core, it is difficult to overestimate the importance to him of the Comstock experience, for it was here that he mastered what became his central literary technique.

Twain ran afoul of the law when he injudiciously challenged another Comstock journalist to a duel, and was obliged to quit Nevada for California. There he subsequently worked for newspapers in San Francisco and Sacramento, while also serving as an *Enterprise* correspondent. He continued to be critical of local injustice and discrimination, and to write with brilliant and sometimes audacious irony and sarcasm. California was less tolerant of his sharpness than Nevada had been (though without the support that Goodman and the *Enterprise* gave him, Nevada also would have been less congenial), and Twain found it prudent to leave San Francisco for a time and visit Tuolumne and Calaveras counties, gold-mining areas on the western slopes of the Sierra Nevada mountains. Staying with friends, he listened attentively to the jokes and humorous tales told by local miners, and recognized them as oral gold which he could polish and use in his own writings. The most famous of these tales was "Jim Smiley and His Jumping Frog," which he converted to written form in 1865. The story became a runaway success, was quickly published all over the country, and made Twain a celebrity. The tale, one of the most subtly brilliant he ever wrote, is a nested series of hoaxes, with both humorous and serious levels (Messent 1995). Jim Smiley is hoaxed, but so are Smiley's dog Andrew Jackson, his frog Dan'l Webster, and the narrator – and the reader. The story also is one of Twain's earliest uses of the mysterious stranger motif, which recurs frequently in his oeuvre, most famously and ominously in the *Mysterious Stranger* manuscripts.

Another California influence on Twain was Bret Harte, whose highly successful short stories in the local color mode Twain studied closely when they came out in 1868–69. According to Bradford Booth, Twain especially noted the accuracy of Harte's rendition of vernacular and portrayal of character, and his skill with language.

In 1866 the Sacramento *Union* commissioned Twain to travel to the Sandwich Islands (Hawaii) as a correspondent. He found much to love and enjoy about those idyllic islands, then still an independent kingdom, but he also recognized that European and American immigrants, particularly missionaries, were fundamentally destroying native Hawaiian culture and replacing it with their own. It was not that he romantically idealized Hawaiian culture – for he knew that it had been bloody, loaded with superstitious taboos, and given to human sacrifice – but that he knew that Europe and the New World culture derived from it had its own even bloodier record of wars and persecution, and in addition was introducing Hawaiians to what Twain considered morally pernicious beliefs in pervasive and unforgivable sin and in inevitable and eternal damnation.

How to consistently represent his own values *against* the general moral consensus was a quandary he contrived to solve in *Roughing It* (1872), the book which fictionally embellished his travels in the American West and Hawaii. The problem was a delicate one, for to openly attack European-American and Christian values from the perspective of his own heretical views would have been to alienate his readership. He managed it mainly by using Artemus Ward's technique of the hoax by indirection in a perfected form, extended beyond any model that Twain encountered on the Comstock. This is made clear in a letter Twain wrote to De Quille in 1875 about a book De Quille was writing – a letter which also casts a great deal of light on Twain's own literary technique in general, and especially on *Roughing It*:

Dan, there is more than one way of writing a book; & your way is *not* the right one. You see, the winning card is to nail a man's interest with *Chapter 1*, & not let up on him till you get him to the word "finis." That can't be done with detached sketches, but I'll show you how to make a man read every one of those sketches, under the stupid impression that they are mere accidental incidents that have dropped in on you unawares in the course of your *narrative*. (Lewis 1947: xviii–xix)

Roughing It wins over readers partly by means of its humor, which makes it, on the surface, one of the funniest books in literature, and partly by means of delicate and exquisite irony. Most readers of the book recognize that Twain the narrator appears to be mocking himself as a terminally naïve outsider. The emphasis is so much on his own follies that it has generally escaped notice that a subdued but very serious recurrent theme in the book is its criticism of human nature. "Silver fever" is depicted in the book, literally, as a malady which, even in its mildest form, deprives its victims of good sense, and at its worst destroys their lives by condemning them to cruelly hard work and single life under a condition of perpetual delusion. The dream, born of cupidity, of instant and easy wealth turns out to be not only fatuous but also in contravention of God's doom that man must earn his bread by the sweat of his brow. Even when some few do acquire wealth they do not also acquire the knowledge of how to use it wisely and to good purpose (Berkove 1998).

Similarly, the hope of finding an Eden here on earth, either in scenic California or idyllic Hawaii, is doomed to disappointment. On close inspection, California turns out to be monotonous in its scenery and weather, and torn up and scarified by the miners. Hawaii has the scorpion, its own version of the snake in the garden, and its people have been victimized first by the priests of their native religion and then by the missionaries of Christianity. *Roughing It*, for all its humor, is, surprisingly, at bottom a gloomy book, whose narrator in its last chapter characterizes as "seven years of vicissitudes" what had begun as a "pleasure trip."

The Westerner in the Old World

Even before *Roughing It*, the influence of the West was manifested in Twain's first major literary success, *The Innocents Abroad, or The New Pilgrims' Progress* (1869). This book may not seem a work of regionalism, but it is useful to regard it as such for two reasons. One is that in 1869 America was still considered by Europe as a "region," a place somewhat remote from the mainstream of culture. It is apparent that Twain was aware of this perception and capitalized on it. The other is that Twain in 1869 was still fresh from the West, and was still under the influence of the attitudes and techniques he learned there. In *Roughing It*, he was to use the standard local color technique of an educated narrator reporting on the doings of the colorful but rough locals, with the Western twist that the locals turned out to be more sophisticated than the narrator. *The Innocents Abroad* is a precursor of that approach. In this case, the locals (Americans) are visiting the center of culture (Europe) and are often less sophisticated than the Europeans, but sometimes more. Bunyan's *Pilgrim's Progress* was an ideal model for Twain to follow, especially since it established a norm for his ironies. The American pilgrims are, for example, mostly well-to-do and traveling in comfort, in contrast to the poor and humble Christian of Bunyan's book, who goes on foot. Many of the Americans are described as pompous and narrow-minded, again in contrast to what a pilgrim should be. In many ways *Innocents Abroad* is a satire on those Americans, and Twain's disdain for their inflexibility and humorlessness is clear in a comment in the penultimate chapter: "The pleasure ship was a synagogue, and the pleasure trip was a funeral excursion without a corpse."

In *Innocents Abroad* Twain vacillates among openly satirizing himself, his fellow pilgrims, and the Old World. He does so by rooting his satire in what can be assumed to be the general moral consensus of his readership. As the book's narrator, Twain himself undergoes a change from naïve credulity to skepticism. Along with a small group of irreverent rebels, for example, he hoaxes the guides, mocks the guidebooks, and ridicules the legends and hyperbole that they attempt to foist on the travelers. He refuses to see Europe and the Holy Land through romantic eyes, and in fact notes their faults and is critical of the immorality he sees in their governments and populations. In this respect, the narrator Twain as Westerner turns the tables on the "cultured" Old World, pointing up *its* naïveté, credulity, vices, and follies, and in the process implying that the Old World might have more to learn from the New than the reverse.

The New York Years

In all three of his formative periods, therefore, Twain proved to be an assiduous student of regionalism, mastering the vernacular and the local customs and mores, learning the regional folklore and humor, and especially absorbing the special techniques of narrative that prevailed in each different locality. His main themes and literary techniques, therefore, were all well established when Twain returned from the West to pursue his career in the East, particularly New York and Connecticut. This is not to say, however, that when he used Eastern localities for some of his subsequent works, the influence on him of those regions was necessarily or invariably superficial.

After Twain married Olivia Langdon, he lived in Buffalo, NY, from 1869 to 1871. In light works such as "A Day at Niagara" (1869) or "John Chinaman in New York" (1870), the New York sites are incidental to the true ironic thrusts of the sketches. Only slightly more apposite is Twain's location of Eden in the vicinity of Niagara Falls in "Extracts from Adam's Diary" (1893). On the other hand, much of Twain's best literature was written in Elmira, NY, where, beginning in 1871, he spent the summers of 20 years at Quarry Farm, the home of his wife's relatives. A study in the shape of a steamboat pilot house was built for him at the farm, and he found the place conducive to rest, reflection, and creativity, gladly returning to it year after year. Elmira was an unusually liberal town, his wife's family were among its intellectual and moral leaders, and the impact of these circumstances on Twain's political and social attitudes, especially in regard to such topics as civil rights, women's rights, and political reform, was extensive and deep (Skandera-Trombley 1994: chs 4 and 5).

Lest the influence upon him of this region be overstated, however, it must be repeated that Twain's personality and character were already formed before he moved to New York state, and that he was selective about what he allowed to influence him, and to what degree. Although, for example, he developed some sympathy for the temperance movement (as expressed, for example, in his negative portrayal of Huck's drunken father) and had friendly associations with members of the Elmira Temperance Society, Twain did not advocate abstinence, and perceptively distinguished between getting alcoholics to sign pledges not to drink, and the more difficult task of getting them to the point where they did not want to drink (Twain 1917: 459). Similarly, although Twain recognized deep obligations to his father-in-law for his understanding and generosity, this did not prevent him from satirizing the hypocritical piety of someone in the same occupation – Abner Scofield, a Buffalo, NY coal dealer – in "Letter to the Earth" (1946).

The Connecticut Experience

Hartford, Connecticut, and more especially its Nook Farm residential community, where Twain lived from 1871 to 1891, was another place where he found intellectual ferment and liberal influences. He soon became part of a circle which included such eminent local personalities as his neighbor, Harriet Beecher Stowe, the Hooker family, the politician and insurance company executive Francis Gillette, the writer C. D. Warner (with whom he co-authored *The Gilded Age*), and the clergyman Joseph Twichell. Additionally, Twain became a member of the Monday Evening Club, whose members prepared papers for presentation to each other (Andrews 1950). Undeniably, this formidable circle challenged and stimulated him, but the view of Connecticut one gets from his works is quite complex. Twain's fundamental and profoundly gloomy conviction that the human race was doubly damned, both for its intrinsic evil and because it was predestined, results in conflicting conceptions of the significance of Connecticut. On the surface, Connecticut culture is progressive and moral, the best face of America, the shape of the world to come. Below the surface, however, all its virtues appear as masks of its deeper and uncontrollable evil.

Twain, for example, occasionally made sport of the importance to Hartford of the Colt Arms factory and its insurance companies, such as when he ironically observed that they complemented each other, the first hurrying people off to the next world, and the second offering them fire protection. The double-layer of this sort of humor, superficially funny but sharply ironic underneath, is repeated in important stories of his Connecticut period. In a tale such as "The Facts Concerning the Recent Carnival of Crime in Connecticut" (1876), the genteel decency of the main character turns out to be veneer, stripped away in his ironically successful battle with a tormenting conscience to reveal a violent and remorseless core personality more vicious than the malevolent conscience (Berkove 2000). The story seems humorous on first reading, but on reflection seriously pessimistic. Similarly, in the first part of *A Connecticut Yankee in King Arthur's Court* (1889), the inferred image of Connecticut, represented by Hank Morgan, is that of a decent and progressive society. By slow and careful degrees this image is replaced in the second part of the book by a reverse and frightening image, that of a prototype of the modern world: industrial, efficient, sharp – and deadly. The technological, "labor-saving" advances that made the Colt Arms factory so successful turn out, terrifyingly at the novel's end, to be means of mass destruction; and Hank, who seems the canny, likeable, democratic hero of the novel in its first part becomes a self-deluded tyrant at the end. Tragically, Hank seems unaware of what is happening to him and the terrible nature of the forces he has unleashed (Berkove 1990).

It would be a mistake, of course, to infer from this discussion of Twain's Connecticut works that his stay in Connecticut was somehow oppressive to him. On the contrary, this was, until the last years, a happy time of his life. In Connecticut he realized his long-time ambition to be a family man; he lived in a beautiful house in an upscale community, he had many friends, and he enjoyed considerable fame and success. The gloom of the Connecticut period was not derived from his environment but from the beliefs he brought with him. Nor was this gloom necessarily intended to be primarily a criticism of Connecticut, America, or the modern world; it was a consequence of Twain's belief that the human race was hoaxed and damned. This can be seen from one last and indirect reference to Connecticut's Colt Arms factory in "The Chronicle of Young Satan" (written 1897–1900), one of the *Mysterious Stranger* (1916) manuscripts. It occurs in an ironic reference by Satan to "progress," that is, the innate human affinity for murder, and to the way armaments have served that instinct with the "five or six high civilizations" of the past five or six thousand years:

> They all did their best, to kill being the chiefest ambition of the human race and the earliest incident in its history, but only the Christian civilization has scored a triumph to be proud of. Two centuries from now it will be recognized that all the competent killers are Christian; then the pagan world will go to school to the Christian: not to acquire his religion, but his guns. The Turk and the Chinaman will buy those, to kill missionaries and converts with. (Twain 1970: 137)

In this passage it is clear that the trouble with the human race goes back to Adam, and that Cain was its first exemplar. Its murderous inclination is only more efficiently cultivated in "high civilizations"; the less developed cultures have the same inherent predisposition. They are as murderous as they can be, and seize with alacrity opportunities to be more so.

CONCLUSION

Although Mark Twain has long been recognized as America's outstanding writer of regionalist literature, and his influence on subsequent regionalist authors is vast and profound, he ultimately does not fit into any neat pigeonhole, including that of regionalist. His was a complex personality; he was also, to some extent, self-contradictory: layered, like his manner of writing. Considering him as a regionalist certainly helps to explain his development, and it usefully illuminates some features of his thought and style, but it is far from constituting a definitive classification. For Twain, there was only one story about the human race, and because whatever region he found himself in had human inhabitants, the story would always be the same.

NOTES

1 I am indebted to Professor Victor Doyno of SUNY-Buffalo for sharing this information with me in several conversations. His research revealed that the Judith Loftus episode is significant in that it reflects the attitude of many citizens of the upper Mississippi area, particularly those from lower-income families, that the laws regarding apprentices were "unjust" and should not be supported. This, together with the divisions that were already in place over the controversial issues of slavery, the Dred Scott decision, and secession, results in the novel's depiction of a society that was deeply troubled and showing signs of stress fractures from internal contradictions.

2 The subject of the ending of *Huckleberry Finn* is the single most vexed issue in the scholarly literature on the book. My position, central to the discussion of Twain in this essay but first presented in "The 'Poor Players' of *Huckleberry Finn*," is that a tragic ending to the novel is a logical consequence of its structure and its deep irony. Once Huck and Jim's raft passes Cairo, the raft drifts every minute deeper into slave territory; while Huck and Jim appear to become freer on the raft, they cannot stay on it for ever, and once they get off the illusory character of their freedom becomes immediately apparent. Also, despite appearances, at the end Jim becomes *not* a free man, but a "free man of color," a shockingly different kind of being. The article explains how the last ten chapters, far from being a disappointing reversion to romantic escape literary devices, are instead the most powerful and tragic in the book, for they detail how Huck and Jim, after having gained enormously in stature and independence up to that point, are systematically diminished to what they were at the novel's beginning; indeed, they are now even worse off, for now both are deluded as to the nature of their "freedom."

3 The pen-name "Mark Twain" derives from this period. The term meant "two fathoms" – safe water for a steamboat. It had been adopted as a pen-name by another Mississippi river pilot during Clemens's piloting years, but Clemens appropriated it early in his Nevada sojourn, and made it famous.

4 In "Dan De Quille and 'Old Times on the Mississippi,'" I have documented how Twain's account of his fellow river pilot Strother Wiley in chapter 14 was inspired by the *first* use of the material in an article by his friend and former room mate, Dan De Quille. In "New Information on Dan De Quille and 'Old Times on the Mississippi,'" I further substantiate this influence and also present evidence that Twain additionally enhanced his entertaining "recollection" of African-American steamboat crew members in chapter 14 by his silent assimilation of another De Quille piece, an 1861 article that was written before the two men met.

5   Edgar J. Burde (1978) assumes these dreams reflected Twain's timidity and insecurity as a pilot, but Edgar M. Branch (1985) persuasively counters Burde's argument.

6   It is not generally known, but Twain earlier recounted his "adventures" in the Civil War in a humorous speech to the Ancient and Honorable Artillery Company of Hartford, Connecticut. The speech was reprinted in the *Detroit Free Press* of Friday, October 5, 1877, p. 3, col. 5, from the *Boston Post* of "Tuesday" (probably October 2). The "Private History" sketch follows it closely, but adds the incident about how a man was shot to death.

REFERENCES

Andrews, Kenneth R. (1950). *Nook Farm: Mark Twain's Hartford Circle.* Cambridge, Mass.: Harvard University Press.

Berkove, Lawrence I. (1968). "The 'Poor Players' of *Huckleberry Finn.*" *Papers of the Michigan Academy of Science, Arts, and Letters* 53, 291–310.

Berkove, Lawrence I. (1980). "The Free Man of Color in *The Grandissimes* and Works by Harris and Mark Twain." *Southern Quarterly* 18: 4 (Summer), 60–73.

Berkove, Lawrence I. (1986). "Dan De Quille and 'Old Times on the Mississippi.'" *Mark Twain Journal* 24: 2 (Fall), 28–35.

Berkove, Lawrence I. (1988). "New Information on Dan De Quille and 'Old Times on the Mississippi.'" *Mark Twain Journal* 26: 2 (Fall), 15–20.

Berkove, Lawrence I. (1990). "*A Connecticut Yankee*: A Serious Hoax." *Essays in Arts and Sciences* 19 (May), 28–44.

Berkove, Lawrence I. (1992). "Mark Twain's Mind and the Illusion of Freedom." Special issue of *Journal of Humanities* [Kobe, Japan] (March), 1–24.

Berkove, Lawrence I. (1993). "Slavery." In J. R. Le Master and James D. Wilson, eds., *Mark Twain Encyclopedia*, 686–9. New York: Garland.

Berkove, Lawrence I. (1998). "The Trickster God in *Roughing It.*" *Thalia* 18, 21–30.

Berkove, Lawrence I. (1999). *Dan De Quille.* (Boise State University Western Writers Series, no. 136.) Boise: Boise State University.

Berkove, Lawrence I. (2000). "Poe, Twain, and the Nature of Conscience." *ESQ* 46: 4.

Booth, Bradford (1954). "Mark Twain's Comments on Bret Harte's Stories." *American Literature* 25 (Jan.), 492–5.

Branch, Edgar M. (1985). "Mark Twain: The Pilot and the Writer." *Mark Twain Journal* 23: 2 (Fall), 28–43.

Burde, Edgar J. (1978). "Mark Twain: The Writer as Pilot." *Proceedings of the Modern Language Association* 93, 878–92.

Goodman, Joseph Thompson (1997). "'An Irregular Correspondent': *The European Travel Letters of Mark Twain's Editor and Friend Joe Goodman,*" ed. and intr. Lawrence I. Berkove. *Mark Twain Journal* 35: 2 (Fall), 1–44.

Kruse, Horst (1981). *Mark Twain and "Life on the Mississippi."* Amherst: University of Massachusetts Press.

Lewis, Oscar (1947). "Introduction." In Dan De Quille, *The Big Bonanza*, vii–xxv. New York: Crowell. (First publ. 1976.)

Messent, Peter (1995). "Caught on the Hop: Interpretive Dislocation in 'The Notorious Jumping Frog of Calaveras County.'" *Thalia* 15: 1 & 2, 33–49.

Skandera-Trombley, Laura E. (1994). *Mark Twain in the Company of Women.* Philadelphia: University of Pennsylvania Press.

Smith, Henry Nash (1967). *Mark Twain: The Development of a Writer.* New York: Atheneum. First publ. 1962.

Twain, Mark (1875). "War times." *Detroit Free Press*, 5 Oct., 3.

Twain, Mark (1917). *Mark Twain's Letters*, 2 vols., ed. Albert Bigelow Paine. New York: Harper and Brothers.

Twain, Mark (1970). "The Chronicle of Young Satan." In *The Mysterious Stranger*, ed. William M. Gibson, 35–174. Berkeley: University of California Press. (First publ. 1916.)

Wecter, Dixon (1952). *Sam Clemens of Hannibal.* Boston: Houghton Mifflin.

29

Willa Cather's
Glittering Regions

Robert Thacker

H. L. Mencken, in the first of two reviews he published of Willa Cather's *My Ántonia* when that breakthrough novel appeared in 1918, offered this assessment in his characteristic style:

> I know of no novel that makes the remote folk of the western prairies more real than *My Antonia* makes them, and I know of none that makes them better worth knowing. Beneath the swathings of balderdash, the surface of numbskullery and illusion, the tawdry stuff of Middle Western *Kultur*, she discovers human beings embattled against fate and the gods, and into her picture of their dull struggle she gets a spirit that is genuinely heroic, and a pathos that is genuinely moving. It is not as they see themselves that she depicts them, but as they actually are. (O'Connor 2001: 88)

Mencken's final sentence, especially, must have pleased Cather; we know that another review of *My Ántonia*, one that appeared in the New York *Sun* and offered much the same sentiment, pleased her so much that she had a copy typed to send to one of her old mentors. An author's pleasure is itself ephemeral, but Mencken's response to *My Ántonia* and Cather's own confirming reaction are indicative and so a fit point of departure here: what Cather sought to do in *My Ántonia* was to create on its pages the very sense that Mencken and others found, that "all this happened!" – as the *Sun* reviewer expressed it. That unnamed reviewer went so far, even, to speak directly to the novel's reader: "You picked up *My Antonia* to read a novel (love story, of course; hope it's a good one) and find yourself enthralled by autobiography" (O'Connor 2001: 80).

As Mencken and a few other critics of the day (H. W. Boynton, Randolph Bourne) quickly appreciated when her first four novels were published during the 1910s, Willa Cather's regionalism was something American literature had not seen before. "Here at last is an American novel," Bourne wrote in his review of *My Ántonia*, "redolent of the Western prairie, that our most irritated and exacting preconceptions

Figure 29.1   Willa Cather at Mesa Verde, 1915.

can be content with" (O'Connor 2001: 84). To them, *My Ántonia* clinched their sense
of Cather's growing achievement.

Beginning this discussion of Willa Cather's regions – her regionalism – with
such contemporary responses, I wish first of all to assert *My Ántonia* as incontrovert-
ible evidence that, with this novel, Cather transformed both prairie writing and, as

Mencken and Bourne had apprehended, American literature. Criticism to one side, the novel's progress with readers confirmed as much: by 1926, Houghton Mifflin had brought out a revised edition with a much-shortened introduction to capitalize on the book's growing "classic" status, and, but for one very brief lapse owing to a printers' strike, the book has never been out of print since. For her part, Cather told a friend in 1938 that "the best thing I've done is *My Ántonia*. I feel I've made a contribution to American letters with that book" (quoted in Woodress 1987: 293). She wrote and told this to others and, though she sometimes gave preference to *Death Comes for the Archbishop* (1927), *My Ántonia* remained a book Cather cherished for the rest of her life.

While this is not the place to explore in detail the basis for such an assessment, Cather's own attitude toward *My Ántonia* reflects clearly its status as the culminating volume of the first stage in her development as an artist. Although she had been writing seriously since the early 1890s – when she was attending the University of Nebraska – *My Ántonia* appeared just before she turned 45; as such, that novel vindicated the struggle she had been engaged in to "make herself born" as a writer (Cather 1915: 150). The elements of that struggle are asserted and validated in all three reviews of *My Ántonia* just cited: the conventional, inherited form of the novel where the reader expects a romance taking place in an imagined world; the suitability of Nebraska – Cather's best-known place – as setting for an American novel; and, finally, the effect of the apparently autobiographical on the way a story is told to a reader.

For Cather, it was the mastery of each of these elements – commingled for the first time in the aesthetic whole that is *My Ántonia* – that had elicited the pleased reactions offered by Mencken and other reviewers. What is more, that mastery recreated on the page Cather's first achieved region – pioneering Nebraska – as a felt place unique to America. And though she is very often seen as a Nebraskan only – it was to that state she and her family emigrated in 1883, when she was nine – it is much preferable to speak of Willa Cather's regions in the plural, since through her art she also transformed the Southwest and Quebec before returning once more to a less immediate Nebraska and, in her last novel, *Sapphira and the Slave Girl* (1940), finally to Back Creek, Virginia, where she had been born in 1873.

In fact, the whole of Cather's work might be seen as a process of finding a voice by finding a place, a region understood as home. Cather's direction in this regard is made clear in a passage from her penultimate novel, *Lucy Gayheart* (1935), where, in detailing Clement Sebastian's malaise as he looks at his life, she wrote: "he was nearing fifty, he was without country, without a home, without a family, and very nearly without friends." More than this, and more to the point, Cather wrote that Sebastian "had missed the deepest of all companionships, a relation with the earth itself, with a countryside and a people. That relationship, he knew, cannot be gone after and found; it must be long and deliberate, unconscious. It must, indeed, be a way of living" (Cather 1935: 78). Writing this, looking back on her own life and her own writing, still heading toward her own homecoming with *Sapphira and the Slave Girl*,

Cather here articulates an aesthetic credo, one found developing through each novel as she creates both character and story by way of the region where each is rooted.

"On the Divide," *O Pioneers!*, and *The Song of the Lark*: Creating Cather's Nebraska

The direction of Cather's development is thrown into relief by looking at the prairie novels of the 1910s in reverse order. Early in *My Ántonia*, Cather writes of her narrator's first glimpse of the prairie landscape that "There was nothing but land: not a country at all, but the material out of which countries are made." There, this narrator, Jim Burden says, "Between that earth and that sky I felt erased, blotted out." There, Burden thinks, "what would be would be" (Cather 1918: 7, 8). Five years earlier, in *O Pioneers!* (1913), Cather made her first extended attempt to render in fiction the Nebraska landscape of her own late girlhood and teenage years. In that novel, however, she began by describing the land itself through a detached third-person narrator; thus *O Pioneers!* opens:

> One January day, thirty years ago, the little town of Hanover, anchored on a windy Nebraska tableland, was trying not to be blown away. A mist of fine snowflakes was curling and eddying about the cluster of low drab buildings huddled on the gray prairie, under a gray sky. The dwelling-houses were set about haphazardly on the tough prairie sod; some of them looked as if they had been moved in overnight, and others as if they were straying off by themselves, headed straight for the open plain. None of them had any appearance of permanence, and the howling wind blew under them as well as over them. The main street was a deeply rutted road, now frozen hard, which ran from the squat red railway station and the grain 'elevator' at the north end of the town to the lumber yard and the horse pond at the south end. On either side of this road straggled two uneven rows of wooden buildings; the general merchandise stores, the two banks, the drug store, the feed store, the saloon, the post-office. The board sidewalks were gray with trampled snow, but at two o'clock in the afternoon the shopkeepers, having come back from dinner, were keeping well behind their frosty windows. (Cather 1913: 11–12)

Such a scene is quite clear, and quite well done, certainly. But the greater appeal of *My Ántonia* owes much, to borrow a phrase from W. H. Auden, to the "human position" of the prairie landscape in that novel. As I have argued elsewhere, with *O Pioneers!* Cather was attempting to teach readers how to best read that landscape – a lesson that in 1913 still very much needed teaching (Thacker 1989: 146–71). She was among the first to undertake that project and, arguably, is still among the very best to have done so. Moreover, with this book Cather – as she was later to argue herself in "My First Novels (There Were Two)" (Cather 1949) – was discovering the material that became her most characteristic. Even so, there is a formal distance in the novel's telling, and in Alexandra Bergson's character, that places it in a lesser position within

Cather's work behind most of its successors, and most especially when seen in relation to *My Ántonia*, a book that also focuses on prairie pioneering as its subject.

That Cather felt the need to address this subject twice is indicative of her development as an artist. Following the writing of *O Pioneers!* Cather undertook a favor during the summer of 1913 for her friend, mentor, and former boss, S. S. McClure: she ghost-wrote his autobiography, a book published under his name in 1914 as *My Autobiography* (Cather 1997). As I have argued elsewhere, this experience had a profound effect on Cather's aesthetic and on her narrative point of view. Completing this task, she turned to her own autobiography in *The Song of the Lark* (1915); and, following that, returned to the prairie-pioneering theme she had already tackled in *O Pioneers!*. But she did so with a difference. No longer were characters seen from the outside by a distant third-person narrator; rather, the narrator speaks with shared history and empathetic feeling for his home and the friends he has had. This was the same relation that existed between Cather herself and S. S. McClure, a person she knew well and sympathized with as he told her his life story in 1913 so that she could write it down (see Thacker 2001). Doing the same with the materials of her own history, Cather humanized the prairie landscape by creating Jim Burden and Ántonia Shimerda and by making that most threatening of landscapes the source of what she calls their shared "freemasonry" (Cather 1918: x). Along with the landscape, Jim and Ántonia also share personal histories and the corporate histories of Black Hawk, Nebraska, as Cather reminds readers once more in the book's final sentence: "Whatever we had missed, we possessed together the precious, the uncommunicable past" (Cather 1918: 360).

As Ántonia and Jim's shared histories demonstrate, Cather's regionalism depends for its effectiveness entirely on a balanced integration of personal history with the region's corporate history, the two held in equilibrium, balanced against one another by Cather's narrative techniques. Yet the achievement of this balance took her considerable time and effort before *My Ántonia*. There were numerous failed attempts early in Cather's career. Many of her early stories, which she did not republish in her lifetime, were concerned with a stark view of her Nebraska plains – indeed, the stories she wrote and published during the 1890s and early 1900s against that setting are unremittingly grim: in "On the Divide" (1896), for example, Cather writes that "It causes no great sensation there when a Dane is found swinging to his own windmill tower, and most of the Poles after they have become too careless and discouraged to shave themselves keep their razors to cut their throats with." Elsewhere in that story she describes Canute Canuteson, the main character, as "mad from the eternal treachery of the plains, which every spring stretch green and rustle with the promises of Eden, showing long grassy lagoons full of clear water and cattle whose hoofs are stained with wild roses. Before autumn the lagoons are dried up, and the ground is burnt dry and hard until it blisters and cracks open" (Cather 1970: 495, 497).

Such stories as this are not only grim, they are also wooden, and so the tracing of Cather's growth to effect as an artist is therefore an examination of the balance she progressively manages to negotiate between the plains as beneficent and the plains as apocalyptic landscape. In contrast to the distance created by third-person narration in *O Pioneers!*, in *My Ántonia* the narrative intimacy borne of Jim's knowledge of Ántonia, as well as the same knowledge shared by the author of the introduction as the person to whom Jim addresses his narrative about "his" Ántonia, mitigates those occurrences that are sorrowful, threatening. Mr. Shimerda commits suicide in the face of "the eternal treachery of the plains," and the tramp throws himself in the threshing machine during the most beautiful, the most bountiful, time of the year. But in these instances, and numerous others like it where Cather incorporates greed, despair, ennui, and other equally positive qualities into *My Ántonia*, her fatalistic grimnesses have given way to vibrant contextualizations – in time, personality, and place – that render such occurrences whole, understandable, integrated into the lives of the characters whom she depicts and whom we understand.

This is, ultimately, the achieved effect of Willa Cather's regionalism. It is first seen fully revealed in *My Ántonia*, as Cather knew, but its gestation lay in the writing she did prior to that novel, most especially the autobiography she ghost-wrote for McClure after she had completed *O Pioneers!*. Applying the lessons she learned there to her own experiences in *The Song of the Lark*, Cather extended them in *My Ántonia* by creating a form that both subverted the conventional novel and made readers feel, as in autobiography, that "all this happened!"

Owing, then, to its position in the progress of Cather's novels, *The Song of the Lark* bears more extended attention here. It is, indeed, a fulcrum text in the progress I have just described. Critics have long seen it as Cather's most autobiographical novel, where she "made her character personal in a way unprecedented in her earlier writing," according to Susan Rosowski, since when "the self is the source of value in an otherwise meaningless world, the prerequisite for the artist is to know that self." Rosowski also notes that Cather, when creating Thea Kronborg's Moonstone, Colorado, "reproduced her hometown so precisely that one could map the stores, churches, houses, and streets of one and find her way in the other," and that Thea "is Willa Cather in essentials, although Olive Fremstad was her external prototype" (Rosowski 1986: 63, 62).

The melding Rosowski speaks of here – the grafting of Cather's own childhood, feelings, and experiences as an incipient artist onto the actual singer Fremstad's experience as an operatic diva – is what gives *The Song of the Lark* its power as a *Künstlerroman*. That is so, certainly; but, as Rosowski also notes, the book's strength flows both from Cather's focus on Thea's "imaginative life" and, implicitly, from those aspects of Thea's life that she omits – formal education, Thea's European training as a singer and, especially, marriage and the possibility of a family of her own (1986: 63).

Thea is marked from the outset. Set apart in her illness as the novel opens, she is of deep concern to Dr. Archie who, for his part, has little sympathy for family fussings among the Kronborgs over the birth of a new baby. Like her creator, Thea knows from early youth that there is something different about her, that she was one set apart, that she "was going to be" Thea Kronborg. Retrospectively, once Thea has achieved acclaim as an operatic diva, Archie thinks back to when she was young and wonders "if it was strange that he should find a child of twelve the most companionable and interesting person in Moonstone" (Cather 1915: 333).

In *The Song of the Lark*, Cather retains the omniscient third person, but there is nothing impersonal about the perspective that voice offers – it moves from character to character, situated most effectively when revealing Thea's (and to a lesser extent, other characters') feelings and thoughts. It is a confiding voice, one which serves to connect Thea's character inextricably with Moonstone, its mores, values, and personalities; an indicative passage reveals Cather's narrator glossing Thea's projected memories of a Moonstone prayer meeting there on a bitterly cold night:

> Thea would have been astonished if she could have known how, years afterward, when she had need of them, those old faces were to come back to her, long after they were hidden away under the earth; that they would seem to her then as full of meaning, as mysteriously marked by Destiny, as the people who danced the mazurka under the elegant Korsunsky [in *Anna Karenina*]. (Cather 1915: 114)

As Cather writes a few chapters later, Thea is seen here and throughout the first two books of the novel – those which detail her time in Moonstone – "being pulled in two, between the desire to go away forever and the desire to stay forever." As her confidant, Dr. Archie, had told her when describing the time available to each individual, once childhood, sleep, and old age had been factored out: "She had only twenty years – no time to lose" (Cather 1915: 122). In the same interview, Archie tried to offer Thea solace over the death of a tramp who, in committing suicide, had tried to get even with the townspeople for the slights they had offered him, Thea among them. Telling her to "Forget the tramp," Archie says that "the failures are swept back into the pile and forgotten. They don't leave any lasting scar in the world, and they don't affect the future. The things that last are the good things. The people who forge ahead and do something, they really count" (p. 121). Caught as she is between Moonstone and the great world outside – it is, of course, the beckoning place where she might do something that really counts – Thea has to choose between the two.

As Cather presents Thea's story, her transformation is not so much a choice as it is an inevitability: like her creator, Thea is also marked with apparent genius, a genius recognized by those around her in Moonstone. In Thea's case, she has a talent for music well above the usual, which eventually draws her east to Chicago for lessons and then, inexorably, to Europe for further training and to a triumphant professional career as a singer, "Kronborg." At each step of the way, Cather invokes Moonstone as either confirmation or contrast. When Thea leaves her discussion of the tramp with Dr. Archie, "the most grown-up conversation she had ever had with him," Cather invokes the familiarity of Moonstone's details before she asserts Thea's feelings: "She left his office happy, flattered and stimulated. She ran for a long while about the white, moonlit streets, looking up at the stars and the bluish night, at the black houses sunk in black shade, the glittering sand hills. She loved the familiar trees, and the people in those little houses, and she loved the unknown world beyond Denver" (Cather 1915: 122).

Moonstone – for Thea – and Red Cloud – for Cather – were home places that, seen retrospectively, defined their very beings, and did so in ways that were both negative and positive. Thea's first winter in Chicago – when she was still studying piano with Harsanyi – found her frustrated, ruing the basic knowledge with which a Moonstone background had not provided her: "Things came too fast for her; she had not had enough preparation. There were times when she came home from her lesson and lay upon her bed hating Wunsch and her family, hating a world that had let her grow up so ignorant; when she wished that she could die then and there, and be born over again to begin anew." When she tells her teacher this, Harsanyi replies, "Every artist makes himself born. It is very much harder than the other time, and longer. Your mother did not bring anything into the world to play piano. That you must bring into the world yourself" (Cather 1915: 150).

Yet once Thea has suffered through many such moments, once her true vocation as a singer is discovered by Harsanyi and, discussed with Thea herself, confirmed (for she had always secretly known), Moonstone looks different to her. Returning from her first winter in Chicago, Thea's thoughts are on her ambitions ("that she meant to grab a few things" [Cather 1915: 185]) and, as the train crosses the Platte River, she is struck by the detail of her home place:

> and the sunlight was so intense that it seemed to quiver in little flames and the glittering sandbars, the scrub willows, and the curling, fretted shallows.

> Thea felt that she was coming back to her own land. She had often heard Mrs. Kronborg say that she "believed in immigration," and so did Thea believe in it. This earth seemed to her young and fresh and kindly, a place where refugees from the old, sad countries were given another chance. The mere absence of rocks gave the soil a kind of amiability and generosity, and the absence of natural boundaries gave the spirit a wider range. Wire fences might mark the end of a man's pasture, but they could not shut out his thoughts as mountains and forests can. It was over flat lands like this, stretching out to drink the sun, that the larks sang – and one's heart sang there too. Thea was glad it was her country, even if one did not learn to speak elegantly there. It was, somehow, an honest country, and there was a new song in that blue air which had never been sung in the world before. It was hard to tell about it, for it had nothing to do with words; it was like the light of the desert at noon, or the smell of the sagebrush after rain; intangible but powerful. (Cather 1915: 186–7)

Having sensed all this detail, having responded to the imaginative effect of the land's details integrated by her sensibility into a landscape, Thea concludes her reverie: "She had the sense of going back to a friendly soil, whose friendship was somehow going to strengthen her; a naïve, generous country that gave one its joyous force, its large-hearted, childlike power to love, just as it gave one its coarse, brilliant flowers"

(Cather 1915: 187). This reverie is then connected to Ray Kennedy, whose friend-ship and generosity made Thea's study in Chicago possible.

Such moments, connected through the character of Thea and by the process of her imaginative and aesthetic growth, allow the reader to trace her progress. Thea's reverie, here, is an imaginative reconfirmation of the aesthetic responses she had had over the winter when she saw Jules Breton's painting, *The Song of the Lark*, in the Chicago Art Institute and, just after, when she heard Dvořák's *New World Symphony* ("the immeasurable yearning of all flat lands" [Cather 1915: 170]). These connec-tions, both aesthetically imaginative and tied to Thea's home place, further inspire her and confirm her direction. At the same time, Thea's return that summer to Moonstone, where she sings at the Mexican dance and, because of that act, suffers the disapproval of her siblings, allows her to recognize that they "were among the people whom she had always recognized as her natural enemies. Their ambitions and sacred proprieties were meaningless to her" (p. 203). Ironically, even though Moonstone and its associations are critical to Thea's developing sense of herself as an artist, she comes to realize – as Cather did herself – that her values and aspirations mean that she can no longer live there.

As such, Cather transforms Thea's Moonstone into a place she carries with her, a central element of her being. Thus, well after she has achieved her success as "Kronborg," Thea tells Dr. Archie that she still "measure[s] high buildings by the Moonstone standpipe" and that, though he tells her that "the old house" in Moon-stone "has been pulled down," "it stands in my mind, every stick and timber." "That's the house I rest in when I'm tired. All the old furniture and the worn spots in the carpets – it rests my mind to go over them" (Cather 1915: 379–80). Thus Thea's Moonstone becomes, for her as a person and within the novel itself, "a glittering idea" (the phrase Scott McGregor uses to describe the long-dead Tom Outland in *The Professor's House* [Cather 1925: 111]). It is part of her being, her consciousness, and this invests Moonstone – Thea's Home Place – with a materiality that exists only through the pages Cather wrote: there is no Thea's Moonstone beyond her own sense of it. A "glittering idea," very much like Thea's central realization as an artist, which comes to her when she is bathing in Panther Canyon off in the Southwest, Moon-stone sustains Thea throughout her life, one lived so far away from the home place. In Panther Canyon, meditating on some shards of ancient broken pottery she has seen, Thea wonders "what was any art but an effort to make a sheath, a mould in which to imprison for a moment the shining, elusive element which is life itself, – life hurrying past us and running away, too strong to stop, too sweet to lose?" (Cather 1915: 254–5). So Moonstone in Thea's memory, Red Cloud in Cather's.

Thea's place-derived epiphany in Panther Canyon, like Moonstone within *The Song of the Lark* generally, sets the stage for *My Ántonia*'s "land mystique" by taking up Cather's own autobiography, and S. S. McClure's too, using a conventional nar-rative form. Ruefully echoing McClure's story, Cather writes of Dr. Archie in a way that anticipates Jim Burden's character and, as well, Burden's relation with "his" Ántonia:

> He fell to looking back over his life and asking himself which years of it he would like to live over again, – just as they had been, – and they were not many. His college years he would live again, gladly. After them there was nothing he would care to repeat until he came to Thea Kronborg.
>
> . . .
>
> It came over him now that the unexpected favors of fortune, no matter how dazzling, do not mean very much to us. They may excite or divert us for a time, but when we look back, the only things we cherish are those which in some way met our original want; the desire which formed us in early youth, undirected, and of its own accord. (Cather 1915: 333, 334)

Such passages as this echo others found in McClure's autobiography and, seen with reference to Cather's next book, may be seen as incipiently defining Burden's entire enterprise in writing his narrative, the text of *My Ántonia* – indeed, the Thea–Dr. Archie relationship is a ready precursor to that between Ántonia and Jim.

As *The Song of the Lark* demonstrates, Cather effected her development as a writer by changing landscape – a scene visualized, made whole by a single person's viewing – into place, a felt environment, one central to the definition of a person's character. That is, it was when landscape ceased being mere backdrop – as it is in "On the Divide" and other early stories – and became integral to the beings of her characters – as in *My Ántonia* and later books – that Cather earned the readers and so the literary prominence that were hers during the 1920s and later. What is more, this process was one of moving from Moonstone as her protagonist's own place – redolent with memories that mean the most to Thea primarily – to Nebraska as a shared, storied region. That is the effect of the progression of novels that followed: *My Ántonia*, *One of Ours* (1922), and *A Lost Lady* (1923). In each of these books, Cather's focus is on the relation between an individual's personal experience and understanding – what she details in *The Song of the Lark* – and the larger community's shared histories. Indeed, the latter two novels may be reasonably seen to be explicitly about the making of shared historical meaning.

Finding a Place: From Nebraska to the Southwest

Reviewing *Death Comes for the Archbishop* upon its publication in 1927, Rebecca West wrote that "The most sensuous of writers, Willa Cather builds her imagined world as solidly as our five senses build the universe around us"; and, later in the review, she speaks of the book's "amazing sensory achievement" (West 1927: 1). What West sees here is the quality that Cather spent her entire career learning how to create, whereby landscape is where representation begins and so roots characters in their imagined regions. What is more, Cather's creative process was one rooted in her own autobiographical places, renderings that make her regional depictions both extended and complex. And once she had "written Nebraska out," so to speak, Cather invested her characters' beings in other, and more complex, regions: the lakeshore of Lake Michigan in *The Professor's House* (1925); New York City, small-town Illinois, and California in *My Mortal Enemy* (1926); the desert Southwest of *Death Comes for the Archbishop* (1927); and the little enclave of French culture that is Quebec in *Shadows on the Rock* (1931). There followed, then, a return to another Nebraska in *Obscure Destinies* (1932) and *Lucy Gayheart* – books set in a place quite different from her earlier renderings of it, as contemporary critics recognized – before she returned to her first home place, Virginia, in her last novel, *Sapphira and the Slave Girl*.

Once she had accomplished *My Ántonia*, Cather may be seen in her 1920s novels to be probing the relation between her characters and their places, asking how the two interact, and demonstrating the symbiotic interrelation between the two. Put in terms of *One of Ours* (1922) or *A Lost Lady*, Cather is detailing how a place has made a Claude Wheeler, or made a Niel Herbert, the person we see him to be in the text. In Claude's case this is straightforward: he is an ill-accomplished farm-boy for whom the 1914–18 war proves an escape from a most unhappy and unsatisfactory life, and to whom an idea of the glories of France gives an abstracted happiness that exceeds all the experiences he had had during the rest of his life.

In Niel's case, the matter is much more complex – his "history" of the Forresters is a parallel to Jim Burden's "history" of his Ántonia – as Joseph R. Urgo notes, "a good deal of Cather criticism argues that Willa Cather saw the present as a falling off from the past, a great decline from the heroic pioneer era when men and women settled, colonized, and personified historical foundation" (1991: 167). Thus the view that Captain Forrester was noble, a person intrinsically "better" than those who, like Ivy Peters, represent the present. As Urgo details, however, this view is Niel Herbert's, not Cather's, and, "By intervening in his material," Niel becomes in the book "representative of the ideological function of narrative history – history in the service of the present" (Urgo 1991: 174). As he seems to narrate – for Cather gives the effect of a first-person narrative by Niel without there being such a narrative – Cather accompanies his narrative with its own undercutting: Niel, like Burden, is believable only if a reader chooses to believe him; but, unlike in Burden's case, few readers are ultimately fully convinced by what he has to say. Especially so, when Niel's evaluations take such form as this piece of "narrative history":

> It was what he most held against Mrs. Forrester; that she was not willing to immolate herself, like the widow of all these great men, and die with the pioneer period to which she belonged; that she preferred life on any terms. In the end, Niel went away with a weary contempt for her in his heart. (Cather 1923: 161)

Such passages – whether acceded to or seen critically – open up the text to a variety of interpretations, and also demonstrate that Cather was not, as critics were to charge in the 1930s, pining nostalgically for a lost pioneering past.

No Cather text demonstrates the complexity of her understanding of contending histories better than her leading modernist experiment, *The Professor's House*. This is the book that offers Cather's most complex view of history, her most subtle use of a single region, and her most artful critique of 1920s America. There, Cather renders the storyteller, Tom Outland, as an affecting presence whose absent being animates the novel's other characters. As noted above, one of them calls Outland "a glittering idea" (Cather 1925: 111), and in so saying it becomes evident that his affecting story owes most to the invisible hand of his creator, Willa Cather. That is, just as Cather, through what she once called "the indirect method," had offered her readers material for other versions of Ántonia, other versions of Marian Forrester and of Niel Herbert, in *The Professor's House* she presents what amounts to Godfrey St. Peter's Tom Outland, itself surrounded by other versions of Outland offered by competing principal characters: each one who knew him has, then, a "my Tom Outland." There is no "objective narrative history" here, despite the Professor's vocation. Although St. Peter is to spend his summer alone editing Outland's Southwest diary while his family is in Europe, he never completes his task; what is more, the reader never sees its execution. "Tom Outland's Story" stands as Tom's story, told in his own words beside a fire on a rainy night to an empathetic audience of one, St. Peter. How it got – still in first-person – from St. Peter to the third-person narrator of the other two books is simply not addressed. Like the unseen but described diary, Tom's own story has weight without definition. Tom is the product of memory and the vexations of Godfrey St. Peter's midlife crisis. As such, Tom never speaks in life, though he seems to; he is memory only.

Writing about what she was trying to do in "On *The Professor's House*," Cather says the book offers "two experiments in form": first, "inserting the *Nouvelle* into the *Roman*," a "device often used by the early French and Spanish novelists." Thus the presence of "Tom Outland's story" as the second book. The second experiment "was something a little more vague"; she continues:

> In my book I tried to make Professor St. Peter's house rather overcrowded and stuffy with new things; American proprieties, clothes, furs, petty ambitions, quivering jealousies – until one got rather stifled. Then I wanted to open the square window and let in the fresh air that blew off the Blue Mesa, and the fine disregard of trivialities which was in Tom Outland's face and behaviour. (Cather 1949: 30–1)

Cather began writing "Tom Outland's Story" – its working title was "The Blue Mesa" – just after she completed *The Song of the Lark*; she envisioned an entire novel of the Southwest to continue from Thea's Panther Canyon epiphany there. But the material proved intractable, so she returned to Nebraska with *My Ántonia* first, and, subsequently, two more novels set there intervened. Yet in returning to the Southwest in *The Professor's House* and, in an extended way, two years later with *Death Comes for the Archbishop*, Cather was detailing a region that had seized her imagination from the time she first visited it in 1912.

Such an imaginative seizure by a region, already used in Thea's story, lies at the center of *The Professor's House*, literally and structurally. And, as Cather's own relation with the Southwest suggests, it derives from what Janet Varner Gunn has called an "autobiographical situation." Such situations, she argues, make "way for thinking about autobiography from three different angles, or in terms of inter-related moments": "the autobiographical impulse, the autobiographical perspective, and the autobiographical response" (Gunn 1982: 12). Each moment may be seen effecting the autobiographical text, bringing it about, and it may further be seen as resident in the intimacy of storytelling in Cather's work, where her placement of "Tom Outland's Story" in *The Professor's House* is its apotheosis. Gunn's ultimate argument, however, has the effect of extending Cather's use of auto-biographical place in her fiction; she writes that "the real question of the auto-biographical self then becomes *where do I belong?* not, who am I? The question of the self's identity becomes a question of the self's location in a world" (Gunn 1982: 23, emphasis in original).

"Where do I belong?", certainly, captures Godfrey St. Peter's predicament as he meditates over the summer of 1920 or '21. He is, after all, a man who cannot leave his family's former home, housing as it does his study – the site of his professional triumph as a historian as well as what he sees as his "real life." And during that summer, with most of his family off in Europe, St. Peter remembers Tom's story as he had told it to him – and only to him – on a rainy night in Hamilton during the summer "after Outland's graduation" (Cather 1925: 175). Tom, of course, went on to die "in Flanders, fighting with the Foreign Legion, the second year of the war," 1915 (p. 40).

For his part, though, Tom – through the story he tells and we read – leaves no question where he "belongs": on the Mesa the first night he spent alone there. As he told St. Peter in 1910:

> This was the first time I ever saw it as a whole. It came together in my understanding, as a series of experiments do when you begin to see where they are leading. Something had happened in me that made it possible for me to co-ordinate and simplify, and that process, going on in my mind, brought with it great happiness. It was possession. The excitement of my first discovery was a very pale feeling compared to this one. For me the mesa was no longer an adventure, but a religious emotion. I had read of filial piety in the Latin poets, and I knew that was what I felt for this place. It had formerly been mixed up with other motives; but now that they were gone, I had my happiness unalloyed. (Cather 1925: 250–1)

Notwithstanding, Tom leaves the Mesa for Hamilton; and, after college, success in his work, and trips to the mesa country with St. Peter, he leaves for the front. Still wondering over his own place, his own being, St. Peter imagines the life awaiting Tom had he lived, a life very much like the one he then finds himself living, and enviously concludes that Tom is better out of it:

What change would have come in his blue eye, in his fine long hand with the backspringing thumb, which had never handled things that were not the symbols of ideas? A hand like that, had he lived, must have been put to other uses. His fellow scientists, his wife, the town and State, would have required many duties of it. It would have had to write thousands of useless letters, frame thousands of false excuses. It would have had to 'manage' a great deal of money, to be the instrument of a woman who would grow always more exacting. He had escaped all that. He had made something new in the world – and the rewards, the meaningless conventional gestures, he had left to others. (Cather 1925: 260–1)

This done, St. Peter undergoes a transformation. He becomes again the "Kansas boy" he had originally been,

not a scholar. He was a primitive. He was only interested in earth and woods and water. Wherever sun sunned and rain rained and snow snowed, wherever life sprouted and decayed, places were alike to him. He was not nearly so cultivated as Tom's old cliff-dwellers must have been – and yet he was terribly wise. He seemed to be at the root of the matter; Desire under all desires, Truth under all truths. He seemed to know, among other things, that he was solitary and must always be so; he had never married, never been a father. He was earth and would return to earth.

"All these recollections," St. Peter concludes, "gave him a kind of sad pleasure" (Cather 1925: 265–6).

In *The Professor's House*, Cather uses her characters' attachment to Tom Outland – of personal connection understood within the family history with him – to undercut any single "objective" version of his significance. She does this by setting contending versions of meaning, of value, against each other over the significance of the Blue Mesa (Mesa Verde), of Tom Outland, and within the small circle of St. Peter's family and professional life. Cather later called the novel a "nasty, grim little tale," but it led her into another more grim and even nastier, *My Mortal Enemy* (1926) (Woodress 1987: 367). Pared down to utter essentials, that brief book offers just three settings: an Illinois home town, Parthia, done deftly without much descriptive detail; New York, precisely rendered; and an apocalyptic version of California. Only the Pacific headland where Myra Driscoll goes to die is offered with any attraction. As such, *My Mortal Enemy* is peopled with placeless characters, wandering without connection to a region of their own. After his wife dies, Oswald Driscoll leaves California for Alaska; Cather's narrator, Nellie Birdseye, is a voice only and unplaced herself. Taken together, *The Professor's House* and *My Mortal Enemy* are novels that demonstrate the importance of regional connection to Cather: St. Peter obtains equilibrium, though not serenity, by confronting Tom Outland and his Mesa so as to return to his own boyhood Kansas place, recognizing again the young person who is still there. That is, St. Peter has a place in this world by the novel's end. Conversely, the placeless people in *My Mortal Enemy*, like Clement Sebastian in *Lucy Gayheart*, are separate and alone, wandering without place or purpose.

These two books, moreover, by their very nastiness seem to have prepared Cather for her most extended meditations on individuated and historicized regions, *Death Comes for the Archbishop* and *Shadows on the Rock*. Cather begins *Death* with an extended prologue, set in Rome, that defines the political circumstances of Cather's story: the just concluded Mexican–American war has brought New Mexico into the United States and, concurrently, made it the responsibility of the American church. The narrative proper, however, begins with the figure of a man in a disorienting landscape:

> He had lost his way, and was trying to get back to the trail, with only his compass and his sense of direction for guides. The difficulty was that the country in which he found himself was so featureless – or rather, that it was crowded with features, all exactly alike. As far as he could see, on every side, the landscape was heaped up into monotonous red-sand hills, not much larger than haycocks, and very much the shape of haycocks. One could not have believed that in the number of square miles a man is able to sweep with the eye there could be so many uniform red hills. (Cather 1927: 16)

This is "Jean Marie Latour, consecrated Vicar Apostolic of New Mexico and Bishop of Agonthonia *in partibus* at Cincinnati a year ago – and ever since . . . he had been trying to reach his Vicarate" (p. 20).

With this abrupt introduction to the Southwest landscape, Cather repeated the disorientation she had first used in *O Pioneers!* and first perfected in *My Ántonia*. Here, however, Latour's discomfort in the face of such a landscape leads him to demonstrate his faith, his most animating belief: he discovers a "cruciform" juniper tree, stops, dismounts, and reads his breviary before it (Cather 1927: 17–18). What Cather is doing here, at the outset of *Death Comes for the Archbishop*, is again tracing the confrontation of an Old World mind with a New World landscape. This was, as her friend Dorothy Canfield Fisher asserted in the 1930s, Cather's great theme – such a confrontation lay at the core of *My Ántonia*, of course, the first-person story of a young boy's arrival to the prairie-plains: the same experience Cather had had herself. But in Latour Cather made her character an acculturated and educated Frenchman, "a priest in a thousand, one knew at a glance" (p. 18), and his task in the text is not so much one of imperially enforcing French religion and culture on the Southwest as it is one of adapting imaginatively and culturally to the place himself. As Cather makes clear, this is a long and complex process for Latour, but it is also one he sets himself to; later, when approaching the Mesa at Ácoma, Latour again meditates on the landscape:

> This mesa plain had an appearance of great antiquity, and of incompleteness; as if, with all the materials for world-making assembled, the Creator had desisted, gone away and left everything on the point of being brought together, on the eve of being arranged into mountain, plain, plateau. The country was still waiting to be made into a landscape. (Cather 1927: 100)

Such a sentence – "The country was still waiting to be made into a landscape" – might well be taken as describing Cather's own imaginative task and, as here, her accomplishment. What is more, Cather wrote of this book that she had all her "life wanted to do something in the style of legend" (1949: 9). Thus Cather's emphasis here is less upon individual stories than it is upon the interleaving of stories, cultures, histories in the Southwest. This is what Cather's Archbishop comes to learn there. Based himself on an historical figure, Latour is shown discovering where he belongs: in Sante Fe, in his Southwest. He confronts a threatening landscape at the novel's beginning and, as his subsequent landscape meditation shows, learns from it. Latour builds a cathedral in the French style in Santa Fe, but he builds from native stone; he remains a missionary, but he recognizes strengths of and respects the beliefs of the Natives, Mexicans, and Americans around him. Although he might have gone back to France when he retired, Latour realizes that Santa Fe is where he belongs, where he should die. In *Death Comes for the Archbishop*, as in its predecessor novels, Willa Cather envisions a disorienting landscape, renders its human value by integrating its history with her character's story, and transforms it into a place, a region redolent of story, history, understanding.

Quebec, Nebraska, and the Place She Started Out From

With *Shadows on the Rock*, Cather's recreation of an extensive place and time is moved from the frontier of the nineteenth-century Southwest to the late-seventeenth-century frontier of New France. Like its immediate predecessor a novel heavily dependent on research, this one represented both a new discovery and a return to the autobiographical. Although a lifelong Francophile, Cather did not visit Quebec City until 1928, when she and Edith Lewis took the Canadian route to their summer cottage on Grand Manan Island, New Brunswick. Seeing Quebec for the first time from the windows of the Château Frontenac, Edith Lewis was later to write, left Cather "overwhelmed by the flood of memory, recognition, surmise it called up; by the sense of its extraordinary French character, isolated and kept intact through hundreds of years, as if by a miracle, on this great un-French continent" (Lewis 1953: 153–4). Having earlier that year lost her father – to whom she had always been extremely close – Cather chose to write *Shadows on the Rock*, a book that recreates an intimate father–daughter bond; this relation, placed within the context of its recreation of frontier Quebec as a precariously small enclave of French culture in North America, "asks what makes a place live" (Skaggs 1990: 141). More than this, in the different points of view Cather creates in Cécile Auclair and her father, Euclide, Cather returns to her perennial place theme, to her own crucial autobiographical experience: the effect of a new land on an old culture. Euclide sees himself still as French – thus his desire to return to France with Count Frontenac – while Cécile, who remembers little of France, is frightened at the very thought – she has become North American, what was then beginning to be called "Canadian" and now is called

"Québecois." Ironically, Cather's depiction of "what makes a place live" in Quebec might well be used to foster the separatist agenda that has characterized Canada's politics in recent years – such is her rendering of its separate history.

Cather's return to Nebraska with *Obscure Destinies* and, following it, with her penultimate novel, *Lucy Gayheart*, was largely rendered through memory. After her mother died in 1931, Cather arranged a family reunion in Red Cloud and spent November through Christmas there; ironically, it was her last visit. *Lucy Gayheart* has gotten very little attention within Cather's works. Merrill Skaggs, however, treats the book's biographical and critical cruxes and concludes, convincingly, that it is a "novel of forgiveness": in it Cather "confronted those things that had wounded or offended her most, and having retaliated or punished, accepted them" (Skaggs 1990: 164). Thus all of the major characters in *Lucy Gayheart* are severely limited personalities and not, clearly, people Cather would have admired herself. The novel's plot – an inversion of *The Song of the Lark* – demanded this and, as Lucy's death asserts and Skaggs explains, through the novel Cather "affirms her *escape* from Red Cloud" (1990: 163). That is, had she stayed there, her own success – just like Thea's – would have been impossible.

Yet just as Clement Sebastian is gauged by his placeless state ("He had missed the deepest of all companionships, a relation with the earth itself, with a countryside and with a people" [Cather 1935: 78]), Lucy Gayheart owes her character to her relation to Haverford. In the first paragraph, the first-person narrator – another spokesperson for the town, as in *A Lost Lady* – the long-dead Lucy is a shared memory: "They still see her as a slight figure always in motion; dancing or skating, or walking swiftly with intense direction, like a bird flying home" (p. 3). Thus told of Lucy's death, we return to her in life at a skating party made of college-age townspeople home for the Christmas holidays, 1901; there, we meet her beau, Harry, and the two are described sitting along the Platte after a skate as the winter's day wanes:

> The red round sun was falling like a heavy weight; it touched the horizon line and sent quivering fans of red and gold over the wide country. For a moment Lucy and Harry Gordon were sitting in a stream of blinding light; it burned on their skates. . . . Their faces became so brilliant that they looked at each other and laughed. In an instant the light was gone; the frozen steam and the snow-masked prairie land became violet, under the blue-green sky. Wherever one looked there was nothing but flat country and low hills, all violet and grey. Lucy gave a long sigh.

The skaters return to the river and "found the river empty, a lonely stretch of blue-grey ice; all the skaters had gone" (Cather 1935: 10). Cather has returned here to her setting prairie sun, a great fact she had used to very different effect with her famous plough against the sun in *My Ántonia*. Of course, though not much named in that text, the ruefulness that characterizes *Lucy Gayheart* is evident there too, since we know of Jim's unhappy marriage. Here, we know, Lucy is gone, a memory only, her life equivalent to the sun's flash or the river as "lonely stretch."

Among the phrases that stand out from *Lucy Gayheart*'s third book – the section that Cather thought its best – is one utterly appropriate in describing Cather's final novel, *Sapphira and the Slave Girl*. While presenting Harry Gordon meditating after Mr. Gayheart's funeral, Cather writes that "the future had suddenly telescoped out of the past, so that there was actually no present" (1935: 220). In myriad ways, that is just what occurs in Cather's last novel. Set in Virginia just before the Civil War, primarily concerned with the evils of slavery, *Sapphira and the Slave Girl* "depicts lives lived in a time when a way of life begins to crumble" (Skaggs 1990: 168). Viewing the world as she did in the late 1930s, with the next great war looming, Cather found in 1850s Virginia an apt parallel to her own time and situation: for her, the future had telescoped out of the past. More than this, though, there is a decidedly personal cast to this novel; in it, Urgo has written, Cather's primary motive "may be the author's own desire to explain her relation to her birthplace" (1991: 159).

This relation needs to be explained. In *My Ántonia*, Cather offers this statement from Ántonia about her first home in Bohemia: " 'Jim,' she said earnestly, 'if I was put down there in the middle of the night, I could find my way all over that little town; and along the river to the next town, where my grandmother lived. My feet remember all the little paths through the woods, and where the big roots stick out to trip you. I ain't never forgot my own country.' " (Cather 1918: 230)

Neither did Ántonia's author. As mentioned above, in 1933 her friend from university days, Dorothy Canfield Fisher, wrote that "the only real subject of all" Cather's "books is the effect a new country – our new country – has on people transplanted to it from the old traditions of a stable, complex civilization" (quoted in Woodress 1987: 452). More recently, Joan Acocella has made something of the same point when she notes that Cather's 1880s Red Cloud and environs "was a world of exiles" (2000: 77). Having focused on these exiles throughout her writing, and having literally been one herself, Cather was ready after *Lucy Gayheart* to confront her own "old traditions of a stable, complex civilization," the American South.

That is just what Cather did in *Sapphira and the Slave Girl*, and she did so audaciously: just a few years after *Gone With the Wind*'s romanticization of the antebellum South, Cather uses the same stereotypes to tell a tale deeply and complexly analytical of the effects of slavery on human motivation and behavior. Sapphira is a character both attractive and repulsive, one whose full motives are never clear. Yet, like all of Cather's major protagonists, she is a character within a text who can be understood, if at all, only through her relation to her region, for its mores, cultural history, and invoked sensual presences have shaped her. Indeed, Sapphira's Back Creek, Virginia – the place, Cather once wrote, she herself started out from – was Willa Cather's first and last region. It is within *Sapphira and the Slave Girl* another "glittering idea," a presence that informs and shapes the story Cather tells. Like Nebraska, like the Southwest, like Quebec, Cather's Virginia glitters as a region of the mind and, perhaps most effectively, as a region of the heart. As artifices created by Cather's arrangement of words in her various texts, her regions glitter by inextricably connecting her characters to their places. They, and their stories, cannot be understood apart from their places. That, finally, is Willa Cather's regionalism, and so her great accomplishment within American letters.

REFERENCES

Acocella, Joan (2000). *Willa Cather and the Politics of Criticism*. Lincoln: University of Nebraska Press.

Cather, Willa (1913). *O Pioneers!*. Lincoln: University of Nebraska Press.

Cather, Willa (1915). *The Song of the Lark*. New York: Penguin.

Cather, Willa (1918). *My Ántonia*. Lincoln: University of Nebraska Press.

Cather, Willa (1922). *One of Ours*. New York: Vintage.

Cather, Willa (1923). *A Lost Lady*. Lincoln: University of Nebraska Press.

Cather, Willa (1925). *The Professor's House*. New York: Vintage.

Cather, Willa (1926). *My Mortal Enemy*. New York: Vintage.

Cather, Willa (1927). *Death Comes for the Archbishop*. Lincoln: University of Nebraska Press.

Cather, Willa (1931). *Shadows on the Rock*. New York: Vintage.

Cather, Willa (1932). *Obscure Destinies*. Lincoln: University of Nebraska Press.

Cather, Willa (1935). *Lucy Gayheart*. New York: Vintage.

Cather, Willa (1940). *Sapphira and the Slave Girl*. New York: Vintage.

Cather, Willa (1949). *On Writing: Critical Studies in Writing as an Art*. Lincoln: University of Nebraska Press.

Cather, Willa (1970). *Willa Cather's Collected Short Fiction, 1892–1912*. Lincoln: University of Nebraska Press.

Cather, Willa (1997). *The Autobiography of S. S. McClure*. Lincoln: University of Nebraska Press (Bison pb). (First publ. 1914 as S. S. McClure, *My Autobiography*.)

Gunn, Janet Varner (1982). *Autobiography: Towards a Poetics of Experience*. Philadelphia: University of Pennsylvania Press.

Lewis, Edith (1953). *Willa Cather Living: A Personal Record*. Lincoln: University of Nebraska Press.

O'Connor, Margaret Anne, ed. (2001). *Willa Cather: The Contemporary Reviews*. Cambridge: Cambridge University Press.

Rosowski, Susan J. (1986). *The Voyage Perilous: Willa Cather's Romanticism*. Lincoln: University of Nebraska Press.

Skaggs, Merrill Maguire (1990). *After the World Broke in Two: The Later Novels of Willa Cather*. Charlottesville: University Press of Virginia.

Thacker, Robert (1989). *The Great Prairie Fact and Literary Imagination*. Albuquerque: University of New Mexico Press.

Thacker, Robert (2001). " 'It's Through Myself that I Knew and Felt Her': S. S. McClure's *My Autobiography* and the Development of Willa Cather's Autobiographical Realism." *American Literary Realism* 33, 123–42.

Urgo, Joseph R. (1991). *Novel Frames: Literature as a Guide to Race, Sex, and History in American Culture*. Jackson: University Press of Mississippi.

West, Rebecca (1927). "Miss Cather's Business as an Artist." *New York Herald Tribune*, 11 Nov., 1, 5.

Woodress, James C. (1987). *Willa Cather: A Literary Life*. Lincoln: University of Nebraska Press.

30

"I have seen America emerging": Mary Austin's Regionalism

Betsy Klimasmith

As a child, Mary Austin recalls, she foresaw her artistic future: "it was clear that I would write imaginatively, not only of people, but of the scene, the totality which is called Nature" (1991: vii). From 1900 until her death in 1934, Mary Hunter Austin published prolifically, authoring more than 30 books in genres including drama, poetry, fiction, literary theory, and nonfiction, as well as over 250 periodical pieces on topics ranging from irrigation to Indians to gender to genius. A century later, we can see that Austin's prophesied "totality" describes her versatility and productivity as a writer. Yet Austin understands her "totality" in terms of place. Toward the end of her autobiography she writes: "my books were always of the West, which was little known; and always a little in advance of the current notion of it. They were never what is known as 'Westerns' . . . I wrote what I lived, what I had observed and understood. Then I stopped" (Austin 1991: 320). Austin's generative connection to the Western landscape is reinforced by the enduring popularity of *The Land of Little Rain* (1903), an episodic, largely nonfictional account of California's Owens Valley. Although Austin wrote perceptively of the various places she inhabited, including Illinois, New York, and California, readers and critics persistently link her work and personality with the arid landscape of the desert West. Identifying Austin with any single geography, however, obscures a theory of environment visible throughout her work.

Austin's focus on the meaning of place, honed by her experiences living in and writing from the southwestern United States, defines a brand of regionalism – and a theory of environment – that surface throughout her œuvre, connecting her widely varied texts and integrating her conception of region with her narrative practice. Austin left a textual legacy including her excellent naturist books *Little Rain* and *Lost Borders* (1909), as well as a theory of regionalism that considers environment more broadly. Her theory of regionalism makes visible the importance of place in all of her work, from the naturist texts to her fantasy, domestic and conservationist novels, to her autobiography.

Before exploring Austin's theory and tracing her practice of regional writing, it is useful to distinguish between her notions of place and environment. Place, considered both as object and as subject, is at the center of Austin's texts. In order to convey the meaning of a place, she believed, a writer needed to reveal its distinguishing qualities. Austin's texts, particularly her naturist works, are characterized by attentive and thorough descriptions of setting that lend an experiential quality to her work. This commitment to place reflected and helped to define the meaning of environment in her day. Austin's persistent grappling with "the land and its meaning" arose from and reinforced a commonly held Progressive Era belief that environments inevitably shaped people, who embodied the places they inhabited. Extending this argument, Austin claimed that a particular landscape should produce its own brand of narrative. Melody Graulich notes that Austin "believed that the desert landscape, the western storytellers and drifters, and the Indians helped her develop her voice, her way of seeing, and her art" (Afterword, in Austin 1991: 384). Austin applied the desert's lessons widely. Living out an inheritance of mobility, Austin followed a trajectory through geography and genre extending that of her pioneer foremothers as she moved from Midwest to West to East to Europe, finally returning to the desert in Santa Fe, New Mexico, where she returned as well to the naturist writing that had initiated her career.

In Retrospect: A Theory of Regionalism

In 1932, living in Santa Fe, writing of the West, and engaged in political activism on behalf of Native Americans, Austin explicated her theory of regional writing in an article titled "Regionalism and American Fiction." She opens by noting the centrality of environment to the human experience and to artistic creativity:

> Art . . . is the response [people] make in various mediums to the impact that the totality of their experience makes upon them, and there is no sort of experience that works so constantly and subtly upon man as his regional environment. . . . It is the thing always before his eye, always at his ear, always underfoot. Slowly or sharply it forces upon him behavior patterns such as earliest become the habit of his blood, the unconscious factor of adjustment in all his mechanisms. (Austin 1932: 97)

Like many of her contemporaries, Austin believed that environments inevitably shaped individuals and cultures; in her work, she constructs "the physical environment as the primary reality which must shape human thoughts and choices" (Buell 1995: 81). Working through the senses and intellect, an environment, whether urban, small-town, or rural, exerts itself upon the body and mind. Physical and emotional responses to particular environments produce the genuine regionalism Austin admires. Regional writing is therefore intensely personal; it must "come up through the land, shaped by the author's own adjustments to it"; it is "deep-rooted" and "intensively experienced" (Austin 1932: 101).

Figure 30.1   Mary Austin.

Because intensive experience is the wellspring of "true" regional writing, only a faithful representation of that experience's particularity can convey the nuances of the region. Austin derives her notion of particularity from a variety of literary sources including Hawthorne's *The House of the Seven Gables* and Cather's *My Antonia*; children's literature offered another powerful model for regional particularity. Labeling children "the most confirmed regionalists," she recalls that in her own childhood, "the best of everything appeared in *St. Nicholas*; and the best was always explicitly localized, dealt with particular birds and beasts, trees and growing things" (Austin

1932: 102). This "explicitly localized" specificity asserts itself throughout Austin's work. Her narrators emphasize the importance, in coming to know place, of time and patience, asserting that in order to understand (and certainly to represent) a region one must experience it both consciously and conscientiously. She notes, "It is not in the nature of mankind to be all of one pattern . . . any more than it is in the nature of the earth to be all plain, all seashore, or all mountains. Regionalism, since it is of the very nature and constitution of the planet, becomes at last part of the nature and constitution of the men who live on it" (Austin 1932: 98). For Austin, regional specificity and variety constitute the core of personal, cultural, and literary experience.

Austin offers several criteria to help readers recognize the type of writing that emerges from such careful attention to the specificity of place. In addition to being *of* rather than *about* the place, she notes, a regionalist narrative will feature the environment as more than backdrop: "The region must enter constructively into the story, as another character, as an instigator of plot" (Austin 1932: 105). Today, readers note her success: "It is a mark of the maturity of her vision . . . that her protagonist is the land" (Buell 1995: 80). Her short stories and novels offer abundant examples of active environments, from the untamed California landscape that produces the cross-dressing rebel heroine in *Isidro* (1905), to the small town that acts as the "villain" in *A Woman of Genius* (1912), to Dulcie Adelaid's personification of the Southwestern desert in *Cactus Thorn* (c.1927, published posthumously in 1988). Whether it produces people in its image, forces people to adapt to its conditions, or destroys people who resist or ignore its demands, the environment acts powerfully, even in texts which are not of the "West" with which Austin remains most frequently associated.

In insisting on the particularity of different regions, Austin emphasizes the heterogeneity of the nation and claims that any national literature must reflect this diversity. Alluding to the "long disappointed expectation of the 'Great American Novel,'" she asserts that an alternative vision of national literature is already at work in the United States, a "genuine" regionalism emanating not from politics or language, but from the "'guts,' the seat of life and breath and heartbeats, of loving and hating and fearing" (Austin 1932: 98). As the source "from which the only sound patriotism springs," a mosaic of texts derived from increasingly particular regions – "the Far West has split into the Southwest, the Northwest, the California Coast and the Movie West" – most accurately reflects the nation's vastly varied geographies (p. 104). Austin's vision of nation, not surprisingly, is "not one vast, pale figure of America, but several Americas, in many subtle and significant characterizations" (p. 98).

While Austin defined regional writing as national writing, the tension between region and nation repeatedly asserted itself as she tried to bring her work to a national audience. Given her readers' insistence on Austin's Western-ness, the bid for national recognition was difficult, a fact emphasized by the caustic tone of her article "New York: The Dictator of American Criticism." In this essay, Austin writes that, according to literary taste-makers, the nation is "centered in New York, with a small New England ell in the rear and a rustic gazebo in Chicago; the rest of it is magnificently predicated through a car window" (Austin 1996a: 58). Reuben Ellis remarks that "ironically Austin, the western regionalist, at times felt herself embattled with a smug Northeastern narrow-mindedness that represented to her the worst of what a regional perspective could be" (Austin 1996a: 55). It is fitting, then, that Austin published both "Regionalism" and "New York" in national periodicals. Although they did not pay well – always a concern for the self-supporting Austin – these periodicals allowed her to engage with a national audience.[1]

Aiming to reach that national audience, Austin offered regional writing as an alternative to the homogenizing forces of modernity. What she called an "automobile eye view" represented a force that privileged homogeneity over specificity, overlooking history and culture as it sped by (Austin 1932: 100). Austin notes, for instance, that the "world of American Indian lore," while literally quite accessible, is almost completely overlooked as an element of regional – and thus national – environment. "This world begins in the dooryard of every American child; it can be fully entered at the edge of every American town, it can be looked out upon from every train window and crossed by every automobile" (p. 104). Paradoxically, the technology that opened new regional worlds to Americans helps to close off the cultural history of place, region, and nation from the careful observation Austin advocates. In regional writing:

> Time is the essence of the undertaking, time to live into the land and absorb it; still more time to cure the reading public of its preference for something less than the proverbial bird's-eye view of the American scene, what you might call an automobile eye view, something slithering and blurred, nothing so sharply discriminated that it arrests the speed-numbed mind to understand, characters like garish gas stations picked out with electric lights. (Austin 1932: 107)

Austin's mission is clear: to identify and perpetuate a national literature made up of intensely regional work that, like the nation it reflects, can be understood only as a collective. Reciprocally, such a literary mosaic will help to produce for the nation a heightened consciousness of history, environment, and self. Investing the time necessary to know a region improves the individual – and thus the nation. Austin notes, "Whoever has lived deeply and experientially into his own environment" may develop the "nimble wit and . . . considerable capacity for traveling in one's mind" required of the regionalist (1932: 105). Self-knowledge and imaginative power serve as antidotes to the blurred vision and decentered self of high modernism.

Austin's vision of environment was not entirely deterministic; in her life and in her writing she asserted that people could escape from difficult or unsympathetic environments and seek out places to which they were better suited. In Austin's case, the desert landscapes of California and New Mexico provided the environment she sought as alternative to the frustrations of her Illinois childhood and the New York of her thirties. With "a mind made to the desert's order," John Farrar stated in a 1923 profile, "Mary Austin went into the southwest and the desert made her life articulate. It has never failed her since, nor freed her" (Farrar 1923: 47). Though Austin chafed at being constrained by her regionalism, she found in the Western landscape inspiration and structure for almost all of her published work.

Encountering the Desert: "One Hundred Miles on Horseback"

Mary Austin's efforts to distance her writing about the West from "Westerns" surface even in her earliest work. In 1889, aged 21, Austin published "One Hundred Miles on Horseback," a travelogue of the final leg of her journey from Carlinville, Illinois to the desert near Bakersfield, California, where her family planned to homestead. Although she was traveling with her mother and brother, here Austin narrates an individual journey in a voice reminiscent of such nineteenth-century diarists and letter-writers as Caroline Kirkland (*A New Home – Who'll Follow?*) and Mary Hallock Foote, whose encounters with Western landscapes were published nationally. Austin shares Kirkland and Foote's task of interpreting an alien region; like them, she is quite literally writing home. "One Hundred Miles" was published in *The Blackburnian*, the literary journal of Austin's alma mater. Although Austin had earlier rejected her mother's advice to become an English major, rebelliously choosing biology instead, she rebelled within the safety of a tiny Presbyterian college in her home town. Blackburn College was an extension of Austin's domestic reality, firmly affiliated with the religious values and moralistic perspective she would later reject. The familiar, epistolary style both recalls domestic narrative forms and presages her observant, descriptive naturist texts. She would later note in her largely third-person autobiography *Earth Horizon* (1932) that when she wrote "One Hundred Miles," "all the derived and imitative influence of academic training fell away, and she wrote for the first time directly, in her own character, much as she did in 'The Land of Little Rain'" (Austin 1991: 189). But the transformation was not quite so sudden, as the essay's content shows.

While Austin would sharpen her precise observations of landscape in her later work, she came to scorn most of the textual reference points she uses in "One Hundred Miles" to orient her Illinois audience to the desert environment. Having arrived in California knowing "nothing except what she read in Bret Harte and Helen Hunt Jackson," Austin uses the Bible, Jackson's *Ramona*, and Harte's Western stories – some of the very texts she would later decry as warping the nation's sense of region – to describe the structures, people, and scenery she encounters (Austin 1991: 177). In her later work Austin would convey the sense that the more deeply one knew the West, the more one could sense its unknowability. Here, however, her narrative voice has the naïve authority of the novice that Austin would later critique and complicate.

Echoing some of her literary sources, Austin's travelogue exoticizes and denigrates the people who make up part of the region. Though in much of her subsequent theory and practice of region Austin was careful, thorough, and generally respectful of the region's people, in "One Hundred Miles" her early textual training in how to frame her encounter with the West is apparent. Unlike the landscape, Westerners neither possess beauty nor inspire awe. She remarks upon the "outlandish-" and "fierce-looking Mexican shepherds," and the "dirty but picturesque children" (1996b: 26–8). This othering depiction of the desert's human and animal inhabitants would almost disappear from Austin's later work as her narrators increasingly integrated themselves into the landscapes they produced. We can see inklings of this heterarchical stance when Austin turns her attention to the domestic spaces of the West.

A vocabulary and perspective more closely linked to her later work surfaces briefly in "One Hundred Miles" when Austin discusses houses and begins to imagine the desert as home: "In each [canyon a] Mexican or Indian has built his hut of adobe or tule, planted his grape-vine and set up his hive of bees" (Austin 1996b: 28). Like her contemporary Edith Wharton, Austin was raised to be attentive to the details of domestic space, and here that intimate understanding brings an imaginative identification otherwise absent from her initial encounter with the landscape. We begin to see how she would imagine her way into the people, animals, and even plants that make up the environment as she focused on the Owens Valley and began to develop her eye for landscape.

The Land of Little Rain: Writing of the Region

Throughout her career, Mary Austin claimed that knowing a region required an intimate knowledge of its particularities. By 1903, when she published *The Land of Little Rain*, she had developed her practice of specificity. Her best-known and most widely available work, the text is a composite of fiction and nonfiction episodes – what Carl Bredahl (1989) terms a "divided narrative" – describing animal, plant, and human life in and around the Owens Valley. Significantly, the narrator does not attempt to speak about or for the West considered broadly, but attends instead to truths evoked by particular places. Only through the effort of intimacy, she implies, can a person begin to see and eventually comprehend a place. She notes, for example, that while the casual visitor may never find a buzzard's nest, the diligent observer will be rewarded: "by making a business of it one may come upon them in wide, quiet canyons or on the lookouts of lonely, tabletop mountains" (Austin 1950: 19). Significantly, this effort at intimacy is not merely visual; the narrator "hunger[s] . . . for bits of lore and 'fool talk'" that will limn the cultural and historical complexities of the landscape (p. 63). Through intimate experience, region is figured on a human scale.

The Land of Little Rain mirrors Austin's efforts to understand the landscape that she had rendered alien in "One Hundred Miles." Austin integrated herself into the landscape in a variety of ways. She remembers ceaselessly observing her new surroundings. At night she would sit and watch "the frisking forms of field mouse and kangaroo rat, the noiseless passage of the red fox and the flitting of the elf owls at their mating. By day she would follow a bobcat to its lair in the bank of the Wash, and, lying before its den, the two would contemplate each other wordlessly for long times" (Austin 1991: 194). Here the facility and vibrancy that characterize Austin's regionalism in *Little Rain* are visible. Further, she notes in her autobiography that she possessed "the scientist's itch to understand by getting inside the material in which he works" (1991: 159). As Austin explored the region, her training in rhetoric and botany led her to see in particular elements of her surroundings the chance for the landscape to "explain itself": "Mary was spellbound in an effort not to miss any animal behavior, any birdmarking, any weather signal, any signature of tree or flower" (1991: 195). Together, these elements become part of the complex system that Austin believed a regionalist must experience personally in order to represent her subject.

As practiced in *Little Rain*, Austin's regionalism integrates both people and nonhuman elements into the place. This literary move was foreshadowed by Austin's own encounters with the people of the Tejon Pass and Owens Valley. Biographer Esther Lanigan calls attention to Austin's productive relationships with older male mentors such as General Edward Beale, who guided Austin's understanding of the Tejon Pass, taking her to Indian villages, telling stories of his long and illustrious past in the region, introducing her to "sheepherders, Indians, and tall Mexican vaqueros," and securing "Government documents, military explorations, agricultural reports . . . [and] geological and botanical surveys" (1997: 197). All of these sources are woven into *Little Rain*, filtered (as Austin's own knowledge was) through the fabric of personal relationships. Similarly, in *Earth Horizon* Austin stresses women's roles in helping her to develop an ear for the stories the place had to tell. Later, when they moved to the Owens Valley, Austin and her husband boarded for three months with a Mrs. Dodge, who "had knocked about the mining country for thirty years and loved talking. Dodge was an old-timer whose every word was interlarded with the quaintest blasphemies, between priceless idioms of the camp. By this time Mary had come to realize that blasphemies were a sort of poetizing" (Austin 1991: 237). Mexican and Indian women, too, live the stories that become the foundation for Austin's knowledge and the material for her representations of the landscape.[2]

In *Little Rain*, environment emerges as a complex system that must be understood both objectively and subjectively. *Little Rain* thus begins the argument that Austin would develop in works like *Lost Borders* and *The Land of Journey's Ending* for the complexity and connectedness of place. These naturist texts attend to connections among animals, plants, geological features, weather, and human culture in the isolated region. Coyotes make the same trails that Austin imagines "very intelligent men" would make (Austin 1950: 11). Animals and people use the water trails that were marked by ancient tribes (p. 16). The environment "breeds in the men, as in the plants, a certain well-roundedness and sufficiency" (p. 33). People learn "direct from the tutelage of the earth" (p. 94). Characterized by connection, the landscape asserts again and again that it can be understood only in all its complexity, a notion Austin emphasizes through her narrative technique.

Although she clearly writes from her own experience, in *Little Rain* Austin rejects the epistolary narration of "One Hundred Miles," diffusing her personal voice. At least three narrative voices are present in *Little Rain* – Austin chooses among an ungendered third-person narrator, a male narrator, and a female narrator given to addressing her audience directly – each helping to initiate the reader into a personal, if textual, experience of the region. This narrative multiplicity implicitly allows narrators to occupy several subject positions at once, a strategy that underpins Austin's conjoined claims in *Little Rain*: first, that the desert landscape can be understood only if it is known intimately, and second, that an intimate knowledge might best be achieved by imaginatively entering into and observing from the perspectives of other desert-dwellers.

While claiming that place knowledge can only develop with time, Austin both offers and denies this knowledge to her readers by manipulating time in the narratives that comprise *Little Rain*. As she notes in "The Basket Maker," "To understand the fashion of any life, one must know the land it is lived in and the procession of the year" (Austin 1950: 59). In "The Streets of the Mountains," the narrator cautions the reader: "Never believe what you are told, that midsummer is the best time to go up the streets of the mountain – well – perhaps for the merely idle or sportsmanly or scientific; but for seeing and understanding the best time is when you have the longest leave to stay" (p. 67).

Here, Austin integrates her readers into her project, assuming either that they come to her text with the same eye she brings to the landscape, or that her text will help them develop this vision. Though she claims that only extended time will allow visitors to understand the mountains, her text immediately sets out to imitate and perhaps offer an alternative to extended experience. Austin plays with time, expanding and contracting it in order to allow her readers an experience of place accessible only via narrative.

> The drone of bees, the chatter of jays, the hurry and stir of squirrels, is incessant; the air is odorous and hot. The roar of the stream fills up the morning and evening intervals, and at night the deer feed in the buckthorn thickets. It is worth watching the year round in the purlieus of the long-leafed pines. One month or another you get sight of the trails of most roving mountain dwellers as they follow the limit of forboding snows, and more bloom than you can properly appreciate. (Austin 1950: 68).

Although the narrator begins watching the mountains during the tourist-approved summer season, the text quickly moves readers into seasons available only to more committed individuals. This "diffusion of narrative angle" allows Austin to manipulate space and time using a technique comparable to time-lapse photography (Buell 1995: 176). The text, then, begins to approximate through narrative the experience of prolonged watching Austin advocates.

Time changes the way in which environment operates in the narrator's mind, shifting memory, altering perception, and precluding the text from replacing – or even fully representing – the experience of intimacy with the landscape. One narrator acknowledges when she sees a place through "a rosy mist of reminiscence" that she "must always see it with a sense of intimacy in the light that never was" (Austin 1950: 31). Lanigan notes, "Her search for the authentic permits her to suspend ordinary consciousness in favor of the nonordinary or heightened consciousness . . . and by so doing, to enter into the spirit of the tale she tells" (1997: 79). Yet Austin is careful to call attention to the positions from which her narrators speak, reminding the reader of the text's constructedness. The meaning of place can be shaped only in reference to experience; if that experience is gained second-hand, through narrative, the meaning of place can never be separated from the narrator's construction.

Like time, intimacy brings with it an emotional attachment that shades the way in which the narrative is produced. When Austin writes, for instance, that "none other than this long brown land lays such a hold on the affections," or that "one finds butterflies, too, about these high, sharp regions which might be called desolate, but will not by me that love them," she reminds the reader of her subjective presence (1950: 6, 75). Austin's technique might be termed relational in that the narrator always writes from – and emphasizes – a personal relationship to the environment he or she describes. This relational quality extends from the land to animals to the people who together comprise the region.

If her narrators emphasize their own feelings about the landscapes they encounter, Austin also effaces the narrators' presence. Narrative is often positioned as hearsay, narrators as interpreters of others' stories. Austin's narrators gain access to the places and people that make up the region through careful observation and perceptive listening. In "The Pocket Hunter," for example, the narrator notes, "I think he said the best indication of small pockets was an iron stain, but I never could get the run of miner's talk . . ." (Austin 1950: 25). Similarly, in "Shoshone Land," Austin undermines her narrator's power when she reminds us that "there was never any but Winnenap' who could tell and make it worth telling about Shoshone Land" (p. 36). This alternate emphasis on and effacement of the narrator's role in constructing the narrative allows Austin to convey the complexity of environment; she would utilize this technique frequently as she began to publish in different genres.

Narrative Multiplicity in *Little Rain* and *Lost Borders*

When writing *Little Rain*, Austin notes, her authorial breakthrough came when she used the rhythms of the environment to structure her work: "She found it at last in the rhythm of the twenty-mule teams that creaked in and out of the borax works, the rhythm of lonely lives blown across the trails" (1991: 296). Graulich notes that for Austin "language and style originate from an understanding of what she would have called the 'landscape line'" (Austin 1991: 384). Austin linked the development of her distinctive style, form, and narration to the particular environments that had shaped her, including the Midwestern landscape that had molded her early life and the various landscapes she moved among as an adult. Given the variety and particularity of place Austin encountered even within a given region, it is fitting that she began her fictional explorations of region with short stories. In those short stories, especially in the collection of linked tales titled *Stories from the Country of Lost Borders* (1909), Austin evokes the particularity and complexity of place using some of the narrative strategies she initiated in *Little Rain*.

In *Lost Borders*, stories are overheard, gleaned from gossip, partially told or retold, recollected from the past. Any narrator's reliability is always open to question; this is just as true of the main narrator as of the desert inhabitants whose stories she relates. Here, the "narrator acts as a filter of the tales related to her by and about the desert's inhabitants" (Lanigan 1997: 107). When we recall Austin's dictum that regional writing considers people as a part of the place, the stories told in this manner have the effect of emerging from the land itself via people who experience the land individually and know the land intimately. Another of Austin's observations in "Regionalism in American Fiction," that the land should be an active element in the narrative, is reflected in way the land acts: "The desert 'herself' enters every story in *Lost Borders* as a character and serves to unify and motivate each one" (Austin 1987: xxx).

We see here the development of a narrative style that takes its cues from the land itself, a strategy introduced in *Little Rain*, where

> Austin allows the book to be taken over by other peoples' stories and her speaker to imagine the desert as it might look through the eyes of birds and animals. In this diffusion of centers of consciousness, and her refusal to maintain an executive control over the perceptual center except at the level of the prescriptive aphorism, Austin adheres to what she sees as the ethic dictated by the place: "Not the law, but the land sets the limit." (Buell 1995: 176)

Austin's narrator plays with the notion of narrative omniscience here, sometimes revealing more than she has promised, remarking on the parts of stories she will never reveal, sharing her frustration when gripping stories refuse to be told. In some stories, like "The Woman at the Eighteen Mile," she does all three. When she hears the woman's story, the narrator recalls: "I sat within the shallow shadow of the eaves experiencing the full-throated satisfaction of old field prospectors over the feel of pay dirt, rubbing it between the thumb and palm, swearing over it softly below the breath. It was as good as that. And I was never to have it" (Austin 1987: 207).

Later, she does learn the details of the woman's story, and while she promises never to reveal what she has learned, she later decides that this pledge "should not mean beyond the term of her life" (Austin 1987: 210). This pattern is repeated and varied throughout the text, and thus, "*Lost Borders*, enmeshing the reader in its web of fact and fiction, of gossip, speculation, and concrete detail, involves the reader in a collaboration with the narrator" (Lanigan 1997: 112). This collaboration gives the narrator a certain freedom and allows Austin to construct for her readers a sense of the region that echoes her own.

In *Earth Horizon*, Austin recalls that stories structured her early experience of the region: "Pete Miller's bear stories, Jerke Johnson's horse stories, sheepherders' tales, deeply touched with a far derived pagan lore, Basque, Mexican, Old French" (1991: 215). It is clear that Austin's West, as critics note of the region today, is a place where many cultures meet.[3] The water trails that interlace through the arid landscape in *Little Rain* become the narrative that webs the region in *Lost Borders*. Stories come and go; told through many mouths, they disperse, change, and return to their initiators in a participatory process that the text both explains and reflects. Austin would return to this form later in her life with *The Land of Journey's Ending* (1924) and *One Smoke Stories* (1934), in which she returns to the practice of writing *of* a region – the New Southwest – by knowing it intimately.

Her narrative strategies in *Little Rain* and *Lost Borders* also allow Austin to undermine and subtly critique conventions of gender. Using a male or gender-neutral narrator let her claim a more culturally powerful voice and distance herself from the nineteenth-century women writers who wrote about their personal encounters with nature (Lanigan 1997: 40). As she notes in *Earth Horizon*, Rudyard Kipling's tales were an early model: "with their slightly mocking detachment, their air of completely disengaging the author from any responsibility for the moral implications of the scene and the people of whom he wrote, [they] had at least pointed the way for a use of the sort of material of which I found myself possessed" (Austin 1991: 230).

Because Austin does not explicitly identify the narrator as herself, she gains the ability to cross boundaries of genre, geography, and gentility more easily than the earlier women writers whose narratives called attention to and were confined by cultural limits. No such limitations seem to be imposed upon Austin's narrator, who is equally comfortable in (and gains apparently unfettered access to) spaces ranging from mining towns to stormy mountain ranges to Mexican villages to Indian campoodies. Intimacy is afforded to a narrator who has become a part of the region.

While we can read Austin's disidentification with the narrator as a rejection of the domestic voice present in "One Hundred Miles," it is perhaps more fruitful to see her narration as an outgrowth of domesticity's intimacy that enables her to convey a deeper sense of place, especially when we note the shift to a consistently female (if still somewhat effaced) narrator in *Lost Borders*. Lois Rudnick claims that "Austin is the first feminist critic to have argued for the importance of what she called the '*home*centric novel.' It was 'stupid and inexcusable,' she told a primarily male audience of critics, to ignore the centrality of women's fiction to an understanding of the development of American culture" (Rudnick 1987: 22, emphasis added).

In making the desert her home, Austin opens domestic modes of perception and communication, such as gossip and the letter, to a broader audience. She uses these forms to redefine both domesticity and the West. Later, Austin would explicitly critique Midwestern domesticity's constraints, particularly in *Earth Horizon* and her largely autobiographical novel *A Woman of Genius*. In her desert texts, however, Austin offers a model for how the ideals and ethics of the home, such as intimate knowledge, sympathetic understanding, acceptance of the unusual, emotional connection, and imaginative identification are the very values that might lead to, or perhaps already characterize, a vibrant national literature.

As Austin's career progressed, *Little Rain*'s blend of place-centered fiction and nonfiction was refracted into the novels, plays, poems, stories, and journalism that comprise her varied œuvre. Because her regionalism aims to encompass both place and people, in much of her work, particularly her more realistic novels, place becomes one factor among many that shape narrative. In her most successful texts, she achieves what she would later term "the first of the indispensable conditions" of regionalism, incorporating environment "constructively into the story, as another character, as an instigator of plot" (Austin 1932: 105). In attempting to render the settings of her fiction recognizable to the inhabitants of that region, whether the region was the California West, New Mexico, or the Midwestern "Ohianna" with which she evoked her Illinois upbringing, Austin does more than account for the visuality of place with which a more touristic eye might be content. Rather, she engages actively with the complex elements that combine to form a particular landscape: its economics, its social and political culture, and its history, along with the physical environment.

Region as Fantasy: *Isidro* and *Outland*

Austin even applies her theory and practice of regionalism to her fantasy novels. She explains: "the countries down the rabbit hole and behind the looking glass never depart for an instant from fidelity to the topsy-turviness of the land of dreams" (1932: 103). Here Austin is describing children's books; but fantasy worlds structure two of her earliest sustained narratives, the novels *Isidro* (1905) and *Outland* (1910, co-written with George Sterling). Straddling two genres, the dime novels Austin read as a child and the utopian fantasies that were a part of the Progressive Era's zeitgeist, these often bizarre texts read as early attempts to translate her practice of regional writing into novels, a form more readily consumed than her less classifiable naturist work (Austin 1991: 63). As she would later write to H. G. Wells, "I agree with you that I can't write novels, but publishers will have them" (Pearce 1979: 107). In addition to their marketability, novels could serve as vehicles for social commentary. The sustained, authoritative narration inappropriate to her desert texts could proclaim that social problems like those she explored in her naturist works should not be dismissed as merely local issues.

Just as exploring and writing from the desert offered Austin a way to rewrite her domestic and narrative inheritance, in her fantasy novels the environment offers alternatives to conventional domesticity. In *Isidro*, for instance, the colonial California setting produces El Zarzo, a slim, heroic lad who becomes Isidro's buddy and partner in adventure until it becomes clear that the lad is in fact a gal. And while the two must marry, as Nicole Tonkovich explains, "she need not be a conventional woman within her home, since her husband (who was once satisfied to enter a celibate fraternity) still prefers to think of her as a lad" (Graulich and Klimasmith, eds. 1999: 14).

If Austin's critique of the constraints of traditional marriage and gender roles is (barely) concealed and (ironically) abandoned in *Isidro*, it is far more obvious in *Outland*, a fantasy novel of warring Indian tribes who live unseen by white people in the forests, mountains, and deserts near the California coast. *Outland* begins with an adult version of the tumble down the rabbit hole: Mona, a professor turned writer, and Herman, her sociologist suitor, follow a woodland trail into the forest realm of the Outlander tribe. As in *Isidro*, *Outland*'s environment has produced a culture that offers alternatives to conventional bourgeois love and marriage. When Mona rejects Herman's marriage proposal at the novel's beginning, she sets the stage for the reader's encounter with Trastevera, the female prophet or *chisera* figure present in stories such as "The Walking Woman" and dramas like *The Arrow Maker* and *Fire*.[4] As the visionary Trastevera charts the course for this unconventional society's survival outside of Anglo political and economic relationships with the land, she maintains an unconventional marriage to a younger man and enforces the tribe's commitment to rituals that require certain attractive young women to postpone marrying for seven years while they serve the tribe as wards. Significant here, as in *Isidro*, is Austin's implicit claim that the pre-Anglo conquest environment has produced female roles much more powerful than those condoned within bourgeois culture. The flip side of this environmental theory of gender surfaces in the novels that move back into more conventional domestic settings.

Modernity and Region: Considering the City

The intimacy with place Austin developed in her naturist texts also structures her novels set in more urban cultural, social, and physical environments. Upon moving to New York in 1910, Austin approached the city much as she had approached the desert. In her effort to "know New York," Austin explored different regions of the city, moving frequently, posing as a typist, working at artificial flowers, and selling pencils and shoelaces (Austin 1991: 352). She writes: "what I was looking for was the web of city life, the cross-ties and interweavings which brought all classes into coalition, made the city unit. . . . I had it in mind that I would make a fiction of my findings, which would do what nobody was doing in fiction for New York, present-ing a closely woven section of the life of the city" (1991: 352). Austin lived in New York for 13 years, but "as a matter of fact," she confesses, "I never found it" (p. 352). While Austin tries to use the tools and practice of environmental intimacy in her new surroundings, the urban landscape eludes representation. Yet her efforts at representing urban landscapes again show how she channels her perceptive practice of experiencing place to criticize and offer alternatives to bourgeois domesticity.

Regionalist theory and practice link Austin's urban domestic novels *Santa Lucia* (1908), *A Woman of Genius* (1912), and *No. 26 Jayne Street* (1920) to her naturist work. First, in all of these texts the environment operates as a force that confronts and shapes the novels' characters, rewarding people who fit it and destroying those who misunderstand it. This role is made explicit in *A Woman of Genius*, the strongest novel of the three; the narrator describes the story as "the struggle between a Genius for Tragic acting and the daughter of a County Clerk, with the social ideal of Taylorville, Ohianna, [the protagonist's home town] for the villain" (Austin 1912: 5). In *Santa Lucia*, a fiction that combines the Western adventure genre (knife fights, ambushes) with the novel of manners (three versions of the marriage plot), Austin exposes the small town's cruelty when the vibrant Julia Stairs, unable to reconcile her passionate nature to the brand of femininity demanded by the college town's moral surveillance, commits suicide. *Jayne Street* tells the story of an idealistic young woman's doomed affair with a womanizing reformer. Here, high-minded political discourse is no match for the moral degradation produced by modernity's urban environment.

In these texts, Austin's treatment of bourgeois domesticity and gender roles reads as an outgrowth of the critiques embedded in *Lost Borders'* stories of cavalier men and the women who suffer them but survive (Lanigan 1997: 108). In *Lost Borders*, the desert becomes an alternative home, where morality is always considered in relation to setting and circumstances. Similarly, in her urban novels Austin imagines alternative homes for her heroines. The stage (*Woman of Genius*), the wilderness (*Santa Lucia*), and Europe (*No. 26 Jayne Street*) all serve as spaces where women may find new homes free from traditional domesticity's constraints. Significantly, both these alternative spaces and the repressive spaces they replace are described with the detail that characterizes Austin's attention to the land in her naturist works.

Although city novels are not usually considered regionalist, in "Regionalism and American Fiction" Austin allows for this possibility. For instance, Austin notes that Edith Wharton's *The House of Mirth* "fulfills the regional test of not being possible to have happened elsewhere" (1932: 100). Austin's urban novels echo *The House of Mirth* in criticizing social realities by describing them explicitly. In addition, the novels allow Austin to maintain her commitment to writing *of* place while fighting one risk of regionalism – that in focusing on the particularities of place, social commentary will be defused and dismissed as anomaly.

Region and the Conservationist Novels

Austin's regionalism is not limited to the aesthetics or visuality of place; region is never divorced from economics or culture, as her conservationist texts emphasize. *The Flock* (1906), *The Ford* (1917), and *Cactus Thorn* (c.1927) differently construct the forces of people, animals, natural resources, and economics in relation to environment. In these texts, as Anne Raine notes of *The Ford*, Austin's "commitment to the human beings who make their living in the landscape insists on the . . . construction of a viable *working* relationship between human and natural economies" (Graulich and Klimasmith eds. 1999: 262). *The Flock* and *Cactus Thorn* present different extremes of the conservationist viewpoint. *The Flock*, a novel describing the lives of sheep and sheepherders, asserts that the people who work the land are its best stewards, and only obliquely criticizes the national forces (here national parks) that contend for rights to the land. In *Cactus Thorn*, however, Grant Arliss, representing an exploitative national politics, is knifed to death by his erstwhile lover Dulcie Adelaid, who strikes on the desert's behalf. *The Ford*'s vision of region falls in between. While these texts may not be completely in tune with equations of "environment" to "wilderness," they persuasively reveal Austin's regionalist commitment to landscape's specificity.

The Ford reads as a revisionist Western romance with a subplot focused on natural resources in an arid California climate. Exploring the issue of how rural communities can negotiate the future in relationship to an increasingly urban economy, the novel asks what constitutes a natural connection with the land and considers how to translate this connection into political, educational, agricultural, or commercial action. *The Ford* traces the economic history of a rural California town increasingly connected to the city by train, car, and telephone, and correspondingly evolving as the city's resource-rich hinterland. Austin's attention to detail leads her to show how modernity reshapes the space of region. The novel's valley-dwellers cling to an idealized vision of the land's power and possibility, despite their lived knowledge of its harshness and vicissitudes. "It had come out so naturally for the bucolic imagination that, as Elwood had lived with the land, he had become possessed of a sense of its possibilities; its voice, so compelling and to them so inarticulate, had spoken to him in terms of canals, highways, towns . . ." (Austin 1997: 272). Though they are able neither to envision nor to mastermind the rural West's transformation, Austin's rural people want development, modernization, and especially the capital that new development may bring. Austin's optimistic attitude in *The Ford* toward modernity and development stems from her version of environmental determinism: that is, that the land determines what is best for it.

In portraying a family learning to read, coming to terms with, and eventually prospering from the particularities of place, *The Ford* articulates a regionalism grounded in realism and emphasizing progress. Both Brent children, the novel's most highly valorized characters, experience the attractions of San Francisco but decide to remain at their family ranch, forestalling the rural community's demise. Of course, the forces of modernity have linked the ranch to the city, offering Kenneth and Anne many more choices than their parents had. When Anne's doomed mother says, "Though I do live in the country, I don't have to be country," we see not only that the previous generation marked sharp delineations between rural and urban, but that ignoring the land's force is fundamentally destructive (Austin 1997: 52). As the boundaries between urban and rural break down, Austin suggests, so do many of the gender restrictions associated with the pioneer generation. Thus, Anne Brent is free not just to choose a successful career as a real estate agent and reject marriage, but to create the terms upon which she relates to the land that is her home. As in her domestic novels, in her conservationist texts Austin writes *of* place in order to re-imagine modernity and home.

Representing the West

Austin's regionalism demanded a thorough and specific knowledge of place accessible only through sustained experience; yet by focusing persistently on particular places she risked both marginalization and limited understanding by the audiences and publishers for whom the regions she described were foreign. Writing in the third person, Austin recalls this difficulty in *Earth Horizon*:

> Mary wrote one of the earliest accounts of it, which in the East nobody would publish until it had long been an old story, seen by a sufficient number of Easterners for an account of it to have credibility in the printed page. That was how it was with a great many things Mary wanted to write about. When they were new and fresh to her, Eastern editors wouldn't believe them, and by the time the East had become aware, Mary had moved on to something new and unauthenticated by New York. (Austin 1991: 213)

Frustrated by this dynamic, Austin would abandon the novel after 1920 and return to the mosaic narrative form she had derived from the Western landscape.[5] Ultimately, it is *Earth Horizon* that brings together her theory and practice of environment, allowing her to say something "new and unauthenticated" about the different environments that had shaped her own life and work.

In *Earth Horizon*, Austin adopts the form of autobiography to depict herself as an embodiment of her theory of environment. She explores the different places that produced her: Illinois, California's Tejon Pass and Owens Valley and Carmel, New York, and New Mexico, showing how and why she committed herself to the settings that best represented who she was and offered what she needed at the time. *Earth Horizon* also details Austin's activity to represent – perhaps even to embody – the West through performance, lectures, and activism, as well as her profound ambivalence about the professional and material consequences of doing so.

Thus, Austin's career underlines how double-edged is the regionalist project. At stake are the pleasure of deep knowledge and the risk of marginalization. Yet her powerful attraction to place – "the land always" – was ultimately stronger than her considerable drive for professional success and recognition. She represents as inescapably visceral her engagement with landscape:

> And still, whenever, out of a car window, over the wall of a rich man's garden, about which I am being proudly shown by the proprietor I get sight of any not utterly ruined corner of it, I am torn in my vitals. This is the way a Naturist is taken with the land, with the spirit trying to be evoked out of it. . . . It is time somebody gave a true report. (Austin 1991: 188)

The powerful, painful nature of engagement with place is present throughout Austin's œuvre, yet only through this intense relation to place, she states at the close of *Earth Horizon*, had she "seen America emerging" (1991: 368). Writing of the subjective experience of the self in environment and seeing beyond the automobile-eye view of the landscape proved irresistible for Austin. The particularity, detail, and multiplicity she saw around her, which she constructed by revising domestic narrative strategies, allowed her to represent place, environment, region, and nation with the complexity and depth she knew they deserved.

NOTES

1   Perhaps this tension between "nation" and "region" led Austin to assert a vision of modernism that ran counter to the high modernism of her peers such as H. D. and Ezra Pound. Dale Metcalfe claims that Austin rejected what she termed the "maimed voices" of modernism, and offered as an alternative a healing modernism arising from the landscape (see Mary Austin, "Fig Leaves," quoted in Dale Metcalfe, "Singing Like the Indians Do: Mary Austin's Poetry" in Graulich and Klimasmith, eds. 1999; see also Graulich's introduction.). As Lois Rudnick notes, like other Southwesterners Austin sought to "heal what T. S. Eliot called *the* disease of modernity: 'the dissociation of sensibility'" (1996: 27). Austin aimed to re-inject sensibility into modern US culture by privileging the particularities of place.

2   See Metcalfe, "Singing Like the Indians Do," and Klimasmith 1995.

3   For recent perspectives on the West as a zone of intercultural contact, see Comer 1999; Lape 2000.

4   For discussion of the *chisera* figure in Austin's plays, see Mark Hoyer, "Ritual drama/dramatic ritual: Austin's Indian plays," in Graulich and Klimasmith, eds. 1999.

5   Austin did write a novella, *Cactus Thorn*, around 1927, but it remained unpublished until 1988.

REFERENCES

Austin, Mary (1905). *Isidro*. Boston and New York: Houghton Mifflin.

Austin, Mary (1906). *The Flock*. Boston and New York: Houghton Mifflin.

Austin, Mary (1908). *Santa Lucia*. New York: Harper & Bros.

Austin, Mary (1912). *A Woman of Genius*. New York: Doubleday Page.

Austin, Mary (1919). *Outland*. New York: Boni and Liverwright. (First publ. 1910.)

Austin, Mary (1920). *No. 26 Jayne Street*. Boston: Houghton Mifflin.

Austin, Mary (1932). "Regionalism in American Fiction." *English Journal* 21, 97–107.

Austin, Mary (1950). *The Land of Little Rain*. Boston: Houghton Mifflin. (First publ. 1903.)

Austin, Mary (1987). *Stories from the Country of Lost Borders*. New Brunswick: Rutgers University Press, intr. Marjorie Pryse. (First publ. 1909.)

Austin, Mary (1988). *Cactus Thorn*. Reno: University of Nevada Press.

Austin, Mary (1991). *Earth Horizon: the Autobiography of Mary Austin*. Albuquerque: University of New Mexico Press. (First publ. 1932.)

Austin, Mary (1996a). "New York: The Dictator of American Criticism." In *Beyond Borders: The Selected Essays of Mary Austin*, ed. Reuben J. Ellis. Carbondale and Edwardsville: Southern Illinois University Press. (First publ. 1920.)

Austin, Mary (1996b). "One Hundred Miles on Horseback." In *Beyond Borders: The Selected Essays of Mary Austin*, ed. Reuben J. Ellis.

Carbondale and Edwardsville: Southern Illinois University Press. (First publ. 1889.)

Austin, Mary (1997). *The Ford*. Berkeley: University of California Press. (First publ. 1917.)

Bredahl, Carl (1989). *New Ground: Western American Narrative and the Literary Canon*. Chapel Hill: University of North Carolina Press.

Buell, Lawrence (1995). *The Environmental Imagination*. Cambridge, Mass.: Harvard University Press.

Comer, Krista (1999). *Landscapes of the New West: Gender and Geography in Contemporary Women's Writing*. Chapel Hill: University of North Carolina Press.

Farrar, John (1923). "The Literary Spotlight; 22: Mary Austin." *Bookman* 53, 47–52.

Graulich, Melody, and Klimasmith, Elizabeth, eds. (1999). *Exploring Lost Borders: Critical Essays on Mary Austin*. Reno: University of Nevada Press.

Klimasmith, Betsy (1995). "Storytellers, Story Sellers: Artists, Muses, and Exploitation in the Work of Mary Austin." *Southwestern American Literature* 20: 2, 21–33.

Lanigan, Esther (1997). *The Song of a Maverick*. Tucson: Arizona University Press. (first publ. 1989.)

Lape, Noreen Groover (2000). *West of the Border: The Multicultural Literature of the Western Frontiers*. Athens, Ohio: Ohio University Press.

Pearce, T. M., ed. (1979). *Literary America 1903–1934: The Mary Austin Letters*. Westport: Greenwood.

Raine, Anne (1999). "'The Man at the Sources': Gender, Capital, and the Conservationist Landscape in Mary Austin's *The Ford*." In Melody Graulich and Elizabeth Klimasmith, eds., *Exploring Lost Borders: Critical Essays on Mary Austin*. Reno: University of Nevada Press.

Rudnick, Lois (1987). "Re-naming the Land: Anglo Expatriate Women in the Southwest." In Vera Norwood and Janice Monk (eds.), *The Desert is No Lady*. New Haven: Yale University Press.

Rudnick, Lois (1996). *Utopian Vistas*. Albuquerque: University of New Mexico Press.

Tonkovich, Nicole (1999). "At Cross Purposes: Church, State, and Sex in Mary Austin's *Isidro*." In Melody Graulich and Elizabeth Klimasmith, eds., *Exploring Lost Borders: Critical Essays on Mary Austin*. Reno: University of Nevada Press.

31

"I have never recovered from the country": The American West of Wallace Stegner

Richard H. Cracroft

> The West at large is hope's native home, the youngest and freshest of America's regions, magnificently endowed and with the chance to become something unprecedented and unmatched in the world.
>
> *Where the Bluebird Sings to the Lemonade Springs*, xv

The American West ran deep and long in Wallace Stegner (1909–93). Intrinsic in the child and father of the man, the West informed his spirit, shaped his intellect, and gave purpose to his writing. And while he initially took umbrage at being labeled a "Western writer," which he saw as a dismissive put-down by provincial Eastern pundits, he came, in time, to see the title as distinctive and positive. He took his place alongside such Western writers as Walter Van Tilburg Clark, Willa Cather, Mari Sandoz, A. B. Guthrie, Jr., Bernard DeVoto, Wright Morris, Norman Maclean, N. Scott Momaday and Larry McMurtry – the latter two former students of his – as a writer who shared not only an understanding of the Western region and its peoples but the responsibility and the challenge of realizing and comprehending a Western past in contexts of an American – and universal – present. In coming to understand the significance of the Western experience, Stegner learned, taught, and wrote that the West was all of a piece with the history of the United States and had played, and continues to play, a major role in shaping the spirit and imagination of the American people.

Wallace Stegner was well suited to his calling as the twentieth-century voice of the American West. No other major modern writer knew so much of the West from personal experience and observation as he. No other modern writer was so steeped in Western history and lore. "What gives his work its essential character," wrote Norman Cousins in 1983, "is a deep familiarity with American historical, cultural, and political terrain. Few writers in the recent past have been able to summon as much knowledge of the main strands of our national life" (Stegner and Etulain 1996:

vii). Certainly no other modern writer has done as much as Stegner, and in so many genres – in the short story, novel, biography, history, and essay – to interpret the West as an essential and integral part of the American experience.

Stegner saw the primary aim of literature as the "celebration of the human spirit as that spirit works itself out in conduct" in the place(es) where one lives out his or her life (1950b: 522). Understanding how the place where one lives has an incalculable effect on that life, Stegner, the quintessential Western regionalist, saw regionality – the acquired, intrinsic, and indelible sense of one's home place – as essential to one's well-being and basic to a writer's kit of tools. He saw the American West in particular as a region among regions – the only geographical region whose name graces a literary genre, the Western – as "the geography of hope" for the nation and the world.

Stegner envisioned the American West, as had Henry David Thoreau, Walt Whitman, John Muir, Theodore Roosevelt, Owen Wister, and Zane Grey, as an ideal and not yet completely jaded stage on which the human spirit could undertake to work itself out, untrammeled, in a land and landscape commensurate with the expansive freedom, vigor, meliorism, and optimism which characterized the American nation. Nick Carraway, in F. Scott Fitzgerald's *The Great Gatsby*, imagining the Dutch sailors' first view of the "fresh, green breast of the new world" off what would become New York, conjectures that "man must have held his breath in the presence of this continent, . . . face to face for the last time in history with something commensurate to his capacity for wonder," filled with "something commensurate with hope" (Fitzgerald 1953: 182), and entranced by what Stegner's friend Robert Frost called, in "The Gift Outright," the *"land vaguely realizing westward, / But still unstoried, artless, unenhanced / Such as she was, such as she would become"* (1969: 424). Stegner saw the American West, geographically and spiritually, as "the New World's last chance "to be something better, . . . the only American society still malleable enough to be formed" (1980: 184).

Through 35 published books, including 15 novels, five works of history, two biographies, several books on conservation, and some 242 articles, 164 first-appearance contributions, and books edited – including forewords, introductions, essay chapters, and critical prefaces (Stegner 1998: xvii; cf. Colberg 1990) – Wallace Stegner has done more than any other American writer to define the American West, explain the Western experience, and show how that experience has helped to shape Americans as people and as a nation. In the process of discovering the West, Stegner shaped, taught, and exemplified his own informal Western literary credo, and in doing so moved beyond "mere" Western regionalism to imagine, embrace, and propound a continental vision of American possibilities for a nation which has likewise enjoyed, often unknowingly, the benefits of "growing up Western."

Growing Up Western

"This is essentially the whole story," writes Stegner: "I grew up western, and the very first time I moved out of the West I realized what it meant to me" (1990: 19). In

Figure 31.1 Wallace Stegner.

acknowledging that "I am a product of the American earth" (1998: 6), and in confessing in a late essay that "I have never recovered from the country" (1998: xi), Stegner acknowledges a childhood which, while difficult in many ways, provided a fortunate beginning for a writer who would recollect and represent, in telling prose, a vanishing West no longer available, save through shared memory and imagination.

In 1914, after moving about in Iowa, North Dakota, and Washington State in tow of his harsh and restless father George H. Stegner, his loving and stabilizing mother Hilda Paulson Stegner, and his brother Cecil, two years his senior, five-year-old Wallace Earle Stegner settled with his family in the tiny village of Eastend, Saskatchewan, Canada, on the Montana–Saskatchewan border. From 1914 to 1920, while George homesteaded on the great plains of Canada, Wally and Cecil lived a frontier "life of the senses . . . , shooting or trapping muskrats, or skating, or driving cows" (Stegner and Etulain 1996: 7). Stegner later described those formative frontier years in his highly autobiographical novel *The Big Rock Candy Mountain* (1943), in *Wolf Willow: A History, a Story, and a Memory of the Last Plains Frontier* (1962), and in a number of autobiographical essays, several of them collected posthumously in *Marking the Sparrow's Fall: Wallace Stegner's American West* (1998). In a memoir of his Saskatchewan childhood, "Child of the Far Frontier," he assessed the elemental formative effect on him of those frontier years:

> The processes of deculturation, isolation, and intellectual schizophrenia that I underwent as a result of being brought up on a belated, almost symbolic frontier were until recently a most common American experience. Like other Americans uncertain of who they are, I take a firm hold on the certainties of where I am from. I can say to myself that a good part of my private and social character, the kinds of scenery and weather and people and humor I respond to, the prejudices I wear like dishonorable scars, the affections that sometimes waken me from middle-aged sleep with a rush of undiminished love, the virtues I respect and the weaknesses I condemn, the code I try to live by, the special ways I fail at it and the kinds of shame I feel when I do, the models and heroes I follow, the colors and shapes that evoke my deepest pleasure, the way I adjudicate between personal desire and personal responsibility, have been in good part scored into me by that little womb-village and the lovely, lonely, exposed prairie of the homestead. (Stegner 1998: 6)

Driven out by drought and hard times, the Stegners moved in 1920 to Great Falls, Montana, where George began to earn his living illegally as a bootlegger while his civilization-deprived family reveled in the luxury of a comfortable home with, for the first time in Wally's young life, a front yard, porch, electricity, and indoor plumbing – complete with tub and toilet (Stegner 1998: 16–28). In 1921, after 15 months in Great Falls, the family moved to Salt Lake City, Utah, where they lived in a dozen houses over the next ten years, while George turned their various living rooms into speakeasys, always just a move ahead of the vice squad. Young Wallace, embarrassed by his father's sordid and illegal business, immersed himself in activities outside the home and came to feel very much at home in the Mormon mecca. As he recalls in several sketches collected in *The Sound of Mountain Water* (1969) and *Marking the Sparrow's Fall* (1998; collected posthumously by his wife and son), and in his novels *The Big Rock Candy Mountain* (1943) and *Recapitulation* (1979), he attended junior high school and East High School, was an active Boy Scout, played on basketball teams sponsored by the Latter-day Saints, learned to play tennis, worked at various jobs, including at Saltair resort on the Great Salt Lake, and hiked the canyons of the surrounding Wasatch mountains.

In 1927 Wally entered the University of Utah, where he majored in English and was encouraged to write by his freshman English teacher, novelist Vardis Fisher. He joined a fraternity and was active in the social, academic, and athletic life of the university, and earned a letter as a member of the tennis team. On graduation from Utah in 1930, Stegner entered graduate school at the University of Iowa on a scholarship, just as Professor Norman Foerster was developing the creative writing program there. At Iowa, he also got his first taste of teaching freshman composition.

After completing his master's thesis, a creative writing thesis, in 1932 ("If I was not the first creative M.A. in the country, I was one of the first two or three," he said later [1988: 49]), he began doctoral work at the University of California at Berkeley; but he left after an uncomfortable year to be with his mother during the final stages of breast cancer. In February 1934, following Hilda Stegner's death, he returned to the University of Iowa to work on his doctorate, which he completed in 1935; his dissertation on Utah naturalist Clarence Dutton was later published as *Clarence Edward Dutton: An Appraisal* (1936). While at Iowa he met Mary Stuart Page, a fellow graduate student, whom he married on September 1, 1934, and received his first full-time teaching appointment: a one-semester stint at Augustana College in Rock Island, Illinois. The couple's only child, Page, was born in 1937.

It was while studying at the University of Iowa that Stegner began to realize, as he later wrote, "how deeply [the West] had been involved in my making" (1990: 17–18). "I began to write my life," he later recalled, "and my life was all western. . . . And every story that crowded to the typewriter evoked the smells and colors and horizons and air and people of the region where I had most lived" (1990: 19). In his association with men and women from across the United States, he soon realized that he was a thoroughgoing Westerner; and he later reflected, in "Living Dry," the first chapter in *The American West as Living Space*,

> If there is such a thing as being conditioned by climate and geography, and I think there is, it is the West that has conditioned me. It has the forms and lights and colors that I respond to in nature and in art. If there is a western speech, I speak it; if there is a western character or personality, I am some variant of it; if there is a western culture in the small-*c*, anthropological sense, I have not escaped it. It has to have shaped me. I may even have contributed to it in minor ways, for culture is a pyramid to which each of us brings a stone. (Stegner 1987a: 4–5)

After his mother, Hilda, and his wife, Mary, whom he acknowledges as the two greatest influences in his life, the other centering and stabilizing force for Stegner, evident in everything he ever wrote, is his sense of place, his rootedness in the American West. In "At Home in the Fields of the Lord," he admits that "I have always envied people with a hometown" (Stegner 1980: 157), and claims, belatedly – and despite being a Gentile in a Mormon sanctuary and thus "forever foreign" (p. 159) – that Salt Lake City, Utah, is his home town, his personal sanctuary, his emotional seat. In the same essay he enumerates the sensory influences on him of specific places and times and experiences while growing up and coming of age in Salt Lake City, and concludes that "Home is what you can take away with you" (pp. 168–9).

The Western writer, Stegner insists – or the New England or Southern or Midwestern writer – "never forgets where he left his heart" (1990: 116). "If you don't know where you are," he affirmatively quotes his former student, Kentuckian Wendell Berry, as saying, "you don't know *who* you are" (1990: 199). He asserts elsewhere, "I believe in the influence of places on personalities" (1980: 166); and he expressed his belief, in "Child of the Far Frontier": "Expose a child to a particular environment at his susceptible time and he will perceive in the shapes of that environment until he dies" (1998: 5).

Stegner's strong sense of his place in the American West, initiated in Eastend, fostered in Salt Lake City, and enhanced and drawn upon right up until his death on April 12, 1993, following an automobile accident in New Mexico, informs his fiction and nonfiction alike. It lends his work its distinctive tone and voice and purpose, and provides a firm *point d'appui* which both centers and frames his Western realism, his Western humanism, his Western values, and his Western spirituality (see Etulain 2001). It shapes the informal Western literary credo that defines the style and the man, and gave him a firm base from which to climb to his broader continental perspective.

Defining the West: Aridity and Space

At the heart of Wallace Stegner's definition of the American West is his well-founded conviction that it is aridity and space, and their effect upon topography, air, light, and life, which make the West unique among North American regions. He first learned about the effects of aridity from Major John Wesley Powell, his personal Western hero whose exploits he would essay in *Beyond the Hundredth Meridian: John Wesley Powell and the Second Opening of the West* (1954), and from Walter Prescott Webb in his classic history, *The Great Plains* (1931), which advocates that aridity west of the ninety-eighth meridian necessitates technological innovations to make agriculture and settlement possible.

While Stegner defines the West geographically, as beginning at the one-hundredth meridian, he claims the actual of demarcation is the isohyetal line, which is

> a perceptible line of real import that roughly coincides with [the one-hundredth meridian], reaching southward about a third of the way across the Dakotas, Nebraska, and Kansas, and then swerving southwestward across Oklahoma and Texas. This is the isohyetal line of twenty inches, beyond which the mean annual rainfall is less than the twenty inches normally necessary for unirrigated crops. (Stegner 1987a: 5)

That peculiar "something that abides, that is different, separate, that is uniquely itself" in the West arises from the unique Western combination of aridity and awesome space, and "makes all the difference" (Stegner 1998: xii). Stegner told Etulain, "There's a very definite constraint upon western growth, and Powell knew why. Aridity is something that you simply cannot fake out. You can only make the maximum use of what water you've got. Beyond that, there isn't any" (Stegner and Etulain 1996: 181). In "I Sing of America," reproduced as the foreword to *Marking the Sparrow's Fall*, Stegner describes some other effects of this "incorrigible aridity" (1990: 111):

> As Walter Webb made clear in *The Great Plains* it is aridity that discourages the growth of turf and substitutes bunchgrass, sage, creosote bush, and bare ground. Aridity clarifies the air and electrifies distances. It dictates the very landscape – the erosional shapes of mesas, buttes, and cliffs; the profiles of canyons; the habits of rivers. It begets a new flora and a new fauna. Aridity inspired barbed wire and the windmill, altered laws and social organization, profoundly affected men, myths, and moralities. (Stegner 1998: xii)

The indisputable fact of this endemic dryness, too often blithely overlooked or ignored by booster, businessman, politician, and historian alike, accounts for the region's distinctive qualities in everything from farming methods, weapons, and tools, to water law, land ownership, and settlement, as well as its people and their attitudes, society, culture, language – and literature.

Hand-in-glove with aridity is the second defining factor of Stegner's West, the "visible, pervasive fact of Western space" (1990: 111–12). "The West is most characterized by its *space*," Stegner told Etulain. "It's what always strikes me coming home, whenever I drive back into it. It's what strikes newcomers most when they come west" (Stegner and Etulain 1996: xiii–xiv). "In the West it is impossible to be unconscious of or indifferent to space," he asserts (1987a: 80). He told Etulain:

> I believe that the awesome space of the West, which is not a fiction, is not going to go away, no matter how badly we abuse it. It is always going to be holding the oases apart because nobody can live there. We can ruin it, tear it up with draglines and bulldozers and ORV's [Off-Road-Vehicles], but there is still going to be space. (Stegner and Etulain 1996: xiv)

The bigness, the sparseness, and the humbling diminution caused by Western scale and distance and shot through with Western aridity affect human beings, conditioning Western perspectives on life, society, culture, and literature. Indeed, he notes, in "Coming of Age: The End of the Beginning,"

> Space does something to the vision. It makes the country itself, for lack of human settlements and other enhancements to the illusion of human importance, into something formidable, alluring, and threatening, and it tends to make human beings as migratory as antelope. Literature reflects this necessity. . . . The country is a very prominent actor in most western writing. It is big and impressive, it is mainly empty, it is unforgiving, it is fragile. (1990: 138)

Teaching Americans to acknowledge, understand, and accommodate these Western realities of space and aridity and their manifold implications for Westerners – and for all Americans, present and future – became Stegner's lifelong spiritual and intellectual mission and his assumed responsibility as a citizen.

Regional Characteristics: The Individual vs. the Community

"If there are such things as regional or national characteristics," Stegner told Etulain in 1980, "you have to try to define them." Aridity and space, those defining qualities which make the West a unique region, are also central to defining and shaping the nature of human experience in the West. If literature is significant human experience expressed significantly, and examines, paraphrasing Stegner, how human lives in particular environments work themselves out in conduct (cf. Stegner 1950b: 522), this explains why much of Stegner's art amounts to his taking "a crack at the society and character the West had created" (Stegner and Etulain 1996: xiv), and identifying, defining, and examining the effects of Western land upon human conduct.

A central theme in his imaginative fiction, as well as in his biographies and histories, is examining, in Western contexts and circumstances, the nature of the universal and timeless tension between the individual and the community, a tension which transcends regional boundaries. As his writing attests, Stegner found both poles in his own life – and he found the Western land a rich proving ground for examining the tension.

The individual

Like most Americans born during the first quarter of the twentieth century, Stegner grew up imbued with the still-green "men to match my mountains" myth of Western independence and self-reliance. This – still vigorous – myth of heroic, rugged, and energetic individualism, personal prowess and unlimited freedom is fostered by the literary tradition which runs through James Fenimore Cooper's Natty Bumppo and George F. Ruxton's LaBonte and Killbuck to Owen Wister's Virginian, A. B. Guthrie's Boone Caudill and Frederick Manfred's Hugh Glass, Jack Schaefer's Shane, and any of Zane Grey's or Louis L'Amour's "tall-in-the-saddle" heroes – and is perpetuated in hundreds of Hollywood Westerns. Although Stegner complains that this stereotypical, mythic figure "has irritated me all my life" (1990: 111) and decries the distortions of the larger-than-life mountain man and "the lone horseman," he admits that, after all,

> there is something to the notion of western independence; there is something about being in big empty space, where people are few and distant, under a great sky that is alternately serene and furious, exposed to sun from four in the morning till nine at night, and to a wind that never seems to rest – there is something about exposure to that big country that not only tells an individual how small he is, but tells him *who* he is. (1990: 9–10)

And *who* he is: is wild and independent and historically and benignly lawless[1] – and enduringly attractive. These attractions, Stegner points out, "did not die with the frontier," and have become of a piece in human mythology with Henry David Thoreau's aphorism, in his essay "Walking," that "all good things are wild and free." And, rightly or wrongly, "we conceive the last remaining home" of wildness and freedom and lawlessness "to be the West" (Stegner 1990: 107).

Furthermore, individuals living in Western land purportedly share – at least in the still vibrant myth – "unrestricted freedom, unlimited opportunity for testings and heroism, a continuing need for self-reliance and physical competence," and also "a family resemblance of energetic individualism, great physical competence, stoicism, determination, recklessness, endurance, toughness, rebelliousness, [and] resistance to control" – traits which continue to be associated with wilderness adventure and "the westering, mythic, civilization-building process" (Stegner 1990: 111). These tendencies, exacerbated by space, emptiness, and distance, "generate a certain mobility among inhabitants of the West" (p. 76) and, in the past at least, perhaps even in the late twentieth century, emphasized and aggrandized individual independence while lessening the sense of any need for settled community life (cf. p. 138). "Being footloose has always exhilarated us," Stegner reminds his readers. "It is associated in our minds with escape from history and oppression and law and irksome obligations, with absolute freedom, and the road has always led west" (p. 71). In the historical West, as in the present, this yearning for Huck-Finn-like freedom and mobility is "physical, familial, social, corporate, occupational, religious, sexual," all confirming and reinforcing what he calls "the illusion of independence" (p. 100) and bespeaking a certain restlessness which is also linked, he told Etulain, to the Western limitations imposed by space and aridity and "altitude, or a combination" (Stegner and Etulain 1996: xvii).

In "History, Myth, and the Western Writer" Stegner discounts the "magic figure of the [lone] horseman" (1980: 188) that has dominated formulaic "Westerns" because it falsifies Western life, remains "rooted in the historic, the rural, the heroic," and does "not take account of time and change" (1980: 199), thereby creating what he terms "a dispossessed past," a romantic, mythic, idealized Never-Never Land out of touch with reality. Still, he admits in his "Variations on a Theme by Crèvecouer" chapter in *The West as Living Space* that the "untrammeled individualist persists partly as a residue of the real and romantic frontiers, but also partly because runaways from more restricted regions keep reimporting him. The stereotype continues to affect romantic Westerners and non-Westerners in romantic ways, but if I am right it also affects real Westerners in real ways" (Stegner 1987a: 80).

And while this myth of "untrammeled" individualism romanticizes and distorts Western life, it also "says something true about western, and hence about American, character" (Stegner 1987a: 80). For space, aridity, and emptiness exert "a continuing influence on . . . minds and senses," and have made, and in certain circumstances continue to make, self-reliance into a social imperative – with social consequences:

> [Self-reliance] encourages a fatal carelessness and destructiveness because it seems so limitless and because what is everybody's is nobody's responsibility. It also encourages,

in some, an impassioned protectiveness. . . . Finally, it promotes certain needs, tastes, attitudes, skills. It is those tastes, attitudes, and skills, as well as the prevailing destructiveness and its corrective, love of the land, that relate real Westerners to the earth. (Stegner 1987a: 80–1)

Stegner's father, George, epitomized for him the "fatal carelessness and destructiveness" of exploitive, self-centered, materialistic, unrestrained individualism, a demon which he exorcized in creating Bo Mason, the driven, blustering, anachronistic father of *The Big Rock Candy Mountain*: "a very western type" who recurs often in Western literature and film (see Stegner 1990: 114).

The community

The contrasting pole to individuality is community. Growing up in Eastend, in the vast Canadian plains, Stegner learned to be "somewhat skeptical of the fabled western self-reliance, because as I knew it, the West was a place where one depended on neighbors and had to give as well as get" (1990: 9). Community and family, made necessary by the imperatives of space and aridity, and exemplified for Stegner in his mother, Hilda, and his wife, Mary, became more important Western values for Stegner than the fabled Western individualism. Indeed, he posits, perhaps more hopefully than realistically, that it is in the small Western villages and families – in community and cooperation – that "the West will realize itself, if it ever does." Families, he asserts, "intimate and interdependent in their shared community, shared optimism, and shared memory[,] . . . are the seedbeds of an emergent western culture" (1990: 116).

Deprived by his father's rampant individualism of the sense of a cohesive family, Stegner first realized the possibilities of community and family and the importance of a sense of place while living in Salt Lake City among large Mormon nuclear families which radiated "the old-fashioned virtues . . . of hospitality and familial warmth . . . and a degree of community responsibility" (Stegner and Etulain 1996: 102). In the communally centered Mormon towns along the Mormon corridor,[2] among the New Mexicans around Taos and Santa Fe and the ranchers of the Absaroka country in Montana, and in small Western cities like Missoula and Bozeman in Montana, Boise in Idaho, Corvallis in Oregon, and Salt Lake City in Utah – towns possessing "their own quality," he told Etulain in 1989 – Stegner saw the future of the West (Stegner and Etulain 1996: xiv).

He especially admired those Western societies, such as the Mormons, that had created unique responses to their regional environments. It was only after he left Utah, notes Dan Flores, that he realized the unique life way that had resulted "from the interplay of Mormon culture and the ranges and canyons of the Intermountain West." *Mormon Country* (1942) was his preliminary examination and appreciation of that interplay, an appreciation "which deepened considerably in *Beyond the Hundredth Meridian*," observes Flores, "when he realized that John Wesley Powell's blueprint for a kind of planned, Darwinian adaptation to the West was based largely on Powell's admiration for the Mormon model" (Meine, ed. 1997: 119).

The pull both ways

Still, Stegner felt the pull both ways. His ambivalence about independence *vis-à-vis* cooperation is seen in *Mormon Country*. While he praises the fruits of Mormon cooperation, order, and efficiency in city planning, irrigation, pioneering, and proselytizing, along with the United Order and family organization, his most striking chapters deal with such Mormon mavericks as J. Golden Kimball, the colorful and profane General Authority ("Sure I'll pray for our enemies! I pray they may all go to hell!" [Stegner 1942: 192]); Jesse Knight, millionaire-miner; Butch Cassidy, lapsed-Mormon outlaw; and Walter Murray Gibson, the fraud who duped the Government, Brigham Young, and King Kalakaua of Hawaii (pp. 128–351) – all of them against-the-grain, individual anomalies in the midst of Mormon communalism.

Stegner's own best literary treatment of the individual vs. community dichotomy is the novella "Genesis," published in "The Whitemud River Range" section of *Wolf Willow*, and regarded by critics as one of Stegner's best pieces of short fiction. Lionel "Rusty" Cullen, a "greenhorn" English immigrant cum heroic, mythic, tall-in-his-stirrups cowboy, endures the taunts of Ed Spurlock, one of the older hands, and the "miraculously beautiful and murderously cold nights" of southern Saskatchewan (Stegner 1962: 163) in hopes that he can prove that he has the right stuff – what Stegner describes elsewhere in *Wolf Willow* as the "specifications for a hero" (pp. 127–38). In the end Rusty saves Spurlock's life during a Canadian Great Plains blizzard and learns that not only are the myths of heroic individualism wrong, they can be dangerous; and that what is more important is heroic, selfless cooperation – that men must work together if they are to survive. Basing "Genesis" as well as "Carrion Spring," "The Wolfer," and "Town and Country" – his other stories in *Wolf Willow* – on the recollections of Corky Jones, an old-time cowboy acquaintance, Stegner describes the cowboys' desperate – and futile – attempts to save their livestock and themselves during the terrible winter of 1906–7. He pits perennial stiff-upper-lip Western optimism against the natural harshness of the environment, and demonstrates that success *in extremis* is possible only when members of beleaguered frontier communities pull together.

In Stegner, it is clear that whether the pendulum swings toward individualism or community, the West is a proving-ground, a country of opportunity and freedom of choice. Here a man like Bo Mason (modeled after Stegner's father, George) or his son Bruce (Wallace), in *The Big Rock Candy Mountain* and *Recapitulation*, or a woman like Susan Burling Ward (Mary Hallock Foote) in *Angle of Repose*, or a hippie like Jim Peck (Ken Kesey) in *All the Little Live Things* – or groups of people, like the Mormons of Orderville, or the tight little families of Montana ranchers or Saskatchewan homesteaders – can test their individual or collective mettle, choose, explore, and follow their bent, and deal with the consequences of those choices. This is a very Western (and, Stegner implies, American) freedom.

Tracing Regional Characteristics: Optimism, Hope, and Responsibility

This intrinsic sense of freedom, implicit in all of Stegner's works and pervasive in Western writing, grows naturally and organically out of the native Western soil of optimism, meliorism, and hope, and out of what Stegner sees as the Westerner's relative innocence, "even dewy innocence, in the teeth of the modern world" (Stegner and Etulain 1996: 123). In his 1964 essay "Born a Square," later collected in *The Sound of Mountain Water*, he asserts: "This western naïvete of strenuousness, pragmatism, meliorism, optimism, and the stiff upper lip is our tradition" (1980: 184) and persists in Western writers and writing because Westerners, full of Western space and freedom, refreshingly naïve, wonderfully square, and *angst*-less, lack "a common conscience, a common guilt, a shared sense of wrong, a Lost Cause, a regional Weltschmerz" found in some other regions (1980: 178); and Westerners believe, contrary to the prevailing mood in midcentury, Cold War America, that "man, even Modern Man, has some dignity if he will assume it, and [insist] that most lives are worth living, even when they are lives of quiet desperation" (1980: 184). In his 1989 update of his conversations with Etulain, although he pointed out that things had improved since midcentury,[3] Stegner still insisted that "Modern literature and western literature are somehow irreconcilable, at least up to now. The kind of western writer who writes modern literature immediately abdicates as a Westerner, and the kind who sticks to the western attitudes is likely to be considered a little backward by the modernists. That dichotomy does persist" (Stegner and Etulain 1996: 123).

Along with this "indigenous optimism," unblinking idealism, the "calm confidence of a Christian with four aces" (Stegner n.d.), and unflappable meliorism, Stegner asserted that Westerners enjoy the certain legacy of "unquenchable hope." Recoiling viscerally, amid the tumultuous 1960s, from a literary generation "that appears to specialize in despair, hostility, hypersexuality and disgust" (1980: 171), Stegner saw the West, among all US regions, as the truly American region, the "geography of hope" (1980: 11). And as late in his life as his introduction to *Where the Bluebird Sings to the Lemonade Springs*, his last collection of essays, he reiterated: "Once I said in print that the remaining western wilderness is the geography of hope, and I have written, believing what I wrote, that the West at large is hope's native home, the youngest and freshest of America's regions, magnificently endowed and with the chance to become something unprecedented and unmatched in the world" (1990: xv).

These Western characteristics of spiritual, emotional, and physical well-being carry with them a keen moral responsibility to which Stegner rose as a profoundly moral writer; and he thought that other Western (and American) writers should be similarly responsible. He confessed in his 1980–1 conversations with Etulain that his early training in responsibility had probably led him "to take a moralistic view of writing – to think of it not only as art, but also as a kind of cultural function" (Stegner and Etulain 1996: 196). He felt that writers are responsible "in a social way – to family, to community, to nation, to whatever else" (p. 198), and that the writer has "the obligation somehow to have some kind of concern for the species, for the culture, *for the larger thing outside of ourselves*" (p. 197, emphasis added).

Irresponsibility – the failure to be culturally responsible – seemed to him "a kind of delinquency" (Stegner and Etulain 1996: 197) and was at the core of his disagreements with his student Ken Kesey, poet Gary Snyder, and the radical student movement of the late 1960s and early 1970s more widely. This clash was part of his reason for taking early retirement from Stanford in 1971.[4] This moral purpose, this "sense in which literature matters," he told Etulain, is "buried not too deeply in most of the books I've written" (p. 197). Indeed, this sense of responsibility is at the core of all his works, nonfiction or fiction, even in the non-Western character Joe Allston, a retired Eastern literary agent transplanted to the California coast (living in a ranchero resembling Stegner's home in Los Altos Hills above Palo Alto) and the crusty protagonist of "Field Guide to Western Birds" (1952), *All the Little Live Things* (1967), and *The Spectator Bird* (1976) – for which Stegner won the National Book Award in 1977. It resides, too, in Lyman Ward – and both of his grandparents, Oliver and Susan Ward – in *Angle of Repose* (1971), for which he won the Pulitzer Prize (1972); and in the transplanted Westerner, Larry Morgan, and his wife Sally, in *Crossing to Safety* (1987), his last novel – a novel set in Vermont but fraught with Stegner's Western values in contrast with the Eastern complexities of the Morgans' close friends, Sid and Charity Lang.

Characteristically, literature about the West, based in the landscape of hope and optimism, anchored in human responsibility and civility, and exuding a sense of affirmation of the essential rightness of the universe, gives rise to a kind of aesthetic, visionary if earth-tethered transcendence. If, as Stegner asserts in his essay "One Way to Spell Man," "The creation and understanding of a piece of literature are mystical experiences [, and] . . . a kind of private insight by which a man gets a 'clear-eyed' view of the ambiguities of human life" (1958: 43), so the Western region and spirit may generate an aesthetic experience, "a private, subjective, mystical experience," writes Stegner critic Sid Jenson, "a sense of being part of something larger than oneself that is 'never quite communicable'" and not really "subject to empirical verification" (Jenson 1974: 249; cf. Stegner 1958: 43). Fleeting moments of this kind of transcendent humanism, a degree less lofty than the ending of Willa Cather's *O, Pioneers!*, recur in Stegner, whether in Joe Allston's recognition of the all-encompassing love embodied in the dying Marian Catlin, in *All the Little Live Things*; or in his description of the ineffable power of the marriage union, at the conclusion of *The Spectator Bird*; or in Lyman Ward's guardedly hopeful end-of-novel dream of his wife's return, in *Angle of Repose*.

Regional Characteristics: Defining and Using
"a personal and possessed past"

Stegner acknowledges that the literature of the American West has, so far, fallen short of the splendor of the Western landscape, and also failed to do justice to the nature of Western men and women. As he identifies it in his essay "History, Myth, and the Western Writer," the cause of this shortfall lies not in the failure of Western writers to match the accomplishments of writers of other regions, but in a decidedly Western dilemma. The problem for both the writer of traditional "Westerns" and the contemporary Western writer is that the traditional writer of Westerns remains inextricably mired in the mythic past, writhing in the grip of historical tyranny, while the contemporary Western writer, also intimidated by the past, avoids the past altogether and writes about a prosaic present untouched and unaffected by history.

Stegner's advice to both the writer of Westerns and the modern Western writer – and instructive for American writers generally – is that they seek the connections between the mythic past and mundane present, to "make the one serve the other," to "find some ordering principle in current change," and to find "a sense of continuity between the real Western past which has been mythicized almost out of recogniz- ability and a real Western present that seems as cut-off and pointless as a ride on a merry-go-round that can't be stopped" (Stegner 1980: 199; cf. Hepworth 1998: 104). To realize this sense of "a personal and possessed past" the Western writer will seek and find universal links in the human character between the rich past and the equally rich present, links which Stegner himself achieves in most of his works, but perhaps most notably in his Pulitzer-winning novel *Angle of Repose*. Historian Lyman Ward, confined by illness and amputation to a wheelchair and embittered by his wife's leaving him for his physician, recreates the trials of his grandparents' East– West marriage and seeks the link between their lives and his twentieth-century present. Lyman discovers a usable and instructive continuity between past and present in his grandfather's inability to forgive his wife for her inadvertent role in the death by drowning of their child. At the conclusion of the novel, Lyman lies in bed, anticipating his wife's return, and "wondering if I am man enough to be a bigger man than my grandfather" (Stegner 1971: 569).

Bearing Witness for the Land

Amid all of his wrestlings with the meaning of the West, Stegner could never forget the very real possibility that the wilderness – that Western "something that abides, that is different, separate, that is uniquely itself" (1998: xii) – is under dire threat of extinction. Over the last 40 years of his life, Stegner became, albeit with professed reluctance,[5] a central figure in the wilderness conservation movement. First sum- moned into the environmentalist trenches by his friend Bernard DeVoto,[6] he devoted his pen to the cause of preserving the Western wilderness for future generations. His books, biographies, and essays comprise the most significant body of conservation writings in environmentalist literature and stand as Stegner's most distinguished and enduring contribution to the West and the nation.[7] Eloquently reaffirming and elucidating Henry David Thoreau's impassioned aphorism, "In wildness is the preservation of the world," Stegner's "Wilderness Letter" of December 3, 1960, became the manifesto of wilderness preservationists: "I want to speak for the wilderness idea," he wrote, "as something that has helped form our character and that has certainly shaped our history as a people." He continues:

> Something will have gone out of us as a people if we ever let the remaining wilderness be destroyed . . . [S]o that never again can we have the chance to see ourselves single, separate, vertical and individual in the world, part of the environment of trees and rocks and soil, brother to the other animals, part of the natural world and incompetent to belong in it. (Stegner 1980: 146–7)

He concludes: "We simply need that wild country available to us, even if we never do more than drive to its edge and look in. For it can be a means of reassuring ourselves of our sanity as creatures, a part of the geography of hope" (1980: 153).

The Legacy of Wallace Stegner

Shortly after Stegner's death, Jackson J. Benson wrote: "He had many roles – novelist, essayist, historian, lecturer, editor, and environmentalist – but perhaps all of them go back to one central role, that of teacher" (Stegner and Stegner, eds. 1996: 2). As a teacher of creative writing Stegner taught and exemplified what would gradually become his literary credo at the Bread Loaf Writers Conference (for eight nonconsecutive summers, 1938–47), and at the universities of Utah, Wisconsin, Harvard, and Stanford. At Stanford University in Palo Alto, California, he directed the creative writing program from 1945 to 1971 and over these 25 years taught several hundred writing students, many of whom would come to be numbered among the most accomplished American writers. In turn, he exposed his students to prominent American writers, most of them his friends, whom he brought to Stanford, including, among many, Elizabeth Bowen, Frank O'Connor, Katherine Anne Porter, and C. P. Snow. His favorite teaching era was the period after World War II, through the mid-fifties to the mid-sixties, when returning veterans brought maturity and eagerness to learn, and a great deal of major talent passed through the Stanford creative writing program. With his assistant, Richard Scowcroft, whom Stegner had taught at the University of Utah, he nurtured the likes of Wendell Berry, Boris Ilyn, Jean Byers, Tillie Olsen, Eugene Burdick, Nancy Packer, Raymond Carver, Peter Beagle, Thomas McGuane, Al Young, Pat Zelver, Evan Connell, Ed McClanahan, Robert Stone, N. Scott Momaday, Larry McMurtry, Ernest Gaines, James Houston, Ken

Kesey, Harriet Doerr, and Edward Abbey. Momaday and McMurtry would both win the Pulitzer Prize. Wendell Berry, a student with whom Stegner found particular affinity in their mutual appreciation for the American land, told Jackson J. Benson during a 1987 interview that Stegner's "very painstaking attempt to understand himself in terms of his own regional sources has been extremely important and confirming to me" (Benson 1996: 261). Some years after leaving Stanford, Stegner grimaced to Richard Etulain about the onerous amount of reading he was still expected to do in behalf of his former students: "I've . . . got about 500 ex-students out there, all of whom it seems to me, write three books a year" (Stegner and Etulain 1996: xv).

Other writers who were not his students confirm Stegner's literary influence. Western naturalist and author Terry Tempest Williams, a friend and colleague in the environmentalist movement, sees Stegner's legacy as teaching "that our birthright is found in the land, in the wilderness, in the geography of hope" (Stegner and Stegner, eds. 1996: 54). Novelist Barry Lopez, who knew Stegner "but slightly," writes: "He encouraged people and assisted them. I think he truly believed the world, or at least the West, could become a better place if people were generous with what they had – if they gave away their time, for example, to a vision larger than any vision they themselves had, or could entirely appreciate" (Stegner and Stegner, eds. 1996: 118). Novelist Gretel Ehrlich, who did not know Stegner personally, said: "His presence was everywhere in the West"; he inspired "all of us, especially those of us who dared to write about the West, the people and the place. Stegner understood what it was to be a westerner" (Stegner and Stegner, eds. 1996: 121–2). Western writer Ivan Doig, who knew him well, writes: "there was a general benefit to me just being in his region of the country and his line of work" (Stegner and Stegner, eds. 1996: 126); and William Kittredge, a friend, author, and a teacher of creative writing, notes that Stegner "reminds us of responsibilities to those things we are willing to name as sacred. He reminds us that we must never let ourselves be talked out of our most central purposes, . . . to work toward cherishing the things we revere" (Stegner and Stegner, eds. 1996: 114). And historian Patricia Nelson Limerick writes of Stegner that: he "challenged western historians to stop amputating the present from the past" (Stegner and Stegner, eds. 1996: 27).

Stegner's son Page, professor emeritus at the University of California–Santa Cruz, notes in his foreword to *Geography of Hope*: "In a sense, it seems, we were all his sons and daughters, uniformly treated by him in equal measures of affection and respect, treated not as acolytes, students, underlings, the less accomplished, but as peers. Because that, indeed, is how he essentially perceived us."

Conclusion: Beyond Westernness

Wallace Stegner, Westerner nonpareil and quintessential, "grew," as Gretchen Holstein Schoff wisely notes, "beyond his westernness" (Stegner and Stegner, eds. 1996: 41) to

Figure 31.2 "Writing class meeting at Wallace Stegner's house, about 1958," by John C. Lawrence.

what Curt Meine astutely calls "Stegner's continental vision" (1997: xx). This "beyond Westernness," this ability to transcend mere regionality to embrace a continental and universal vision, has made Stegner's a major voice in twentieth-century American letters and culture.

Although, as Wendell Berry said of his mentor in 1985, "As a regional writer, he seems to me exemplary," Stegner was super-regional and continental in his scope and vision. This remarkable "product of the American earth" (Stegner 1998: 6) was driven by a transcendent literary ambition, claimed Arthur Schlesinger, Jr., "to make sense of an ordinary American life, to delineate the historic continuities between past and present and thereby to help transform natural chaos into human order" (Stegner and Stegner, eds. 1996: 20).

Human is the key word in fathoming Stegner. He believed that literature is the "celebration of the human spirit," a record of human conduct under fire (Stegner 1950b: 522), and that one of the proper functions of literature – in whatever environment a human being lives – is to reveal character through action. As even a cursory reading of his corpus attests, he wrote about people – not just Western people – working out their lives, and about human values and the meaning of human life. "If fiction isn't people," he writes, "it is nothing, and so any fiction writer is obligated to be to some degree a lover of his fellowmen; though he may, like the Mormon preacher [J. Golden Kimball?], love some of them a damn sight better than others" (quoted in Jenson 1974: 254). His work reflects his love of people as viewed through the lenses of his realistic, hopeful, values-centered Western humanism.

Regionalism, then, is not enough to explain Stegner. While his Westernness was his literary and philosophical point of departure, it was not his destination. "If regionalism is a launching pad," he told Etulain, "it's all to the good" (Stegner and Etulain 1996: 125); but a solid sense of one's home place must be only a launching pad toward a universal and humane literature which is at once "the source of wisdom and the receptacle of values" and not an end in itself (Stegner 1958: 10).

Stegner saw the contemporary American writer as assuming the responsibilities which formerly belonged to religion, becoming a kind of seer in the tradition of Ralph Waldo Emerson, whose duty is to remind readers of the larger picture, of timeless values, the old verities, the possibility of hope, and of the necessity of belief in something larger than the merely human. His books, whether set in Canada, Montana, Utah, Idaho, California, or Vermont, reach beyond the merely regional to the wise and witty human universal, and are expressions of a brilliant, quick, retentive, educated, and cultivated mind. Deliciously resonant with literary allusion, cultural density, and a broad swath of human wisdom, Stegner's books give the reader a sense of being in conversation with a lively, incisive, culturally rich mind.

Writing from a worldview that was at once Western, American, and continental in its scope, Stegner soared beyond all of his would-be definers to achieve a human and humane literature of universal dimensions. In his novels, short stories, biographies, and essays, he undertook not only to define and understand the Western experience, and to remind "his nation of what it owed to the West," as Schlesinger insisted, but to transform that experience into creative, coherent, penetrating, and powerful expression of the American experience and the human condition, reminding "the West what it owed to the nation" and the world. "And he did this," concludes Schlesinger, "with keen intelligence, poetic apprehension, and a serenity that will long abide" (Stegner and Stegner, eds. 1996: 20).

NOTES

1 "Benignly lawless" in the sense of Robin Hood and his Merry Men or the film *Butch Cassidy and the Sundance Kid*, a literary and cinematic benignity which wrongly and pleasantly colors, for example, the careers of Jesse James and Billy the Kid. For discussion of Western lawlessness see Robinson and Robinson 1977: 71.

2 The Mormon corridor, as Stegner (almost) frames it in *Mormon Country* (1942: 21, 34–5), begins in southern Alberta, Canada, skips to both sides of the border of western Wyoming and eastern Idaho, includes all of Utah, eastern and southern Nevada, a strip of southwestern Colorado and northwestern New Mexico, northern, eastern, and southeastern Arizona, crosses over the Mormon Road from Las Vegas to San Diego and San Bernardino, and includes the Mormon colonies of northern Chihuahua state, Mexico. Stegner overlooked southern Alberta and northern Chihuahua, the top and bottom of the Mormon corridor.

3 In their recorded conversations held in 1980–1 (and updated in 1989), Richard W. Etulain asked Stegner if he would change anything he said in "Born a Square," which he wrote in the turbulent late 1960s. Stegner responded: "I'm sure I would change it some, because events move on, and opinion with them. I doubt that the literature of the country is quite as sick as I thought it then, and the publishing situation has changed somewhat. But the basic stance from which I wrote the article remains the stance from which I still see things" (Stegner and Etulain 1996: 128).

4 See Stegner's *All the Little Live Things* (1967) for his fictional treatment of the hippie movement as embodied in Jim Peck, who resembles the late Ken Kesey, the prototypical hippie guru. For discussion of Stegner's response to hippies such as Alan Watts, Allen Ginsberg,

Gary Snyder, and Kesey, see Benson 1996: 312–20, and on Kesey in particular 248–57 *passim*. Benson sums up Stegner's antipathy: "In the long run what irritated Stegner about Kesey were the values that his life and work endorsed, which in many instances were diametrically opposed to his own. For a man dedicated to the ideal of cooperation, the advocacy of anarchy was outrageous. Much of his life. . . . Stegner fought a battle to dispute the Western myth of rugged individualism, particularly as it has been embodied in the lone horseman. Kesey fondly embraces that myth, which Stegner found so destructive of the people and the land, and used it in his work" (Benson 1996: 254).

5 He told T. H. Watkins, long-time editor of *Wilderness*, "Actually I would like, and would always have liked, nothing better than to stay home and write novels and histories, and when the compulsions of some book get too strong for me, I have a history of backing way from environmental activism. . . . I am a paper tiger, Watkins, typewritten on both sides." The Sierra Club felt otherwise, awarding him the John Muir Award in 1982 (T. H. Watkins, "Reluctant Tiger: Wallace Stegner Takes Up the Conservation Mantle," in Meine, ed. 1997: 156).

6 See DeVoto's three essay collections: *Forays and Rebuttals* (Boston: Little, Brown, 1936); *Minority Report* (Boston: Little, Brown, 1940); and *The Easy Chair* (Boston: Houghton Mifflin, 1955). His Western histories are: *The Year of Decision: 1846* (Boston: Little, Brown, 1943); *Across the Wide Missouri* (Boston: Houghton Mifflin, 1947); and *The Course of Empire* (Boston: Houghton Mifflin, 1952). The two principal biographies of DeVoto are Stegner's (1974) and Orlan Sawey, *Bernard DeVoto* (New York:

Twayne, 1969). For a very useful tandem treatment of DeVoto and Stegner see Thomas
(2000).

7   DeVoto first enlisted Stegner in the battle
to preserve Dinosaur National Monument;
Stegner and others edited *This Is Dinosaur:
Echo Park Country and Its Magic Rivers* (1955).
Stegner's important contributions to the literature of conservation include his biographies of
Powell (1954) and DeVoto (1974); his edition
of *The Letters of Bernard DeVoto* (1975); the six
essays which launch *The Sound of Mountain*

Water (1969; Stegner 1980); his lecture/essays
"Living Dry," "Striking the Rock," and "Variations on a Theme by Crèvecoeur," which comprise *The American West as Living Space* (1987a)
and were reprinted, along with "Thoughts in
a Dry Land" and "A Capsule History of Conservation," as the "Habitat" section of *Where
the Bluebird Sings to the Lemonade Springs* (1990);
and his hard-hitting indictment of Western
land policy, "The Spoiling of the American
West," which appeared in the *Michigan Quarterly Review* (1987).

References

Benson, Jackson J. (1996). *Wallace Stegner: His Life and Work*. New York: Viking Penguin.

Colberg, Nancy (1990). *Wallace Stegner: A Descriptive Bibliography*. Lewiston, Idaho: Confluence.

Cracroft, Richard H. (1991). "'A Profound Sense of Community': Mormon Values in Wallace Stegner's *Recapitulation*." *Dialogue: A Journal of Mormon Thought* 24: 1 (Spring), 101–13.

Cracroft, Richard H. (2001). "'Meliorism, Optimism, and the Stiff Upper Lip': Wallace Stegner's Western Naif and Judith Freeman's *Set for Life*." In Richard H. Cracroft, Jane D. Brady, Linda Hunter Adams (eds.), *Colloquium: Essays in Literature and Belief*, 403–20. Provo, Utah: Center for the Study of Christian Values in Literature, Brigham Young University.

Etulain, Richard (2001). "Wallace Stegner and Western Spirituality." *Literature and Belief* 21, 255–72.

Fitzgerald, F. Scott (1953). *The Great Gatsby*. New York: Charles Scribner's Sons. (First publ. 1925.)

Flora, Joseph M. (1970). "Vardis Fisher and Wallace Stegner: Teacher and Student." *Western American Literature* 5 (Summer), 122–8.

Flora, Joseph M. (1988). "Wallace Stegner." In Thomas J. Lyon, et al. (eds.), *A Literary History of the American West*, 971–88. Fort Worth: Texas Christian University Press.

Flora, Joseph M. (1997). "Wallace Stegner: An Update and a Retrospect." In Thomas J. Lyon, et al. (eds.), *A Literary History of the American West*, 836–53. Fort Worth: Texas Christian University Press.

Frost, Robert (1969). *The Complete Poems of Robert Frost*. New York: Holt, Rinehart & Winston.

Hepworth, James R. (1998). *Stealing Glances: Three Interviews with Wallace Stegner*. Albuquerque: University of New Mexico Press.

Jenson, Sid (1974). "The Compassionate Seer: Wallace Stegner's Literary Artist." *BYU Studies* 14: 2 (Winter), 248–62.

Lewis, Merrill (1982). "Wallace Stegner." In Fred Erisman and Richard W. Etulain (eds.), *Fifty Western Writers*, 456–76. Westport: Greenwood.

Lewis, Merrill, and Lewis, Lorene (1972). *Wallace Stegner*. (Boise State Western Writers Series, no. 4.) Boise: Boise State College.

Meine, Curt, ed. (1997). *Wallace Stegner and the Continental Vision: Essays on Literature, History, and Landscape*. Washington DC: Island.

Robinson, Forrest G., and Robinson, Margaret G. (1977). *Wallace Stegner*. Boston: Twayne.

South Dakota Review (1985). Stegner Issue. 23 (Winter).

Stegner, Page, and Stegner, Mary, eds. (1996). *The Geography of Hope: A Tribute to Wallace Stegner*. San Francisco: Sierra Club.

Stegner, Wallace (1942). *Mormon Country*. New York: Duell.

Stegner, Wallace (1943a). *The Big Rock Candy Mountain*. New York: Duell.

Stegner, Wallace (1943b). *One Nation* (with the editors of *Look*). Boston: Houghton Mifflin.

Stegner, Wallace (1950a). *The Preacher and the Slave*. Boston: Houghton Mifflin; republ. 1969 (Garden City: Doubleday), as *Joe Hill: A Biographical Novel*.

Stegner, Wallace (1950b). "Variations on a Theme by Conrad." *Yale Review* 49 (March), 512–23.

Stegner, Wallace (1954). *Beyond the Hundredth Meridian: John Wesley Powell and the Second Opening of the West.* Boston: Houghton Mifflin.

Stegner, Wallace (1958). "One Way to Spell Man." *Saturday Review* 41 (May 24), 8–11, 43–4.

Stegner, Wallace (1962). *Wolf Willow: A History, a Story, and a Memory of the Last Plains Frontier.* New York: Viking.

Stegner, Wallace (1964a). "Born a Square," *Atlantic* 213 (Jan.): 46–50; repr. in *Sound of Mountain Water* (1980), 170–85.

Stegner, Wallace (1964b). *The Gathering of Zion: The Story of the Mormon Trail.* New York: McGraw, Hill.

Stegner, Wallace (1967). *All the Little Live Things.* New York: Viking.

Stegner, Wallace (1971). *Angle of Repose.* New York: Doubleday.

Stegner, Wallace (1974). *The Uneasy Chair: A Biography of Bernard DeVoto.* Garden City: Doubleday.

Stegner, Wallace (1976). *The Spectator Bird.* New York: Doubleday.

Stegner, Wallace (1979). *Recapitulation.* New York: Doubleday. Passages cited here are from the Fawcett-Crest edn. (1979).

Stegner, Wallace (1980). *Sound of Mountain Water: The Changing American West.* New York: Dutton. (First publ. 1969.)

Stegner, Wallace (1981). *American Places,* text by Wallace and Page Stegner and photographs by Eliot Porter. New York: Dutton.

Stegner, Wallace (1987a). *The American West as Living Space.* Ann Arbor: University of Michigan Press.

Stegner, Wallace (1987b). *Crossing to Safety.* New York: Penguin.

Stegner, Wallace (1988). *On the Teaching of Creative Writing.* Hanover, NH: University Press of New England.

Stegner, Wallace (1990). *Where the Bluebird Sings to the Lemonade Springs: Living and Writing in the West.* New York: Random House.

Stegner, Wallace (1998). *Marking the Sparrow's Fall: Wallace Stegner's American West,* ed. Page Stegner. New York: Henry Holt.

Stegner, Wallace (n.d.). "Notebook – Ideas and Themes for Speeches . . . ," Wallace Stegner Papers, Box 109, Folder 1, Marriott Library, University of Utah, Salt Lake City.

Stegner, Wallace, and Etulain, Richard W. (1996). *Stegner: Conversations on History and Literature,* rev. edn. Reno: University of Nevada Press. (First publ. 1990.)

Thomas, John L. (2000). *A Country in the Mind: Wallace Stegner, Bernard DeVoto, History, and the American Land.* New York: Routledge.

Topping, Gary (1999). "Wallace Stegner." In Richard H. Cracroft (ed.), *Dictionary of Literary Biography: 20th Century American Western Writers,* 1st ser., vol. 206, 294–302. Detroit: Bruccoli-Clark-Layman.

Index

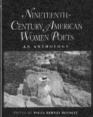